The Agile Guide to Business Analysis and Planning

The Agile Guide to Business Analysis and Planning

From Strategic Plan to Continuous Value Delivery

Howard Podeswa

✦✦ Addison-Wesley

Boston • Columbus • New York • San Francisco • Amsterdam • Cape Town
Dubai • London • Madrid • Milan • Munich • Paris • Montreal • Toronto • Delhi • Mexico City
São Paulo • Sydney • Hong Kong • Seoul • Singapore • Taipei • Tokyo

For information about buying this title in bulk quantities, or for special sales opportunities (which may include electronic versions; custom cover designs; and content particular to your business, training goals, marketing focus, or branding interests), please contact our corporate sales department at corpsales@pearsoned.com or (800) 382-3419.

For government sales inquiries, please contact governmentsales@pearsoned.com.

For questions about sales outside the U.S., please contact intlcs@pearson.com.

Visit us on the Web: informit.com/aw

Library of Congress Control Number: 2020952174

Cover image: Kornn / Shutterstock
Lightbulb icon: Irina Adamovich / Shutterstock

ISBN-13: 978-0-13-419112-6
ISBN-10: 0-13-419112-9

1 2021

The book is dedicated to my parents: my late father, Yidel Podeswa, a professional artist whose creative talent and life force have been an everlasting inspiration to me, and my mother, Ruth Podeswa, who, through her encouragement and example, instilled in me the confidence to take on new challenges.

Contents

Foreword

There are three things Howard and I have in common: our passion for business analysis, our enthusiasm for painting, and our love of good food and conversation.

Several years ago, I worked at one of the largest banks in Canada as the center of excellence (CoE) lead for requirement management/business analysis. I held the responsibility for advancing the requirement management capabilities for the organization's IT & Operations unit, including the training curriculum for business analysis. It is there that I met Howard as we collaborated, mapping the bank's business analysis competencies in the development of a new training curriculum for the bank's business analysts. I was immediately impressed by Howard's ability to understand what I was trying to achieve. He understood well the role of the business analyst and the knowledge and experience business analysts must have to be efficient in their position. His recommendations to augment the curriculum's quality were to the point, and his willingness to collaborate and adjust his course offerings to fit my needs was essential to me.

We subsequently met several times, through formal business meetings, discussing how his courses were performing for us. These were also excellent opportunities to discuss how we could collaborate to advance the training curriculum further. I eventually moved to a different position. Howard and I stayed in contact. We met regularly on a casual basis, catching up, and often ran into each other at industry conferences where Howard presented.

We collaborated through the International Institute of Business Analysis (IIBA). I served in various capacities for fifteen years, initially as a volunteer in multiple roles, including chair of the board of directors. I also led the association as interim president and CEO in 2013–2014. I covered various roles and functions afterward, including director of business and corporate development, where I established multiple strategic alliances with other professional associations.

I established a formal relationship with the Agile Alliance. I negotiated with them a collaboration to develop the second edition of the *Agile Extension to the BABOK Guide, v3.0*, which successfully launched in August 2017. It is an excellent publication. The book tells you what you need to know about agile analysis—it lays out the land, if you wish; it describes the concepts and techniques practitioners should know. Howard has mapped them all out for you in this publication plus many others. However, in my opinion, the real value this book provides, and the reason I don't hesitate telling you to invest in it, is the way Howard interlaces, using a running case study, dozens of scenario-based examples, tools, and techniques. Furthermore, Howard describes them all across the product development lifecycle and how they apply to the most common agile industry frameworks.

Over the last twenty-plus years in business analysis covering various functions, I saw firsthand how difficult it has been for many organizations to transition from a waterfall or some form of iterative development approach to agile. To my chagrin, I saw many organizations debating whether the role of the business analyst still had a place in an agile environment. I witnessed how challenging it has been for many seasoned business analysts to upskill their agile competencies to continue to bring value to their organization. There has been much progress since then, and business analysts have emerged as essential contributors to agile initiatives. Today, organizations with a high level of maturity in product development understand the critical importance that business analysts bring to their agile practices. But for many other organizations, there are still significant challenges as organizations try to fit bits and parcels of two or three agile frameworks to meet their internal processes and ways to manage projects. And this is where the real value of this book comes in. Howard has laid out more than 175 tools and techniques, examples, and guidelines that product owners and business analysis practitioners can readily apply.

Howard's involvement with IIBA is also important to note, as an overall supporter of the association, as a contributor in the review of *BABOK v3: A Guide to the Business Analysis Body of Knowledge*, and sometimes as a gadfly, provoking the organization toward continual improvement. During my tenure at IIBA, I had the privilege to cochair the IIBA official annual Building Better Capability global conference over the course of five years. I had the opportunity to see Howard present in person. The subjects of his presentations were always pertinent, and the delivery always professional, valuable, and enthusiastically well received.

Throughout the years, the relationship I had with Howard evolved into a friendship, as we shared similar passions and interests. I have the highest respect and admiration for Howard. As this book demonstrates, he is the consummate business analysis professional and a recognized leader in the field. He is also an accomplished artist, having exhibited his work in several galleries throughout the world. And he certainly knows how to pick the perfect restaurant for a great meal and conversation.

Howard is a pioneer in the field of business analysis. His first book, *UML for the IT Business Analyst: A Practical Guide to Object-Oriented Requirements Gathering*, was published in 2005 as business analysis fully emerged as a profession. His second book, *The Business Analyst's Handbook*, published in 2009, has become a business analysis staple for both seasoned and aspiring business analysts throughout the world. *The Agile Guide to Business Analysis and Planning* represents a culmination of his vast experience in both agile and business analysis.

What is unique about this book is how Howard treats the subject. It is also how he presents himself. The book has a personal feel to it. It's rather uncommon for a business publication to include several pages dedicated to the author's particular interest, in this case, Howard's passion for painting. But by doing so, Howard connects with the reader on a more personal level, demonstrating how his artistic capabilities add to the richness of his persona and how creativity can be a catalyst for problem solving and innovation, which Howard describes across the book.

With his vast experience in the field, Howard demonstrates how business analysis and agile practitioners can apply fundamental business analysis practices and techniques across the most widely used agile frameworks—including Scrum, Kanban, SAFe, DevOps, XP, lean software development, lean startup, and continuous delivery (CD)—and across all the product development lifecycle activities.

Whether you are new to agile practices or a seasoned business analyst transitioning from traditional business analysis to agile analysis, you will learn which tools to use and when to use them. Howard provides step-by-step guidance for performing your analysis work across the entire product development lifecycle, advice and guidance you can use immediately to be more confident and productive from day one on an agile project. Product owners will gain confidence in interacting with agile teams as they carry out the high-level agile planning analysis activities. Furthermore, they will be able to leverage Howard's guidance to manage stakeholder expectations and keep them involved and engaged throughout the product development process.

I don't pretend to be an expert in agile analysis and planning. I know enough about it to understand how valuable this book is for anyone involved in an agile initiative. I have seen the challenges many practitioners are facing when embarking on a new agile initiative. This book will become a staple reference that both product owners and business analysis practitioners should have by their side.

I am grateful that Howard asked me to write this foreword and thankful for the trust he put in me in helping him wherever I can to bring this publication to fruition. I know you will enjoy reading it and get great value from it.

Happy reading.

—Alain Arseneault
Former IIBA Acting President & CEO, and
President & CEO of TheBAExecutive™

Preface

> "The green reed which bends in the wind is stronger than
> the mighty oak which breaks in a storm."
> —Confucius

This book aims to help enterprises become nimbler and more effective in responding to a rapidly changing environment by assisting them in establishing a reliable, agile analysis, and planning competency. **Agile analysis and planning** is defined in this book as an organizational competency concerned with the *examination of a business* or any aspect of it (including culture, organizational structure, processes, and products) to *learn what needs to change and when* in order to achieve a desired outcome, in a context that places a high premium on *adaptability, resilience,* and *continuous innovation and value delivery.* Key activities within the competency include analyzing who the product is for (the stakeholders), defining their requirements, determining when the capabilities will be delivered, and estimating costs and resources.

Why I Wrote This Book

In my many years of consulting with IT organizations, I've seen practitioners of agile analysis and planning struggle to find a hands-on book that provides guidance they could readily use on the job. Current books on the subject lay down the framework for the competency. International Institute of Business Analysis (IIBA)'s *Agile Extension to the BABOK Guide*, published in association with the Agile Alliance, provides a foundation that describes, in broad terms, how to apply techniques and principles at different planning horizons. Project Management Institute (PMI)'s *Agile Practice Guide* provides a valuable overview, from the perspective of project leaders and project teams. There are also essential books that provide detailed guidance on specific aspects of the discipline, such as Humble's excellent books on DevOps, Cohn's books on user stories, and books devoted to specific frameworks, such as *The Scrum Guide.* I saw a gap in the market, though, for something built on the foundation of those books but that goes further. I realized there were hardly any publications that *connected the dots across these essential techniques* while providing guidance specific enough for the practitioner to adapt and apply them on the job. I wrote this book to fill that gap. It offers actionable advice backed up by specific examples that illustrate how to use and adapt agile practices in different scenarios.

The guidance in the book is supported by more than 175 tools, techniques, examples, diagrams, templates, checklists, and other job aids, making it an essential tool kit for any business analysis practitioner or product owner. It synthesizes the analysis and planning guidance of the most widely used agile frameworks and distills the lessons I've learned from the last twenty to thirty years working with agile teams. Over time, I've made my share of mistakes—failing, trying again, and failing better (to paraphrase Samuel Beckett). Along the way, I've learned what works and what doesn't. This book incorporates the lessons learned from those mistakes so that you don't have to learn them the hard way.

The guidance you'll find in this book draws from the collective wisdom of those I've worked with over the years: my colleagues and clients at REI Co-op, Covance, LabCorp, US Food and Drug Administration (FDA), Intact Insurance, TD Bank, BMO Bank of Montreal, Rogers Corp, TELUS, Canada Mortgage, Housing, True Innovation Inc., and many others. I am grateful to them for trusting me to work with them and sharing their lessons learned with me so that I could pay it forward and share them with you.

Agile analysis and planning focuses on improving communication with customers and users so that the business can anticipate and respond effectively to changes in customers' habits and behaviors *even under extreme uncertainty*. At no time in my memory has this felt as important as today. As I complete this book, a pandemic is raging across the globe, and the world is facing a long-overdue reckoning with the consequences of racial and economic disparity. Everything at this moment seems uncertain, from the profound to the mundane. What will society be like at the end of these changes? Will we come together or be further divided? Will the shift from real-world engagement toward online life be permanent? Will remote work become the norm? What about distance learning and online shopping? It's a time of great challenge but also an opportunity for reinvention. It is my wish that this book will help you and the organizations you work for navigate these changes, adapt, and even thrive in these incredibly uncertain times—and in the "new normal" that is to follow.

State-of-the-Art Guidance across Agile Frameworks

This is my third book on business analysis. My earlier books, *UML for the IT Business Analyst* (2005, 2009) and *The Business Analyst's Handbook* (2008), described how to carry out the business analysis function within an iterative-development lifecycle. It's been very gratifying to witness the international success enjoyed by those books, including a Spanish and Portuguese edition and a second release of the UML book. If you liked those books, I am confident you will enjoy this new publication as well. Much has changed, though, since my first publication. This book returns to similar ground but with a refreshed perspective on today's most successful and widely used agile and analysis frameworks and practices. These include:

- DevOps
- SAFe
- Kanban

- Scrum

- Lean software development

- Lean startup and minimum viable product (MVP)

- User stories, Extreme Programming (XP)

- Continuous integration/ continuous delivery (CI/CD)

- Test-driven development (TDD), acceptance test–driven development (ATDD), and behavior-driven development (BDD)

- Full-potential plan

- Discovery-driven planning

- Circumstance-based market segmentation

- Agile Fluency model

In addition, the book is aligned with the following professional certification guides:

- PMI: *Agile Practice Guide*

- IIBA: *Agile Extension to the BABOK Guide v2*

- PMI: *Business Analysis Practice Guide*

- IIBA: *BABOK v3: A Guide to Business Analysis Body of Knowledge*

What Makes This Book Unique?

Unlike many other guides, this book contains everything you need *in one place* to practice effective agile analysis and planning:

- **Detailed guidance:** It's a practical manual that tells you what to do *and* shows you how to do it.

- **Integration with business analysis:** Most books on agile analysis focus solely on agile techniques, overshadowing the use of valuable business analysis techniques such as business rules analysis and process modeling. This book shows you how to insert legacy analysis techniques into an agile process to increase an agile team's productivity.

- **Broad coverage of agile approaches and frameworks:** The book incorporates best practices from today's most widely used agile frameworks, including lean, SAFe, Kanban, and Scrum, enabling you to be effective in any agile environment.

- **Experience-based guidance:** This book is based on years of experience working with companies and teams on improving agile analysis and planning in their organizations, learning what works and when. It's *informed* by today's most effective agile frameworks but *is beholden to none*.

- **Context-based just-in-time learning:** The book presents you with techniques and guidelines in the context in which you'll be using them across the development life-cycle. You learn what you need to know and when you need to apply it.

- **Extensive job aids:** The book includes more than 175 valuable job aids to increase your understanding and effectiveness. These include:
  - Concrete examples and templates that you can use to create analysis and planning artifacts, such as the product vision statement, product roadmaps, story maps, epics, features, spikes, stories, and acceptance criteria
  - Sample diagrams and diagram legends
  - Meeting agendas and other facilitation aids
  - Checklists

- **Contiguous end-to-end case study:** An end-to-end case study runs through the book, enabling you to see exactly how the steps and artifacts feed into each other over the course of an agile development lifecycle.

Furthermore, the book provides clear evidence of the value of business analysis in an agile organization—demonstrating how traditional business analysis combined with agile analysis and planning techniques can produce higher-performing agile teams.

Why Agile Analysis and Planning Is Important for the Enterprise

We know that organizations that adopt an agile approach experience significant benefits. For example, their projects are 37 percent faster to market than the industry average (QSM),[1] and their productivity increases by 16 percent.[2] But we also know that an agile organization can dramatically *improve* its success rates by enhancing its level of competency in analysis and planning.[3] The "Business Analysis Benchmark"[4] showed that project success rates for agile organizations *more than doubled* from 42 percent at the lowest maturity level (level 1) for the competency to 91 percent at the highest maturity level (level 4). Moreover, it found that even modest increases in maturity levels could have a significant impact. For example, a half-step increase from level 2 to 2.5 led to a rise in success rates from 62 percent to 74 percent for agile organizations. (More on this research is presented in Chapter 2.)

---

1. Quantitative Software Management Associates (QSMA), "The Agile Impact Report. Proven Performance Metrics from the Agile Enterprise," QSMA for Rally Software Development Corp., 2009, 1.

2. QSMA, "Agile Impact Report," 1.

3. The report correlated success to the maturity level of the requirements process, roughly equivalent to what I refer to as *analysis and planning* in the book. The report looked at the impact of maturity level on success rates for different development approaches, including agile.

4. Keith Ellis, "Business Analysis Benchmark—The Impact of Business Requirements on the Success of Technology Projects," IAG Consulting, 2009.

Problems that can be addressed by having effective agile analysis and planning capabilities in your organization include the following:

- Added costs for rework because requirements were sufficiently understood up front
- Delays due to poor team planning and coordination
- Reduced team productivity because work is not being well prioritized across the product
- Poorly managed stakeholder expectations
- Underresourced, overworked product owners
- Challenges scaling agile development because cultural issues within the organization are not appropriately addressed

Today, agile analysis and planning is recognized as an effective approach for addressing these issues and more. Organizations who already have business analysts experienced in traditional business analysis are upskilling them with agile competencies and embracing them as valuable contributors. At the same time, startup technology companies that began their agile journey without a strong business analysis competency are now adding it to their organizations. As they mature, they're finding that the skillset is becoming more relevant to them because of the increased levels of complexity in the business domains they address and in their products' underlying architecture.

The benefits to the business of establishing an effective agile analysis and planning competency include the following:

- *Enhanced ability to anticipate customer need*: Agile analysts use a wealth of techniques to gain a deep understanding of the customer. Root-cause analysis and circumstance-based market segmentation identify the underlying needs of customers and the root causes of the problems they are experiencing. Kano analysis helps the business forecast the capabilities customers would embrace. MVP testing reveals which proposed features are most valuable to customers and validates hypotheses in order to direct development resources.

- *Improved ability to manage change*: Agile analysis increases the ability of teams to *sense and respond to change* and make the appropriate adjustments along the way.

- *Ability to plan effectively:* The competency enables an organization to plan effectively for the short term and long term, whether under conditions of extreme uncertainty or when conditions are well known.

- *Reduced time to market:* Time to market is reduced because agile analysis focuses development effort on a minimal set of high-value features that are further evaluated and enhanced over time.

- *Data-informed decisions:* Agile analysis and planning practices enhance the ability to make *data-informed decisions* by using the lean startup MVP process, A/B testing, and actionable metrics.

- *Reduced rework and delays:* Agile analysis reduces rework and unnecessary delays because the right amount of analysis is performed at the right time.

- *Improved team productivity:* Productivity improves because the team is always working on items of the highest value across the product.

- *Improved stakeholder engagement:* Stakeholders are more engaged due to an incremental, rolling analysis process that involves them throughout the lifecycle.

- *Product owner support:* With a well-developed agile analysis competency, product owners are provided with the support they need to be effective in their jobs. Agile analysis and planning practitioners take on requirements and day-to-day communication with the team so that product owners can focus on the outward-facing aspects of the role.

- *Ability to leverage the business analysis (BA) experience*: By upskilling their existing business analysts and incorporating them into agile organizations, companies can *leverage the experience of seasoned business analysts* to improve team performance on agile initiatives.

Who Should Read This Book

The intended readers for this book can be broadly grouped as follows:

- Business analysis practitioners and product owners
- IT directors and leaders of centers of excellence (CoEs) in business analysis, agile practice, and DevOps
- Educators

The benefits for each type of reader are as follows.

Business Analysis Practitioners and Product Owners

The primary reader for this book is the working professional—a person responsible for the analysis, planning activities, or both, in an agile software development organization. The job titles of those who perform this work vary widely among organizations, as does the distribution of responsibilities between those titles. They include business analysts, team analysts, product owners, proxy product owners, and product managers. This book is for *anyone* responsible for this work in an agile organization—regardless of job title.

If you are a product owner, you can use the knowledge in this book to learn how to

- Organize and coordinate agile teams for peak effectiveness.
- Analyze the market for the product.
- Develop a compelling product vision statement.

- Plan and estimate requirements implementation at all planning horizons.

- Plan MVPs to test hypotheses for the product and make data-informed decisions.

- Prioritize epics and features across the product.

If you're a business analyst, you can use this book to communicate the product vision to the team and help them translate that vision down to smaller requirements units and specifications (e.g., features, stories, and their acceptance criteria). Within these pages, you'll also find detailed guidance on maintaining the product backlog, tracking the progress of stories, story preparation, and estimation. Senior business analysts will learn how to prepare and tailor the agile analysis process for their situation—including setting up the product backlog, gaining consensus on the definition of ready, setting Kanban work-in-progress limits, and determining capacity.

If you're responsible for analysis and planning at any level in your organization, the information in this book will provide you with the confidence and skills to work effectively within any of the popular agile frameworks and practices in use today. If you're an entry-level business analyst or team analyst, you'll appreciate the chapter on fundamentals, the detailed guidance on feature and story preparation, and the wealth of job aids in the book. If you're a product or higher-level business analyst, you'll benefit from the book's strategic guidance dealing with culture, stakeholder analysis business objectives, strategic planning, and scaling considerations.

IT Directors and Leaders of CoEs in Business Analysis and Agile Practice

IT directors and CoE leaders in business analysis and agile practice can leverage the information contained in this book to

- Develop and customize an agile analysis and planning framework that's right for the organization.

- Build a library of CoE resources for analysts and planners using the book's templates, checklists, and examples.

- Craft a strong value proposition to communicate the benefits of agile analysis and planning competency in the organization.

Educators: College or Corporate Trainers or Learning Directors

If you're an educator, you can use this book as a basis for building a curriculum in agile analysis and agile development that incorporates today's most popular proven concepts, tools, and techniques. Each chapter describes clearly defined objectives and summaries, leveraging a running case study with sample solutions that you can use for group workshops.

If you are interested in using the book to build a training curriculum, please contact me for additional content and services, including PowerPoint presentations, eLearning offerings, and in-house training. Send email inquiries to info@nobleinc.ca or check online at https://www.nobleinc.ca.

How This Book Works

Think of this book as the voice of a coach in your ear as you walk through the agile analysis and planning process. Each chapter guides you through the activities performed at that point in the agile development cycle. The steps are illustrated with a running case study so that you can see how analysis and planning artifacts evolve the course of development and how they connect to each other. Additional examples are provided so you can see how to apply the techniques to other situations.

I should note that the sequencing of analysis activities in the chapters is only a rough guide because agile analysis and planning is not a sequential process. You rarely complete a planning or analysis activity in one step; more typically, you perform some of it up front and the rest of it in a rolling fashion. Moreover, activities are often carried out concurrently. For the most part, the chapters are sequenced based on the order in which activities are *first* performed.

How to Read the Book

There are two ways to read this book:

1. The traditional way, front to back. That's what I'd advise if you're new to agile or business analysis.

2. By skipping to the parts that are most important to you. You may prefer to read the book this way if you have some agile experience and want to fill in your knowledge gaps. In that case, I'd recommend you

   - First scan Chapter 3 to fill gaps you may have in fundamental concepts.
   - Next, read Chapter 4 to gain a bird's-eye view of the agile analysis and planning activities covered in this book.
   - Then go to the chapters that deal with the activities that interest you. Each chapter is self-contained, dealing with one or more analysis or planning activities. When it refers to a topic that was introduced earlier in the book, I've included a cross-reference in case you're reading the book in a nonsequential manner.

Overview of Chapters

The following is a brief description of each chapter:

Chapter 1, The Art of Agile Analysis and Planning	Presents a brief, personalized look at the art of agile analysis and planning based on lessons learned from my life both as an artist and as an analyst. It explains why I believe the agile approach is conducive to the creative process.
Chapter 2, Agile Analysis and Planning: The Value Proposition	Presents the value proposition for developing an effective competency in agile analysis and planning in an organization.
Chapter 3, Fundamentals of Agile Analysis and Planning	Explains the principles, frameworks, concepts, and practices that underlie the agile analysis and planning competency and the rest of this book, such as lean, Kanban, Scrum, DevOps, and user stories.
Chapter 4, Analysis and Planning Activities across the Agile Development Lifecycle	Provides an overview of planning and analysis activities across the agile product development lifecycle. Three scenarios are covered: short-term initiatives with planning horizons up to three months, long-term initiatives up to five years, and scaled agile initiatives. The Agile Analysis and Planning Map in this chapter provides a bird's-eye view of the process. This map is referenced in later chapters so that you can see where you are in the development process as you progress through the book.
Chapter 5, Preparing the Organization	Explains how to prepare an organization for agile software development, including guidance on forming effective agile teams, managing stakeholders' expectations, and guidelines for governance, finance, and marketing groups. (Please note that guidelines specific to scaled organizations are covered in Chapter 17.)
Chapter 6, Preparing the Process	Describes how to prepare the agile analysis and planning process. Senior analysts and CoE leads will learn how to customize the right agile framework and practices for their situation and how to fine-tune process parameters like work-in-progress limits and the definition of ready to optimize team productivity.
Chapter 7, Visioning	Covers early analysis activities to envision a new product or significant enhancement. Product owners can use the information in this chapter to craft effective product and epic vision statements and specify objectives. Analysts will learn to communicate the product vision to the team and continue the visioning process through root-cause and stakeholder analysis. The chapter also covers the specification of "leap of faith" hypotheses in preparation for MVP planning.

Chapter 8, Seeding the Backlog—Discovering and Grading Features	Focuses on the discovery and specification of the initial items in the product backlog. Analysts and product owners should read this chapter to learn how to prioritize and specify features and nonfunctional requirements for the product or release backlog. Prioritization tools covered in this chapter include Kano analysis, cost of delay, and weighted shortest job first (WSJF).
Chapter 9, Long-Term Agile Planning	Explains how to perform long-term planning for horizons of six months to five years. Product owners and business analysts can use the information in this chapter to create a long-term product roadmap, specify goals, objectives, assumptions, and metrics for the planning period. The chapter explains the full-potential plan—an approach for planning transformative change over a three- to five-year period. It describes the agile approach to planning using MVPs to test assumptions and determine what to include in the product. The chapter also explores deployment strategies and options for the long-term implementation plan, including guidelines for when to use narrow and deep versus wide and shallow approaches.
Chapter 10, Quarterly and Feature Preparation	Describes how to prepare upcoming features. When the team is using a Kanban approach, this preparation occurs on a rolling basis. When a timeboxed planning approach is used, it occurs before quarterly planning for the group of features lined up for the quarter. This chapter applies to both approaches. The chapter includes both agile and legacy tools, including the feature definition of ready, ATDD, specification of feature acceptance criteria using BDD, value stream mapping, journey mapping, and process modeling.
Chapter 11, Quarterly and Feature Planning	Describes how to plan an upcoming feature or quarter. The chapter applies to teams that use timeboxed planning approaches (in which case all features for the quarter are planned together) and those that use a single-item flow-based approach (in which case a single feature is planned). The chapter begins with guidance on when to use which approach. It explains how to plan and estimate features using methods and approaches such as the Planning Game, Planning Poker, Delphi estimation, story points, ideal developer days, as well as the no-estimating approach.

Chapter 12, MVPs and Story Maps	Demonstrates how to use MVPs and story maps to plan the delivery of learning and value within short time-frames. MVPs are minimal versions of the product that enable the product owner to test hypotheses and make data-informed decisions about development investment and resource allocation. Story maps are visual representations of the plan that indicate the operational and implementation sequencing of stories.
Chapter 13, Story Preparation	Covers the analysis of stories before implementation. This preparatory work occurs on a rolling basis if the team is using Kanban. It is performed before iteration planning when a timeboxed approach such as Scrum is used. This chapter covers both contexts. Tools covered include the INVEST story-writing guidelines, patterns for splitting stories, and the specification of story acceptance criteria using BDD and the Gherkin syntax.
Chapter 14, Iteration and Story Planning	Covers planning for a short-term horizon of one week to one month. The chapter explains how to determine team capacity and how to forecast which stories will be done. Planning tools covered in this chapter include the iteration backlog, developer task board, and Kanban board.
Chapter 15, Rolling Analysis and Preparation—Day-to-Day Activities	Describes day-to-day rolling analysis and planning activities. The chapter includes guidance on ongoing story and feature preparation, the daily stand-up, updating the developer task board, burndown chart, cumulative flow diagrams, and more.
Chapter 16, Releasing the Product	Covers the final preparations for general availability (GA), also known as production release. The chapter includes guidance on operational preparations, value validation, alpha testing, and beta testing. It also examines the pros and cons of using a hardening iteration before GA.
Chapter 17, Scaling Agility	Describes the analysis and planning challenges faced by large agile organizations. It provides actionable guidance for scaling the agile organization, the process, and the product backlog. This chapter explains and incorporates best practices for scaled agile development, including DevOps, CI/CD, ATDD, BDD, and SAFe.
Chapter 18, Achieving Enterprise Agility	Explores agile analysis, planning, and product development from the enterprise perspective—beyond the IT context that has been the main focus of the rest of this book. The chapter includes thirteen practices for optimizing an enterprise's responsiveness to change.

Appendixes	Provide a collection of useful tools for the agile analyst and planner, including checklists, templates, and agendas for easy reference on-the-job or during training. Also included is a detailed case study illustrating discovery-driven planning—the financial planning counterpart to the data-driven development approach described in the rest of this book.

Repeating Book Features

This book contains several repeating features to make it easier to find what you need. They are identified with icons as follows:

 Checklist: Useful lists for the practitioner (e.g., a checklist of stakeholders)

 Example: A concrete example of an artifact

 Template: A template for creating an artifact (text or diagram)

 Tips and Guidelines: Useful tips, guidelines, and formulae for the practitioner

 Cross-reference: Cross-reference to another book section, where you can learn more about a topic

Introducing the BLInK Case Study

This book follows one case study through the product development lifecycle, from visioning to continuous value delivery. The case study is included so that you can immediately see how to apply the techniques and to connect them over the course of product development. (If you're not a fan of case studies, you can skip or quickly scan those sections. I won't be offended, and you won't miss any new concepts.)

Many people learn best by doing. I am one of them. If that describes you, I urge you to actively work through the case study sections yourself, comparing your deliverables with those I've provided in the book. It's perfectly okay for your deliverables to be different from those in the book or for you to come up with different results. The outputs will depend on the conversation you have (or *imagine* having) with stakeholders and how you choose to document them. What's important is that you can justify any decisions you've made.

The example I've chosen for this book revolves around a fictionalized insurance company called Better Living (BL) Inc. As the case study opens, BL is looking to develop a usage-based insurance (UBI) product that uses data from Internet of Things devices to personalize health insurance costs and benefits. The product is to be named BLInK —Better Living through Insurance Knowledge.

One reason I chose this case study is that it's current: as I started work on this book, I was working with an insurance client on a similar product. But the main reason I chose it is that it involves the analysis of an innovative product within a mainstream business— just the type of initiative where one is most likely to find an agile business analyst. As the case study opens in Chapter 7, the product is in its early visioning phase. Throughout the rest of the book, we follow the agile analysis and planning of this product through to implementation and delivery.

Certification Information

This book is mapped to the following professional certification guides:

- *BABOK v3: A Guide to the Business Analysis Body of Knowledge*
- *Agile Extension to the BABOK Guide v2*
- *The PMI Guide to Business Analysis*
- *The Agile Practice Guide*

For a detailed mapping of chapters to the guides, please see Appendix A.2.

Register your copy of *The Agile Guide to Business Analysis and Planning* on the InformIT site for convenient access to electronic templates, updates, and/or corrections as they become available. To start the registration process, go to informit.com/register and log in or create an account. Enter the product ISBN (9780134191126) and click Submit. Look on the Registered Products tab for an Access Bonus Content link next to this product and follow that link to access any available bonus materials. If you would like to be notified of exclusive offers on new editions and updates, please check the box to receive email from us.

Thanks

No person gets anywhere on their own; we all do it with the help and mentoring of others. First and foremost, I want to thank the many colleagues and mentors who have generously shared their knowledge throughout my career. A special thanks to Alain Arseneault, with whom I worked closely at BMO Financial Group and in many other contexts. He has been enormously instrumental in the development and success of business analysis internationally through his pioneering work developing the bank's competency and later through his involvement with IIBA in multiple capacities, including acting CEO. Alain has been incredibly generous with support and guidance over the years, and he has gone beyond-the-beyond with this assistance on this book. I can't thank him enough.

Often, transformative change is the result of a change *agent*—an individual with vision and a strategy for executing it. I've met these talented individuals in many organizations, and they've often wielded influence far beyond their formal titles, largely as a result of the respect in which they are held by their peers. In this regard, I want to thank Abhijeet Mukherjee, with whom I worked at UST Global to raise the maturity level of business analysis across the corporation. Thanks, too, to Saurabh Ranjan, who was UST's COO at the time and a champion and primary sponsor for Global BA and Strategic Consulting CoE-related programs and initiatives. I also want to thank three other leaders of change in their organizations—Trenton Allen at REI Co-op; Andre Franklin at Covance; and Dana Mitchell, agile practice lead for agile transformation at TD Bank Securities—for trusting me to work with their teams and for sharing their insights about agile analysis and planning practices.

A big shoutout as well to the *early agile adopters*, clients who saw the promise of iterative, incremental development right from the beginning and were true pioneers in business domains that were not particularly open to agile development and analysis at the time. Foremost among these was John Beattie, former VP at TELUS—an agile visionary and someone with whom I had the immense pleasure of working. I'd also like to thank Tim Lloyd from True Innovation for his helpful encouragement and collaboration over many years.

Special thanks to Karl Wiegers, whose early writing on requirements spurred my interest in business analysis, for sharing his experience and guidance as a writer and analyst. He is a living example of the principle of paying it forward. Thanks also to Christopher Edwards for his valuable input and detailed notes on the last chapters. Without all of these people, and many others too numerous to name, this book would not exist in its current form.

Thanks also to my technical editors, Ron Healy, for the care he took to consider the guidance in this book against his own experience, and to Clifford Berg, who encouraged me to expand the coverage of DevOps practices and challenge my own assumptions, and helped me find the most useful guidance to highlight in several of the book's key chapters. Both editors gave me precisely what I was looking for—*a hard time*—and the book is much better for their efforts. Thanks also to Tracy Brown, my development editor, for her support and guidance. A huge shoutout to Haze Humbert, executive editor at Pearson, for cajoling, encouraging, and generally kicking my ass to get this book done, and to everyone else on the Pearson team, including Rachel Paul, Menka Mehta, Julie Nahil, and Carol

Lallier. Thanks, as well, to Christopher Guzikowski, my first editor at Pearson during the early days of the book, for believing in the book and supporting it when it counted most.

This book is especially indebted to the almost weekly telephone calls about its themes over the four years of its making with a lead developer at Hootsuite, one of Canada's most innovative agile companies. His input and insights are so interwoven into this book that he is very much a collaborator. It is an added pleasure that he is also my son, Yasha Podeswa.

About the Author

Howard Podeswa is an established author, professional artist, and sought-after speaker at international conferences. His paintings have been shown in numerous exhibitions across Canada and internationally, including the United States, Italy, and South Africa. His work is held in numerous private and public collections.

Podeswa's career in software development began when an academic background in nuclear physics led to a job working on a nuclear-accident simulation program for Atomic Energy of Canada Ltd. Since then, he has been enthralled by software development and often found himself on the cusp of change as a developer of innovative systems in transportation, laboratory automation, and communications. From the 1990s onward, he has been helping large organizations transition their planning, analysis, and requirements engineering (RE) processes to agile practices across a broad range of sectors, including telecommunications, banking, government services, insurance, and healthcare.

He plays a leading role in the industry as a designer of agile and business analysis (BA) training programs for companies and higher education institutions, including Boston University Corporate Education Center and Humber College; as a reviewer of the BA profession's standard books of best practices (*BABOK* [IIBA] and *Business Analysis for Practitioners—A Practice Guide* [PMI]); and as an author whose books have become staples in many BA libraries: *The Business Analyst's Handbook* and *UML for the IT Business Analyst*.

Podeswa, through his role as director for Noble Inc., has provided agile and BA training programs and consulting services to clients across the globe in the private and public sectors. Companies that have benefitted from his services include the International Standards Organization (ISO), Moody's, the Mayo Clinic, TELUS, UST Global, BMO, TD Bank, Intact Insurance, Labcorp, the US Food and Drug Administration (FDA), Canada Mortgage and Housing Corporation (CMHC), Bell Nexia, and Thomson Reuters.

Chapter 1

The Art of Agile Analysis and Planning

This chapter provides a personal introduction to agile analysis and planning from my perspective as an artist and IT professional. It explains how the approach supports creativity and responsiveness. The chapter uses storytelling to introduce the main themes of the book, with two narratives that illustrate the value that the competency brings to the business.

1.1 Objectives

This chapter will help you

- Understand how agile analysis and planning supports a creative, adaptive process of product development.

- Understand through examples, how the competency benefits the business.

1.2 On Art and Agile Analysis

I come from a family of artists: my grandfather, uncle, and father were painters. (One of my father's works is shown in Figures 1.1.) I am one, too. Throughout most of my time in software development, I've had a parallel life as a professional artist.

From my art practice, I've learned a valuable lesson about the creative process. If you want to create a good painting every time reliably, you need to plan and execute each step very carefully. First, you prepare the canvas, then you make a complete drawing of the final image, and only then do you start to apply paint. I created the painting in Figure 1.2 using that process.

Figure 1.1 *Yidel Podeswa, Apples, 2012, oil on canvas. (Photo by Toni Hafkenscheid.)*

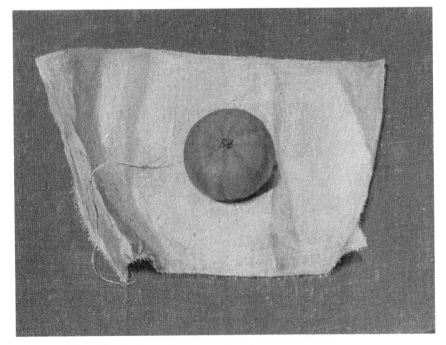

Figure 1.2 *Howard Podeswa, Clementine, 2019.*

However, if you want to create something truly innovative, something original that has never existed before, you can't use that process because you don't know beforehand what the result is going to look like. It's something you figure out in the making. And so, you just start with a rough vision of what you want; then you have to experiment—iteratively refining that vision over time through a process of trial and error. Figures 1.3 through 1.5 illustrate how I used this process to create the painting series, *A Brief History*, exhibited in the Koffler Gallery (Toronto, Ontario) in 2016 and Kelowna Art Gallery (Kelowna, British Columbia) in 2017. Figure 1.3 is an installation view of the two main paintings, *Heaven* (2015) and *Hell* (2013).

Figure 1.3   *Howard Podeswa,* Heaven *and* Hell, *installation view, 9 ft × 15 ft, Koffler Gallery, 2016. (Photo by Howard Podeswa.)*

When I began work on the series in 2012, I had a rough vision for the exhibition and the two central paintings in it. I wanted viewers to have to make a choice—to face Heaven or Hell—and to have an immersive experience whichever choice they made. I wanted that experience to invoke a reflection on where we are headed—the future. The series and exhibition title, *A Brief History*, is an allusion to Stephen Hawking's writings on this question from the point of view of astrophysics. I had a rough concept for the *Hell* painting: a vortex suctioning in the dark images that were beginning to fill our newsfeeds. And finally, I knew the constraints with which I had to work—such as the dimensions of doors and elevators the paintings had to pass through and the height of the gallery. I left everything else to be worked out through prototyping and trial and error. Figure 1.4 shows an early prototype for the painting.

Figure 1.4   *Howard Podeswa,* Hell, *2012 (work in progress, prototype), 6 ft × 9 ft. (Photo by Howard Podeswa.)*

Figure 1.5 shows the final version of the painting.

Figure 1.5   *Howard Podeswa,* Hell, *2013 (final state), 9 ft × 15 ft. (Photo by Toni Hafkenscheid.)*

Comparing the two versions, you can see that some of the features that were present in the early prototype have been retained: the circular composition, the central perspective point inside the circle, as well as the overall tenor of the images. Nevertheless, the final result is significantly different from earlier versions. One feature—the circle motif—has become much more emphasized. All of the details have changed. This process is strikingly similar to the agile analysis and planning process you'll be reading about in this book: It begins with a broad vision of the product and how users will experience it. It continues with an analysis of constraints and context for the usage of the product. It proceeds with a series of prototypes and "sketches" to test out hypotheses about the product. And it uses an iterative process based on intervention (trying something out), measurement (gathering user feedback), and adjustment to determine the features that make their way into the product.

What is true in art is true in software development: the traditional, step-by-step approach to analysis and planning—what software developers refer to as the *waterfall* approach—works pretty well when you are working on something routine. But when you're working on something truly innovative, about which little can be known in advance with certainty, it's more effective and natural to adopt an experimental approach—the agile analysis and planning approach that is the subject of this book. As we'll see, this approach even has benefits for noninnovative development, too. For example, it shortens time to market by focusing effort on high-value features, using data to inform decisions.

1.3 I Work for a Mainstream Company! What's This Got to Do with Me?

Some readers might now be thinking, "I work in a mainstream business. I'm in insurance/finance/government (fill in your business domain), where it's all about *reliability*. What does 'agile' have to do with me? We don't *do* trial and error!"

Here's an example of why agile development is still relevant in these contexts. These days, I'm working with teams on a usage-based insurance (UBI) product. The product will base costs and benefits on customer behaviors: what times of day they drive, how they accelerate and brake, where they travel, and so on. It's a very controversial product to develop because of privacy issues. And that's the point. There's so much uncertainty about what features and inducements customers will and won't accept that if analysts specified *all* the requirements upfront, much of their work would likely end up on the cutting room floor. Instead, they are using an approach similar to the one I've described for creating novelty in art—one that begins with a broad vision and gradually brings features into focus through a process of experimentation: trying something out and making adjustments based on the response. That is the agile approach.

This kind of product development is not an anomaly today in mainstream businesses. As new data sources and Internet of Things (IoT) devices proliferate, so, too, do opportunities for innovation, even in traditional business domains. Add in the accelerated pace of change all businesses are experiencing today, and it's no wonder that the adoption of agile approaches is now widespread even in mainstream business domains. Since these traditional business domains also happen to be the natural habitat for business analysis (BA), two disciplines—BA and agile development—are now in close contact with each other in ways they rarely used to be. The result is the emergence of an agile analysis and planning competency—BA, as practiced in an agile context, in line with agile planning approaches. Why analysis *and* planning? In agile development, the two activities are too tightly intertwined to be effectively separated: the backlog is in a continual state of flux, with changes affecting both the *analysis* of requirements items (epics, features, and stories) and the *plan* for rolling them out. Consequently, a single paradigm is needed that encompasses both: Agile business analysis and planning. For convenience, I'll also be referring to the competency by the slightly shorter term, "agile analysis and planning."

Let me give you a personal perspective on the evolution of the competency. I started out in IT as a developer for Atomic Energy of Canada (AECL) and eventually moved on to systems design and analysis. In the late 1990s, my clients began asking me for help developing a new competency—business analysis—one that repurposed many of the techniques I had used in the technical realm for the analysis of a business and its needs. Through this work, I became an early contributor to the emerging field of BA: I created Boston University Corporate Education Center's first BA certification program, acted as the BA subject matter expert for the National IT Apprenticeship System (NITAS) BA program (an apprenticeship program from the US Department of Labor and CompTia), and created internal BA training programs for companies such as TELUS, Rogers Cable, Bank of Montreal (BMO), and Moody's. As the discipline evolved, I came to see it as being about much more than requirements. Today I would describe it informally as follows:

> Business analysis is the examination of a business (or any other organization), or an aspect of it, in order to understand what needs to change to achieve a desired outcome.

From my development experience, I knew that iterative-incremental development (a process involving short development cycles, or *iterations*) and the broader agile approach that grew from it were the way of the future. I intuited early on, though, that the BA competency was going to have to adapt to this newer way of working. I was fortunate to have a number of clients who felt similarly and who trusted me to help guide them on that journey. Many of these clients, such as Willy Rose at the Canadian Imperial Bank of Commerce (CIBC), were true pioneers—early adopters (back in the late 1990s) of iterative-incremental practices in mainstream businesses. That work resulted in my first book, *UML for the IT Business Analyst*.[1]

In those early days of agile development, most of the organizations I worked with were islands of agility within their companies; the larger enterprise still operated along traditional lines. That all changed when I was called into a meeting in 2013 by a vice president at a large telecom company. Here's what he told me: "Howard, in five or six years, the

---

1. Howard Podeswa, *UML for the IT Business Analyst: A Practical Guide to Object-Oriented Requirements Gathering* (Boston: Thomson Course Technology, 2005).

whole organization will be agile. You've been working with our business analysts. What do you think's going to happen to them? I've got agile consultants running around saying you don't need analysts in agile. If that's the case, what am I supposed to do with all my analysts?"

I immediately recognized this meeting as a pivotal moment. This executive wasn't talking about an *island* of agility but the transformation of an *entire enterprise* in a traditional business sector—the natural habitat of the business analyst. Either BA was going to adapt, or it would disappear. It was not yet clear at the time whether BA *would* survive, as it wasn't just the consultants at this one company who had been dismissing analysis. I still own a copy of *Agile Software Development with Scrum*[2]—the book that introduced the agile Scrum framework to the world in 2002. About the only reference to requirements analysis I can find in it is the advice *not* to spend too much time on it![3] Yes, the book does deal with product backlog items—work items that can represent requirements. But it is as though those items just show up magically in the product backlog. There is very little about the planning and analysis work required to get them there.

The same year that I met with the telecom executive, 2013, I delivered a talk on agile BA at the Norway Developers Conference (NDC). Mine was the only one of about fifty presentations to address agile BA. It simply wasn't on the radar for most agile practitioners. It was entirely reasonable to believe that BA and business analysts would not survive the transition to agile practices.

You may be wondering what happened after that conversation with the vice president. Over the next couple of years, I worked with the company's teams across the country on the analysis aspects of their agile transition. The company ended up keeping its business analysts and includes them today on most agile teams. Why? The analysts have proven their worth by filling a competency gap on agile teams—contributing soft skills, elicitation skills, domain knowledge, and valuable analysis expertise in areas such as workflow modeling, domain modeling, and business rules. Right across the agile development lifecycle, business analysts have been critical to ensuring *business value is maximized* whenever decisions are made. (We look further at the broader research on this topic and the value proposition for agile analysis in Chapter 2, "Agile Analysis and Planning: The Value Proposition.")

In keeping with the agile preference for communicating through stories, the following are two "truthy" (with thanks to Stephen Colbert) stories about agile analysis and planning. They are based on real events, but I've changed the details for reasons of pedagogy and confidentiality. One story gets into the weeds of agile analysis techniques, and the other deals with agile culture. Together, I hope they give you a feel for the value that agile analysis brings to an agile development organization and the business as a whole.

---

2. Ken Schwaber and Mike Beedle, *Agile Software Development with Scrum* (Upper Saddle River, NJ: Prentice Hall, 2002), 92–93.

3. Schwaber and Beedle, *Agile Software Development*. The reference is to "If too much time is spent thinking about requirements, competition gets to the market first" (p. 92). The authors also discuss the relationship between requirements uncertainty and "noise" (p. 93) in their argument for using empirical processes when requirements are volatile.

1.4 Story 1: It's Not My Problem

This story is called "It's Not My Problem"—but, really, it's a morality tale about why you shouldn't skip BA in agile development.

I became involved in this story when one of my clients, a company in the healthcare sector, asked me to advise it regarding some recurring issues the company was experiencing. During a break in one of our meetings, a high-level manager pulled me aside to tell me, "There's a problem here that everyone recognizes, but no one wants to talk about in public." That problem was that, time and again, stories that performed well on their own would fail during end-to-end user acceptance testing (UAT). Since UAT usually happened late in the release cycle, it inevitably led to last-minute panic and missed deadlines or a release with missing features.

Figure 1.6 illustrates the issue the company faced.

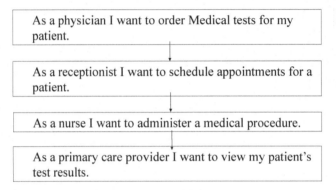

Figure 1.6 *User acceptance testing for managing medical laboratory tests*

Each rectangle represents a requirements item—a user story or feature. The stories are shown in the order they are usually performed by users: first, a physician orders a medical test, then a receptionist schedules an appointment for the procedure, and so on. During implementation, each team in the group would focus on a different user role (physician, receptionist, etc.). As each team finished a user story, the story was tested against its acceptance criteria. Once all the stories were completed and individually tested, QA pulled them together for UAT in the sequence shown in Figure 1.6. It's at that point that the test would fail.

I had a strong hunch about what was wrong: I guessed that the analysis of the end-to-end process for ordering and administering a medical procedure must have been skipped over during the preparations prior to development. The manager confirmed that this was, indeed, the case. The trouble was that *she couldn't convince the team to do anything about it*. She offered several reasons why. Fundamentally, many of her developers seemed to believe that you don't have to do process analysis in agile. She thought some of the outside agile consultants who had been working with the teams might have spread this view. Another issue was that the analysis of the end-to-end process didn't fall within any particular team's wheelhouse, since each team was focused on only one user's perspective. Anyone who *might* have wondered about it simply assumed that another team was doing the analysis.

I first addressed the mistaken impression that team members had about analysis in agile development and explained that the competency is widely accepted as an essential activity in agile development today. (*The Scrum Guide*[4] today refers to this work as product backlog *refinement*.) Then I offered three mechanisms for ensuring that the scenario she described wouldn't recur. The first was for her analysts to adopt the acceptance test–driven development (ATDD) practice of specifying end-to-end tests for features up front.[5] To ensure that this work occurs before feature implementation, I suggested that her teams define and use a feature definition of ready (DoR). The DoR is a set of rules—a checklist of characteristics—that an upcoming requirements item must have. To avoid the type of scenario she described, I suggested she include the following condition in the feature DoR:

> The end-to-end process or value stream for the feature has been analyzed enough to determine the sequencing of steps (stories), the integration points, and determine the UAT required to test the feature.

Finally, to ensure this analysis work was taken into account during planning, I suggested her analysts capture it in a functional spike (referred to as an *enabler story* in the Scaled Agile Framework [SAFe])—a special kind of story reserved for the analysis of upcoming user stories.

In this book, you'll find guidance on each of these issues. For example, in Chapter 6, "Preparing the Process," you'll learn what to include in a feature DoR. In Chapter 13, "Story Preparation," you'll learn how to specify and use spikes. In Chapter 17, "Scaling Agility," you'll learn about ATDD and how to use the DoR during refinement events.

1.4.1 Conclusions

Here are the key points covered in this story:

- The agile analyst helps prevent last-minute integration issues through ATDD and behavior-driven development (BDD) practices.

- The agile analyst prepares features before implementation to avoid unnecessary rework.

---

4. Ken Schwaber and Jeff Sutherland, *The Scrum Guide: The Definitive Guide to Scrum—The Rules of the Game* (ScrumGuides.org, 2020), 10, https://www.scrumguides.org

5. The common way to do this is to create a feature file for the whole process or value stream in the backlog and specify end-to-end test scenarios using the Gherkin syntax. See Jens Engel, Benno Rice, and Richard Jones, "Feature Testing Setup," GitHub, © 2012–2019, https://behave.readthedocs.io/en/latest/gherkin.html

1.5 Story 2: The Cantankerous Customer

This story is about how you can get all the details right about agile practice but still fail if you don't pay sufficient attention to culture. The story began when I got some pushback from a director at a financial institution over some guidance that I had given her teams about estimation methods: I had advocated for the use of real-time estimates over a more abstract metric—story points. (I've since shifted my position on this issue.) As we were discussing the pros and cons of the approaches, I learned about the real problem behind this discussion: acrimonious planning meetings. I was told that during these meetings, the customer would often challenge individual developers on their estimation of effort. It was this friction that had caused her to abandon the use of real-time estimates.

When I first heard this, my initial reaction was, "There's nothing necessarily wrong with some friction. In agile development, the customer is *supposed to* negotiate and challenge the developers to find better ways to deliver value with less effort." But I found out that's not what was happening here. The customer and the team weren't negotiating about trade-offs; business stakeholders simply didn't *believe* the estimates given by the developers and testers. Now, this is *not* the kind of challenge that is encouraged in agile practice. To create an environment for requirements to emerge organically, you need, instead, to nurture a *collaborative* culture between business stakeholders and development. Each party is expected to respect, not challenge, the other's area of expertise.

Because of this negative experience, the director had become a strong advocate of story points—a relative versus absolute metric. As she explained it, story point estimation removed one of the most acrimonious issues from discussions—how much *time* a requirement item should take. In its place, it focused discussions on a much less controversial topic—the *relative effort* to implement one requirement item versus another.

I agreed with the director that the use of story points was a useful quick fix. However, to address the problem at its root, I suggested she look at the cultural issues at play. I advised she gain consensus on a bill of rights and responsibilities for the customer and the development team. One of those rights is the sole right of those *performing* the work to estimate the effort to do it. Balancing this right, customers have the right to decide what the requirements are and how to prioritize them in light of business value and cost. Customers also reserve the right to change their minds about that until implementation, without undue penalties. When rights and responsibilities are agreed upon up front, I argued, future confrontations can be avoided. In this book, you'll find detailed guidance on these issues. For example, in Chapter 5, "Preparing the Organization," you'll learn about customers' and developers' rights and responsibilities. In Chapter 11, "Quarterly and Feature Planning," and Chapter 14, "Iteration and Story Planning," you'll learn how to plan requirements with those rights in mind. And in Chapter 18, "Achieving Enterprise Agility," you'll be provided with a more expansive look at agile culture and what it means from an enterprise perspective.

1.5.1 Conclusions

Here are the key points covered in this story:

- Getting the culture right is key to success in any agile endeavor.

- Foster collaboration between the customer and developers by gaining consensus on a bill of rights and responsibilities for each side in the relationship.

- Those doing the work have the sole right to estimate the work, while the customer has the exclusive right to prioritize it.

1.6 Chapter Summary

Here are the key points covered in this chapter:

- Agile analysis and planning is about beginning with a vision and allowing detailed requirements to emerge through a process of iterative experimentation and feedback.

- Agile analysis reduces unnecessary rework by ensuring that integration issues are identified up front.

- Agile business analysts are critical to propagating cultural change.

1.7 What's Next?

Chapter 2 explores the fundamental concepts that underlie the agile business analysis competency and the rest of this book. The aim of that chapter is to level-set readers. If you already have a strong background in those areas, skip ahead to Chapter 3, "Fundamentals of Agile Analysis and Planning."

Chapter 2

Agile Analysis and Planning: The Value Proposition

Chapter 1, "The Art of Agile Analysis and Planning," presented my personal perspective on agile analysis and planning. This chapter examines the origin of the competency and the research concerning its efficacy. It first presents the parallel histories of the approaches that gave birth to agile analysis and planning: agile development and business analysis. It then reviews the research on the value proposition for a company developing the competency.

2.1 Objectives

This chapter will help you

- Understand the histories of business analysis, agile development, and agile analysis and planning.
- Know the benefits of business analysis and agile development.
- Understand the value added by including an effective agile analysis competency in an agile organization.

2.2 What Is Agile Analysis and Planning?

The short definition of agile analysis and planning is that it is business analysis (BA) plus planning as practiced in an agile context. That definition only helps, though, if you know what the individual terms mean. The following is a more formal definition based on the description introduced earlier in the book:

> **Agile analysis and planning** is the examination of a business or any aspect of it (culture, organizational structure, process, products, and more) to learn *what* needs to change and *when* in order to achieve a desired outcome in a

context that places a high premium on adaptability, resilience, and continuous innovation and value delivery. It includes analyzing who the product is for (the stakeholders), defining their requirements, determining when the capabilities will be delivered, and estimating costs and resources.

As explained in Chapter 1, I bundled BA together with requirements implementation planning because both are in a continual state of flux in agile development and therefore are inextricably linked. Changes to requirements and priorities affect the implementation plan, and changes to the plan affect the timing of the analysis. A more precise term for the discipline is *agile business analysis and planning*, since *analysis* without that qualifier could refer to any sort of analysis (e.g., financial, data, or systems analysis). For brevity, however, I more often use *agile analysis and planning* in this book. You'll occasionally see the even shorter term, *agile analysis*. Don't attach any special meaning to these variants; they all refer to the same competency.

As the definition points out, agile analysis and planning occurs in an environment that places a high value on adaptability and continuous delivery (CD). This context distinguishes it from traditional analysis and planning, where the business sets a higher value on *predictability* and sticking to a preset plan. This shift in context has a profound impact on the way the competency is carried out. For example, in a waterfall context, the requirements specifications and requirements implementation plan are frozen prior to development. Changes can be made but only after following a rigorous change management process. In agile development, however, we expect and even encourage changes to the requirements and plan because they enable the business to respond quickly to learning and adapt to the market.

You might think that the kinds of businesses that would value adaptability and continuous delivery—and thus be natural candidates for agile development—would be disruptive innovators. You'd be partially right: those companies use the approach because it enables them to test hypotheses for the product and respond effectively to learning. But agile development is also widely practiced by established companies because it provides them with the strategic capability to react to changes in the market and technology without sacrificing reliability.

2.3 Who Is a Business Analyst?

This book is primarily concerned with agile BA as a competency and a practice and is less concerned with the title of the person doing the work. Unless otherwise specified, when I use the term *business analyst* in this book, I mean *any* person engaged in BA activities, regardless of their formal title. In practice, those who perform these activities may have the title of business analyst, IT business analyst, team analyst, business systems analyst—or even a non-BA title such as requirements engineer, product owner, data analyst, tester, UX professional, or programmer.

This usage is in line with the International Institute for Business Analysis (IIBA), which defines a business analyst as follows: "any person who performs business analysis tasks described in the *BABOK® Guide*, no matter their job title or organizational role. Business analysts are responsible for discovering, synthesizing, and analyzing information from a variety of sources within an enterprise, including tools, processes, documentation, and stakeholders."[1]

In practice, organizations often use more fine-grained role names for subsets of BA responsibilities. For example, in many of the organizations with which I work, the business analyst is typically someone concerned with high-level business requirements, whereas the team analyst is concerned with detailed product requirements. As a general rule, I avoid these distinctions in this book: a business analyst, or analyst, is simply any practitioner of BA. The exception is a context where it's important to specify the role. For example, I may use the term team analyst when discussing guidelines that apply only to business analysts at the team level.

2.4 Why Agile Analysis and Planning?

In this chapter, you'll be looking at the research on the benefits of agile analysis and planning. To give you a more tangible feel, let's follow the story of one specific, fictionalized company: Customer Engagement One (CEO) Inc.

CEO is developing an app, also called CEO, that enables any business to manage its engagements with customers across multiple platforms. The early version of the app was built as a simple, monolithic system using an agile methodology. The typical change request could be accommodated by a single agile team working independently. Consequently, teams got by with minimal preparation and planning.

As the product grew, however, it became more complex. A typical change now required more competencies than could fit within a single agile team. Teams now needed to collaborate more frequently, but doing so was difficult with their current minimal approach. They began to suffer from bottlenecks as they waited for others to perform work they were dependent on. Features delivered by individual teams were inconsistent, leading to rework and delays. Stories couldn't be completed on time because there were essential requirements that were not well enough understood at the time estimates were made. The user experience of the app became fractured because teams didn't have a shared understanding of the vision for the product. The company had tried to launch a product-wide, strategic initiative to provide a more consistent experience but had given up because there never seemed to be enough teams ready at the same time to pull off a change of that size.

At this point, the development lead for CEO realized that the organization needed to spend more time on analysis and planning and develop more effective processes for carrying it out. Staff were trained in the competency and deployed to agile teams. Product owners were more productive because they could focus on market-facing responsibilities while team-level analysts took the lead on day-to-day team-facing activities.

The planning process in the organization was changed so that a portion of each team's budget was now reserved for strategic initiatives. These were planned quarterly. The rest of the budget was earmarked for customer-generated requests. These were planned using the Kanban approach to enable fast response to learning and customer feedback. Business

---

1. International Institute of Business Analysis (IIBA), *BABOK v3: A Guide to the Business Analysis Body of Knowledge*, 3rd ed. (Toronto, Canada: IIBA, 2015), 2–3.

analysts started to prepare features and user stories in advance of planning, resulting in improved estimates. This practice allowed teams to forecast completion dates better and coordinate their work in advance. As a result of these changes, the CEO was now able to take on large initiatives.

The previous story is not as fictional as I suggested. Other than the name, it's the story of an actual company. The agile analysis benefits that it describes are available to any company willing to spend the time and energy to develop the competency.

2.5 The Parallel Histories of Agile and Business Analysis

Agile analysis and planning is, as noted earlier, a hybrid of two disciplines: agile planning and development and BA. Figure 2.1 indicates how these two approaches co-evolved from the 1940s to 2017. Significant events in agile development are indicated in roman; events in BA are indicated in italic; those related to agile BA are shown in bold.

1940s: Kanban for Manufacturing

1950s: Lean Thinking (Toyota)

1980's: Objectory process, Boehm's Spiral Model

1991: Continuous Integration (CI) by Grady Booch

1994: DSDM Atern

1996: Scrum first developed

Late 90s: BA begins to appear in the wild

1999: Extreme Programming, User Stories

2001: Agile Development with Scrum published

2001: Agile Manifesto; Agile Alliance formed

2002: Test-Driven Development

2003: Lean Software Development

2003: IIBA founded

2005: LeSS (Bas Vodde & Crag Larman)

2005: IIBA CBAP certification implemented; BABOK 1 released

2006: International Requirements Engineering Board (IREB) founded in Germany

2007: Kanban for Software Development

2009: DevOps

2009: Lean Startup

2010 Jez Humble and David Farley introduce Continuous Delivery (CD)

2011: SAFe, **Use Case 2.0**

2015: PMI-PBA Certification introduced

2015: **Agile Extension to the BABOK Guide V1.0** published by IIBA

2017: **Agile Extension to the BABOK Guide V2.0** published by IIBA and Agile Alliance

2017: PMI publishes *Guide to Business Analysis* and Agile Practice Guide

2018: Jeff Sutherland releases the Scrum@Scale Guide

2020: The Scrum Guide, 2020; SAFe 5.0

Figure 2.1 *Agile business analysis timeline*

Following is a brief survey of that history, as summarized in the figure. We focus first on the history of BA, then on the concurrent evolution of agile development.

2.5.1 A Brief History of Business Analysis

Business analysts began to appear during the late 1990s when companies began to introduce the role into their software development organizations. The early focus of business analysts was on requirements—specifically, the discovery, creation, communication, management, and validation of software requirements. Today the BA competency covers a much broader scope up to and including enterprise and strategy analysis. *BABOK v3: A Guide to the Business Analysis Body of Knowledge (BABOK Guide)*, third edition, defines the practice as follows: "**Business analysis** is the practice of enabling change in an enterprise by defining needs and recommending solutions that deliver value to stakeholders. . . . Initiatives may be strategic, tactical, or operational."[2]

In 2005, the IIBA began to offer professional BA certification based on the *BABOK v3*. Other bodies soon followed suit: the International Requirements Engineering Board (IREB) introduced its Certified Professional for Requirements Engineering (CPRE) certification in 2007. The Project Management Institute (PMI) offered its PMI Professional in Business Analysis (PMI-PBA) certification in 2015.

2.5.2 A Brief History of Agile Development

The origins of agile development can be traced back to the 1940s and 1950s with the introduction of Kanban and lean thinking. Surprisingly, though these practices have become foundational to agile software development, they were developed for an entirely different business context—the manufacture and design of automobiles—and only later adapted for software.

As Figure 2.1 indicates, the spiral model and the objectory process (later known as Rational Unified Process [RUP]) were introduced in the 1980s. These processes were based on *iterative development*—the development of software in short cycles or iterations—an approach that was to become a central practice in agile development.

Two iterative frameworks were added in the mid to late 1990s: Scrum and Extreme Programming (XP). Both used a *timeboxed approach to planning*, whereby all the work for an upcoming iteration (the timebox) is committed to upfront. Today, Scrum is one of the most widely used agile frameworks—and even those who don't adopt the entire framework often use concepts and events popularized by Scrum, such as velocity and the daily standup. XP has contributed practices, such as pair programming. Its most significant impact on agile analysis and planning is the use of stories, story point estimation, and the Planning Game.

These various precursors to agile development came together in 2001 when seventeen people met in the Utah mountains and emerged with *The Agile Manifesto* and

---

2. IIBA, *BABOK v3*, 2.

12 *Principles behind the Manifesto.* Later that year, some of its authors and others formed the Agile Alliance, a nonprofit organization, to promote agile practices. Today, the organization has more than seventy-two thousand members.[3]

Since the writing of the Manifesto, many other frameworks and practices have been added to the agile family. These include test-driven development (TDD) and its extension, acceptance test–driven development (ATDD), and the Scaled Agile Framework (SAFe) for scaled agile organizations, released in 2011.

In 2009 and 2010, two essential practices were introduced that made it possible to deploy updates frequently without sacrificing reliability: DevOps and continuous delivery. These practices have enabled agile development to fully achieve its promise, as stated in its original principles, "to satisfy the customer through early and continuous delivery of valuable software." Using DevOps/continuous delivery practices, product improvements can be safely released multiple times per day instead of once every two to three months, as used to be the case when I was working in the 1990s when RUP was prevalent.

In practice, BA and agile development have been merging since the mid-1990s, when IT departments in large companies began to experiment with iterative development methodologies such as RUP. I worked with waterfall business analysts at that time to help them transition to an iterative-incremental approach using techniques such as use-case scenarios to plan requirements implementation. The official merger of the two streams happened in 2015 with the publication of the *Agile Extension to the BABOK Guide v1.0*, soon followed by a second version, jointly published by the IIBA and Agile Alliance in 2017. That same year, the PMI published the *Agile Practice Guide* for project leaders and project teams.

2.6 Two Diagnoses for the Same Problem

It's not entirely a coincidence that agile software development and BA both began around the same time—the 1990s and early 2000s. Both were responses to the same problem vexing software engineers at the time: a disturbingly high number of software projects were deemed failures. For example, the Standish Group's 1995 CHAOS Report found that 31.1 percent of projects were canceled before they were completed and that only 16.2 percent of software projects were completed on time and on budget.[4] Others reported that 64 percent of features were never, or rarely ever, used.[5] Business analysis and agile development were both proposed as ways to resolve this issue. However, they proceeded from different diagnoses of the underlying problem. Let's look at each diagnosis and the evidence regarding its success.

---

3. "About Agile Alliance," 2020, https://www.agilealliance.org/the-alliance

4. Project Smart, *The Standish Group Report: CHAOS* (Standish Group, 1995/2014), 3.

5. Mary Poppendieck and Tom Poppendieck, *Lean Software Development: An Agile Toolkit* (Boston: Addison-Wesley, 2003), 32. The authors quote a Standish Group study reporting 45 percent of developed features never used and 19 percent rarely used.

2.7 The Business Analysis Diagnosis

Business analysis began with the hypothesis that the root cause of project failure was communication—specifically, *poor communication* between business stakeholders and solution providers. There was ample research to back up this hypothesis. For example, the Standish Group reported at the time on the top ten causes of challenged projects.[6] The top two factors pointed to poor communication problems: lack of user input and incomplete requirements and specifications.[7] So did four other factors in the list: *unrealistic expectations, unclear objectives, changing requirements*, and *unrealistic timeframes*.

To address this root cause, some IT organizations began to define a new role—the IT business analyst. Initially, many business analysts were former systems analysts. I was one of those who made the transition—intrigued by the new competency because it included the stakeholder interactions I had come to enjoy as a systems analyst but without the technical aspects of the role. After years working at the cutting edge of technology, I was burning out and ready to make the switch.

Many other former IT developers did the same, but just as many moved to BA from business operations. The first business analysts that I trained were social workers who were about to be assigned to work as business analysts on a project to replace the case-management system they had been using. Today, I'd estimate that about half of today's business analysts come from the business side. That's a good thing because it means that those with in-depth knowledge of the users and business context for a software product can take a leadership role concerning its requirements.

2.8 The Business Analysis Track Record

The data indicate that the BA approach has been highly successful. Let's begin with growth metrics. In 2004, one year after IIBA was founded, it had thirty-seven members. Today it has almost thirty thousand members, more than one hundred twenty chapters in over forty countries.[8] PMI reports that "business analysis has become a competency of critical importance to project management."[9] It's doubtful we would be seeing this kind of growth and acceptance unless the BA competency was providing significant value.

What do software development organizations themselves think about the importance of BA to their success? Some insight is provided by the Standish Group's *CHAOS Report 2015*, which lists the main factors cited by organizations for project success. Table 2.1 summarizes the study's results.

---

6. Project Smart, *CHAOS*, 9.

7. Project Smart, 9.

8. IIBA, "About IIBA," 2020, https://www.iiba.org/about-iiba

9. Project Management Institute, "PMI Professional in Business Analysis (PMI-PBA)®," 2020, https://www.pmi.org/certifications/business-analysis-pba

Table 2.1   *CHAOS Factors of Success*

Factors of Success	Points	Investment
Executive Sponsorship	15	15%
Emotional Maturity	15	15%
User Involvement	15	15%
Optimization	15	15%
Skilled Resources	10	10%
Standard Architecture	8	8%
Agile Process	7	7%
Modest Execution	6	6%
Project Management Expertise	5	5%
Clear Business Objectives	4	4%

Source: Adapted from Standish Group International, *CHAOS Report 2015* (Standish Group, 2015), 11.

While the study doesn't explicitly call out BA, three of the top ten factors listed are directly addressed by the competency:[10]

1. *User Involvement:* Including user feedback, requirements review, basic research, prototyping, and other consensus-building tools.

2. *Clear Business Objectives:* The development of a shared understanding across all stakeholders and participants about the purpose of the project and how it aligns with the organization's goals and strategy.

3. *Optimization:* A structured process for improving business effectiveness.

You might have noticed that one of the other factors is *agile process.* We'll get back to that later in this chapter.

What does the data say about the impact of BA on cost? One of the most scientifically rigorous studies of its kind, the Business Analysis Benchmark,[11] found that organizations using poor requirements practices spent *62 percent more* on similarly sized projects than organizations using the *best* requirements practices.[12] Figure 2.2 illustrates how this added cost, referred to by the study's authors as the *requirements premium*, decreases to zero as requirements quality increases.

---

10. Shane Hastie and Stéphane Wojewoda, "Standish Group 2015 CHAOS Report—Q&A with Jennifer Lynch," 2015, https://www.infoq.com/articles/standish-chaos-2015

11. Keith Ellis, *Business Analysis Benchmark—The Impact of Business Requirements on the Success of Technology Projects* (Toronto, Canada: IAG, 2009), 2–3.

12. Ellis, *Business Analysis Benchmark.* Specifically, the study found that an organization with best requirements practices spent on average $3.63 million on a project originally estimated at $3 million, while an organization with poor requirements practices paid $5.87 million for a project estimated at $3 million—representing a 62 percent cost increase.

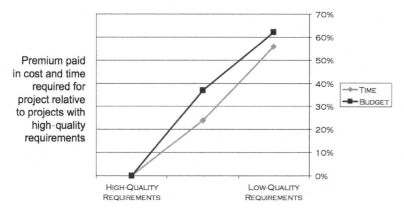

Source: IAG Business Analysis Benchmark, 2008

Figure 2.2 *Business requirements premium: average increase in the overrun on time or cost versus projects that used high-quality requirements. N = 109. (Source: Keith Ellis,* Business Analysis Benchmark—The Impact of Business Requirements on the Success of Technology Projects *[Toronto, Canada: IAG, 2009], 9.)*

The benefits don't end there. The report found that *every measure* in its study improved as requirements discovery and management maturity levels rose. These include:

- Percentage of projects delivered on time
- Percentage of projects delivered on budget
- Percentage of projects delivering all required features
- Percentage of projects deemed successful

The following are some of the other conclusions of the study regarding the benefits of BA:[13]

- In companies that have only an average level of requirements competency, the lack of excellence will consume approximately 41.5 percent of the IT development budget on strategic projects.
- Companies in the upper third of requirements capability report 54 percent of projects on time, on budget and on function and pay 50 percent less for their applications. In contrast, companies with a poor requirements capability had three times as many project failures as successes.
- Companies with excellent requirements processes reported that over 70 percent of their projects were successful.

Importantly, these benefits apply across all software development approaches. So, if your team is already experiencing the benefits of agile development, it will experience even more benefits by adding an effective BA capability.

---

13. Ellis, 8.

2.9 The Agile Diagnosis

In the late 1990s and early 2000s, as BA was being established, another hypothesis for project failures was evolving. It proposed that the root cause was the waterfall development process widely in use at the time and that the solution was to replace it with an approach referred to as *agile* development. *Waterfall* development is a predictive, sequential process wherein each step is completed before the next begins: first, a comprehensive needs and requirements analysis is performed up front; then a complete design is created and is followed by implementation, testing, and finally, release into production. Plans are made up front on the basis of requirements and other factors, and success is measured based on conformance to the plan. When projects failed, the waterfall answer was to enforce the process more strictly: do *even more* comprehensive analysis up front to ensure no critical requirements were missed and impose *stricter* controls on requirements changes. The problem was that no matter how hard companies tried, this approach didn't do much to move the needle. (Recall that disappointing 1995 *CHAOS Report*.)

The early agilists began to wonder if the problem wasn't with waterfall's assumptions of stability and predictability—noting that the opposite assumption is more often true: that software development often occurs under *volatile, unpredictable* conditions. Requirements often change after they've been baselined because of changing customer behaviors, market competition, new technology, new learning, and other factors. Instead of spending more time on upfront analysis and planning, the agilists proposed spending *less*. Instead of relying on a preset plan that was doomed to obsolescence the moment it was signed, they offered an adaptive approach that uses feedback to revise planning decisions throughout development to optimize *agility*—the ability to create and respond to change in order to succeed in an uncertain and turbulent environment.[14] The adjective *agile* can be used to describe a development process or organization that is responsive to change.

The agile toolkit draws from many sources. It includes workflow-management practices pulled from Kanban, guidelines for reducing waste from lean software development; events and techniques from the Scrum and XP frameworks; and scaled agile techniques from SAFe, DevOps, and continuous integration and continuous delivery (CI/CD). In the next chapter, we'll look at all these foundational approaches and their impact on the practice of agile analysis.

2.10 The Agile Track Record

Agile development is no longer an interesting theory; it's accepted practice. The *14th Annual State of Agile Report*[15] found that "95% of respondents report their software organizations practice Agile development methods" and that 61 percent have been doing so for three or more years. Fifty-one percent of respondents reported that more than half

---

14. Derived from Agile Alliance, *Agile 101* (Agile Alliance, 2020), https://www.agilealliance.org/agile101/

15. Digital.ai, *14th State of Agile Report*, 2020, 8, https://explore.digital.ai/state-of-agile/14th-annual-state-of-agile-report

or all of their teams were agile. Today, it is the presumed approach in most development organizations that I encounter.

Agile process was also cited as one of the top ten success factors for software development initiatives in the Standish Group's *CHAOS Report 2015*, as shown in Table 2.1. Table 2.2 summarizes the report's findings concerning the success of projects using agile versus waterfall approaches.

Table 2.2 *CHAOS Resolution by Agile versus Waterfall*

Size	Method	Successful	Challenged	Failed
All size projects	Agile	39%	52%	9%
	Waterfall	11%	60%	29%

Source: Adapted from Standish Group International, *CHAOS Report 2015* (Standish Group, 2015), 7.

As the table indicates, the use of an agile versus a waterfall method more than tripled the percentage of projects considered successful and reduced the percentage of failures to one-third that of the waterfall rate.

Agile development has also been shown to have a positive impact on productivity, with a 2015 QSM Associates study, commissioned by Rally Software, finding that "Agile projects experienced a 16% increase in productivity compared to [the] industry average."[16] It's worth noting, though, that this metric doesn't quite match the more extravagant claims made by Scrum's authors when the framework was introduced: "When we say Scrum provides higher productivity, we often mean several orders of magnitude higher, i.e., several 100 percents higher."[17]

One reason for the discrepancy is that if you do a feature-by-feature comparison, agile development probably costs almost as much as waterfall because savings are mostly offset by rework involved in agile's trial-and-error approach. Its benefit, however, lies elsewhere: in the effectiveness of the investment. Agile methods help the business quickly determine *which* features to develop and then get that minimum marketable product (MMP) to market quickly. In that respect, agile has been highly successful: according to a QSMA study, "Agile projects are 37% faster to market than [the] industry average."[18]

The evidence also suggests that agile development is leading to better products. In one study,[19] a full 78 percent of participants believed that using agile had led to higher stakeholder satisfaction.

---

16. Melinda Ballou, "As Agile Goes Mainstream, It's Time for Metrics," Rally Software Development, 2008, https://www.broadcom.com/products/software/agile-development/rally-software

17. Ken Schwaber and Mike Beedle, *Agile Software Development with Scrum.* (Upper Saddle River, NJ: Prentice Hall, 2002), viii.

18. QSM Associates, *The Agile Impact Report, Proven Performance Metrics from the Agile Enterprise* (Boulder, CO: Rally Software, 2015), 4.

19. A *Dr. Dobbs Journal* survey quoted by Mike Cohn reported that *78 percent of participants believed that using agile had led to higher stakeholder satisfaction.* See Mike Cohn, *Succeeding with Agile* (Boston: Addison-Wesley, 2010), 16.

2.11 Why Agile Teams Should Include an Effective BA Competency

With such a strong case for BA and agile development individually, you'd think the case for a competency that combined the two would be a slam dunk. The research bears this out. According to the *Business Analysis Benchmark*,[20] requirements maturity is closely correlated with success outcomes across all development approaches, including agile. Figure 2.3 illustrates its findings for organizations using agile development.

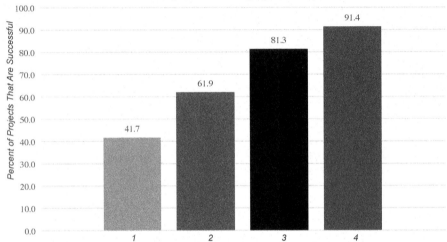

Source: Business Analysis Benchmark, 2009. IAG Consulting.

Figure 2.3 *Percentage of projects successful versus requirements maturity level for agile organizations. N = 437. (Source: Keith Ellis,* Business Analysis Benchmark—The Impact of Business Requirements on the Success of Technology Projects *[Toronto, Canada: IAG, 2009], from a file provided by the author summarizing research for the* Business Analysis Benchmark.)

The figure clearly shows that if your agile team doesn't yet include a strong BA competency, it should introduce one. For example, if your team is currently at the *lowest* requirements maturity level, it stands to *more than double* its success rates by moving

---

20. Ellis, *Business Analysis Benchmark*, from a file provided by the author on research for the report.

to the highest maturity level. A single-step increase from level 1 to level 2 results in a 49 percent increase in success rates.[21]

Interestingly, the report also showed that the impact on success rates of requirements maturity level alone was far more significant than the effect of development methodology alone.[22] If you hold the maturity level constant, the *maximum* improvement for organizations using agile versus waterfall methods is an 11.6 percent increase in project success rates (at maturity level 2)—not nearly as high as the doubling of rates that are possible when improving requirements maturity levels alone.

2.12 Chapter Summary

Here are the key points covered in this chapter:

- Agile development was launched with the publication of *The Agile Manifesto* in 2001.

- IIBA was founded in 2003.

- Research shows that increasing BA maturity levels results in improvements in the percentage of projects delivered on time, percentage of projects on budget, and percentage of projects delivering all required features.

- Research shows that an agile team that goes from a low requirements maturity level can double its success rates.

2.13 What's Next?

In this chapter, we looked at the business case for agile analysis and planning. In Chapter 3, "Fundamentals of Agile Analysis and Planning," we look at the fundamental concepts behind the competency.

---

21. Ellis, *Business Analysis Benchmark*.

22. According to the report, the greatest improvement for organizations using agile versus waterfall methods occurs at maturity level 2, where there is an 11.6 percent increase in project success rates (from 54.77% to 61.94% successful). The benefit is down to 4.4 percent at level 3, while at the extremes (levels 1 and 4), agile success rates are actually slightly worse than those of waterfall.

Chapter 3

Fundamentals of Agile Analysis and Planning

This chapter presents a crash course in the fundamentals of agile analysis and planning, including the concepts, frameworks, practices, professional organizations, and terminology that underlie the competency. For readers who are new to business analysis (BA) or agile development, it provides a foundational understanding for the rest of the book, introducing the International Institute for Business Analysis (IIBA), Project Management Institute (PMI), the Agile Alliance, Scrum, lean software development, Kanban, Scaled Agile Framework (SAFe), user stories, and more.

3.1 Objectives

This chapter will help you

- Understand the concepts, frameworks, and practices that underlie agile BA and the rest of this book.

- Understand how epics, features, and stories are used to represent requirements.

- Understand the two main approaches to agile planning: flow-based planning and timeboxed planning.

- Understand Kanban, Scrum, and Extreme Programming (XP).

- Understand the agile analysis contribution to eliminating the seven wastes identified in lean software development and to supporting lean practice.

3.2 What the Agile Manifesto Means for Business Analysis

In the previous two chapters, we learned that BA is practiced differently in an agile context than in a traditional waterfall process. To fully comprehend the impact of agile development on BA, you have to begin at the beginning, with the Agile Manifesto and "12 Principles behind the Agile Manifesto."

3.2.1 Agile Manifesto

The *Agile Manifesto*[1] lists the four core values of agile development:

> We are uncovering better ways of developing software by doing it and helping others do it. Through this work we have come to value:
>
> | | | |
> |---|---|---|
> | Individuals and interactions | over | processes and tools |
> | Working software | over | comprehensive documentation |
> | Customer collaboration | over | contract negotiation |
> | Responding to change | over | following a plan |
>
> That is, while there is value in the items on the right, we value the items on the left more.

As the last line of the Manifesto indicates, the Manifesto is a declaration of *relative* values, not *absolutes*: its aim is to minimize "items on the right," such as processes and documentation, not to *prohibit* them. It's an important distinction because if you believe there should be *no* planning in agile, then agile analysis and planning would not be a competency—it would be an oxymoron. Fortunately for its practitioners (and for you, if you are one), that's not the case.

3.2.2 The Impact of the First Value on Analysis

The first core value of the Manifesto is, "Individuals and interactions over processes and tools." In line with this value, agile requirements communication and management is lightweight, with a preference for direct, personal interactions with stakeholders and developers over formal procedures.

3.2.3 The Impact of the Second Value on Analysis

The second line of the Manifesto values "working software over comprehensive documentation." If you're a waterfall business analyst transitioning to agile, it means you'll be writing less requirements documentation than you're used to. Because the requirements

---

1. Agile Alliance, *The Agile Manifesto*, 2001, https://www.agilealliance.org/agile101/the-agile-manifesto

are captured and communicated just before they're needed, you don't have to write as much down to avoid misunderstandings.

3.2.4 The Impact of the Third Value on Analysis

The third line of the Manifesto values "customer collaboration over contract negotiation." If you've formerly been a waterfall business analyst, this value represents a fundamental shift in how you interact with solution providers and business stakeholders. Instead of providing comprehensive specifications up front that can be used as the basis for contractual commitments, your focus shifts to helping business and development collaborate throughout development on requirements discovery.

3.2.5 The Impact of the Fourth Value on Analysis

The fourth line of the Manifesto values the "ability to respond easily to change over following a plan." This value has a profound impact on requirements change management and implementation planning. If you're working on a waterfall project, the requirements and the implementation plan are frozen before implementation. Any changes after that trigger a formal change process. On an agile initiative, you don't freeze the requirements, and only a lightweight process is needed to change them.

3.3 What the Twelve Principles Mean for Business Analysis

The Agile Alliance backed up the Manifesto with the following twelve principles. I've used *italics* to highlight areas of particular interest to BA.

1. Our highest priority is to satisfy the customer through e*arly and continuous delivery of valuable software.*

2. *Welcome changing requirements*, even late in development. Agile processes harness change for the customer's competitive advantage.

3. *Deliver working software frequently*, from a couple of weeks to a couple of months, with a preference for the shorter timescale.

4. *Business people and developers must work together daily throughout the project.*

5. Build projects around motivated individuals. Give them the environment and support they need, and trust them to get the job done.

6. The *most efficient and effective method of conveying information* to and within a development team is *face-to-face conversation.*

7. Working software is the primary measure of progress.

8. Agile processes promote sustainable development. The sponsors, developers, and users should be able to maintain a constant pace indefinitely.

9. Continuous attention to technical excellence and good design enhances agility.

10. *Simplicity—the art of maximizing the amount of work not done—is essential.*

11. The best architectures, requirements, and designs emerge from *self-organizing teams.*

12. At regular intervals, *the team reflects on how to become more effective*, then tunes and adjusts its behavior accordingly.[2]

Principle 1 emphasizes that delivery must have value. As an agile business analyst, you help the team follow this principle by helping ensure it is always occupied with work of the highest value. For example, you negotiate with developers to explore alternatives that deliver similar value at lower cost. Agile Principles 2, 4, and 6 revisit BA issues raised in the Manifesto: changing requirements, customer collaboration, and reliance on conversation over documentation.

Principle 3 is to deliver software frequently. While this principle doesn't refer explicitly to analysis, it has a profound impact on how you practice it: because of agile's frequent delivery cycles, you have to decompose requirements into units small enough to be developed within a short timeframe. This decomposition isn't trivial. It turns out to be one of the most challenging problems business analysts face when they begin practicing in an agile development environment. We deal at length with this issue in Chapter 13, "Story Preparation."

Principle 10 is "Simplicity—the art of maximizing the amount of work not done—is essential." As an agile business analyst, you practice this principle by minimizing upfront analysis and delaying all analysis until the *last responsible moment*—the point at which the cost of a further delay outweighs the benefits. In so doing, you reduce wasted effort on requirements that will later be changed or abandoned.

Principle 11 calls for *self-organizing teams* and shared team responsibility. With self-organization, the team decides who takes on which role depending on the work being done—and this can change from day to day. What that means for you is that you or any other team member with the necessary skills might be doing analysis one day and something else, such as testing, on another day.

I should point out, though, that this principle is rarely practiced in its pure form. In the absence of a formal leader, an informal leader often emerges. Rather than full self-organization, today's agile teams are self-managing under the direction of a leader who serves (aka a servant-leader). In this model, the leader's purpose is to provide vision, serve team members, and support their growth as persons.[3]

For more on agile leadership, see Chapter 17, section 17.6.1, and Chapter 18, "Achieving Enterprise Agility."

2. Agile Alliance, "12 Principles behind the Agile Manifesto," 2001, https://www.agilealliance.org/agile101/12-principles-behind-the-agile-manifesto

3. Robert K. Greenleaf Center for Servant Leadership, "The Servant as Leader," 2016, https://www.greenleaf.org/what-is-servant-leadership

Principle 12 calls for self-reflection by the team. As an agile business analyst, you support this principle during team retrospectives by providing team members with an external perspective on the team's performance, as seen by business stakeholders and customers.

3.4 Practices, Standards, and Frameworks

Let's now turn from the Agile Manifesto and the twelve principles to other practices, standards, and frameworks that underlie agile analysis and planning.

3.4.1 Business Analysis Standards

Agile BA is an extension of a more general competency, business analysis. As a working professional in this area, you should understand the basic concepts, standards, and professional bodies that underlie and govern the discipline. The following is an overview of those items.

3.4.1.1 BABOK *(IIBA) and Business Analysis Practice Guide (PMI)*

BABOK: A Guide to the Business Analysis Body of Knowledge (BABOK Guide) is IIBA's guide to the BA discipline and a basis for its certification path. Its most popular professional certification is the *Certified Business Analysis Professional (CBAP)*. As an agile business analyst, you'll also be interested in *The Agile Extension to the BABOK Guide*, copublished by IIBA and the Agile Alliance, to address BA in the context of agile development.

Following IIBA, the PMI developed its own BA certification—the *PMI Professional in Business Analysis (PMI-PBI)*—and published its BA guide, the *Business Analysis Practice Guide*. The PMI also worked with the Agile Alliance to publish *The Agile Practice Guide*, focusing on the project leader and project team perspective. The *International Requirement Engineering Board (IREB)* offers the *Certified Professional for Requirements Engineering (CPRE)*, a certificate aimed at those working in requirements engineering, BA, and testing. (Full disclosure: I have acted as a reviewer for both IIBA's *BABOK Guide* and PMI's *Business Analysis Practice Guide*.)

IIBA and PMI guides break down the BA competency into domains of expertise. As you'll see, there's a lot of similarity between the two main guides.

3.4.1.2 BABOK *Knowledge Areas*

The third edition of *BABOK Guide* divides the BA competency into six knowledge areas (KAs):

1. *Business Analysis Planning and Monitoring*: Planning and coordinating analysis activities

2. *Elicitation and Collaboration*: Eliciting requirements from stakeholders and collaborating with them throughout the lifecycle

3. *Requirements Lifecycle Management:* Managing and tracing requirements and changes across the development lifecycle

4. *Strategy Analysis:* Identifying strategic business needs and developing strategies to address them

5. *Requirements Analysis and Design Definition:* Organizing, specifying, and modeling requirements

6. *Solution Evaluation:* Evaluating solution performance

3.4.1.3 PMI Guide Domains

PMI's *Business Analysis Practice Guide* specifies five BA domains:

Domain 1—Needs Assessment: Analyzing the problem or opportunity, goals, objectives, business case, organizational changes

Domain 2—Business Analysis Planning: Planning the Business Analysis Approach; analyzing stakeholders

Domain 3—Requirements Elicitation and Analysis: Eliciting, analyzing and creating high-quality requirements in an iterative-incremental manner

Domain 4—Traceability and Monitoring: Managing requirements and requirements attributes; managing changes to requirements; tracing requirements

Domain 5—Solution Evaluation: Evaluating a solution

IIBA and PMI guides define several terms that underlie BA practice—a baseline of concepts for the practicing analyst. These are summarized next.

3.4.2 Requirements-Related Terminology

You'll be encountering various BA and requirements terms throughout this book. These terms are often used in different ways by different people. To avoid confusion, let's clarify how they will be used in this book.

3.4.2.1 Product Vision Statement

The **product vision statement** is a single sentence or phrase that describes the reason for creating the product.[4]

3.4.2.2 Business Goal

A **business goal** is something the business aspires to. Goals should be measurable and timebound. For example, a goal may relate to revenue, profitability, customer service, or customer retention.

---

4. Roman Pichler, "8 Tips for Creating a Compelling Product Vision," October 8, 2014, https://www.romanpichler.com/blog/tips-for-writing-compelling-product-vision

Example business goals:

- Increase sales by 10 percent by the end of the year
- Grow membership by 8 percent by date X.
- Establish an enterprise-wide assortment planning capability by the end of the year.

Goals may be expressed for various levels. A business goal refers to a desired high-level outcome at the C-level (executive) or below.

3.4.2.3 Business Objective

A **business objective** is a lower-level outcome (i.e., below the enterprise level). Objectives should also be measurable and timebound.

Example business objectives:

- Provide the ability to promote services and benefits by the third quarter.
- Merchandising will drive top-line sales by 2.5 percent due to the ability to establish localized assortments, by X.

3.4.2.4 Requirements

A **requirement** is "a usable representation of a need. . . . The nature of the representation may be a document (or set of documents), but can vary widely depending on the circumstances."[5] Requirements should be measurable, testable, and timebound. *BABOK Guide* describes four requirements types: business requirements, stakeholder requirements, solution requirements, and transition requirements. I like to add another: user requirements. These are described in the next sections.

3.4.2.5 Business Requirements

Business requirements are high-level needs, goals, and objectives of the organization. They should express *what* needs to happen, not *how*. They should be measurable and timebound.

Example business requirement:

Provide a directory of services by the end of the quarter.

---

5. International Institute of Business Analysis (IIBA), *BABOK v3: A Guide to the Business Analysis Body of Knowledge*, 3rd ed. (Toronto, Canada: IIBA, 2015), 15.

3.4.2.6 Stakeholder Requirements

Stakeholder requirements describe the "needs of stakeholders that must be met in order to achieve the business requirements."[6] The analysis is typically midlevel—not detailed enough for designing a solution.

3.4.2.7 User Requirements

User requirements describe the user's experience *using* the product. User requirements should be solution-agnostic. They act as a bridge between higher-level stakeholder requirements and more detailed solution requirements. User stories and use cases are examples of ways to represent user requirements.

User requirements per se should not include design or detailed functional specifications, but you can use them as a frame upon which to hang those specifications. For example, a user story or use case for a search function may include a link to a performance requirement.

3.4.2.8 Solution Requirements

Solution requirements describe the characteristics of a solution in enough detail to design a solution. Two subcategories of solution requirements are functional requirements and nonfunctional requirements.

3.4.2.9 Functional Requirements

Functional requirements (FRs) describe the required behaviors of the solution. These are often expressed from the perspective of the system.

Example FRs:

- The ability to search by product code, name, or category
- Compliance with specified business rules
- Expected system behavior when a precondition or system fails
- Data validation rules

3.4.2.10 Nonfunctional requirements

Nonfunctional requirements (NFRs) are so called because they do not directly specify functionality. Rather, they describe how well the system must perform in its intended environment and how it should respond to constraints on its behavior. NFRs are also called **service-level requirements** (SLRs), **supplementary requirements**, and **quality requirements**. There are many different kinds of NFRs. Let's look at the common ones.

---

6. IIBA, *BABOK v3*, 16.

Scalability is the ability of the solution to grow and accommodate increased demand or scope. For example, "The solution should be built to accommodate twice the current volume while still meeting performance requirements."

Reliability describes the level of resiliency of the system. For example, "Mean time between failures (MTBF) shall not exceed X."

Availability is the ability of the solution to perform its agreed function when required. It includes the specification of when and how the business can access the solution. For example, "System should be available 24/7 during year X."

Recoverability describes how quickly the solution should be made available following an outage. For example, "Time to restore service following an outage shall not exceed 1 hour."

Capacity is the amount of data or services that the solution can manage. For example, "The system will maintain 5 years of historical data" and "The system will support 1,000 simultaneous users."

Maintainability is the ability of the system to be changed or repaired easily and its ability to react to an expanded user base or new business units. For example, "The system will be configurable to support new business units without additional coding."

Security is the ability to ensure the confidentiality, integrity, and availability of assets, information, and services. For example, "The system will authenticate all users via XYZ single sign-on (SSO)."

Data integrity is the ability to manage data consistency across the business. For example, "All APIs will follow architecture best practice to ensure data structures are aligned across consuming systems."

Interoperability is the ease with which the solution may be used with other software systems. For example, "The solution will be compatible with X."

Usability is the extent to which its intended users can use the solution with effectiveness, efficiency, and satisfaction. For example, "The solution shall prompt users to confirm financial transactions after successfully entering transaction details."

Other examples of NFRs include **performance requirements, compliance** with industry standards, and **redundancy requirements.** The management of NFRs within an agile requirements process is discussed in Chapter 8, "Seeding the Backlog—Discovering and Grading Features."

3.4.2.11 Transition Requirements

The last requirements type, **transition requirements,** are requirements that describe how the solution will be deployed and released into production—such as migration and training requirements.

3.4.2.12 Why Terminology Is (and Is Not) Important

The main benefit of knowing these requirements types is to help you ensure that someone (even if it's not you) is responsible for capturing them. That said, it's *not* worth spending precious hours debating whether a requirement belongs to one category or another; the important thing is to ensure it is included somewhere!

3.4.2.13 Trace Goals to Requirements

An important aspect of your responsibilities as an analyst is to trace requirements items and other BA information to other items. An item may be traced to an item of the same type (e.g., goal to goal, requirement to requirement), to items below it (e.g., objective to user requirement), and to items above it (e.g., functional requirement to business requirement).

Figure 3.1 is an example of a goal to grow membership and its relationships with the requirements that support that goal.

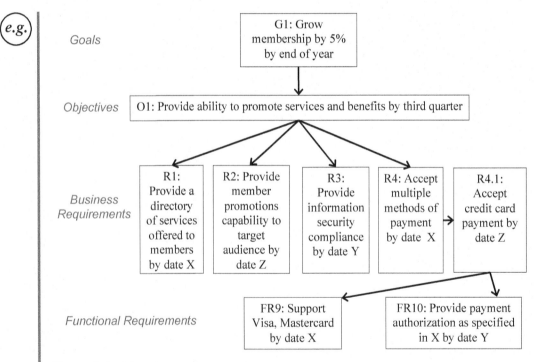

Figure 3.1 *Mapping goals to requirements*

3.4.2.14 Assumptions

An **assumption** is "an influencing factor that is believed to be true but has not been confirmed to be accurate, or that could be true now but may not be in the future."[7] In traditional

---

7. IIBA, 441.

waterfall BA, you would remove assumptions before development. In agile development, you treat assumptions that can't be verified up front as hypotheses to be tested through experimentation.

3.4.2.15 Constraint

A **constraint** is "an influencing factor that cannot be changed, and that places a limit or restriction on a possible solution or solution option."[8] Constraints may be business constraints—such as cost limits—or technical ones, such as constraints on supported platforms and programming languages.

3.4.2.16 Business Rule

A **business rule** is "a specific, practicable, testable directive that is under the control of the business and that serves as a criterion for guiding behavior, shaping judgments, or making decisions."[9]

Business rules are not "requirements" in and of themselves because they are inherent properties of the business: they would exist independently of a software development initiative. However, they become tied to the requirements when a solution is required to *comply* with them.

BABOK v3 differentiates between two kinds of business rules: behavioral and definitional. **Behavioral business rules** are rules that the organization chooses to enforce as a matter of policy. An example is the rule that an insurance policy must be verified before an adjustment is performed on a claim. Behavioral business rules covered in this book include decision tables that proscribe the required response to various input conditions.

Definitional business rules describe business concepts and objects and their relationships with each other as well as calculations and derivation methods (e.g., how to derive a student's final grade). Definitional rules are expressed in the structural model—sometimes referred to as the *business domain model*, *class diagrams*, or *business-perspective entity-relationship diagram* (ERD).

3.4.2.17 Milestone

A **milestone** is a significant event or achievement.

Examples milestones:

- We will be using the planning tool for ski and winter sports items by the end of the first quarter.

- Use of the planning tool will spread to travel and kids' items by the end of the second quarter.

---

8. IIBA, 444.

9. IIBA, 443.

3.4.2.18 Requirements Units

In agile analysis, you decompose requirements into small items that can be developed within a short time—anywhere from a day or two to about eight days, depending on the practice. What you call these items depends on the framework you're using. Scrum refers to them as **product backlog items (PBIs)**; XP calls them **stories**; Kanban refers to them as **work items**. In *Use-Case 2.0*,[10] they're referred to as *use-case slices*. The most commonly used term is *story*.

Requirements items—or work items—that are bigger than the story size limit are referred to by names that indicate their size. Although there is no single consensus on terminology, the usage that follows is common. It's the one I use in this book.

3.4.2.19 From Epics to Features to Stories

Figure 3.2 illustrates the relationship between epics, features, and stories. An epic is decomposed into features, and each feature is decomposed into stories.

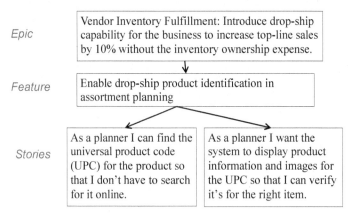

Figure 3.2 *Decomposing an epic*

3.4.2.20 Epics

In its original usage, *epic* simply meant a requirements item larger than a story. However, today it's common to reserve the term for the largest work items. The following definition is in line with that usage: an **epic** is a large, product-level work item that may require multiple teams over multiple quarters. The value delivered by an epic represents a high-level capability of the product affecting a user or group of users. For example, an epic may deliver

- A top-level menu item on the user interface (e.g., customer management, suppliers, orders).

- A functional area of a product.

---

10. Ivar Jacobson, Ian Spence, and Kurt Bittner, *Use-Case 2.0: The Guide to Succeeding with Use Cases* (London: Ivar Jacobson International SA, 2011).

- The expansion of an existing capability.

- A business process, or a step in a process or value stream.

- A project.

- Internal improvements.

3.4.2.21 Feature

A **feature** is a product-level work item that can be completed by one or more teams within one quarter, release cycle, or SAFe Program Increment (PI). A feature should represent a characteristic of a product that a user or group of users or customers care about. It is not a fine-grained requirement, but rather something significant enough to be highlighted to customers in marketing materials.

The above definition is in line with frameworks such as SAFe and *Use Case 2.0*. Note, though, that others may use the term differently. For example, in XP, a feature is a story; others use the term to refer to a set of user stories that should be released at the same time.

3.4.2.22 Story

Let's now return to the term *story* and define it more precisely. A **story** is a work item that *delivers value*, sized so that it can be implemented by a single team within a short period of time. The story size limit may vary from a day or two to about two weeks, depending on the approach and the team.

3.4.2.23 User Story

The recipient of the value delivered by a story—the actor who wants it—may be a user, a technical architect, sponsor, marketing representative, or software component. When the entity who wants the story is a user, the story is referred to as a *user story*.

A user story is "something a user wants,"[11] described from the user's perspective. Like any story, a user story must be small.

A User Story Is a Reminder to Have a Conversation

A User Story is not a requirement in the traditional sense. It is only a *reminder* to talk about a requirement; the details are expected to come out in the conversation itself. You may or may not be writing down the result of that conversation. For example, you might document it on a Note physically posted onto a Story card, document it elsewhere, or not document the conversation at all and rely on verbal communication.

User Story Templates

You should express stories in the language of the customer. You don't have to follow any particular format, but one template has become popular because it captures the main

---

11. Mike Cohn, "User Stories, Epics and Themes," Mountain Goat Software, October 24, 2011, https://www.mountaingoatsoftware.com/blog/stories-epics-and-themes

points about a story. It's referred to as the **Role-Feature-Reason,** or **Connextra,** template, and it looks like this:

"As a [user role] I want [function] so that [business value]."

3.4.2.24 Acceptance Criteria

Supply each feature and story with acceptance criteria that describe the conditions required for the stakeholder to consider the requirement "done." You can write acceptance criteria in an informal manner (e.g., "I can search by title"), or you can follow a template, such as the Gherkin template, discussed in Chapter 13, section 13.10.9.

3.4.2.25 Themes

Sometimes you're going to want to group stories for reasons other than that they are all components of a feature or epic. In that case, you can group them into themes. A **theme** is a grouping that may be based on any criterion. Typically, a theme represents a business objective communicated to customers (e.g., image recognition, two-factor authentication).

3.4.2.26 Story Estimation

One way to estimate a story is to use **story points,** a relative measure of effort. Alternatively, you can use time-based units, such as **ideal developer days** (IDDs). **Velocity** refers to the number of these units a team delivers within a given amount of time (e.g., within a two-week iteration).

Points and IDDs are usually allocated using the Fibonacci series: 0, 1, 2, 3, 5, 8, 13, and so on. At the start of a new venture, a point is typically set to be roughly equal to one IDD. The maximum story points for a story is often set to 8, representing the number of available days in a two-week period, or iteration. (Two of the ten workdays are assumed to be lost to planning and other work not directly related to feature implementation.)

3.4.2.27 Feature Lifecycle

As discussed earlier, a feature is a large requirement item, big enough to matter to customers. In agile processes, each feature goes through something like its own waterfall lifecycle—first analyzed, then coded, tested, and deployed. Unlike waterfall, though, this lifecycle is iterative and "porous" in that there is overlap between the steps. Figure 3.3 illustrates the lifecycle of a feature, using the feature statuses proposed by Jacobson.[12]

The figure illustrates the following lifecycle:

- A feature begins as a *requested* item, at which time it is in the backlog but is not yet active, sequenced, or estimated.

- The feature is considered *ready* once it has been prepared well enough for implementation to begin. If the organization is practicing quarterly planning, a feature must be in the ready state before you can include it in the quarterly plan.

---

12. Ivar Jacobson, "Feature State Cards," Ivar Jacobson International, https://s3.amazonaws.com/ss-usa/companies/MzawMDE1MTI2AwA/uploads/Feature_State_Cards_3_9.pdf

- A feature is considered *committed* when it has been assigned to a lead team, and all teams required for its implementation have committed to it.

- A feature is considered to be *previewed* once it has been discussed. This preview discussion typically begins about one or two iterations before implementation. The feature is then decomposed into stories.

- Once enough of a feature's functionality has been implemented to satisfy the customer, the feature is deemed *accepted*. Accepted doesn't necessarily mean that *all* the feature's stories have been implemented—only that *enough* have been implemented for the feature to be releasable (i.e., that it would deliver significant value to the customer if released to the market).

- Once the feature is accepted, it may quickly transition to the deployed state (presuming continuous delivery capabilities are available), or its deployment may be delayed so it can be released with other features at the end of the quarter.

Once the feature has been deployed into production and delivered to the user, the feature is considered *released*. Once a feature's value has been proven in the marketplace, the feature moves to the *validated* state, after which it undergoes continuous improvement.

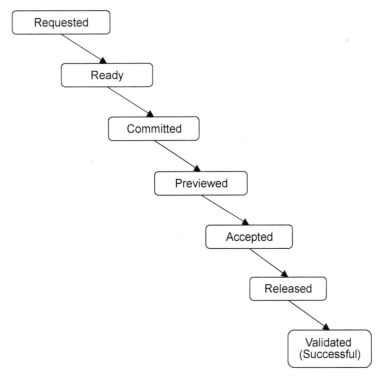

Figure 3.3   *Feature lifecycle*

3.4.3 Agile Planning

Agile planning is particularly challenging because it has to accommodate late changes. The way you do that is by delaying planning decisions as much as possible so that they can be made on the basis of the most current information possible. There are two broad agile planning approaches for carrying this out: the flow-based approach (e.g., Kanban), in which commitments are made just before the implementation of each item, and time-boxed planning (e.g., Scrum), in which commitments are made earlier, at the start of the planning period. As we'll see, a good rule of thumb is to use a mix of the two approaches: flow-based planning for smaller, customer-driven work items that affect one or two teams and timeboxed planning for strategic, product-level initiatives. Let's explore each of these options further.

3.4.3.1 Flow-Based Planning

In single-item flow-based planning (e.g., Kanban), you commit to features and stories on an item-by-item basis just before implementation. This approach provides the most adaptability because the customer can reprioritize a requirement right up until its implementation. It's the preferred approach for customer-driven work items, especially when they involve local changes that can be accomplished by one or two teams (e.g., a story to change the options for viewing a user's messages). This approach is also recommended when developing novel products because it accelerates learning.

The downside is that if you use only this approach, you can find yourself in a situation where teams are rarely free at the same time to take on large product-level work items, since each one is working to the beat of its own drummer. As a result, strategic initiatives can end up sitting on the shelf for long periods. For that reason, most large organizations should reserve some of their teams' budgets for timeboxed planning, as discussed next.

3.4.3.2 Timeboxed Planning

In timeboxed planning (e.g., Scrum, SAFe), all of the work items for a given period (the timebox) are committed to up front at the same time. It's common to define a long timebox of about a quarter and smaller timeboxes within it of about one to two weeks, referred to as iterations (or sprints in Scrum). Typically, this plays out as follows: All teams within a group meet at the start of each quarter to plan and commit to multiteam features over the quarter. They meet again at the start of each iteration to commit to the team-level stories that they'll be working on.

This is the preferred approach for large, strategic initiatives involving multiple teams because it ensures that all teams are free to take on large work items at the same point in time. An example of a product-wide initiative that benefits from this approach is the implementation of a consistent user experience across the product. Frameworks that use the timeboxed approach include Scrum, XP, and SAFe. The Scrum framework includes sprint planning but not quarterly planning.

I don't recommend quarterly planning, however, for localized, customer-driven features. The reason is that it requires commitment at the start of the quarter based on the information available *at that time* rather than the more current information available just prior to implementation. It's true that even with this approach, all parties are *supposed* to agree that upfront commitments to features are provisional, not absolute—and that last-minute changes *should* be accommodated. In practice, though, teams tend to be reluctant to make changes once a plan is written down. Consequently, if the customer wants to add a new feature based on learning that occurred partway through the quarter, the feature often has to wait until the start of the next quarter. Even worse, if the learning occurs in the latter half of a quarter, the new feature won't be included until the following two quarters because the upcoming quarter will already have been planned.

3.4.3.3 Why a Mixed Planning Approach Is Preferred

As noted earlier, organizations that use flow-based (Kanban) planning for all of their work can find that big initiatives end up sitting on the back burner. Their products also tend to become disjointed because each team is focusing only on localized issues. On the other hand, organizations that rely too heavily on timeboxed planning suffer from inordinately long learning cycles and decision-making that isn't based on the most current knowledge. For these reasons, as a rule of thumb, most large development organizations do best with a mix of the two approaches.

For more on agile planning in a scaled organization, see Chapter 17, section 17.9.

3.4.3.4 What About the Delivery Cadence?

Everything we've been talking about relates specifically to the intake side of the equation: the acceptance of requirements items into an implementation plan. The considerations are very different with respect to the output side—the delivery of releasable items to the customer. On that score, the recommendation is more straightforward: wherever possible, use the flow-based approach to deliver requirements items. With this approach, each work item is integrated and tested as soon as it's done, so that it is in a releasable state should the customer choose to deploy it immediately to the market. To accomplish this at scale with confidence, the organization needs to adopt continuous integration and continuous delivery (CI/CD) and DevOps practices. If these capabilities are not present, it may be necessary to wait until the end of the iteration, quarter, or release cycle to integrate and test completed stories.

For more on DevOps, see Chapter 17, section 17.5.2.1

3.4.4 Agile Frameworks

Let's now turn to the agile frameworks you need to know about and their impact on analysis and planning. Keep in mind that it's most likely that your organization will be using a hybrid of best practices from various sources as opposed to strictly adhering to a single framework. For example, it might use Kanban's approach to flow-based planning, add in Scrum tools such as daily standups and burndown charts to monitor progress, and use XP stories to specify work items.

3.4.4.1 Kanban

Kanban was developed in the 1950s for automobile manufacturing and is now widely used for software development. For example, Kanban is listed as one of the twenty-two tools of lean software development. Kanban doesn't include the concept of fixed iterations, since items progress on a piece-by-piece basis.

One of the important insights of Kanban is that simple rules and visual cues can effectively govern sophisticated behavior. The Kanban process plays out as follows: You represent each work item (e.g., a feature or story) as a card on a Kanban Board. You create a column, or *queue*, for each status that needs to be differentiated and tracked. Then you move the cards across the columns from left to right, as their status changes. You move them up or down within a column to indicate relative priority.

The flow across the columns is governed by a few simple rules: A work-in-progress (WIP) limit is set for each queue. Whenever the number of items in a queue falls below the WIP limit, a developer associated with the queue pulls the topmost work item from the queue to its left. Once the number of items in a queue reaches the WIP limit, no more items may be added to the WIP column until an item has left the queue.

3.4.4.2 Scrum

Scrum was created by Ken Schwaber and Jeff Sutherland and was presented at the OOPSLA (Object-Oriented Programming, Systems, Languages, and Applications) conference in 1995. Its creators describe Scrum as "a lightweight framework that helps people, teams and organizations generate value through adaptive solutions for complex problems."[13] The approach is defined in the *Scrum Guide*, which you can download for free at Scrum.org.

Scrum is very popular in IT departments of mainstream businesses. Its popularity is likely due to a confluence of factors:

- The Scrum process provides a structure for planning and status reporting.

- Scrum sets a development cadence (one or two weeks to one month) that many mainstream organizations can comfortably live with.

- Scrum has a well-marketed certification process.

Scrum is out of favor in some agile quarters because items are committed at the start of an iteration (referred to as a *sprint*) rather than later on the basis of more current priorities. Another complaint has been that the framework is overly accepting of longer delivery cycles rather than viewing CD as the norm, though this concern has been addressed in the 2020 Scrum Guide.[14]

Despite these objections, Scrum is an excellent choice for large product-level work items because it results in teams who are free at the same time (the start of a sprint) to

---

13. Ken Schwaber and Jeff Sutherland, *The Scrum Guide: The Definitive Guide to Scrum—The Rules of the Game*, Scrumguides.org, 2020, 3, https://www.scrumguides.org
14. "The Sprint Review should never be considered a gate to releasing value." *Scrum Guide*, 12.

make commitments. If you choose Scrum, use timeboxing to govern the flow of items going *into* an iteration (sprint)—but not to delay the flow of items through integration and testing at the tail end of their lifecycle.

Even if your organization does not explicitly use the Scrum framework, it likely uses some of its elements and ceremonies, such as the daily standup, product backlog, and retrospectives. These are summarized next.

The Sprint

Scrum uses the term **sprint** to refer to an iteration. (In this book, unless referring specifically to Scrum, I use the more generic term *iteration*.) A sprint is a period of up to one month during which a potentially releasable increment is created. Typical sprint durations are one or two weeks. An **increment** is an updated version of the software containing all the enhancements implemented during the sprint and including enhancements made in all previous sprints.

Note that an increment does not *have* to be released to the general market by the end of every sprint; it just has to be potentially *releasable*. For example, it might be released into a staging environment or released into production but with the changes concealed from the general user population until a later date. You might decide to delay exposure to the user because the feature is not yet competitive enough for general release or because a completed feature is not marketable until other stories in the value stream are also available.

The Product Backlog

In Scrum, requirements reside in a product backlog. The **product backlog** is "an emergent, ordered list of what is needed to improve the product. It is the single source of work undertaken by the Scrum Team."[15]

Each requirement item in the backlog is referred to as a **product backlog item** (PBI). Scrum places few restrictions on what a PBI can be or how it should be documented. The product backlog is a dynamic artifact, with requirements items added, dropped, re-sequenced, and refined throughout the development cycle.

Scrum and the Business Analysis Competency

Scrum does not allow designated roles for team members because this would run counter to its support for self-organizing teams. However, it does refer to the team's responsibility for activities within the BA domain, such as "stakeholder collaboration, verification."[16]

The Product Owner and Business Analysis

The product owner (PO) is accountable for managing and prioritizing the product backlog. While backlog management responsibilities largely overlap with those of BA, the prioritization of backlog items lies outside its scope.

---

15. Schwaber and Sutherland, *The Scrum Guide*, 10.
16. Schwaber and Sutherland, 5.

The ScrumMaster and Business Analysis

The focus of the ScrumMaster role is to ensure that the Scrum guidelines are carried out and that impediments are removed from the team's path. Responsibilities that overlap with BA include "helping find techniques for effective . . . Product Backlog management" and "facilitating stakeholder collaboration."[17] We look at these more closely in the section on BA roles in agile.

Transparency

In place of control through comprehensive planning, Scrum offers control through **transparency**.[18] Examples of transparency in Scrum include its requirement that working code be demonstrated every sprint and that the progress of PBIs be visible to the business and team members.

> Recently I learned that a group of stakeholders were told by developers that they wouldn't be able to see the product backlog because "you don't use one in agile." I later found out that there *was* a backlog but that developers were hiding it from stakeholders to avoid being harassed about timelines. This is a prime example of how *not* to practice transparency.

Definition of Done

The **definition of done (DoD)** is a set of conditions that must be satisfied for a requirements unit to be considered completely implemented—or "done." The DoD acts as a minimum set of conditions that *every* PBI must comply with; in addition, each individual PBI also has its own acceptance criteria. Common DoDs include that the requirement be discussed with users, coded, tested and that the code be checked in, refactored, and integrated.

Readiness

Scrum requires that PBIs be *ready* prior to their selection in sprint planning. In Scrum, **ready** means that the PBI is sufficiently prepared to be immediately worked on and completed by the team within a single sprint.

Many organizations go further and define formal **definitions of ready (DoRs)** to specify the conditions that must be true before teams commit to a work item. You can define a DoR at the feature level to specify what must be true before a feature is accepted into the plan and at the story level to clarify what must be true before a team commits to a story.

If the organization is using Scrum with quarterly planning, verify all features under consideration against the feature DoR before quarterly planning; check stories against the story DoR before iteration (sprint) planning. If the organization is using flow-based planning (e.g., Kanban), check each feature and story individually against the corresponding DoR as it comes up in the backlog.

---

17. Schwaber and Sutherland, *The Scrum Guide*, 7.
18. Schwaber and Sutherland, 3.

Sprint Goal

The sprint goal "is the single objective for the Sprint. . . . The Sprint Goal also creates coherence and focus, encouraging the Scrum Team to work together rather than on separate initiatives."[19] As an analyst, you help the customer and development team collaborate to craft the sprint goal. If the goal is in jeopardy at any time once the sprint is underway, you work with the business and developers to explore options to deliver it in other ways (e.g., by delaying all or part of a PBI to a later sprint).

Backlog Refinement

The work to prepare PBIs for implementation is referred to, in Scrum, as **backlog refinement**. In the rest of this book, however, unless referring to Scrum, I use the more generic term **preparation** (e.g., backlog preparation, feature preparation, story preparation). Scrum defines **backlog refinement** as "the act of breaking down and further defining Product Backlog items into smaller more precise items. This is an ongoing activity to add details, such as a description, order, and size."[20] A rough guideline is that a maximum of 10 percent of the team's time be spent on backlog refinement.

Refinement in Scrum is an ongoing, collaborative process between the PO and the development team. Refinement activities include all preparation work needed for the PBI to be actionable—such as removal of dependencies and initial design work. Much of the work is analysis related: incrementally adding granularity to PBI requirements and acceptance criteria as implementation nears.

The goal of refinement in Scrum is to prepare PBIs in the backlog enough that they are "ready" to be included in sprint planning. (If you're using a Kanban approach, you also prepare work items. However, you do so individually, as each individual item comes up in the backlog, as opposed to preparing a group of items for the sprint.)

Sprint Planning

A **sprint planning** event is held before each sprint to determine what will be accomplished during the upcoming sprint and how. In the rest of this book, I use the more generic term **iteration planning** to refer to the activity. During the event, the team creates a *sprint backlog*—a plan for what will be accomplished in the next sprint and how it will be accomplished. The *what* is expressed in the sprint goal and a set of requirements items (PBIs) for the sprint. The *how* is expressed in a list of **developer tasks** to implement those items—with owners and estimates assigned. Developer tasks include *all* work done on PBIs—not only design and coding but also analysis and testing. For example, during the event, you plan for any remaining analysis work on PBIs planned for the current sprint as well as for analysis work on upcoming PBIs to make them ready for a future sprint.

Daily Scrum, or Daily Standup

The **daily scrum**, commonly called the **daily standup**, is a short meeting to plan the day's work. It should be held at the same time every day—often occurring in the morning. All

---

19. Schwaber and Sutherland, 11.
20. Schwaber and Sutherland, 10.

team members meet to discuss what they have done toward the sprint goal since the last meeting, what they will do until the next meeting, and any impediments they foresee. As an analyst, you update the team on analysis activities related to the work that is being implemented. *The Scrum Guide* is strict about applying a 15-minute time limit to the standup, but you should extend the meeting if the update requires a longer discussion.

Keep in mind that the standup is only meant for updates; hold a follow-up meeting, if necessary, to resolve issues that have arisen during the standup. In contrast to the standup, only those members who can contribute to a solution should attend the follow-up.

 For more on the daily standup, see Chapter 17, section 17.9.9.

Sprint Review and Retrospective

At the end of every sprint, a **sprint review** is held to review and demonstrate the work that was done and to readjust the product backlog as necessary.

A **sprint retrospective** is held afterward as an internal meeting to support continual improvement. As the business analyst, you're an important attendee at the retrospective, contributing an external perspective on the team's performance.

3.4.4.3 Extreme Programming

XP is an iterative-incremental framework for software development developed in the 1990s by Kent Beck and described in his book, *Extreme Programming Explained.*[21] As a timeboxed framework, XP shares many features with Scrum. Differences include its greater focus on technical issues and its short iterations of approximately one week. In addition, while Scrum does not address planning beyond the sprint, XP includes quarterly planning.

Primary practices of XP include the following:

- Pair programming—two programmers working together
- Sitting together as a team in an open space without cubicles
- Energized work—sustainable work hours, with avoidance of regular overtime
- Slack—allowance for nonstructured time
- Test-first programming—writing the test before the code
- Continuous integration (CI)
- Incremental design—designing for current needs and growing the design as the business grows
- Automated testing

Many of these primary practices are widely accepted today, even in organizations that haven't adopted XP as their framework.

---

21. Kent Beck and Cynthia Andres, *Extreme Programming Explained: Embrace Change*, 2nd ed., The XP Series (Boston: Addison-Wesley, 2005).

A number of XP's techniques relate directly to agile analysis and planning. These include

- The practice of organizing small, vertically integrated teams (referred to as **whole teams**) of no more than twelve members.[22]

- The use of stories as a basic unit for requirements management.

- **Informative workspaces** whereby an observer can get an idea of the project in fifteen seconds. Examples of this practice in this book include the use of the product canvas, story maps, and the GO (goal-oriented) product roadmap.

- XP's **Planning Game** guidelines that set out the terms for quarterly and iteration planning.

3.4.4.4 *Rational Unified Process (RUP)*

The Rational Unified Process (RUP) is an iterative-incremental process developed by the Rational Corporation in the late 1990s and is based on the objectory process. Objectory was created by Ivar Jacobsen in the late 1980s.

In the RUP, analysis, design, coding, and testing occur during all phases of development—although the relative effort varies over time. The RUP lifecycle begins with a short **inception** phase during which the business case and high-level use-case model are created, and prototypes and proofs of concept are built. Next is an **elaboration** phase during which the majority (often up to 80%) of the requirements are analyzed up front, and the architecture is tested and established. In this phase, most of the use-case scenarios are specified. It's followed by a **construction** phase during which the remaining analysis, design, and implementation activities occur in an iterative, incremental fashion over a number of iterations. Finally, a **transition** phase occurs during which the solution is migrated to production.

3.4.4.5 *Use Cases*

The use-case approach was developed by Ivar Jacobson and described in his 1992 book, *Object-Oriented Software Engineering.*[23] Use cases have since become a popular tool for analyzing requirements—absorbed as part of the Unified Modeling Language (UML) standard. They are the basis for many widely used iterative-incremental software development lifecycle frameworks and methods, such as RUP.

A use case is defined as follows: "A use case is all the ways of using a system to achieve a particular goal for a particular user. Taken together, the set of all the use cases gives you all of the useful ways to use the system and illustrates the value that it will provide."[24] A

---

22. Beck and Andres, *Extreme Programming Explained*, 9. The authors reference Malcolm Gladwell's *The Tipping Point*, which sets twelve as the maximum number of people who can comfortably interact with each other in a day.

23. Ivar Jacobson, *Object-Oriented Software Engineering: A Use-Case Driven Approach* (Reading, MA: Addison-Wesley, 1992).

24. Jacobson et al., *Use-Case 2.0*, 4.

simple way to think of a use case is that it represents a user task—a unit of work, or goal, that a user expects to accomplish through an interaction with the system.

A **use-case narrative** (also referred to as a use-case *specification*) is a "description of a use case that tells the story of how the system and its actors work together to achieve a particular goal. It includes a sequence of actions (including variants) that a system and its actors can perform to achieve a goal."[25] The narrative may be specified at various levels of granularity depending on circumstances—from briefly described (where only the user and goal are specified) to fully described (where a comprehensive description is provided).

An entire use case, containing *all the ways* to achieve a goal, usually takes longer than a single iteration to implement. Consequently, rather than assigning an entire use case to an iteration, you assign specified scenarios of the use case. A **use-case scenario** is a complete pass through a use case, describing one way it might play out.

Jacobson adapted the use-case approach for agile development with *Use Case 2.0*. One of its additions to the original approach was the invention of the **use-case slice** as the primary atomic requirements unit for planning. A use-case slice is "one or more stories selected from a use case to form a work item that is of clear value to the customer."[26] To be suitable for inclusion in iteration planning, a use-case slice must be small enough to be implemented within a single iteration.

Use Cases versus User Stories

Any requirements unit that would qualify as a small-sized use-case slice would also qualify as a user story in XP's approach. In an ideal world, I would prefer to see the use-case slice used as the atomic agile requirements unit because it always provides a usage context (the use case) for a requirement. Another reason is that the approach provides a single, unified framework for organizing requirements, not only during development but after development as well—something for which user stories are not well suited. However, in the real world—and this book—I most often use user stories during development because they are much more widely used by agile teams and better supported by agile tools.

Post-implementation, the better requirements unit to use for **persistent** (long-lasting) documentation is the use case because user stories are too small to be used as an effective reference. For example, consider that one user story in a backlog might allow a shopper to order gift-wrapping, another might add the option for drone delivery, and a third might have nothing to do with shopping. For reference purposes, it's useful to gather all the stories in the backlog related to purchasing under one roof. That's precisely what happens when you consolidate them into a *Purchase items* use case. (You can achieve a similar effect by gathering stories into feature files.)

3.4.4.6 Lean Thinking

Lean thinking was developed by Taiichi Ohno and Shigeo Shingo at Toyota in the 1950s. It is the source of many guidelines that have found their way into agile practice, such as small batch sizes, just-in-time production, and short cycles.

---

25. Jacobson et al., 51.
26. Jacobson et al., 15.

Lean thinking underlies the agile principle, "Simplicity—the art of maximizing the amount of work not done—is essential."[27] In lean thinking, this guidance is expressed in its aim of reducing *muda* (waste) in the value stream.

3.4.4.7 Lean Software Development

Lean software development, first coined in 1992, is an approach pioneered by Bob Charette for achieving perfection by eliminating waste.[28] It has been developed further into various branches by contributors such as Tom and Mary Poppendieck, who laid out their framework in 2003 in their book *Lean Software Development: An Agile Toolkit*.[29] The toolkit includes seven lean principles and twenty-two **thinking tools**, many of which have a direct bearing on BA and the guidance in this book.

The first and central principle is to *eliminate waste*. In lean software development, waste is "anything that does not add value to a product, value as perceived by a customer."[30]

The Seven Wastes

Lean software development recognizes seven "wastes":

1. Partially done work

2. Extra processes

3. Extra features

4. Task switching

5. Waiting

6. Motion

7. Defects

Let's examine these wastes and how you can reduce them through effective agile analysis and planning.

1. Partially Done Work[31]   Work that has begun but that may never be completed by the time it's needed is considered wasteful. The same is true if the partially done work will be out of date by the time it's needed. In agile analysis, this waste is minimized using a just-in-time approach—delaying the analysis until just before implementation, when we can be sure it will be current and when the immediacy of the upcoming development means that stakeholders are more likely to give the item the attention it needs.

---

27. Agile Alliance, "12 Principles."

28. David J. Anderson, "Lean Software Development," 2015, https://msdn.microsoft.com/en-us/library/hh533841(v=vs.120).aspx

29. Mary Poppendieck and Tom Poppendieck, *Lean Software Development—An Agile Toolkit* (Boston: Addison-Wesley, 2003).

30. Poppendieck and Poppendieck, *Lean Software Development*, xxv.

31. Poppendieck and Poppendieck, 5.

2. Extra Processes   The waste of extra processes[32] is minimized in agile analysis through the use of low-overhead processes for managing and changing requirements, the elimination or reduction of requirements sign-offs, and reliance on direct interactions over extensive documentation to communicate requirements.

3. Extra Features   Extra features[33] represent the wasted effort to develop features that are never used. Agile analysis reduces this waste by using a data-informed approach to decide which requirements to invest in and which to drop. Waste in the form of extra features is also reduced through just-in-time analysis, since analysis effort is spent only on requirements that have current value and prioritization decisions are based on up-to-date information.

4. Task Switching   Task switching represents the effort wasted when a worker switches back and forth between different work items. In agile analysis, this waste is minimized by defining small stories that can be developed one after the other rather than concurrently and by keeping work-in-progress limits low.

5. Waiting   Waiting represents waste caused when work cannot proceed until something else occurs. Agile business analysts reduce waiting by defining minimally dependent stories and by preparing features and stories before implementation so that all dependencies are identified and planned for in advance.

6. Motion   Motion[34] represents the movement of people and artifacts. Agile analysis reduces motion through the use of *information radiators*—publicly posted displays of information—to communicate requirements information freely to the team and by eliminating or reducing handoffs and sign-offs. Information radiators are discussed further in the next section.

7. Defects   Defects are reduced in agile analysis through the early definition of acceptance criteria—ensuring that the developers know what test scenarios to look out for before they begin. Wasted effort due to defects is also reduced by decomposing requirements into small units that can be developed and tested quickly, thereby exposing bugs early when they are easiest to fix.

Tools of Lean Software Development

The Poppendiecks' approach to lean software development contains twenty-two "thinking tools." In the following sections, we focus on some of the tools that relate most strongly to agile analysis and planning.

Tool 1: Seeing Waste   The first step in removing waste is to see it. In the previous discussion of the seven wastes, you learned how agile BA helps the team see each of these kinds of waste.

---

32. Poppendieck and Poppendieck, 5.
33. Poppendieck and Poppendieck, 6.
34. Poppendieck and Poppendieck, 7.

Tool 2: Value Stream Mapping   Value stream mapping is the charting of steps in an end-to-end process in order to optimize it (e.g., by reducing wait times). As an agile business analyst, you perform value stream mapping on *operational* business processes in order to improve them. You may also perform value stream mapping on the *development* process itself in order to identify bottlenecks and inefficiencies in the development lifecycle.

Tool 3: Feedback   As an agile business analyst, you support fast feedback by defining short, valuable stories that can be implemented and tested out within a single iteration.

Tool 4: Iterations   As an agile business analyst, you support the guidance "to implement a coherent set of features in each iteration"[35] by using visual tools like customer journeys, process maps, and story maps to ensure the stories in each iteration fit well together.

Tool 7: Options Thinking   Options thinking means keeping one's options open by delaying irreversible decisions until uncertainty is reduced and by investigating alternatives (e.g., co-developing two options). You practice options thinking by facilitating the exploration of alternative ways to deliver value and delaying requirements analysis and commitment to the last responsible moment.

Tool 8: Last Responsible Moment (LRM)   Delay decisions to the LRM, defined as "the instant in which the cost of the delay of a decision surpasses the benefit of delay, or the moment when failing to take a decision eliminates an important alternative."[36] The agile business analyst practices LRM by minimizing upfront analysis and delaying detailed analysis until close to implementation—when any further delay would incur unacceptable costs.

Tool 10: Pull Systems   Lean development favors pull systems in which workers determine what work to do next rather than rely on centralized command-and-control systems that don't respond well to change. Lean uses signs (placards), known as Kanbans, to represent work items. As a work item advances from station to station, so, too, does its Kanban card. Workers at each station make their own decisions about advancing work items based on simple rules. In agile analysis, you use this approach to manage the progression of features and user stories across their development lifecycle.

Tool 12: Cost of Delay   In SAFe, the cost of delay represents the value of a work item, taking into account time criticality. Time criticality is the difference in value between an initiative that is started immediately and the same one begun after a delay. Time criticality is an especially significant concern when profitability depends on being first to market. In agile analysis, you determine the cost of delay of PBIs and use it to help determine an item's priority sequence in the backlog.

For more on the cost of delay, see Chapter 6, "Preparing the Process," section 6.5.4.4.

Tool 20: Testing   As an agile business analyst, you support testing by following acceptance test–driven development practice—negotiating and crafting acceptance criteria for features and stories before their implementation and teaching others to do so. At

---

35. Poppendieck and Poppendieck, 29.

36. Lean Construction Institute, "LCI Lean Project Delivery Glossary," 2017, https://www.leanconstruction.org/media/docs/LCI_Glossary.pdf

the feature level, you specify acceptance criteria for user acceptance testing (UAT) and describe how much of the feature must be implemented before the feature as a whole is considered done. You also specify acceptance criteria at the story level to determine the tests that an individual story must pass in order to be considered done.

Principles of Lean Software Development

Lean software development also includes a set of principles. We've already examined the impacts of many of these have on BA, such as to eliminate waste and to decide as late as possible, so I focus here on principles that provide additional guidance.

Deliver as Fast as Possible.   This principle advises that features be delivered to customers immediately, or as close to immediately as possible. Speed is highly valued because it enables many other lean principles, such as "decide as late as possible." As an agile business analyst, you contribute to this principle by specifying small Stories that can be implemented and delivered quickly. At the product level, you contribute by helping the customer and team define a minimum marketable product (MMP) that can be released rapidly into the market. For the whole team and organization, it means using CI/CD, and DevOps practices to provide the capacity to deliver changes reliably as soon as the business wants them released.

Build Integrity In.   This principle means that the software, architecture, and interfaces should possess coherence, with all parts working together cohesively as a whole. As an agile business analyst, you actualize this principle using story maps to ensure that the stories implemented within each iteration add up to useful functionality.

See the Whole.   This principle states that teams should focus on optimizing the whole product, not just the aspects of the product within their areas of expertise. You support this principle by organizing teams around value to the business (vs. competencies), by supporting team ownership of commitments, and through such practices as the use of a single product backlog and product owner across all teams working on a product.

Information Radiators

An **information radiator** is "a display posted in a place where people can see it as they work or walk by. It shows readers information they care about without having to ask anyone a question."[37] In lean terms, information radiators lessen the *waste* of *motion* by reducing handoffs and sign-offs.

The audience for information radiators is not only internal—it's for those outside the teams as well, to provide answers to questions without having to interrupt those doing the work.

Cockburn describes the following attributes of a good information radiator:

- Legible at a distance
- Easy to understand at a glance

---

37. Alistair Cockburn, *Crystal Clear: A Human-Powered Methodology for Small Teams*, (Boston: Addison-Wesley, 2004), 54.

- Updated continually

- Posted in a public place

- Is (ideally) a physical artifact (e.g., flipchart or whiteboard). Large display monitors may also be used (e.g., to communicate status information).

When working with non-colocated teams, you need to slightly adapt the guidance about a physical artifact. In such cases, members and stakeholders should first assemble in the real world for planning purposes if possible. During this phase, they use physical flipcharts. After they disperse, the flipchart content is transferred to digital form and posted online so that all interested parties have access to the same version.

As an agile business analyst and planner, you use information radiators extensively. We'll be using the following radiators in this book:

- Product portrait (or product canvas), providing an overview of the product

- GO (goal-oriented) product roadmap, indicating long-term implementation plans

- Story maps, showing incremental rollout of stories across a release (program increment) cycle

- Developer task boards, showing task assignments and progress

- Kanban boards, indicating the current status of work items

3.4.4.8 Lean Startup

Lean startup was developed by Eric Ries and described in his book *The Lean Startup*.[38] The lean startup approach is based on validated learning, whereby investment decisions are based on feedback from controlled experiments in the marketplace. Despite its name, the approach doesn't apply only to organizations customarily thought of as startups. It can also refer to established telecommunications companies, insurance companies, and even government agencies. What's important is that the organization is developing a product or service that is novel.

Lean startup practices that are incorporated in the analysis guidance within this book include the following:

- Minimum viable product (MVP): The minimal version of a product needed to facilitate learning in the marketplace

- Actionable metrics: Metrics that provide actionable guidance on where next to invest

- Leap of faith hypotheses: Unproven theories about a product's value and growth that need to be tested quickly

---

38. Eric Ries, *The Lean Startup* (New York: Crown Publishing Group, 2011).

3.4.4.9 Test-Driven Development, Acceptance Test-Driven Development, and Behavior-Driven Development

Test-driven development (TDD) refers to a "style of programming in which three activities are tightly interwoven: coding, testing (particularly, unit testing) and design."[39] TDD was popularized by Kent Beck in *Test-Driven Development: By Example*, published in 2002. According to TDD, tests are written before programming so that they may focus the work of developers. The TDD process begins with writing a unit test, followed by a failed execution of that test. Coding is performed until the software passes the test, and finally, refactoring is carried out to clean up the code. **Acceptance test–driven development (ATDD)** extends this practice beyond unit and low-level integration testing to include full end-to-end user interface testing. The tests are often automated.

As an agile business analyst, you practice ATDD by specifying acceptance criteria for features and stories before implementation in collaboration with business stakeholders, quality assurance (QA) team, and developers. These collaborations are often referred to as the Triad meetings.

Before coding begins, you collaborate to create executable specifications for feature-level acceptance criteria in feature files, for example, using the BDD Gherkin syntax.

For more on BDD, see Chapter 13, section 13.10.9. For more on the Triad, see Chapter 13, section 13.6.3.

3.4.4.10 DevOps

DevOps is an approach for reducing time to delivery by minimizing bottlenecks in the delivery pipeline. The guidelines focus on automating the build/test/deploy so changes can be made frequently and reliably. DevOps is recommended for all scaled agile organizations because its practices, particularly its guidelines for automating the build, test, and deploy steps, are essential for safe, rapid deployment at scale. It's also key to enabling many of the other agile practices and benefits described in this book. For example, by shortening the development cycle through automation, DevOps accelerates learning and supports evidence-based MVP planning.

DevOps guidance is to shift left: to move activities, such as testing and deployment, to an earlier stage in the delivery pipeline in order to find problems earlier, when they are easier to correct. As an agile business analyst, you support this practice by defining acceptance criteria for features and stories before implementation. The criteria are not only sources for test specification but also serve as requirements, guiding the work of developers through specific examples. You specify the acceptance criteria in feature files using the BDD Gherkin syntax—a natural-language format that facilitates test automation.

3.4.4.11 SAFe

The Scaled Agile Framework (SAFe) was developed by Dean Leffingwell as a framework for applying agile, iterative development to large enterprises. We look at SAFe more closely in Chapter 17. Since we'll be using some SAFe terms in this book, and because

---

39. "TDD," *Agile Glossary*, 2015, https://www.agilealliance.org/glossary/tdd

SAFe concepts are pretty widely used even by organizations that haven't adopted the framework, we'll preview some of the terminology here.

SAFe Concepts and Terms

SAFe planning is built around the **program increment (PI)**. A PI is a planning cycle of about eight to twelve weeks—typically a period of four 2-week iterations followed by one 2-week iteration for innovation and planning. It's roughly equivalent to a quarter or release cycle. One advantage of calling it a PI is that you can separate the planning period (the duration of the PI) from the release schedule. For example, you can develop requirements implementation plans based on a ten-week horizon so that teams have enough notice to commit and coordinate plans for large work items. At the same time, you can release on a different schedule based on business and market concerns.

The **program** level represents a long-range enterprise mission that spans multiple teams.

In SAFe, teams aligned to a common mission are organized into a long-lived team of teams, referred to as an **Agile Release Train (ART)**. Teams across an ART synchronize their planning, test the product's conceptual integrity, and so on, at each PI.

SAFe defines a **feature** as a work item that can be implemented within a single PI by one ART (team of teams).[40]

SAFe and This Book

This book applies to those working in SAFe organizations. Following is a mapping of terms used in the book to SAFe terms:

- A quarter is equivalent to a SAFe PI.
- The quarterly events described in this book correspond to SAFe's PI events.
- Quarterly planning and preparation activities described in the book correspond to the PI planning activities that typically occur in SAFe's innovation and planning (IP) iteration. However, the default practice presumed in the book is that these activities are not performed in a reserved iteration, but in parallel with development, toward the end of the prior planning period.
- This book uses the term **product area** to refer to a group of teams dedicated to a subset of the product. It's roughly equivalent to a SAFe ART.

3.4.4.12 Domain-Driven Design

Domain-driven design (DDD) was developed by Eric Evans[41] in 2003. The approach has been experiencing a resurgence lately, possibly as a reaction to the haphazard design

---

40. "A feature is sized or split as necessary to be delivered by a single Agile Release Train (ART) in a Program Increment (PI)." Richard Kastner and Dean Leffingwell, *SAFe 5.0 Distilled* (Boston: Addison-Wesley, 2020), 270.

41. Eric Evans, *Domain-Driven Design: Tackling Complexity in the Heart of Software* (Boston: Addison-Wesley Professional, 2003).

choices that have sometimes been made in agile development. In DDD, the business domain drives the design so that the resulting code will closely match the structure and terminology of the business—making it easier to adapt the software over its lifespan to changing requirements. As an agile business analyst, you support the DDD approach by providing an analysis of the business vision, stakeholder goals and objectives, and business-perspective models such as value stream maps that drive design models. A fuller consideration of DDD, including class diagrams and coding implications, is beyond the scope of this book. For more on business-domain object-oriented modeling, see my earlier book *UML for the IT Business Analyst*.[42]

3.4.4.13 *UML and Business Process Modeling Notation*

The UML is a broad modeling standard that covers everything from domain models for real-world organizations and processes to technical models that describe design issues. Aspects of the standard relevant to your work as a business analyst include UML's domain models, such as UML's business domain class diagrams and activity diagrams, and use-case models that illustrate the user's view of a product or system.

The Business Process Modeling Notation (BPMN) is a widely used standard for modeling business processes. In this book, you'll learn how to use BPMN models to construct story maps and, in the reverse direction, to use story maps to build BPMN process models for reference on future change initiatives.

For more on BPMN, see Chapter 10, section 10.16.

3.5 Overview of Agile Roles and the Business Analyst

For most of this book, our focus will be on the agile analysis competency, not the role. I want to address it here because you might be concerned with this issue, especially if you are a business analyst with waterfall experience wondering where you'll end up after an agile transition. You might also be responsible for organizing agile teams—and wondering how your agile business analysts fit in.

Figure 3.4 is an overview of agile roles and functions related to agile BA.

As indicated in Figure 3.4, roles and functions that overlap strongly with BA include the business analyst, team analyst (unsurprisingly), PO, and proxy PO. Roles with some BA overlap include the facilitator and coach ("free-floating" roles often not dedicated to a particular team), proxy user (representing a group of users), user experience (UX) designer, ScrumMaster, QA professional, and data analyst.

The development team includes all functions necessary to deliver work items (stories). The term **developer** is used in a generic sense to refer to any member of the team. The **extended team** includes nondedicated members, such as business analysts, who are made available to multiple teams. **Scrum team** refers to the development team plus the PO and ScrumMaster.

42. Howard Podeswa, *UML for the IT Business Analyst*, 2nd ed. (Boston: Cengage Learning PTR, 2009).

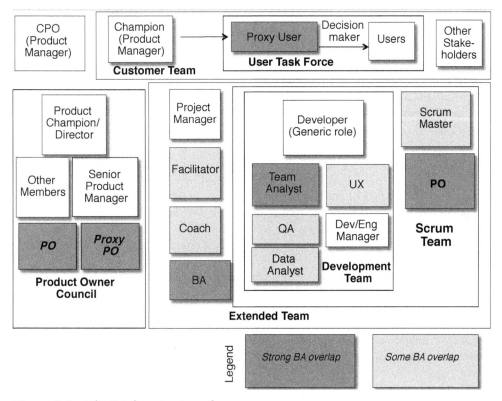

Figure 3.4 *The BA function in agile*

3.5.1 The Product Owner's BA Responsibilities

Most agile development organizations include a role that works closely with development to represent the business. The role is referred to by different names, including the PO (*product owner* comes from the Scrum framework), customer (an XP term), and product manager. I'll be referring to the role as the PO.

The PO has both inward- and outward-facing responsibilities. Inward-facing responsibilities include

- Developing and communicating the product goal.
- Creating, communicating, and ordering product backlog items.
- Maximizing the value of work performed by the development team.
- Ensuring transparency and clarity of the backlog.[43]

Outward-facing responsibilities include meeting with customers, marketers, sales representatives, and strategic planners.

---

43. Schwaber and Sutherland, *The Scrum Guide*, 5–6.

Many POs are chosen for their outward-facing competencies. They tend to be product managers from the business side and business subject matter experts (SMEs) who may have minimal background in requirements management. The solution to this competency gap is to either provide them with coaching and training in agile analysis or to support them with a business analyst well-versed in the competency. Often, there aren't enough POs to fill the role at the team level. As a business analyst, you might help solve that problem by acting as team PO or proxy PO, while the SME serves as area PO over a group of teams.

3.5.2 The Agile Team Analyst

According to frameworks such as Scrum, the team analyst is viewed as a competency, not a formal, dedicated role. On agile teams in the new-technology sector, the analysis competency is often filled by someone other than a dedicated analyst (e.g., the PO or members of the development team who have other primary areas of expertise, such as in data analytics or UX design).

Mainstream businesses often include a designated analyst on their agile teams—either as a dedicated member or as a member of the extended team, shared among a group of teams. As someone in this role, you support the PO by eliciting and managing detailed requirements—a responsibility similar to the IT business analyst role in traditional organizations. We look at considerations for and against dedicated business analyst roles later in this chapter.

3.5.3 The ScrumMaster's BA Responsibilities

While the main focus of the ScrumMaster (a role within the Scrum framework) is on coaching the team on the Scrum process and removing impediments, many aspects of the role overlap with BA:

- Finding techniques for effective product backlog management
- Helping the Scrum team understand the need for clear and concise product backlog items
- Helping establish product planning in an empirical environment
- Helping the team create high-value increments[44]

3.5.4 Proxy User

When there are many diverse users, a user task force may be formed to represent a *group of users*, with a proxy user as its head, representing the group's needs. Because the required competencies overlap with BA, business analysts often occupy this position. The proxy

---

44. Schwaber and Sutherland, 6–7.

user also has final decision-making authority on behalf of the group—something outside of the traditional BA function.

3.5.5 BA Responsibilities of the Product Champion (Director)

The customer team (an XP entity) is a body that includes everyone needed to ensure the software meets the needs of stakeholders. Members may include the product manager, proxy product owners, users, QA professionals, and UX designers. The product owner council (POC) is a similar organization, consisting of the POs and proxy POs that lead the teams working on an initiative.

A customer team or POC is led by a product champion (also known as a director)—a first among equals. The product champion often has to resolve prioritization conflicts between the technical and business sides (e.g., when deciding how much time to spend on technical debt vs. new product development). For this reason, the champion is often some-one with a foot in each world. Many are former software developers who have moved over to the business side. This is also the background of many business analysts, making them a natural fit for this role.

For more on the POC, see Chapter 17, section 17.8.8.

3.5.6 Coach

Coaches are assigned to work with new agile teams until they are able to go it alone—at which point the coach gradually hands off control to a local member (e.g., a ScrumMaster). Many aspects of the role relate to BA issues, such as guiding the team on how to represent requirements and when to analyze them.

3.5.7 When Are Dedicated Business Analysts Advised?

The short answer is "often." Here's why: An agile organization requires more resources from the business side than waterfall does because it requires one business decision maker per agile team of about seven to ten people and because they are involved *throughout* development instead of only at its endpoints. There are often insufficient business decision makers, such as product and program managers, to fill these positions. If you're responsi-ble for organizing the teams, what do you do? There are many solutions to this problem, but most involve the inclusion of an agile business analyst in some capacity.

3.5.7.1 Dedicated Team Analyst as Assistant to the Rotating PO

One effective solution was first described to me by Angus Muir of Travelers Insurance. I've been recommending it to teams ever since. Find business SMEs to serve as *rotating* team POs and empower them to make decisions and set priorities. This frees the more senior product managers to act as area POs across a group of teams. At the same time, the rotation of SMEs in and out of the team-level PO role prevents them from going stale and losing touch with the market.

The disadvantage of this approach is that a new, inexperienced SME is continually moving into position as a team PO. The team analyst, in this case, provides continuity with respect to the requirements, jockeying the requirements through the development process as POs are swapped in and out. The analysts provide each new PO with an understanding of why stories have been prioritized the way they have, what business objectives they support, the dependencies between them, and the processes and tools used to manage the requirements.

3.5.7.2 Business Analyst as Proxy PO

A different solution is to assign a proxy PO rather than a full PO to each team. The proxy PO is similar to a PO but with limited authority to make local prioritization decisions. Business analysts are often chosen to fill the role because they have the necessary requirements-analysis capabilities.

3.5.7.3 Team Business Analyst Supporting a Shared PO

Another solution advocated by scaled agile approaches such as LeSS is to do away with the team-level PO. Instead, one PO, shared among several teams, focuses on the role's outward-facing aspects. Detailed requirements analysis is offloaded to the team, making it especially important that it includes someone with strong analysis competencies.

3.5.7.4 Other Scenarios Where a Dedicated Business Analyst May Be Advised

Other scenarios where high-performing business analysts are especially valuable include

- Complex business initiatives, such as mergers, transformative changes, and process reengineering initiatives, that demand in-depth analysis skills.

- Third-party or vendor solutions where the financial risk is heavily front-loaded.

- Large, multiple-team initiatives where business analysts help track and manage requirements dependencies and communicate requirements across all teams.

3.5.8 Business Analysts Provide Requirements Leadership

As an agile business analyst, your function is to provide leadership in the BA competency to the rest of the team: you facilitate requirements workshops with business stakeholders and developers present, and you coach other team members in agile requirements activities—such as writing, splitting, and negotiating stories. You are also engaged in analysis tasks, such as eliciting and defining the business rules for a story. During Triad meetings, you work with the PO, testers, and developers to

- Define acceptance criteria for features and stories.

- Challenge developers to explain which aspects of a story's requirements contribute most to high estimates.

- Consider workarounds that achieve similar business goals at lower cost.

Throughout the development process, you help ensure that the team is working on the requirements of the highest value to the business.

3.5.9 The Distinction between Business Analysts and Business Systems Analysts

Many organizations have different types of business analysts—such as **business analysts** (when referring to analysts with a higher-level business perspective) and **business systems analysts (BSA)** (for those with a more technical orientation) as well as varying levels of analysts (e.g., senior, intermediate) within each type. I try to avoid spending too much time distinguishing between these roles, as the effort goes against the cross-functionality preferred in an agile organization. In general, though, if these subroles are used in your agile organization, the "business" business analyst is usually the person responsible for product visioning, the business case, and defining business goals and objectives (i.e., the higher-level business requirements for an initiative). The IT business analyst or the BSA is responsible for the more detailed IT requirements (functional requirements) while working daily with the team. As a BSA, you are usually expected to have some technical background. For example, you may be asked to map required data fields to existing data tables.

3.6 Soft Skills of the Agile Business Analyst

So much of this book is concerned with tools such as user stories and story maps that you might think that BA is all about technique. It's not. It's very much a *people* competency. In fact, the most common reason reported to me for including business analysts on agile teams is that they fill a *soft skills* gap. Many of the sharpest technical minds I've worked with in the industry were missing these qualities—and turned out to be poor business analysts despite their exemplary qualifications. One BA had rare technical expertise in precisely the geographical mapping systems my customer was looking for but had a terrible way with people. Another had a strong background working on scaled agile projects, but stakeholders perceived him as arrogant. I never worked with either of them again and have since learned to screen much more carefully for soft skills.

If you're selecting people to fill the BA competency on an agile team, look for the soft skills described in the following sections.

3.6.1 Making the Unconscious Conscious

It's not a coincidence that business analysts and psychoanalysts both have "analyst" in their names. The main job in both cases is to *make the unconscious conscious*. A good business analyst can take knowledge that is deep inside the brains of customers and stakeholders and bring it into conscious expression so that developers are able to act on it.

3.6.2 Curiosity

A great business analyst should be naturally curious about people, their needs, and how they do things. Avoid candidates who like to dominate conversations. Prefer candidates who spend more time asking questions and listening to others.

3.6.3 Agent of Change

Business analysts are change agents. Great business analysts have the strength of personality and self-confidence to challenge assumptions, even when the issue at hand is "above their pay grade."

3.6.4 Political Intelligence

Business analysts can get themselves into trouble if they aren't quick to pick up on the politics of a situation. One business analyst who used to work for me reported to a high-level executive who was feared by the people under him. A business analyst with good political intelligence would have talked to his staff in private. This business analyst interviewed them as a group. Unfortunately, stakeholders held back information, and there were serious gaps in the solution that was developed. Those gaps added a lot of unexpected costs.

Political intelligence also means knowing what to say and what not to say—and to whom. You don't want a business analyst who betrays confidences or makes offhand commitments to the business without checking first with the team.

3.6.5 Works Well with Difficult People

Business analysts are rarely able to choose the stakeholders and developers they work with. They need to be able to manage people—regardless of the personality type in front of them. (By the way, this is one of those situations where growing up with a difficult parent can provide benefits later on in life.)

3.6.6 Negotiation Skills

Business analysts must often work with opposing parties to bring them toward shared goals and requirements priorities—whether it's business stakeholders with conflicting priorities for the product or it's "business vs. development" with business stakeholders pushing to prioritize new features while developers favor technical enhancements.

3.6.7 Facilitation

Business analysts need excellent communication and facilitation skills: They need to be ready to facilitate requirements workshops as needed, present requirements to the team, and facilitate planning sessions such as big room iteration planning events.

3.6.8 Adaptability

You'd think agile consultants and analysts would be the most adaptable people in the world. After all, they specialize in agility! Surprisingly, they can sometimes be quite rigid and doctrinaire in their views. That's not a desirable trait for agile business analysts because they often have to work in a context that isn't the ideal agile environment. For example, the organization may not have the technical infrastructure for the DevOps practices that enable agile's short development cycles. In this case, you want business analysts who have the flexibility to adapt to the situation and recommend the best approach given the context.

3.6.9 Not Afraid to Ask Questions

A good business analyst is not afraid to ask "dumb" questions. These often turn out to be the very questions that many others also don't understand but are embarrassed to ask about. A great business analyst knows her primary value is not that she knows the business better than anyone else, but that she knows what questions to ask and when.

3.6.10 Sense of Humor

Business analysts often have to deal with contentious situations (e.g., when managing conflicting priorities or when diffusing tension between the business' and developers' estimates of effort). Humor is often the key that opens the door to resolution.

3.7 13 Key Practices of Agile Analysis and How They Differ from Waterfall

Let's summarize some of the key practices and properties of agile analysis and how they differ from BA as practiced in a waterfall context.

3.7.1 A Competency, Not a Role

In waterfall, BA is often carried out by a dedicated role, such as a business analyst, IT business analyst, or BSA. In agile development, BA is a team *competency*, but it may be a formal role. Formalized roles within the team are discouraged because they lead to bottlenecks.

3.7.2 A Facilitator, Not a Messenger

On waterfall projects, business analysts are often seen as intermediaries who "throw the requirements over the fence" to the developers. As an agile business analyst, your role is to be not a messenger, but a *facilitator*, enhancing the quality of direct discussions between business stakeholders and solution providers.

3.7.3 Changes to Requirements Are Welcomed

In a waterfall process, you freeze requirements before development and strictly control subsequent changes. As an agile business analyst, you welcome changes to the requirements at any time with minimal ceremony.

3.7.4 Collaboration with Developers vs. Contractual Relationship

As an agile business analyst, your goal is to support a collaborative relationship whereby the customer and solution provider collaborate throughout development to find the best solution that delivers the desired business outcomes. It's not to lay down a set of comprehensive requirements that can serve as the basis for a contract, as is the case for waterfall development.

3.7.5 Just-In-Time Requirements Analysis

As an agile business analyst, you analyze requirements incrementally at the LRM—as close as possible to when they will be implemented. This is in contrast to waterfall development, where the requirements are analyzed upfront.

3.7.6 Conversation versus Documentation

In a waterfall process, you rely on written specifications as the primary means for communicating requirements to developers. As an agile business analyst, you rely primarily on conversation. This reduces waste (the added effort to create and maintain the documents), speeds the development process, and enhances the ability to respond to change, since it is much easier to change direction when little is written down. This doesn't mean you won't create any requirements documentation in agile, just less of it.

3.7.7 Specification by Example: Acceptance Test–Driven Development

As an agile business analyst, specific examples and narratives are your preferred vehicle for explaining requirements and test cases. You specify acceptance criteria for each requirements unit before implementation so that the criteria can be used as input to the developers. The acceptance criteria also serve as the basis for specifying automated and manual tests.

3.7.8 Small Requirements Units

As an agile business analyst, you split requirements into small units (user stories) that can be comfortably implemented and delivered within a short period. There is no need for this activity in a waterfall approach.

3.7.9 Vertical Slices of Functionality

Because agile processes aim for each requirements unit to deliver real value to the user, aim to specify each requirements unit so that it provides a "vertical slice" of functionality. For example, a vertically sliced requirements unit would call for implementing a couple of fields right through the architecture (UI layer, business layer, database layer) rather than all the fields of a single layer, such as the graphical user interface.

When complex products are involved, one small agile team is often unable to include all the necessary competencies to deliver value. Consequently, you may need to define the vertical slice at the higher level of a feature (multiteam) and then split it into smaller team-level stories.

3.7.10 Lightweight Tools

Agile analysis favors lightweight solutions to requirements management problems over solutions that require extensive overhead. For example, in this book, you'll learn of two approaches for managing requirements dependencies between two teams. The heavy-weight solution is to track dependencies using a requirements management tool. The light-weight solution is to assign someone to sit in on the other team's planning meetings—an investment of about fifteen minutes per day that achieves the same objectives.

3.7.11 Business Analyst and Business Stakeholder Engagement across the Complete Development Lifecycle

Because analysis proceeds incrementally over the course of an initiative, you need to pre-pare stakeholders to be involved *throughout* the development lifecycle, not only at its ends, as is the case for waterfall development.

3.7.12 Mix of BA Classic and Agile BA Tools

To be effective as an agile business analyst, you need to be familiar with a mix of agile requirements techniques and tools—such as story maps and user stories—as well as tradi-tional BA tools, such as domain modeling and business process modeling.

3.7.13 Meet Them Where They Are

In the course of your work as an agile analyst, there are many opportunities where you'll need to choose between options that seem to work best for the situation and those that are more ideologically pure from an agile standpoint. You should certainly not lose sight of the optimum solution and should advocate for it as a long-term solution. But for imme-diate guidance, choose the option that provides the best value to the business based on where the business is right now. Remember that in any given situation, *the goal of the agile business analyst is to do well by the business—not to do well by agile.*

3.8 Agile Business Analysis Rules of Thumb

Whenever I work with a group that is new to agile, many of the same questions pop up time and again. How many user stories are typical for an iteration? How many acceptance criteria are typical for a story? How many points are typical? I've assembled many of these questions and their answers in the rules of thumb listed in Appendix A.2.1. Keep in mind that these are broad guidelines, not strict rules. They are particularly valuable as a quick reference when you're starting out as an agile analyst and don't have a guide for what would be "normal" in an agile development organization. They will give you an idea about what's typical for velocity, story sizes, iteration length, and other parameters. Once you've been at it for a while, let experience be your guide, since practices will vary according to circumstances.

3.9 Chapter Summary

Here are the key points covered in this chapter:

- The atomic requirements unit in agile development may be known as a product backlog item (Scrum), story (XP), or use-case slice (*Use Case 2.0*). The most widely used unit is the story.

- A feature is a requirement item that may be delivered by one or more teams within a quarter, release cycle, or program increment. A story is a work item that is small enough to be implemented by a single team in about one or two weeks.

- To be accepted, a story must satisfy its acceptance criteria as well as the definition of done (DoD).

- Analysts contribute formally to an agile organization as dedicated team analysts, proxy POs, and extended team members.

3.10 What's Next?

In this chapter, we looked at the fundamental concepts behind agile BA. In Chapter 4, "Analysis and Planning Activities across the Agile Development Lifecycle," we focus on how to put these ideas and related techniques into practice over the course of an agile development lifecycle.

Chapter 4

Analysis and Planning Activities across the Agile Development Lifecycle

This chapter provides an overview of the agile analysis and planning process. It begins with the Agile Analysis and Planning Map, depicting analysis and planning tools used during an agile product development lifecycle. The tools include activities, artifacts, and events. Figure 4.1 illustrates the activities and tools of agile analysis and planning across the agile development lifecycle.

The map is divided vertically into zones of activity—clusters of related work. For example, the Quarterly Inception zone includes activities to launch the quarter, such as quarterly planning and story mapping. Horizontally, the map is divided into three lanes:

- Short Lane, for planning horizons up to about six months
- Long Lane, for horizons from two quarters (six months) to five years
- Grand Lane, for large-scale agile organizations.

The chapter explores each lane through a narrative that illustrates what to do when, as development progresses.

4.1 Objectives

This chapter will help you

- Understand how the activities and artifacts of agile analysis and planning fit together across the agile development lifecycle.

- Understand what activities apply to short-term and long-term planning horizons and the additional activities needed for scaled agile organizations.

- Understand how to use the map to plan analysis and planning activities for a given situation.

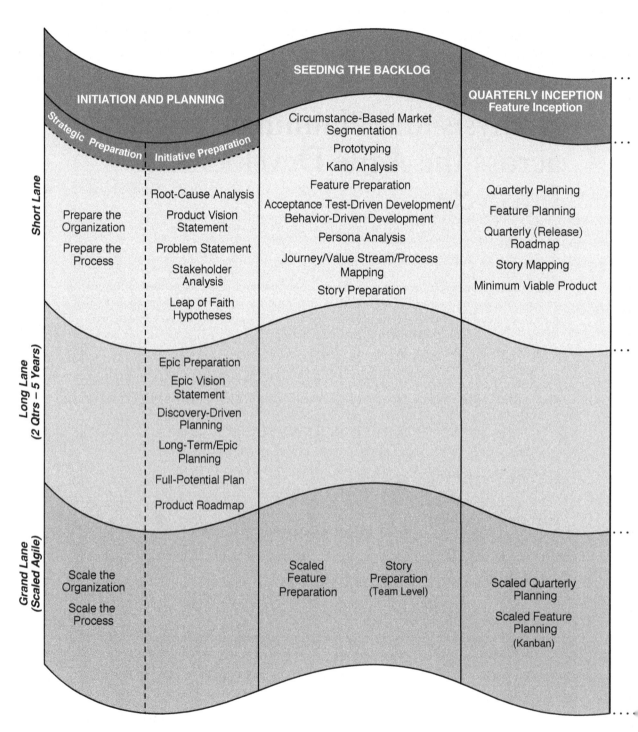

Figure 4.1   *Agile Planning and Analysis Map*

ITERATION INCEPTION	DAILY ACTIVITIES			ITERATION CLOSEOUT	QUARTERLY CLOSEOUT Epic, Feature Closeout
Iteration Planning	Daily Standup Requirements Analysis & Documentation Code, Build, Test, Deliver Acceptance Test-Driven Development/ Behavior-Driven Development Minimum Viable Product, Split Testing Epic, Feature Preparation Story Preparation			Iteration Review Iteration Retrospective	Prepare for General Availability Quarterly Retrospective Epic, Feature Retrospective
					Pivot or Persevere
Scaled Iteration Planning Iteration Planning (Team Level)	Product Owner Council Meetings DevOps	User Task Force Meetings Scaled Feature Preparation (Kanban)	Integration Meetings Story Preparation (Team Level)	Scaled Iteration Review Scaled Iteration Retrospective Iteration Retrospective (Team Level)	DevOps Scaled Quarterly/Feature Retrospective

4.2 Overview of the Agile Analysis and Planning Map

Figure 4.1 is divided vertically into zones and horizontally into lanes. Each zone represents a set of related analysis and planning activities, events, and artifacts. For example, the Quarterly Inception zone includes the story map and minimum viable product (MVP)—both of which are used to plan the quarter. I refer to these as **zones**, rather than phases, because agile development is not sequential: activities and artifacts are not performed to completion before the next one begins; they are refined incrementally over time. The progression is not always from left to right, either; it may reverse itself at any time. For example, an individual story may move from the testing activity back to detailed requirements analysis if testing reveals that more work is required to satisfy the customer.

A zone's left-to-right position does provide, however, a *rough* indication of when it is carried out *for the first time* and when it *primarily* occurs. For example, the release roadmap is created at the start of the quarter, though it is updated as needed. If an activity is used in two key contexts, I've listed it twice. For example, story preparation is an aspect of seeding the backlog. It is also performed as a daily activity once the initiative is underway. To make that clear, story preparation appears in both the Seeding the Backlog and the Daily Activities zones on the map.

Each horizontal lane in Figure 4.1 represents a particular scenario. Across the lane, you'll find activities and artifacts useful for the corresponding situation. For example, in Figure 4.1, the Grand Lane includes product owner (PO) council meetings, indicating that the activity is relevant to a large-scale agile organization.

The zones and lanes form a grid: based on the position of an item, you can see which scenario to use it for and the zone it belongs to. For example, in Figure 4.1, integration meetings are shown in the Grand Lane, indicating the tool is used for scaled organizations. It appears in the Daily Activities zone, indicating that these meetings are ongoing.

4.3 The Zones

The map in Figure 4.1 contains seven zones of activity:

- **Initiation and Planning:** Activities, artifacts, and events to prepare and plan for new product development or an epic—a significant change to an existing product. This zone also contains activities to improve the organization's maturity level in agile development and analysis.

- **Seeding the Backlog:** Activities to create and prepare the initial set of work items (epics, features, and stories) in the backlog.

- **Quarterly Inception (Feature Inception):** If the organization is using flow-based planning (e.g., Kanban), this zone covers activities to plan an upcoming feature, including estimation, team commitments, and agreement on a roadmap for delivering stories.

If the organization is using a timeboxed approach, this zone covers activities to plan all the features that will be delivered in the upcoming quarter.

- **Iteration Inception:** This zone includes activities for launching an iteration—a short planning cycle of about one to two weeks. The zone applies to organizations using a timeboxed planning approach, such as Scrum or XP.

- **Daily Activities:** This zone is for ongoing analysis and planning activities, such as daily standups and detailed requirements analysis. Following best practices, stories should be continuously delivered as they are done. To deliver a story means to provide it in a deployable state. Actual deployment to production or the market can occur at the time it is delivered or be delayed at the customer's discretion until a planned release date.

- **Iteration Closeout:** Final activities at the end of an iteration. This zone applies to organizations using a timeboxed planning approach, such as Scrum or XP.

- **Quarterly Closeout (Epic, Feature Closeout):** Final activities at the end of a long planning cycle—a quarter, release cycle, epic, or feature. The zone includes activities to prepare for general availability (GA), also known as a production release.

4.4 The Lanes

The map in Figure 4.1 contains three lanes, each depicting activities, events and artifacts for a particular scenario.

- The **Short Lane** applies to a scenario with planning needs up to the next quarter, release, or program increment (PI). A PI is a SAFe planning cycle of about eight to twelve weeks. For brevity, I often use the term *quarter* as shorthand for any of these periods—a calendar quarter, release cycle, or PI.

- The **Long Lane** applies to a scenario with planning horizons of two quarters to five years.

- The **Grand Lane** applies to a scaled agile organization. Some items on this path are referred to as *scaled* events. A scaled event is one with representation from all collaborating teams, such as the teams within a product area or a SAFe Agile Release Train (ART). If the development organization has only one level of collaborating teams, the term applies to all the teams working on the product.

The lanes are not exclusive. If you have long-term planning needs, you also have short-term planning needs. Consequently, you'd use the tools in the Short and Long lanes. If the organization is large and has long-term planning needs, you'd use tools from all lanes.

Use the map as a checklist of tools to consider when customizing the right process for your situation. Once the process is in action, use the map to find the right tools based on where you are in the development cycle, such as iteration closeout.

The map tells you what tools to *consider*. The tools you *select*, though, will depend on your situation. Be a minimalist: use a technique only if you can specify at least one problem that it solves. Don't use it just because it's on the map.

4.5 A Story in Three Acts

Now that we've reviewed the process, let's see how to carry it out by returning to Customer Engagement One (CEO) Inc. (see Chapter 2, "Agile Analysis and Planning: The Value Proposition," section 2.4), the company developing the CEO app—a product that enables companies to manage their engagements with customers across multiple platforms from a single interface.

In our retelling of the story, you have been asked to take on agile analysis and planning responsibilities during the company's early phase as a young startup. In real life, numerous individuals and roles might carry out these responsibilities, such as business analysts, business systems analysts (BSAs), team analysts, proxy POs, and POs. In this story, we simplify things by collapsing them into a single role: the analyst. To make it more realistic, let's assume you'll fill the role initially, with the expectation that, as the company grows, you'll become a lead in the competency, and others will be hired as needed.

We follow the CEO story in three acts, each focusing on one lane of the map and highlighting some of its main activities. We begin with Act 1. It illustrates the Short Lane, the first row in Figure 4.1.

4.6 Act 1: The Short Lane

You have been informed that CEO is to be based on a freemium business model. Users will be offered a complimentary version, which they can use until the number of collaborating users reaches a preset maximum. To go beyond this number, they will be required to upgrade to a premium, paid subscription. In the early releases, the free and premium versions will have the same capabilities, except for the cap on users in the free version. The plan is to eventually add additional features to the premium version for enterprise-wide use.

The marketing team intends to use a bottom-up strategy to sell the product—pitching the product first to support agents who engage with end customers. The assumption is that enough users within a company will want to collaborate to trigger conversion to the premium version.

Your first focus is on initial preparation and planning, the Initiation and Planning zone on the map in Figure 4.1.

4.6.1 Initial Preparation and Planning

Because there is so much uncertainty about the requirements, you recommend that a prototype be tested as soon as possible. The testing is carried out, and results indicate that the most popular capabilities are the ability to manage communications across multiple platforms without having to "hop in and out" of separate social networks and the ability to analyze trends across platforms. Based on the positive response to the prototype, the company secures funding to develop CEO First Generation (CEO-1G)—the first version of the product to be released to the market.

You learn from the development lead that CEO-1G will be built as a monolithic system—simple enough for one team of eight to ten members to contain all the required competencies needed to deliver stories. Due to the volume of work, two to three of these teams will be needed (Prepare the Organization in Figure 4.1).

You choose a flow-based (Kanban) planning process because it accelerates learning at a time when there is high uncertainty about the product (Prepare the Process in Figure 4.1). You choose the Short Lane because planning needs do not extend beyond a few months at a time.

Since there is no vision statement for the product, you facilitate a workshop with stakeholders to create one (Product Vision Statement in Figure 4.1). Together, you craft the following product vision statement: "To connect companies with their customers, anywhere, anyhow." You perform a stakeholder analysis to understand users, customers, suppliers, and other stakeholders and their objectives for the product. These include customer support agents, marketers, sales agents, and data analysts.

Next, you convene a group of business stakeholders and developers to explore the unproven assumptions that are key to the product's viability (Leap of Faith Hypotheses in Figure 4.1). You identify the following hypotheses:

- Support agents will use the product to collaborate with other agents on messages from customers.
- Users will invite enough of their colleagues to trigger conversion to the premium model.
- Enough companies will move to a subscription model for the product to reach profitability within five years.

You advise the group that it will be designing MVPs to test these hypotheses.

4.6.2 Seeding the Backlog

Next, you coach marketers to use *circumstance-based market segmentation* to anticipate the ways that people will use the product. Using the technique, they learn that the high-level usages for the product are, in order of preference, as follows:

- **Manage Messages:** Provide the ability to respond to customer messages (through support agents).
- **Marketing Campaigns:** Push marketing messages out to the community.

- **Sales:** Sell goods and services to customers.
- **Analytical Reporting:** Data analytics about engagement with the app, how marketing campaigns are performing, and so on.

You create a feature for each of these usages and add it to the backlog. You turn your attention to the first feature in the backlog: *manage messages*. To prepare it for implementation, you facilitate a value stream mapping workshop (Feature Preparation in the Seeding the Backlog zone in Figure 4.1). Attendees include business subject matter experts (SMEs) and representatives of the user roles that participate in the workflow for managing a message.

With your coaching, the group develops a workflow model that indicates the following steps:

- The system *ingests* messages.
- A Tier 1 support agent
  - *views* a message,
  - *triages* it,
  - *tags* it according to the topic,
  - *responds* to it, *resolves* it, or *assigns* it to a Tier 2 agent or queue.
- A Tier 2 agent may resolve the message or pass it to a Tier 3 agent or queue.

Following behavior driven development (BDD) practices, you specify end-to-end user acceptance testing (UAT) to validate that this sequence of steps can be carried out correctly (Behavior-Driven Development in the Seeding the Backlog zone in Figure 4.1).

You meet with the PO, team, and stakeholders to estimate the feature and develop a plan for implementing it (Feature Planning in the Feature Inception zone in Figure 4.1), focusing on the MMF—the minimum functionality for the feature to deliver significant value. During the meeting, you determine the following stories for the Manage Messages feature:

- As a Tier 1 support agent, I want to ingest messages from platform X so that I can see what customers are saying about the product.
- As a Tier 1 support agent, I want to view messages with simple formatting so that I can see what customers are saying about the product.
- As a Tier-1 support agent, I want to assign a message to a Tier 2 agent or work queue so that someone with more knowledge than me can collaborate on its resolution.
- As a Tier-2 support agent, I want to assign a message to a Tier-3 agent or queue so that difficult technical support issues are addressed by someone with the necessary expertise.
- As a support agent (all tiers), I want to respond to an assigned message so that I can advance it toward resolution.
- As a support agent (all tiers), I want to resolve an assigned message so that the issue may be closed.

You identify other, lower-priority stories for the feature, such as the following:

- As a support agent, I want to assign a tag (topic) to a message so that topic-based analytics can be generated and so that the message can be routed to the agent with the appropriate expertise.

Business stakeholders have indicated that this last story is a "nice-to-have" but that the MVP as a whole would be valuable without it. Consequently, you add the story to the bottom of the backlog and don't include it among the test scenarios required for feature acceptance.

You prepare the first stories in the backlog during the Triad sessions with business stakeholders, quality assurance (QA) professionals, and developers. You specify story acceptance criteria. Developers gain sufficient understanding of the story to estimate it reliably.

4.6.3 Daily Activities

Planning and coordination occur daily as you and the rest of the team meet for a 15-minute daily standup (Daily Standup in Daily Activities zone in Figure 4.1). Throughout the day, you meet with users to analyze the remaining requirements for current stories and to test stories as developers implement them. When a user story has met its acceptance criteria and developers have confirmed that the definition of done has been satisfied, the user story is considered done. Stories are continuously integrated and tested, with much of the work automated (Code, Build, Test, Deliver in Figure 4.1).

As the feature is nearing completion, you begin preparations on the next feature in the backlog (Feature Preparation under Daily Activities in Figure 4.1). The next feature is for an MVP to validate whether customers will invite enough of their colleagues to trigger conversion to the premium model. You work with the development team and business SMEs to split the feature into the following stories:

- As a user, I want the capability to invite my colleagues to use the product so that I can receive loyalty rewards.

- As a prospective customer, I want to respond to the invitation so I can begin using the product.

- As a data analyst user, I want to view metrics by message topic so I can detect negative comments and reviews that are at risk of going viral.

Developers flag an impediment. The data analyst's story is dependent on the following story:

- As a support agent, I want to assign a tag (topic) to a message so that topic-based analytics can be generated.

Currently, the latter story is sequenced far down in the backlog. Everyone agrees to move the story to the top of the backlog in order to remove the impediment.

You continue to prepare stories on a rolling basis, as each story nears the top of the backlog (Story Preparation in the Daily Activities zone in Figure 4.1). To prepare a story, you meet with the PO, QA, and developers to determine its acceptance criteria and develop wireframes. Each story then undergoes coding, integration, testing, and deployment to a select group of users.

4.6.4 Feature Closeout: Prepare for GA

As soon as enough stories in a feature are done for the feature to satisfy its acceptance criteria, the feature is released for GA. You continue to prepare features and stories on a rolling basis as they come up in the backlog.

4.6.5 Quarterly Inception, Iteration Inception

Some time has passed, and you are reconsidering the analysis and planning process because of changing circumstances. For one thing, the product is now integrated with third-party providers who require a long lead for change requests. For another, the marketing team wants releases to come on a three-month cycle so they have enough lead time to plan campaigns. To accommodate these needs, you advise that each team reserve a portion of its time for initiatives planned on a quarterly basis. The remainder of the team's time will be retained for flow-based (Kanban) work items to preserve the ability to respond quickly when necessary.

At the start of each quarter, each development team convenes to determine the features it will implement over the quarter and specify the plan for rolling them out (Quarterly Planning in the Short Lane in Figure 4.1). They reconvene every two weeks to plan stories for the upcoming iteration (Iteration Planning in the Short Lane in Figure 4.1.)

4.6.6 Iteration Closeout

At the end of each iteration, the team, PO, and interested stakeholders meet for an iteration review to demonstrate the completed stories to stakeholders. Next, the team meets for an iteration retrospective to explore what has been working well and what practices need to be changed (Iteration Closeout in Figure 4.1).

4.6.7 Quarterly Closeout

At the end of the quarter, you facilitate a quarterly retrospective to review how things went and make recommendations (Quarterly Closeout in the Short Lane in Figure 4.1). QA reports it is struggling to meet the demands of development teams to create and run automated tests. The DevOps lead suggests that the solution is not more testers but better coaching, so that developers can create and run tests on their own.

4.7 Act 2: The Long Lane

The free version of CEO is now well established. It includes rich features for replying to customer support messages. The company has now secured longer-term funding to develop new features over the three years in the premium version to support marketing and sales, and analytical reporting. There are now more teams, but the product is still simple enough that each team can operate, for the most part, as a self-sufficient unit. You decide to update the process to include techniques from the Long Lane.

You meet with stakeholders to develop a long-term plan for rolling out features (Long-Term Planning in the Long Lane in Figure 4.1). During this activity, you create a product roadmap, outlining the goals, dates, and features for releases over the next three years. Attendees agree to extend customer-support capabilities to additional social networks in the first release. Marketing features will be added in the release that follows; sales and analytical reporting features will be added in a later release.

At the start of each quarter, you review the product roadmap with stakeholders and adjust it as necessary. You carry out daily analysis and planning activities, as described for the Short Path.

4.8 Act 3: The Grand Lane

The company has now been in business for a few years. The CEO app has grown from a simple, monolithic product to a complex system with multiple microservices and architectural tiers. It's no longer possible to cover all the required competencies within a single team. As a result, multiple teams often have to work closely together to deliver value. You decide to add tools from the Grand Lane to the analysis and planning process because they support the coordination of multiple teams.

4.8.1 Scale the Organization

You facilitate a meeting to discuss how the teams should be organized (Scale the Organization in Figure 4.1). One lead developer argues that teams be formed on the basis of competencies—one for user experience, one for the business layer, one for the database layer, and so on. You argue, instead, that teams be organized around *value* to minimize coordination overhead. You gain agreement that there should be four groups of teams, each focused on a distinct product area, or *usage* of the product:

- Customer support
- Marketing campaigns
- Sales
- Analytical reports

Each feature team will include business and technical competencies to deliver features within its product area. Component teams will be set up to own commonly used micro-services and software interfaces. Teams within a product area will collaborate with each other and with component teams, as necessary, to deliver value.

POs will be allocated as follows: each team will have a team-level PO, each product area will have an area PO, and there will be a product-level PO for the product as a whole. Additional business analysts will be brought in at the team level and as extended members at the product area level, as needed. You will focus on product-level needs and act as lead analyst for the customer-support product area.

4.8.2 Scaled Quarterly Planning

You convene all teams in your product area at the start of each quarter for a two-day multiteam quarterly planning session to determine the features that will be delivered during the quarter (Scaled Quarterly Planning in the Grand Lane in Figure 4.1).

4.8.3 Scaled Iteration Planning

At the start of each iteration, you bring all teams together within your product area for scaled iteration planning, using the "Big Room" approach (Scaled Iteration Planning in the Grand Lane in Figure 4.1). Working closely with each other, the teams plan the stories they will implement in the upcoming iteration. During the session, they check in with each other regularly to ensure their plans align.

As the teams determine what work will be done over the next two weeks, feature team POs advocate for new capabilities, while component team POs promote technical improvements. With the engagement of the product-level PO, you help bring everyone toward a consensus, guided by a company rule of thumb to spend approximately 75 percent of the budget on feature development and 25 percent on technical improvements.

4.8.4 Daily Planning and Analysis

Each day begins with a team-level daily standup. Prioritization conflicts raised during the standup are addressed in the PO council meetings that convene two or three times per week.

Starting around the second week of each iteration, the team analysts in your product area focus on preparing stories for their next iteration planning session.

4.8.5 Iteration Closeout

At the end of each iteration, you gather all the teams in your product area for a scaled iteration review and retrospective.

4.8.6 Quarterly Closeout

At the end of the quarter, you bring together all the teams in your product area for a scaled quarterly retrospective to review how the past quarter went and begin preparations for the next one.

4.9 Chapter Summary

Here are the key points covered in this chapter:

- The Agile Analysis and Planning Map is divided into zones and lanes.
- Each zone (e.g., Initiation and Planning, Quarterly Closeout) groups related activities, events, and artifacts.
- Each lane describes a scenario. It illustrates the activities and artifacts used in the scenario and when to use them.
- The Short Lane is for agile projects that require planning for a horizon up to about three months and do not require coordination between teams.
- The Long Lane is for initiatives that require long-term planning.
- The Grand Lane is for large-scale initiatives that require coordination between teams.

4.10 What's Next?

This chapter provided a brief overview of the whole process. Now, we're going to rewind and start again—this time pausing to learn how to use the tools that apply at each step along the way. That's the subject of the remaining chapters—beginning with Chapter 5, "Preparing the Organization."

Chapter 5

Preparing the Organization

This chapter provides guidelines for preparing small development organizations for agile software development. It includes preparations for a new agile initiative and general guidelines for transitioning organizations toward higher maturity levels of agile analysis. Figure 5.1 highlights the activities covered in the chapter.

The chapter explains how to structure teams by value so that each team can deliver capabilities to customers and users with minimal dependencies on others. The chapter also explains why team dependencies cannot be entirely eliminated. It includes guidelines for forming feature teams and component teams. Also included are guidelines for preparing non-IT divisions new to agile, including the marketing team, financial planners, and compliance officers.

This chapter focuses on small agile organizations of up to ten teams that do not require much inter-team coordination. For guidance on scaled development organizations of collaborating teams, see Chapter 17, "Scaling Agility."

For guidelines on scaling the agile organization, see Chapter 17, section 17.8. For guidance on preparing the enterprise beyond the context of software development, see Chapter 18, "Achieving Enterprise Agility."

5.1 Objectives

This chapter will help you

- Use the purpose alignment model to determine whether a product or capability should be developed in-house or delivered by a third party.

- Prepare departments and stakeholders new to agile development for an agile initiative.

- Determine an organization's target agile maturity level and its readiness for agile development.

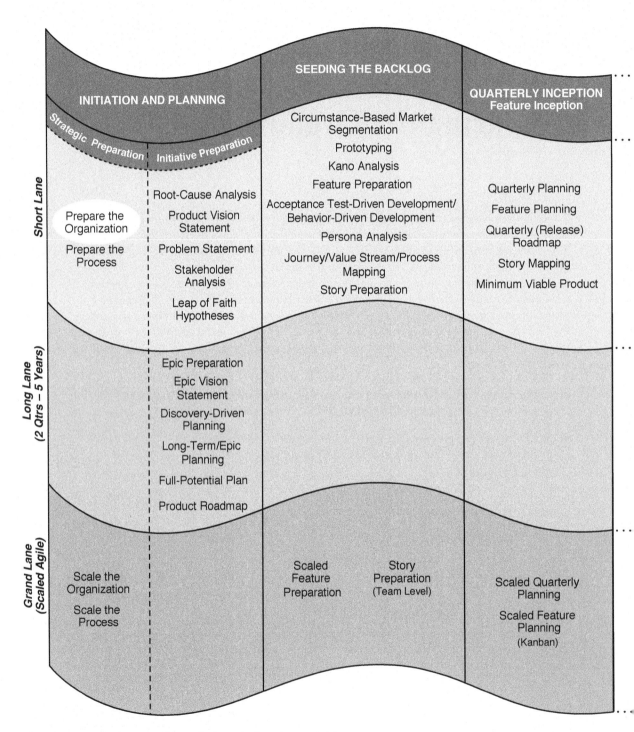

Figure 5.1   *Chapter 5 agile analysis and planning activities*

DAILY ACTIVITIES

QUARTERLY CLOSEOUT
Epic, Feature Closeout

ITERATION INCEPTION

ITERATION CLOSEOUT

Daily Standup

Requirements Analysis & Documentation

Code, Build, Test, Deliver Acceptance
Test-Driven Development/
Behavior-Driven Development

Minimum Viable Product,
Split Testing

Epic, Feature Preparation

Story Preparation

Iteration Planning

Iteration Review

Iteration Retrospective

Prepare for General Availability

Quarterly Retrospective

Epic, Feature Retrospective

Pivot or Persevere

Scaled Iteration Planning

Iteration Planning (Team Level)

Product Owner Council Meetings

DevOps

User Task Force Meetings

Scaled Feature Preparation (Kanban)

Integration Meetings

Story Preparation (Team Level)

Scaled Iteration Review

Scaled Iteration Retrospective

Iteration Retrospective (Team Level)

DevOps

Scaled Quarterly/Feature Retrospective

- Know what structural changes to champion if the organization is not at its target maturity level.

- Understand Kotter's eight steps for accelerating change in an organization.

- Use your knowledge of the ways the product is used to optimize productivity by organizing cross-functional teams around usage.

- Manage the expectations of stakeholders new to agile development.

5.2 This Chapter on the Map

As shown in Figure 5.1, we'll be examining Prepare the Organization, an activity performed as part of the first zone, Initiation and Planning.

5.3 What Is Initiation and Planning?

In Chapter 4, "Analysis and Planning Activities across the Agile Development Lifecycle," we grouped analysis and planning work into zones of related activities—the vertical columns in Figure 5.1. The Initiation and Planning zone covers initial analysis and planning activities for new product development or a significant change to an existing product. The activities in this zone include organizational preparation, calibration of the analysis and planning process, product visioning, initial stakeholder analysis, and the development of a product roadmap for the venture. This chapter focuses on organizational preparation.

Many of the analysis activities in this book presume that the enterprise is already following an agile approach. For organizations that have not yet reached an acceptable level of maturity in agile development or business analysis, this zone also includes activities to get them there.

If a transformation is required, it's unlikely that it will lie within your official sphere of responsibility as a BA, but that doesn't mean it's not your concern. As we'll see in this chapter, your effectiveness as an analyst or consultant lies in the ability to *influence* change to provide better results for the business. This chapter describes *what* changes to champion and introduces some of the approaches you can use to effect change in the organization. For a fuller treatment, I encourage you to explore books devoted to the topic, such as the following recommended titles:

- *Leading Change: Why Transformation Efforts Fail*[1]

- *ADKAR: A Model for Change in Business, Government and Our Community*[2]

---

1. John P. Kotter, *Leading Change: Why Transformation Efforts Fail* (Boston: Harvard Business Review Press, 2012).

2. Jeffrey M. Hiatt, *ADKAR: A Model for Change in Business, Government and Our Community* (Loveland, CO: Prosci Learning Center Publications, 2006).

- *The Heart of Change: Real-Life Stories of How People Change Their Organizations*[3]
- *Changing the Way We Change: Gaining Control of Major Operational Change*[4]
- *Change Management: The People Side of Change*[5]
- *Master Change, Maximize Success: Effective Strategies for Realizing Your Goals*[6]

5.4 How Long Should You Spend Up Front on Initiation and Planning?

As a rule of thumb, the time spent upfront on initiation and planning activities should not exceed 10 percent of the planning horizon. So, if the planning horizon is ten months, as a *general rule*, you wouldn't spend more than one month preparing and planning for it. In practice, take the time you need. But if that turns out to be more than three months, start a separate project for initiation and planning.

At the start of every quarter or significant change, revisit the activities in the Initiation and Planning zone. Make adjustments in light of experience and changing circumstances. For example, it may be necessary to add feature teams or reallocate resources due to changing demand.

5.4.1 The Greater the Anticipated Risks, the Greater the Need for Upfront Planning

Generally speaking, the higher the risks anticipated for a venture, the more upfront analysis and planning will be needed. For example, a high-cost, fixed-contract initiative with an external solution provider exposes the business to the risk of high, unexpected costs: missed requirements can result in cost overruns, missed launch dates, and risks to the customer experience. To mitigate these risks, you need to extend activities in the Initiation and Planning zone to allow for a comprehensive risk analysis in the plan.

5.4.2 What's Past Is Prologue[7]

Tap into the collective wisdom of the organization regarding similar initiatives when determining how long to spend on preparation and planning activities. Reach out to key

---

3. John P. Kotter and Dan S. Cohen, *The Heart of Change: Real-Life Stories of How People Change Their Organizations* (Boston: Harvard Business Review, 2012).

4. Jeanenne LaMarsh, *Changing the Way We Change: Gaining Control of Major Operational Change* (Upper Saddle River, NJ: Prentice Hall PTR, 1995).

5. Jeffrey M. Hiatt and Timothy J. Creasey, *Change Management: The People Side of Change* (Loveland, CO: Prosci Research, 2012).

6. Rebecca Potts and Jeanenne LaMarsh, *Master Change, Maximize Success: Effective Strategies for Realizing Your Goals* (San Francisco: Chronicle Books, 2004).

7. "Whereof what's past is prologue." See William Shakespeare, *The Tempest*, act 2, scene 1, line 217, PlayShakespeare.com, https://www.playshakespeare.com/the-tempest/scenes/act-ii-scene-1

individuals who were involved in these activities in the past. Ask them which activities can be safely postponed until development and which, in their view, should be performed up front because the cost of delaying them would be prohibitive to a successful outcome.

One of the most extreme examples of excessive upfront planning concerned a communications company that asked my company to assess its requirements before it decided on a replacement for its geographic information system (GIS). It didn't take me long to recognize the primary problem: the upfront analysis had gone on for *six years*, and yet nothing had been decided! As Tom Peters (author of *In Search of Excellence*) puts it, "Have a bias for action." Yes, it's vital to spend the necessary time to identify and mitigate risks. But at the same time, you have to realize that you will never have *all* the facts. At some point, you have to dive in with what you know, because the cost to delay the decision any further becomes too high.

5.5 The Purpose Alignment Model

Before you start developing a new product or capability—and even before creating the vision for a new product—how do you know if developing it is the best strategy? Use Niel Nickolaisen's purpose alignment model,[8] illustrated in Figure 5.2, for guidance on this question.

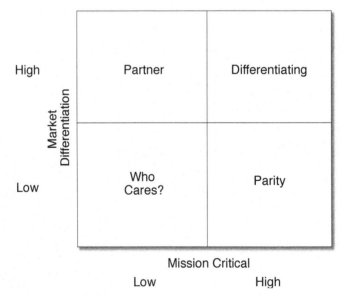

Figure 5.2 *The purpose alignment model*

8. Niel Nickolaisen, "Breaking the Project Management Triangle," InformIT, August 20, 2009, p. 2, https://www.informit.com/articles/article.aspx?p=1384195

The model can be used to evaluate an entire product, service, or capability of a product or service.

If the product or capability already exists and the question is whether to improve it, determine if it is currently at, above, or below parity with similar capabilities available in the market. If it is below parity and improvements are being considered, or it's a new product or capability, determine which quadrant it belongs to, as indicated in Figure 5.2, based on mission criticality and market differentiation. Then use the guidelines for the corresponding quadrant to determine whether to maintain parity, develop the capability in-house, outsource it, or develop it in partnership with another company.

5.5.1 Differentiating Quadrant (Top Right)

The model includes four quadrants based on levels of market differentiation and mission criticality. Use the top-right quadrant in Figure 5.2 for mission-critical products or capabilities that are market differentiators. Items landing in this category should be developed in-house by long-lived teams because they have to be continually improved for the product to remain competitive.

5.5.2 Parity Quadrant (Bottom Right)

The bottom-right quadrant in Figure 5.2 is for mission-critical capabilities that are not core differentiators. *Parity* with the market standard is sufficient for these items, since excellence is unlikely to affect customer choice.

Develop items in this quadrant in-house, or outsource them. Weigh the immediate savings of outsourcing against future costs. Keep in mind that choices made early on can have a significant impact on the cost of future changes.

> As a general rule of thumb, use the following guidelines for capabilities in the quadrant:
>
> - Use an outsourced solution if the product or capability is a novel innovation. Outsourcing enables accelerated learning by providing the ability to test the market for the capability quickly at a low cost.
> - Use an in-house solution if uncertainty is low and high volumes are expected—for example, when improving an established product with a large customer base. While upfront costs and time to market are higher with an in-house solution than with outsourcing, total costs will be lower once volumes are high.

One example of a parity capability is eBay's payment processing. Payment processing is a parity capability for eBay because it's mission-critical but not a differentiator. Early on, when the business case for eBay was, as yet, unproven, it outsourced payment processing to PayPal in order to deliver the capability quickly with minimal upfront investment. By

2002, eBay's volume grew to the point where it no longer made financial sense to out-source the service, and the company brought it in-house by purchasing PayPal.

Many businesses face a similar decision regarding cloud services, such as AWS (Amazon Web Services). At the outset of product development, the use of these services speeds time to market, provides scalability, and doesn't require a substantial upfront investment. However, once the business grows, the cost of these services often tips the scale in favor of in-house development.

If an outsourced solution is to be used, explore ways to reduce future costs in case the solution needs to be replaced when volumes rise. Costs can be significantly reduced by building adaptability into the design from the start, such as through strategies like service-oriented architecture (SOA) and the use of outgoing APIs for messages to third-party services.

5.5.3 Partner Quadrant (Top Left)

Use the top-left quadrant in Figure 5.2 for capabilities and products that are differen-tiators but outside the company's core mission and competency. For example, consider a training company whose value lies in its intellectual content—the courseware, work-books, and so on, that it provides to its customers. Suppose that it decides to launch an eLearning platform. The platform is not the company's core competency, but it is a crucial differentiator. The preferred option is to develop the services collaboratively through a long-term partnership with a third party. That option provides a stable basis for ongoing innovation in a critical area without diverting the company from its core mission.

5.5.4 Who Cares? Quadrant (Bottom Left)

Use the bottom-left quadrant for capabilities that have low mission-criticality and market differentiation. Spend as little resources as possible on these capabilities. Consider exclud-ing them from product development due to their low value to the business.

5.6 Preparing the Infrastructure

For the full potential of agile development to be realized, you have to ensure the right development and testing infrastructure exists—one that supports DevOps and continuous integration and continuous delivery (CI/CD) practices, including automated testing, auto-mated builds, and provisioning. Figure 5.3 illustrates what happens when that infrastruc-ture is lacking. Unfortunately, I still see this situation in some development organizations.

In Figure 5.3, user stories undergo unit tests and low-level integration tests as soon as they're completed. Once they pass those tests, they are tested against their acceptance criteria in the presence of the development team. If the story fails its acceptance criteria or just does not "feel right" to users, it is sent back for immediate rework. Once the story is accepted (and satisfies the definition of done), it is considered done. So far, so good. However, in this scenario, because the final build-and-test steps involve time-consuming manual tasks, they are delayed until the end of the release cycle.

Manual Test and Deploy with Delayed Integration and Release

| Code + Compile | → | Unit Test | → *Deploy to Staging* → | Low-level Integration Tests | → | User Story Testing (Acceptance Criteria) | → | Final Build and Test (UAT) | → *Deploy to Production* → | Deployment |

Development Environment — *Staging Environment* — *Production*

←---- During Iteration ----→←---- Prior to Release ----→

Figure 5.3 *Testing without automation*

This approach is better than pure waterfall because low-level technical testing occurs continuously and early instead of at the end of the development lifecycle. But it's not the ideal approach because it delays testing under realistic production conditions until the end of the release cycle—a period of up to three months. In addition, this approach doesn't provide the option for the timely release of changes the business wants to implement immediately, such as bug fixes and small enhancements to existing features.

The *recommended* agile approach, instead, is to use DevOps, incorporating CI and CD practices. With this approach, a work item undergoes its build and final testing steps automatically, as soon as the item has been coded and has passed its initial tests. This automation enables changes to be delivered frequently and reliably to the customer, while actual market deployment is based on the demands of the business. For example, the company may want to hold back a feature until it is mature enough to be competitive in the marketplace or until there are enough supporting features to allow a user to have a better experience.

For more on DevOps and other technical practices, see Chapter 17, section 17.5.2.1.

5.6.1 Transitioning from Manual to Automated Testing

Test automation is key to enabling a company to deliver changes to the market with speed and confidence. If your organization is transitioning toward automated testing, use the test pyramid in Figure 5.4 as a guideline to determine where to focus the automation effort for maximum benefit.

The figure illustrates the relative prevalence of tests by test type. The type with the most tests is at the bottom of the pyramid. The type with the fewest is at the top. (Other versions of the pyramid, such as Martin Fowler's, may vary from that shown in Figure 5.4.)[9]

---

9. Martin Fowler, TestPyramid, MartinFowler.com, November 15, 2017 (originally published May 1, 2012), https://martinfowler.com/bliki/TestPyramid.html

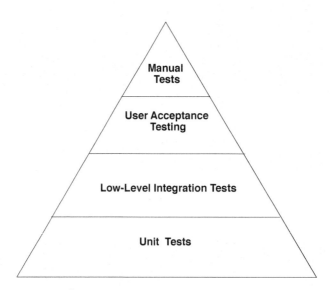

Figure 5.4 *Test pyramid*

At the top of the pyramid are manual tests. These should be the least numerous because they are the most time consuming and expensive to run.

Next are automated user acceptance tests. There should be fewer automated tests of this type than the types below it on the pyramid. There are several reasons for this:[10]

- User acceptance testing (UAT) tends to be brittle. Changes to the user interface can easily break existing tests.

- Automated UAT scenarios are expensive to write.

- User acceptance tests have a propensity for nondeterministic behavior (i.e., they provide inconsistent results for the same test, making them difficult to diagnose).

Automated lower-level integration tests verify the connection between one software component and another, such as the connection between a programming unit and an API to which it sends messages. These automated tests should be more numerous than user acceptance tests because they are less brittle. Most automated tests should be unit tests, because

- There are more low-level units to test than higher-level components.

- Unit tests are frequently reused in regression testing and are a critical capability for enabling reliable, continuous delivery.

- Automated unit tests are less subject to change than other test types.

---

10. Fowler, TestPyramid.

Use the testing pyramid to guide the transition to test automation for software that's *already* been written:

- Focus test automation, at first, on end-to-end UAT (at the top of the pyramid), since you won't need many of these relative to other types of tests.

- Next, focus on automating lower-level integration tests.

- Finally, create automated unit tests (bottom of the pyramid) for existing software units.

When prioritizing the automation of *new* software units, advance through the pyramid in the opposite direction, from the bottom up. Developers should begin creating automated unit tests and low-level integrations tests as part of their coding process. All new software units should include these tests and pass them before being accepted. Expect testing-automation activities to take up about 50 percent of a developer's coding time. As an analyst, you collaborate with others to specify UAT.

5.6.2 Timing the Automation of the Build and Distribution Processes

When transitioning to automated build and distribution processes, focus investment on new products, because decisions made early in the product's lifecycle have a disproportionate impact on future automation costs. For example,

- A system designed at the outset to use Web Services (e.g., AWS) for its build and distribution processes can be built and scaled later at much less cost than one that relies heavily on manual intervention.

- New releases of a product designed at the outset as a website are easier to distribute reliably than a product designed as a mobile app or as a laptop application. The former requires updates only at the server end, whereas the latter involves users' participation—introducing unreliability because some users may not participate.

5.7 Organizing Development Teams

I once attended an address given by a vice president of software development before his retirement. "If I had to do it all over again," he said, "I would have organized teams differently." He had realized that he had made a mistake organizing his teams by competency: one team for business analysts, a data layer team, an interface team, and so on. This approach had caused team dependencies that, in turn, led to delays whenever a team had to wait for others before it could deliver stories into production. In this section, we look at the guidelines for forming agile teams that reduce dependencies and optimize productivity.

5.7.1 Guidelines for Forming Agile Teams

> Use the following guidelines to form teams that can respond quickly to change.
>
> - Everyone works for the customer
> - Foster a whole-team culture
> - Maximize self-sufficiency
> - Self-management
> - Keep teams small
> - Favor full-time membership

5.7.1.1 Everyone Works for the Customer

Encourage a culture where all team members, whether they're business SMEs or programmers, work for the *customer*, not for internal stakeholders or departments.

5.7.1.2 Foster a Whole-Team Culture

Encourage a *whole-team* culture—where the *entire team* is responsible for reaching team goals, and everyone, regardless of job title, shares responsibility for success and failure. Encourage team members to have a collaborative mindset in which everyone contributes to shared goals according to their skill set, not their formal roles.

5.7.1.3 Maximize Self-Sufficiency

Where possible, form teams that include the competencies (skills, knowledge, and abilities) required to deliver value. Include business stakeholders and practitioners on the *same* team. Based on their knowledge and experience, business stakeholders may participate as SMEs, business analysts, testers, or product owners.

By including as many business and technical capabilities as possible within the team, you reduce dependencies and handoffs and accelerate decision-making. The cross-functional composition of the team also prevents the emergence of silos and the tendency to create factions.

Note that in many cases, you may need to share resources between teams. For example, there may not be enough work to occupy a UX designer or business analyst on a full-time basis, so that person may be made available to a group of teams. These shared team members form part of the **extended team**.

Some agile frameworks, such as Scrum, advise that team dependencies be eliminated by organizing self-sufficient teams, where each team contains all the skills required to deliver value.[11] In practice, though, it's usually not possible to remove all dependencies because of several factors:

- Features are intentionally designed to be well-integrated. This results in dependencies between the feature teams that support them.

- The product is often too complex for any single team to contain all the competencies required to deliver value.

- Component teams are often formed to maintain commonly used software components. This results in dependencies between feature and component teams.

5.7.1.4 Self-Management

Each team should make tactical decisions and decide for itself how to, when to, and who will carry out the work, while leaving bigger, strategic decisions to senior-level decision makers.

5.7.1.5 Keep Teams Small

Each agile team should consist of about five to ten members. At least some of these members should be jacks-of-all-trades, adaptable enough to pitch in as needed (e.g., performing QA, BA, and UX tasks as required).

5.7.1.6 Favor Full-Time Participation

As a general guideline, members should be fully dedicated to one team so they can focus entirely on the team goal and reduce time lost to task-switching between teams. It is likely, though, that some members will have to be shared, perhaps due to a lack of resources or because there isn't enough work in a competency to justify a full-time person. Cohn recommends that teams form a consensus on simple rules regarding sharing, such as "No person can be assigned to more than two projects" or "Everyone on the team must be at least x% dedicated to the team."[12]

5.7.2 Organize around Value

Organize teams around value, not competencies, so that each team can deliver value to an end user or customer with minimal dependencies on other teams. Figure 5.5 is an example of teams organized around value in a small development organization.

In the example in Figure 5.5, the product is small enough for each team to be able to contain all the required competencies.

---

11. For example, the Scrum Guide states, "Scrum Teams are cross-functional, meaning the members have all the skills necessary to create value each Sprint." Ken Schwaber and Jeff Sutherland, *The Scrum Guide: The Definitive Guide to Scrum—The Rules of the Game*, Scrumguides.org, 2020, 5, https://www.scrumguides.org

12. Mike Cohn, *Succeeding with Agile* (Boston: Addison-Wesley, 2010), 196–197.

Note that the boxes within each team in Figure 5.5 refer to competencies, not individuals. An individual may have more than one competency, and a competency may be practiced by more than one individual on the team.

The benefit to the business in organizing by value is that it can adapt the product quickly and reliably in response to changing circumstances, new opportunities, and threats.

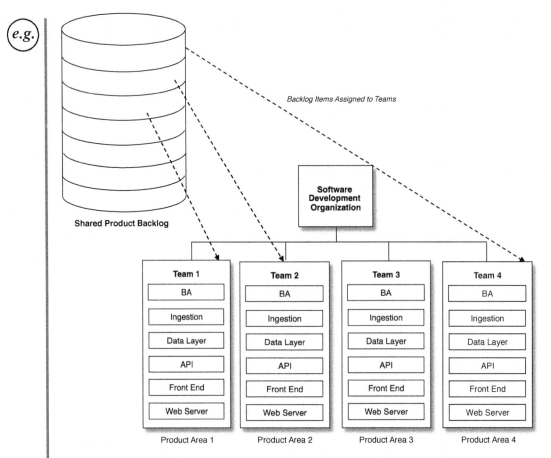

Figure 5.5 *Teams organized by value*

5.7.3 Feature Teams versus Generic Teams

As a general rule, the best organizational strategy is to create long-lived **feature teams** that each specialize in a product area. A **product area** is a subset of the product representing a high-level use case (usage) or feature set. Over time, the team gains expertise in its product area, resulting in optimized performance and reduced turnaround time. For an example of teams of teams by product area, see Figure 17.4 in Chapter 17.

The exception is during the early stages of new product development when teams should be generic. Generic teams at that time enable managers to allocate resources dynamically in response to changing demand. Once the product has stabilized, though, and demand is more predictable, teams should organize into long-lived feature teams.

5.7.4 The Extended Team

Once a product matures and becomes more complex, you typically can't contain all the required competencies within a small agile team of about ten or fewer members. Fully self-sufficient teams are no longer possible. Instead, teams need to collaborate. They often need to share members, too (as noted in section 5.7.1.6).

Figure 5.6 illustrates the structure of a feature team for a mature product, highlighting dedicated and shared team members. The following is one example. It's not a general prescription. Individual team structures will vary.

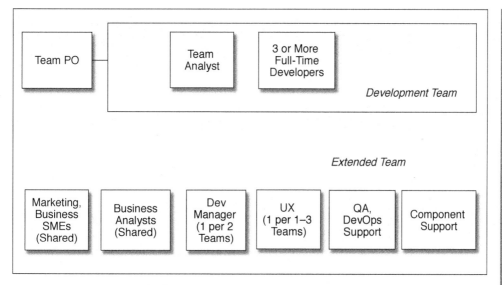

Figure 5.6 *Structure of a feature team*

The core development team in Figure 5.6 consists of one team analyst and three or more full-time developers. The **extended team** includes shared members: these are marketing and business SMEs, high-level business analysts, a development manager shared among no more than two teams, a UX designer shared among one to three teams, QA and DevOps professionals to coach the team in automated testing and integration, and support for the software components used by the team.

See Chapter 15, "Rolling Analysis and Preparation—Day-to-Day Activities," section 15.3, for more on organizing teams in scaled agile organizations.

5.7.5 Why Organizing by Competency Is Bad for the Business

As noted earlier in the chapter, it's a common mistake to organize teams by competency instead of by value. Team organization may sound like an issue of little concern to the business or business analyst, but it's not, because poor organization delays time to market.

Figure 5.7 illustrates why. It depicts a development organization for a messaging product, organized by competency.

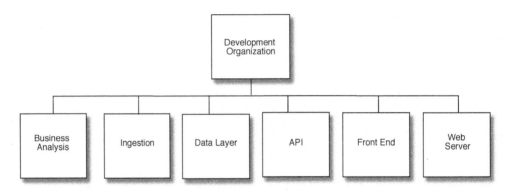

Figure 5.7   *Teams organized by competency (not advised!)*

In Figure 5.7, there is one team to handle high-level BA and a team for each technical layer of the application: ingestion (loading messages into the app), data layer, API, front end, and Web server. The trouble with this arrangement is that no single team can deliver value on its own. For example, a feature to add a new message type requires

- Analysis by the BA team.
- Work by the ingestion team to load the new message type into the system.
- Work by the data layer team to enable the new message type to be stored in the database.
- Work by the front-end team to allow the new messages to be displayed.

If any of these teams finishes early, the feature can't be released any sooner. The feature is only releasable once *all* the other teams have completed their work. This structure also increases the number of handoffs and approvals per feature. Each handoff introduces a time lag to wait for approvals, to plan, and to allocate tasks for the next team—increasing the overall time it takes to bring change requests to the market. If teams are currently organized this way, champion transformational change to prevent these negative impacts. As we've seen, that means organizing teams by value into feature teams.

5.8 Managing Stakeholder Expectations about Agile Development

If you set appropriate expectations about agile development from the start, stakeholders are more likely to take the long view when problems arise (as they inevitably will). Let's look at examples of common stakeholder expectations and how to manage them.

5.8.1 The Negative Expectation That Requirements Delayed Are Requirements Denied

A common expectation of stakeholders new to agile development is that requirements that don't make it into the first cycle will never get implemented. Stakeholders have often learned this lesson from negative experiences with waterfall development. The consequence is stakeholders who assign high priorities across the board to requirements items. This outcome is anathema to agile development, since the approach is based on the phased rollout of requirements over time.

To head off this problem before it becomes an issue, meet with stakeholders early on to explain the agile trade-off: the customer gets the benefit of shortened time to market and continuous delivery of features instead of the long lag time that is typical of waterfall processes. However, to obtain those benefits, business stakeholders have to prioritize some requirements over others because agile development is, by nature, incremental. Another advantage of agile development to stakeholders is that they can change their minds at any time and reprioritize requirements based on changing circumstances.

> To help stakeholders focus on what's most important, *ask them to imagine what core features they would want to deliver if the initiative ran out of time or money at some point in the development cycle.*

Sometimes it helps to flip the terminology: instead of speaking about *prioritizing* requirements, talk about *sequencing* them—reframing the conversation from one about *values* to a practical one about *problem solving.*

Make sure stakeholders also understand that they don't have to make prioritization decisions on entire features. For example, they may decide to implement some stories of Feature X first, followed by some stories for Feature Y, followed by more stories for Feature X.

There's nothing more persuasive than the evidence of one's own eyes, though, to convince stakeholders that agile's incremental approach works and that requirements delayed are not requirements denied. Provide opportunities for stakeholders to meet teams and customers who have been using agile development successfully. Arrange for experienced agile teams to invite new stakeholders to sit in as observers during product demonstrations.

5.8.2 Productivity Expectations

A few years ago, I was speaking with an executive about his company's planned agile transition. He told me that stakeholders were very enthusiastic about "agile getting their products to market much quicker." I should have been pleased, but I was concerned. Business stakeholders sometimes mistake agile's promise of *early delivery* to mean that they can get *all* the requirements they want in much less time than waterfall. The reality is not so straightforward. For example, in Chapter 2, "Agile Analysis and Planning," I quoted a QSM study that found that agile projects received a 16 percent productivity increase compared to the industry average.[13] It is a significant benefit—but far from the expectations of "several 100 percent" gains in productivity made in the early days of Scrum.[14]

On the other hand, the same study found that "Agile Projects are 37% faster to market than [the] industry average."[15] How can agile development result in faster time to market without corresponding increases in productivity? The answer lies in *what* is delivered: agile development enables a business to bring *something* to market quickly—but not the whole wish list. What agile development delivers quickly is a *minimum marketable product* with a limited set of features. Make sure stakeholders understand that the approach speeds time to market by focusing effort on the *highest-value* features, not by delivering the *same* set of features in less time. The value of agile development lies in learning that *not all the requested features are actually needed*—or that less-costly versions will be able to get the job done just as well.

Another common but incorrect expectation is that productivity improvements will come quickly as an organization transitions to agile development. More commonly, it can take a few months to a few years for teams to get good enough at agile development for improvements to be realized.

Stakeholders also can have mistaken expectations about what will be delivered frequently. Many expect that software updates will be delivered to the *market* at least every one to two weeks (the length of a typical Scrum sprint). That may be the case for some updates, but it's often not so for major features. Although deployment to a *testing* environment occurs continuously, it can often still take two to three months to deploy significant changes to the *market*. The benefit of agile development, in this case, is that the delivered solution will be

- More *relevant*—since it is based on current priorities and requirements.

- More likely to *delight the user*—since it relies on user feedback throughout the development process.

---

13. QSM Associates, *The Agile Impact Report, Proven Performance Metrics from the Agile Enterprise* (Boulder, CO: Rally Software, 2015), 5, https://www.rallydev.com/sites/default/files/ Agile_Impact_Report.pdf. Productivity was measured as an aggregate of tooling and methods, technical difficulty, personnel profiles, and integration issues.

14. Ken Schwaber and Mike Beedle, *Agile Software Development with Scrum* (Upper Saddle River, NJ: Prentice Hall, 2002), viii.

15. QSM Associates, *The Agile Impact Report*, 4.

- More cost-efficient—because it weeds out low-value requirements and eliminates administrative waste.

5.9 Preparing the Customer–Developer Relationship

In Chapter 1, "The Art of Agile Analysis and Planning," you read about a company whose meetings kept ending in acrimony because business stakeholders didn't believe the developers' estimates. The problem, at its heart, had to do with the relationship between business stakeholders and the development organization. In this instance, the relationship was contractual. In a truly agile organization, it's collaborative, with both sides working together to problem-solve as circumstances change.

Prepare both parties in the relationship by gaining early consensus regarding norms of behavior. Following XP guidance, coach them to codify this consensus in a bill of rights and responsibilities for the customer and the development team. The *customer*, in this context, refers to the entity representing customers and stakeholders (e.g., a Scrum product owner (PO) or a customer team).

5.9.1 Customer's Bill of Rights and Responsibilities

Following is an example of a customer bill of rights and responsibilities.

Customer Bill of Rights

The customer has ultimate responsibility for managing and prioritizing the stories in the product backlog, subject to the following constraints:

- The customer does so with the approval of stakeholders and in collaboration with development and operations.
- If a conflict can't be resolved through collaboration, a higher-level role may be called upon to make a decision.
- The customer may add, drop, and change stories and acceptance criteria.
- The customer may change priorities and functionality without undue penalties.

If the organization is using iterations for planning (e.g., as indicated by Scrum), these rights are subject to the following limitations.

The customer

- May not add stories, acceptance criteria, or functionality to an iteration once it begins unless the development team agrees.
- May not change the length of an iteration once it begins.

---

e.g.

> **Customer Responsibilities**
>
> The customer agrees to
>
> - Accept the estimates of the development team.
> - Participate in team planning.
> - Respond to developers' questions in a timely fashion.
> - Collaborate with developers to explore options.

5.9.2 Developers' Bill of Rights and Responsibilities

Following is an example of the developers' bill of rights and responsibilities.

> **Developers' Rights**
>
> The development team
>
> - Has the sole right to make and update estimates.
> - Has the right to add technical stories to the backlog.
>
> **Developers' Responsibilities**
>
> The development team agrees to
>
> - Deliver a potentially shippable integrated increment with each work item.
> - Accept the priorities assigned by the customer to backlog items.
> - Be transparent with the customer about progress.
> - Alert the customer if goals are endangered.
> - Collaborate with the customer to explore alternatives and trade-offs.

5.10 Agile Financial Planning

Prepare financial planners for changes in the way planning is performed on agile initiatives in contrast to traditional waterfall projects. Following is an overview of those differences.

5.10.1 Measuring Success

In traditional waterfall project management, you measure success by the degree to which the solution delivers specified outputs (the *deliverables*) at a given cost within a specified time. You can't use this approach on agile software initiatives because there is no base-lined set of requirements to be delivered: by intention, agile requirements are subject to change at any time.

Agile initiatives measure success on the basis of desired business *outcomes*[16] rather than prespecified outputs. You don't ask, "Did the customer receive a product with the specified features on time and budget?" Instead, you ask, "Did the customer increase market share as much as expected?" or "Did it get the expected return on investment?"

5.10.2 Discovery-Driven Financial Planning

Traditional financial planning approaches rely on past data to make projections into the future. This approach doesn't apply when the product is novel because there is no historical or trend data to draw from. In such circumstances, financial planning methods need to take uncertainty into account and bake it into the plan.

One approach to doing that is by **discovery-driven planning**. With this method, instead of projecting an expected bottom line from historical trends, you begin by specifying the bottom line that must be achieved for the venture to be successful. Then you work *backward* to identify the assumptions you need to make to get there (e.g., assumptions about the price customers will pay and support costs). These assumptions then drive the planning process: you create a plan to test critical hypotheses as early as possible.

For more on discovery-driven planning, see Chapter 18, section 18.10.2, and Appendix B.

5.11 Preparing the Marketing and Distribution Teams

If the marketing team is new to agile development, you'll need to help it prepare for changes resulting from the approach. Prepare marketers to expect that only the release date and goals may be committed at the start of a release cycle; the features may not be determined until close to the scheduled release date. As a result, marketers may not be able to specify the content of advertising copy until close to the release date.[17] This is in contrast to traditional waterfall development, where marketing teams obtain a list of committed features with a comfortable lead time.

In many organizations, this plays out as follows: The marketing group sets the release date based on business conditions. It sends marketing representatives to the feature teams as extended team members. They collaborate with developers to establish the lead time

---

16. Michael F. Hanford, "Program Management: Different from Project Management," IBM Developer Works, May 14, 2004, http://www.ibm.com/developerworks/rational/library/4751.html
17. Cohn, *Succeeding with Agile*, 39.

required before a general release to allow for marketing, testing, and deployment activities. They then work backward from the release date to set a cut-off date that provides the necessary lead time. When the cut-off date arrives, only those features deemed *done* are included in the release and promoted in advertising.

Prepare the marketing team for changes at the front end of development as well. Explain that they will need to use new methods to analyze the market because traditional research methods don't apply to novel products. The product class may be so new that there are no comparable products to compare it to, and customers can't reliably predict what they'll want. Discuss the use of **circumstance-based market segmentation**. The approach is based on the insight that "People don't want to buy a quarter-inch drill. They want a quarter-inch hole."[18] In other words, they're not really looking for a product; they're looking to get a job done. Following the approach, researchers recruit customers in the field and interview them to learn what jobs they are trying to accomplish, the constraints that influence their choice of product, and what other products they've sometimes purchased for the same job.

For more on circumstance-based market segmentation, see Chapter 8, section 8.4.

5.12 Preparing Channels and Supply Chains

If the company is an established incumbent developing a novel product, it should plan for changes to its existing distribution and supply channels. An established company's current market, distribution channels, and supply chains often are not appropriate for the new product and must be developed in an iterative, agile manner, just like the product itself.

5.13 Preparing Governance and Compliance

Governance is concerned with overseeing an initiative by monitoring its progress and expenditures to determine how well it is adhering to its plan. *Compliance* is concerned with ensuring the initiative conforms to standards and guidelines—both internal to the company and external (e.g., ISACA/CMMI Institute's Capability Maturity Model Integration [CMMI], Institute of Electrical and Electronics Engineers [IEEE], Information Technology Infrastructure Library [ITIL], and Sarbanes-Oxley Act [SOX]).

Agile development includes some practices that, at least at first glance, appear to run counter to governance and compliance in traditional organizations. Examples of these agile practices include minimal documentation, lack of formal sign-offs and the postponement of decisions to the last responsible moment. Despite this apparent conflict, agile

---

18. Harvard Business School professor Theodore Levitt, as quoted in Clayton M. Christensen, Scott Cook, and Taddy Hall, "What Customers Want from Your Products," *Working Knowledge*, January 16, 2006, https://hbswk.hbs.edu./item/what-customers-want-from-your-products

development can usually be brought in line with governance and compliance regulations if the appropriate preparations and adaptations are made.

If governance and compliance officers are new to agile development, use the following strategies to prepare them for an agile initiative.

5.13.1 Challenge Compliance Assumptions

Be willing to challenge assumptions about compliance rules. There is often much more room for give-and-take than you might first expect. The following real example is instructive: A company was planning to use a third-party vendor for new product development. The auditor was concerned that the vendor might change agreed-upon requirements. This concern was expressed in the following rule: "If a vendor logs in to the requirements repository, the vendor is prevented from changing requirements." The lead analyst determined that the rule would not be easy to enforce, so he pushed back. They agreed that only a "controlled environment" would be needed for compliance—and that the unique, trackable login identification already provided by the repository on changes was sufficient.

5.13.2 Do Compliance *After* Process Design

One of the most useful pieces of advice regarding compliance and agile development comes from Andre Franklin, a process and systems analysis expert in drug research and development services—a highly regulated sector—who provided this guidance: Don't have auditors determine what the process should be. Design the process first the way you want it. Then bring the process to auditors for approval. That way, practitioners do what they do best—design processes—"and auditors do what they do best—audit processes for compliance."

5.13.3 Focus on Goals, Not Means

Another effective strategy is to argue that though an agile process may use nontraditional lightweight methods, it still achieves the goals behind compliance regulations.

For example, it is sometimes assumed that testing standards strictly govern the testing process, whereas they often only define *goals* for testing; that there must be a well-defined testing process in place; that it must be followed; and that it must lead to a low defect rate. There is often a great deal of latitude, however, on *how* to achieve those goals. The DevOps automated environment used in agile development often achieves the goals of standards, because it results in high levels of testing, leading to low defect rates. For example, Cohn reports that CMMI compliance up to level 5 has been achieved with agile frameworks.[19]

The same is true concerning documentation: while the *types* of documents required for compliance are often nonnegotiable, there is often flexibility regarding the *form* the

---

19. Cohn, *Succeeding with Agile*, 400. Cohn lists Philips Research and Systematic as examples of companies achieving CMMI compliance with agile processes.

documentation takes. Even minimalist documentation, in the form of photo images of whiteboard designs, can be sufficient to satisfy compliance regulations.

Concerning ISO 9001, a study of agile organizations concluded that "an agile process [can] produce documents that can be used (1) as proof of conformance and that (2) can be reviewed as part of ISO 9001's verification and validation" and that "there will be no problems whatsoever when a company wants to use agile development and still keep its ISO 9001 certificate."[20]

5.13.4 One-Time Experiments

If you aren't successful at gaining governance and compliance adaptations for agile development at the enterprise level, try negotiating such governance changes as one-time experiments.

5.14 Preparing for Increased Demand on Resources

If the organization is new to agile development, engage functional groups and alert them to expect an increased demand for human resources to support agile methods. If the resources are required across multiple initiatives and projects, the organization may need to follow an extensive process to review the request against workforce capacity. A central body such as the project management office (PMO) may need to be called in to help with the allocation of talent.

Following is an example of the number of resources that might be expected to support an agile development initiative (individual cases will vary):

- One business stakeholder, who is comfortable making decisions, for each team of five to ten people, acting in the role of team-level PO.

- Business SMEs, as needed, dedicated to feature teams or shared among a group of teams as extended team members. These individuals must be prepared to make themselves available throughout the development cycle rather than only at its ends, as is the case with waterfall development.

- Business analysts dedicated or shared among a group of teams.

In addition to these requirements, technical competencies will also be required. They may be fully dedicated to a team or shared as part of the extended team, as indicated in the example in Figure 5.6.

---

20. Tor Stålhane and Geir Kjetil Hanssen, "The Application of ISO 9001 to Agile Software Development" (conference paper, Product-Focused Software Process Improvement, 9th International Conference, PROFES 2008, Monte Porzio Catone, Italy, June 23–25, 2008), p. 14.

5.15 Preparing an Enterprise for Agile Development

In the preceding sections, we focused on preparation for a specific agile initiative—a new product or significant capability. But these guidelines presume that the organization already has some degree of maturity using agile as an approach for product development. If the organization is not yet there, you, as a business analyst, should take steps to influence change. (This added work will not be necessary, however, if the organization's maturity level is high.) Start the process by preparing the business case for transitioning to a higher level of maturity in agile development and analysis. Use the recommendations in this chapter to identify the current and target levels of agility. Include industry statistics and the benefits of agile development, and find an executive who will champion the effort.

A critical strategic planning activity when transitioning to agile development is the development of a change management approach. It should describe how the change will be communicated to the organization, how people will be trained in agile techniques, how resistance to change will be managed, and how roles and responsibilities will be defined. If you're a team-level analyst, these issues are unlikely to fall within your formal sphere of duties, but they do fall within your sphere of influence. That's because, as an analyst, your role is to be an agent of change within your organization. It is your ability to influence and convince others (e.g., through stealth change management) that makes you effective. That power often extends beyond your formal duties.

I feel passionately about this issue because so much of the organizational change I have been involved in has been due to visionary BA practitioners wielding outsized influence because of the high regard in which they were held by their peers. It's worth noting, though, that while you, as an analyst, are a *catalyst* for change, the change must be supported by a coalition of committed executives across the organization and by representatives at all levels for it to be sustainable—and this support must be consistent and long-lived. Without a broad and deep commitment, it's difficult to maintain successes over the long period, and old habits eventually return—an unfortunate situation I have seen in other organizations.

If the organization's level of maturity in agile development is already high, a full change management process may not be needed. If an extensive transformation is called for, then a process should be instituted with a full-time change management lead. The following sections describe some of the activities to consider in your change management approach.

5.15.1 Agile Fluency Model

The first step in getting from a current to a desired level of agility is to determine what those levels are. Use the agile fluency model, devised by Shore and Larsen,[21] to grade your

---

21. James Shore and Diana Larsen, "The Agile Fluency Model: A Brief Guide to Success with Agile," ThoughtWorks, March 6, 2018, https://martinfowler.com/articles/agileFluency.html

organization's current and target levels of agile fluency. It characterizes each successive level as a zone, as follows:

- Zone 1: *Focusing.* Teams produce business value.
- Zone 2: *Delivering.* Teams deliver value on market cadence (i.e., based on demand from the market).
- Zone 3. *Optimizing.* Teams lead their market.
- Zone 4. *Strengthening.* Teams make their organizations stronger.

Zone 4 is the highest agility level, but it's not necessarily the correct destination for every organization. Your goal should be to choose the right target zone (or zones) for the situation. The entire enterprise doesn't need to set the same target. Guidelines for assigning zones are provided in the following sections.

5.15.1.1 Zone 1: Focusing

Assign the Zone 1, Focusing, level if teams have absorbed agile fundamentals and can work collaboratively and transparently. These teams are benefiting from agile practice, but their processes are not repeatable. Zone 1 is an appropriate target for teams at the start of an enterprise transition when they are experimenting with the process. This zone is also a sufficient target level for teams working on short-lived software systems.

5.15.1.2 Zone 2: Delivering

Assign the Zone 2, Delivering, level if processes are repeatable, benefits are sustainable, and productivity and adaptability are high. This zone is an appropriate target for teams that will be working on systems or products that will be enhanced over a long period.

5.15.1.3 Zone 3: Optimizing

Assign the Zone 3, Optimizing, level if the organization is developing disruptive products and services. Advancement to this level typically requires structural change.

 See Chapter 17, section 17.8, for guidance on structuring organizations in this zone.

5.15.1.4 Zone 4, Strengthening

Zone 4, Strengthening, is for organizations using innovative approaches to management theory and practice.

 See Chapter 18 for guidance on applying agile approaches at the enterprise level.

5.15.2 Transitioning the Team

If the development team has not practiced agile development before, a coach should mentor the team for the first couple of months, after which you (the analyst) or another full-time team member, such as a ScrumMaster, should take over the role. At this time, the coach moves to the sidelines, returning to work with the team as needed.

The aim should be to advance the team's agile fluency level to the desired target zone, according to the agile fluency model. The focus should be on improving the structural aspects of the team. The Tuckman model,[22] which describes the stages of a maturing team, may be used to guide these improvements at the team level. Teams should be guided through the *forming* stage (where there is a high dependence on the leader), to *storming* (where team members jostle for position), to *norming* (where consensus forms), to *performing* (where the team is united in purpose and self-sufficient).

5.15.3 Transition Activities at the Enterprise Level

If the organization is new to agile development or is practicing it but struggling with the approach, a full change management process will be needed to improve agile practices across the enterprise. The following sections provide guidelines for creating and accelerating that change according to Kotter's eight-step process.

5.15.3.1 Kotter's Eight Steps for Accelerating Change

John Kotter has described the following eight steps for accelerating change in an organization:[23]

- "Create a sense of urgency." Generate and sustain a sense of urgency about the transformation. Identify and communicate a big opportunity that is available today but may be gone tomorrow. Explain what steps need to be taken to get there, the advantages in succeeding, and the costs of failure.

- "Build a guiding coalition." Create a diverse coalition to guide the transformation. Seek out change agents. The alliance should represent all levels of the organization, functions, and locations.

- "Form a strategic vision and initiatives." Strategic initiatives are "targeted and coordinated activities that, if designed and executed fast enough and well enough, will make your vision a reality."[24] The vision communicates how the future will improve upon the present, motivates product developers and stakeholders, and helps them align their efforts toward a common purpose.

- "Enlist a volunteer army." Create a movement of people within the organization motivated by the vision for change. Kotter reports that 15 percent of an organization adopting the change is enough to generate momentum. At 50 percent, the change is sustaining.[25]

---

22. Denise A. Bonebright, "40 Years of Storming: A Historical Review of Tuckman's Model of Small Group Development," *Human Resource Development International* 13, no. 1 (2010): 111–120, https://doi.org/10.1080/13678861003589099

23. John Kotter, *8 Steps to Accelerate Change in Your Organization: With New Insights for Leading in a COVID-19 Context*, Kotterinc.com, 2020, pp. 10–38, https://www.kotterinc.com/wp-content/uploads/2020/06/2020-8-Steps-to-Acceperate-Change-eBook-Kotter.pdf

24. Kotter, *8 Steps*, 18.

25. Kotter, 24.

- "Enable action by removing barriers." Remove bureaucratic practices that deter and decelerate change. Find out which barriers have stood in the way of past improvement efforts.

- "Generate short-term wins." Generate and communicate tangible, small wins that customers and stakeholders care about in order to motivate volunteers.

- "Sustain acceleration." Sustain a sense of urgency over the long term until the vision is achieved.

- "Institute change." Create lasting change. Where existing frameworks are effective, graft the changes onto existing structures. A center of excellence (CoE) supports, disseminates, and sustains best practices.

The approach used to integrate agile practices depends on the organization's agile maturity level. If the organization is successfully using agile methods, the integration will have already occurred. If the organization is using agile methods but is struggling, coaches should be brought in to identify and improve practices, and a CoE should be created (if one does not exist) to promote best practices. A change management process should be instituted to determine the target agility level (or levels) and manage the transition of the organization to the desired future state.

5.15.3.2 Organizations with No Agile Experience
If the organization has no experience, institute a full change management process for the transformation with a lead change manager to head the transformation. A CoE should be created to support and sustain the change.

The best results come from using both a bottom-up and top-down approach to the transition:

- Prove the value proposition with a few pilot initiatives.

- Gain executive support at the highest levels of the organization, up to the CEO, in order to communicate the strategic importance of the transformation to the company. Develop a community of volunteers as described by Kotter to drive the change (see section 5.15.3.1).

- Let the first teams experiment with practices to learn what works best and when.

- Communicate and sustain best practices through tools, techniques, and training provided by the CoE.

The ideal pilot initiative is small and mostly self-contained—able to be implemented by a team or small group of teams with minimal inter-team dependencies. Give the first agile teams a high degree of freedom to experiment with agile development frameworks and practices. Encourage them to hold open houses to share their experiences and successes. Iteration reviews are an excellent opportunity for these events.

During the broader rollout, teams should focus on improving processes so they are repeatable and sustainable. As the lead on agile analysis and planning, you support this objective by developing techniques, tools, practices, and processes in the competency. These tools should be disseminated and maintained by a CoE in business analysis or agile development.

Don't aim for uniformity across teams. For example, teams working primarily on customer-generated requests may choose a Kanban process because it is optimized for learning. In contrast, teams working on strategic product-wide initiatives may choose a timeboxed approach because it ensures that all teams will be free at the same time to make commitments.

In the final phase, extend the agile transition out to the development organization as a whole. During this phase, establish a standard set of agile analysis and planning techniques, tools, practices, and processes.

5.15.4 Transition Timeline

It can take six months or more to get good enough at agile development to begin to realize improvements. The timeline for a complete enterprise transition varies widely according to the organization's culture, structure, and level of competency in agile development. To give you one example of how such a transformation can play out, the following is a case study, as it unfolded for one of my clients. The client reported these results at the end of Year 2 in the timeline.

5.15.4.1 Initiation (Year 0)
At the start of the transition, the total number of teams in the organization was one thousand. Five hundred of these were software teams. Aside from a few teams, none were agile. The plan was to transition all one thousand teams.

5.15.4.2 Years 1 and 2
The transition began with a single business area. At the six-month mark, the rest of the enterprise started to transition. By the end of the second year, the organization had transitioned at least seventy teams to agile development.

5.15.4.3 Year 3
In Year 3, the organization plans to bring a further thirty-five teams to Zones 1 and 2 of the agile fluency model. During this time, it will be focusing on the standardization of practices.

5.15.5 Communications Plan

The change management plan should contain a communications plan. The plans should be supported by an active and committed coalition of sponsors and volunteers. Measures in the change management plan, such as stakeholder analysis and the identification of resistance, should drive the communications plan.

The communication plan should describe the communication methods to be used. Aim to optimize the quality of communications within the team, between teams, and between teams and business stakeholders. Use the highest-quality mode possible. In order of preference, these modes are

- In-person conversation.
- Video call.
- Virtual meeting.
- Asynchronous communication: Methods include wikis, SharePoint, messaging services, email, and updates made through software applications and services.
- Conference call (audio).

Teams are increasingly synchronizing their efforts through the asynchronous approach: when CI/CD is practiced (as is advised), then updates to version control and code repositories serve to communicate changes across teams. Changes to requirements, their priorities, and their statuses can also be tracked through requirements management tools.

If teams are colocated, use in-person communication as your preferred method of contact; use the lower forms only when necessary. If teams are distributed, favor video calls because members can see who's speaking and read body language. The next best option is Web conferencing that enables shared presentations and communication via text or voice. Examples are WebEx and GoToMeeting. This is a good option if the conversation is mostly one-way (e.g., a status update). Use telephone conference calls only as a last resort.

5.15.6 Agile Enterprise Transition Team

If there is no other body in place to do so (such as an agile CoE or a PMO), create an agile enterprise transition team to champion agile practices within the organization and provide resources for those who need assistance applying them. The team should meet regularly (about every two weeks) and keep its own backlog of work items. More information on the enterprise transition team can be found in *The Enterprise and Scrum*, by Ken Schwaber.[26]

5.16 Determine Organizational Readiness

The following checklist summarizes many of the organizational issues discussed in this chapter. It may be used to verify whether an organization is ready for agile development and to identify readiness gaps that still need to be addressed. The evaluation should be made by a change manager, the PMO, or a CoE with the input of seasoned agile practitioners.

---

26. Ken Schwaber, *The Enterprise and Scrum* (Redmond, WA: Microsoft Press, 2014).

5.16.1 Organizational Readiness Checklist

Use the following checklist of key questions to determine organizational readiness for agile initiatives.

- ☐ Does the culture invite change and innovation and support a customer focus?   ☑
- ☐ Does the culture actively encourage participants to challenge assumptions, decisions, and the status quo?[27]
- ☐ Does the current organizational structure minimize inter-team dependencies?
- ☐ Do IT and the business sit on the same teams?
- ☐ Do IT team members report primarily to the business side (vs. IT)?
- ☐ Are team members encouraged to contribute any way they can regardless of job title?
- ☐ Do people from the business side feel comfortable leading development teams and making decisions for them? Are there enough of these people available for one to be allocated per agile development team (five to ten members)?
- ☐ Are all parts of the organization (funding, marketing, supplier relationship management, etc.) prepared for frequent rollouts and ongoing changes to the requirements?
- ☐ Is the technical infrastructure in place to facilitate accelerated time to market? Is test automation supported? Are the build and deploy processes primarily automated?

5.17 Chapter Summary

Here are the key points covered in this chapter:

- Use the purpose alignment model—a chart mapping criticality against market differentiation—to develop a high-level strategy for new features (e.g., whether to develop features in-house, through partnerships or outsourcing).

- Organize teams by *value*. Each team should be as self-sufficient as possible, self-managing, and small (five to ten members).

- Establish an agile culture through customer and developer bills of rights: the customer is the sole person responsible for managing and prioritizing the stories in the product backlog; the development team has the exclusive right to make and update estimates.

- Use circumstance-based market segmentation to analyze the jobs customers might want to use the product for. Organize teams around those jobs.

---

27. Thanks to Ron Healy for suggesting this question.

- Integrate and test continuously, but expose features to the market based on the demands of the business.

- Use the agile fluency model to grade an organization's level of agility as focusing (teams produce business value), delivering (value delivered on market cadence), optimizing, or strengthening.

5.18 What's Next?

This chapter focused on *organizational* preparations for agile development. In Chapter 6, "Preparing the Process," we focus on preparing the *process*—that is, the steps to set up the agile analysis process for an upcoming initiative.

Chapter 6

Preparing the Process

In Chapter 5, "Preparing the Organization," we examined organizational preparations for agile development. This chapter covers process preparation and offers guidelines for selecting the planning approach, agile framework, techniques, and artifacts for the initiative. The chapter describes how to tune or calibrate the chosen process by customizing the product backlog, including the specification of product backlog item attributes, such as cost of delay and weighted shortest job first (WSJF). It also includes guidelines for planning requirements traceability, specifying the definition of done (DoD) and definition of ready (DoR), forecasting team capacity, and setting Kanban work-in-progress (WIP) limits.

6.1 Objectives

This chapter will help you

- Determine the right mix of agile practices for the circumstance, including considerations for low-risk and high-risk initiatives.
- Set up the product backlog for new product development.
- Determine the attributes that will be used to describe backlog items.
- Prepare for requirements traceability.
- Specify DoD, DoR, and initial Kanban parameters (e.g., WIP limits).
- Forecast initial team capacity (velocity).

6.2 This Chapter on the Map

Figure 6.1 highlights the activities covered in the chapter.

As shown in Figure 6.1, we'll be examining *Prepare the Process*. This activity is performed as part of the first zone, Initiation and Planning.

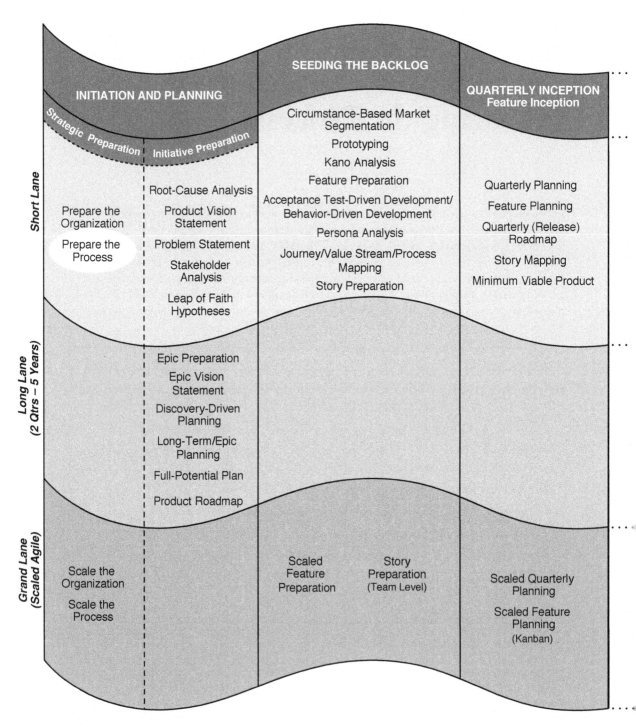

Figure 6.1 *Chapter 6 on the map*

QUARTERLY CLOSEOUT
Epic, Feature Closeout

DAILY ACTIVITIES

ITERATION INCEPTION

ITERATION CLOSEOUT

Daily Standup

Requirements Analysis & Documentation

Code, Build, Test, Deliver Acceptance
Test-Driven Development/
Behavior-Driven Development

Minimum Viable Product,
Split Testing

Epic, Feature Preparation

Story Preparation

Iteration Planning

Iteration Review
Iteration Retrospective

Prepare for
General Availability

Quarterly
Retrospective

Epic, Feature
Retrospective

Pivot or
Persevere

Scaled
Iteration
Planning

Iteration
Planning
(Team Level)

Product
Owner
Council
Meetings

DevOps

User Task
Force
Meetings

Scaled
Feature
Preparation
(Kanban)

Integration
Meetings

Story
Preparation
(Team Level)

Scaled Iteration
Review

Scaled Iteration
Retrospective

Iteration Retrospective
(Team Level)

DevOps

Scaled
Quarterly/Feature
Retrospective

6.3 Process Preparation

Before embarking on new product development, numerous issues about the process must be addressed. Should teams use a flow-based or timeboxed approach to planning? Which estimation units should they use—story points or real-time estimates? Should teams use a feature DoR, and if so, what conditions should it specify? These are the issues included in the activity Prepare the Process—the subject of this chapter.

In the following sections, we look at two sides of this preparation: tailoring and tuning the process. **Tailoring** means fitting the agile analysis and planning process to the circumstance (e.g., selecting the right agile framework, techniques, and artifacts). **Tuning** means calibrating the chosen process to optimize desired outcomes. Tuning activities include setting up the product backlog, determining the PBI (requirements item) attributes that will be tracked, planning how requirements items will be traced, specifying the DoD and DoR, and setting up a Kanban board to manage the workflow of requirements items (features and stories).

6.4 Tailoring the Agile Practice to the Context

Agile development is not a one-size-fits-all proposition: practices that work well in one situation may not work well in another. To *tailor* the practice is to adapt it to its context—taking it in a little here, by pulling back on an agile method, and taking it out a little there, by extending it. For example, on a fixed-contract project, you may choose to customize a hybrid analysis and planning process—one that uses a continuous deployment approach at the back end to deliver reliable improvements quickly to the market but a waterfall approach at the front end to mitigate risk. You can't use a one-size-fits-all process because there are benefits *and* costs to agile development, and they change depending on the context. In any given circumstance, you need to tailor the process to maximize the net benefit. Let's begin with the potential costs.

6.4.1 Costs of Agile Development

In agile development, the initial implementation is based on an incomplete understanding of the requirements, with the expectation that the requirements will be clarified over a number of cycles analysis, implementation, and testing. This rework adds to the cost of product development relative to a waterfall approach, where implementation occurs only after a comprehensive analysis.

Another drawback of agile development is the cost to clean up—or **refactor**—software to remove deficiencies, such as redundancies and unreachable and inefficient code. Agile development creates refactoring work because early versions of the software are often meant to deliver learning and quick wins, not market-level quality or maintainability. Agile practitioners can, however, minimize this effect by refactoring continuously rather than allowing the work (also known as *technical debt*) to build to the point where it is difficult to manage.

6.4.2 Benefits of Agile Development

Agile development—and agile analysis and planning in particular—reduces costs because it enables the business to quickly determine a product's most valuable features and focus investment there, where it will have the most impact. Agile analysis also leads to *reduced* rework, because it occurs at the last responsible moment—as close as possible to implementation when it is most current. In contrast, waterfall analysis is more likely to be out of date by the time it's used because it is performed and completed up front.

Agile development also improves the business's ability to respond quickly to change because its methods shorten time to market. Another benefit of the approach is that it creates solutions that match or exceed expectations because it incorporates continuous feedback throughout the product's lifecycle.

6.4.3 Finding the Best Trade-Off of Costs and Benefits

The costs and benefits discussed in the preceding sections will vary by circumstance. For example, iterative-incremental development provides a higher net benefit if there is extreme uncertainty about the product than if it is well-established. The challenge in any situation is to find a mix of practices that provides the best trade-off of costs and benefits.

Figure 6.2 illustrates how context affects the overall target level of analysis and planning agility from lowest to highest expected agility.

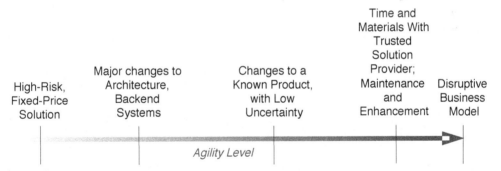

Figure 6.2 *Target agility level by context*

The figure is a general guide. Assess each situation according to its own merits. Let's examine some scenarios.

6.4.3.1 *High-Risk, Fixed-Price Solution*

The first scenario is a high-risk initiative to purchase a commercial-off-the-shelf (COTS) solution or a fixed-price customized solution. The risk to the business may be high because of a high upfront cost, the absence of a track record with the solution provider, or both. The target agility level for this scenario is low because incremental analysis would expose the customer to unacceptable financial risk: the customer would bear the full cost of any missed requirements not supported in the delivered product. On the other hand, an in-depth upfront analysis protects the business by minimizing the chance it will purchase a product that doesn't satisfy its needs and by transferring the consequences of a low estimate to the solution provider. Use the agile practice of incremental *implementation*, however, wherever practical. For example, a COTS eLearning product may contain components such as a community billboard, registration, academic reporting, and course development that can be turned on incrementally. The advantage of incrementally deploying these components is that exposure to risk is reduced if significant problems arise navigating to the new software. This advantage should be weighed against the possible benefits of the alternative—a Big Bang, all-at-once deployment. The latter approach can prevent costly workarounds often associated with partial deployments. For example, two systems may have to be maintained during an incremental transition, leading to inefficiencies such as double entries.

6.4.3.2 Changes to Architectural and Backend Systems

When the initiative is a change to a legacy architecture or backend system, the target agility level will be low for technical reasons. It's usually more costly and less efficient to make architectural changes incrementally (the agile way) than it is in a single pass. However, other agile practices are advised for this scenario: use the minimum viable product (MVP) process to verify leap-of-faith design hypotheses. Use continuous integration and (CI/CD) practices to enable speedy, reliable delivery of software changes.

6.4.3.3 Changes to a Known Product with Low Uncertainty

What about a change to a well-understood product or service, where there is low uncertainty about the requirements and the requirements are nonvolatile (unlikely to change)? An example is a change to an insurance product that expands coverage. This scenario requires a medium target agility level. Analyze high- to midlevel requirements up front to ensure the solution covers essential capabilities and to provide enough information for a reliable cost and time estimation. However, you should perform *detailed* requirements analysis incrementally to reduce the lag time before implementation and shorten time to market for the most valuable features. Aim for a high agility level with respect to deployment: use DevOps and CD/CI practices to gain the benefits of early and frequent testing and delivery.

6.4.3.4 Time and Materials with Trusted Solution Provider; Maintenance and Enhancement

The cost–benefit calculation is different for a time-and-materials contract with a trusted developer—for example, ongoing maintenance and enhancement (M&E) by an internal IT department or long-term partner. The target level of agility should be high in this case because there is a foundation of trust, and the financial risk is spread out over time, not frontloaded.

6.4.3.5 *Disruptive Business Model*

The rightmost scenario in Figure 6.2 represents initiatives where there is extreme uncertainty. The product, service, or technology may be novel and the business model in doubt. This scenario calls for the highest level of target agility. In this circumstance, it's not just software development but the *entire* business ecosystem that is characterized by uncertainty. The affected areas can include marketing departments, distribution channels, and supply chains. As a result, **enterprise agility** is called for—the extension of agile principles and practices beyond the development team to the entire company. Enterprise agility practices for developing a business under conditions of extreme uncertainty include lean startup, discovery-driven planning, and circumstance-based market segmentation.

For more on enterprise agility, see Chapter 18.

6.4.4 Determining the Framework

The next step in process tailoring is to determine the approach and framework that will be used. We'll be focusing on analysis and planning issues. Technical practices such as CD and DevOps are also prepared at this time.

For guidance on technical practices, see Chapter 15, section 15.8.

In Chapter 3, "Fundamentals of Agile Analysis and Planning," we looked at flow-based versus timeboxed agile processes. In flow-based planning (e.g., Kanban), each work item is addressed as it reaches the top of the backlog and progresses independently through the development lifecycle. In a timeboxed approach (e.g., Scrum), all items for a period are accepted into the plan at the start of the period. As a general guideline, select a flow-based approach to plan customer-driven features because it provides greater adaptability. Use a timeboxed approach to plan large strategic initiatives because it's easier to align teams when everyone is available at the same time. Use a mix of both approaches if teams will be involved in both kinds of initiatives. Keep in mind that these considerations apply to the intake of work items. Once a work item is implemented, it should be delivered continuously following CI/CD practices.

For more on flow-based vs. timeboxed planning, see Chapter 3, section 3.4.3, and Chapter 17, 17.4.

Once you've decided on the approach, choose a framework that supports it. For flow-based planning, use Kanban. Frameworks that support a timeboxed approach include Scrum, Extreme Programming (XP), and Scaled Agile Framework (SAFe).

Most organizations choose a hybrid process that uses elements from various frameworks. For example, the process may be based on Kanban, with added Scrum ceremonies such as the daily standup and the retrospective. Alternatively, it may be based on Scrum, with work planned on a two-week basis, but also include Kanban tools to manage the workflow of stories once they have entered a sprint.

6.5 Tuning the Process

Once you've determined the framework—the instrument you will use for analysis and planning—you need to calibrate it to optimize performance. Let's look at how you tune the adjustable parameters of the process, such as cadence, requirements attributes, and the DoR.

6.5.1 Business Analysis Information Artifacts and Events

If the determination has not yet been made, you'll need to select the business analysis and planning artifacts that will be used for the initiative. *BABOK v3* refers to these artifacts as **business analysis (BA) information**—"the broad and diverse sets of information that business analysts analyze, transform, and report . . . information of any kind . . . that is used as an input to, or is an output of, business analysis work."[1] These artifacts include features, stories, functional requirements, business rules, business cases, and organizational models.

6.5.2 Checklist of Agile BA Information Artifacts

Following is a checklist of the agile BA information artifacts discussed in this book. Use the list to *consider* artifacts for the initiative, but don't expect to produce every artifact on every occasion.

- ☐ Product vision statement
- ☐ Product canvas
- ☐ Vision statement
- ☐ Stakeholder analysis
- ☐ Goals
- ☐ Objectives
- ☐ Leap of faith hypotheses
- ☐ Metrics
- ☐ Minimum Marketable Features (MMF), Minimum Marketable Product (MMP)
- ☐ Product roadmap
- ☐ Product backlog
- ☐ Iteration backlog
- ☐ Story map
- ☐ Stories: Themes, epics, features, user stories, functional spikes, bug-fix stories, technical stories

1. International Institute of Business Analysis (IIBA), *BABOK v3: A Guide to the Business Analysis Body of Knowledge*, 3rd ed. (Toronto, Canada: IIBA, 2015), 14–15.

☐ Functional requirements

☐ Nonfunctional requirements (NFRs)

☐ Business rules: Behavioral rules (decision tables); definitional rules (data model, data dictionary)

☐ Business process models

☐ Use-case models

☐ Reverse income statement (for discovery-driven planning)

☐ Assumptions checklist

☐ Milestone planning chart

6.5.3 Defining Requirements Types

Define requirements types early. It establishes a common lexicon, ensuring that everyone means the same thing when using a term such as *business requirement*. Moreover, once you've created a set of requirements types, you can use them as a checklist to ensure you haven't missed anything in your analysis.

6.5.3.1 Checklist of Requirements Types

Use the following checklist to determine whether you've considered all requirements types. It incorporates *BABOK v3* requirements types with the addition of user requirements.

☐ Business requirements   ✔

☐ Stakeholder requirements

☐ User requirements

☐ *Solution requirements* with two subcategories:

   – Functional requirements

   – Nonfunctional requirements

☐ Transition requirements

See Chapter 3, sections 3.4.2.4 to 3.4.2.11, for more on requirements types.

6.5.3.2 Why Types Matter (and When They Don't)

When you get into the weeds, defining requirements types can be difficult, and I've often seen lead business analysts struggle with this issue. For example, I've heard (and participated in) arguments regarding whether NFRs should even exist as a type, since you implement them with functional requirements. Should user requirements be a type in its own right or a subtype of stakeholder requirements—or should it be a subtype of solution requirements? I've learned not to indulge these arguments for too long because they usually have little impact on outcomes.

So, why bother with requirements typing at all? It's not as much about *how* you categorize requirements; it's about *doing* it. By defining types and verifying that you've addressed them in your analysis, you reduce the risk of unexpected costs due to missed requirements (e.g., unexpected integration, data conversion, and transition costs). You can also use requirements types as a basis for

- Mapping out which roles will be primarily responsible and accountable for which type.
- Determining how each requirement type will be represented.
- Specifying the point in the development lifecycle at which each requirement type will be tested and how.

6.5.4 Tuning the Backlog

As noted in Chapter 3, the product backlog is the repository of requirements items and other work. You need to set up the backlog at the start of new product development and tune it to optimize it for your circumstance. This setup includes determining what kind of information it will track and how to organize the backlog to support multiple teams. Let's look at some guidelines for carrying out these activities.

 For product backlog guidelines for scaled agile organizations, see Chapter 17, section 17.7.

6.5.4.1 General Guidelines for Setting Up the Product Backlog

Use the following guidelines and principles when setting up the product backlog.

Single Source of Truth

The backlog is a *single* source of truth across all teams. A single product-level backlog

- Supports a whole-product view.
- Simplifies prioritization decisions: the product-level product owner (PO) can view and prioritize across teams while individual feature teams can view items within their domains.
- Simplifies the tracking of dependencies across teams

Specify a PBI attribute to identify the team to which the PBI is assigned. Each team can view its PBIs. Mike Cohn recommends that the number of items viewable to any team be limited to about 100 to 150.[2] This maximum is based on Dunbar's number of 150,[3] presumed to be a limit to the number of relationships a person can maintain.

---

2. Mike Cohn, *Succeeding with Agile* (Boston: Addison-Wesley, 2010), 331–333.

3. Aleks Krotoski, "Robin Dunbar: We Can Only Ever Have 150 Friends at Most," *The Guardian*, March 13, 2010, https://www.theguardian.com/technology/2010/mar/14/my-bright-idea-robin-dunbar

For more on establishing product backlogs for scaled agile organizations, see Chapter 17, section 17.7.

Varying Levels of Granularity and Sizes

At any time, items in the backlog will be at varying levels of granularity. In general, the closer a PBI is to the front of the backlog (i.e., the nearer it is to implementation), the higher the level of detail.[4] PBIs also vary in size from large epics to small stories. PBIs near the top of the backlog should be small: the estimate to implement a PBI that is close to implementation should not exceed the size limit for a story.

The Backlog Is Dynamic

The backlog is a dynamic, not static, list. It is expected that, over time, items will be removed, re-sequenced, changed, and added to the backlog.

The Backlog Is Comprehensive

The backlog includes requirements in the form of epics, features, and stories as well as other items, such as the product goal, bug fixes, and technical debt payment.

6.5.4.2 Physical Form of Backlog Items

During planning, represent PBIs using physical cards if the teams are physically together; otherwise, use virtual cards. Cards are recommended at this time because they are intuitive, easy to create, and easy to move around. They also feel temporary, so the team is less likely to see them as set in stone than if they were entered into a requirements tool. If it's a small initiative and team members are colocated, continue with physical cards throughout development. Otherwise, transfer the items to a requirements management tool, once the planning session is over, to provide visibility across teams and locations.

6.5.4.3 Defining PBI Attributes

Determine the attributes (fields) that will be tracked for each item in the backlog. Consider the following checklist of PBI attributes.[5]

- ☐ Item type: Feature epic, user story, functional spike, and so on
- ☐ Description: Text description of the requirement (e.g., use the Role-Feature-Reason format where appropriate)
- ☐ Acceptance criteria
- ☐ Estimate
- ☐ Order: Sequence in the backlog (assigned by the PO)

---

4. Ken Schwaber and Jeff Sutherland, *The Scrum Guide: The Definitive Guide to Scrum—The Rules of the Game*, Scrumguides.org, 2020, 10–11, https://www.scrumguides.org.

5. Scrum offers the following guidance: PBI details include "description, order, and size. Attributes often vary with the domain of work." See Schwaber and Sutherland, *The Scrum Guide*, 10.

□ Value: The value delivered by the item; may be expressed in "so that" clause

□ WSJF prioritization (see section 6.5.4.5)

□ Cost of delay: Value of the item, taking into account time criticality (see section 6.5.4.4)

□ Owner: Person with primary expertise and sign-off authority for the item

□ Planned quarter/release cycle/program increment (with timeboxed planning)

□ Designated iteration (with timeboxed planning)

□ Projected delivery

□ Designated team

□ Designated developer(s)

□ Status (e.g., ready, done)

□ Dependencies and other relationships: Dependencies and relationships with other PBIs and configuration items

□ Change log: Record of changes to the item

6.5.4.4 Determining Cost of Delay

In SAFe, the **cost of delay** expresses the relative value of a backlog item, taking into account time criticality. Determine the cost of delay for an item as follows:

[Cost of Delay] = [User and Business Value] + [Time Criticality] + [Risk Reduction and Opportunity Enablement Value (RE & OE)]

where

- **Time criticality** is a measure of the decay of value over time.
- **RE & OE** account for the value of the feature in reducing risk or due to an opportunity it enables.

In the pure form of the WSJF method, you assign a relative point value for each term, in much the same way you do for estimating effort with story points.

6.5.4.5 Determining WSJF

To determine an item's priority based on its cost of delay, calculate its **weighted shortest job first** (WSJF) value according to this formula:

WSJF = [Cost of Delay] / [Job Duration]

The higher the WSJF of the item, the higher its priority sequence in the product backlog. (In other words, the PBI with the highest WSJF is sequenced first.)

Popularized by SAFe, WSJF is a useful and recommended aid to prioritization, particularly for features. Use it as a guide to *inform* decisions, though, not to dictate them, because the approach doesn't account well for all scenarios, especially black swan events[6]—relatively rare but impactful occasions when a feature is wildly over- or underestimated. (For example, a black swan may occur when significant technological problems only become apparent once development is underway.)

Some have proposed adaptations to WSJF to make it useful not only for prioritization but also for financial planning.[7] Dahlstrom and Lund recommend that the WSJF method be adapted for this purpose as follows:

- Establish standard values at the enterprise level for each term in the formula.

- Use a prioritization model that uses absolute, monetary values for cost of delay evaluation at the strategic level but uses relative estimates (e.g., points) at the operational level.

According to their report, these adaptations improve the percentage of satisfied requirements from "50% to 89% on a strategic level and from 85% to 90% on an operational level."[8]

6.5.5 Determining Requirements Granularity Levels

The reason the level of granularity provided for each item in the backlog varies over time is that you perform agile requirements analysis incrementally. The lean principle applies: wait until the last responsible moment (LRM) to perform analysis tasks. If the development organization uses flow-based planning (e.g., Kanban), wait to prepare large features until about six weeks before their planned implementation, two to four weeks if they're small. Begin to prepare stories one to four weeks before implementation.

If the organization uses timeboxed planning (e.g., SAFe, XP, Scrum), begin preparing features for the next quarter (or SAFe PI) about halfway into the previous one. Begin story preparation about one or two iterations before the planned implementation.

The risk when postponing preparation past these guidelines is reduced team productivity because teams don't understand requirements items well enough to reliably estimate them or correctly implement them.

---

6. "SAFe and Weighted Shortest Job First (WSJF)," Black Swan Farming Inc., 2017, https://blackswanfarming.com/safe-and-weighted-shortest-job-first-wsjf

7. Gustav Dahlström and Jesper R. Lund, *Is It SAFe to Use WSJF for Prioritisation in Financial Software Development? A Case Study of Prioritisation Needs at a Swedish Bank* (master's thesis, KTH Industrial Engineering and Management Industrial Management, 2019), 5, http://www.diva-portal.org/smash/get/diva2:1372030/FULLTEXT01.pdf

8. Dahlström and Lund, *Is It SAFe*, 5.

Because they are prepared incrementally, the items in the backlog will vary significantly in granularity. The following granularity levels have been adapted for stories from the *Use Case 2.0* guidelines for specifying use cases.[9]

- Briefly described

- Bulleted outline

- Steps outlined (essential outline)

- Fully described

Let's examine these granularity levels and when they are advised.

6.5.5.1 *Briefly Described*

Use this level for low-order items at the end of the backlog. At this level, only a short description of the item is provided. The text may be informal (e.g. "Submit order") or may follow a template (e.g., "As a customer, I want to submit an order so that I can receive my requested items").

6.5.5.2 *Bulleted Outline*

To achieve this granularity level, outline the item in enough detail to estimate its size and complexity. Specify acceptance criteria indicating the scenarios to test and the expected outcomes. Prepare stories to this level of granularity prior to commitment—approximately one to four weeks before their planned implementation (one or two iterations, if the organization is using a timeboxed framework such as Scrum). If the team is in close collaboration with the business, this target level of documentation granularity may suffice, with the remainder of the understanding achieved through conversation, user testing, and discussions among the Triad—business, quality assurance (QA), and developers.

6.5.5.3 *Steps Outlined (Essential Outline)*

At this level of granularity, you provide detailed story acceptance criteria and low-level (step-by-step) test-case specifications. If you're using *Use Case 2.0*, you reach this level by specifying the steps in use-case flow specifications. This target level is appropriate when working with third parties that don't have a close, long-term relationship with the product, such as offshore third-party solution providers.

This level is usually not required if there is a long-term relationship with the solution provider, such as a partner or internal IT department, since developers have a good understanding of the business and there is more likely to be a foundation of trust.

---

9. Ivar Jacobson, Ian Spence, and Kurt Bittner. *Use-Case 2.0: The Guide to Succeeding with Use Cases* (London: Ivar Jacobson International SA, 2011), 47–48.

6.5.5.4 *Fully Described*

To reach this level, add detailed notes and functional requirements to the requirements item. Use this level of granularity

- To communicate complex requirements and business rules related to a feature or story.

- Where the relationship between the solution provider and the business is short term.

- When required by regulatory and compliance regulations.

6.5.6 Tracing Requirements and Other Configuration Items

At various points in the life of a story, you need to be able to answer questions such as the following: What objectives does the story support? What tests were run against it? Which stories are affected if we deprioritize it? You use **traceability** to answer these questions. To **trace** an item is to link it with another item. Each traceable item is referred to as a **configuration item**.

You can set up a traceability system to trace a story to configuration items, such as the story's owner, stakeholders, business objectives, tests, graphic user interfaces (GUIs), software components, data tables, and other stories with which it has dependencies.

6.5.6.1 *Provide Just Enough Traceability*

Traceability's benefits come with a cost—the administrative effort required to keep relationships up to date. On an agile initiative, this can add up to a significant effort, since requirements are continually in flux. Use automated methods whenever possible. Only trace an item if doing so serves a purpose. If you can't identify at least one important question you can answer by tracing an item, don't trace it.

Once you've identified the questions, determine what you need to trace to what in order to answer them.

6.5.6.2 *Provide Traceability in Different Directions*

You can trace a configuration item in three directions: downstream (forward), upstream (backward), and cross-stream (horizontally). Let's look at these kinds of traceability and the benefits they provide.

Downstream (Forward) Traceability

To trace an item **downstream** is to link it to configuration items further along in the development cycle. For example, you can trace a user story downstream to the GUIs, test cases, databases, microservices, and software components created, changed, or used as a result of the user story.

Use downstream traceability to answer the following kinds of questions:

- To which team, release, iteration is the story assigned?

- Which software components will be affected by the user story?

- What test cases were run for the user story? What were the test results?
- What actions were taken relative to the story?
- At the beginning of each day: Which user stories are ready for testing?

Upstream (Backward) Traceability

Trace an item **upstream** to link it back to an earlier item. For example, you can trace a user story upstream to business objectives, personas, business stakeholders, business processes, features and epics, and objectives.

Use upstream traceability to answer the following questions:

- Why was this feature added to the backlog?
- What business objectives does it support?
- What feature does this story support?
- What business process does this feature support?

Cross-Stream (Horizontal) Traceability

Cross-stream traceability links items of similar types to each other. For example, you can trace stories to other stories they depend on.

Provide cross-stream traceability stories to answer the following kinds of questions:

- If we delay the implementation of a user story, what other user stories will it hold up?
- If we postpone story X, what other stories could be delayed as a result?
- If we deliver story Y, what stories do we need to regression-test as a result?

You can also trace a story to the business rules it supports, its functional requirements, and its NFRs. In addition, you can trace the history of changes that were made to a configuration item over time, by whom, and why.

6.5.6.3 Determining Traceability Mechanisms, Tools

We've talked about the *relationships* that should be traced. If a mechanism has not yet been established, the next step is to determine *how* traceability will be implemented. Before we explore the options, let's summarize the main guidelines for a typical, large distributed agile development organization.

If the organization is practicing DevOps/CD, provide traceability wherever possible through the configuration management system (CMS) and version control in order to obtain current and reliable information with minimal overhead. If CMS tracing is unavailable or inadequate (e.g., it doesn't provide the necessary granularity), use a requirements management tool.

During colocated planning sessions, manual traceability approaches are best. For example, SAFe uses red strings to trace dependencies between stories. Once teams disperse, however, enter stories and their relationships into the CMS or requirements tool to provide access across all locations, as described previously.

Now let's explore the mechanisms further. Use the leanest traceability mechanism for the situation—one that delivers the information, accuracy, and access needed with the minimum overhead cost.

Traceability through the CMS

If the development organization follows best practices in CI/CD, traceability between configuration items is provided by the CMS and version control. A history of changes to configuration items is also provided.

Each traceable configuration item is represented as a record (row) in the configuration management database (CMDB). The CMS maintains relationships between configuration items by managing the connections between corresponding records in the database.

Figure 6.3 is an example of relationships maintained between configuration items on a claims project. The configuration items include user stories, requestors, objectives, and software components such as classes, services, and subsystems.

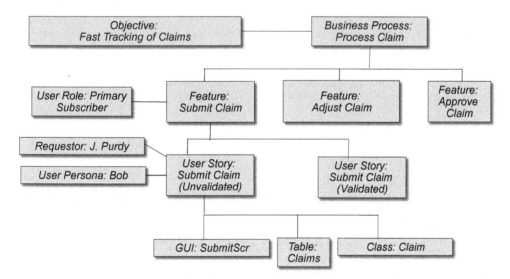

Figure 6.3 *Tracing configuration item relationships in a configuration management database for a claims project*

Traceability from features to automated tests (not shown) is achieved by organizing behavior-driven development test specifications into feature files.

For more on behavior-driven development, see Chapter 10, section 10.9.5.

Traceability through Requirements Management Tools

As noted earlier, when a CMS is not available or does not provide sufficient traceability, use a requirements management tool. Aside from traceability, requirements management tools also offer the capability to generate burndown charts and support Kanban workflow management processes and artifacts. One of the most popular tools for agile teams is Jira Software by Atlassian.

 For guidance on selecting requirements management tools, see Chapter 17, section 17.10.

Traceability Spreadsheets

If the preceding methods are unavailable or their cost is prohibitive, a simple, low-cost solution is to trace requirements elements using a spreadsheet application such as Excel or Google Sheets. Table 6.1 is an example of a traceability matrix for BLInK, the insurance product in our case study that provides benefits to customers based on their behaviors.

Table 6.1 shows that story PBI1030 supports business rule BR012 and that implementing the story affects the subscription data table and an application table.

Now let's turn to some lightweight, manual traceability options.

Visual Cues

With this approach, you represent stories as cards (or their virtual equivalents), and use *visual cues* to signal their relationships. The most common use of a visual cue is the placement of a story on a story map: stories are generally dependent on stories placed above them and the stories to their left.

Other visual cues include the use of color-coded dots and red strings to indicate dependencies on a program board.

 For more on dependencies on story maps, see Chapter 12, section 12.5.4. For more on the red string and colored dot approaches, see Chapter 11, section 11.11.3.5.

Conversation

The most lightweight manual option for managing dependencies is through conversation. Those working on related items communicate directly to each other about their plans and progress. Use discussion to communicate inter-team dependencies during *big room iteration planning meetings*. As dependency issues arise, people move between teams to notify those affected and resolve problems. Another conversation option is for teams to send envoys to sit in on the planning sessions of those they work with closely or for collaborating teams to conduct their planning sessions together.

 For more on lightweight solutions for coordinating dependent teams, see Chapter 17, section 17.11.

Table 6.1 *Product Backlog Item (User Story) Traceability Matrix*

PBI/Story	Sequence	Description	Estimate	User	Team	Business Rules	User Interface	Tables
PBI100	1	Receive BLInK marketing on invoices	2	Primary subscriber	Orange		RF003	
PBI030	2	Earn premium reduction for sign-up	3	Primary subscriber	Orange	BR012	UI004	Subscription table Application table
PBI022	3	Offer BLInK with Quick Quote to select, preapproved customers	5	Broker/agent	Blue	BR012	UI030	

6.5.7 Setting Process Parameters

An agile analysis process has configurable parameters—such as cadence, the DoD, and WIP limits. Tune these parameters for optimal performance at the start of an initiative, and readjust them over time.

6.5.7.1 Determining the Cadence

If the teams are using a timeboxed planning approach (e.g., Scrum), they need to decide on the duration—or cadence—of the timeboxes. This step does not apply if teams are using a flow-based planning framework (e.g., Kanban), because work is not planned by time period but by work item.

Two timeboxes to consider are the iteration and quarterly. The iteration cadence is typically one or two weeks. The maximum duration of an iteration varies by framework. In XP, it's one week. Scrum sets an upper limit of one month. Most timeboxed frameworks (such as XP, SAFe, and Scrum) recommend that the iteration length (cadence) be fixed.[10]

The iteration cadence determines the planning horizon—how far ahead you're planning. However, it should *not* determine when stories are delivered. Stories should be delivered continuously, as they are completed, not at the end of the iteration. Note that to *deliver* a story is to provide it in a releasable state; however, the customer may decide to delay its release into production until a later date.

If your development organization has not adopted DevOps practices, it may not be able to integrate and test stories reliably at that pace. In that case, the cadence acts as an upper limit on delivery. Development commits to deliver a releasable integrated increment *at least* once per iteration.

If there are longer-term planning needs, you will need to set a cadence for the longer horizon. You can set it to the duration of a release cycle (one to six months), the length of a SAFe program increment, or a calendar-based period (e.g., a quarter). For simplicity, I refer to the long-term planning horizon as a **quarter**. When you see the term in this book, it means any of these variations.

6.5.7.2 Set Estimation Standards (When Relative Estimation Units Are Used)

You can use the following method regardless of the estimation approach. It applies to story points, ideal developer days (IDDs), Gummi Bears, and Nebulous Units of Time (NUTs).[11] Let's assume the unit is the story point—the most popular choice. Gain consensus from the team on a story, or a set of stories, as the standard for a 1-point requirement item. If you're using story points or IDDs, the story should require one day's effort by one dedicated developer with the appropriate skills for the work item. Teams may also find it useful to establish an 8-point standard so that they can better gauge where a given story lies within the acceptable point range of 1 to 8.

---

10. "They are fixed length events of one month or less to create consistency." Schwaber and Sutherland, *The Scrum Guide*, 7.

11. "Points (estimates in)," *Agile Alliance Glossary*, 2020, https://www.agilealliance.org/glossary/points-estimates-in

Once the team has established a standard, estimate the other stories in relation to it using Fibonacci numbers. For example, the team assigns 3 story points to story X, indicating that they estimate the effort to implement it to be three times that of the standard one-unit story.

It's worth noting at this point the secret about these estimation units. Unless you're using real-time estimates, it doesn't matter, in the end, what standard you used to represent one unit of effort. Within a few weeks or iterations, the team establishes a record of the number of units it *actually* can deliver in a given timeframe. That's what you use—not the original time associated with a one-unit story—to make forecasts once some time has passed.

6.5.7.3 Determining Initial Capacity (Velocity)

The team's **capacity**, or **velocity**, is the number of estimating units (e.g., story points or IDDs) that it can deliver within a given period. Calculate velocity on a per-team basis, not for the entire group of teams.

You can determine velocity for various estimation units and planning horizons. The most common usage is to measure the total number of story points a team delivers per week or iteration.

Use velocity for forecasting purposes; don't use it as a performance metric or to compare teams. Following is a simple-to-use formula for converting estimates to time:

(Remaining Time) = (Remaining Estimating Units) / Velocity × Cadence

For example, suppose there are 400 remaining story points in the product release backlog, the velocity is 40 story points per iteration, and the cadence is two weeks/iteration. The remaining time is 400/40 × 2 = 20 weeks.

For a more accurate forecast, make projections based on the team's burndown chart.

For guidance on forecasting using a burndown chart, see Chapter 15, section 15.7.5.5.

If the team is using a timeboxed planning approach (e.g., Scrum), you need to know the team's past velocity going into iteration planning, since you use it to forecast future capacity—the number of estimating units that the team will deliver in the upcoming iteration. To quote Shakespeare, "The past is prologue."[12] The best forecast for what the team *will* achieve is based on what it achieved in the past. If the team has worked on a comparable initiative, set the initial velocity for the new venture based on what it accomplished previously, adjusting for changes in team sizes, holidays, availability, and so on.

If the team is new or hasn't worked on a comparable initiative before, use one of the methods that follow to forecast capacity.

---

12. William Shakespeare, *The Tempest*, act 2, scene 1, line 217, PlayShakespeare.com, https://www.playshakespeare.com/the-tempest/scenes/act-ii-scene-1

Determining Initial Capacity, Method 1: Based on Availability

Base your projection on experience, if possible, but if there is no comparable example to draw from, you may use the following formula:

(Initial Capacity) = (Total Potential Person-Days) × (Availability) − (Slack)

The **total potential person-days** represents the entire budget if all members are fully dedicated to the work. For example, for an eight-person team and a two-week cadence (ten working days), the potential person-days are 8 × 10 days = 80 days. **Availability** is the fraction of time members can spend on the planned work while accounting for time lost to other activities and events. It includes time lost to work on other projects, meetings, demos, illness, vacations, unplanned bug fixes, administrative activities, and email. A rough guideline is to initially forecast availability to be about 60 percent of potential time and then rely on your own measurements.[13] Following lean guidance,[14] you should also set aside some **slack** time so that team members will be available to pitch in and unplug bottlenecks when they occur.

Determining Initial Capacity, Method 2: Guesstimate and Decompose

An alternative method for forecasting the initial velocity (see Cohn)[15] is to guesstimate how many stories can be delivered and verify the guesstimate by decomposing the stories into tasks. To use this method, proceed as follows:

- Ask the team to review the first stories in the product backlog—items that have been sequenced and estimated.

- Ask the team to guess how many of these stories they will be able to deliver in the first iteration.

- Ask them to decompose each story into individual tasks and estimate the time to perform each task.

- Add up the task times for all the selected stories.

- If the sum of the task times exceeds the available time in the iteration, drop stories from the back of the list until the total task time is within the available time.

- Set the initial capacity to the sum of the points given to the stories that remain.

This alternative process may seem like a lot of extra work, but it's not. Many teams would be decomposing stories into estimated tasks, in any case, during iteration planning.

---

13. Mike Cohn, *User Stories Applied: For Agile Software Development* (Boston: Addison-Wesley Professional, 2004), 104. Cohn cites a range between one-third to one half the number of developer days in the iteration, but about 60 percent is more typical.

14. Mary Poppendieck and Tom Poppendieck, *Lean Software Development: An Agile Toolkit* (Boston: Addison-Wesley, 2003), 81.

15. Mike Cohn, "How to Estimate Velocity as an Agile Consultant," Mountain Goat Software, July 25, 2013, https://www.mountaingoatsoftware.com/blog/how-to-estimate-velocity-as-an-agile-consultant

Adjusting Capacity Once Implementation Begins

Once the first period or iteration has passed, forecast future capacity according to the following formula:

[Capacity] = [Past Velocity] ± [Changed Circumstances]

As the formula indicates, the future capacity is based on past performance (past velocity), making adjustments for changed circumstances such as holidays, illness, changes to team composition, and technical challenges.[16]

For forecasting purposes, use *recent* velocities achieved by the team during the past three or four iterations. Don't use a historical average because the team's performance can be expected to vary, fluctuating at first but settling down after three to six iterations.

Estimation and Velocity for Multiple Teams

When working with multiple teams, have all teams meet at the start of the initiative to agree on a standard story or stories to represent a 1-point estimate. You can also establish standard stories for an 8-point story. Afterward, the team that is likely to implement an upcoming story estimates it relative to this standard.

Velocity has relevance only at the team level. Where there are multiple teams, each team tracks its own velocity and uses that to determine team capacity—the number of estimation units it can accept into the iteration.

Estimating Features versus Stories

The preceding considerations about estimates are primarily a concern at the story level. When estimating features, it's often sufficient for a team to specify the number of iterations or weeks it will take to deliver the item.

For more guidance on estimating features, see Chapter 11, section 11.11.2.

6.5.7.4 *Tuning the Definition of Done*

The **DoD** specifies conditions that must be true before a story can be considered "done." It applies to all stories. In addition to the DoD, each story must satisfy its acceptance criteria to be deemed done. By specifying a DoD and enforcing compliance with it across all stories, the organization achieves a consistent level of quality for all delivered requirements.

Work with the development organization to specify a DoD if one does not yet exist. Review it and update it over time to achieve higher levels of quality. For example, at the start of a transition to automated testing, the following condition is added to the DoD: "Automated unit and low-level integration tests have been created and passed." Later in the transition, another condition is added: "Automated UAT tests have been created and passed."

---

16. While slack is incorporated indirectly in the above formulation as a component of past velocity and changed circumstances, there is an argument for explicitly subtracting slack when forecasting capacity based on past velocity to ensure the team isn't always operating at peak capacity and to account for unknown unknowns. (Karl Wiegers in personal communication with the author.)

Review the effectiveness of the DoD and consider improvements during the iteration retrospective[17] and quarterly retrospective.

Definition of Done Examples

There is no standard DoD that works for all organizations; it will depend on circumstances, such as the degree to which CI/CD and DevOps are practiced. At a minimum, the DoD should stipulate that the story has been demonstrated and tested by the customer.

The following is an example of a DoD.

- Coding is complete.

- The code has been checked in.

- Automated tests created: unit tests, integration tests, UAT.

- The story has passed tests satisfactorily: unit-tests, low-level integration tests, functional tests, acceptance criteria, end-to-end integration testing, system testing (e.g., regression testing, performance testing).

- Compliance, governance, and NFRs have been satisfied.

- The code has been refactored.

6.5.7.5 Tuning the Story Definition of Ready

Deem a requirements item **ready** when it is understood well enough for the team to make an informed commitment and begin implementation without undue delay or need for subsequent rework. It's a good idea to formalize what "well enough" means by specifying conditions in a DoR. In Kanban, you can indicate that a work item has satisfied these conditions by moving it to a Ready column.

If your team uses timeboxed planning, require that stories must pass the DoR to be considered for iteration planning.

To enable high team productivity, stories should be more than "simply items on a list."[18] They should satisfy additional conditions, such as being estimable. To propagate best practices and to ensure a standard level of preparation, specify these conditions in a story DoR.

Definition of Ready Example

The following DoR example incorporates INVEST guidelines and others.[19,20]

---

17. Schwaber and Sutherland, 10.

18. Jeff Sutherland, "Scrum: What Does It Mean to Be Ready-Ready?" (OpenViewVenture, 2011), https://www.youtube.com/watch?time_continue=3&v=XkhJDbaW0j0

19. Sutherland, "Scrum."

20. For example, Roman Pichler, "The Definition of Ready in Scrum" [blog post], December 16, 2010, http://www.romanpichler.com/blog/the-definition-of-ready

INVEST is a mnemonic for writing quality stories. The acronym stands for independent, negotiable, valuable, estimable, sized-appropriately, testable. For more on INVEST guidelines for stories, see Chapter 13, section 13.12.1.

- The story is independent.
- The story is refined.
- The story is well articulated.
- The story is actionable.
- The story is negotiable.
- The story is contextualized.
- The story is unique.
- The story is consistent with other stories.
- The story's value is known.
- The story has been discussed and prioritized recently.
- The story is estimable.
- The story is testable.
- The story is small.
- The story is vertically sliced.
- The story is non-solutionized.
- The story is complemented with supporting documentation, including a wireframe.
- The story and acceptance criteria have been approved.
- The customer and team have confirmed that the story satisfies the previous conditions.

Let's look more closely at these DoR conditions to understand them better.

The Story Is Independent.   The story has minimal dependencies on other stories. Independent stories reduce waste because they remove the administrative cost of tracking dependencies. In addition, they prevent delays that occur when a story isn't done in time for another that depends on it.

The Story Is Refined.   The story has been sufficiently analyzed and understood for planning and implementation to begin.

The Story Is Well Articulated.   The story is described in a way that clarifies who wants it and what they want. You can satisfy this condition through the use of a standardized template, such as the Connextra template, "As a [user role], I want [function] so that [business value]." A template helps remind story writers to articulate critical issues, but its use should not be enforced too strictly: it's not worth the effort trying to fit every story into a predetermined format if you can more clearly and naturally express it in another way.

For more on story templates, see Chapter 13, section 13.9.2.

The Story Is Actionable.   The story must be immediately **actionable** by the team:

- It should have no outstanding dependencies on other stories that would delay implementation.

- Preparatory analysis and technical work for the story are complete enough for the story to be completed during the implementation iteration or within the time estimate.

- The **architectural runway**, including specification of service communication protocols, creation of infrastructure, and identification of components, has been sufficiently prepared.

The Story Is Negotiable.   The story is ready to be negotiated. The PO and team agree that the requirements for the story are not fixed but will evolve on the basis of on dialogue. Business stakeholders and the development team understand the value and costs of the story well enough to negotiate trade-offs.

The Story Is Contextualized.   The context for the requirement is clear. As an example of a story with unclear context, consider "As a customer, I want the system to present the service fee to me up front." It's unclear what the user is doing while this requirement is active. To contextualize the story, be specific: "As a Web banking customer, I want the system to present the transaction service fee up front whenever I perform a banking transaction."

The Story Is Unique.   The requirements in the story should not duplicate those in another story. Duplication leads to overestimation of work and duplicated effort.

The Story Is Consistent with Other Stories.   The requirements in the story do not contradict those in another story. Inconsistencies in the requirements result in discrepancies in the product if they're not caught and rework if they are.

The Story's Value Is Known.   Mary and Tom Poppendieck quote statistics[21] that show that 45 percent of developed features are never used, and 19 percent are rarely used—adding up to a whopping 64 percent of features with no or minimal value. Sutherland[22] has reported that, if one were to examine a typical backlog, at least one-third of its items

21. Mary Poppendieck and Tom Poppendieck, *Lean Software Development: An Agile Toolkit* (Boston: Addison-Wesley, 2003), 32. The statistic is attributed to the Standish Group.
22. Jeff Sutherland, "Scrum: What Does It Mean to Be Ready-Ready?" (OpenViewVenture, 2011), https://www.youtube.com/watch?time_continue=3&v=XkhJDbaW0j0

would be "junk stories"—stories that have no value that anyone can identify. To improve these statistics, the value of a story must be clear before the team commits to it.

You can communicate the story's value qualitatively through the "so that" clause of the Connextra template. You can also specify it quantitatively by calculating the story's cost of delay—its overall value—as described in section 6.5.4.4.

The Story Has Been Discussed Recently. It's not enough to determine a story's value when it was written. Its value may have changed over time. To be ready, the story must have been discussed and its value confirmed *recently* by business stakeholders.

The Story Is Estimable. The story is understood well enough to be estimated by the team if called upon to do so. It isn't necessary that the story actually has been estimated—just that it *could* be.

The Story Is Testable. The story's acceptance criteria are understood well enough so that tests can be specified, a sufficiently reliable estimate can be made, and implementation can begin.

It is expected that acceptance criteria will evolve. The higher the uncertainty about the product or feature, the more general the acceptance criteria should be to allow more room for the customer to determine what is acceptable through trial and error.

The Story Is Small. The story fits within the maximum limit set for a story. A common restriction is for most stories not to exceed 5 story points, with a strict maximum of 8 points. Where timeboxed planning is practiced (e.g., Scrum), there is the added stipulation that the story must be small enough to be comfortably implemented during an iteration.

One useful tip for keeping stories small is to include only one distinct capability per story. Not only does this practice help limit size, but it also makes it easier to cost and prioritize each capability individually.

The Story Is Vertically Sliced. The story is structured so that, to the degree possible, it cuts a vertical slice through architectural layers to deliver usable functionality to the user with minimal or no dependencies on other stories.

The Story Is Non-solutionized. The story has been written in a non-solutionized manner to leave room to determine what solution works best through trial and error. The story should describe need and value rather than a design solution. For example, the story "As a customer, I want to be able to search for products by type" is better than "As a customer, I want the system to present a dropdown box of product types."

The Story Is Complemented with Supporting Documentation, including a Wireframe. Other artifacts required for the team to begin implementing the story, including wireframes, are available. A **wireframe** is a rough layout of the screen, showing items and how they will be grouped, without indicating design choices.

The Story and Acceptance Criteria Have Been Approved. The story, including its functionality and acceptance criteria, has been approved according to the agreed-upon approval mechanism. That mechanism may be anything from an informal discussion to a formal sign-off by a designated authorizer, such as the PO or superuser.

The Customer Has Confirmed That the Story Meets the Preceding Criteria.   When I ask teams about their DoRs, they often show me very well-articulated ones. The trouble is that they don't use them! Require that every story be evaluated against the DoR before it is accepted into the iteration plan and development.

How to Avoid Gating in the Definition of Ready

A poorly expressed DoR runs the risk of becoming a gating mechanism[23] nudging the team back toward a sequential waterfall approach. To avoid this tendency, define conditions that do not require completion but instead allow for concurrency. Rather than stating a flat rule that a particular activity or artifact must *always* be complete for the story to be ready, state the *circumstances* in which the rule applies, and describe the desired *degree of completion*. For example, consider the following DoR condition: "If the story is part of a larger process, the process has been analyzed well enough to understand the impact on other stories and other steps of the process." This condition specifies the circumstance ("If the story is part of a larger process") and the degree of completion required ("enough to understand").

6.5.7.6 *Tuning the Feature Definition of Ready*

Use a **feature DoR** to specify the conditions a feature must satisfy before it is included and committed in the plan. When the team is using a flow-based approach such as Kanban, this commitment occurs feature by feature, as each one nears the top of the backlog. When it is using timeboxed planning, features are committed to as a group at the start of the quarter, release cycle, or PI.

The following feature DoR incorporates guidelines from Ivar Jacobsen[24] and others.

- The feature has no (or minimal) dependencies on other features.

- All dependent teams are committed: All teams upon which delivery of the feature is dependent have committed to the feature. No feature is accepted into a quarter (or release cycle) unless this condition is met.

- The feature is negotiable: All parties understand that everything is negotiable concerning the feature—its priority, functionality, acceptance criteria, and estimate. The costs and benefits of the feature are understood well enough for trade-offs to be negotiated during PI/release planning.

23. Mike Cohn, "The Dangers of a Definition of Ready" [blog post], Mountain Goat Software, August 9, 2016, https://www.mountaingoatsoftware.com/blog/the-dangers-of-a-definition-of-ready

24. Ian Spence, "Preparing Features for PI Planning—What Does It Mean for a Feature to Be Ready?" Ivar Jacobson International, https://www.ivarjacobson.com/publications/blog/preparing-features-pi-planning-what-does-it-mean-feature-be-ready

- The feature is valuable: The feature would deliver significant value if released, and its value has been confirmed recently through discussion with the customer.

- The feature is estimable: The feature is understood well enough to be estimated. The closer the feature is to implementation, the more accurate the estimation.

- The feature is right-sized: The feature is small enough to be implemented within a quarter by one or more teams, yet significant enough to be of value if released to the market.

- The feature is testable: Acceptance criteria for the feature are known. The feature's acceptance criteria communicate how far the feature's implementation must go for it to be releasable. Business stakeholders, QA, and developers share an understanding of how the feature as a whole (vs. its individual stories) will be tested and the test procedures that will be used.

- The feature is clear: The customer can explain the feature to the team.

- The feature is feasible: It is possible to implement the feature within the time frame provided by the estimate. Financial and technical risks are understood and within acceptable limits.

- The feature is owned: Someone has been designated as the primary person for discussing and approving the feature.

- Stakeholders are engaged: Stakeholders impacted by the feature have been identified and commit to being involved in its development.

- The cost of delay for the feature is understood. (See section 6.5.4.4 for cost of delay calculation.)

- The feature is prioritized: Priority sequencing may be determined using the WSJF method. (See section 6.5.4.5 for WSJF calculation.)

- If the feature impacts a business process, the process is well-enough understood to identify dependencies on other stories and effects on other steps in the process.

6.5.7.7 Tuning Workflow Parameters (Kanban)

The Kanban approach contains several configurable parameters. These include target *item sizes*, the *states* that will be tracked (columns of the Kanban Board), and *WIP limits*.

Determining Item Size

Kanban's guideline regarding work items is that they be sized so that they are *understandable* and *doable*. Typical sizes in Kanban range from about half an hour to two days, with a preference for items sized at one day or less.

In a context where the work items represent stories, the item sizes are often larger. As we've seen, a story can take up to five days to implement (and even eight days, on occasion) because it has the added constraint of delivering useful value—and that's not always possible within a limit of one or two days.

Determining Kanban States (Columns)

Kanban does not specify the states that must be tracked for a work item. Typical statuses for a story are *Backlog* (i.e., the item is present in the backlog but not yet ready), *Ready* (satisfies the DoR), *In Progress*, and *Done*. Other statuses often added before *Done* include *Code Review* and *Test*. Table 6.2 is an example of a Kanban board to track the states of stories as they make their way through their lifecycle.

Table 6.2   *Example of Kanban Board*

Backlog	Ready	In Progress	Code Review	Testing	Done
PBI101	PBI045	PBI077	PBI057	PBI088	
PBI087	PBI099	PBI127	PBI152	PBI126	
PBI141		PBI131		PBI044	

For examples of Kanban boards used in conjunction with timeboxed iteration planning, see Figures 14.5 and 14.6 in Chapter 14, "Iteration and Story Planning."

Determining WIP Limits

Once you've determined the Kanban columns, you need to set a WIP limit for each one. The following are guidelines for setting WIP limits in software development.

Keep the WIP limit for the *In Progress* column lower than the number of team members to reduce inefficiencies. This practice limits the need for multitasking and allows for slack time so that someone is more likely to be available to help unplug bottlenecks.

When using timeboxed planning, make sure the WIP limit for the Ready column (containing stories queued up for iteration planning) does not exceed the number of team members. Anything higher would result in more ready stories than the team can work on, assuming each member takes one story. That, in turn, would mean you had prepared more stories to be ready for the iteration than you needed to—violating the last-responsible-moment principle.

Start with What You Do Now: Agree to Pursue Incremental, Evolutionary Change

In setting WIP limits, follow the Kanban principles: "Start with what you do now" and "Agree to pursue incremental, evolutionary change."[25] Begin by letting the development process play out, tracking the movement of work items across the Kanban board without seeking to intervene. Once you've allowed the process to run for a while, set WIP limits by observing the number of items that have tended to accumulate in each state. Over time, make changes to WIP limits and work item sizes with the aim of reducing the time items spend in each state.

---

25. "Kanban," Agile Alliance Glossary, 2020, https://www.agilealliance.org/glossary/kanban/
#q=~(infinite~false~filters~(postType~(~'page~'post~'aa_book~'aa_event_session~'aa_experience_
eport~'aa_glossary~'aa_research_paper~'aa_video)~tags~(~'kanban))~searchTerm~'~sort~false~
sortDirection~'asc~page~1)

6.6 Optimizing the Process Using Value Stream Mapping

Once the development process is up and running, use value stream mapping to locate opportunities to remove waste.

To use this lean technique, first determine the steps that a work item (e.g., user story) goes through as it passes through the development process, then research how long it spends at each stage. Figure 6.4 is an example of a value stream map resulting from this analysis.

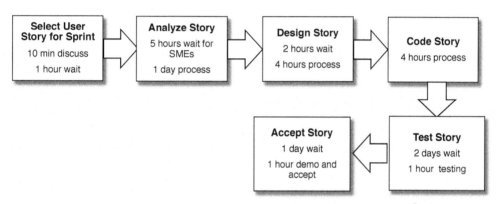

Figure 6.4 *Value stream map for implementing a user story*

Figure 6.4 indicates two significant sources of waste in the development process: five hours in Analyze Story (while the analyst waits for SMEs to become available) and two days in Test Story (while a story waits to be tested). The first can be improved by managing stakeholder expectations up front regarding participation and working with managers to obtain the required time commitment. The second waste item may be an indication that more testers are needed on the team.

6.7 Determining Process Readiness

Use the following checklist to determine whether the agile planning and analysis process is ready. Create a plan to address any remaining gaps.

☐ Has a base process been developed or selected (e.g., Kanban, Scrum) and tailored ☑
to the context?

☐ Has a product backlog been set up, and is it ready to be used?

☐ Have standard requirements types and attributes been established?

☐ Has a traceability process been established?

☐ Have BA artifacts and events for the process been established?

☐ Have Kanban workflow parameters and artifacts been set or initialized (e.g., WIP limits)?

☐ For timeboxed planning, has the cadence been determined?

☐ Has a shared DoD been established?

☐ Has a shared DoR been established?

6.8 Chapter Summary

Here are the key points covered in this chapter:

- Trace stories backward to features, business objectives, business processes, and so on; horizontally to other stories; and forward to tests, software components, and so on.

- Specify a DoD to indicate conditions that must be satisfied before a story is accepted as complete.

- Specify a DoR to indicate conditions that must be satisfied before committing to a story during planning.

- Forecast capacity based on past velocity, adjusting for changing circumstances.

6.9 What's Next?

This chapter focused on *process preparation*—preparing the agile process that will be used to analyze and manage requirements. In Chapter 7, "Visioning," we begin that process by working with stakeholders and developers to envision the product and its impact on customers and the business.

Chapter 7

Visioning

This chapter examines visioning activities. In visioning, stakeholders articulate a vision of the future state that will be realized by the product or endeavor and the reason for embarking on the initiative. Visioning is carried out when developing a new product or undertaking a major change. It is revisited quarterly and as required by changing circumstances, such as a new market opportunity—or loss of an opportunity—due to unexpected regulatory changes. Figure 7.1 highlights the activities included in this chapter.

The chapter begins with the first step in the process, root-cause analysis. Root-cause analysis is a set of methods for tracing the causes of an effect back to a root cause. An example of an effect is poor customer retention. An example of a root cause is an *inefficient customer-service process*. Root-cause analysis techniques covered in this chapter include Five Whys and cause–effect diagrams. The chapter explains how to use this analysis to inform the crafting of product vision statements, epic vision statements, and problem statements. The identification of root causes helps direct development investment to areas that have the greatest potential to impact outcomes.

Stakeholder analysis begins as early as possible in the initiative and is continually updated and developed as more stakeholders are discovered and their needs become better understood. The chapter includes guidelines, templates, and checklists for performing this analysis and using it to inform the communication plan.

The next step covered in the chapter is the identification of leap of faith hypotheses— critical assumptions that underlie the vision and must be valid for the undertaking to be viable (e.g., the hypothesis that users will pay for a subscription to a new service). Leap of faith hypotheses are identified and tested early so the company can decide whether to invest its resources in the endeavor or pivot to another hypothesis. The chapter explains the agile approach for doing so using the minimum viable product (MVP) process. An MVP is a low-cost version or facsimile of the proposed product or feature used for learning. Customers interact with MVPs, and their feedback is used to test hypotheses, features, changes, and design solutions.

The chapter ends with guidelines for specifying metrics to validate hypotheses and measure progress toward goals and objectives. It explains how to define **actionable metrics**— measurements that can be used to make data-informed decisions.

The chapter also marks the beginning of the BLInK case study workshops that run throughout the book. Each workshop provides a snapshot of agile analysis and planning tools as you step through the development lifecycle.

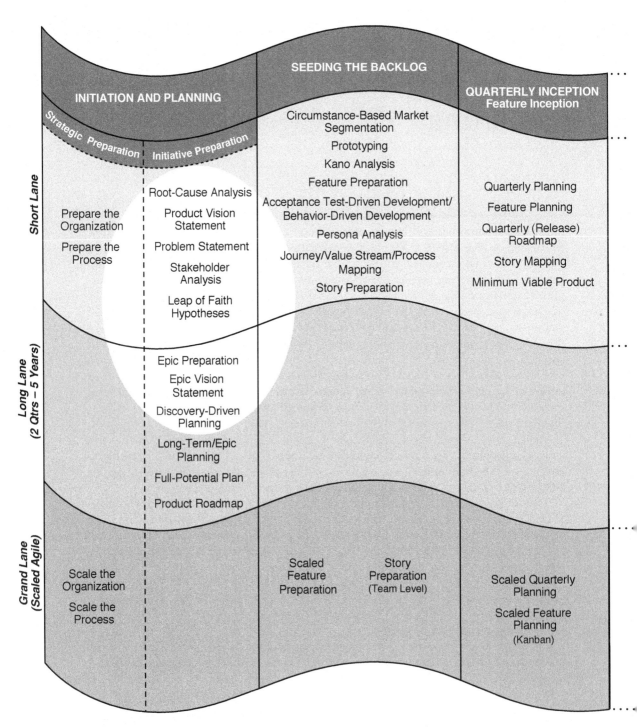

Figure 7.1   *Chapter 7 on the map*

| ITERATION INCEPTION | DAILY ACTIVITIES | | | ITERATION CLOSEOUT | QUARTERLY CLOSEOUT Epic, Feature Closeout |

DAILY ACTIVITIES

Daily Standup

Requirements Analysis & Documentation

Code, Build, Test, Deliver Acceptance Test-Driven Development/ Behavior-Driven Development

Minimum Viable Product, Split Testing

Epic, Feature Preparation

Story Preparation

ITERATION INCEPTION

Iteration Planning

ITERATION CLOSEOUT

Iteration Review

Iteration Retrospective

QUARTERLY CLOSEOUT
Epic, Feature Closeout

Prepare for General Availability

Quarterly Retrospective

Epic, Feature Retrospective

Pivot or Persevere

Scaled Iteration Planning

Iteration Planning (Team Level)

Product Owner Council Meetings

DevOps

User Task Force Meetings

Scaled Feature Preparation (Kanban)

Integration Meetings

Story Preparation (Team Level)

Scaled Iteration Review

Scaled Iteration Retrospective

Iteration Retrospective (Team Level)

DevOps

Scaled Quarterly/Feature Retrospective

7.1 Objectives

This chapter will help you to

- Identify root causes and needs.
- Articulate the vision statement for the product or epic.
- Craft a problem statement.
- Analyze stakeholders, goals, and objectives.
- Discover leap of faith hypotheses.
- Specify the actionable metrics that will be used to validate hypotheses.

7.2 This Chapter on the Map

Figure 7.1 highlights the visioning tools we cover in the first zone, *Initiation and Planning*. These are root-cause analysis, product vision statement, epic vision statement, stakeholder analysis, problem statement, leap of faith hypotheses, and circumstance-based market segmentation.

7.3 Overview of Product Visioning and Epic Preparation

In visioning, stakeholders articulate a shared vision of the future and the reason for undertaking the endeavor. This activity is performed at the product level (product visioning) to communicate the rationale for building the product. It also occurs at the epic level to articulate the rationale for a major change initiative and prepare the epic for planning and implementation.

Visioning occurs primarily at the beginning of an undertaking, but the activities are revisited quarterly and as required by changing circumstances (e.g., because a hypothesis for the product no longer holds true or because of a new opportunity or threat).

Individuals typically responsible for product visioning include the following:

- Director of product
- VP of product
- Chief product officer
- Product-level product owner (PO), Portfolio
- Senior business analyst

Junior business analysts are not typically involved in the *formation* of the product vision, but they share the responsibility to *communicate* the product vision and objectives to the team.

Visioning is an essential activity for achieving any bold target that requires sustained effort, such as Nike's moonshot challenge to "double business with half the [environmental] impact."[1]

The envisioned target may be for

- an enterprise (enterprise visioning),

- a product (product visioning), or

- an epic or change initiative (**epic visioning**).

In this chapter, we focus on product and epic visioning.

The result of visioning is a vision statement. Internally, a product vision statement motivates the team and supports the development of a cohesive product. Externally, the product vision statement communicates the product's potential value to investors and early adopters (earlyvangelists) at the start of a venture and drives marketing messages to customers. Similarly, epic vision statements and problem statements communicate the reason for a change initiative.

7.3.1 An Example of Product Visioning and Why It's Important

A couple of years ago, I worked with a team of consultants tasked with choosing an incident management solution for a public transportation agency. The incidents ranged from small schedule delays to fatal accidents. (Suicides were a particularly common and unsettling incident type; one unfolded in real-time as I was viewing the monitoring system with the team.)

After I'd introduced the consultants to the benefits of visioning, they realized that they had never gone through this vital step even though they were well into the preliminary analysis. And so, they convinced their manager to convene a visioning workshop with stakeholders. During the workshop, the participants defined a vision of the product that was very different from the one assumed by the consultants. The participants expressed a vision of a solution that would free up customer support agents from the mundane incidents that occupied most of their time so that they could focus on those tasks best handled by humans. The consultants, on the other hand, had been working under the assumption that the vision was of an all-encompassing tool that could manage *any incident* an agent might have to deal with. This insight resulted in significant savings because it meant that the team could now exclude incident types that required integration with police and government systems. As it turned out, those were the types that had contributed most to the initial cost estimates.

---

1. "NIKE, Inc. Sets Bold Vision and Targets for 2020" [press release], *Business Wire*, May 11, 2016, https://www.businesswire.com/news/home/20160511005885/en/NIKE-Sets-Bold-Vision-Targets-2020

7.3.2 Visioning Checklist

By the time you get involved with the initiative as a business analyst, the product vision may already have been defined or completely missed, as was the case in the preceding example. If you were not part of the initial analysis, your first step should be to check if any steps in the product visioning process were skipped. Use the checklist in Appendix A.4 to determine if that's the case.

As a business analyst, you are a change agent. If you discover that important steps were missed during product visioning, it is your responsibility to raise your concerns, highlighting the risks of not carrying them out. Though you may lack the authority to act on those concerns, you *can* influence those who do.

7.3.3 Initial Stakeholder Identification

As soon as possible, identify the primary individuals and groups affected by the initiative and those who impact it, such as approvers. Key stakeholders include business subject matter experts (SMEs) in the areas affected by the initiative, the PO, sponsor, and steering committee members.

Stakeholder identification and analysis is ongoing. As the initiative progresses, expect to discover more stakeholders and learn more about their needs. We examine these activities more fully in section 7.9.

7.3.4 Facilitation Tips

Product visioning and root-cause analysis workshops typically take place through group facilitation led by a PO or business analyst. As a facilitator, the soft skills you bring to the table to these events are at least as important as the analysis techniques covered in this book. Tips for facilitating stakeholder events can be found in the appendix.

 See Appendix A.3 for tips on facilitating events.

7.4 Root-Cause Analysis

If you don't diagnose the real cause of a problem, you can't solve it. Use Lean Six Sigma's **root-cause analysis** techniques early in the development process to aid in the diagnosis. For example, following a merger of two banks, data discrepancies keep appearing despite repeated efforts to fix them. Root-cause analysis traces the problem back to data duplication between the two banks' systems. The problem is solved by normalizing the data or merging the systems.

Sometimes a need that stakeholders bring forward is really a proposal for a solution. In this case, you use root-cause analysis to identify the underlying need. For example, one of my clients was a software consulting company looking to enhance a software system used by its compliance auditors. The auditors had told analysts they needed reporting features they'd seen in a competitive product. Root-cause analysis revealed the *real* need: to mitigate the risk of missing the opportunity to bid on government contracts if the company didn't meet a compliance deadline. Once this problem was correctly identified, the team was able to focus enhancements on those features the software system needed for compliance, significantly reducing the risk of missing the deadline. A similar approach can be used to trace an opportunity back to a core benefit (e.g., tracing the opportunity presented by new mobile payment technologies to greater customer convenience).

Table 7.1 is an overview of the root-cause analysis approach.

Table 7.1 *Root-Cause Analysis: At a Glance*

What?	**Root-cause analysis:** A set of techniques for uncovering the root causes of a presenting symptom. The approach encompasses a family of tools such as Five Whys (asking Why? repeatedly) and cause–effect diagrams.
When?	At the start of an initiative.
Why?	Ensure the real problem is addressed so that symptoms do not recur.
Tips	Create analysis artifacts live, during facilitation events, so that attendees can visualize cause–effect relationships as they are discovered.
Deliverables	Root causes, Five Whys graph, cause–effect diagram, cause–effect tree

We look at the following root-cause analysis tools:

- Five Whys
- Cause–effect diagrams
- Cause–effect trees

7.4.1 Five Whys

The Five Whys method is just what it sounds like. You ask, "Why?" repeatedly until a root cause is found. There is nothing magic about the number five; it's just a rough approximation of the number of times one has to ask the question to get to the root cause.

As an example, suppose stakeholders present the problem of decreasing revenues. You ask the first why question: "Why has the decrease occurred?" You learn that it's mostly due to an increase in voluntary churn (customers choosing to leave the company). Next, you ask, "Why has voluntary churn increased?" You learn that it is because customer loyalty is weak. Again, you ask why. You learn that competitors have more robust customer loyalty programs. Figure 7.2 shows the Five Whys diagram you create during this conversation.

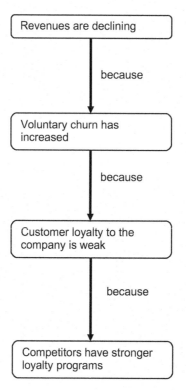

Figure 7.2 *Example of a Five Whys diagram for decreased revenue*

The figure illustrates the train of causes from the effect "Revenues are declining" back to the root cause of the problem, "Competitors have stronger loyalty programs." In a similar way, you can trace an expressed want back to a root need.

Since root-cause analysis is one of the first analysis activities in new product development, it's also a fitting place for our case study to begin. We follow this case through most of the book as we walk through the Agile Analysis and Planning Map (see Chapter 4, "Analysis and Planning Activities across the Agile Development Lifecycle," Figure 4.1).

BLINK CASE STUDY PART 1

Five Whys

Background

In the introduction to the book, we learned of Better Living (BL) Inc., a company that offers insurance products in personal and commercial lines. The commercial lines products offer employer-sponsored group health insurance to employees. Employees enroll in a group insurance plan. All those in the plan pay a community rate, set for the group on the basis of factors such as age, geography, and smoking habits. The premium is sponsored by the employer, with the employee paying any remaining costs.

According to industry reports, costs to cover an employee and family with group health insurance have nearly tripled in the last fifteen years.[2] To slow this increase, the federal government (in our fictional example) has passed legislation that permits insurance companies to provide enrollees with insurance benefits, such as rate reductions, for making healthier lifestyle choices. This presents BL with the opportunity to develop innovative usage-based insurance (UBI) products that personalize benefits on the basis of healthful behaviors.

The Ask

As a senior business analyst, you've been asked to facilitate a meeting of product managers, marketing executives, the sponsor, and other business stakeholders to identify the potential benefits of exploiting the opportunities provided by the new legislation.

> **Tip**
>
> Use the Five Whys approach to structure your questions during the event. Record responses live during the event using a Five Whys diagram.

Preparation

To prepare for your meeting, review the business-domain terminology that follows. (It is used in this and subsequent case studies.)

Business Terminology

- *Group insurance*: Insurance provided to a group of people (e.g., employees of an organization) under a joint group plan
- *Policy owner*: Person who pays for the policy
- *Subscriber*: Someone covered under an insurance policy
- *Loss ratio:* The total amount paid out to subscribers divided by the amount paid in

What Transpires

You begin by asking attendees why the opportunity to offer behavior-based insurance products benefits BL. Stakeholders reply that it would provide a treasure-trove of behavioral data on enrollees.

You ask, "Why does behavioral data benefit the business?" You learn it's because it improves BL's ability to predict undesirable health events.

You ask, "Why does a better ability to predict health events benefit the business?" You learn that it allows BL to forecast loss ratios for different premium price points more reliably.

---

2. Christina Merhar, "Small Business Q&A's: How Group Health Insurance Works," PeopleKeep Inc., March 25, 2015, https://www.peoplekeep.com/blog/small-business-health-insurance-qa-guide

You ask, "Why does reliable loss-ratio forecasting benefit the business?" You learn that getting the loss ratio right is the key to competitiveness and profitability in the industry: If it's too low, you lose customers to competitors. If it's too high, you lose money on each customer.

Deliverables

Deliverable 1: Five Whys Diagram

You create the deliverable shown in Figure 7.3 during this step, based on stakeholder answers to your questions. You identify the root benefit as *increased competitiveness and profitability due to better loss ratio forecasting*.

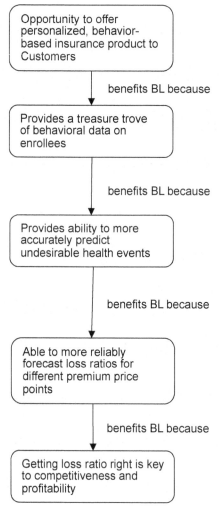

Figure 7.3   *BL insurance: Five Whys diagram*

Case Study Retrospective

As a result of this root-cause analysis, it is now clear that the core business benefit to the company is increased competitiveness and profitability due to the enhanced capability to forecast loss ratios. The analysis will help direct future development on features that generate rich datasets that will improve financial forecasting.

7.4.2 Cause–Effect Diagrams

Whenever you ask why, you can get more than one answer—and those answers may lead to more questions with more answers. Though elegant in its simplicity, the Five Whys method doesn't have a way to map multiple causes. A **cause–effect diagram** does. Use it when there are multiple answers to the question, "Why?"

The diagram is also referred to as an **Ishikawa diagram** or **fishbone diagram**. Figure 7.4 is a template for this type of diagram.

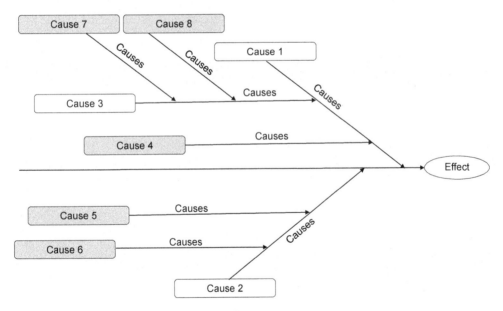

Figure 7.4 *Cause–effect diagram template*

7.4.2.1 Facilitation Tips

Start the diagram by drawing a horizontal line—the spine—with an ellipse at one end—the fish head (indicated at the right edge of Figure 7.4). Ask stakeholders to specify the **effect**—the presenting symptom that triggered the initiative. The effect can be an undesirable symptom you wish to trace to its root causes, a presenting opportunity traced to root benefits, or an expressed want traced to a core need. Indicate the effect inside the head of the diagram, as indicated in Figure 7.4.

Now, ask stakeholders *why* the effect occurs. For each cause you discover, draw a new line away from the spine. Label the tip of the new line with the cause, as shown for causes 1 and 2 in Figure 7.4.

Next, ask stakeholders why *each* of these items occurs and map those answers as indicated in Figure 7.4 for cause 1 (shown to be due to causes 3 and 4) and cause 2 (linked to causes 5 and 6).

Continue asking about each cause until you come up against a dead end. For example, causes 7 and 8 are dead ends. Additional why questions do not yield useful knowledge. For example, any further causes are outside of the organization's sphere of influence.

The dead ends on the diagram are the *root causes*. In Figure 7.4, they're the shaded causes: 4, 5, 6, 7, and 8.

7.4.2.2 Example of a Cause–Effect Diagram

Let's suppose you've convened a group of stakeholders to examine the reason for declining revenues. You soon learn there are multiple causes, so you use a cause–effect diagram for the analysis. Figure 7.5 illustrates the diagram developed during the meeting.

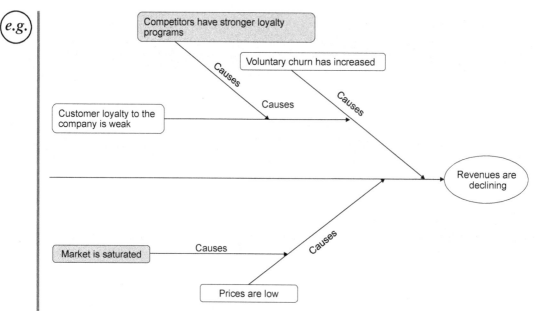

Figure 7.5   *Cause–effect diagram declining revenues example*

Figure 7.5 traces declining revenues to two root causes: the market is saturated and competitors have stronger loyalty programs. The company may decide to address these causes by seeking out new markets and by strengthening its loyalty programs.

Cause–Effect Analysis

Background

Recent industry reports have highlighted growing concerns in the public about rising healthcare costs. BL Inc. is searching for ways to attract new customers and improve customer retention by addressing those concerns through novel product offerings.

The Ask

You've been asked to facilitate a meeting of business SMEs to identify the root causes of rising healthcare costs.

Following are the deliverables for the event:

- Deliverable 1: Cause–effect diagram tracing the causes of rising healthcare costs
- Deliverable 2: List of root causes

Tip

Use a cause–effect diagram instead of Five Whys whenever there is likely to be more than one reason for an effect, as is the case here with respect to rising healthcare costs.

What Transpires

As attendees arrive, you draw the spine of the diagram, writing "Rising healthcare costs" at its head.

You ask stakeholders, "Why are healthcare costs rising?" A data analyst replies that it's because of an *increase in the average number of claims per individual*. You indicate this cause on the diagram.

Others point out that there's also been an *increase in the average cost per health event*. You add the cause to the diagram. You ask, "Why is there an increase in the average cost?" The only answers you receive have to do with pricing factors over which BL has no influence, so you end that line of questioning.

Pointing to the first cause, you ask, "Why has there been an increase in the average number of claims?" Stakeholders reply that this is because of the declining health of enrollees. You continue this process until all branches lead to dead ends—signaling that the root causes have all been found.

Deliverables

Deliverable 1: Cause–Effect Diagram

Figure 7.6 is the cause–effect diagram resulting from the analysis.

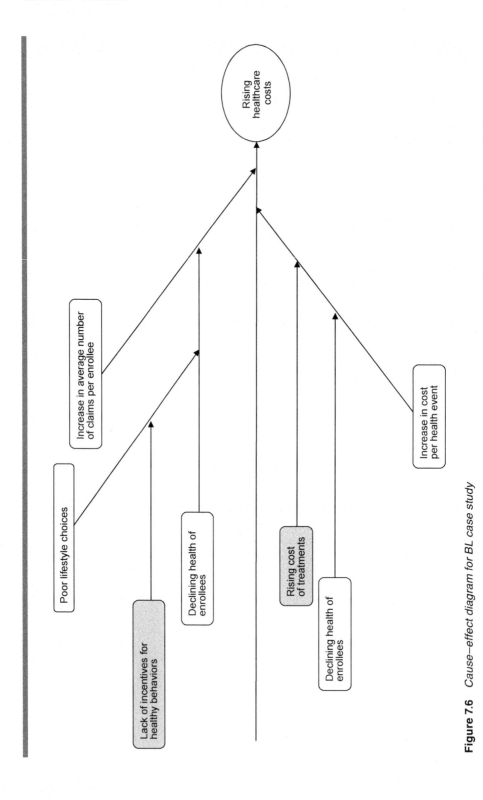

Figure 7.6 *Cause–effect diagram for BL case study*

Deliverable 2: List of Root Causes

- Lack of incentives for healthy behaviors
- Rising costs of individual treatments (drugs and procedures)

Case Study Retrospective

Of the two root causes, lack of incentives for healthy behaviors is determined to be the area in which BL can have the most significant impact. The company will investigate the opportunity to attract and retain customers by helping them lower their healthcare costs through products that incentivize healthy behaviors.

Case Study Epilogue

Following this investigation of the root causes of rising healthcare costs and the earlier Five Whys analysis of the opportunity to develop personalized products, BL has decided to proceed with the development of a new commercial line product, **BL**In**K**, **B**etter **L**iving through **In**surance **K**nowledge. The new product uses personalized data to encourage customers to adopt healthy behaviors. The advantages to the insured are lower healthcare costs as a result of improved health and rewards for healthy behaviors, such as reductions in gym memberships. The benefit to BL is improved loss-ratio forecasting due to data harvested from the product, resulting in higher profitability.

7.4.3 Cause–Effect Trees

You may have noticed that in Figure 7.6, *declining health of enrollees* appeared twice. This duplication occurred because it was a cause that had two different effects. Cause–effect diagrams don't have any explicit mechanism for indicating this kind of relationship or for showing other complex relationships—such as instances where *multiple* causes have to occur together before an effect can happen. **Cause–effect trees** address these shortcomings. Use them if you need to analyze several presenting problems holistically because their causes are intertwined. The trees also enable stakeholders to identify areas of improvement that have the potential to address multiple issues simultaneously.

7.4.3.1 Legend

Figure 7.7 shows a cause–effect tree legend that is adapted from the original form invented by Eliyahu M. Goldratt.[3]

Each rounded rectangle on the diagram represents an entity. An **entity** is an item that may be a cause, an effect, or both, based on its relationship to other entities. Each arrow points from a cause to an effect (e.g., in Figure 7.7, C causes A). If an effect has more than one cause, more than one arrow will point to it. When these arrows are unadorned, they

---

3. James F. Cox and John G. Schleier, *Theory of Constraints Handbook* (New York: McGraw Hill, 2010).

represent on OR relationship, meaning either entity, on its own, causes the effect. For example, if either B or E occurs, then UDE 2 will happen. When two or more arrows are lassoed by an oval (a bar may also be used), an AND relationship is indicated, meaning *all* of the causes must occur to generate the effect.

The diagram includes special entities referred to as **undesirable effects** (UDEs). These represent unacceptable symptoms.[4] Examples of UDEs are high defect levels, undesirable turnaround times, low market share, bugs, and any functionality that does not operate as expected. You may use parenthesis to indicate the stakeholder affected by the UDE—for example, *UDE 1: (Patient) Lack of access to medical reports.*

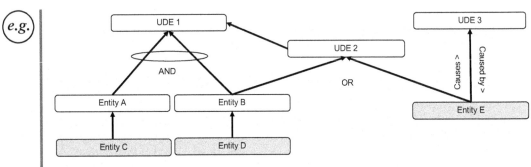

Figure 7.7 *Cause–effect tree legend*

7.4.3.2 Creating the Diagram

Begin the analysis by asking stakeholders to identify the symptoms that the business is experiencing. As these symptoms are detected, add them as UDEs near the top of the diagram. For each UDE, identify the stakeholder concerned about it (e.g., customer, business, or employer).

Tracing back from these UDEs, ask stakeholders to identify their causes—adding them to the diagram as they are discovered.

If there is more than one cause for an effect, ask if they both need to happen for the effect to occur. Use the appropriate notation to document the response. Once no more causes are discovered, review the diagram with stakeholders and list the dead-end entities as root causes.

> Always choose the root-cause-analysis tool that can handle just as much complexity as you need for the situation—but no more. If there is only one problem under consideration, use the Five Whys method for a preliminary analysis. Use cause–effect diagrams if you need to do a deeper dive. If there are multiple, interrelated problems, use cause–effect trees.

---

4. Cox and Schleier, *Theory of Constraints*, 394–395.

Cause–Effect Tree

Background

The prior cause–effect analysis has sparked a conversation within BL about other issues and problems the company is dealing with and whether it might be possible to address them, as well, during the upcoming initiative.

The Ask

You've been asked to bring stakeholders together to broaden the root-cause analysis.

Following are the deliverables for the event:

- Deliverable 1: Cause–effect tree mapping the undesirable effects brought up during the meeting to their root causes
- Deliverable 2: A list of UDEs and the stakeholders affected by them
- Deliverable 3: A list of root causes and the UDEs they contribute to

Preparation

To prepare for your meeting, transpose the causes and effects from the cause–effect diagram you created previously (see Figure 7.6) to a draft of the new deliverable, a cause–effect tree.

Tips

Use a cause–effect tree for this event because you'll be examining multiple problems that are likely to be interrelated.

Begin the meeting by reviewing the cause–effect tree draft you created in preparation for the meeting. Revise the tree as needed on the basis of the review. Ask stakeholders about any other problems they are aware of, and add these to the model as UDEs. Ask why these UDEs occur, and map the resulting relationships. Continue as described in the preceding section until the root causes have been found.

What Transpires

You review the draft diagram. You ask attendees to cite any other problems they are aware of, from the standpoints of BL Inc. and its customers:

- A representative of BL's financial division reports that the business is concerned about decreasing profitability.
- Underwriters mention undesirable loss ratios—the amount paid out vs. paid in.
- A data analyst brings up another disturbing trend for the company—the increase in the average amount paid out per subscriber.

You represent these as UDEs on the cause–effect tree diagram.
You ask attendees about customer issues:

- A customer relations manager offers that employers have identified increased absenteeism as a primary concern.

- A marketing manager notes that subscribers are increasingly concerned about their declining health.

You add these UDEs to the diagram.

Working backward, you ask "Why?" for each UDE now on the diagram, adding each cause and its relationships to other entities you discovered.

You ask what causes the first UDE, *decreased profitability*, and learn that it is due to three issues:

- Undesirable loss ratio. (You previously identified this item as a UDE.)
- Pricing is not competitive enough to attract and retain customers.
- Low brand loyalty

You ask stakeholders if any of these causes would be enough on its own to decrease profitability:

- Stakeholders tell you that the loss-ratio issue reduces profitability.
- However, they also offer that the last two issues—uncompetitive pricing and low brand loyalty—must both be present.

You "lasso" these causes, indicating an AND relationship.

You continue with this process, asking "Why?" about each entity until you reach dead ends (root causes).

Deliverables

Deliverable 1: Cause–Effect Tree
Figure 7.8 illustrates the diagram developed during this meeting.

Deliverable 2: UDEs
The following UDEs are identified:

- UDE 1: (BL) Decreased profitability
- UDE 2: (BL) Undesirable loss ratio
- UDE 3: (Subscriber) Rising healthcare costs
- UDE 4: (BL) Increased average payout per subscriber
- UDE 5: (Employer) Increased absenteeism
- UDE 6: (Subscriber) Declining health

Deliverable 3: List of Root Causes
The following root causes are identified:

1. Compliance constraints—contributing to UDE 1 and UDE 2
2. No BL technical capabilities for interfacing with Internet of Things (IoT) devices to access data—contributing to UDE 1 and UDE 2
3. Company does not offer attractive incentives or rewards—contributing to UDE 1
4. Lack of incentives for healthy behaviors—contributing to UDE 3, UDE 4, UDE 5, and UDE 6
5. Rising cost of treatments—contributing to UDE 3

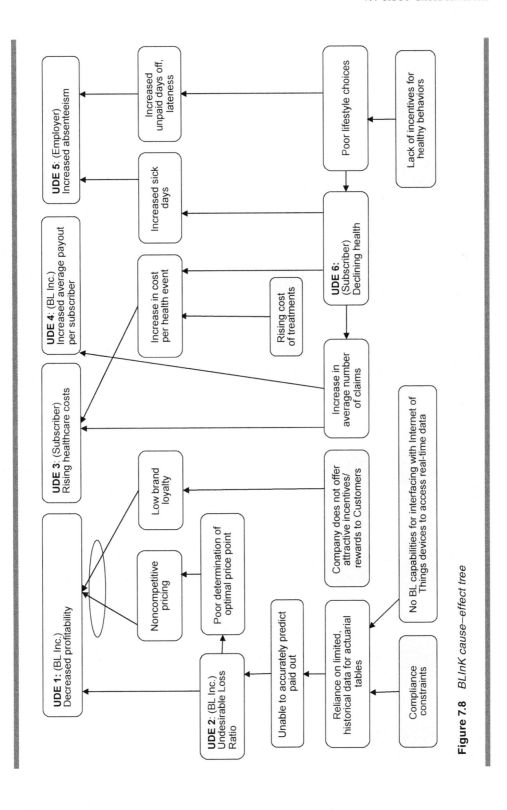

Figure 7.8 *BLInK cause–effect tree*

Case Study Retrospective

The analysis strengthened the business case for BLInK—broadening the range of problems it would address. The analysis points product development in the direction of features that provide a rich source of data that can be used for actuarial tables, encourage healthy behaviors, and contribute to a more attractive rewards program.

Case Study Epilogue

After the meeting, stakeholders review their conclusions. They exclude root cause 1, *compliance*, because of recent legislation that has removed compliance as an area of concern.

Reviewing the proposed BLInK program, you note that that the product will use a subscriber's health data to encourage healthy behaviors by offering benefits for healthy choices. You facilitate an examination of the program's impact on the remaining root causes.

Root causes 2, 3, and 4 are all found to be areas in which BLInK would have a positive impact. The product would provide the technical capabilities required to collect data from IoT devices. Moreover, it would deliver an attractive rewards program to customers, thereby increasing loyalty and providing incentives for healthy choices.

Based on the analysis, you conclude that BLInK promises to improve outcomes for the following UDEs:

- UDE 1: (BL) Decreased profitability

- UDE 2: (BL) Undesirable loss ratio

- UDE 3: (Subscriber) Rising healthcare costs

- UDE 4: (BL) Increased average payout per subscriber

- UDE 5: (Employer) Increased absenteeism

- UDE 6: (Subscriber) Declining health

7.5 Specifying a Product or Epic

You can use the Connextra template to summarize the understanding you reached through root-cause analysis for a new epic or product. For example, in the BLInK case study, you understood the core benefit of the product: increased competitiveness and profitability due to better loss-ratio forecasting. In the Connextra format, you express this as follows: "As a group insurer, I want to gather lifestyle data so that I can improve loss-ratio forecasts." In one sentence, this formulation identifies the primary beneficiary, the primary functionality, and the beneficial outcome. Another example is the epic "As a supply chain manager, I want to introduce dropship capability so that top-line sales can be increased without the inventory expense."

Specify acceptance criteria for an epic that describe, at a high level, the minimum requirements for completion. The following example expresses the business objective that must be achieved: "Legacy system can be retired."

> **Epic:** Modernize customer loyalty program
>
> **Acceptance Criteria:** Implementation of this epic means that the legacy system can be retired.

We examine acceptance criteria for epics and features at greater length in Chapter 10, "Quarterly and Feature Preparation," section 10.9.

7.6 The Problem or Opportunity Statement

The problem or opportunity statement is a less concise but more informative summary of the business case for a product or change initiative, such as an epic.

The statement addresses the following **Five W** questions:

- *What* is the root problem (or opportunity)?
- *Whom* does it affect?
- *Where* does the problem occur?
- *When* does it occur?
- *Why* should we care?

You can articulate the problem statement in a paragraph, a section of a business case, or a sentence or two, using the following template:

> The problem/opportunity of [*what?*] affects [*who?*] [*where?*] [*when?*], the impact of which is [impact on the customer or business—the *why*].

In the template, the **impact** refers to the undesirable effect or symptom; the **problem** is the root cause of those effects.

You can add a sentence that turns toward a solution as follows: "A successful solution would [benefits]."

In Scaled Agile Framework (SAFe), a similar format is used as part of the epic hypothesis as follows:

> "For [customers (the *who*)] who [do something (the context, or *when*)], the [solution] is a [something (the *how*)] that [provides this value]; unlike [competitor, current state], our solution [does something better (the *why*)]."[5]

The SAFe epic hypotheses template contains the following items:[6]

- Date of entry
- Epic name
- Epic owner
- Description—elevator pitch for the epic
- "For . . . who" template, as described earlier
- Business outcomes (objectives)
- Leading indicators that will be used to validate hypotheses
- Nonfunctional requirements

BLINK CASE STUDY PART 4
Problem Statement

Background
Following up on the previous root-cause analysis workshops, you invite stakeholders to a meeting to craft the BLInK problem statement.

The Ask
The objective is to craft the following deliverable: problem statement.

Tips
Use the Five W questions *(who, what, where, when, why)* to structure your conversation with stakeholders. Discuss the deliverables of the prior case study. Write up the root causes identified in the analysis as *problems* in the problem statement. Identify the UDEs as *impacts*.

What Transpires
You review the results of the previous analysis with stakeholders, using the problem statement template to guide your questioning. You begin by asking stakeholders,

5. Richard Kastner and Dean Leffingwell, *SAFe 5.0 Distilled: Achieving Business Agility with the Scaled Agile Framework* (Boston: Addison-Wesley, 2020), 154.
6. Kastner and Leffingwell, *SAFe 5.0 Distilled*, 154.

"*What* are the root causes that BLInK is expected to address?" Stakeholders concur on the following causes:

- Rising healthcare costs
- Increased average payout per subscriber
- Increased absenteeism
- Declining health

Next, you ask, "*Who* is affected by these symptoms?" Attendees concur that, as indicated in the prior analysis, the affected stakeholders for these root causes are employers, subscribers, and the business (BL). You learn that all of these stakeholders are affected nationwide.

You ask *when* the problems impact stakeholders and learn that they do so on a daily basis. You ask *why* stakeholders are concerned, as you review the UDEs discovered in the prior analysis.

Deliverables

The following deliverable was created:

Deliverable 1: Problem Statement

The problems of rising healthcare costs, increased average payout per subscriber, increased absenteeism, and declining health affect employers, subscribers, and the business (BL) nationally every day, the impact of which is declining health, double-digit increases in healthcare costs for the average subscriber, and lost productivity due to absenteeism for the employer. A successful solution would incentivize healthy behaviors, resulting in reduced healthcare costs and absenteeism due to illness while providing BL Inc. with more accurate data with which to price premiums and a competitive edge in the marketplace.

Case Study Retrospective

The *problem statement* communicates a shared understanding of the problems BLInK is expected to solve and the stakeholders who will benefit.

7.7 The Product Portrait

We're about to evolve the understanding we've been developing into a product vision statement, customer objectives, stakeholder analysis, and many other informative BA information artifacts. These artifacts should be transparent to business stakeholders and members of the development organization in order to promote a shared understanding of the product. The **product portrait** is a publicly posted chart—or information radiator—that provides that transparency. It also reduces time lost to interruptions by answering critical questions about the product.

Table 7.2 provides an overview of the tool.

Table 7.2   *The Product Portrait at a Glance*

What?	Product portrait: An overview, displayed in a public space, that provides a snapshot of the product. Based on Roman Pichler's product canvas.
When?	Create the portrait during initial preparation for a new product or significant change. Update it as needed.
Why?	• Promotes transparency. • Reduces interruptions to the team.
Tips	Use the portrait to facilitate visioning workshops, working through the template from left to right to support a customer-driven analysis. Post it in a public place and update it often.
Deliverables	Product portrait includes vision statement, stakeholders, objectives, assumptions, metrics, design sketches, and features.

7.7.1 The Product Portrait Template

Figure 7.9 is a product portrait template. The template is based on Roman Pichler's product canvas,[7] with added elements from lean startup and other sources. Adapt it according to your needs.

Use the product portrait as a *facilitation tool* during visioning workshops, advancing from the top to the bottom and left to right. Follow this sequence: vision, stakeholders, goals, objectives, assumptions, metrics, and so on. In this way, the product portrait supports a customer-focused process.

Use the sketch pad area of the product portrait to communicate visual artifacts developed during the product's analysis and design. Pictures have significant benefits over words: they take advantage of our natural ability to use "parallel processing" when handling visual input. The sketch pad may include artifacts such as the following:

• Customer and user journeys

• Process models

• Wireframes and other user interface design items

• Charts and tables

---

7. Roman Pichler, "The Product Canvas" [blog post], July 16, 2012, https://www.romanpichler.com/blog/the-product-canvas

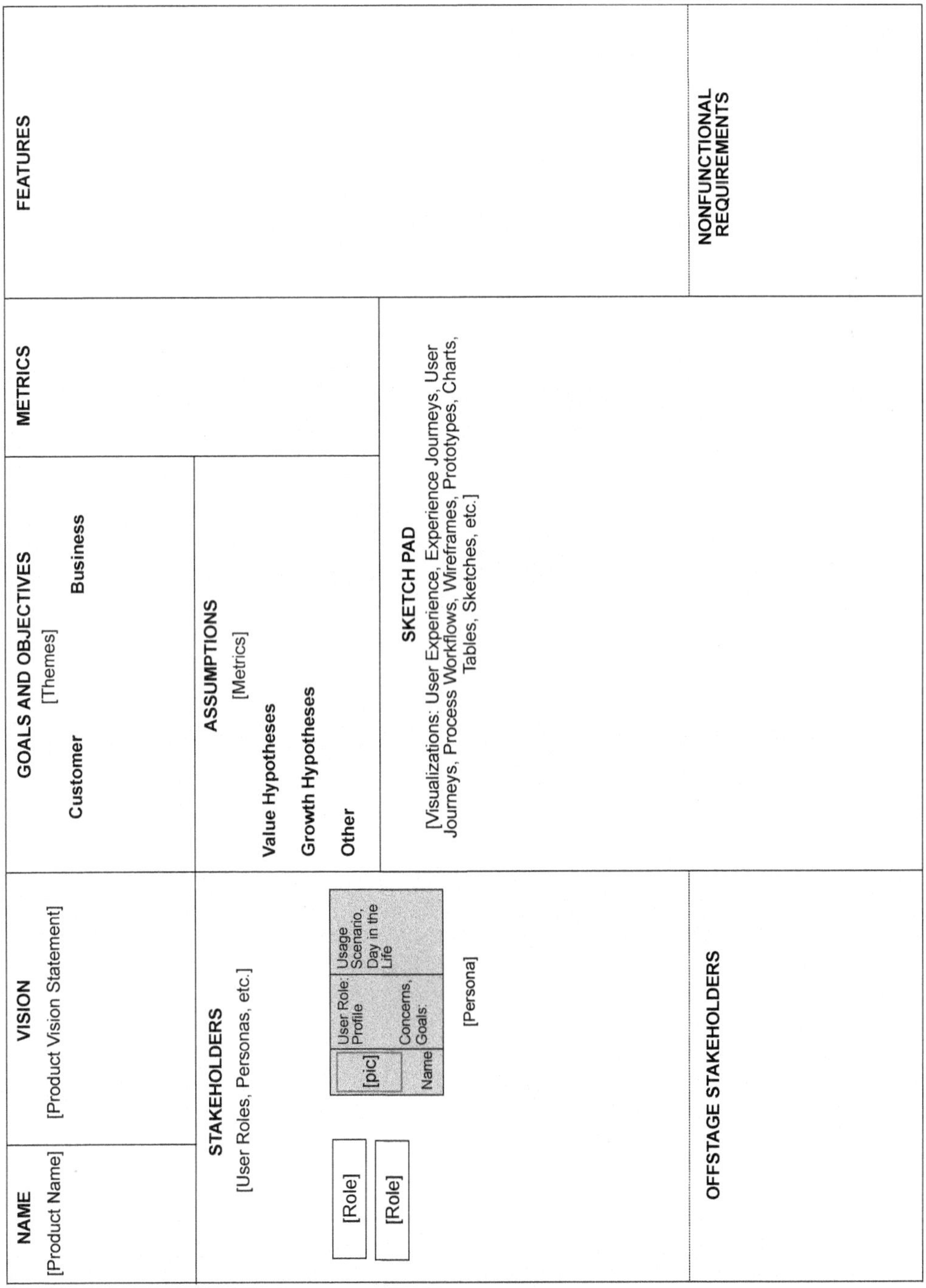

Figure 7.9 *Product Portrait Template (adapted from Pichler's Product Canvas)*

7.8 Crafting the Product and Epic Vision Statements

Root-cause analysis looks backward to understand the underlying causes of problems. Vision statements look forward.

7.8.1 The Product Vision Statement

The **product vision statement** looks forward, describing the change users will experience when the product is deployed to the market and what the company hopes to accomplish by developing it. The responsibility to articulate the product vision statement and supporting objectives belongs to product-level POs and business analysts. A team-level analyst is responsible for understanding the product vision and objectives, communicating them to the team, and ensuring that the requirements support them.

7.8.2 The Epic Vision Statement

Similarly, an **epic vision statement** describes the future state after an epic—a significant change to an existing product. Within the problem statement format, the epic vision statement can serve in place of the final sentence, "A successful solution would. . . ." Use the epic vision statement for the elevator pitch within the SAFe epic hypotheses template. The articulation of the epic vision statement is the responsibility of the area PO or product-level PO, depending on the scope of the change. A team-level analyst is responsible for communicating the epic vision and its objectives to the team and ensuring that the requirements support them.

7.8.3 Properties of Well-Crafted Product and Epic Vision Statements

The product vision statement should express the product's most inspiring purpose rather than its more mundane objectives.[8] In line with full-potential planning (see Chapter 9, "Long-Term Agile Planning," section 9.4), it should be bold and innovative (e.g., to be first in customer service or to dramatically increase market share within three to five years). Similarly, an epic vision statement expresses an inspiring reason for a change initiative rather than describing an incremental improvement.

A vision statement should be short so that it can be easily remembered and propagated throughout the organization and out into the market. John Kotter identifies the following properties of a well-crafted vision statement:[9]

- Communicable
- Desirable

---

8. Roman Pichler, "8 Tips for Creating a Compelling Product Vision," October 8, 2014, https://www.romanpichler.com/blog/tips-for-writing-compelling-product-vision

9. John Kotter, *8 Steps to Accelerate Change in Your Organization*, Kotter Inc., 2020, https://www.kotterinc.com/wp-content/uploads/2020/06/2020-8-Steps-to-Acceperate-Change-eBook-Kotter.pdf

- Creates a verbal picture

- Flexible

- Feasible

- Imaginable

- Simple

An *agile* vision statement articulates a view that leaves ample room for **emergence**, whereby new features are discovered by observing how customers use the product rather than predetermining what will be useful. To allow for emergence, don't specify features in the vision statement; focus, instead, on the raison d'être for the product or change. For example, Instagram's product vision statement is about "capturing and sharing the world's moments." Note how this statement describes the *value* of the product but does not specify whether those moments are captured as photos, video, or virtual reality. This lack of specificity is deliberate because it does not place unnecessary constraints on how the product will evolve. Had Instagram's vision statement specified photos, it would have limited the potential scope of the product in the minds of users, the business, and product developers.

The product vision statement should be designed for longevity. However, it should be revised if the company wishes to reorient the product in a fundamental way in response to changes in the market or public perception of the product. For example, Facebook changed its product vision statement in 2017 from "making the world more open and connected"[10] to the statement "to give people the power to build community and bring the world closer together."[11] As this example also illustrates, it's not enough to change the vision statement. The change has to percolate down to changes in the product and the culture of the development organization.

7.8.4 Vision versus Mission Statements

Some organizations have vision *and* mission statements. The product vision statement describes an envisioned future, while the mission statement focuses on what the company has to do *today and every day* to get there. In other words, the vision statement is *aspirational*, whereas the mission statement is *operational*. As former International Institute for Business Analysis (IIBA) acting CEO Alain Arseneault puts it, it's the difference between having a *vision* of a healthy environment and a *mission* to clean and sanitize every room frequently.

For example, Zappos's vision (an online store service) is the aspirational view that "One day, 30% of all retail transactions in the US will be online. People will buy from the company with the best service and the best selection. Zappos.com will be that online

10. Nick Statt, "Mark Zuckerberg Just Unveiled Facebook's New Mission Statement," *The Verge*, June 22, 2017, https://www.theverge.com/2017/6/22/15855202/facebook-ceo-mark-zuckerberg-new-mission-statement-groups

11. Facebook, "About," https://www.facebook.com/pg/facebook/about

store."[12] Its day-to-day mission is expressed in its tagline, "POWERED by SERVICE,"[13] and through one of its core values, "Deliver WOW through service."[14] The mission statements communicate the strong service orientation of the company in its daily operations.

- In practice, these nuances are not always observed. For example, Uber's stated *mission* is "to bring transportation—for everyone, everywhere"[15]—a statement that is more an aspirational *vision* of the future than an operational directive for the present (although that's quickly changing).

BLINK CASE STUDY PART 5

Product Vision Statement

Background
You've completed a root-cause analysis for the BLInK product identifying the problems the product should address.

The Ask
As a senior-level business analyst, you have been asked by senior management to facilitate a visioning workshop to craft the product vision statement for BLInK.

Preparation
You prepare the following deliverables and distribute them to participants:

- List of UDEs and the stakeholders affected by them (Case Study Part 3, Deliverable 2)
- A list of root causes and the UDEs they contribute to (Case Study Part 3, Deliverable 3)
- Problem statement (Case Study Part 4, Deliverable 1)

What Transpires
You open the meeting by explaining how to create a well-crafted product vision statement, provide examples, and review input artifacts. You ask stakeholders to envision a future where BLInK has been rolled out successfully. How will things change for the better?

One stakeholder notes that, by incentivizing healthy behaviors, BLInK reduces absenteeism (a problem experienced by employers), improves health and decreases

---

12. Zappos.com, "About Zappos," https://www.zappos.com/marty/c/about-zappos

13. Zappos.com, "What We Live By: Our Core Values," https://www.zappos.com/about/what-we-live-by

14. "How to Write Mission and Vision Statements for B2B: And Why It Matters," Blender, https://www.themarketingblender.com/vision-mission-statements. See especially "Vision Statement Examples (A to Z)" and "Mission Statement Examples (A to Z)."

15. Uber Newsroom, "Our Mission," Uber Technologies Inc., 2018, https://www.uber.com/en-CA/newsroom/company-info

healthcare costs (addressing concerns of employees), and at the same time reduces payouts and increases profitability (concerns of BL Inc.). You challenge stakeholders to focus on the most vital concern.

Deliverable

During the meeting, you develop the following deliverable.

BLInK product vision statement: "To incentivize customers to make healthy choices and reward them when they do."

Case Study Retrospective

Product owners and business analysts at various levels will communicate the product vision statement throughout the development organization, to business stakeholders, and to customers, where it will guide product development and marketing efforts.

7.9 Stakeholder Analysis and Engagement

A **stakeholder** is any person or group that has an impact on an initiative or is impacted by it. Stakeholder **analysis** is a process used to identify stakeholders and analyze their needs, attitudes, influence, and the initiative's impact on them. Stakeholder **engagement** includes developing a strategy and timelines for collaborating and communicating with stakeholders and the ongoing activities to carry them out.

The business analyst has primary ownership of the stakeholder analysis and engagement process. These duties include developing, conducting, and managing the process; determining the participants and timelines, and establishing procedures for maintaining stakeholder analysis information.[16] Perform a comprehensive stakeholder analysis to ensure all stakeholders are considered and as a first step in determining the requirements for a product or initiative.

Stakeholder analysis and engagement includes the following activities:[17]

1. Identify and analyze stakeholders.

2. Plan stakeholder collaboration.

3. Plan stakeholder communication.

4. Facilitate and conduct ongoing engagement and analysis.

---

16. Alain Arseneault, in an editorial note to the author, July 2020.

17. International Institute of Business Analysis, "Plan Stakeholder Engagement," in *BABOK v3: A Guide to the Business Analysis Body of Knowledge*, 3rd ed. (Toronto, Canada: IIBA, 2015), 31–35. The steps in the book are derived from activities in *BABOK v3*, section 3.2.

7.9.1 Identify and Analyze Stakeholders

The first step is to identify the stakeholders. At this point in visioning, you've begun to do that in the problem statement. If you're an outside consultant like me, you might start with one stakeholder—the person who first contacted you, such as the sponsor or the champion for the product. That person then leads you to the next interviewees, who lead you to others.

7.9.1.1 Stakeholder Checklist

If you rely solely on this process, however, you can miss essential stakeholders. For example, early in my BA career, I was so focused on users of the product, I neglected to interview the steering committee that would be reviewing my recommendations. As a result, I was unprepared for the questions they asked me during my final presentation about the project's financial justification. Since the legacy software was no longer supported, I had assumed the financial justification was so obvious it didn't need to be addressed. Had I thought to interview the committee members beforehand, I wouldn't have been blindsided during my presentation. Fortunately, I was saved by the product's champion, who explained why there was no choice but to move ahead. Ever since, though, I've made a habit of using a checklist to make sure I *consider* every kind of kind of stakeholder—even though I don't expect to include them all. See Appendix A.5 for a checklist of stakeholder types and their contribution to the analysis. Other sources of information for identifying stakeholders include company websites, internal corporate groups, organization charts, process maps, and documentation from previous initiatives.[18]

7.9.1.2 Stakeholders List, Roles, and Responsibilities Table

Refine the stakeholder analysis by investigating the involvement of each stakeholder in the initiative and with the product. Table 7.3 is an example of **stakeholder lists, roles, and responsibilities**, an artifact used to document the results of stakeholder analysis.

Use techniques like *user role modeling workshops* and *user personas* to refine the stakeholder analysis further.

 To read about personas, see Chapter 10, section 10.12. To learn about user role modeling, see Chapter 10, section 10.18.

7.9.2 Plan Stakeholder Collaboration

Next, determine how each stakeholder or stakeholder type will collaborate with the development team.

Gain agreement on the following points:

- Forum for the collaboration: the method of engagement, such as requirements workshops, focus groups, wikis, scheduled meetings (real and virtual), Web conference, conference calls

- Location

---

18. Arseneault, personal communication, 2020.

Table 7.3 *Stakeholders List, Roles, and Responsibilities*

Stakeholder Group (User Group, Business Function, Title, etc.)	Contact	# in Role	Location	Impact on Stakeholder		Involvement of Stakeholder with Initiative		Attitude toward Change (e.g., Supports, Resists)	Expectations of Stakeholder	Expectations of Team toward Stakeholder
				Level	Primary Impact	Level	Primary Function with Respect to Initiative (e.g., Investor, Shareholder, Vendor, Proxy User)			
Director of new product development	R. Hamdi	1	Dallas	H	Improved analytics for data-informed decision-making	H	Sponsor			
Chief financial officer	H. Groot	3	Los Angeles	L		H	Steering committee member (approve budget, monitor progress)			
Marketer	J. Gupta	10	New York, Dallas	H	Ability to launch campaigns across multiple platforms	M	Business SME, user			

e.g.

- The expected type of involvement (e.g., as an active collaborator, tester)
- Time expectations (e.g., full-time team member, one hour per week)
- Responsiveness (e.g., same-day response to urgent queries)

> **TIP**
>
> Don't wait until the initiative is underway to address expectations; do it as soon as possible. I learned this lesson the hard way from a former client, who continually interrupted me throughout a project for progress reports for upcoming meetings. All too often, the work was pointless, since the meetings didn't occur. Worse—it was time-consuming work I hadn't planned for when setting timelines. Prevent conflict by managing expectations up front.

7.9.3 Plan Stakeholder Communication

Use the preceding analysis to create a stakeholder communication plan that specifies the following:

- Informational requirements—information needed by the stakeholder from the team (e.g., status updates) and by the team from the stakeholder
- Forum or method of communication (e.g., summary reports, status update meetings, email, wiki, website)
- Timing, frequency of communication
- Level of granularity required
- Audience level (expert, general)
- Preferred communication style (formal, casual)

 For guidelines on choosing the best means of communication, see Chapter 5, section 5.15.5.

7.9.3.1 Stakeholder Impact/Influence Matrix

Use a *stakeholder impact and influence matrix* to determine the communication strategy. Table 7.4 illustrates the four quadrants in the matrix.

Table 7.4 *Stakeholder Impact and Influence Matrix[19]*

<table>
<tr><td rowspan="5" style="writing-mode:vertical">Influence of Stakeholder</td><td>High</td><td>Ensure stakeholder concerns are addressed. Keep stakeholders abreast of issues and overall progress.</td><td>Consult stakeholders regularly about features, business objectives and targets. Keep stakeholder abreast of issues and overall progress.</td></tr>
<tr><td>Low</td><td>Communication can be summary (e.g., public announcements).</td><td>Consult stakeholders on targeted areas where new features or changes will impact them.</td></tr>
<tr><td></td><td>Low</td><td>High</td></tr>
</table>

Impact on Stakeholder

Place each stakeholder or role in the appropriate quadrant based on the nature of their involvement, then plan a communication strategy for each stakeholder using the guidelines in the corresponding section, as shown in Table 7.4.

7.9.4 Facilitate and Conduct Ongoing Engagement and Analysis

Execute the plan. Facilitate collaboration between stakeholders and the team and communicate with stakeholders as described in the plan. Stakeholder analysis is iterative and ongoing. As you learn more about stakeholders and discover new ones, update information and plans as required.

BLINK CASE STUDY PART 6

Identify Stakeholders

Background
Now that you've identified the main stakeholders, the next step is to analyze their relationships to the initiative and devise a strategy for communicating with them.

The Ask
You have been asked to produce the following deliverable for the BLInK venture:

- List of stakeholders, roles, and responsibilities (Draft)

Tips
Review the cause–effect tree you created in Case Study Part 3 (Deliverable 1, Figure 7.8). Look for references to stakeholders and the UDEs that affect them. Focus on UDEs that the product is intended to address. These will suggest stakeholder interests.

---

19. IIBA, *BABOK v3*, 345.

Then review the stakeholder checklist in Appendix A.5 to see if there are any stakeholders you missed. Document what you learn in a draft of the Stakeholders List, Roles, and Responsibilities table (Table 7.3). Do not be concerned about completing the table or including all the columns at this time.

What Transpires

You review the results of the root-cause analysis and the stakeholder checklist with attendees to derive a list of stakeholders. These include the policyholder and employer. You learn that the policyholder of group insurance plans usually is the employer. You gain consensus from SMEs to treat them as one role type, with *Policyholder* as the primary name.

You investigate other impacted stakeholders, documenting your results in a Stakeholders List, Roles, and Responsibilities table. Next, you review your list with attendees—using the Stakeholder Influence and Impact Matrix (Table 7.4) to categorize stakeholders. Finally, you discuss each quadrant and confirm the high-level communications strategy to be used for the stakeholders within.

Deliverables

Deliverable 1: BLInK Stakeholders List, Roles, and Responsibilities

You produced Table 7.5 as a result of this preliminary analysis.

Table 7.5 *BLInK Stakeholders List, Roles, and Responsibilities*

Name(s), Main Contact	Stakeholder Role (Type)	Impact on Stakeholder	Involvement of Stakeholder with Initiative (Responsibilities, Authority Level)
M. Grande	Policyholder (employer): Pays for the policy	Lower premiums; decreased absenteeism	Consulted
R. Hinkle	Primary subscriber (employee): Main person named under the policy	Reduced healthcare costs; improved health	Consulted
H. Groot, F. Hill	Subscriber (also called enrollee, member): Any person covered under the policy	Reduced healthcare costs; improved health	Consulted
R. Norman, Z. Branitsky	Broker: Sells policies, represents buyer	Higher revenue from new business	Consulted

Name(s), Main Contact	Stakeholder Role (Type)	Impact on Stakeholder	Involvement of Stakeholder with Initiative (Responsibilities, Authority Level)
X. Krieg	Agent: Sells insurance policies, represents one or more insurance companies	Higher revenue from new business	Consulted
A. G. Houseman	Underwriter: Adjudicates insurance applications, determines coverage and premiums	Better targeted pricing and coverages	Consulted
M. Lautrec	Legal and compliance auditors		Approvals
Y. Hendles	Actuary: Analyzes financial risk	More accurate forecasting and risk assessment due to a richer, more personalized dataset	Consulted, informed
Z. Nguyen	Vendor	Responsible for devices and data services	Consulted, informed
R. Yang	Sponsor	Improved profitability, loss ratio; decreased average payout per subscriber	Formal approvals
V. Chretien	Product owner		Responsible for prioritizing product backlog

Case Study Retrospective

As a result of the stakeholder analysis, you are now able to construct a communication plan that includes the voices of all key customers and stakeholders.

7.10 Analyzing Goals and Objectives

The next step is to translate the product or epic vision statement into goals and objectives. Consider the perspectives of the business and the end customer: What does the company gain by developing the product or carrying out the change initiative? What are the benefits to the purchaser and the user?

Since we're about to focus on goals and objectives, let's review what we know about them from Chapter 3, "Fundamentals of Agile Analysis and Planning." A **business goal** is something to which the enterprise aspires to, such as

Establish an enterprise-wide assortment planning capability by the end of the year.

A **business objective** is an outcome below the enterprise level (e.g., Provide the ability to promote services and benefits by the end of the third quarter). The objective can be a **learning objective,** for example, to test the hypothesis that, if users are warned before they share an article or video they haven't viewed, they can be incentivized to view the content and form their own opinion before sharing it. Companies should maintain a learning mindset throughout their lifespans.

Goals and objectives should be measurable and time-bound (e.g., the business goal to increase sales *by 10 percent* by the *end of the year*).

 See Chapter 3, sections 3.4.2.2 and 3.4.2.3, for more on goals and objectives.

7.10.1 Use Circumstance-Based Market Segmentation as a Basis for Goals and Objectives

Use circumstance-based market segmentation to identify the **jobs** that customers hire the product to do—the high-level **usages** of the product (e.g., launch a marketing campaign). If a new product is being developed, represent these usages as customer goals and objectives. For example, one job or customer goal for a gaming app is to babysit toddlers so that their parents can have some personal time.

Once the product is established, continue using circumstance-based market segmentation to reveal opportunities for new usages of the product and to improve the way they are currently implemented. For example, after the gaming app in the preceding scenario is released, further market analysis reveals a new "job" customers want to carry out through the product: parents want to protect their children from viewing harmful content while interacting online. This insight is the basis for an epic—a change initiative whose objective is to provide protection across the platform by a given date.

 See Chapter 8, section 8.4, for more on circumstance-based market segmentation.

As noted earlier, goals and objectives must be measurable. Define the metrics that will be used to measure progress. In line with full-potential planning guidelines (discussed Chapter 9, section 9.4), specify metrics that represent *real-world outcomes*, such as

increased market share and compound annual growth rate (CAGR), rather than process metrics such as total lines of written code or velocity. A success metric for the gaming app in the previous example might be a 50 percent reduction in the average time between episodes of whining.

7.10.2 Representing Goals and Objectives within the Story Paradigm

The following are guidelines for representing goals and objectives within the story approach. The benefit of doing so is that you can use a single paradigm to trace the entire evolution of a goal to detailed requirements items. However, if your organization already has an effective way to manage goals and objectives, there is no need to change it.

7.10.2.1 Represent User Capabilities as Epics and Features

If the goal or objective is to implement a high-level usage (a *job* a user can do with the product), create an epic or feature to deliver it, depending on the estimate for the item. An epic may require multiple teams over multiple quarters. A feature must be implementable within a single quarter; it may include multiple teams.

7.10.2.2 Represent Other Goals and Objectives as Themes

Represent any other goal or objective as a theme. A **theme** is a mechanism for clustering epics, features, and stories by any topic across organizational lines, product areas, and products. A single epic, feature, or story may belong to multiple themes.

Consider, for example, the objective of highlighting a new offering in all communications with customers. This objective is not in itself something users do with the product, but it affects many of the capabilities they use, such as generating customer invoices and renewals. Consequently, you treat the objective as a theme and the work to change the capabilities as epics, features, and stories.

BLINK CASE STUDY PART 7
Craft Goals and Objectives

Background
Now that you've identified BLInK stakeholders, you invite them to an exploratory meeting to discuss the goals and objectives for developing the product.

The Ask
You've been asked to facilitate an investigation into two perspectives on goals and objectives for the product—the viewpoint of customers and the viewpoint BL Inc.
Following are the deliverables of this step:

- Deliverable 1: Customer goals and objectives (with metrics)
- Deliverable 2: Business goals and objectives (with metrics)
- Deliverable 3: List of metrics

What Transpires

You convene a meeting of sponsors, program managers, product managers, customer relationship managers, and marketing executives. You begin by summarizing the undesirable effects (UDEs) uncovered by the prior root-cause analysis. You note the issues of *poor health outcomes* and *rising healthcare costs* and suggest a subscriber objective to *improve health outcomes* and *lower costs*.

You invite those with a knowledge of the market to consider these and other customer objectives. You ask business stakeholders to describe business-side objectives. Once you've identified the goals and objectives for the product, you facilitate a discussion about the metrics that will be used as success indicators.

Deliverables

Deliverable 1: Customer Goals and Objectives (with Metrics)

- Reduce insurance premium contribution (policyholder). Metric: Percentage premium change (M7)
- Empower customers to control premium (subscriber). Metric: Satisfaction survey (M14)
- Reduced healthcare costs (subscriber). Metric: Subscriber annual payout (M15)
- Improved health (subscriber). Metrics: Number of claims per person (M4); Average annual amount claimed per subscriber (M5)

Deliverable 2: Business Goals and Objectives

- Reduce churn. Metric: Voluntary churn rate (M10)
- Increase market share. Metric: Market share (M11)
- Reduce loss ratio. Metric: Loss ratio (M3)
- Reduce the number of claims. Metric: Claims per policy (M12)
- Increase the predictive capability for risk. Metric: Loss ratio (M3)
- Attract customers. Metric: Growth rate (M13)

Deliverable 3: List of Metrics

- M3: Loss ratio
- M4: Number of claims per person
- M5: Average annual amount claimed per subscriber
- M7: Percentage premium change
- M10: Voluntary churn rate
- M11: Market share
- M12: Claims per policy
- M13: Growth rate
- M14: Satisfaction survey
- M15: Subscriber annual payout

Case Study Retrospective

The goals and objectives for the product will be used to guide the prioritization of features. The metrics will be used to gauge the success of the venture.

7.11 Analyze Leap of Faith Hypotheses

The next step is to consider how the vision and value proposition for the product will be validated. In traditional product development, this can be achieved by using historical data to make projections. If the product is novel, you can't use this approach, because there is no history of products in its class. Instead, you validate the business case using an experimental, evidence-based approach—running low-cost MVP experiments to test the hypotheses that underlie the vision.

7.11.1 What Is a Lean Startup?

Leap of faith hypotheses and MVPs are critical tools in the lean startup approach devised by Eric Reis. Before you say, "That's not for my organization; we're not a startup," let me clarify the term. A **lean startup** is "an organization designed to create new products and services under conditions of extreme uncertainty."[20] The critical factor is not the age of the business—it's the level of uncertainty regarding the product. In fact, many of the lean startup organizations I work with are not startups in the popular sense of the term. They're in mainstream business sectors such as insurance, telecom, finance, and government. But they're involved in lean startup ventures because the products they're developing are novel. The following are some real examples of lean startups:

- A telecom developing a self-service site for customers to customize their own plans, where there is extreme uncertainty regarding whether customers will want to use the site.

- An insurance company developing products that use data from IoT devices to personalize rates and benefits (as in our BLInK case study). In this instance, there is extreme uncertainty regarding whether customers will be willing to set aside privacy concerns.

- A government agency considering offering a loan risk-assessment service. This is a lean startup for the organization because it has traditionally provided this service for free as part of the application process for its core products. Though there was data to indicate that customers would want the service, there was extreme uncertainty about whether they would pay for it.

7.11.2 What Are Leap of Faith Hypotheses?

The MVP process begins with identifying **leap of faith hypotheses**—critical assumptions about the product that must be true for the venture to be successful. In Chapter 9, "Long-Term Agile Planning," and Chapter 12, "MVPs and Story Maps," you'll learn to use these hypotheses to drive MVP planning, with the objective of testing critical assumptions as quickly and inexpensively as possible.

---

20. Eric Ries, *The Lean Startup* (New York: Random House, 2011), 34.

7.11.2.1 Hypotheses for Change Initiatives

Hypothesis testing is not exclusive to the start of new product development. Continue running experiments to test hypotheses throughout the product's life. For example, Twitter is currently experimenting with a feature for shared items: the user will see one post with a similar point of view, one with a slightly different point of view, and one that is completely different.[21] The learning objective is to test the hypothesis that if users see these different takes, they'll want to dig deeper into the article or watch the full video. The benefit of running controlled experiments first is that there may be other assumptions and effects the company hasn't anticipated. Experimentation brings those effects to light so that they can be addressed before the changes are widely released.

7.11.3 Value Hypotheses

The lean startup approach identifies two broad categories of leap of faith hypotheses: value and growth hypotheses. **Value hypotheses** are critical, unproven assumptions about the product's value.

Following are examples of value hypotheses:

- Customers will want to use this product once they see it; they just don't know it yet, because it's the first of its class.

- Customers will be willing to put up with a lower-quality product than is currently available in exchange for a low price or high convenience.

- Customers will engage heavily with the product.

7.11.4 Growth Hypotheses

You can have a product that delivers value to customers yet still does not achieve a fast-enough **growth rate** to succeed. Fast growth is especially important for new entrants because they need to capture the market quickly before incumbents have a chance to respond. The growth assumptions that must be true for the venture to succeed are referred to, in lean startup, as **leap of faith growth hypotheses.**

Following are examples of growth hypotheses:

- Each user will refer at least x users (viral company model).

- The right proportion of buyers to sellers will be achieved (marketplace company model)

---

21. From an interview with Jack Dorsey. Michael Barbaro, "Jack Dorsey on Twitter's Mistakes," *The Daily* [podcast], August 7, 2020, https://podcasts.apple.com/ca/podcast/the-daily/id1200361736?i=1000487397342

7.11.5 Specifying Metrics

Often, teams consider metrics only after the feature has been implemented. That's too late to inform development decisions because, by then, critical decisions have already been made. It's the responsibility of the PO with the support of the business analyst to persuade stakeholders and developers to specify metrics early in the process so that the data can be used to inform investment. The metrics should be refined over time (e.g., as MVPs are planned and tested).

Determine the metrics that will be used to validate hypotheses and measure progress toward goals and objectives. Choose metrics that measure outcomes over ones that measure process steps. For example, measure quality, cost, and hospital readmission rates rather than time to complete medical procedures.

Lean startup provides guidance for defining **actionable metrics** that isolate the impact of change, as opposed to **vanity metrics**—measurements that seem to suggest improvement but are, in fact, inconclusive. Let's examine those guidelines.

7.11.5.1 Vanity Metrics

Suppose a newspaper business decides to launch a project to boost advertising revenues. To assess the program's success, it measures the publication's monthly advertising revenue before, during, and after the campaign. Sure enough, revenue rises. They conclude that the program was a success. Were they right?

Not necessarily. There could have been other reasons for the rise, such as the closing of a competing publication. The metric they chose made people *feel good* about the project but didn't prove anything. In lean startup, such metrics are referred to as **vanity metrics**.

7.11.5.2 Actionable Metrics and Split Testing

In contrast to vanity metrics, **actionable metrics** provide the business with measurements it can act on to make decisions. The problem with the previous metric example was that it didn't mask out the background noise of everything else happening in the environment. To do that, you need to add a control group subject to the same context as the test group, except that it doesn't experience the intervention you're measuring. This approach is referred to as **split testing** or **A/B testing**.

Returning to our newspaper example, we could expose the new program to a small group (cohort) of customers while leaving another group unexposed—and measure the *difference* between ad revenue gains for each group. If there is a net improvement in revenue for the test group but not for the control group, the increase must be due to the program, since environmental changes would have affected both groups equally.

You can use this approach with more than two groups as well. For example, you can measure the conversion rates for two groups—each exposed to a different change in a user interface—and compare those measurements against a control group that doesn't experience any change.

Metrics to test value hypotheses include the following:

- Number of daily active users or number of monthly active users (a measure of stickiness)

- Conversion rate from free trial to subscription

- Frequency of opens

- Average session length

- Total time in the application (daily, weekly, monthly)

- Engagement retention (percentage of initial users who return to the application within a given period)

To block out environmental factors, perform split testing and take care to measure the *differences* in values between test groups and control groups.

Metrics for growth include the following:

- Referral rate: Average number of referrals made by each user.

- Net promoters NP = % Promoters − % Detractors,[22] where
    - % Promoters = percentage of customers who respond with a 9 or 10 to the question, "On a scale of 0 to 10, how likely is it that you would recommend the product to a friend or colleague?"
    - % Detractors = percentage of customers who respond with a 0 to 6.

Research shows a correlation[23] between high NP scores and growth. High NP also means a low cost to acquire a customer (CAC)—since existing customers do much of the marketing at no cost.

- Growth rate of monthly active users (MAU), where MAU = # unique users who have visited a site or used an application at least once during the month

- Bounce Rate: % of customers who visit and leave immediately

7.11.5.3 Actionable Metrics for Enhancements

The preceding guidelines about metrics also apply once the product is established and undergoing continual improvement. Specify actionable metrics to measure the value of proposed features or revisions. As the feature is developed, test out solutions with users and collect actionable metrics. Use the resulting data to evaluate the effectiveness of alternative solutions for the feature. During beta testing, collect and analyze actionable metrics to validate the feature and determine whether or not to include and support it.

---

22. Frederick F. Reichheld, "The One Number You Need to Grow," *Harvard Business Review*, December 2003, https://hbr.org/2003/12/the-one-number-you-need-to-grow.

23. See Reichheld, "The One Number You Need."

7.11.6 Hypotheses in Discovery-Driven Planning

Financial planners face the same challenge as do product developers when dealing with an innovative product: how to create a plan when there is extreme uncertainty surrounding the product and the market for it. **Discovery-driven financial planning** extends the MVP approach into the realm of financial planning. The financial planner works backward from the outcomes deemed necessary for a venture to be successful in order to determine the financial hypotheses or assumptions that must be made. Then the planner devises a strategy to test those assumptions in the market as quickly as possible. The steps in this process are as follows:[24]

- Identify the required future outcomes (targets).
- Identify the assumptions that must be made for those targets to be met by preparing a reverse income statement.
- Create a plan to test those assumptions in order of importance.
- Implement the plan: Test the assumptions.
- Learn: Make strategic investment decisions based on test results.

Examples of financial assumptions discovered and tested through this process include the following:

- Cost of production
- Cost to acquire a customer
- Price that customers will be willing to pay for the product
- Packaging and shipping costs
- Product lifespan

For a more detailed description of discovery-driven planning, see Chapter 18, section 18.10.2, and Appendix B.

7.11.7 Assumption Checklist

Provide more information about hypotheses or assumptions in an assumptions checklist. Table 7.6 illustrates an example.

---

24. Based on the process described by Christensen and Raynor, with some changes made to the number of steps and their activities. Clayton M. Christensen and Michael E. Raynor, *The Innovator's Solution* (Boston: Harvard Business Press, 2003), 227–229.

Table 7.6 *Assumptions Checklist*

ID	Assumption	Measurement (Target)
1	Return on sales (ROS) will be high	ROS (≥16%)
2	Fewer customers will decide to leave	Voluntary churn (10% reduction)

7.11.8 Using a Milestone Planning Chart to Plan Assumption Testing

Use a *milestone planning chart* to plan the timing of assumption testing. Table 7.7 illustrates some examples of milestones.

For a complete example, see Appendix B, section B.8.

Table 7.7 *Milestone Planning Chart*

Milestone Event Completed	Assumptions to Be Tested
Prototypes created	(A1) A price advantage of 10 percent will be enough to lure customers away from incumbent suppliers.
Pilot production	(A2) Production costs can be kept below $100/unit.

BLINK CASE STUDY PART 8
Analyze Assumptions

Background

Having analyzed goals and objectives, you prepare to investigate the assumptions (leap of faith hypotheses) that must be true for those objectives to be attained. You invite stakeholders to a brainstorming session to identify those hypotheses and the metrics used to test them.

The Ask

Following are the deliverables of the analysis:

- Deliverable 1: Assumptions checklist (indicating metrics)
- Deliverable 2: List of metrics

What Transpires

You review the goals and objectives of the product (see deliverables of Case Study Part 7). You explain that you will be asking stakeholders to consider what assumptions must be valid for these goals and objectives to be achieved.

For the objective *increase predictive capability*, you discover the value hypothesis, "Customers will want to continue with the program after a six-month trial." For the objective to improve health, you discover the value hypothesis, "Behaviors will improve as a result of the program." Attendees continue discussing objectives and their related assumptions until no new assumptions come up.

Next, you facilitate a review of the assumptions. You ask stakeholders to sequence them in order of criticality—with the intention that those listed first will be tested earliest. After that, you discuss the metrics that will be used to test the assumptions that have been identified.

Deliverables

Deliverable 1: Assumptions Checklist

Value Hypotheses

- (A1) Customers will want to continue after a six-month trial. (M1)
- (A2) Behaviors will improve. (M2)
- (A3) Accuracy of risk, payout predictions will improve. (M3)
- (A4) Health will improve due to participation. (M4, M5)
- (A5) Customers will like the product when they see it. (M6, M16)
- (A6) Premium will go down. (M7)
- (A7) Reluctance to share data can be overcome when a benefit is shown immediately. (M8)

Growth Hypotheses

- (A8) Subscribers will refer others. (M9)
- (A9) Acceptance will grow once use becomes widespread—at which time large immediate discounts will no longer be required. (M8, M13, M16)
- (A10) BLInK will lead to improved customer retention. (M10)

Deliverable 2: List of Metrics

Metrics

- M1: BLInK renewal rate
- M2: Lifestyle score
- M3: Loss ratio
- M4: Number of claims per person
- M5: Average claimed amount
- M6: Response rate
- M7: Percentage premium change
- M8: Penetration rate
- M9: Referral rate
- M10: Voluntary churn rate
- M13: Growth rate
- M16: Post-trial conversion rate

7.12 Chapter Summary

Here are the key points covered in this chapter:

- Root-cause analysis is a set of techniques for tracing effects back to their initial causes. The approach includes the Five Whys technique and cause–effect graphing.

- The product vision statement is a short description of a future when the product is used by its target market.

- Perform stakeholder analysis as early as possible and continue it incrementally throughout the development lifecycle.

- Represent business goals and objectives as themes.

- Represent customer objectives as epics and features.

- Leap of faith hypotheses are assumptions that must be true for the product to be viable. Identify them at the start of a venture so you can plan to validate them in the market as soon as possible.

7.13 What's Next?

In Chapter 8, we'll look at activities associated with *seeding* the backlog—the determination and specification of the features and other work items associated with the product.

Chapter 8

Seeding the Backlog—
Discovering and Grading
Features

Previous chapters were concerned with developing a vision for a product or change initiative. This chapter explains how to identify and analyze the initial set of features to support that vision and plant the first seeds in the product backlog. Figure 8.1 highlights the activities, events, and artifacts included in this chapter.

The chapter begins with the discovery of the product's high-level use cases using circumstance-based market segmentation. For example, the high-level use cases for a social network include "Stay in touch with my friends" and "Get my news." Each use case is represented in the backlog as an epic or feature, depending on its size. (An epic may span multiple quarters; a feature may not.) The chapter contains guidelines for representing these items in the product backlog using the Role-Feature-Reason (Connextra) template.

The chapter explains how to assess the value and cost of backlog items and how to use these measures to determine the item's priority sequence in the backlog. The chapter describes how to use Kano analysis to grade customer value, determine the cost of delay (total value of the item), and use those results to determine the item's weighted shortest job first (WSJF)—an indication of its priority sequence.

The chapter concludes with guidance on specifying and managing nonfunctional requirements (NFRs) within an agile analysis framework.

8.1 Objectives

This chapter will help you to

- Use the results of circumstance-based market segmentation to seed the backlog with features.

- Use Kano analysis to grade the customer value of proposed features.

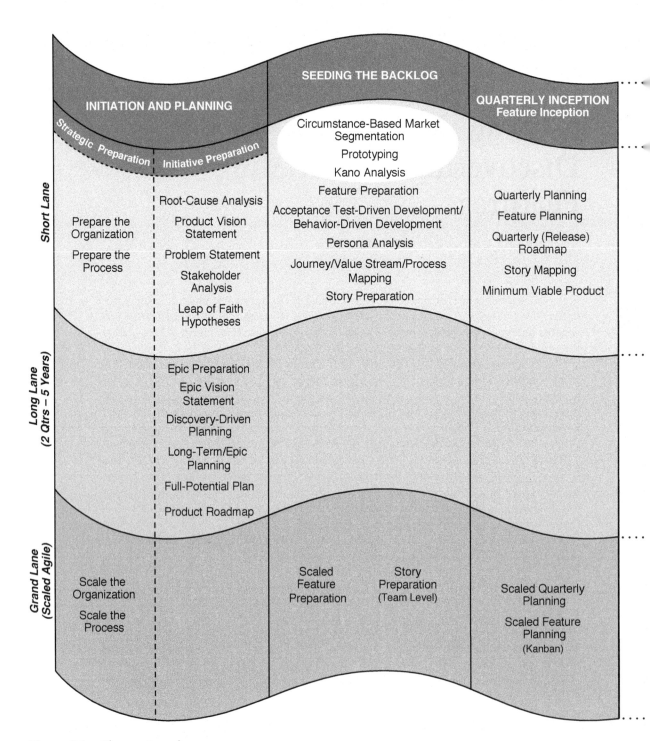

Figure 8.1   *Chapter 8 on the map*

**ITERATION
INCEPTION**

DAILY ACTIVITIES

**ITERATION
CLOSEOUT**

**QUARTERLY
CLOSEOUT**
Epic, Feature Closeout

Daily Standup

Requirements Analysis
& Documentation

Code, Build, Test, Deliver Acceptance
Test-Driven Development/
Behavior-Driven Development

Minimum Viable Product,
Split Testing

Epic, Feature Preparation

Story Preparation

Iteration
Planning

Iteration Review

Iteration Retrospective

Prepare for
General Availability

Quarterly
Retrospective

Epic, Feature
Retrospective

Pivot or
Persevere

Scaled
Iteration
Planning

Iteration
Planning
(Team Level)

Product
Owner
Council
Meetings

DevOps

User Task
Force
Meetings

Scaled
Feature
Preparation
(Kanban)

Integration
Meetings

Story
Preparation
(Team Level)

Scaled Iteration
Review

Scaled Iteration
Retrospective

Iteration Retrospective
(Team Level)

DevOps

Scaled
Quarterly/Feature
Retrospective

- Use WSJF and cost of delay to inform sequencing decisions.
- Know how to manage NFRs within an agile process.

8.2 This Chapter on the Map

As indicated in Figure 8.1, we'll be examining the following items in the Seeding the Backlog zone: circumstance-based market segmentation, prototyping, and Kano analysis.

8.3 Overview: Seeding the Backlog

If, like most analysts, you are not directly involved in higher-level visioning and planning, your active responsibilities begin with activities in the Seeding the Backlog zone: the determination of the initial set of features, their value to the customer, and their sequencing in the backlog.

 The first items in backlog need to be prepared further so they will be ready for planning and implementation. We cover feature preparation in Chapter 10, "Quarterly and Feature Preparation," and story preparation in Chapter 13, "Story Preparation."

8.3.1 Definitions: Epics and Stories

As we're about to discuss large work items, let's review some relevant definitions from Chapter 3, "Fundamentals of Agile Analysis and Planning."

- An **epic** is a large work item. It may require multiple teams over multiple quarters and span multiple product areas. It should represent a high-level capability of the product affecting a user or group of users. For example, an epic may deliver a top-level menu item (e.g., Orders), a functional area of the product, the expansion of an existing capability, a business process, a project, or internal improvements.

- A **feature** is a work item that can be completed within one quarter by one or more teams. A feature should represent a characteristic of a product that a user, customer, or group of them cares about.

8.3.2 How Many Features Should You Seed Up Front?

As a rule of thumb, aim to limit the initial set of features to fifteen to twenty in order to avoid overplanning and analysis-paralysis. This is also the number of items that can be comfortably analyzed and prioritized using Kano analysis. We'll learn about Kano analysis in section 8.11.

The higher the uncertainty and the more novel the product, the less you should ana-lyze and determine up front about its features. If the product is novel, allow the feature's requirements to emerge and evolve through customer usage. Because the conception of the product may change significantly over time, focus the initial analysis on near-term features and defer the analysis for items further back in the backlog. On the other hand, if the product is well-established, and uncertainty is low, the requirements are less likely to need significant revision (or be abandoned) during the development lifecycle. In that case, there can be a net benefit in performing a more extensive upfront analysis, since it provides more information on which to base cost estimates and implementation decisions. This reduces the need for rework otherwise needed when early implementations are based on an incomplete understanding of requirements.

8.3.3 Whom to Invite to Backlog Seeding

As a rule, don't invite investors to backlog seeding workshops, as their focus tends to be on targets and the plans for reaching them—not on product requirements. Do consider inviting the following attendees:

- Stakeholders who will benefit directly or indirectly from the product's features
- Those with prioritization and approval authorities
- Those who will be doing the development work (for input on estimation and alternatives)

Roles to consider include:

- Product owner (PO) council members
- Senior product manager
- Product-level PO, area POs, team-level POs
- Architects
- Development managers
- Developers, QA, analysts, and other team members

The elicitation may take the form of group meetings, individual interviews, or informal discussions.

8.4 Circumstance-Based Market Segmentation for Feature Discovery

How do you forecast which features of a novel product will be valued by customers when there are no existing products to compare it to? Christensen[1] advises the use of *circumstance-based market segmentation* for this purpose—a technique first introduced in Chapter 7, "Visioning." The process begins with field research to determine the **jobs** people hire the product for—the *objectives* (desired outcomes or benefits) that a customer has in mind when deciding to purchase the product. Each job represents a high-level capability or usage of the product. Once you identify the jobs, you work with customers and stakeholders to explore the specific features required to perform them well.

For example, consider the CEO case study mentioned earlier in the book—a product that manages a company's engagements with customers across social media platforms. Field research indicates that customer relations specialists would use the product to keep abreast of what customers are saying about the product, so that the company can respond before negative mentions go viral. Investigating further to discover what features users would value for that purpose, you identify the following items:

- Provide the capability to aggregate all hashtag mentions of the product across social media platforms.

- Use AI capabilities to automatically label favorable and unfavorable mentions so that they can be triaged.

- Alert support staff when unfavorable mentions risk going viral.

8.5 Other Ways to Discover Initial Features

You also discover features as you use the agile analysis techniques and tools discussed in upcoming chapters. For example, through process modeling, you identify the user tasks in an end-to-end business process to apply for a new service offering. One task is for an end customer to submit an application for the service. Another is for an approver to approve it. Those tasks represent use cases (usages) of the system. Since an entire use case typically requires more effort than the maximum allowed for a user story, it is typically classed as a feature. Recall that a feature may require multiple teams and up to a quarter to implement; a user story must be implementable by a single team and cannot exceed eight days (or less, depending on the practice).

---

1. Clayton M. Christensen and Michael E. Raynor, *The Innovator's Solution: Creating and Sustaining Successful Growth* (Boston: Harvard Business Press, 2013), 77–79.

For more on analysis and planning techniques that generate features, see Chapter 10, section 10.14, "Journey Mapping," section 10.15, "Value Stream Mapping," section 10.16, "Business Process Modeling," and section 10.17, "Use-Case Modeling."

8.6 Feature Independence

Define features so that they are as independent of each other as possible. Doing so simplifies requirements management significantly because it allows features to be prioritized and reprioritized without concern for the impact on other items in the backlog.

The CEO features we just looked at are good examples of independent features because they can be implemented in any sequence. Suppose the first feature, the ability to aggregate hashtag mentions across platforms, is not yet implemented, and only one platform is supported. Nevertheless, the second feature, to automatically tag favorable and unfavorable mentions, could still be implemented, delivering value to the user. Even if neither of these features is implemented, the last feature to alert support staff can still be implemented and deliver value: it would just be based on manual labeling and a single platform.

8.7 Using the Role-Feature-Reason Template to Represent Epics and Features

The Connextra (aka Role-Feature-Reason) template, introduced in Chapter 2, "Agile Analysis and Planning: The Value Proposition," may be used for any item size: epic, feature, or story.

> Connextra Template
>
> As a [user role], I want to [function] so that [business value].

It's not crucial, however, to write up items in this format. Use what works best. Whether or not you use the template, make sure that there is a common understanding of its elements: who the users are, what they want to do, and why they want to do it (the value).

On a large initiative, you often begin with short, informal wording during planning sessions and translate these into the Connextra template when you transfer the items to an electronic product backlog. It's better to use a template at that point. Otherwise, the original meaning of the items can get lost once everyone has dispersed—especially if there is a long lag until implementation. A template makes sure that crucial information is preserved when the item is captured.

8.8 Specifying Emergent Features

If the product is highly emergent, it is best to word features so they focus on the desired outcome rather than on the capability itself in order to leave as much flexibility as possible regarding the solution. For example, rather than specifying the feature, "As a customer, I want an alert when my order arrives at each new stage in the workflow," specify, "As a customer, I *want to have confidence* that my order is being processed." The latter allows for greater experimentation. An alert may be what customers *think* they want, but it may turn out that a map that tracks the order in real time is what they *really* want, once they've had the opportunity to experiment with options. (What they get, in the end, will depend on what can be achieved in the time budgeted for the feature.)

8.9 Physical Representation of Features

A small, colocated team should use physical cards as its backlog. A large organization, with multiple non-colocated teams, should first bring everyone together for planning sessions using physical cards. However, as discussed earlier, they should transfer the cards to an electronic product backlog in order to provide members at all locations with real-time access to the same requirements registry.

 We look further at product backlogs for multiple teams in Chapter 17, "Scaling Agility."

BLINK CASE STUDY PART 9

Seed the Product Backlog

Background
You invite user representatives and business stakeholders who have a close familiarity with the market to brainstorm features for BLInK.

The Ask
The deliverables planned for the event are as follows:

- Deliverable 1: Sequenced list of initial features

Preparation
You prepare handouts for attendees indicating the goals and objectives for BLInK. (See Chapter 7, Case Study 7, Deliverables 1 and 2.)

What Transpires
You review the vision statement, goals, and objectives for BLInK, distributed in the handout and posted on the product portrait. You use the goals and objectives to drive the discussion, asking attendees what features the product would need to include for the business and customers to achieve their objectives. Once these

features are identified, you facilitate a discussion about sequencing, with those items implemented first placed at the top of the list.

Deliverables

Deliverable 1: Sequenced List of Features

- Play competitive health games with other members to win extra Health Rewards and benefits.
- Redeem rewards for healthful items at my local supermarket (partner with chain).
- Earn Health Rewards for healthy behaviors, referrals, and renewals so that they can be redeemed for healthy products.
- Redeem rewards for healthy benefits (gym, yoga sessions, athletic gear, dental/eye examinations, vaccinations, flu shots).
- Accurately estimates risk and costs using behavioral data.
- Receive a discount on my insurance premium for making healthy choices.
- Receive an immediate incentive benefit for consenting to BLInK.
- Members can cancel BLInK after a trial period while retaining earned benefits.
- Receive benefits for continuing after a trial period.
- Get reports and recommendations regarding my progress toward my health goals.

8.10 Feature Attributes

As you seed the backlog with features, you need to consider the PBI attributes of the items, based on those you decided to track. In Chapter 6, "Preparing the Process," we looked at common product backlog item (PBI) attributes. These include

- Description
- Acceptance criteria
- Estimate
- Order
- Value (The value delivered by the item; may be expressed in "so that" clause.)
- WSJF prioritization
- Cost of delay

See Chapter 6, section 6.5.4.3, for more on the attributes of a backlog item.

To establish the feature's order (sequence number) in the backlog, you need to know its relative priority—or WSJF. To determine its WSJF, you need to know the effort to implement it and its value to the customer and user. Let's look at an approach for ascertaining that value using Kano analysis.

8.11 Determining Customer and User Value with Kano Analysis

Kano analysis[2] is an approach developed by Noriaki Kano that uses specially designed surveys to research proposed features to assess their value to customers and users and determine how much effort (if any) to spend developing them. The following is an overview of the Kano process:[3]

- Select the target features.

- Select the customers.

- Create the questionnaire.

- Create prototypes.

- Test the questionnaire internally.

- Conduct the survey.

- Grade the features.

Let's examine these steps.

8.11.1 Select the Target Features

First, select the features to be included in the survey. The recommended number of features for a Kano survey is fifteen to twenty.[4] Include only those features that the customer will experience and benefit from. Exclude other work items (e.g., a technical work item to refactor the code).

---

2. Hasan Akpolat, *Six Sigma in Transactional and Service Environments* (Burlington, VT: Gower, 2004), 22–23. Also see Peter S. Pande, Robert P. Neuman, and Roland R. Cavanagh, *The Six Sigma Way: How GE, Motorola, and Other Top Companies Are Honing Their Performance* (New York: McGraw-Hill, 2000), 193, 194.

3. This process is based on steps described by Daniel Zacarias. See "The Complete Guide to the Kano Model: Prioritizing Customer Satisfaction and Delight," Folding Burritos, https://foldingburritos.com/kano-model

4. Cary-Anne Olsen-Landis, "Kano Model—Ways to Use It and NOT Use It," *IBM Design*, March 23, 2017, https://medium.com/design-ibm/kano-model-ways-to-use-it-and-not-use-it-1d205a9cf808

8.11.2 Select the Customers

The next step is to select customers for the survey. Sample sizes may vary (e.g., fifty to three hundred).[5] The larger the sample size, the lower the margin of error. Use the following guidelines when selecting customers:

- *Group customers according to target market segments.* For example, a social networking app may have two very distinct markets, commercial and personal, with very different views about features: commercial customers use it primarily for customer outreach; personal users use it for communicating with friends. Don't include both kinds of customers in the same survey.

- *Separate customers with different levels of exposure to the product.* Separate customers already using the product (or a similar one offered by a competitor) from customers who are not. Their expectations can differ significantly. Something seen as an *excitement feature* by someone new to the product might be considered a *basic feature* by a customer who uses it regularly.

8.11.3 Create the Questions

Next, create the questions that will appear on the questionnaire. For each feature, create a functional and dysfunctional question.[6] Each question should refer to one feature only. The functional question is, "How would you feel if you had feature X?" The dysfunctional question is, "How would you feel if you did not have feature X?"

Ask respondents to select one of the following responses to each of the questions:

- I like it this way.

- I expect it this way.

- I am neutral.

- I can live with it this way.

- I don't like it this way.

8.11.3.1 Self-Stated Importance Question

A third question is often added to the original couplet, called the **self-stated importance** question. For each feature, this question asks: "How important is it, or would it be, that the product support feature X?" Respondents are asked to grade their answers on a scale from 1 to 9 (1 = not at all; 9 = extremely important).

---

5. Measuring U, "Kano Modeling: The Method," https://measuringu.com/approach/kano-modeling

6. Ori Zmora, "Feature Grading: An Introduction to the Kano Model," *UserFocus*, September 1, 2014, https://www.userfocus.co.uk/articles/kano-model.html

8.11.4 Create Prototypes

As the first rule of writing states, "Show, don't tell." In Kano analysis, the best option is to provide a prototype for each feature in the questionnaire. Prototypes are especially valuable when assessing new-market innovations because it's difficult for customers to imagine how they would use a product until they begin working with it. Then next-best options are a wireframe or sketch presented above the question set, followed by text only. If you use text, specify what the customer can *do* with the feature rather than a property of the product. For example, it's better to ask, "How would you feel if you were able to chat immediately with our support staff?" than to ask, "How would you feel about our proposed Insta-Chat button?

8.11.5 Test the Questionnaire Internally

First, test the questionnaire internally by asking team members and others to complete it and provide additional comments. Rephrase any question that people find confusing or that leads to conflicting results (e.g., a preponderance of cases where respondents like *having* and *not having* a feature).

8.11.6 Conduct the Survey

Distribute the survey online, by email, in a test lab, or in person. Collect responses.

8.11.7 Grade the Features

For each questionnaire, assign a grade for each feature based on the answers given by the respondent to the two Kano questions (functional and dysfunctional). To determine the grade, use the Pouliot[7] table, a revision of the original Kano evaluation table.[8] The Pouliot table is shown in Table 8.1.

The grades stand for

- Q: Questionable (results are unclear)

- B: Basic (respondent expects the feature)

- E: Excitement (a "wow" feature)

---

7. David Walden (Ed.), "Kano's Methods for Understanding Customer-Defined Quality," *Center for Quality of Management Journal* 2, no. 4 (1993): 28–36 (special issue on Theoretical Issues of Kano's Methods), http://walden-family.com/public/cqm-journal/2-4-Whole-Issue.pdf

8. Fred Pouliot revised the Kano table by changing two of the grades along its diagonal. Pouliot's version indicates that when a respondent has the same response, whether positive or negative, to both having and not having a feature, the evaluation is *Questionable* (unreliable) vs. *Indifferent* (the customer doesn't care). The one exception along the diagonal is when a respondent is neutral to both having and not having a feature—in which case the grade is Indifferent.

- I: Indifferent (respondent doesn't care)
- R: Reverse (respondent doesn't want the feature)

Table 8.1 *Revised Kano Evaluation Table[9]*

		Dysfunctional				
		1: I like it	2: I expect it	3: Neutral	4: I can live with it	5: I don't like it
Functional	1: I like it	Q	E	E	E	P
	2: I expect it	R	Q	I	I	B
	3: Neutral	R	I	I	I	B
	4: I can live with it	R	I	I	Q	B
	5: I don't like it	R	R	R	R	Q

Next, assign a final grade to each feature by selecting the grade with the highest number of occurrences across the questionnaires. Reevaluate any feature with a lot of Qs by crafting a clearer set of questions and including them in a follow-up survey. If two or more grades are tied for highest frequency, the following rule applies: *Basic* wins out over *Performance*, which wins out over *Excitement*, which wins out over *Indifferent*.[10] Use Table 8.2 to work this out for each feature. The spreadsheet lays out the grades from left to right in the order in which they override each other. (If there is a tie, the leftmost grade wins.)

Table 8.2 includes two examples. Feature 1 received 5 *Basic* grades and 5 *Performance* grades: the assigned grade is the leftmost grade—Basic. Feature 2 received 7 *Excitement* grades; that's more than any other grade, so it is assigned an *Excitement* evaluation.

Table 8.2 *Kano Grading Spreadsheet*

Feature	Basic	Performance	Excitement	Indifferent	Reverse	Questionable	Assigned Grade	Self-Stated Importance Question (1–9)
Feature 1	5	5	2	1	1	1	Basic	
Feature 2	3	2	7	2	1	0	Excitement	
...								
...								

To grade the self-stated importance questions for a feature, simply calculate the average score for the feature across all questionnaires.

---

9. Walden, "Kano's Methods," 34.
10. Zacarias, "The Complete Guide to the Kano Model," 11.

Once you've assigned a Kano grade to each feature, create a sequenced list based on their assigned grades according to the following order: Basic, Performance, Excitement, Indifferent, Reverse, Questionable. If two features are assigned the same grade, sequence the one with the highest self-importance grade first. This sorted list indicates the relative customer and user value of the features in the backlog. (See section 8.12.1 for other factors that contribute to value.)

8.11.8 Interpreting the Kano Grades

The Kano grades assigned to a feature provide insights into customer preferences, as described in the following sections.

8.11.8.1 Basic

Basic features are also known as *expected features, requirements without voice,* and *dissatisfiers.* The **Basic** grade represents a must-have—a feature so basic that customers don't even ask for it because they take it for granted. For example, a basic feature when reserving a flight is that there be a restroom onboard. Customers don't choose a flight on the basis of this feature but would reject one that didn't have it.

Bring features in this grade up to customers' expectations. Improvements to a feature in this category *beyond* that level should not be prioritized, since they are unlikely to affect a customer's purchasing decisions.

8.11.8.2 Performance

Performance features are also known as *variable requirements, one-dimensional features, spoken needs, requirements with voice,* and *satisfiers.* After basic features have been brought to an acceptable level, the business should prioritize initiatives to improve performance features. **Performance features** represent wants—features customers typically ask for. They're also referred to as variable requirements because of the correlation between performance and customer evaluation: the higher the performance, the higher the customer's evaluation of the product. Examples of performance features are competitive pricing (the more competitive the price, the higher the evaluation) and speed.

8.11.8.3 Excitement

Excitement features are also known as *attractive features, delighters, subconscious requirements, latent requirements,* and *wow features.* They embody the spirit of *omotenashi*—a Japanese hospitality principle based on anticipating another's needs. Malcolm Gladwell describes a penultimate case of *omotenashi* involving the early sales of Toyota's Lexus LS.[11] In response to flaws discovered in only two or three of the eight thousand

---

11. Malcolm Gladwell, "Revisionist History Presents: Go and See" [podcast], Pushkin Industries, 2016, https://podcasts.apple.com/gb/podcast/revisionist-history-presents-go-and-see/id1119389968?i=1000467526588

cars it had initially sold, the company sent a letter to every customer, stating that someone would be picking up the car and leaving a loaner. The company not only fixed the cars free of charge (as would be expected), it cleaned them, returned them with a tank full of gas—and left a gift on the front seat. In another example of *omotenashi*, an airline company researched passengers' Christmas gift wishes before takeoff and delivered personalized gifts when the flight arrived. These are examples of excitement features—features that make customers go "Wow!" Customers don't think of asking for these features, but they are surprised and excited when they receive them.

While you should, in general, prioritize basic and performance features over excitement features, you should try to include *some* excitement features in an early release. This can be especially important when developing a new-market innovation, in order to test the value hypothesis that people will love the product once they see what they can do with it and to build an initial group of enthusiastic customers.

8.11.8.4 *Indifferent*

An indifferent feature is one the customer doesn't care about either way. As you might expect, these features should not be prioritized.

8.11.8.5 *Reverse*

Two other useful categories arise from the analysis process itself, though they are not considered formal Kano grades: Reverse and Questionable.

A *reverse* feature is one that customers *don't* want included in the product. This grade is given when respondents say they dislike having a feature and like not having it. Many Instagram users (such as this author) would include its curated newsfeed as a feature in this category.

8.11.8.6 *Questionable*

This category arises when the respondent gives conflicting responses—such as liking (or disliking) both the functional and dysfunctional questions about the feature. If a feature is assigned this grade, it may be a sign that the question needs to be rephrased.

8.11.9 Satisfaction versus Fulfillment Graph

Figure 8.2 plots customers' satisfaction level with the product as requirements are increasingly met—indicating a separate trajectory for each Kano category. For example, satisfaction levels for basic features tend to remain constant once an expected level is reached, while performance features see their satisfaction levels continue to rise as the feature is more fully implemented.

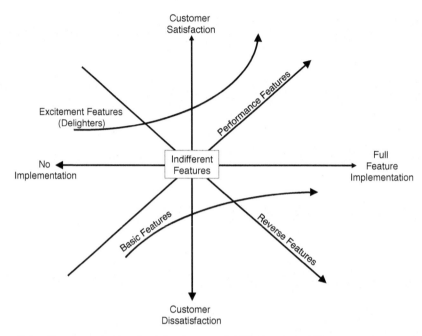

Figure 8.2 *Kano analysis—Satisfaction vs. fulfillment graph[12]*

8.11.10 The Natural Decay of Delight (and Its Opposite)

The categorization of a feature is not stagnant. A feature that was once an exciter typically becomes a basic feature once it becomes commonplace—a phenomenon that has occurred with many of the features introduced in the original iPhone. This change over time is referred to by Daniel Zacarias as "the natural decay of delight."[13]

There are reverse situations where customer expectations have been *lowered* due to low-end disruptions and other marketplace changes. As a result, what was once a basic feature becomes an exciter. Such is the case with free meals and free baggage on flights—features that were once expected but would now be exciters if offered today by an airline.

8.11.11 Continuous Analysis

Mike Timko has recommended using a continuous grading system in place of the discreet grades provided by the Kano evaluation chart. The approach is complex but aided by spreadsheets provided for this purpose. For a description of continuous analysis, see "Kano's Methods for Understanding Customer-Defined Quality."[14]

---

12. Based on a diagram by Chandra Munagavalasa. See "Excite and Delight Your Customers by Using the Kano Model," *Agile Connection*, April 28, 2014, https://www.agileconnection.com/article/excite-and-delight-your-customers-using-kano-model

13. Zacarias, "The Complete Guide to the Kano Model," 11.

14. Walden, "Kano's Methods," 17–25.

BLINK CASE STUDY PART 10

Kano Analysis

Background

With a list of proposed features for BLInK in hand, the next step is to conduct Kano analysis to grade their value.

The Ask

You've been asked to design a Kano survey to explore customer attitudes toward the following proposed BLInK features:

- Earn Health Rewards for healthy behaviors, referrals, and renewals so that they can be redeemed for healthy products.
- Redeem rewards for healthy benefits (gym, yoga sessions, athletic gear, dental/eye examinations, flu shots).
- Receive discount on my insurance premium for making healthy choices.
- Members can cancel BLInK after trial period while retaining earned benefits.
- Receive benefits for continuing after trial period.
- Play competitive health games with other members to win extra Health Rewards and benefits.
- Redeem rewards for healthful items at my local supermarket.
- Get reports and recommendations regarding my progress toward my health goals (summaries, metrics, recommendations, etc.).
- Receive an immediate incentive benefit for consenting to BLInK.

You are to distribute this survey to a small group of 150 customers and summarize the results on a Kano grading spreadsheet. You will assign a Kano grade to each feature on the basis of these results. Finally, you'll create a sequenced list of features based on their grades according to the following sequence: Basic, Performance, Excitement, Indifferent, Reverse, Questionable. If two features are assigned the same grade, the one with the highest self-importance evaluation will be sequenced first.

Following is the deliverable of this step:

- Kano grading spreadsheet indicating features in order of suggested priority

What Transpires

You design a Kano questionnaire asking the three Kano questions about each of the features. Once the survey is conducted, you assign a Kano grade to each feature. You sequence the features on the basis of their Kano grades.

Deliverables

Deliverable: Kano Grading Spreadsheet

Table 8.3 shows the resulting Kano grading spreadsheet with a sequenced list of features for BLInK based on Kano grades.

Table 8.3 *BLInK Kano Grading Spreadsheet (Final)*

Feature	Basic	Performance	Excitement	Indifferent	Reverse	Questionable	Grade	Self-Stated Importance Question (1–9)
Earn Health Rewards for healthy behaviors, referrals and renewals so that they can be redeemed for healthy products	75	45	22	8	0	0	Basic	8
Redeem rewards for healthy benefits (gym, yoga sessions, athletic gear, dental/eye examinations, vaccinations, flu shots)	85	43	15	7	0	0	Basic	7
Receive discount on my insurance premium for making healthy choices	50	60	0	30	0	10	Performance	9
Members can cancel BLInK after trial period while retaining earned benefits	52	70	0	28	0	0	Performance	8
Receive benefits for continuing after trial period	40	89	20	1	0	0	Performance	6
Play competitive health games with other members to win extra Health Rewards and benefits	25	45	50	20	2	8	Excitement	3

Feature	Basic	Performance	Excitement	Indifferent	Reverse	Questionable	Grade	Self-Stated Importance Question (1–9)
Redeem rewards for healthful items at my local supermarket	39	20	70	20	1	0	Excitement	2
Get reports and recommendations regarding my progress toward my health goals (summaries, metrics, recommendations, etc.)	30	15	80	20	5	0	Excitement	1
Receive an immediate incentive benefit for consenting to BLInK	20	40	55	15	10	10	Excitement	9

Case Study Retrospective

As a result of Kano analysis, you now have a basis for determining customer value and prioritizing features. All other things being equal, basic features will be prioritized over performance features, which will be prioritized over excitement features. In line with lean startup guidance, you also suggest including some excitement features as early as possible.

8.12 Sequencing Epics and Features in the Backlog

One of the essential attributes of a feature is its order in the backlog. The backlog sequence determines the implementation sequence: items at the top of the backlog are implemented first; those at the bottom are last. The ordering of backlog items is a responsibility of the PO, carried out with the support of business analysts.

An item's position in the backlog reflects its relative priority. (Highest priority items are implemented first.) When features are initially considered, they should be assigned general priority levels—for example, High (must have), Medium (should have), and Low (nice to have). Once some preliminary analysis and estimation has been done, you can determine priority more accurately by considering the total value of the feature relative to its cost.

The first step is to determine the customer value of a feature. To do that, you can use the Kano method we have been following. To review, analyze the results of Kano surveys. List basic features first, then performance features, and a few excitement features. Sort features within a particular grade on the basis of self-stated importance question ratings.[15]

All other things being equal, you would use the resulting sequence to order the features in the backlog. But all other things are not equal. An item's position also depends on other factors, such as the cost to implement the feature and the opportunity cost if the item is delayed. Use the cost of delay/WSJF method to accommodate these factors, as described in the following sections.

8.12.1 Determining Cost of Delay

The full value of a feature is expressed in its **cost of delay**, according to the following formula:

Cost of Delay = User and Business Value + Time Criticality + Risk Reduction and Opportunity Enablement Value (RR&OE),

where

- **User value** represents the value of the item to the end user or customer. It may be determined through surveys (e.g., using the Kano method described in this chapter).

15. Walden, "Kano's Methods," 17–25.

- **Business value** represents the value to the organization paying to develop the feature.
- **Time criticality** is a measure of the decay of the feature's value over time.
- **RR&OE** account for the value of the feature in reducing risk or enabling an opportunity.

For planning purposes, use relative values for each of the terms in the preceding formula. Use a similar point-based approach as that used to estimate the size of a story. For example, determine a standard for a 1-point RR feature; then assign RR values to other features based on the standard, using the revised Fibonacci series: 0, 0.5, 1, 2, 3, 5, 8, 13, 20, 40, 80, 100.

The resulting cost of delay is a measure of the total value of the feature.

8.12.2 Determining WSJF

To prioritize a feature, you need to balance its total value (cost of delay) against the cost to implement the feature. This measure is referred to as **weighted shortest job first** (WSJF).

Calculate WSJF according to the formula:

$$\text{WSJF} = \text{Cost of Delay} \div \text{Job Duration}$$

Job duration is the estimate for implementing the feature, typically measured in story points. When estimating, ensure that everyone obeys XP's Planning Game rule that only those doing the work are allowed to provide an estimate. This means the developers—not the business—have the final say on how long something will take.

For more on estimating features, see Chapter 11, section 11.11.2.

Use WSJF values as the basis for sequencing items in the backlog, with the highest WSJF items at the top.

WSJF is a valuable method for determining the implementation sequence. Its main benefit is that it reminds you to consider the component factors that should play into prioritization decisions. However, take care not to place too much confidence in the calculations, as the method doesn't take every kind of scenario into account.

8.12.3 Prioritization Tips

The following are tips and guidelines for prioritizing features.

8.12.3.1 Use the Purpose Alignment Model

Don't forget to address the elephant in the room—*whether a feature should be developed at all* or the company should instead rely on a third-party service or partner.

In Chapter 5, "Preparing the Organization," we learned how to evaluate this question at the product level using the purpose alignment model. Use the alignment model at the *feature level* to inform the decision about whether or not to develop features in-house based on their degree of mission-criticality and market-differentiation.

 See Chapter 5, section 5.5, for more on the *purpose alignment model*.

8.12.3.2 Use Broad Estimates at the Start of an Initiative

At the start of new product development or a change initiative, as you seed the backlog, ask developers to provide ballpark effort estimates for the top features in the backlog (maximum fifteen to twenty). Because the estimates at this point are used only to inform prioritization decisions, not for forecasting, it's sufficient to use broad estimates, such as days (for anything that takes up to two weeks), weeks (for anything from two weeks to a year), and years. Another approach is to use T-shirt sizes, such as extra-small, small, medium, large, extra-large, double extra-large.

8.12.3.3 Prioritization and Estimation Go Hand in Hand

Most people would love to have high-end products but don't prioritize them because they cost too much. This principle is embedded within the WSJF approach that uses both value and cost to prioritize an item. The rule of thumb, therefore, is to prioritize and estimate at the same time with business and developers present. If the estimate is too high for a valued feature, stakeholders can negotiate on-the-spot changes that might lower the feature's cost and therefore raise its priority—or WSJF value.

The downside to doing both at precisely the same time, is that business stakeholders won't have much interest in developers' internal deliberations regarding estimation. To avoid this problem, have business stakeholders meet first to set broad initial priorities, then ask development to provide reasonable cost estimates. Business stakeholders then reprioritize the features, taking those estimates into account.

8.12.3.4 Prioritizing Features That Support High-Priority Strategic Goals

In the case of features that support strategic goals, it's often better to prioritize up front and delay estimation until closer to implementation. For example, in our CEO case study, a decision is made at the executive level to favor features that integrate the product with a third-party provider in order to strengthen the partnership between the two companies. You add an epic to integrate with the product and assign it a high-priority sequence. However, you determine what features will be included and the estimates for those features closer to implementation.

8.12.3.5 Prioritizing Market versus Technical Risk

There has been an evolution of thought about risk prioritization since my early days in iterative development using Rational Unified Process (RUP). In those days, we often implemented features that exposed technical risk first. Today, because development is often characterized by high market uncertainty, we tend to prioritize market risk—the argument being that if there's no market for the product, it doesn't matter whether the technology is viable. If there is high uncertainty about the market, prioritize features that expose market risk early (e.g., by implementing "juicy bits")[16] in early MVP versions. However, if there is minimal uncertainty about the market and high uncertainty about the proposed technology, prioritize features that expose technical risk.

8.12.3.6 Prioritize for the Right Mix of New Development and Technical Debt Payment

Not all work items before a team relate to new feature development and bug fixes. Some of it should be aimed at technical improvements such as technical debt payment—stabilizing the code so that it is easier and safer to maintain in the future. As a general rule, when prioritizing upcoming work, it's best to stick with a sustainable split of about 75 percent of available time spent on new features and bugs and 25 percent on technical improvements.

Sometimes, though, you'll need to shift the split temporarily in reaction to circumstances. For example, the business decides it needs to respond to market challenges with a big push to develop new features. The company is comfortable allowing technical debt to build up for a time to achieve this objective. Once technical debt reaches unacceptable levels, the organization changes the split to favor code stabilization. When the debt is cleared, the organization returns to a 75/25 split of new features versus technical improvements.

8.12.3.7 Don't Forget Operational Costs

When determining a feature's priority, it's not just the cost associated with development that you need to consider. You also have to consider the operational cost. For example, a feature to provide bonus reward points to preferred customers might be inexpensive to code and deploy but costly to carry out.

8.13 Writing Feature Acceptance Criteria

In agile analysis and acceptance test–driven development (ATDD) guidance, you specify feature acceptance criteria before implementation so they can serve not only as the basis for tests but also as specifications by example—scenarios that communicate requirements to developers and stakeholders.

Following is an example of high-level descriptions of feature acceptance criteria. This level of detail is appropriate for a feature on entry to quarterly planning.

---

16. Mike Cohen, *User Stories Applied: For Agile Software Development* (Boston: Addison-Wesley Professional, 2004), 101–103.

> **Feature**
> As an incident manager, I want to manage incidents from a single interface so that I can view and prioritize issues across all sources.
>
> **Acceptance Criteria**
>
> I can view and manage scheduling delays.
>
> I can view and manage nonemergency incidents.
>
> I can filter/sort/rank all incidents by defined attributes.

Acceptance criteria specification is part of a larger activity for which you are responsible—feature preparation. Features should be prepared before they are accepted into the development plan. If the organization is doing quarterly planning, this preparation must occur before the quarterly planning meeting for all features in the plan. If the organization is practicing flow-based planning, it takes place on an item-by-item basis before the feature is accepted into development.

 For more on specifying feature acceptance criteria, see Chapter 10, section 10.9.

For more on Triad meetings, see Chapter 13, section 13.6.3.

8.14 Analyzing Nonfunctional Requirements and Constraints

Not all requirements result in observable functionality. Some, such as security and performance requirements, relate to the quality of the product. As we saw in Chapter 3, these are referred to as nonfunctional requirements (NFRs). That chapter also introduced the concept of constraints—influencing factors "that cannot be changed," and that place "a limit or restriction on a possible solution or solution option."[17] Ensure that NFRs and constraints are identified as you prepare for development—and that plans are in place to test compliance. NFRs and constraints may be documented in a separate artifact, such as RUP's supplementary requirements or in a service level requirements (SLR) specification. They are included in the product portrait in the bottom right region of the template.

NFRs may be verified through compliance audits or by running system tests (e.g., system tests to verify performance NFRs). If an NFR applies to all stories, include it in the definition of done.

---

17. International Institute of Business Analysis (IIBA), *BABOK v3: A Guide to the Business Analysis Body of Knowledge*, 3rd ed. (Toronto, Canada: IIBA, 2015), 444.

8.14.1 Do NFRs Go in the Backlog?

If the NFR requires work, add it to the backlog; if it doesn't, don't add it. For example, a compliance NFR stating that an application must be written in a specific coding language requires a simple inspection: the code either does or does not comply. However, an NFR requiring that a system accommodate 1 million users when the current one supports only 100,000 *does* require development work. In the latter case, add a technical story for scaling the system to the product backlog to account for the effort to comply.

8.14.2 NFRs and Constraints Checklist

Use the checklist in Appendix A.6 to make sure you haven't forgotten any critical NFRs or constraints.

BLINK CASE STUDY PART 11

Completing the Product Portrait—
Prioritizing Features and Specifying NFRs

Background

With the BLInK Kano grading spreadsheet (Table 8.3) in hand, you now plan to review the results with stakeholders and developers. First, you'll meet with attendees to discuss the features that were surveyed. Then you'll be asking developers to provide rough estimates.

The features have already been assigned an initial sequence based on their Kano grades. You'll be advising attendees to adjust this sequence according to what they learn about the estimated cost. As well, you'll be encouraging attendees to consider moving some excitement features forward.

Finally, you will be reviewing the NFRs and constraints checklist to determine which, if any, apply to the BLInK initiative.

The Ask

Following are the deliverables for this activity:

- Deliverable 1: Sequenced list of features with rough estimates
- Deliverable 2: NFRs and constraints
- Deliverable 3: Updated product portrait

What Transpires

For the most part, attendees decide to stay with the initial Kano sequencing. The exception to this rule is the feature for an immediate incentive on consenting to BLInK: as this is an excitement feature, with a high self-stated importance and low cost, stakeholders are inclined to move it forward. You warn them that though this feature has a low development cost, its *operational* cost is high—since every BLInK customer receives a benefit. Nevertheless, business stakeholders prioritize the feature because the incentive is seen as key to overcoming resistance due to privacy concerns.

Stakeholders propose adding a feature excluded from the Kano analysis (which focused on customer-facing features) to support internal business objectives: the capability to accurately estimate risk and costs using personalized behavioral data. The feature is added to the backlog.

Deliverables

The following deliverables were produced.

Deliverable 1: Sequenced List of Features with Rough Estimates

- Receive an immediate incentive benefit for consenting to BLInK (days)
- Earn Health Rewards for healthy behaviors, referrals, and renewals, so that they can be redeemed for healthy products. (weeks)
- Redeem rewards for healthy benefits (gym, yoga sessions, athletic gear, dental/eye examinations, vaccinations, flu shots). (months)
- Accurately estimates risks and costs using behavioral data. (months)
- Receive a discount on my insurance premium for making healthy choices. (weeks)
- Members can cancel BLInK after the trial period while retaining earned benefits. (days)
- Receive benefits for continuing after the trial period. (days)
- Play competitive health games with other members to win extra Health Rewards and benefits. (weeks)
- Redeem rewards for healthful items at my local supermarket (partner with chain). (weeks)
- Get reports and recommendations regarding my progress toward my health goals (summaries, metrics, recommendations, etc.). (months)

Deliverable 2: NFRs and Constraints

- National Association of Insurance Commissioners (NAIC) Corporate Governance Annual Disclosure (CGAD) model
- Department of Labor (DOL) Fiduciary Rule ("The Rule")
- Complies with external design document X1

Deliverable 3: Updated Product Portrait

Figure 8.3 illustrates the product portrait at the end of the visioning workshops.

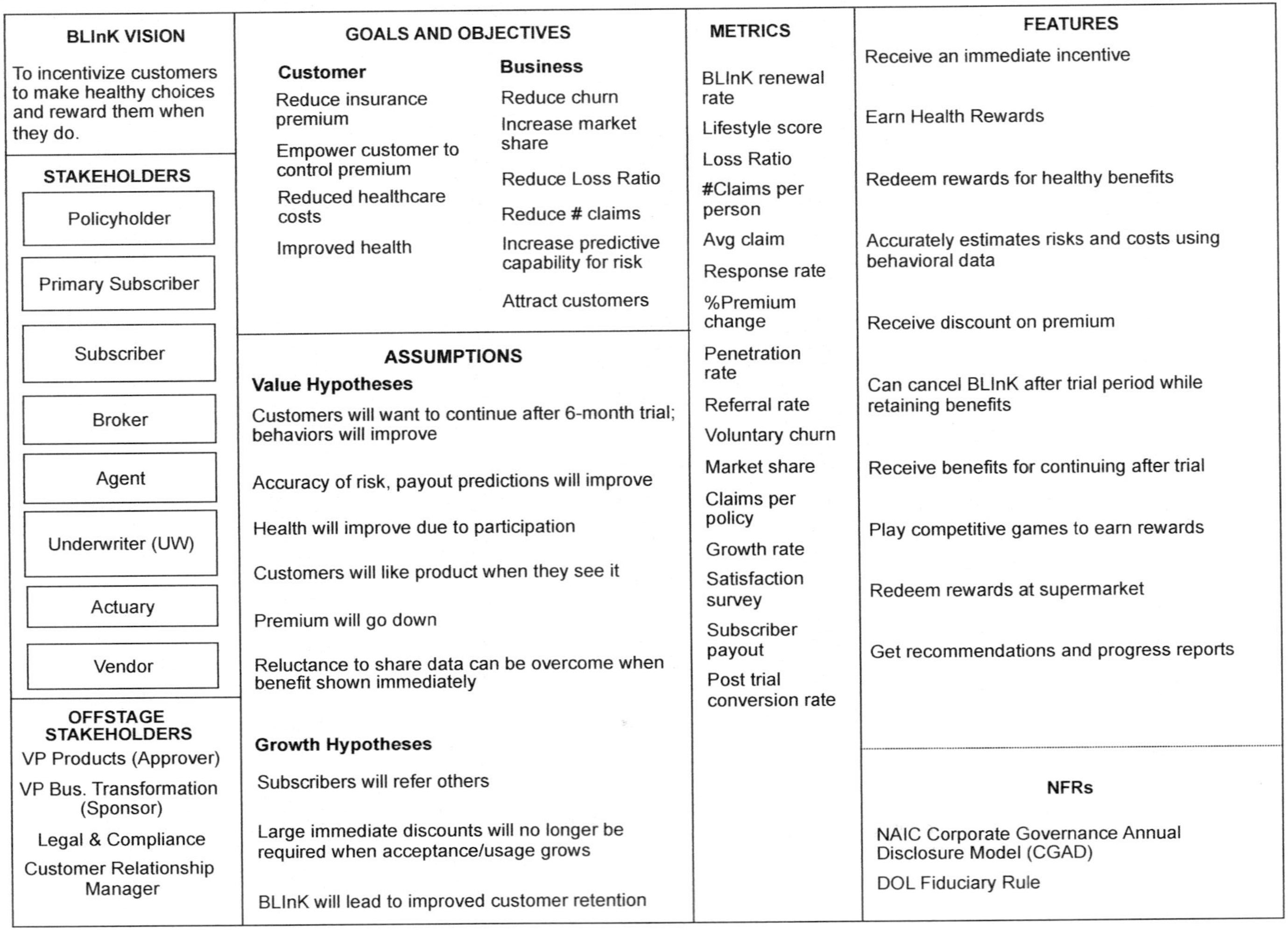

BLInK VISION

To incentivize customers to make healthy choices and reward them when they do.

STAKEHOLDERS

- Policyholder
- Primary Subscriber
- Subscriber
- Broker
- Agent
- Underwriter (UW)
- Actuary
- Vendor

OFFSTAGE STAKEHOLDERS

- VP Products (Approver)
- VP Bus. Transformation (Sponsor)
- Legal & Compliance
- Customer Relationship Manager

GOALS AND OBJECTIVES

Customer
- Reduce insurance premium
- Empower customer to control premium
- Reduced healthcare costs
- Improved health

Business
- Reduce churn
- Increase market share
- Reduce Loss Ratio
- Reduce # claims
- Increase predictive capability for risk
- Attract customers

ASSUMPTIONS

Value Hypotheses
- Customers will want to continue after 6-month trial; behaviors will improve
- Accuracy of risk, payout predictions will improve
- Health will improve due to participation
- Customers will like product when they see it
- Premium will go down
- Reluctance to share data can be overcome when benefit shown immediately

Growth Hypotheses
- Subscribers will refer others
- Large immediate discounts will no longer be required when acceptance/usage grows
- BLInK will lead to improved customer retention

METRICS

- BLInK renewal rate
- Lifestyle score
- Loss Ratio
- #Claims per person
- Avg claim
- Response rate
- %Premium change
- Penetration rate
- Referral rate
- Voluntary churn
- Market share
- Claims per policy
- Growth rate
- Satisfaction survey
- Subscriber payout
- Post trial conversion rate

FEATURES

- Receive an immediate incentive
- Earn Health Rewards
- Redeem rewards for healthy benefits
- Accurately estimates risks and costs using behavioral data
- Receive discount on premium
- Can cancel BLInK after trial period while retaining benefits
- Receive benefits for continuing after trial
- Play competitive games to earn rewards
- Redeem rewards at supermarket
- Get recommendations and progress reports

NFRs

- NAIC Corporate Governance Annual Disclosure Model (CGAD)
- DOL Fiduciary Rule

Figure 8.3 BLInK product portrait

Case Study Retrospective

As a result of the analysis, the team now has a prioritized, roughly estimated list of features with which to seed the product backlog.

8.15 Chapter Summary

Here are the key points covered in this chapter:

- Use Kano analysis to determine customer value and grade features according to the following categories: Basic, Performance, Excitement, and Indifferent.

- A basic feature is expected by the customer. The customer would not choose a product without the feature, but higher feature performance beyond an expected level does not equate to higher customer satisfaction.

- A performance feature is one for which customer satisfaction increases with performance.

- An excitement feature is one the customer does not expect but would be excited by if included in the product.

- An indifferent feature is one the customer does not care about.

- Cost of delay is a measure of the total value of the item, including user (customer) value, business value, time criticality, risk reduction, and opportunity enablement.

- WSJF is a measure of an item's relative priority sequence based on the total value of the item (cost of delay) and job duration.

8.16 What's Next?

This chapter and those that preceded it focused on the analysis of goals, objectives, hypotheses, and features. In Chapter 9, "Long-Term Agile Planning," we examine how to plan hypothesis testing and the delivery of proposed features, long-term goals, and objectives over the next three to five years.

Chapter 9

Long-Term Agile Planning

This chapter examines long-term planning for a product or epic for the next two or three quarters to five years. It begins with the full potential plan—an approach for planning transformative change over a three to five year period. Next, the chapter provides an overview of the agile approach to planning using minimum viable products (MVPs)—market experiments to test assumptions and determine the highest-value features to include in the product. Also included is an overview of the capabilities required for effective MVP implementation, such as continuous delivery capabilities. Figure 9.1 highlights the activities, events, and artifacts included in this chapter.

The chapter explores deployment strategies and options for the long-term plan. It includes guidelines for when to use narrow and deep versus wide and shallow approaches and when to defer deployment (e.g., because features aren't yet competitive in the marketplace).

Once an organization has considered these strategies and options, the next step is to create a detailed plan. The chapter explains how to use a product roadmap to guide the conversation and specify quarterly goals, objectives, assumptions, metrics, and features across the planning period.

9.1 Objectives

This chapter will help you

- Understand how to use a full-potential plan to deliver transformative change.

- Understand the MVP process.

- Understand the capabilities required for effective MVP implementation, including DevOps and continuous delivery.

- Understand wide and shallow versus narrow and deep deployment options and when to use them.

- Know when to defer feature deployment.

- Facilitate long-term planning workshops using a product roadmap.

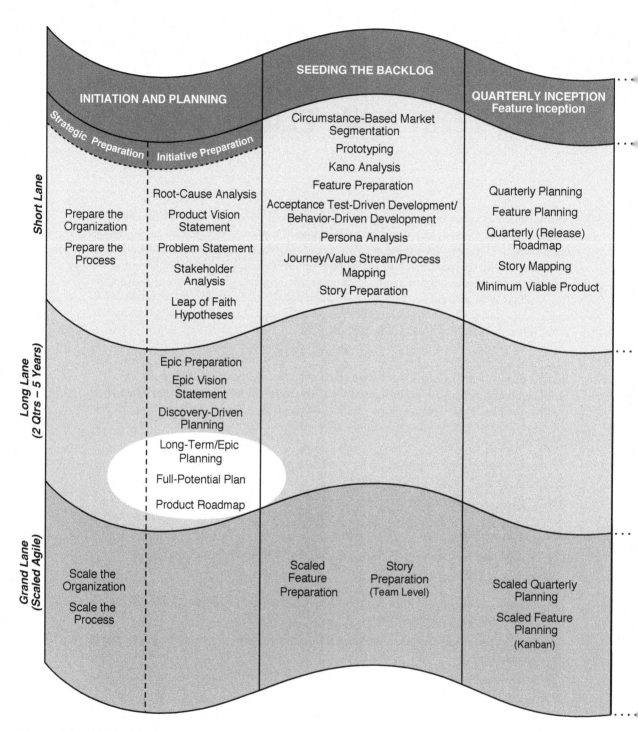

Figure 9.1   *Chapter 9 on the map*

ITERATION INCEPTION

DAILY ACTIVITIES

ITERATION CLOSEOUT

QUARTERLY CLOSEOUT
Epic, Feature Closeout

Daily Standup

Requirements Analysis
& Documentation

Code, Build, Test, Deliver Acceptance
Test-Driven Development/
Behavior-Driven Development

Iteration
Planning

Minimum Viable Product,
Split Testing

Epic, Feature Preparation

Story Preparation

Iteration Review

Iteration Retrospective

Prepare for
General Availability

Quarterly
Retrospective

Epic, Feature
Retrospective

Pivot or
Persevere

Scaled
Iteration
Planning

Iteration
Planning
(Team Level)

Product
Owner
Council
Meetings

DevOps

User Task
Force
Meetings

Scaled
Feature
Preparation
(Kanban)

Integration
Meetings

Story
Preparation
(Team Level)

Scaled Iteration
Review

Scaled Iteration
Retrospective

Iteration Retrospective
(Team Level)

DevOps

Scaled
Quarterly/Feature
Retrospective

9.2 This Chapter on the Map

As indicated in Figure 9.1, we'll be examining the following items in the Initiation and Planning zone: long-term planning, epic planning, full-potential plan, and the product roadmap.

9.3 Overview of Long-Term Planning, Epic Planning, and MVP

The planning horizon for long-term planning is two or three quarters to five years. Initiatives covered by long-term planning may span the product and value streams (e.g., an initiative to redesign the user experience across the product). The full-potential planning approach is used for this planning horizon. We examine this approach in the next section.

You manage the requirements items in the plan as epics, features, and stories, depending on their size. The items do not have to be contained within a high-level work item; they may simply sit as product backlog items at the product or product-area level. However, you can encompass them in an epic (e.g., a SAFe portfolio epic[1]—a high-cost initiative that can extend over multiple program increments [PIs; quarters] and value streams).

Agile long-term planning may sound like an oxymoron, since agile principles favor "responding to change over following a plan." That's true, but a company often needs to plan long term if it wishes to accomplish ambitious goals. For example, a business may see a significant market opportunity in its space and realize it won't be a dominant player unless it has a bold vision for where it wants to take the product and a plan for getting there. Furthermore, without a long-term vision and plan for a product, piecemeal improvements can lead to a fractured user experience.

What differentiates agile long-term planning from traditional planning is that it uses an adaptive approach rather than a predictive one. Unlike its waterfall counterpart, an agile plan is not predetermined up front. Instead, it is a best-guess forecast—with the expectation that it will be amended on the basis of changing circumstances.

Another way the agile plan differs from a waterfall plan is that it does not try to dictate upfront which features to prioritize. Instead, it relies on MVP experiments—low-cost versions of the product that customers interact with. The first quarters in the plan include MVPs to validate hypotheses about the product or change initiative before committing significant resources to it and to determine the minimum set of features, or **minimum marketable features** (**MMFs**), for the first market release. An MMF is the smallest version of a feature that would be viewed as valuable by customers if released to the market. The value of this process is that it allows the company to focus development resources on a small set of high-value features rather than attempting to "boil the ocean" by implementing a host of features customers rarely use.

You review the long-term plan with the teams and stakeholders at the beginning of every quarter to remind everyone about the broader plans for the product that should be considered during shorter-term quarterly planning. At this time, you may also revise

---

1. Scaled Agile, "Epics," August 20, 2020, https://www.scaledagileframework.com/epic

the long-term plan on the basis of learning, experience, and changes in the market. For example, stakeholders and developers may agree to push back timelines due to unexpected technical challenges, reprioritize goals and features as a result of an unexpected opportunity, or pivot to a new hypothesis if an existing one has been invalidated. When an epic's hypothesis is invalidated, create a new epic based on the new hypothesis.[2]

9.4 The Full-Potential Plan

Companies use **full-potential planning** to achieve bold goals within the time-frame we've been discussing—up to three to five years. For example, a private equity firm may use a full-potential plan to grow an acquired company from a half-million dollars annual revenue to 100 million dollars in five years.

Following this approach, the organization sets **bold goals** for the next three to five years and determines achievable **quick wins** for the first twelve to eighteen months. An example of a bold goal is, "Advance from the fourth to top quartile for total shareholder return (TSR) in five years." An example of a quick win is "Reduce costs by 12 percent in one year by switching to digital invoicing." The plan uses the MVP process described in the preceding section during the early stages to test hypotheses and determine the features that will be developed. As an analyst, you don't determine the plan but you do facilitate it and contribute to its success. We look further at your contribution in section 9.4.4.

First, let's summarize the approach. The phases of the plan are as follows:[3]

- Phase 1: Define bold targets.
- Phase 2: Create detailed plans.
- Phase 3: Deliver quick wins.

9.4.1 Phase 1: Define Bold Targets

Phase 1 typically takes place over four to six weeks. During this phase, the organization sets bold targets and identifies three to five high-priority initiatives as described below.

9.4.1.1 Set Bold Targets

The company sets bold targets immediately to communicate that transformational change is occurring. Following are examples of bold targets:

- Expand market share from 10 percent to 80 percent in five years.
- Increase revenues by 75 percent in three years.
- Become a Fortune 500 company in four years

---

2. Scaled Agile, "Epics."

3. Daniel Schroer, Till Boluarte, and Steffen Simon, "How Full-Potential Plans Help PE-Owned Companies Outperform in Medtech," Boston Consulting Group, 2019, https://www.bcg.com/en-ca/industries/health-care-payers-providers/how-full-potential-plans-help-pe-owned-companies-outperform-in-medtech

9.4.1.2 Select Three to Five High-Priority Initiatives

Next, the company performs a comprehensive analysis of the business, focusing on areas with the best and worst performance and opportunities for disruptive improvement. It decides on three to five Big Bets: a **Big Bet** is an initiative that will deliver a *high* or *fast impact*.

Examples of **high-impact Big Bets** include

- Mergers and acquisition (M&A).

- Expanding into new geographical locations.

- Product innovation.

Examples of **fast-impact Big Bets** include

- Procurement.

- Pricing innovations.

- Operational excellence initiatives.

- Product innovation.

9.4.2 Phase 2: Create a Detailed Plan

Phase 2 typically takes place over eight to ten weeks. During this phase, the company creates a detailed plan for achieving the Big Bets.

First, it performs a detailed examination of the three to five Big Bets selected in Phase 1. Then, it creates an implementation plan for each Big Bet. A typical Big Bet may take twelve to eighteen months to implement. In agile analysis, a product-innovation Big Bet is managed as an epic. During phase 2, you develop the detailed implementation plans for these Big-Bet epics.

During this phase, the company also establishes a body, such as a project management office (PMO), to champion and sustain the Big-Bet initiatives and foster talent. This body assesses the capabilities of managers in the key areas affected by the change to determine whether they align with the goals of the plan. The company responds quickly to any gaps by training or replacing resources. Entrepreneurship, not just functional competency, is sought after.

9.4.3 Phase 3: Deliver Quick Wins

Phase 3 typically occurs over twelve to eighteen months. In this phase, the company launches the three to five high-impact initiatives—the Big Bets. The company uses the early wins to build confidence in the full-potential plan and fund the longer-term investments. The plan uses the MVP approach to test hypotheses and learn what customers value. The company then uses that learning to build out the product.

Throughout the period covered by the plan, a governing body (e.g., the PMO) tracks progress toward the bold goal, such as a goal to increase revenues by 75 percent in three years. The metrics must measure real-world outcomes (e.g., quality and cost targets) versus process metrics (e.g., time to complete a task). A system is established to warn of deviations from the plan so that course corrections may be made quickly.

9.4.4 The Business Analyst's Contribution to a Successful Full-Potential Plan

In the video "The CEO Agenda: Full Potential Plan," Bain partners James Markey and others reviewed the top priorities for leaders looking to execute a full-potential plan successfully. As an analyst, you support the plan and are fundamental to its success. Let's look at some of the critical success factors identified by Bain and your contribution to them as an analyst:[4]

- *Knowing where to play:* Successful leaders know the right products, markets, and channels their companies should engage in.[5] As an analyst, you use tools such as circumstance-market segmentation to find the right markets and techniques such as Kano analysis and the MVP process to find the right products and features.

- *Knowing how to win:* Successful interventions mobilize the right capabilities, get the right resources to the right places, and get teams excited about the mission.[6] You contribute to the latter by communicating the product vision statement and high-level goals to the teams and helping them translate the vision and goals into product requirements.

- *Understanding customers and their needs better than competitors and delivering those needs better:*[7] As an analyst, you contribute by performing a rigorous stakeholder and requirements analysis. You use root-cause analysis to understand core needs. You use MVP experiments to learn what customers value by exposing them to low-cost versions of the product.

- *Continuously cultivating customer relationships:* Another critical factor is soliciting continual feedback and bringing that learning into the organization so that it can adapt, change, and improve to serve the customer better.[8] As an analyst, you contribute to this success factor by collecting and analyzing customer feedback

4. James Allen, Rob Markey, Manny Maceda, Julie Coffman, Patrick Litré, Laura Miles, Raj Pherwani, Michael Mankins, Henrik Poppe, and David Harding, "The CEO Agenda: Full Potential Plan," Bain and Co., September 30, 2016, https://www.bain.com/insights/the-ceo-agenda-full-potential-plan-video
5. Allen, et al., "The CEO Agenda."
6. Allen, et al., "The CEO Agenda."
7. Allen, et al., "The CEO Agenda."
8. Allen, et al., "The CEO Agenda."

regularly from MVP experiments and through ongoing data collection and analysis to inform future requirements and adjust priorities.

- *Managing internal risk:*[9] Of the 12 percent of CEOs who succeed in implementing the full-potential plan, the most correlated factor is the ability to anticipate and mitigate risk. You support this capability by facilitating a **premortem** to anticipate what can go wrong with the transformation and develop a plan for dealing with it. As part of the process, you walk through a checklist of risk factors to assess in the premortem. You update the list regularly on the basis of lessons learned from impediments that have arisen in past change initiatives. For example, the checklist may include the question, "Have we convinced the organization that the current state of affairs is unacceptable?" with boxes for high-, medium- and low-risk assessments.

- *Choreography:* Successful leaders know not only what steps to take but how to sequence them, taking into account interdependencies. As an analyst, you contribute by tracing dependencies among work items. You may also work with stakeholders to develop a workflow model for implementing the plan.

- *Mergers and acquisitions (M&A) strategy:* Companies that achieve top-quartile returns (top quarter against others in its category) have a strong M&A strategy.[10] They perform comprehensive financial and commercial due diligence. In addition, they have a well-considered integration plan, so they know how the companies will fit together. You contribute to the integration plan by analyzing the current processes of the acquiring and acquired companies, identifying gaps and modeling to-be processes.

9.5 Using MVPs to Validate the Assumptions behind the Plan

As we saw earlier, agile epic and long-term planning uses the MVP process during the early phases of product development to test hypotheses and determine the features that will be built. This plan is revisited quarterly in light of customer feedback and is revised as necessary. You also use the MVP process to market-test new features and solution options at low cost before developing them at higher cost for general availability. We've learned a bit about this process. In this section, we examine it further.

9.5.1 Overview

The MVP approach begins with identifying leap of **faith hypotheses**—critical assumptions that must be true for the product or initiative to be viable. In Chapter 7, "Visioning," you learned to discover these hypotheses. The next step is to plan the testing of the hypotheses using MVPs (low-cost versions used for learning) over several Build-Measure-Learn

---

9. Allen, et al., "The CEO Agenda."
10. Allen, et al., "The CEO Agenda."

cycles. You use the feedback from the process to validate the hypotheses and determine what features to concentrate on first, focusing on the minimum functionality required for each feature to deliver significant value. As we saw earlier, these are the MMFs.

The point of the approach is to avoid implementing a bucket list of features, many of which are rarely used. Instead, the strategy is to release a minimal product quickly, aimed at **earlyvangelists**.[11] Earlyvangelists are people who face a critical problem addressed by the product, are actively looking for a solution, and are willing to overlook initial flaws because they believe in the product's vision. As you implement the plan, you grow the market out from this initial group. You continue to use MVPs to test assumptions about new features, new markets, and design options.

9.5.2 What Is an MVP?

Eric Ries, the inventor of the MVP approach, defined the minimum viable product as follows: "The MVP is that version of the product that enables a full turn of the Build-Measure-Learn loop with a minimum amount of effort and the least amount of development time."[12] MVPs are "experiments to learn how to build a sustainable business."[13]

The core insight of the MVP approach is that if you want to know what customers want, it's better to put the product in front of them and let them use it than it is to whiteboard a solution. The customers may interact with the MVP in a controlled test lab or as beta testers in the market. They may even be able to purchase it.

Ries used the MVP process to develop IMVU, a gaming app.[14] In the first MVP for the game, the avatars were all stationary because the company didn't have the technology needed to create seamless movement. Feedback from customers indicated that avatar movement was highly valued. Rather than release a feature that was uncompetitive, the company decided to MVP-test a low-cost alternative—teleporting. Teleporting was a solution they could implement well, since the avatar merely had to disappear and reappear somewhere else without traversing the intermediate terrain. Customers not only tolerated this solution, they perceived it to be more advanced than that offered by its main competitor.

9.5.3 The MVP Process

The steps of an MVP process can be summarized as follows:

- Determine what needs to be learned.
- Determine what to measure.
- Determine what to build.
- Build.

11. Steven Blank, "Perfection by Subtraction—The Minimum Feature Set" [blog post], Word Press, March 4, 2010, https://steveblank.com/2010/03/04/perfection-by-subtraction-the-minimum-feature-set

12. Eric Ries, *The Lean Startup* (New York: Random House, 2011), 77.

13. Ries, *The Lean Startup*, 75.

14. Ries, 108.

- Measure.

- Learn.

- Pivot or persevere.

9.5.3.1 Determine What Needs to Be Learned

Determine the leap of faith hypotheses behind the product vision. Identify the value and growth hypotheses, as described in Chapter 7, section 7.11. An example of a leap of faith value hypothesis is the assumption that vendors will want to sell the product. However, an assumption that advertisers will pay for customer attention is not a leap of faith hypothesis because it is well supported by historical evidence.[15]

9.5.3.2 Determine What to Measure

Determine the metrics to collect to validate the leap of faith hypotheses. Define actionable metrics (vs. vanity metrics), as described in Chapter 7, section 7.11.5. For example, the percentage of customers who return to the product daily is an actionable metric for the value hypothesis "Customers will value the product."

9.5.3.3 Determine What to Build

Determine the MVP, specifying the features it will include in order to test the hypotheses.

9.5.3.4 Build

Build the MVP prototype as soon as possible. It should include low-cost versions of features required for learning. It may exclude many of the essential features needed in a marketable product.

9.5.3.5 Measure

Put the MVP in front of customers, as described earlier—in a test lab or the market. You might even attempt to sell the MVP version to determine if customers will value the product enough to pay for it. Collect actionable metrics during this period to validate hypotheses, test design options, and determine the features customers value most.

9.5.3.6 Learn

Assess the feedback and use it to make adjustments to the next version of the MVP or, if a leap of faith hypothesis is disproven, to discontinue under the current hypothesis.

9.5.3.7 Pivot or Persevere

Use the feedback from the MVPs to determine whether to pivot or persevere. If a leap of faith hypothesis has been invalidated, discontinue investment or pivot to a new hypothesis. If the leap of faith hypotheses have been proven, proceed to develop the MMFs.

---

15. Ries, 81.

9.6 Capabilities for Effective MVP Implementation

To enable the MVP process and quick feedback loops described in the preceding sections, an organization must have the necessary capabilities. For example, it must have a corporate culture that sees learning as a valid business benefit and the technology to enable frequent and dependable build-test-deploy cycles. The required organizational capabilities include

- Technical capabilities such as the necessary development and deployment environments.
- Development and delivery approach (e.g., DevOps, continuous integration [CI], and continuous delivery [CD])
- Deployment options and potential issues (e.g., knowing when to use a wide and shallow vs. narrow and deep implementation strategy, when to defer deployment, and when to deploy continuously).
- A culture that supports collaboration.

In the following sections, I introduce the first three items. In Chapter 18, "Achieving Enterprise Agility," we examine corporate culture.

For guidelines on developing a culture that supports MVP experimentation and agile product development, see Chapter 18, sections 18.6 through 18.9.

9.6.1 Technical Capabilities

To allow for a short turn of the Build-Measure-Learn cycle, as required by the MVP process, an organization must have the necessary environment types, and it must be able to deploy to them frequently, with confidence and with minimal manual intervention. Typically, the environments are virtual, set up on demand using automation with limited human interaction.

Figure 9.2 is an example of the environment types a change may pass through on its way to being deployed in production.

Figure 9.2 *Deployment environment types*

The figure illustrates one possible configuration; others are possible. The arrows describe the general progression of a change through the environment types, but the movement is not one-directional. For example, it may reverse direction from staging back to development in response to errors.

The three environment types in Figure 9.2 are as follows:

- **Development (dev) environment:** This is the environment accessed by developers. Services deployed to the dev environment are accessible from the local versions of code created by developers on their local machines. Unit testing and low-level integration tests are run in this environment.

- **Staging environment:** Next, the code is deployed to staging. Automated integration tests, as well as manual testing/acceptance testing, are run in this environment. If the code doesn't pass the tests, the change is rolled back, and the developer continues to work on it locally. The staging and dev environments are kept separate to avoid false failures during testing.

- **Production environment:** Once all automated and manual tests are passed, the changes are deployed to production. The PO may decide to give users broad access to the change at this time. Alternatively, the PO may choose to hold back access until the feature is rich enough to be competitive. In this case, the new functionality may be deployed into production but hidden from general use (e.g., placing it behind a feature flag).

Other configurations and environments are possible. For example, a performance testing environment is sometimes established for performance and volume testing.

9.6.2 Deployment and Delivery Approach

The MVP approach depends on a fast turn of the build-test-learn cycle. This requires a deployment and delivery approach that enables versions of the product to be released frequently and safely. Not only does such a capability accelerate MVP learning; it also shortens time to market, enables faster bug fixes, and increases the company's ability to respond quickly to feedback and changing market conditions. Let's look at deployment and delivery practices that provide this capability: DevOps, CI, and CD.

9.6.2.1 DevOps

The DevOps approach accelerates the Build-Measure-Learn loop by reducing the time from ideation to deployment, principally through automation and cloud services. It addresses cultural and technical practices, including CI/CD, discussed in the following sections.

 For more on DevOps, see Chapter 17, section 17.5.2.1.

9.6.2.2 Continuous Integration

Continuous integration provides the capability to integrate the work of multiple developers frequently, with confidence, using automated unit and integration tests. CI automation does not include deployment and high-level integration testing.

9.6.2.3 Continuous Delivery

Continuous delivery is a set of practices for deploying software changes to the market quickly, reliably, and sustainably. CD extends CI by adding practices for user-acceptance testing and deployment to production that use minimal human involvement.

With the CD approach, changes are **delivered** as soon as they are produced. This means they are *potentially* shippable: they can be **deployed** into production, *subject to approval from the business*. In section 9.6.3, we examine when it's better to defer deployment of a delivered feature.

> **Deliver versus Deploy**
>
> As this section explains, there's a difference between delivering a change and deploying it:
>
> - To **deliver** a product or change is to provide it in a potentially shippable form.
> - To **deploy** a product or change means to ship it, open it, and put it to use. One can deploy to any physical or virtual environment, such as a staging or production environment.

Looking under the Hood: How CI/CD Works

CI/CD practices are so critical to the performance of an agile organization that all business analysts (even those without technical responsibilities) should have at least a high-level understanding of how they work from a technical standpoint. Implementations will vary, but the following is an overview of one typical scenario.

Two version control management systems, Git and GitHub, are used to track changes when editing code. Git is used by developers to manage and track changes locally. The developer uses Git to create a **branch**—an independent line of development. The developer also creates a pull request in GitHub to request that the changes be merged with the **master branch**—the master version of the product. The pull request may require the approval of one or two developers. When executed, the request merges the developer's branch with the master branch and runs automated integration and system tests.

The process described to this point enables CI. The CD process extends this continuous, automated capability for advancing the changes through the build, test, and deploy steps. For example, GitHub notifies the CD servers (often using webhooks) whenever a line of development is integrated with the master through the CI process (i.e., a branch has been merged with a master branch). CD servers respond by kicking off the build, test, and deploy steps. These steps rely heavily on automation with minimal human intervention.

For example, human approvals may be required for deployment to production after the automated tests have passed, but the deployment steps themselves are automated.

 For a more in-depth discussion on DevOps/CI/CD, see Chapter 17, section 17.5.2.1.

9.6.3 Deployment Options and Potential Issues

As you develop a detailed long-term implementation plan, you'll need to decide between deployment options and address potential issues, such as the following:

- How will you time the deployment? Will you deploy changes to the market as soon as they are available, delay deployment, or deploy them first to a sacrificial product to protect the brand?

- How will you phase in the features planned for the product? Will you go wide and shallow or narrow and deep?

In this section, we look at those questions.

9.6.3.1 *When to Plan for Deferred versus Immediate Deployment*

As noted earlier, CD delivers *potentially* shippable changes on a continuous basis. However, the timing of their deployment is subject to the approval and demands of the business. Let's look at some common types of changes—and whether it's in the business interest to deploy them immediately or defer.

When a Feature Doesn't Deliver Sufficient Value
One of the most common reasons to delay deployment of a change is because it is part of a larger value stream or workflow but doesn't, on its own, deliver sufficient value to the customer to be useful or competitive. Let's look at an example to explain.

Suppose that Customer Engagement One (CEO) Inc. wanted to add a capability to create standardized replies to common questions from customers. A customer service representative (CSR) will be able to view and select these replies when addressing support questions from customers. The first feature to be delivered implements a flow for creating and saving a reply and corresponding title (question), such as "What happened to my parcel?" Although this feature is potentially shippable, it doesn't deliver value on its own because the user can't use the stored reply. It's in the business interest to defer deployment of the feature because, if it *were* deployed, it would be viewed by customers as an **amateur-hour** solution, risking the brand's reputation.

How long should CEO Inc. wait before it finally deploys features to the market? Let's suppose that after the first feature to create and save a reply is implemented, the remaining features in the backlog are as follows:

- View saved replies.
- Search the list of replies for keywords.

- Edit a saved a reply.

- Delete a reply.

The first of these, to view all of the replies, adds some value but not enough to be useful. Only once the second feature enabling searches is available is the feature set rich enough for a closed beta release to select customers and, if successful, deployment to the market.

It's worth noting that although the deployment to the market is deferred, each feature can still be used and tested by users as it becomes available. For example, the feature may be deployed to a test lab to obtain customer feedback or included in a sacrificial product. (We explore options for doing that in the next section.)

> As an analyst, you support the capability to deliver releasable features by specifying each feature as a "full-stack" work item that cuts through frontend and backend layers of the software.

In the preceding CEO example, deployment was delayed because the changes would be viewed as an amateur-hour solution by customers. However, there are ways to gain the learning benefits of frequent customer feedback without risking a brand's reputation. Let's look at two of these: sacrificial product and beta customers.

Deploying to a Sacrificial Product

One option is to create a **sacrificial product**—a side product used to test new functionality. Once features have proven themselves in the side product, they are added to the primary product. Once the side product has served its purpose, it is sacrificed. In this way, the business benefits from rapid learning, while the brand is unaffected if things go wrong.

For example, Google's policy has been to change Gmail slowly over time. In 2014, to quickly test new features rapidly in the marketplace without affecting Gmail's reputation, Google created Inbox—an experimental product aimed at early adopters. Once changes had proven themselves in Inbox, they were added to Gmail. Eventually, in April 2019,[16] Inbox was sacrificed. Having served its learning function, it was dropped from Google's product line.

Deploying to Beta Customers

Another option is to release the product first to a closed group of carefully selected **beta customers** and use their feedback to make improvements. The use of beta customers is important not only for highly innovative features but also as an essential step in the rollout of any new feature or improvement.

For more on beta testing, see Chapter 16, section 16.5.3.

---

16. "Inbox by Gmail," Wikipedia, August 16, 2019, https://en.m.wikipedia.org/wiki/Special: History/Inbox_by_Gmail

To illustrate the use of beta customers, suppose that CEO Inc. is considering adding a new feature to its product: "As a marketer, I can view responses to an ad campaign from multiple sources in a single place." This feature would be particularly valuable to users in companies with multiple Facebook pages and a high volume of traffic—so much so that they would use it even if implemented with limited functionality. Consequently, CEO searches its database for customers with the targeted characteristics (those who work at a company with multiple pages and high volume). CEO contacts the selected customers, asking if they would be excited about the opportunity to use leading-edge technology and wouldn't mind being called for feedback. Those that respond positively become beta customers. The beta customers benefit from using new capabilities before the general public, and CEO benefits from rapid learning without risking the brand's reputation.

Deploying Major Features and Enhancements

Most companies wait to deploy major features and enhancements to the end of a release cycle; a period that is typically about three months but may range up to six. Marketing, sales, and operations often prefer this cadence, as it provides them with the necessary lead time to prepare for major changes.

Deploying Bug Fixes and Minor Changes

Bugs fixes should be deployed as soon as they are delivered so users can benefit quickly. Deploy a group of bug fixes together if they are related.

Deploy small changes frequently to deliver quick wins and build confidence and funding for larger improvements.

Impact of Regulatory Constraints on Deployment

Features developed for regulatory compliance may need to be deferred until the time the regulations come into effect. Nevertheless, try to deliver some features as soon as possible, to provide confidence that the full-scale deployment will go through successfully when the time comes.

Deferred Deployment Due to Technical Limitations

A common reason for deferring deployment is that the organization's testing, building, and deployment processes are mostly manual and too time consuming for changes to be released frequently and safely into production. Until CI/CD practices are instituted, the only viable option may be to queue up changes and deploy them together at the end of a quarterly release cycle. As noted across this book, it's your responsibility as an analyst to meet the people where they are: support the organization in being as effective as possible using its current processes, but at the same time, be an agent of change championing a transformation to CD practices.

Should You Defer Deployment Due to Concerns about Breaking a Flow?

I have often seen teams deferring deployment of a feature until the larger workflow it belongs to has also been adapted. They do this, generally, out of a concern that deploying the feature on its own might break the flow of information between steps. However, this should not be a reason to defer deployment. To understand why, let's examine two kinds of changes: a change that adds a shared data item to an application programming interface (API), and one that removes a shared data item. The addition of an item does not introduce data-chain errors because existing clients are not expecting the new data to be there. While they won't be able to use the new data, they won't be harmed by its presence. The removal of a shared item, though, would appear to be riskier. However, it can be addressed in a couple of ways.

If the item is being removed from an API whose clients are third-party companies, you address the problem by versioning the API. You notify the third-party clients that they must move to the new version within a given deadline, after which the old version will no longer be supported. Typically, clients are given about two years to transition to the new version, after which the old version is no longer supported.

A well-known example of the removal of shared data was Facebook's decision to stop sharing likes with third-party clients due to privacy concerns. In this particular case, clients were given only two weeks to adjust to the removal of the data from Facebook's API, because it was determined that the information should never have been shared in the first place.

When a data item is to be removed from the API of an internally used microservice, a different approach is taken. In this case, it's usually preferable to move everyone over to the new version together, due to the expense of maintaining multiple API versions. To prevent breaks in the chain, you first change the clients of the API, so they stop using the data in question. Once that is complete, the data item can be safely removed from the API.

Addressing Customer Concerns about Deployment Frequency

A development manager recently spoke to me about his teams' adverse reactions to agile development. The company's software systems relied heavily on third-party software services provided by a partner. Ever since the partner had switched to agile development, the company's internal teams were unhappy about the disruption caused by frequent updates. They longed for the pre-agile days when new versions were delivered less frequently—about once a year.

As in the preceding scenario, the answer lies with API versioning, not in slowing down deployment. The partner should continue to deploy a new API frequently but support old versions for a couple of years to allow the client company to transition at a comfortable pace. At the same time, following CD practices, the client company should use a repository to direct deployment to use the appropriate version of the API.

9.6.3.2 When to Use a Narrow and Deep versus Wide and Shallow Implementation Approach

As you consider the detailed long-term implementation, you need to determine the approach you'll use to roll out features. There are two primary options in this regard: the narrow and deep and the wide and shallow. Let's look at those options and when to use them.

Narrow and Deep

With the **narrow and deep** approach, you focus first on providing deep functionality for a point solution before broadening out. A **point solution** is a narrow context for development. It may be focused on

- One delivery platform out of many that will be supported.

- One use case for the product (e.g., using the CEO app to launch a marketing campaign).

- A particular submarket (e.g., private bank customers vs. corporate customers).

- A specific line of products (e.g., limiting a new insurance program to group insurance products while excluding personal insurance).

Benefits

The main benefit of the narrow and deep approach is that by nailing one case first, you gain a solid understanding of user needs from which to build out the product. At the same time, you create a core base of enthusiastic users from which to grow the market.

This option also results in an internal team of highly skilled specialists at all levels of the organization—from product development to customer service. This optimizes responsiveness because specialists are usually more efficient than generalists. Another benefit is faster time to market, since developers don't have to contend with costly efforts to generalize a solution out of the gate.

Wide and Shallow

In the **wide and shallow** approach, you focus first on bringing to market a broad-based solution that consolidates the capabilities of multiple products under one roof. The solution is often inferior, at first, to a product that is more narrowly focused. However, it delivers benefits specifically related to its breadth.

Examples of broad-based solutions include those implemented across multiple delivery channels, platforms, markets, and lines of products. The breadth may be achieved through any combination of internal development, third-party services, partnerships, and acquisitions.

Benefits

The primary benefit to the user of the wide and shallow approach is efficiency. The user is able to perform operations from a single place instead of transferring in and out of separate applications. Another benefit is that a consolidated solution provides a "true north" for data—a single source of truth that eliminates the discrepancies that occur when data resides in separate solutions. The approach also offers testing benefits: the same functionality can be tested simultaneously across multiple platforms, reducing wasted time due to context switching.

Which Approach to Use When

There are no hard and fast rules governing which approach to use for a given circumstance. Try experimenting with both approaches to see which works best. There are some questions, though, that can help guide the choice:

- *What is the image of the company?* If the company is known as a specialist, the narrow and deep approach is favored; if it's known as a generalist, use a wide and shallow approach.

- *What is the key differentiator for the product?* If the product's differentiator is that it works across a broad spectrum (e.g., spanning different input sources, channels, product types, customer types), the wide and shallow approach is preferred. If the differentiator is the product's richness of features for a core group of users, use the narrow and deep approach.

- *Who are the most important customers for the product?* If those customers are willing to sacrifice depth for the benefit of having everything under one roof, use a wide and shallow approach. If not, use a narrow and deep approach.

- *What are the most critical hypotheses?* Use the approach that tests those assumptions first. For example, use a wide and shallow approach for products whose value hypothesis is based on the breadth of the product. That way, you can quickly test the technical viability of the proposition.

Facebook is an example of a company that used a narrow and deep strategy to grow, focusing early development on providing a rich user experience to a small but fiercely loyal customer base of college students. In time, these early adopters' enthusiasm brought the product to the attention of a broader market.

In the CEO Inc. case study, the company would choose a wide and shallow approach for initial development because the product's differentiator is its ability to manage customer engagements from a single interface. CEO might first focus on providing a thin set of features for two message sources to demonstrate the viability of a broad-based product.

For the initial version, the company might choose two message sources, email and Zendesk, a cloud-based ticketing system. The first release would deliver a minimally functional version that supports the two message sources across an end-to-end workflow as follows:

- Ingest message

- View message

- Triage message

- Tag message

- Respond to message

- Assign message

- Resolve message

The decision about which approach to use isn't always binary. Sometimes, it's best to use a narrow and deep approach for some items but wide and shallow on others—or use different approaches during different stages of product development.

The preceding discussion provides only a brief introduction to the topic. If you're interested in learning more, I encourage you to research sources devoted to the issue, such as Goldman[17] and Fauska, Kryvinska, and Strauss.[18]

Earlier, we learned that phase 2 of the full-potential plan is to create a detailed implementation plan. Now that we've looked at approaches that *guide* the development of that plan, let's turn to its actual creation.

9.7 Overview of the Product Roadmap

Use a product roadmap to plan the implementation of

- A product.
- A Big Bet in the full-potential plan.
- A long-term epic.
- A quarter or release cycle.

Table 9.1 provides a summary of the artifact.

Table 9.1 *The Product Roadmap at a Glance*

What?	**The product roadmap:** An overview of the plan for the product describing the rollout of goals, objectives, and other planning items across the planning horizon. Used to plan products and epics over the long term (up to five years). Also used for quarterly planning.
When?	Create a long-term product roadmap at the start of the planning period. Review it at the beginning of each quarter and in response to changing circumstances.
Deliverables	Long-term plan including timelines, goals, tested assumptions, metrics, and features for each interim planning cycle.

The template illustrated in Figure 9.3 is adapted from Roman Pichler's version—the GO product roadmap.[19]

---

17. Goldman's article, though focused on online advertising, makes important arguments that relate to strategic agile planning. Aaron Goldman, "Narrow & Deep or Wide & Shallow: How Does Your Tech Partner Roll?" InsidePerformance, March 27, 2013, https://www.mediapost.com/publications/article/196700/narrow-deep-or-wide-shallow-how-does-your-tec.html#axzz2OmYyNuax

18. P. Fauska, N. Kryvinska, and C. Strauss, "Good & Service Bundles and B2B E-Commerce by Global Narrow-Specialized Companies," 15th International Conference on Information Integration and Web-based Applications & Services (iiWAS2013), December 2013, Vienna, https://doi.org/10.1145/2539150.2539169

19. Roman Pichler, "The GO Product Roadmap," November 25, 2013, http://www.romanpichler.com/blog/goal-oriented-agile-product-roadmap

Planning Horizon: [Period covered by the Roadmap]

Duration of an Interim Period : [Time covered by one column (e.g., one quarter, release cycle, program increment, date range, iteration, x months]]

Interim Period				
Name				
Goals and Objectives				
Assumptions Tested				
Metrics				
Milestones, Events				
Sequenced Features				

Figure 9.3 *Product roadmap template*

As an analyst, you use the product roadmap as a facilitation tool during planning events and as an information radiator to communicate those plans afterward. You review the roadmap at the beginning of each quarter and revise it when circumstances change.

9.8 Planning the Interim Periods

Decompose the long-term planning horizon into interim periods or timelines. An interim period may represent a quarter (three months), a release cycle, a PI or any other interval. A program increment is defined in SAFe as a "planning interval during which an Agile Release Train (ART) delivers incremental value in the form of working, tested software and systems. PIs are typically 8–12 weeks long. The most common pattern for a PI is four development Iterations, followed by one Innovation and Planning (IP) iteration."[20]

The next task is to plan each interim period, with decreasing detail for more distant periods. Use the product roadmap as a facilitation tool: proceed down the column and ask attendees about each item as follows:

- Specify the interim timeline
- Craft interim goals and objectives
- Specify assumptions and metrics

20. Richard Kastner and Dean Leffingwell, *SAFe 5.0 Distilled: Achieving Business Agility with the Scaled Agile Framework* (Boston: Addison-Wesley, 2020), 274.

- Specify events and milestones
- Specify features

These are described in the following sections.

9.8.1 Specify the Interim Timeline

Gain consensus from business stakeholders and developers on a timeline or release date for the interim period. You may specify a quarter (e.g., Q2), a date, a date range, or *x* months after the prior release. The benefit of the latter option is that if one of the timelines is missed, the subsequent ones don't have to be revised.

Remind stakeholders that this is an *agile* plan: it invites change. Only the roadmap's dates are true commitments; everything else is a best forecast *at this point in time*. Features in the plan are expected to change as a result of learning and changing conditions.

This style of commitment can represent a significant cultural shift from the more binding commitments stakeholders may expect on the basis of their experience with waterfall development. As an analyst, you play a crucial role in explaining the business benefits of the agile approach in terms of shortened time to market, more efficient allocation of resources, greater transparency—and, most important, *better products* because they're built using continual feedback from customers.

9.8.2 Craft Interim Goals and Objectives

Goals and objectives drive planning. Begin with a discussion of the goals and objectives for the interim period (e.g., Q1). Ask stakeholders to consider learning goals in addition to business and customer goals and objectives. Learning goals in the early periods enable the company to test hypotheses and determine the MMFs—the features customers most value. Advise stakeholders that interim goals will be reviewed regularly and revised as necessary.

When specifying a goal or objective, avoid naming features so as not to constrain development. Examples of well-worded quarterly goals and objectives include the following:

- (Learning goal) Test the value hypothesis that customers are willing to overlook privacy concerns in exchange for immediate benefits.
- (Learning goal) Test the value hypothesis that customers will engage heavily with the feature.
- (Business objective) Decrease voluntary churn by *x* amount.
- (Customer objective) Provide first-call response.
- (Business/customer objective) Widen product availability to region X.

A goal or objective may be *supported by* multiple features. For example, the business objective to decrease voluntary churn is supported by features enabling customers to earn and redeem rewards. Note how the objective—decrease churn—doesn't specify the features. It focuses on the outcome—the *reason* for the features.

9.8.3 Specify Assumptions and Metrics

An agile plan uses continual feedback to test assumptions about the product, features, and design solutions. The roadmap embeds the practice into the template. Facilitate a discussion about the next item—the assumptions that will be tested during the period. Then discuss the metrics that will be collected to validate the assumptions and measure progress toward the goal.

Gain stakeholder consensus that the chosen metrics are meaningful in validating the assumptions being tested. Make sure progress metrics track real-world outcomes (e.g., churn rates).

For more on specifying value and growth hypotheses and metrics, see Chapter 7, section 7.11. For guidance on metrics for validating hypotheses, see section 7.11.5.

9.8.4 Specify Events and Milestones

Specify the important events and milestones for the interim period. A **milestone** is an achievement that occurs at a point in time and is used to mark progress. Examples of milestones are funding approvals, the launch of a marketing campaign, the release of an increment into the market, and the completion of user acceptance testing. An **event** is any other occurrence, such as a compliance audit.

9.8.5 Specify Features

Finally, specify the features that will be implemented during the period. Include features that will be prototyped and tested in MVPs.

As an analyst, it's your responsibility to clarify to stakeholders that all features and timelines for their implementation represent best-guess forecasts, not commitments. Coach attendees to name features by focusing on the value they provide vs. how they will be implemented. For example, *"As a traveler, I can specify the rating of the hotel I want to stay at"* is better than *"I can select a rating from a drop-down list."*

See Chapter 8, "Seeding the Backlog—Discovering and Grading Features," section 8.7, for more on writing epics and features.

BLINK CASE STUDY PART 12

Long-Term Planning—
Creating the Product Roadmap

Background

With BLInK's vision, goals, and objectives analyzed, the focus turns toward developing a long-term plan for realizing them.

The Ask

You are tasked with facilitating long-term planning workshops with business stakeholders and developers. Attendees will include the program and product managers, customer relationship managers, senior product manager, chief product owner

(CPO) / director, architect, POs of the development teams, development managers, and the development team (UX, analysts, programmers, etc.).

The deliverable from this activity is a BLInK product roadmap. For each release within the long-term plan, the roadmap will indicate the following items:

- Release goals and objectives
- Assumptions
- Metrics
- features

Tips

Carry out the following steps:

- **Preparation:** Ensure the product portrait is visible during the long-term planning session so that stakeholders can refer to it.
- **Review vision, goals, and assumptions:** Open the planning session by reviewing the product portrait, with a discussion of the following items: goals, objectives, assumptions, and features.
- **Review planning horizons.**
- **Review implementation strategy** (e.g., narrow and deep vs. wide and shallow).
- **Plan the interim periods:** Beginning with the first interim period (e.g., Q1), proceed down the corresponding column, asking about goals, riskiest hypotheses, metrics, milestones, and features. Repeat for remaining columns, with diminishing detail for distant periods.

What Transpires

Review Product Vision, Goals, and Assumptions:

A senior product manager reviews recent changes in the market and changes to strategic objectives. There is consensus that no revisions are required to the product portrait.

Review Planning Horizons

Stakeholders agree that planning will look ahead to the next year, with interim planning periods of three months, timed to align with release cycles.

Review Implementation Strategy

Stakeholders agree to begin with a narrow and deep approach, focusing first on developing a rich set of group insurance features. Rewards offered to customers will focus first on benefits that Better Living (BL) Inc. can provide on its own. Later, rewards will include benefits involving partnerships with third parties, such as medical/dental service providers and grocery-chain partners.

Plan the Interim Periods

Attendees highlight the risk that customers will not be willing to share their data because of privacy concerns. You suggest that testing this assumption be the central goal of the Q1 release. Stakeholders agree. Next, you ask about customer goals and objectives. You learn that, at a minimum, the first release should deliver a customer goal to sign up for BLInK. Marketers report that an initial analysis indicates that offering an immediate discount at sign-up might be enough to overcome a customer's reluctance to share data. Stakeholders agree that the precise incentives will be worked out during the quarter on the basis of feedback from MVP experiments.

Moving down the Roadmap, you focus on assumptions. Referring to the product portrait, you ask attendees about leap of faith hypotheses that should be tested during the first quarter. The discussion yields the following list, in order of importance:

- Reluctance to share data can be overcome when a benefit is shown immediately.
- Customers will agree with behavior-based pricing.
- Behaviors will improve.
- Health will improve.
- Subscribers will refer others.

Developers confirm that it would be feasible to create MVPs to test these assumptions with select customers during the first quarter.

Continuing down the roadmap, you discuss the metrics that will be used to test the assumptions and measure progress toward goals. You begin with metrics for the hypothesis that customers' reluctance to share data can be overcome if benefits are shown immediately. Attendees agree that a meaningful metric for validating this hypothesis should be penetration rate, defined as

Total # Policies including BLInK ÷ Total # Policies

The metric will be measured for various incentive options to determine those that are most effective. You continue in this way, discussing other assumptions and objectives and how they will be measured.

Finally, you ask attendees to consider the features that will be developed to test the assumptions and achieve the goals identified for the release. You ask developers to provide rough estimates for prioritization purposes and work with business stakeholders to sequence the features.

There is a consensus that the top two features are

- Immediate incentive for consenting to BLInK (days)
- Earn rewards for healthy behaviors (weeks)

You continue listing other features for the release. You repeat the process for the remaining interim periods in the roadmap.

Deliverables

Deliverable 1: BLInK Product Roadmap

Figures 9.4 and 9.5 illustrate the product roadmap for BLInK for the next four quarters.

Planning Horizon: 12 months, January 1 to December 31

Interim Planning Cycle (one column): one quarter = one release cycle

Release Date:	March 31	June 30
Release Name	**BLInK1: MyBLInK**	**BLInK2: MyDiscount**
Release Goals	• Learn whether customers will be willing to share data when provided with the right incentive • Enable customer to enroll in BLInK and immediately begin earning rewards	• Determine whether customers will continue after trial • Provide behavior-based premium discounts to BLInK customers
Assumptions Tested	(A7) Reluctance to share data can be overcome when benefit shown immediately (A5) Customers will like the product when they see it (A2) Behaviors will improve (A4) Health will improve (A8) Subscribers will refer others	(A1) Customers will continue after 6-month trial (A2) Behaviors will improve (A6) Premium will go down
Metrics	• Voluntary churn (O1,A10) • Penetration rate (Total policies with BLInK /total policies) (O2) (A7) • Avg claims rate: #claims/# policies (O4) • Lifestyle score (A2, O3) • # emergency room admissions; # claims; health claim costs (A4, O4) • Response rate (A5) • Referral rate (A8) • Growth rate (O6) • Survey: Customer-empowered rates (O8) • Life-style risk factors; # emergency room visits (O10)	• BLInK continuation rate (O1) • Voluntary churn rate (A10) • Lifestyle score (A2) • Average premium change (A6, O7) • Loss ratio (O5)
Milestones, Event	• Prototype produced • Launch marketing campaign • First release deployed to market	• Long-term funding secured • New risk model deployed • Second release deployed to market
Features	• Ability to enroll in BLInK [months] • Immediate incentive for consenting to BLInK [days] • Earn rewards for healthy behaviors [weeks] • Regular feedback to customer on health [weeks] • Redeem rewards for gym, yoga sessions [weeks] • Refer friends for rewards [days]	• Benefits offered for continuing after trial [days] • Model analyzes risk and prices premiums using behavioral data [weeks] • BLInK monthly premium discount available to customer [weeks] • Policy holder able to cancel BLInK after trial [days]

Figure 9.4 *BLInK product roadmap (Q1 and Q2)*

Planning Horizon: 12 months, January 1 to December 31

Interim Planning Cycle (one column): one quarter = one release cycle

Release Date	September 30	December 31
Release Name	**BLInK3: MyGames**	**BLInK4: MyPartner**
Release Goals	• Demonstrate that behaviors can be improved through rewards for healthy choices • Customer can earn rewards by playing games that incentivize positive behaviors	• Partner with food retailer to promote healthy choices through rewards program • Increase community awareness of program
Assumptions Tested	(A2) Behaviors will improve	(A3) Better data leads to more accurate risk assessment and pricing (A6) Premium will go down (A9) Acceptance will grow once use becomes widespread (large immediate discounts will no longer be required) (A10) BLInK will lead to improved customer retention
Metrics	Lifestyle score (A2)	• Voluntary churn (O1) (A10) • Market penetration (O2) • Loss ratio; predicted vs. actual outcomes (sickness, death) (A3) • Average premium change (A6, O7) • BLInK penetration rate (A9)
Milestones, Events	• Third release deployed to market	• Fourth release deployed to market
Features	• Redeem rewards for dental and eye exams [days] • Gamification: Compete against your peers (steps, etc.) [weeks] • Daily bonuses [days]	• Partnership with major grocery chain [weeks] • BLInK renewal benefits [days] • BLInK analytics reports (profitability, trend analysis [weeks]

Figure 9.5 *BLInK product roadmap (Q3 and Q4)*

Case Study Retrospective

In this workshop, you facilitated collaboration between the business and solution providers in order to develop a long-term plan. You specified the goals and objectives for each release and a forecast of features that will be implemented to support those goals. You ensured that all parties understand that the plan is provisional subject to change based on what is being learned as the product is tested through use.

9.9 Using the Product Roadmap for Shorter Planning Horizons

The roadmap is a simple planning tool that organizes work items in one-dimensional lists according to relative priority. In this chapter, we focused on its use for long-term planning. You can also use roadmaps for shorter planning horizons (e.g., to plan iterations across a single release cycle or to plan the rollout of a feature).

 To indicate the relationships between features, use a story map, a finer-grained planning tool, explored in Chapter 12, "MVPs and Story Maps."

9.10 Chapter Summary

Here are the key points covered in this chapter:

- A full-potential plan is a plan for transforming an organization by setting bold goals for the next three to five years. It includes detailed planning for three to five Big Bets that will result in quick wins within eighteen months.

- Plan to use MVPs to test leap of faith hypotheses and assumptions, to determine the MMFs that will be included in the product, and to test solution options.

- Use a *narrow and deep* strategy to build a fiercely loyal following by developing a rich set of features for a narrow slice of the product.

- Use a *wide and shallow* strategy if the business case is based on the breadth of the product.

- Use a *product roadmap* for long-term planning. It indicates the timelines, goals and objectives, assumptions, metrics, and features across the planning horizon. The plan is a forecast, not a commitment.

9.11 What's Next?

In this chapter, we focused on long-term planning. In Chapter 10, "Quarterly and Feature Preparation," we narrow our gaze to the upcoming quarter or feature set and the analysis work to prepare for it.

Chapter 10

Quarterly and Feature Preparation

The previous two chapters examined the planning and specification of features. This chapter focuses on analysis activities to prepare features for development. If the teams are using a flow-based (Kanban) approach, feature preparation occurs as each feature approaches the top of the backlog. If they're using a timeboxed planning approach, the set of features lined up for the next quarter is prepared before the quarterly planning meeting. Figure 10.1 highlights the activities, events, and artifacts included in this chapter.

First, the chapter explains the business case for feature preparation. It includes a checklist of preparation activities and guidelines for managing those activities in the backlog as functional spikes. The rest of the chapter provides detailed guidelines for performing the analysis activities of feature preparation. These include the specification of feature acceptance criteria, Minimum Marketable Features (MMFs), journey mapping, value stream mapping, process analysis, use-case modeling, and user-role modeling workshops.

10.1 Objectives

This chapter will help you

- Support hyper-productive teams and continuous, reliable delivery through effective feature preparation.

- Specify Minimum Marketable Features (MMFs) and feature acceptance criteria (AC) in accordance with ATDD/BDD in order to enable fast learning and deliver quick wins.

- Assess the current state and determine the future state of a process or business area using journey maps, value stream maps, data flow diagrams, and Business Process Modeling Notation (BPMN) process models.

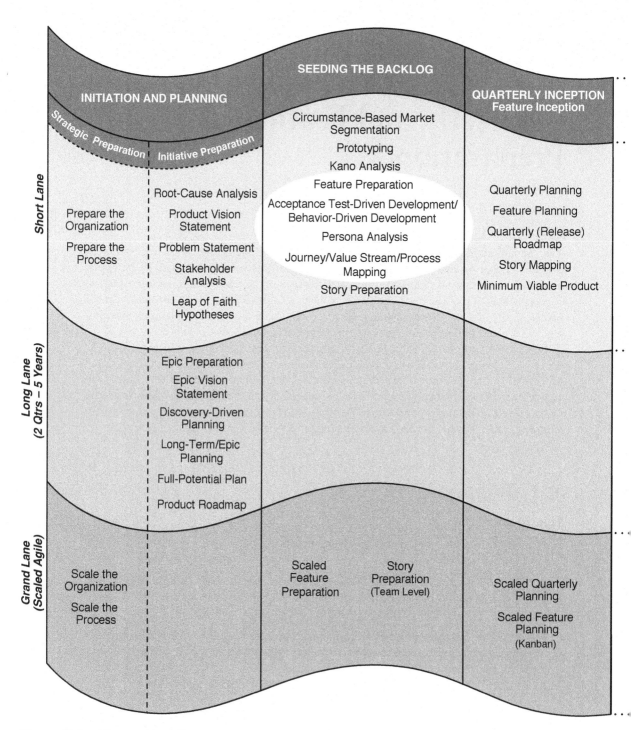

Figure 10.1 *Chapter 10 on the map*

QUARTERLY CLOSEOUT
Epic, Feature Closeout

DAILY ACTIVITIES

ITERATION INCEPTION

ITERATION CLOSEOUT

Iteration Planning

Daily Standup

Requirements Analysis & Documentation

Code, Build, Test, Deliver Acceptance
Test-Driven Development/
Behavior-Driven Development

Minimum Viable Product,
Split Testing

Epic, Feature Preparation

Story Preparation

Iteration Review

Iteration Retrospective

Prepare for
General Availability

Quarterly
Retrospective

Epic, Feature
Retrospective

Pivot or
Persevere

Scaled
Iteration
Planning

Iteration
Planning
(Team Level)

Product
Owner
Council
Meetings

DevOps

User Task
Force
Meetings

Scaled
Feature
Preparation
(Kanban)

Integration
Meetings

Story
Preparation
(Team Level)

Scaled Iteration
Review

Scaled Iteration
Retrospective

Iteration Retrospective
(Team Level)

DevOps

Scaled
Quarterly/Feature
Retrospective

10.2 This Chapter on the Map

As indicated in Figure 10.1, we'll be examining the following items in the Seeding the Backlog zone: epic preparation, feature preparation, acceptance test–driven development (ATDD) / behavior-driven development (BDD), persona analysis, journey mapping, value stream mapping, and process mapping.

10.3 Overview of Features

Since we're about to focus on features, let's quickly review some fundamental concepts about them.

A **feature** is a product-level work item that can be completed by one or more teams within one quarter or release cycle. The feature may be expressed in the Connextra format—for example, "As a member, I want to receive messages and notifications so that I can respond to issues that require my immediate attention."

A feature is bigger than a story but smaller than an epic. The relationships can be summarized as follows:

Epic > Feature > Story

Features often begin as epics. As we learned earlier, in Chapter 7, "Visioning," an **epic** is a product-level work item that may require multiple teams over multiple quarters and may span product areas, business areas, and value streams. An example of an epic is the introduction of home delivery across a product line to increase sales revenues by 20 percent. Chapter 7 explains how to prepare an epic by articulating the epic vision and leap of faith hypotheses. It also explores the MVP process for determining the minimum marketable features (MMFs)—the high-value features to develop. The next step is to prepare the upcoming features. This chapter focuses on that preparation.

10.3.1 Examples of Feature-Length Change Initiatives

As discussed in previous chapters, you decompose large work items into stories—small work items that deliver value but require no more than a few days' work—in order to shorten the feedback cycle and smooth the flow of work. If that's the case, why not dispense with epics and features and treat all requirements as stories? You can, if the team is exclusively tasked with small enhancements and bug fixes. Frequently, though, teams are asked to work on items that exceed the maximum size for a user story. A larger container—an epic or feature—is required to encapsulate the high-level functionality and objectives that it will deliver. Epics and features also include acceptance criteria (AC) that describe the product's behavior when stories are strung together in an end-to-end workflow. Examples of work items larger than a story include the following:

10.3.1.1 *Deliver a New or Improved Value Stream or Process*

A work item to create a new process or value stream—or reengineer an existing one—typically exceeds the maximum size of a user story and must be managed as a feature. Feature preparation activities may include value stream mapping and modeling of the current and future processes.

10.3.1.2 *Nontrivial Change to a Mature Product*

When a product is young, it's relatively easy to add a new capability because there aren't too many existing ones that the new capability might affect. However, as the product matures and accumulates a broader range of capabilities and components, it becomes harder to add or change a capability because it can affect so many existing parts. As a result, the change request must be classified as a feature.

Consider Customer Engagement One (CEO), the app being developed by our example company, CEO Inc.[1] Suppose the first version of the product allows customer support agents to view messages from two sources—each with its own format and rules. If the product owner (PO) wants to add a third message source, such as email, doing so affects only one function—viewing. This requirement is achievable within a few days, so you manage it as a user story.

Now suppose CEO has grown into a mature product with features to ingest, view, triage, tag, respond to, assign, and resolve messages. It's much more difficult to add a new message source because all of the existing features have to be adapted. A change of this type now takes weeks to implement and involves multiple teams. Consequently, you treat it as a feature (or epic, if it spans quarters), not a user story.

10.3.1.3 *Implementing a Use Case*

A use case is a usage of the product or system, typically sized to deliver a goal a user can accomplish through a single interaction with the product. Examples of use cases include the following:

- Submit a college application.

- Open an account.

- Place an order.

Each use case represents all the ways the interaction can play out, including successful and unsuccessful scenarios that the solution must support. The effort to implement all the scenarios of a use case typically exceeds the maximum story size. Consequently, you manage the use case as a feature and each scenario or set of related scenarios as a story. For example, you represent the *Place an order* use case as a feature. The user stories for the feature include the following, expressed in an informal format:

- Place an order (basic flow: no options).

---

1. This example was adapted from one provided by Yasha Podeswa in a conversation with the author, August 2019.

- Place an express order.
- Place a backorder.

10.4 Benefits of Feature Preparation

Sometimes I have to convince teams that feature preparation is not only allowed in agile development but should be encouraged and included in the plan. By preparing features before quarterly planning sessions begin, you facilitate improved capacity planning: developers can provide better estimates because they have a clear understanding of what's being requested. Furthermore, by preparing features before their implementation, you enable hyperproductive teams.[2] Developers can begin work on the solution without having to wait for key information or technical preparations. Collaborating teams can work in parallel with confidence because the feature's acceptance criteria (AC) and process models specify how the pieces must fit together when assembled. If integration errors show up, they're caught quickly because the feature AC are also used as the basis for specifying and executing automated high-level integration tests.

10.5 Feature Preparation Activities

This chapter focuses on *preparation*, while the next chapter focuses on *planning*. There is no strict line between the two, but in general, **planning** is about commitment—determining what features and goals will be delivered and gaining the commitment of collaborating teams to do the work. **Preparation** is the work to make an item ready for planning and implementation.

The outcome of feature preparation is a **ready** feature—one that is suitable for quarterly planning and able to be implemented without undue delay or rework. For example, a ready feature is prioritized and can be accomplished in three months or less by one or more teams.

Feature preparation activities include analysis and technical preparation. The analysis activities may include the items summarized in the following checklist.

✓ **Checklist of Feature Preparation Analysis Activities**

☐ Specification of features and AC

☐ Context analysis

☐ Stakeholder analysis

☐ Persona analysis

---

2. Jeff Sutherland, "Scrum: What Does It Mean to Be Ready-Ready?" (OpenViewVenture, 2011), https://www.youtube.com/watch?time_continue=3&v=XkhJDbaW0j0

☐ Journey mapping

☐ Value stream mapping

☐ Process modeling

☐ Use-case modeling

☐ User-role modeling workshops

☐ Initial splitting into stories

This chapter covers all of the items in the preceding list except for the last. The decomposition of features into stories (aka story splitting) is covered in Chapter 13, "Story Preparation."

To be clear, you don't perform *all* of the preparatory activities in the preceding checklist for every feature. The chapter provides guidance on activities to *consider* doing—but only do what's necessary for the situation.

Guidelines for splitting features into user stories are provided in Chapter 13, section 13.13. Additional guidelines for preparing features on a scaled initiative can be found in Chapter 17, section 17.9.12.

Technical preparation involves the drafting of a solution design, creation and testing of proofs of concept and prototypes, and readying the **architectural runaway**—a task that includes the specification of service communication protocols, identification of components, and creation of infrastructure. While this book focuses on analysis issues, we do review some of the models used in technical preparation that you should be familiar with as an analyst. These include the following:

• Context diagrams

• Communication diagrams

• Data-flow diagrams

• Block diagrams

10.6 Timing of Feature Preparation

When do you begin the preparation of features? The lean guideline is to wait until the last responsible moment (LRM)—the point at which any further delay would result in unacceptable costs. How you apply this principle depends on the planning approach you're using.

In a Kanban system, you prepare each feature as it approaches the top of the backlog, with a lead time of about six weeks for large features and two to four weeks for smaller ones.

If the teams are using the alternative planning approach—timeboxing—you prepare the group of features lined up for the upcoming quarter starting about halfway (six weeks) into the prior quarter. Some organizations prepare these features in a reserved iteration (e.g., SAFe's Innovation and Planning [IP] Iteration),[3] but this is generally not advised. We look at arguments for and against reserved iterations (aka hardening iterations) in Chapter 17.

10.7 Assessing Readiness

Use the checklist in Appendix A.7 to assess whether or not teams are ready for quarterly planning. Conditions in the checklist include that a vision, roadmap, and impacted users have been specified and that sufficient features (about ten to twenty) are ready.

10.7.1 Using the Feature Definition of Ready (Feature DoR)

Use the **feature definition of ready (DoR)** to determine if a feature is ready to be included in the quarterly plan or (in Kanban) to advance on to development.

The following are examples of the feature DoR conditions we saw in Chapter 6, "Preparing the Process."

- The feature is right-sized: The feature is small enough to be implemented within a quarter by one or more teams.

- The feature has no (or minimal) dependencies on other features.

- The feature is valuable.

- All teams are committed.

- The feature is estimable: The feature is understood well enough to be estimated.

 For more on the feature DoR, see Chapter 6, section 6.5.7.6.

10.8 Accounting for Preparation Work: Tasks and Spikes

Once you've flagged the need for preparatory analysis, how do you account for that work in your plans? If the analysis will be performed during the iteration in which it's flagged, represent it as a developer task. A **developer task** is a work item carried out by an individual team member. (The term *developer* is deceiving. Analysis, design, testing, and coding are all treated as developer tasks.) Developer tasks are posted on a developer task board.

 We look at developer tasks and developer task boards in Chapter 15, sections 15.4, 15.6, 15.7.3, and 15.7.5.

---

3. Richard Kastner and Dean Leffingwell, *SAFe 5.0 Distilled: Achieving Business Agility with the Scaled Agile Framework* (Boston: Addison-Wesley, 2020), 262.

If you plan to defer the analysis work to a future iteration, you'll have to add it to the product backlog. However, you can't represent it as a user story because it doesn't result in working code. Instead, you manage the analysis as a **functional spike**, also known as an **enabler story**. We'll look at functional spikes in Chapter 13. Figure 10.2 is an example of one.

> **[5]**
>
> Functional Spike:
>
> As an analyst, I want to investigate pricing rules so that the story to *order a product* may be enabled.

> Acceptance Criteria
>
> 1. A set of input conditions affecting pricing
>
> 2. Business rules, verified by customer, specifying how a product is to be priced on the basis of input conditions

Figure 10.2   *Example of a functional spike*

Figure 10.2 illustrates the functional spike to investigate pricing rules. The value that it delivers is expressed in the "so that" clause: the spike enables a future story to order a product. The spike is assigned five story points, indicating the estimate and time limit for the analysis.

Once you've identified the analysis activities required to prepare the feature, the next step is to perform them. The following sections provide guidelines for performing feature AC specification, persona analysis, journey and value stream mapping, and process and use-case modeling.

10.9 Specifying Features and Their Acceptance Criteria

Meet with business representatives, developers, and testers (sometimes called "the Triad") to describe the feature in a way that clearly communicates the requirement. Chapter 8, "Seeding the Backlog—Discovering and Grading Features," section 8.7, provides guidelines for specifying features using the Role-Feature-Reason (Connextra) template. Coach stakeholders and the team to use the template, but don't force its use where the resulting wording is unnatural and impedes understanding.

Then, specify feature AC. AC play a central role in agile analysis: they serve as requirements and as the basis for user acceptance testing (UAT). For the first release of the feature, specify just enough AC to define an MMF—the minimum functionality required to deliver value that the customer would view as significant.

As an analyst, you support feature AC specification. You support ATDD guidance by ensuring AC are specified before work on the feature begins so that they can serve as **specifications by example**. The AC tell the developers how much functionality must be delivered for the item to be releasable—providing them with the information they need to estimate the feature for capacity planning. The AC also serve as test scenarios to validate the solution. These scenarios describe how the product must behave when user stories are strung together in a larger workflow or value stream. A common approach is to specify the AC in a feature file in the Gherkin syntax so they can be interpreted by a test automation tool such as Cucumber.

AC and estimates are so intertwined that you should encourage stakeholders to discuss them at the same time with developers and QA professionals so trade-offs can be explored. This is the principle behind the Triad approach, discussed in Chapter 13.

For more on the Triad, see Chapter 13, section 13.6.3.

10.9.1 Specifying Epic Acceptance Criteria

Specify epic AC that communicate, at a high level, the minimum requirements for completion. In Chapter 7, we saw the following epic example. Its AC expresses the epic's business objective, "legacy system can be retired."

> **Epic:** Modernize customer loyalty program.
>
> **Acceptance Criteria:** Implementation of this epic means that the legacy system can be retired.

The following AC examples specify minimum capabilities for an epic.

> **Epic:** As a planner, I want to introduce dropship capability to increase top-line sales without the inventory ownership expense.
>
> **Acceptance Criteria:**
>
> Provide the ability to identify dropship-eligible product.
>
> Enable financial reporting (sales $/units, sell-through %, inventory ownership) for all dropship-eligible products.
>
> Identify when dropship-eligible product is no longer available for sale.
>
> Provide the ability to execute a clearance (markdown) price change for dropship-eligible product.

> **Epic:** Implement payment platform.
>
> **Acceptance Criteria:** Completing this epic allows multiple payment types to be used interchangeably.

10.9.2 Specifying Feature Acceptance Criteria

Like epic AC, feature AC do not have to cover all possible scenarios. Instead, begin by specifying an MMF that includes only the minimum level of functionality needed for the feature to be seen as valuable by customers.

Following is an example of feature belonging to the epic we saw earlier: "As a planner I want to introduce dropship capability to increase top-line sales without the inventory ownership expense." Its AC are specified in brief descriptive text, also known as scenario titles.

Feature: Enable dropship product identification in assortment planning.

Acceptance Criteria:

Scenario: Specify a dropshipped product. (success)

Scenario: Specify a product ineligible for dropshipping. (failure)

Scenario: Search for dropshipped products satisfying search attributes.

Following is an example we saw in Chapter 8.

Feature:

As an incident manager, I want to manage incidents from a single interface so that I can view and prioritize issues across all sources.

Acceptance Criteria:

I can view and manage scheduling delays.

I can view and manage nonemergency incidents.

I can filter/sort/rank all incidents by defined attributes.

10.9.3 The Analyst Contribution

As an agile analyst, you support ATDD by facilitating Triad conversations between stakeholders, QA, and developers about AC and by specifying AC, as discussed earlier. However, you should review and adjust your contribution over time based on experience. Options for your involvement in feature AC include the following:[4]

- You own the feature files—or the team as a whole owns them.

- You write the AC, scenario titles, and Gherkin given/when/then specifications—or you write AC and scenario titles, and QA professionals write the given/when/then specs.

---

4. Ian Tidmarsh, "BDD—An Introduction to Feature Files," Modern Analyst, https://www.modernanalyst.com/Resources/Articles/tabid/115/ID/3871/BDD-An-introduction-to-feature-files.aspx

10.9.4 Analyze AC During Triad Meetings

Analyze AC for epics and features incrementally, through collaborative sessions with business stakeholders (representing the customer), testers, and developers—the Triad.

Before committing a feature to development, facilitate Triad discussions to specify high-level AC in the language of the business. The AC and conversations clarify the requirements to stakeholders, testers, and developers. Continue to meet with the Triad to refine the AC with more specific test scenarios.

 See Chapter 13, section 13.6.3, for more on the Triad.

This chapter focuses on feature preparation, but you also need to prepare stories and their AC. Story preparation and AC are discussed in Chapter 13.

10.9.5 Specifying AC in the BDD Gherkin Syntax

The Gherkin syntax is widely used because it can be easily interpreted by stakeholders, testers, and test automation tools. Typically, you begin by writing story AC informally; then, as the story approaches development, you specify test scenarios in Gherkin feature files. Gherkin includes keywords such as *given*, *when*, and *then* to identify standardized aspects of test scenarios.

> **Gherkin Template**
>
> **Scenario:** <<scenario title>>
>   **Given** <<precondition>>
>   **When** <<trigger>>
>   **Then** <<postcondition>>

For example, you create the following feature to introduce dropship capabilities.

> **Feature: Introduce Dropship Capability**
>
> As a planner, I want to introduce dropship capability for the company to increase top-line sales without the inventory ownership expense.
>
> **Acceptance Criteria**
>
> * Provide the ability to identify dropship-eligible product.
> * Provide the ability to execute a clearance (markdown) price change for dropship-eligible product.
> * Enable financial reporting (sales $/units, sell-thru %, inventory ownership) for all dropship-eligible products.
> * Identify when dropship-eligible product is no longer available for sale.

> *Following is an example of a Gherkin scenario specification.*
>
> **Scenario:** Provide the ability to identify dropship eligible product
> > **Given** I am signed in as Mandy Jackson
> > **When** I query product SKU: UPL1283
> > **Then** I should see "This item is dropship eligible."

10.9.6 Specifying UAT for End-to-End Workflows

If the feature or epic results in a new or reengineered process or value stream, specify end-to-end tests that describe how the product behaves across the workflow. Following ATDD guidance, do this before implementation. For example, you specify the following scenarios in the preceding example, **Introduce Dropship Capability**, to test the end-to-end workflow for the feature:

- Identify a dropship-eligible product
- Execute a markdown for it
- Create financial reports
- Identify when the item is no longer available.

Various tools may be used to specify the tests. As noted earlier, one recommended approach is to specify them in Gherkin feature files. If you're going to be using feature files and are not familiar with them, read the following technical description. Otherwise, you may want to skip to the next section.

10.9.6.1 Specifying End-to-End UAT Using Feature Files

With this approach, before implementation (and continuing as new AC and stories are added) you collect the AC specifications for the stories of the feature into a feature file so they can be executed together (e.g. the four scenarios in the preceding example).

You tag different parts of the feature file to control which parts are activated. Doing so enables you to specify AC scenarios up front and activate them only once the corresponding user stories are ready.

The developers write step definitions for the scenarios in source code. The feature files are stored in a repository, placed under version control, and executed automatically during the build. After the feature is deployed, you reuse the automated tests for regression testing. As the feature AC evolve, you revise the specifications in the feature files.[5]

10.10 Context Analysis

BABOK v3: A Guide to the Business Analysis Body of Knowledge third edition *(BABOK v3)*, defines **context** as the "circumstances that influence, are influenced by, and provide

---

5. Tidmarsh, "BDD."

understanding of the change. . . . The context is everything relevant to the change that is within the environment. Context may include attitudes, behaviors, beliefs, competitors, culture, demographics, goals, governments, infrastructure, languages, losses, processes, products, projects, sales, . . . and any other element meeting the definition."[6] In this chapter, we focus on attitudes, behaviors, beliefs, culture, demographics, goals, and processes.

10.11 Stakeholder Analysis

If you don't have a good understanding of customers and their motivations, you can't create a product that meets (or exceeds) their expectations. Consequently, your analysis begins with the stakeholders—the people affected by the planned feature or features.

In Chapter 7, we covered the preliminary stakeholder analysis that occurs at the genesis of the initiative. That analysis is refined over time. First, we focus our analysis on the users affected by an upcoming feature or (if the teams are planning quarterly) by the group of features lined up for the next quarter. In the next section, we examine how to refine that analysis through the use of personas. Later in this chapter, we explore another stakeholder analysis technique—user-role modeling workshops.

 For more on stakeholder analysis, see Chapter 7, section 7.9.

10.12 Persona Analysis

A **persona** is an imaginary proxy or **archetype** for a user or customer—a named individual with a personal backstory and motivation for using the product. Personas are used as stand-ins for the user when designing products. Personas are effective because of a simple truth known to creatives: *it's easier to create for an audience of one than it is for an audience of everyone*. Table 10.1 summarizes the persona technique and its usages.

Table 10.1 *Personas at a Glance*

What?	**Persona:** A proxy for the user.
When?	Create personas during quarterly preparation and feature preparation, focusing on users who will be prioritized during the change.
Why?	Specific examples bring user analytics to life in a way that numbers do not.

---

6. International Institute of Business Analysis (IIBA), *BABOK v3: A Guide to the Business Analysis Body of Knowledge*, 3rd ed. (Toronto, Canada: IIBA, 2015), 13.

Tips	• Derive personas from data and interviews; don't create them out of thin air.
	• Refer to personas when prioritizing features, creating journey maps, and writing user stories.

Deliverables   Personas identifying biography, goals, and high-level use cases.

10.12.1 History of Personas

In his book *The Inmates Are Running the Asylum*,[7] Alan Cooper traces his invention of personas to his time working on Plan*IT—a project-management critical path tool. When he was interviewing stakeholders about requirements, he got to know one user particularly well. When she was not around, he found it helpful to imagine himself having conversations with her. The *imagined* person had become a proxy for the *real* user when the real user was not available. Though Cooper didn't have a name for it yet, he had created his first persona.

Later, in 1995, when working on a business intelligence tool, Cooper became frustrated by the way developers responded when asked to describe how the product would be used. They would explain all the options included in the product, but they couldn't provide him with a picture of how a *specific person* might use it. When he interviewed the users himself, he found that they could be grouped into three buckets based on their high-level usage of the product. He created a proxy—or persona—for each bucket. One persona used the tool to create templates, another used templates created by others to create reports, and a third optimized templates but didn't create them. Cooper kept these personas in mind when considering features. He often referred to the personas when presenting designs to the team, and soon the whole team began using them. Ultimately, the product included three different interfaces—each designed from the point of view of one persona.

You may have noticed how, in this origin story, each persona created by Cooper represents a distinct *usage* of the product, more so than a specific user *type* or demographic. This is the best way to create personas. Each one should do things with the product that others do not do.

In my experience with development organizations, personas have a mixed reputation. Most of the teams I work with do not use them (or, at least, don't use them regularly), finding the technique too contrived. Others have found it extremely useful in anticipating the needs of different kinds of users. An example is a financial company developing an interface for two different types of borrowers. My advice is to experiment with the technique to see if it is useful in your environment.

> If personas feel too contrived, try using a real user instead of a fictional character. Don't overelaborate the backstory; keep it simple.

7. Alan Cooper, *The Inmates Are Running the Asylum: Why High-Tech Products Drive Us Crazy and How to Restore Sanity* (Indianapolis: Sams–Pearson Education, 2004).

10.12.2 Persona Examples

Let's illustrate the use of personas with some examples.

10.12.2.1 Personas for the CEO Case Study

Let's return to CEO Inc., the company creating an integrated customer engagement platform. Based on initial market testing, CEO has found four different kinds of users who use the product in distinct ways. To personify these usages, you create the following personas:

- *Jorge the CSR:* Jorge is a customer service representative (CSR) for one of CEO's clients, Magnum Robotics. He uses the product for day-to-day customer support. The product's main attraction for him is that it pools all his incoming support messages into a single inbox.

- *Magda the Marketer:* Magda works in marketing for Magnum Robotics. She uses the product to launch and manage ad campaigns. The most exciting feature for her is the ability to post public announcements on multiple platforms from a single interface.

- *Tupac the Sales Manager:* Tupac manages sales of products and services for Magnum Robotics. For Tupac, the product's main attraction is the ability to view and analyze sales across multiple social media platforms.

- *Ayala the Data Analyst:* Ayala is a data analyst for Magnum Robotics. She uses the product to analyze brand mentions on social media. Ayala is most excited about its ability to pick up on trending issues before they go viral.

During quarterly preparation for the next CEO release, you refer to the personas when considering which goals, objectives, and features to prioritize. For example, you may decide to prioritize the goals and features favored by Jorge because analytics show that customer support is one of the most popular usages among early adopters. For the longer term, forecasts indicate that the product's data analytics features have the highest growth potential. When those features are developed in a future release, Ayala will be prioritized.

10.12.2.2 Personas in Mainstream Business Applications

The following are some recent examples of how teams I work with have been using personas in mainstream business sectors.

Jane the Primary Borrower, Joe the Co-Borrower

Teams at a financial firm I'm working with are currently developing a self-service website for borrowers. They've created a persona, *Jane*, who represents the primary borrower listed on a loan, and another persona, *Joe*, who represents a co-borrower. When designing the interface, they ask: "What should Jane see?" "What should Joe see?" For example, Jane should see an option to add a co-borrower; Joe should not. The personas are helping the teams tease out detailed requirements and rules for different kinds of users. The personas are also guiding the design of two versions of the user interface: one for primary borrowers and one for co-borrowers.

Pat, Jody, and Taylor—The Insurance Customers

An insurance company is developing a quick-quote site for customers. Its teams are currently working with the following personas:

- *Pat* personifies a *low-risk* business insurance customer. He owns a hair salon, which he runs out of a suite in a commercial property. He wants small-business insurance for his salon.

- *Jody* personifies a *medium-risk* customer. Jody is Pat's building owner. Jody is seeking property insurance for the building.

- *Taylor* is a *high-risk* customer. She is a metalworker who uses heavy machinery on the property. Taylor is seeking to purchase property and liability insurance.

The user interface will ask different questions for different types of risks. The teams are using the personas to sort out who sees which questions. For example, the question, "How many units do you rent out?" is relevant only to Jody, the building owner.

10.12.3 Creating Personas

The following sections describe the steps for identifying and specifying personas. The steps are as follows:

- Research users.

- Divide users into buckets based on usage.

- Refine the personas.

10.12.3.1 Research Users

Explore how current users use the product, using data analytics, surveys, and interviews. For example, data analytics highlight a subset of customers who are high-frequency users of a feature similar to one being proposed. You use the attributes of that subset to locate individual customers and interview them about their needs and how they use the product. In step 2, you use those insights, along with analytical data, to develop a persona for the subset.

Another source of information for personas is *circumstance-based market segmentation* (discussed in Chapter 7). With that approach, you analyze the *jobs* customers hire the product to do by researching customers in the field. Each job is a high-level use case that may be represented as a persona.

10.12.3.2 Divide Users into Buckets Based on Usage

Divide users into distinct buckets based on the high-level use cases for the product. Represent each bucket as a persona. Every persona uses the product in ways that others do not. A typical number is three or four personas for each high-level feature, with one acting as the primary persona for a quarter or release cycle.

10.12.3.3 Refine the Personas

Describe the goals each persona has in purchasing or using the product. Flesh out the persona with some personal background, such as relevant aspects of the persona's demographics, state of mind, pain points, and values. Attach a photo or sketch to the persona. Finally, identify scenarios in which the persona would use the product.

10.12.4 Documenting Personas

Each persona you specify should provide enough information to allow the team to picture an individual along with his or her backstory and unique perspective on the product relative to other personas. Figures 10.3 and 10.4 are two examples of templates for specifying personas. Figure 10.3 is more formally laid out; Figure 10.4 is informal.

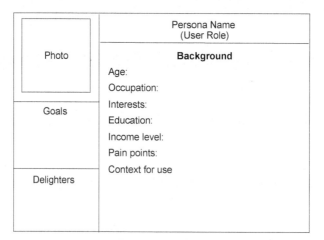

Figure 10.3 *Formal persona template*

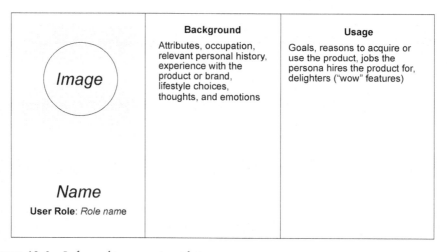

Figure 10.4 *Informal persona template*

Identify the **persona's goals** in using the product. The goal may be a high-level outcome, such as *reduce costs*, or a job (high-level use case) the user does with the product, such as *manage my finances*.

Identify the persona's **delighters**—excitement or "wow" features the customer does not expect but would be delighted to find.

See Chapter 8, section 8.11, for more on Kano analysis and delighters.

Pain points are issues that frustrate the persona. For example, a pain point for Magda the Marketer is the difficulty she has synchronizing posts across multiple social media platforms.

Specify **contexts for use**—the situations in which the persona uses or would use the product. For example, Magda would use CEO when she wishes to distribute the same product announcement to customers across multiple social media platforms.

Add other demographic information (e.g., occupation and educational level), as needed, to help flesh out the user interface and priorities for the persona.

10.12.5 Working with Personas

Once you've defined personas, you can use them in various ways, as described in the following sections.

10.12.5.1 Use Personas to Determine Priorities

Refer to personas when discussing which features to prioritize during the quarter or release cycle. For example, ask, "What does Marie the Manager need?" to determine which features to prioritize for a manager.

10.12.5.2 Use Personas to Guide User Interface Design

Use personas to guide the design of the user interface. Consider creating a distinct user interface for each persona to support the different ways of using the product. Ask what information each persona would want to view and update.

10.12.5.3 Use Personas to Guide Journey Mapping

Identify the primary persona(s) being addressed in the upcoming quarter or change initiative. Refer to the primary persona during journey mapping to explore the customer's actions, thoughts, and feelings as he or she is introduced to, acquires, uses, and promotes the product.

10.12.5.4 Use Personas with User Stories

Specify a persona in a user story to provide a more vivid picture of the user who benefits. Include the persona in the Connextra template, as follows:

- As [persona], I want [feature] so [reason].

For example, "As *Mike the Subscriber*, I want to customize my smoking cessation program so I can quit smoking at my own pace."

BLINK CASE STUDY PART 13

Personas

The Ask

As the team analyst, you've been asked to facilitate a workshop to develop personas for BLInK. The deliverable from the event will be

- **Deliverable 1:** BLInK personas representing key users

Preparation

You invite marketing SMEs, the product manager, data analysts, sales personnel, and the team. You've asked them to be prepared to discuss what is known about the customer from market surveys and in-depth interviews.

What Transpires

During the workshop, you learn that potential customers for BLInK can be grouped into two buckets, as follows.

Bucket 1

The first group are current customers of Better Living (BL) Inc. who could be motivated to purchase BLInK coverage because of general concerns about their health. Market research suggests that this group represents the largest potential pool of early adopters.

Analytics indicate that the majority in this group have white-collar jobs. They self-report as being highly sedentary. On surveys, they agree strongly that exercise and improved diet are "very important." They tend to rate their ability to delay short-term gratification for long-term benefits as "very poor."

According to market analysts, Kano questionnaires indicate that if an immediate benefit were offered during sign-up with no obligation to commit, it would be a wow feature for this target market.

Bucket 2

Another bucket of potential customers exists among those who are not currently BL customers but who work at companies that offer BL group insurance. Kano analysis indicates that smoking-cessation programs would be an excitement feature for this target market. Demographic data shows that most individuals in this bucket work in blue-collar jobs.

You create personas for Buckets 1 and 2. Stakeholders agree to focus the initial release on the needs of Bucket 1 (current BL customers)—identified by market analysis as the subset with the highest interest in early releases of the product.

Deliverables

Deliverable 1: Personas

Figure 10.5 is the persona created to represent Bucket 1— BL customers concerned about declining health and interested in using BLInK to improve it.

	Aisha is a 55-year-old business analyst at RxCRO, where she participates in a BL group life insurance plan. Her doctor has told her she is at risk of developing severe medical conditions unless she gets more exercise and improves her diet. She wants to act on her doctor's advice but hasn't been able to summon the motivation to commit to short-term pain for a long-term gain.	Aisha is excited by the way the program incentivizes her to improve the quality of her diet and get more exercise. She would be a frequent user of the meal and nutrition programs and group exercise classes included in BLInK. Aisha would be amazed by immediate benefits on sign-up that don't require a long-term commitment.
Aisha (Primary Subscriber)		

Figure 10.5   *BLInK persona: Aisha*

Because of the high number of potential customers in this category, Aisha will be a *strategic persona*—the primary focus of the first release.

The second persona, Mike, is illustrated in Figure 10.6. Mike represents customers who would use BLInK as an incentive to quit smoking.

	Mike is a 25-year-old engineer. BL group health insurance is offered through his employer, MacDougal's, but Mike is not currently a BL customer. He is a heavy smoker who is worried about the long-term effects of his habit. He is "not a fan" of support groups and other public smoking-cessation programs. As he often says, "I'm not a joiner."	Mike is looking for a smoking-cessation program that he can follow privately. He would be excited by BLInK's customizable programs and its rich set of personal incentives geared toward smoking cessation.
Mike (Primary Subscriber)		

Figure 10.6   *BLInK persona: Mike*

Case Study Retrospective

In this workshop, you created two personas, representing two ways of using the BLInK program. These personas can now be used to explore customer journeys, features, and design options.

10.13 Overview of Journey, Process, and Value Stream Maps

Having examined the product's users, we now turn the analysis toward the ways users engage with the product. We explore the following tools, used in this context:

- Journey mapping

- Value stream mapping

- Process analysis (process modeling)

- Use-case modeling

Use the techniques to analyze a current state, determine a future state, and perform a gap analysis.

Journey mapping examines customers' thoughts, feelings, and actions as they engage with the brand or product across channels (e.g., using social media, email, websites, and direct messaging). Use this technique to identify touchpoints between customers and the product, and **moments of truth**—opportunities to make lasting impressions on customers.

The touchpoints may trigger a business process or occur during a process. For example, a touchpoint where a customer submits an order triggers a process to receive and manage the order. Use **value stream mapping** to optimize the flow of materials or information required to deliver value to the customer (e.g., to respond to an incident). The value stream map indicates the sequence of steps and the metrics at each step, such as time spent actively working on an item and time spent waiting.

Compared to value stream maps, process models include a richer set of elements for specifying workflow rules. Use **process modeling** to analyze a workflow that must be carried out consistently according to defined rules. A **process model** is a visual representation of that workflow. For example, you use process modeling to analyze the current fraud-detection processes at two banks undergoing a merger. Then, you perform a gap analysis to identify inconsistencies and develop future-state process models to address the gaps.

10.14 Journey Mapping

Let's begin then with the big-picture model—the journey map. Suppose you've identified a target user and have represented her as a persona. What is the sequence of events that would lead that persona to purchase and use the product? That's the story told by a journey map. Table 10.2 summarizes journey mapping and its uses.

Table 10.2 *Journey Maps at a Glance*

What?	**Journey map:** A model that provides an in-depth view of a customer's engagement with a company or product over time. A journey map describes how customers decide to purchase a product, use it, and become loyal repeat customers.
When?	Create journey maps in preparation for a large change initiative (epic or large feature), quarter, or release cycle.
Why?	• Brings customer behavioral data to life. • Provides insight into customers' motivations. • Indicates moments of truth where intervention can significantly alter the customer's perception of the brand.
Tips	Use journey maps to • Highlight opportunities to create positive moments of truth. • Identify gaps during transitions between channels, devices, and departments. • Provide a consistent customer experience regardless of channel, device, or department.
Deliverables	Journey map: Stages, actions, touchpoints, thoughts, and feelings of the customer.

10.14.1 Overview of the Customer Journey Map

A customer journey map is a model that provides a 360-degree view of a customer's engagement with a company or product over time. Customer journey maps depict the

- Steps taken by the customer.
- Touchpoints between the customer and the company (or product).
- Goals, thoughts, and feelings of the customer at each step and transition.

The customer experience depicted on the map should be based on market research data so that it accurately reflects customer attitudes. The value of journey maps is that, like personas, they bring this data to life. By telling the story of a customer's interactions with the product over time, a journey map provides insight into customer motivations and highlights opportunities to improve the customer experience.

10.14.2 Customer Journey Map: Mortgage Example

The following is an example of journey mapping by teams currently working on an automated self-service website for home-mortgage applications. The site's objectives are to reduce costs to the bank through automation and increase revenues by attracting more customers. No customers will be forced to use the new system: it is hoped that a significant portion will do so voluntarily because of the convenience it provides. The teams are developing a customer journey for each of two personas, *Mary the Existing Customer* and *Joan the Prospect*.

Mary represents an existing customer who already has a mortgage with the bank. Mary's journey map describes her migration to the self-service site as her mortgage comes up for renewal. Through journey mapping, the group hopes to discover opportunities to maximize customers' conversion rate from the old to the new system and ease the transition.

Joan represents a prospect with no current business with the bank. Joan's journey map describes the stages she goes through as she searches for a competitive mortgage and submits a mortgage application using the new site. By analyzing Joan's journey, the group hopes to create customer experiences that will increase the number of new customers brought into the company.

10.14.3 Components of a Journey Map

There is no single, universal template for drawing a journey map. However, there are some common components:

- A lens or persona
- Stages
- Touchpoints
- Thoughts and feelings
- Opportunities (pain points, moments of truth)

Figure 10.7 is an example of a journey map template that incorporates common elements.

The stages in Figure 10.7 indicate high-level customer activities (e.g., researching and purchasing). The rows describe aspects of the customer experience (e.g., thinking and feeling). Let's look at the meaning of these elements and how you use them to develop the map.

10.14.3.1 Determine the Scope of the Map

The first step in developing a journey map is to determine its **scope**. Examples of scope for a journey map include

- An entire customer lifecycle from the customer's first contact with the brand to customer offboarding.
- The steps leading up to a decision to purchase.
- The response to an event or incident report.

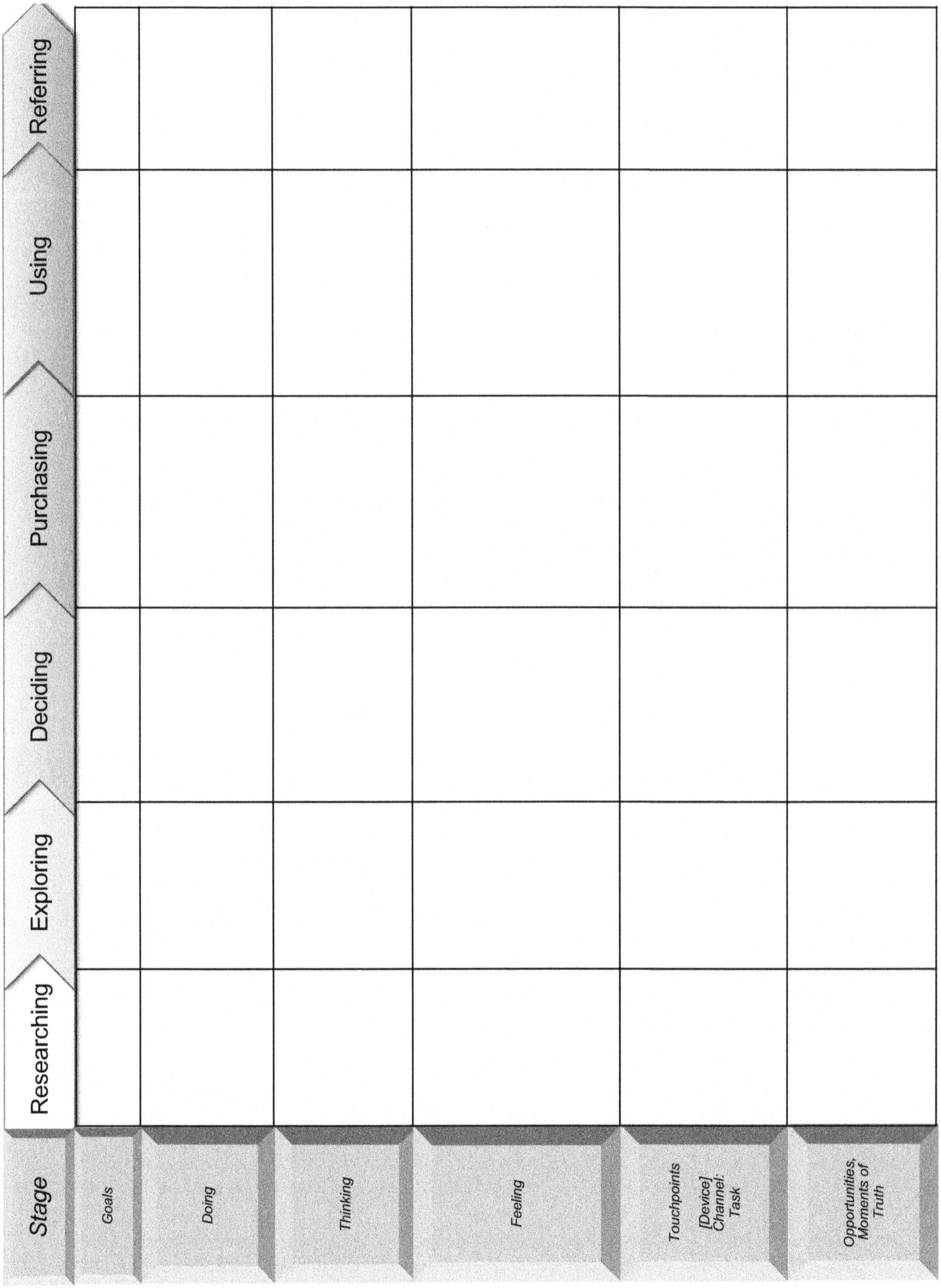

Stage	Researching	Exploring	Deciding	Purchasing	Using	Referring
Goals						
Doing						
Thinking						
Feeling						
Touchpoints [Device] Channel: Task						
Opportunities, Moments of Truth						

Figure 10.7 *Journey map template with stages based on activities*

10.14.3.2 Lens or Persona

The **lens** is the "filter"[8] through which the customer journey is experienced. Specify a *persona* as the lens if the purpose of the exercise is to explore the experiences of a subset of customers and measure them against customer expectations. You may also specify the following as the lens:

- A user role (e.g., sales agent, manager)

- Target market

- Participant in a business process (e.g., approver)

The lens in all of the preceding examples represented a segment of the market. What if the objective is to explore touchpoints common to *all* customers? In that case, specify the perspective from which the touchpoints will be evaluated, such as the company's commitment to empower its care professionals "to do what's right for the customer."[9]

10.14.3.3 Stages

Next, determine the **stages**, or phases, along the journey. There is no rule about how to name these stages. The stages may be named after high-level customer activities (e.g., researching) or high-level goals and outcomes (e.g., find the best price). Alternatively, a stage may refer to a customer state (e.g., loyal customer) or a phase of the customer lifecycle. Following is an example of a journey map's stages, based on customer lifecycle phases. The first five stages are noted in "Understanding the Customer Lifecycle Management Process in 5 Easy Steps":[10]

- Reach: The company reaches out to the prospect (e.g., through ads and email).

- Acquisition: First contact is made between the prospect and the company.

- Conversion: The prospect is converted into a customer; a sale is made.

- Retention: The customer is engaged in continuing business with the company.

- Loyalty: The customer is an active ambassador for the company.

---

8. Chris Risdon, "The Anatomy of an Experience Map," UIE, November 30, 2011, https://articles.uie.com/experience_map

9. "To do what's right for the customer" is reported to be a value of American Express. See interview with Raymond Joabar, EVP, Global Servicing Network, American Express Company: Micah Solomon, "American Express's Customer Service Approach: What Customers Care about Today," *Forbes*, December 15, 2017, https://www.forbes.com/sites/micahsolomon/2017/12/15/american-expresss-customer-service-secrets-consulting-with-amex-on-what-makes-a-difference/#31065f9b40ff

10. Jessica Wise, "Understanding the Customer Lifecycle Management Process in 5 Easy Steps" [blog post], Live Help Now, July 2, 2019, https://www.livehelpnow.net/blog/understanding-customer-lifecycle-management-5-easy-steps

- Loss: The customer is lost, whether voluntarily or otherwise. Include the loss stage to ensure the impact of a change on terminated customers is considered (e.g., so that terminated customers don't continue to receive announcements).

Following is an example of a journey map's stages based on the *activities* the customer is engaged in:[11]

- Researching: The customer researches competitors across attributes such as cost, features, ratings, and reviews.
- Exploring: The customer explores the features of the product or service.
- Deciding: The customer decides to acquire the product or service.
- Purchasing: The customer pays for the product or otherwise completes the transaction to order the product (e.g., by committing to a monthly subscription).
- Using: The customer uses the product. The experience builds loyalty toward the company and product.
- Referring: Due to positive customer experiences, the customer refers others to the product.
- Leaving: The customer is leaving the company (e.g., canceling the account or subscription).

Use the preceding examples as a rough guide, keeping in mind that actual stage names may differ according to the map's nature and scope.

10.14.3.4 Actions (Doing)

Next, investigate the **actions** the customer is taking at each stage, such as the following:

- Email the company
- Speak to friends
- Search for the product on the Web
- Call customer service
- Place an order
- Report an incident

Describe these actions using text or graphics. The benefit of text over graphics is that it's easy to document. Use graphics to convey nonsequential flows (e.g., loops, concurrency).

---

11. See Visual Paradigm, "What Is Customer Journey Mapping?" https://www.visual-paradigm.com/guide/customer-experience/what-is-customer-journey-mapping. Also see Margaret Rouse, Lauren Horwitz, and Jesse Scardina, "Customer Journey Map," Tech Target, June 2017, https://searchcustomerexperience.techtarget.com/definition/customer-journey-map

10.14.3.5 Touchpoints

Define the touchpoints for each stage. A **touchpoint** is an interaction a customer has with the company or product. Characterize each touchpoint according to its device, channel, and task.

> The **device** is the apparatus used during the interaction—such as a laptop, mobile device, or tablet. Each device may support multiple channels.

> A **channel** is a mechanism used for the interaction, such as a website, an app, direct messaging, a social media platform, live chat, or email.

> A **task** is the specific user activity being performed on the channel, such as "Submit an order."

10.14.3.6 Thoughts and Feelings

Provide insight into customers' motivations as they interact with the product at touchpoints along the journey map. What are their rational **thoughts**? For example, are they evaluating the company's reputation for service against competitors?

Describe what the customer is **feeling**. For example, the customer may feel disrespected because turnaround time is so poor.

Insights about thoughts and feelings help guide the determination of which touchpoints to focus on during the quarter or release cycle.

10.14.3.7 Opportunities (Pain Points, Moments of Truth)

Specify opportunities to improve the experience, such as pain points and moments of truth. A *moment of truth* is a critical interaction between the customer and the company or product that forms a lasting impression.

10.14.4 Using the Journey Map

Use journey maps for the following analysis purposes:

- *To inform investment in product development*—journey maps help business stakeholders make better investment decisions. They do so by providing a holistic view of the customer experience over time across channels and highlighting moments of truth.

- *To identify gaps* as the customer transitions between channels, devices, and departments.

- To provide a *consistent customer experience* across touchpoints.

- To discover opportunities to *improve conversion rates* (browsers to shoppers) and *increase referral rates*.

- *To improve the customer experience* when a customer reports an issue or incident.

- *To build story maps*: Story maps are tools for planning an upcoming quarter or feature set. Use the journey map's **actions** as the basis for constructing the story map's **backbone**—the section that lays out user tasks in the order they are typically performed.

- *To flag the need for process improvement*—for example, the map may indicate customer frustration due to long turnaround times at a touchpoint where an incident is reported. This, in turn, flags the need to analyze and improve the company's incident management process.

Revisit the journey map after the change has been implemented. Has the intervention moved the needle? Are there touchpoints that still need to be improved? Revise the journey map in line with the new data. Repeat the process.

BLINK CASE STUDY PART 14

Journey Maps

Background

The business has decided that the focus of the next release will be on converting those who are currently BL customers to the BLInK program.

The Ask

As team analyst, you've been asked to facilitate a workshop to create a journey map. It will explore opportunities to optimize the customer experience in order to maximize the conversion rate. The deliverable from the workshop will be

- **Deliverable 1:** Journey map describing the journey from prospect to customer.

Preparation

You invite Marketing SMEs, the product manager, data analysts, and the team to the workshop.

As inputs to the meeting, you post the personas previously developed for the initiative (Figures 10.5 and 10.6) and the proposed goals and features for the release, as indicated on the product roadmap.

Before the meeting, you prepare a blank journey map according to the template in Figure 10.8.

What Transpires

You first explain the purpose of the meeting—to create a journey map to guide product development.

Journey Map Preparation

You begin by facilitating a discussion of the scope. Attendees agree that they want the map to examine the BLInK customer lifecycle through to the stage where customer loyalty has been attained.

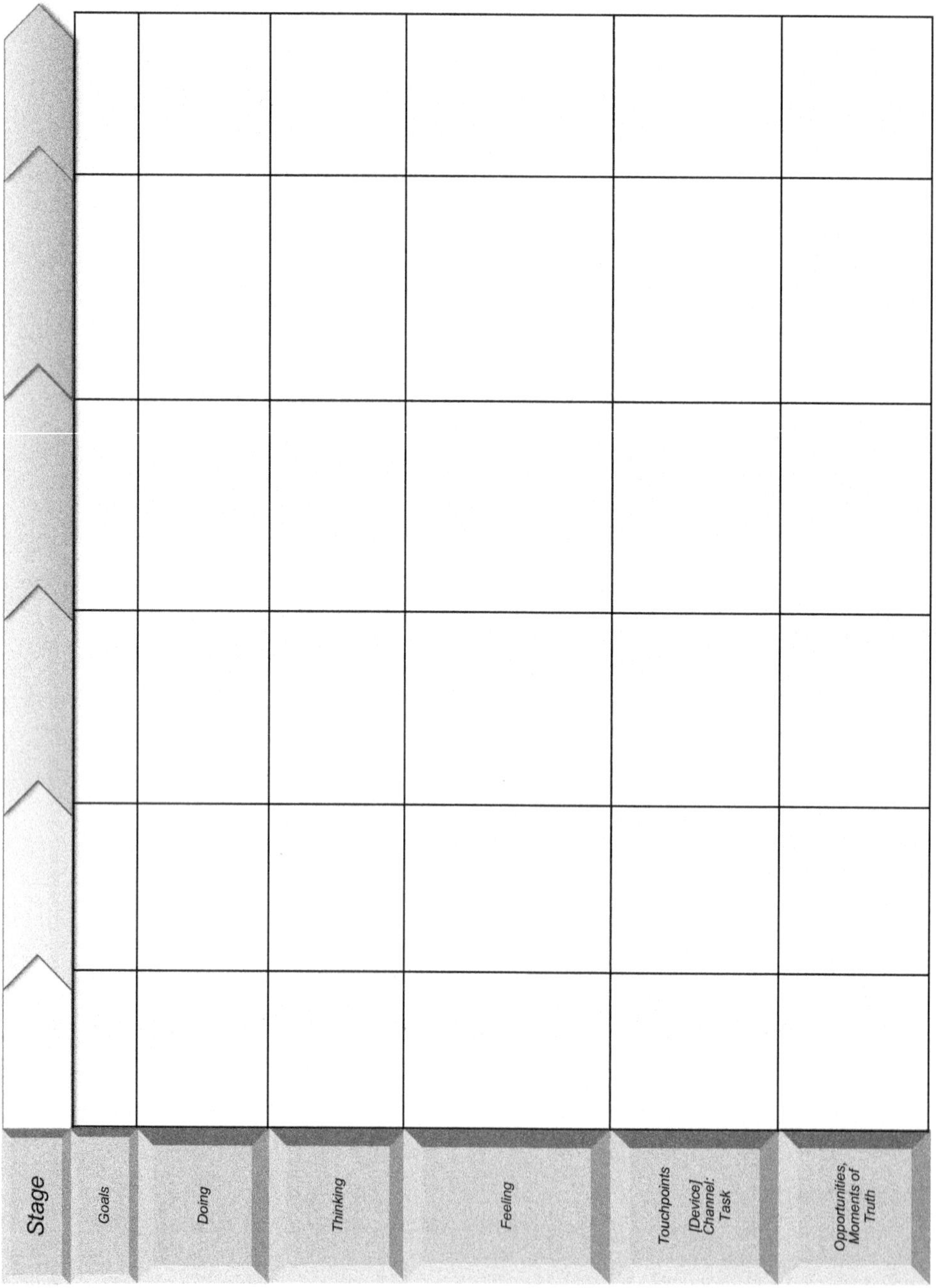

Figure 10.8 *Journey map template with unnamed stages*

The journey map template columns are labeled: Stage, Goals, Doing, Thinking, Feeling, Touchpoints [Device] Channel; Task, Opportunities, Moments of Truth

Determining the Lens

You move on to a discussion of the lens. You review the Aisha persona, a current BL customer interested in improving her diet and exercise, and Mike, a heavy smoker who is not currently a BL customer.

Attendees agree that the release should focus on current BL subscribers. Accordingly, the Aisha persona is chosen as the lens.

Since the journey taken by noncustomers is quite different, another journey map will be created for the Mike persona. However, that map will be deferred until a later release, when the analysis will be more relevant.

Determining the Stages

Next, you turn to the stages of the journey. Attendees agree to name the stages according to Aisha's high-level goals. The stages are as follows:

- *Research the market* to learn about available options for improving her diet and exercise levels.
- *Assess the solution* to see if it is right for her.
- *Start a trial.* Accept an offer to try the program with no obligation to commit.
- *Try the offering.* Use BLInK over a six-month evaluation period.
- *Enroll.* Commit to the BLInK offering.
- *Post-sales.* Become a loyal ambassador for the program.

Analyzing the Stages

With the stages identified, you facilitate a discussion of each of the columns for Stage 1: Research the market. You review the customer's goals for this stage. A primary goal is to research health-improvement options. Marketers suggest a touchpoint: BL would reach out to Aisha through emails with links to learn more about the program. You ask the group to consider Aisha's thoughts and feelings at this touchpoint. You learn from data analysts that Aisha wants to improve her health but currently lacks the motivation to make the first move. Attendees note that this is a moment of truth to excite the customer with an offer that provides an immediate incentive for positive action. You continue in this way with the rest of the stages until the journey map is complete.

Deliverables

You produce the following deliverable:

Deliverable 1: Aisha's Journey Map

The journey map for Aisha is shown in Figure 10.9.

Case Study Retrospective

Through this analysis, you learned that existing BL customers are concerned about data privacy protection and that the provision of immediate benefits would be an excitement attractor at this touchpoint. Insights such as these will help direct the prioritization of features for the upcoming release and those that follow.

Stage	Research market	Assess solution	Start trial	Try offering (6-month evaluation)	Enroll	Post-sales
Goals	Research health-improvement options	Determine if BLInK is right for me	Accept trial	Start using BLInK to make improvements	Make decision to extend program beyond trial	Maintain fitness goals
Doing	• Web search • Talk with colleagues • Respond to email invite	Attends lunch meeting at work about BLInK	• Visits site • Requests free trial • Verifies acceptance	• Walks more • Enters meals • Tracks daily progress • Works out at gym	• Opts in to permanent program	• Continues workout • Joins food-retailer program • Refers others
Thinking	• How effective is this? • What are costs and benefits?	• How long until I earn benefits, improve fitness? • What rewards can I earn?	• Why should I do this now? • How easy will it be to opt out?	• Am I reaching my fitness goals? • How many calories did I burn? • How many rewards have I earned?	• Did I reach my goals? • What financial benefits did I receive? • How do I cancel if I decide I want to quit?	• Am I gaining weight? • How do I stick with it for the long haul?
Feeling	• Wants to do improve health but lacks motivation • Worries about "body-shaming"	• Insurance companies don't have my best interests at heart • Apprehensive about privacy invasion	• This will fail like everything I've tried in the past • Hesitant about signing up for something she may regret	• Apprehensive about starting an exercise program after years of neglect	• Happy with progress to date • Still apprehensive she might regret her decision later	• So excited by her progress that she wants to tell others about the program
Touchpoint [Device] Channel] Task	• Email: "Learn more" link • Portal, email: Event signup • App: Install; notification	• Lunch meeting (on-site)	• Portal, app: sign up for free trial	• [Digital scale]: weight tracker • [Fitness tracker]: Step count, calories • App: View fitness levels; manage goals	• Automatic conversion at 6 months • Portal, app: Manage my account	• [Point of sale (barcode)] • App: Track calories; weekly offers • Email: Special offers
Moment of Truth	• Highlight inclusive, anti-body-shaming culture • Highlight immediate benefits	• Speakers who have benefited • Privacy guarantees by trusted third party	• Immediate and permanent rate reduction at sign-up	• Offer the best gym membership discounts in the market	• Free diet and exercise consult on enrollment • No cancellation penalty	• Free gear for referrals • Weekly discounts at participating retailers

Figure 10.9   BLInK journey map (Aisha)

10.14.5 More on Journey Maps

For more information and examples regarding customer journeys, see "The Customer Journey,"[12] "Customer Journey Mapping Examples,"[13] and "How to Create a Customer Journey Map."[14]

10.15 Value Stream Mapping

A **value stream map** is a lean model used to highlight and reduce waste, shorten cycle times, and optimize processes.[15] A **value stream** is an end-to-end workflow that begins with a trigger (e.g., a customer requests a product) and ends in value delivery. It includes the sequence of steps for delivering value and the people required to carry them out. **Operational value streams** deliver value to an end user of the product (e.g., a product is delivered to a customer). **Development value streams** deliver solutions that enable operational value streams (e.g., delivery of an order-processing system).[16]

Similar in form to a block diagram, a value stream map illustrates a progression of steps or stations connected by arrows. Value stream maps also include metrics for the time spent productively and unproductively at each station. Table 10.3 summarizes the technique.

Table 10.3 *Value Stream Maps at a Glance*

What?	Value stream map: A lean, SAFe tool used to model and measure a workflow that ends with value delivery.
When?	When preparing to optimize a business process.
Why?	Identifies waste so it can be removed.
Tips	Use analytics and interviews to gather metrics about activity times.
Deliverables	Value stream map, identifying the steps of the process, time spent actively working and waiting at each step.

---

12. Christine Churchill, "The Customer Journey" [blog post], Customer Service Institute of America (CSIA), October 20, 2017, https://www.serviceinstitute.com/2017/10/20/the-customer-journey

13. Roxana Nasoi, "6 Customer Journey Mapping Examples: How UX Pros Do It" [blog post], CXL Institute, August 31, 2018, https://cxl.com/blog/customer-journey-mapping-examples

14. Megan Grocki, "How to Create a Customer Journey Map," UX Mastery, September 16, 2014, https://uxmastery.com/how-to-create-a-customer-journey-map

15. "What Is Value Stream Mapping (VSM)?" American Association for Quality, 2020, https://asq.org/quality-resources/lean/value-stream-mapping

16. "Identify Value Streams and ARTs," Scaled Agile Inc., September 28, 2019, https://www.scaledagileframework.com/identify-value-streams-and-arts

Reasons for performing value stream mapping include the following:

- Process optimization and reengineering

- Process automation

- Compliance requirements (e.g., conformity with a General Data Protection Regulation [GDPR] requirement to respond to a subject access request [SAR] within a month of receiving it)

When using value stream mapping for process optimization, first create a current-state model to highlight bottlenecks and opportunities for improvements. Then develop future-state models to simulate and evaluate solution proposals.

10.15.1 Developing a Value Stream Map

To create a value stream map, first determine the steps or stations in the workflow (e.g., submit an order, assemble an order, pick up an order). Next, interview workers at each station and collect metrics. Track the time spent at each station *actively* working (performing activities that add value) and *waiting* (representing waste).

Adjust the process to reduce waste. Collect metrics again, and analyze the results to gauge the effectiveness of the intervention. Repeat until the process has been optimized.

Figure 10.10 illustrates a value stream map for processing an order.

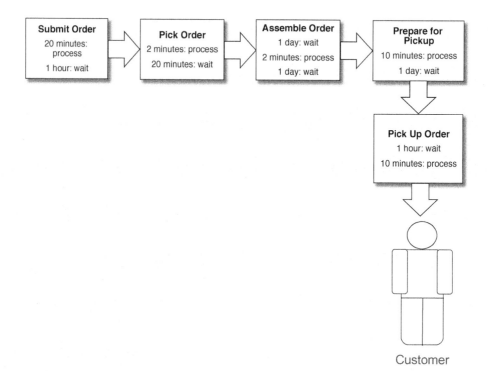

Figure 10.10 *Value stream map for placing an order*

According to Figure 10.10, the turnaround time for an average order is approximately three days, only 44 minutes of which are spent actively processing the order. The rest is waste. The most promising opportunities to reduce turnaround time are Assemble Order and Prepare for Pickup, since they are the primary contributors to waste in the process.

10.16 Business Process Modeling

The modeling elements of value stream mapping are sufficient for indicating overall workflow. However, they lack nuance regarding the timing rules and conditions that govern its steps. Use business process models to express those nuances when a workflow must be rigorously followed (e.g., to comply with government guidelines). Let's examine one of the most widely used standards, **Business Process Model and Notation** (BPMN). Table 10.4 summarizes the technique.

Table 10.4 *Process Models at a Glance*

What?	**Business process model:** A representation of a business process, typically in the form of a diagram. The model indicates the workflow (sequencing of activities) within the process.
When?	To prepare for process optimization or the implementation of a new process.
Why?	For gap analysis. To prepare for a process optimization initiative. To merge two processes (e.g., due to a business merger). To document standard operating procedures.
Tips	Don't try to boil the ocean. Do just enough analysis for the next one or two quarters or release cycles.
Deliverables	*Public and private process models.* Public models depict the external façade (touchpoints) of the process. Private models describe internal steps.

10.16.1 Bring Process Participants Together

It often takes multiple participants to carry out a process. While each may understand their part of the process, their understanding of other aspects can be limited. As an analyst, this presents a challenge, because you have to put together a comprehensive picture of the whole process from these disjointed views. It's like the fable in which people are asked to describe an elephant after feeling one part of it in the dark. The most efficient way to address this issue is to bring together representatives of all process participants so that their perspectives can be consolidated and reconciled on the spot.

10.16.2 What Situations Call for Process Modeling?

One of my aims in writing this book is to reintroduce "classic" but valuable analysis tools, such as process modeling, to agile teams that don't yet use them. Reasons for using process modeling include:

- **To prepare end-to-end UAT:** Model an end-to-end process in order to identify integration points, and specify scenarios for integration testing and end-to-end UAT.

- **To prepare for process optimization/reengineering:** Model a current process to highlight bottlenecks and opportunities for efficiency improvements. Then, create to-be models to simulate and evaluate solution proposals.

- **When changing a step in a larger process:** Model a complete process to assess the impact of a change on other steps in the workflow.

- **To merge processes:** Model each of the processes that will be merged. Perform a gap analysis to identify discrepancies and recommend solutions. Create a to-be model for the merged process. Contexts for merging processes include
  - A merger between companies that use different systems or processes.
  - To replace multiple data sources with a single source of truth.
  - To eliminate the overhead of supporting multiple systems.
  - To design new business processes.

- **When outsourcing an existing service or process:** Create models that communicate message and data flows between internal systems and third-party services.

- **Internet of Things (IoT) development:** Use process maps such as block diagrams and Unified Modeling Language (UML) communication diagrams[17] to specify how devices will interact with each other.

- **To document standard operating procedures:** Use process models to analyze and communicate standard operating procedures to support repeatability.

10.16.3 Screenshots Do Not a Process Model Make

It's tempting to use screenshots of existing systems as current-state process models, but they don't serve the same purpose, as the following story illustrates. My company was asked by a communications company to review requirements specifications for replacing its geographical information system (GIS). The system was used by many business processes, for example, to plan the installation of communication towers. Our consultant asked if he could view models of the affected processes. He was assured that the models existed, but they were never presented to him, so he noted the omission as a requirements risk. We later learned that the purported models were screenshots. Unfortunately,

---

17. For more on UML diagrams, see Howard Podeswa, *UML for the IT Business Analyst: A Practical Guide to Object-Oriented Requirements Gathering*, 2nd ed. (Independence, KY: Cengage, 2009).

screenshots don't replace process models. In one sense, they are too *detailed*—since they show user interfaces that can't easily be compared to another solution. At the same time, they don't tell you enough—since they only indicate what the user *experiences*, not what is going on behind the scenes. The omission resulted in missed integration requirements that the company had to pay dearly for when it discovered, after purchasing a solution, that the system only supported asynchronous integration, whereas synchronous (real-time) integration was required. Had a few days been spent modeling the processes that used the GIS, the analysis would have revealed the missing integration requirements so that they could be included in the specifications.

10.16.4 Do Just Enough Analysis for Your Purposes

Try not to spend too much time on the as-is model; focus most of your effort on the to-be model because that's where the value lies.

Adjust the level of analysis to the circumstance. If you're building a process model to understand dependencies for release planning, you probably don't need to include precise workflow logic. But if you're reengineering a business process whose workflow rules must be consistently enforced, you'll need to build a more detailed model.

10.16.5 Models with and without Swimlanes

Most process modeling notations provide the option of reserving a column or row for each participant. These are referred to as **lanes**. A process model with lanes is sometimes referred to as a **swimlane-workflow** or **multifunctional flowchart** diagram. Each activity is placed in the lane of the participant who performs it. A **participant** may be a human role or a software system.

10.16.6 BPMN

The most widely used standard[18] for drawing business process workflow models is BPMN, maintained by the Object Management Group (OMG). It's worth noting, though, that the most popular *practice*—at least based on my own unscientific observation—is not to use *any* standard at all and rely on informal flowcharting symbols such as diamonds and arrows. This practice is adequate for many business analysis purposes, but if you need precision, use a standard, since it's not open to misinterpretation.

Reasons to select the BPMN standard over others include the following:

- BPMN has a rich symbol set that elegantly handles a broader range of situations than most other standards.

- BPMN is widely used—meaning it has strong support in terms of software tools and analysts who know how to use the models.

---

18. Object Management Group, *Business Process Model and Notation (BPMN™)*, January 2014, https://www.omg.org/spec/BPMN

BPMN offers a number of ways to model a process. Chief among them are the *public process model*, providing a high-level external view, and the *private process model*, providing a more detailed internal view. Typically, you begin with a public process model and, if necessary, refine it over time into a private process model.

10.16.6.1 BPMN Public Process Model

The **BPMN public process model** is an external view of a process. It focuses on touchpoints between the business and external entities while hiding internal steps. An **external entity** may be any organization, person, or system outside the organization (or system) under discussion (e.g., a customer, a supplier, an external system, or a third-party software service).

The organization (or system) under discussion is represented as a **pool**, as are the external entities it interacts with. A pool is indicated as a large rectangle.

A **message flow** (shown as a dashed arrow with a triangular arrowhead) indicates communication between pools. A message flow may represent a service request or information sent electronically or manually (e.g., snail mail).

Public Process Model Examples

Figure 10.11 is an example of a public process model depicting the process for handling an insurance claim. It illustrates the main elements of a public process model.

There are four **pools** in the figure—the claims system under development, the customer, the policy management system, and finance. A thin-lined circle indicates the start of the process. This element is referred to as the **start event**. Endpoints—referred to **end events**—are indicated by a thick-lined circle. You can include more than one start and end event in the model. For example, a replenishment process may have two start events: it is invoked by an internal user and automatically triggered when inventory falls below a trigger level. It may also have two endpoints—one ending successfully and the other unsuccessfully.

Each rounded rectangle depicts an **activity**. Solid-lined arrows represent **sequence flows**, indicating the direction of time. The diamond is a **gateway**—a decision point in the process. I've included one in the example because it makes the model more understandable, but gateways are commonly absent from public models.

The model in Figure 10.11 describes how external entities experience the business process for managing a claim. The first touchpoint is when a customer sends a claim to the claims organization. The receipt of the claim triggers the process. The next touchpoint occurs during the verify policy coverage step: claims sends a message to policy management with a request to check coverage. At other touchpoints toward the end of the process, claims sends claim resolution messages to the customer. Finally, in cases where a claim is covered, claims sends a message to finance to issue payment against the claim. There are other steps internal to the process, but they are not included in the public model because external entities don't experience them.

Figure 10.12 is an example of a public process model for the CEO example we've been following. An analyst at CEO has created the model in preparation for a release that integrates the product with two third-party entities—Zendesk and email.

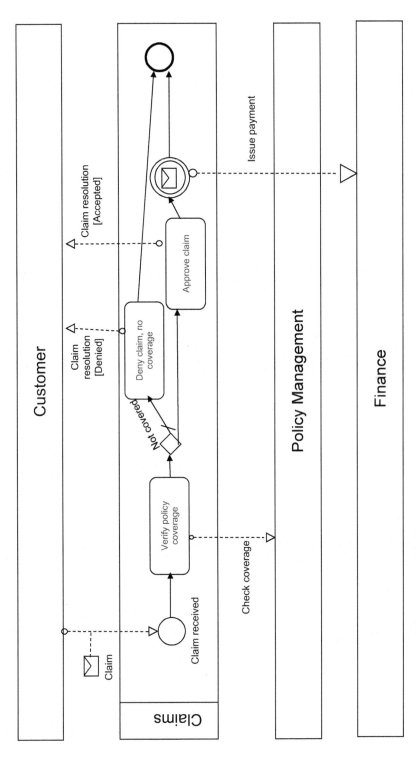

Figure 10.11 *Public BPMN model for claims system*

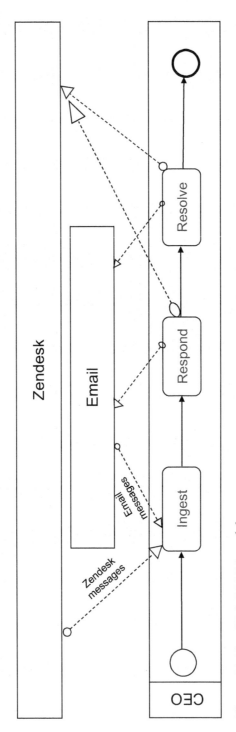

Figure 10.12 *CEO BPMN model*

The model presents just enough information to identify the touchpoints between CEO and the third-party entities, the overall sequencing of these touchpoints, and the possible dependencies among them. For example, *Resolve* is dependent on *Respond*, which is dependent on *Ingest*.

BLINK CASE STUDY PART 15

BLInK Public Process Model

Background

On the journey map you created earlier (Figure 10.9), you identified a touchpoint, *Sign Up for Free Trial*. Business stakeholders now want to implement this touchpoint in the first release. The goal of the release is to implement the entire end-to-end process it triggers—even if only for a narrow scenario—right through to the point when the end customer receives an activated BLInK device. A device may be any object (e.g., fitness tracker, app-enabled mobile phone) used to transmit health data.

The Ask

The PO has asked you to do a first-pass analysis of this process in preparation for the first release cycle. The team will use the deliverables to design proofs of concept to validate the viability of proposed integration mechanisms. The expected deliverable is

- **Deliverable 1:** BPMN public process model for processing BLInK application

What Transpires

You invite the product manager, process owner, and SMEs with insight into device vendors and interfaces to attend a group workshop to analyze the end-to-end BLInK application and activation process.

During the workshop, you learn that the vendor will be responsible for managing the device and detailed data collection and analysis. BL Inc. will receive only summaries of this information. The process begins when BL receives an Application and Health Assessment from a primary subscriber. The vendor plays a part in validating eligibility for the device. At the end of the underwriting step, a request is sent to the vendor to initialize the device. Later, another request goes out to the vendor to begin streaming data to the device.

Deliverables

The following deliverable was created:

Deliverable 1: BLInK Public Process
Figure 10.13 illustrates the BPMN public process model for the process "Enroll in BLInK Program."

Case Study Retrospective

As a result of the process analysis, you specify that the solution must have the capability to interface with the vendor in the provision of three services—to validate eligibility, initialize the device, and begin data streaming.

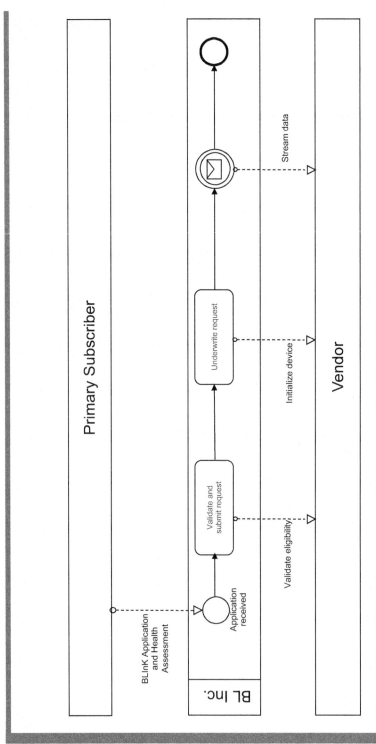

Figure 10.13   BPMN public process model for the process "Enroll in BLInK Program"

10.16.6.2 BPMN *Private Process Model*

What if a process change results in new or changed internal steps that the solution must support? In that case, analyze how the steps connect *before* implementation begins so you can ensure that they'll fit together when assembled. To do that, you need to construct a private process model because it includes internal steps.

Private Process Model Example

Figure 10.14 illustrates a proposed to-be claims process whereby customers submit claims through a self-service site.

The top pool models the workflow of the customer: The customer logs in and manages her profile. Next, she submits a claim. During this user task, a *message* is sent to policy management to verify coverage (e.g., to check if the policy covers the claim category). Also, the claim is sent to the claims department at this time and picked up by a claims supervisor.

From the perspective of the claims department, the first step is for adjusters to post their availability so that they may be assigned to a claim. Next, they view their schedule for the day. A claims supervisor queries the claims sent from the customer through the self-service site. The supervisor schedules adjusters to work on the claims. The adjuster reviews the claim, submits an adjustment, and may revise it. Then, a claims manager performs a final adjudication, at which time a message is sent to the customer regarding the resolution of the claim. If the claim has been approved, a message to issue payment is sent to the finance department.

10.16.6.3 BPMN Modeling Elements

Figure 10.14 includes some of the main components of a BPMN model:

- **Start Event:** Begins the process. There may be multiple start events, one for each way the process may be triggered (e.g., a process may be activated in response to a customer request or internally triggered).
- **End Event:** Ends the process. There may be multiple end events, one for each possible ending (e.g., transaction successful, transaction rejected, and transaction canceled).
- **Intermediate Event:** A point at which the process sends an event or receives an event. A symbol may be placed inside an event to characterize the event type (e.g., the envelope symbol may be used inside an intermediate event to indicate the sending or receiving of a message).
- **Sequence Flow:** Indicates the sequence in which elements are executed.
- **Activity:** Work performed in a process. It may be a task—an atomic step—or a complex subprocess decomposed into tasks.
- **Exclusive Gateway:** Decision.
- **Message Flow:** Indicates communication between two pools.
- **Pool:** Independent organization, external software system or component.
- **Lane:** Indicates a process participant within a pool (organization).

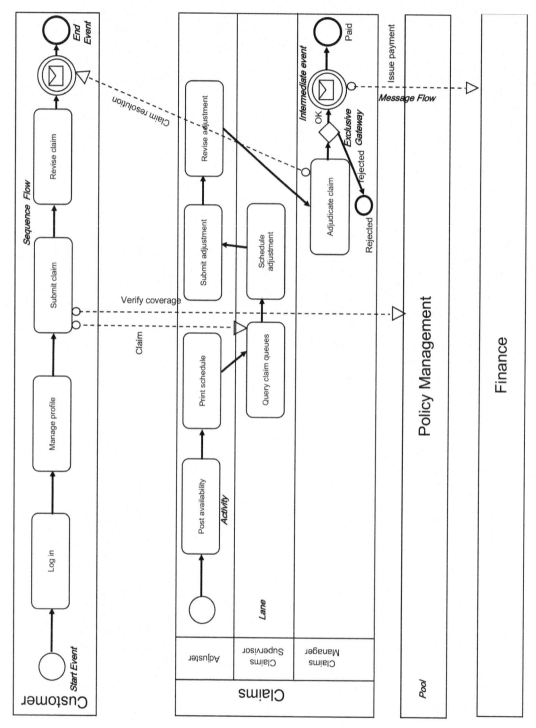

Figure 10.14 *Private BPMN model for claims process*

Note also how Figure 10.14 models an entire end-to-end value stream: it begins with a customer goal—a request to process a claim—and ends with that goal being satisfied. This is precisely the scope you should be first considering when analyzing processes, since it is only when the goal is reached that the process ends from the customer point of view.

If you discover a complex activity within the process, indicate it as a subprocess using the collapsed subprocess icon (a plus sign inside a square). Describe the subprocess in its own diagram.

Figure 10.15 illustrates a few more BPMN symbols that are useful as you add more detail to the model.

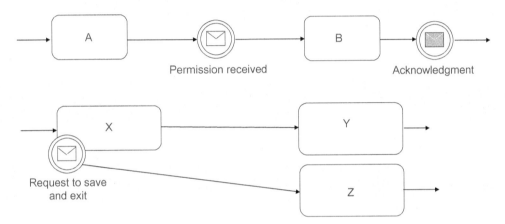

Figure 10.15 *BPMN events*

Symbols illustrated in Figure 10.15 include the following:

- **Catch Event:** Indicates that an event (e.g., a message) is received. For example, in the figure, "Permission received" is a catch event. To model a catch event, place a line-drawing version of the event icon at the center of the symbol.

- **Send Event:** Indicates a point in the process where an event is sent out—for example, data is transmitted or a digital request is sent to a software interface. To indicate a send event, draw the icon in the center of the event as a solid symbol, as shown for "Acknowledgment" in Figure 10.15.

BPMN provides the ability to model nuances in the timing of caught events. For example, in the upper diagram of Figure 10.15, activity A runs to completion before the process responds to the message "Permission received." The activity isn't interrupted—even if the message arrives in the middle of it.

In the lower diagram, however, the response to an incoming message is immediate: at *any point during* activity X, if the message "Request to save and exit" arrives, the activity is interrupted, and Z is executed. On the other hand, if the message does not arrive, X continues to completion, followed by activity Y. The catch event *Request to save and exit* is referred to as a *boundary event*. As its name suggests, it's drawn on the boundary (border) of the activity it interrupts.

BLInK Private Process Model

Background

In the first release, teams will be implementing the process to apply for the BLInK program.

The Ask

You have been asked to model the BLInK application process, so that it is well-enough understood for release planning to commence. The deliverable of the analysis will be used to plan the implementation of user tasks in the upcoming release cycle.

- **Deliverable 1:** BPMN private process model for the end-to-end process to enroll in the BLInK program

Preparation

As input for the analysis, you use the public process model for enrolling in the BLInK program, derived previously (see Figure 10.13).

Taking a lean approach, you plan to do only enough process analysis to support release planning needs. You'll focus on the overall sequencing of activities and handoffs but avoid detailed workflow analysis for now.

The first release will deliver operational BLInK devices to customers. Accordingly, you set the analysis scope to cover all steps from the submission of a BLInK application until the delivery of a working device.

What Transpires

You begin by interviewing SMEs about the participants required to process a BLInK application. You learn that these include the primary subscriber (an external participant) and the underwriter, actuary, and agent (internal participants). From your prior analysis, you learned that the device vendor also participates in this process to validate eligibility, initialize the device, and send a trigger to the device to begin streaming data.

You convene a process analysis workshop, inviting the product-level PO, process owner, and representatives of underwriters, actuaries, agents, team POs, and vendor SMEs.

With their input, you build a consolidated model of the process. You learn that the customer's first touchpoint is with the agent who receives the BLInK Application and Health Assessment. The agent validates the request using a vendor service. If the customer has a negative record resulting from prior device usage, the service invalidates the request, and the device is not issued. If the request is valid, the agent submits it forward for the next step, underwriting.

After an underwriter underwrites the application, a request is sent out to the vendor to initialize the device, followed by a message to begin streaming data—at which point the process ends. Actuaries report that they will need to set BLInK risk and pricing guidelines before the underwriting of BLInK applications begins.

Deliverables

The following deliverable was created:

Deliverable 1: BPMN Private Model—Enroll in BLInK Program

Figure 10.16 illustrates the BPMN private process model for the process "Enroll in BLInK program."

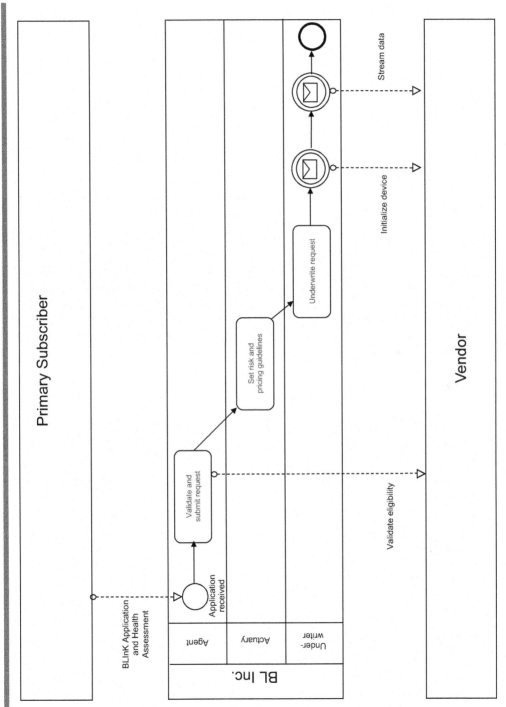

Figure 10.16 BPMN private process model for the process "Enroll in BLInK program"

Case Study Retrospective

In this workshop, you performed just enough preliminary analysis to understand the main user activities and handoffs for managing a BLINK application—the process planned for the next release. The deliverable you've created will be used during release (quarterly) planning to develop a story map and plan the incremental implementation of user tasks to support the process.

10.17 Use-Case Modeling

A **use-case model** consists of diagrams and supporting specifications. A **use-case diagram** is a picture that associates user roles and external systems with their usages of the product. In other words, the diagram shows who does what. On a use-case diagram drawn from a system perspective, each use case represents a user task—a unit of work (or goal) that a user expects to achieve during a single interaction with a software system or product. (The preceding definition applies to a typical use case. Use cases can also be defined for higher- and lower-level goals.) The full set of use cases for a product represents all the ways that the product is used. Each use case may be further described in a use-case specification—documentation that may include a combination of text and diagrams.

The best way to use use-case modeling in agile development is to develop the model first and use that to plan and drive development, revising the model as you go. This is the approach I often used in the past when working with Rational Unified Process (RUP) teams. I believe it's still a valuable approach because it provides an overview of product usage and a framework from which to build out and organize features and stories. You represent each use case as a feature, for example, creating a Gherkin feature file for it. You represent the smaller work items to implement them as user stories or use-case slices (using the terminology of Use Case 2.0). However, in practice, I've observed that the process usually happens the other way around: the use-case models and specifications are created *after* implementation—to be used for future reference. It's useful but not ideal. At the very least, the analyst should endeavor to ensure the diagrams and specifications are updated as each story is done rather than wait until a production release.

If you're preparing a change to an existing product, check to see if use-case models already exist. If they do, review them. They'll help you determine which users will be affected by changes to the product. The specifications tell you which flows are currently supported and how. Update the model to indicate the future state, including new use cases and user roles that will be supported.

10.17.1 Use-Case Modeling Example: Claims

Let's return to the claims processing private model depicted in Figure 10.14. Based on the process model, you create a use-case model summarizing the user tasks (use cases) that will be supported by the solution. The model is shown in Figure 10.17.

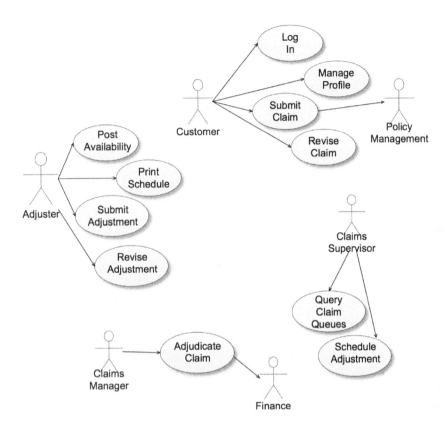

Figure 10.17 *Claims use-case model*

10.17.2 Use-Case Modeling Elements

Figure 10.17 illustrates the main modeling elements of a use-case diagram. Each user role interacting with the product or system is modeled as an **actor**—indicated as a stick figure. You may also use the generic object symbol—the rectangle. Any external system that interacts with the product or system is also shown as an actor (e.g., *policy management* and *finance*).

Model each user task as a use case, depicted as an oval. Draw an arrow from an actor to a use case to indicate that the actor is a **primary actor**—the entity that initiates the task. Draw an arrow from the use case to an actor to indicate a **secondary actor**—involved after the use case is triggered.

As you add new user tasks and new users to the system, you update the use-case models continuously so they can remain useful for future maintenance and enhancement (M&E) initiatives.

10.18 User-Role Modeling Workshops

A user-role modeling workshop is a group-interview method that employs silent brainstorming to discover user roles for an upcoming planning period.[19] The approach is particularly useful when the group is large. The duration of a typical user-role modeling workshop is one hour. Attendees invited to the workshop include the PO, the complete development team, process owners, and other SMEs who would know about users affected by the proposed changes.

10.18.1 Agenda

During the workshop, the following steps are carried out:

1. Brainstorm the Roles

2. Organize the Roles

3. Consolidate the Roles

4. Refine the Roles

10.18.1.1 Brainstorm the Roles

This step takes approximately fifteen minutes. Distribute blank sticky-backed cards to participants. Inform the group that anyone can write a role on a card, post it to the wall, and announce it. No other discussion is allowed at this time. Use the *popcorn rule* to determine when to stop: quit if a time limit passes without any more roles popping up on the wall.

Figure 10.18 illustrates what the user roles for an incident management system might look like at this point.

10.18.1.2 Organize the Roles

This step takes approximately 15 minutes. Ask attendees to arrange cards so that related roles are grouped together. The more that roles *functionally* overlap, the more they should *physically* overlap.

Figure 10.19 illustrates how the roles might be arranged at this point.

Note that the cards for user and incident reporter are almost entirely overlapping, indicating they likely refer to the same role. The Tier 1 service agent and customer service representative roles also overlap, as do incident manager and incident supervisor. The three tiers of service agents have a slight overlap.

---

19. Mike Cohn, *User Stories Applied: For Agile Software Development* (Boston: Addison-Wesley Professional, 2004), 33.

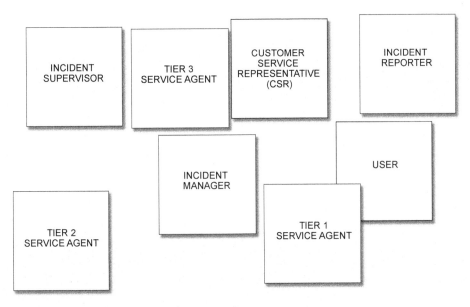

Figure 10.18   *Initial user roles for an incident management system*

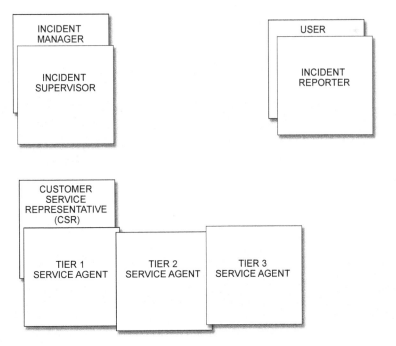

Figure 10.19   *Organized user roles for an incident management system*

10.18.1.3 Consolidate the Roles

Focusing first on cards that completely overlap, ask each card's author to describe the role and how it differs from the others. If it turns out that there are roles that are entirely equivalent, ask attendees to decide on one as the primary. The other names may be listed as aliases or dropped.

Next, turn to cards that have some partial overlap or are positioned close to each other. Ask their authors about the user tasks each role should be able to perform. If the tasks are identical, keep only one card. If there are some common tasks and some that are specific to each role, keep the individual cards and add a generic role to represent the commonality. (In the UML standard, this new actor is referred to as a **generalized actor**.) For example, the two roles retail customer and wholesale customer may have some usages in common but others that are specific to each role. You add a new actor, customer, to represent a generic customer. The value in creating the generic role is that if there is a user story that is valued by both kinds of customers, you will be able to specify "As a customer, I want to . . ." instead of stating "As a retail or wholesale customer, I want to. . . ." The same is true for other requirements artifacts and rules. This practice also helps with prioritization, since a feature or story that meets the needs of multiple users (represented by the generic actor) is potentially more valuable than a story that meets the needs of only a subtype—all other things being equal.

Set aside any cards representing roles outside the scope of the change or the release; they'll be useful later when planning subsequent changes and releases.

Figure 10.20 illustrates how the roles we've been looking at might be consolidated at this point. The incident supervisor and customer service representative cards have been eliminated. In addition, the user card was eliminated in favor of the incident reporter because the latter better described the role's relationship to the product.

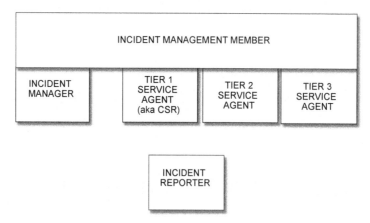

Figure 10.20   *Consolidated user roles for an incident management system*

A new role, incident management member, was created to represent anyone working in incident management—an incident manager or service agent at any tier. It was felt this role would be useful because there are numerous features that everyone in that business area needs access to.

10.18.1.4 Refine the Roles

Now that you have pruned and organized the user roles, the next step is to refine them by investigating and documenting their attributes. Following are examples of user attributes:

- **Goal for using the product:** What is the user trying to achieve with the software? What jobs is the customer hiring the product to do?

- **Frequency of use:** How often does the user use the application?

- **Level of domain expertise:** How well does the user understand the business domain?

- Add other user attributes specific to the product (e.g., on an HR site, add an attribute that specifies the types of jobs users are searching for, such as full time or part time).

Table 10.5 illustrates role attributes for the incident management product we've been examining.

Table 10.5 *Refined User Role Table*

User Role	Frequency of Usage	Technical Proficiency with the Product	Business Domain Expertise	Goal in Using Product or System
Incident manager	Daily	Medium	High	Manage workflow. Make sure no incidents get bottlenecked in the system.
Tier 1 service agent	Daily	Low	Low	Respond quickly to an incident—either directly or by assigning it to someone who can.
Tier 2 service agent	Daily	Medium	Medium	Provide product-specific assistance.
Tier 3 service agent	Daily	High	Low	Provide third-party technical expertise.

BLINK CASE STUDY PART 17

Role-Modeling Workshop

Background

You've been asked to facilitate a user-role modeling workshop to discover user roles impacted by the upcoming BLInK release. Your aim is to cover all users involved in the end-to-end process of activating a new BLInK subscriber.

The Ask

The deliverable for this analysis activity will be

- **Deliverable 1:** User-role cards with refinement notes

Preparation

You decide to invite a diverse group to the user-role modeling workshop in order to ensure all users are considered. Because of the large number of participants, you choose to use silent brainstorming as an efficient way to extract the collective knowledge of the group.

You prepare an agenda that lists the four steps of a user-role modeling workshop:

1. Brainstorm the Roles
2. Organize the Roles
3. Consolidate the Roles
4. Refine the Roles

At the start of the workshop, you explain the process to participants and hand out sticky notes.

What Transpires

During Step 1, *Brainstorm the Roles*, participants post user roles covering a broad range of potential users, including those who set underwriting policies, those who execute them, the employers who offer the policies to their employees, and the employees who purchase group insurance. Figure 10.21 indicates the user roles posted during Step 1.

Figure 10.22 shows the cards as they appear after Step 2, Organize the Roles.

The remaining steps of the user-role modeling workshop are performed until a set of refined user roles is agreed on.

Deliverables

Deliverable 1: User Roles

For the upcoming release, the group has identified and described the user roles in Figure 10.23.

Figure 10.24 illustrates other user roles that were discovered during this workshop but found to be beyond the scope of the upcoming release.

Policyholders other than the master policyholder will not be addressed in the first release. Marketing analyst users also will not be accommodated until BLInK has begun to generate useful data.

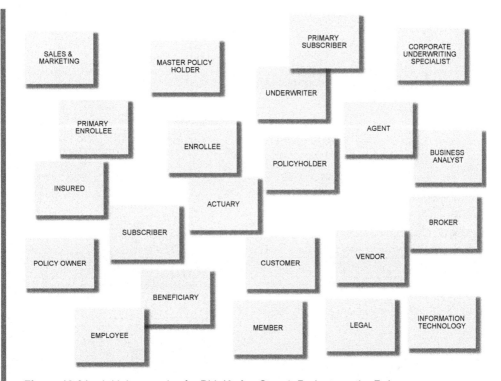

Figure 10.21 *Initial user roles for BLInK after Step 1, Brainstorm the Roles*

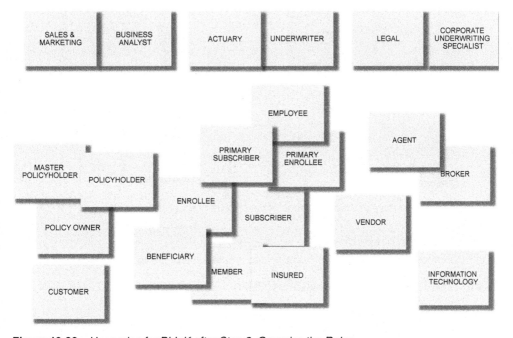

Figure 10.22 *User roles for BLInK after Step 2, Organize the Roles*

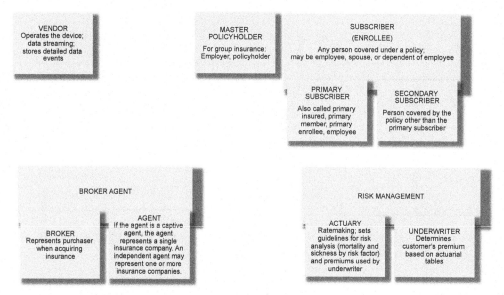

Figure 10.23 *Final user roles for upcoming release of BLInK*

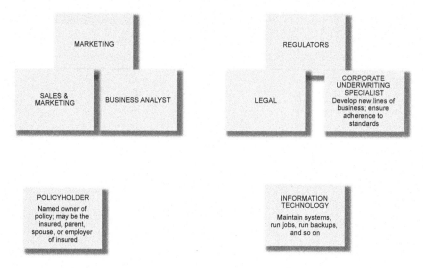

Figure 10.24 *User roles beyond the scope of the upcoming BLInK release*

Case Study Retrospective

In this workshop, you identified user roles for the first release of the BLInK initiative.

10.19 Review the Architecture

As an analyst, your responsibilities don't always stop at the requirements; you may also be expected to map those requirements to software components and review design solutions. This is especially true if you are a business *systems* analyst. The following sections discuss some other models you may be asked to review in preparation for an upcoming change.

10.19.1 Context Diagram

Create or review a context diagram to analyze and model a system's high-level data integration requirements. A **context diagram** (also known as *level 0 data flow diagram [DFD]*) provides a high-level view of a system in its environment. It indicates data inputs to the system and their sources and the data outputs from the system and their destinations.

A context diagram may be drawn from a business or technical perspective. A **business-perspective context diagram** models data flows to and from a business organization. A **technical-perspective context diagram** models the flow of data between the software product or component under design and the external software entities and users it interacts with.

10.19.1.1 Context Diagram Example

Figure 10.25 is a context diagram that describes the high-level data integration requirements for a proposed claims management system.

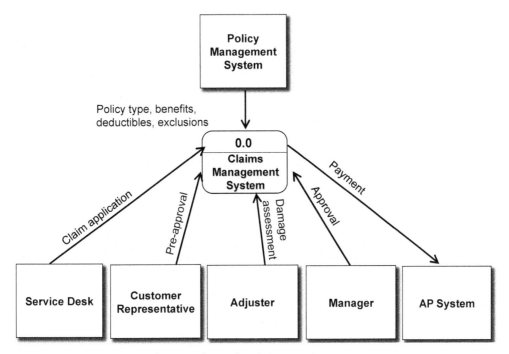

Figure 10.25   *Context diagram for to-be claims system*

The software system under discussion is represented by a single **process** icon—a rounded rectangle. The shaded rectangles represent **external entities**—objects outside of the system, such as human users and external software systems. The connecting lines or arrows are referred to as **data flows**—pipes along which information travels. Incoming arrows to the system indicate **data inputs**. For example, the diagram shows that the input data "Damage assessment" is supplied by an adjuster.

Outgoing arrows from the system indicate its data outputs. For example, the system generates a payment electronic financial transaction (EFT), which it sends to the accounts payable (AP) system.

10.19.2 UML Communication Diagram

A context diagram focuses on data integration issues. Systems and services that communicate in real-time don't just pass data to each other, however. They pass **messages**—requests to *do* things with that data—for example, a synchronous message to a rating service to look up a customer's credit rating based on a social insurance number. Messaging integration requirements may be modeled with a high-level **UML communication diagram**. For more on communication diagrams, see *The Business Analyst's Handbook*[20] or the official standard at the Object Management Group website, www.omg.org.

10.19.3 Data Flow Diagrams

Level 1 DFDs are used to model the movement of data to and from the main processes of a system or software product. The system under design is decomposed into smaller components, each representing one of its **processes**. The diagram indicates the flow of data to and from each process.

Datastores may also be shown on the diagram. A *datastore* is a place where data is saved for later use. Datastores are often implemented as data tables.

Each process on a level 1 DFD can be decomposed into subprocesses on a level 2 DFD and down to more levels as needed.

10.19.3.1 Level 1 DFD Example

Figure 10.26 is a level 1 DFD for the claims processing system we saw in Figure 10.25.

The external entities we saw earlier on the context diagram (see Figure 10.25) system reappear on the level 1 DFD. The rounded rectangles on the DFD represent the processes implemented by the system:

- *Submit Claim*—to input a claim application into the system
- *Review Claim*—an initial review of the claim (e.g., to ensure all required fields are present)
- *Assess Damage*—to evaluate the damage for which the claim is being made
- *Approve Payout*—final approval of payment to the customer against a claim

---

20. Howard Podeswa, *The Business Analyst's Handbook* (Boston: Course Technology PTR, 2008).

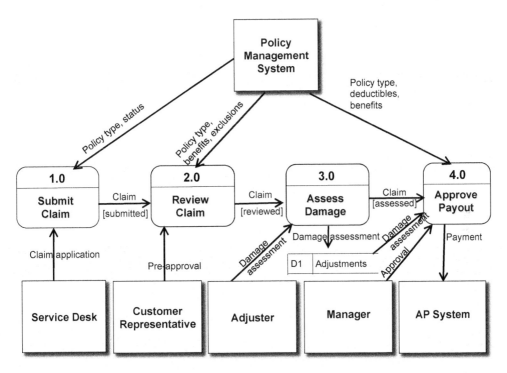

Figure 10.26 *Level 1 DFD for to-be claims system*

As in the context diagram, data flows indicate where data is input to and output from a process. The figure also contains the datastore D1: Adjustments, displayed as an open rectangle.

As you can see from the example, a level 1 DFD clarifies where data is generated and consumed with more granularity than the context diagram shows. This added detail allows you to identify dependencies between processes, data omissions, and gaps in the data requirements.

For example, Figure 10.26 indicates that the data item Damage assessment is output from the process Assess Damage and that this data is required by the process Approve Payout. In traditional implementation planning, we'd implement the assess feature before the approve feature. However, in agile planning, we may decide to implement the approve feature first—to deliver a "quick win" or plan an MVP. In that case, we know from the diagram that we'll need to create a workaround to account for the missing data damage assessment that would otherwise have been provided by the assess feature.

10.19.3.2 *Benefits of DFD Models*

Use DFDs for the following purposes:

- Identify the processes impacted by data changes.

- Prepare for data transformations and migrations.

- Identify data dependencies.

- Track the source of data errors.

- Ensure that every item of data that is needed somewhere is collected somewhere.

10.19.4 Architecture (Block) Diagrams

An **architecture model** is very similar to a level 1 DFD in that it indicates components that make up a large system and the connections among them. On a DFD, these components are processes and subprocess. On architecture diagrams, they can represent other objects as well (e.g., software services, application programming interfaces [APIs], and IoT devices). A simple **block diagram** is often used for this purpose, but more formal diagrams, such as the UML communication diagram, may also be used. For more on communication diagrams and other UML models, see *UML for the IT Business Analyst.*[21]

Figure 10.27 is an example of an architecture block diagram for a network of interconnected IoT home devices. It indicates high-level integration points for the components: A thermostat downloads an HVAC schedule from a mobile application interface (House-Mate API) and reports energy usage data back to the API. A fire/smoke detector informs the API of low-battery alerts and alarms. The detector can also send a message to turn on a sprinkler and is able to place emergency calls.

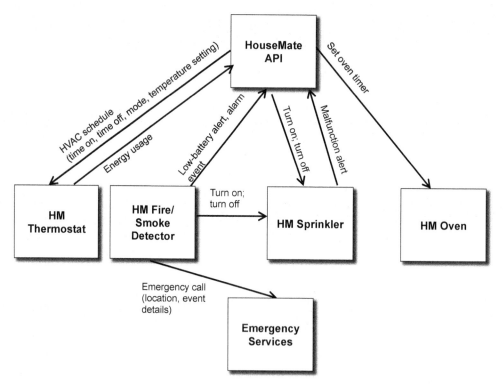

Figure 10.27 *Architecture diagram for a network of home IoT devices*

---

21. Podeswa, *UML for the IT Business Analyst.*

BLINK CASE STUDY PART 18
Architecture Diagrams Maps

Background

To address technological risk, the BLInK team is planning to design and test proofs of concept and prototypes for the IoT devices used at a gym during training.

The Ask

You have been asked to meet with stakeholders and designers to prepare high-level integration requirements for the devices. The deliverable will be

- **Deliverable 1:** Architecture block diagram for BLInK IoT devices used at the gym

What Transpires

You begin by asking the group to identify the gym IoT devices that are to be incorporated as well as any software components (applications, APIs, etc.) they need to be able to communicate with.

You learn that in the first implementation, the plan is to incorporate the gym kiosk card reader, swiped by customers on entry and exit, into the IoT network. Gym machines used for workouts will also be connected.

The high-level design is as follows: IoT devices will access BLInK data and services (such as activity analyses) over the Internet using a Web API, to be known as BWAPI (BLInK Web Application Programming Interface). They will also be able to communicate directly with the customer's mobile device using BMAPI—BLInK's mobile API.

You model the interconnecting devices and interfaces and now turn the attention of the group to their connections. The proposal is for the kiosk card reader to send data about the duration of each visit to BLInK over the Web (through BWAPI) so that customers do not have to have their mobile devices on hand when exiting the gym.

You learn that the plan for the workout machines, though, is for them to communicate directly with the user's mobile device (through BMAPI) in order to retrieve workout programs and send back exercise data such as the machine model number, calories consumed, and exercise duration and steps. The customer's mobile device app will upload exercise data to BLInK over the Web.

Deliverables

The following deliverable was produced:

Deliverable 1: BLInK Architecture Diagram for Gym Context
Figure 10.28 is the deliverable that resulted from this analysis.

Case Study Retrospective

Based on the high-level model produced in this activity, designers can begin designing proofs of concept and creating prototypes to determine the feasibility of connecting the devices according to the proposed solution. If initial testing reveals unexpected problems, the team will make adjustments or pivot to a new design before too much effort is wasted on a nonviable design.

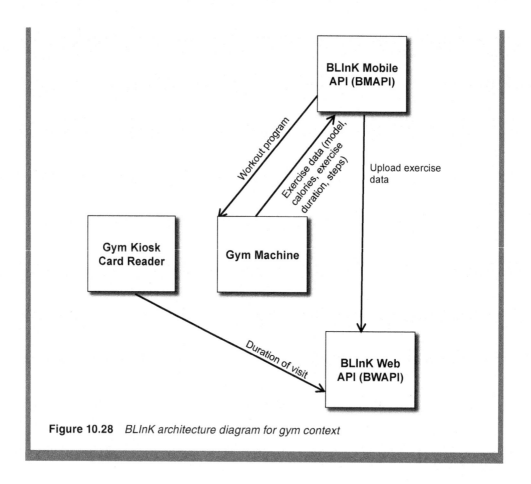

Figure 10.28   *BLInK architecture diagram for gym context*

10.20 Chapter Summary

Here are the key points covered in this chapter:

- Following ATDD/BDD practice, specify AC before implementation to guide developers. If using Gherkin, specify AC scenarios at the feature level in Gherkin feature files.

- Use personas to personalize user analytics when prioritizing features and designing user interfaces.

- Use journey maps to understand customers' thoughts and feelings as they interact with the brand or product.

- Use value stream mapping and process maps when designing, changing, or optimizing a process or part of a process.

- Use a context diagram and data flow diagrams to model data integration requirements.

10.21 What's Next?

This chapter focused on the preliminary analysis you carry out before accepting features into the implementation plan. In Chapter 11, "Quarterly and Feature Planning," we turn the planning process itself—the determination of the goals and features that will be delivered over the upcoming quarter. At this time, the first stories within those features are also broken out and prepared. See Chapter 13 for guidance on the preparation, splitting, and writing of stories.

Chapter 11

Quarterly and Feature Planning

This chapter covers quarterly planning and feature planning. It applies to teams that use a timeboxed planning approaches, including quarterly, release, and program increment (PI) planning (SAFe). It also applies to teams that use a single-item flow-based approach (e.g., Kanban) to plan a feature—a large requirements item that may require multiple teams up to three months to complete. Flow-based feature planning is similar to quarterly planning except that its scope is an upcoming feature instead of all the features for an upcoming quarter. Figure 11.1 highlights the activities covered in the chapter.

The chapter begins with guidance on when to use which approach—quarterly planning or flow-based feature planning—and when to do neither and limit planning to shorter terms (iterations and stories).

The chapter explains the meaning of commitment in agile planning and the view of both the quarterly plan and feature plan as a hypothesis and forecast. It includes general guidelines based on Extreme Programming (XP)'s Planning Game and detailed guidance for delivering event outputs, including specification of goals, capacity planning and estimation, roadmapping, and commitments.

The chapter provides guidance for the facilitator-analyst, including entry conditions for the planning event, whom to invite, topics, and event deliverables. It explains feature estimation in detail, including how to estimate features using story points, ideal developer days (IDD), Planning Poker, Delphi estimation, and the Fibonacci series. The chapter concludes with guidelines for reviewing and revising the plan once development is underway.

Quarterly planning guidance continues in the next chapter with a deep dive into two other techniques used in agile planning: minimum viable products (MVPs) and story mapping.

11.1 Objectives

This chapter will help you

- Know when to plan quarterly and when to use a flow-based approach (Kanban).
- Facilitate quarterly and feature planning meetings.
- Apply XP's Planning Game rules to quarterly planning.

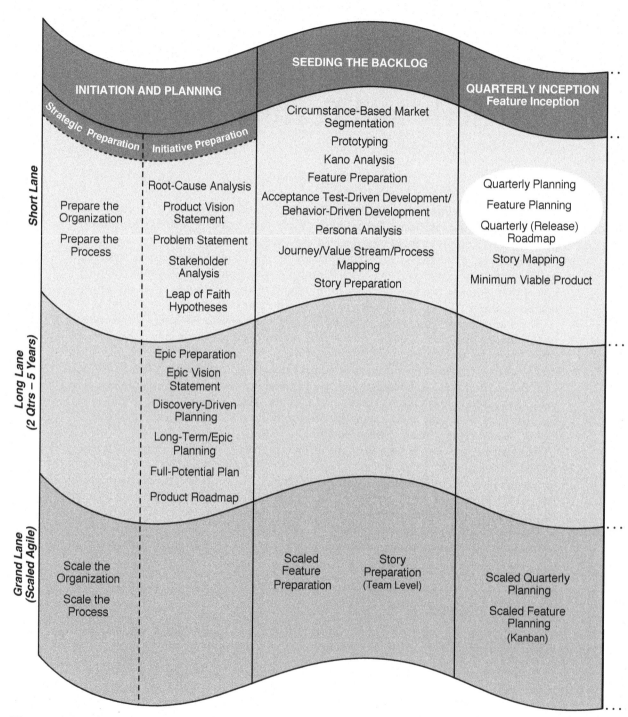

Figure 11.1 *Chapter 11 on the map*

DAILY ACTIVITIES

QUARTERLY CLOSEOUT
Epic, Feature Closeout

ITERATION INCEPTION

ITERATION CLOSEOUT

Daily Standup

Requirements Analysis & Documentation

Code, Build, Test, Deliver Acceptance
Test-Driven Development/
Behavior-Driven Development

Iteration Planning

Minimum Viable Product,
Split Testing

Epic, Feature Preparation

Story Preparation

Iteration Review

Iteration Retrospective

Prepare for
General Availability

Quarterly
Retrospective

Epic, Feature
Retrospective

Pivot or
Persevere

User Task
Force
Meetings

Product
Owner
Council
Meetings

DevOps

Scaled
Feature
Preparation
(Kanban)

Integration
Meetings

Story
Preparation
(Team Level)

Scaled Iteration
Review

Scaled Iteration
Retrospective

Iteration Retrospective
(Team Level)

DevOps

Scaled
Quarterly/Feature
Retrospective

Scaled
Iteration
Planning

Iteration
Planning
(Team Level)

- Prioritize features for the planning period.

- Understand how and when to use real-time estimation units, story points, and IDDs.

- Use Planning Poker and Delphi estimation to estimate features in the plan.

- Create a roadmap for an upcoming quarter, release, PI, feature, or feature set.

- Revise the quarterly and/or feature plan once development is underway.

11.2 This Chapter on the Map

As shown in Figure 11.1, the chapter examines quarterly planning, feature planning, and the quarterly roadmap—items in the Quarterly Inception /Feature Inception zone.

11.3 Overview of Quarterly Planning

Quarterly planning is the act of forecasting what will be delivered over the next quarter (the scope) and developing a roadmap for getting there. The term *quarterly planning* is used in this book as a shorthand that includes quarterly planning, planning for similar periods (approximately two to six months), release planning, and PI planning.

During a quarterly planning event, collaborating teams (e.g., teams within a product area or Agile Release Train [ART]) meet with business stakeholders to plan the quarter's scope, matching the effort to implement planned features against the team's capacity. They also develop an implementation roadmap for the quarter indicating when goals, objectives, and features will be delivered.

An agile quarterly plan is not static. It is revised on the basis of new learning, data, changing behaviors, and market conditions. We look at guidelines for updating the quarterly plan in section 11.12.

11.4 Overview of Flow-Based Feature Planning

If the teams are using a single-item, flow-based approach (e.g., Kanban), they plan on a per-feature basis: all the teams collaborating on an upcoming feature meet to plan the feature. A feature is a work item that may require multiple teams and up to a quarter to implement. A **feature set** may also be planned. A feature set is a group of related features meant to be released together. You can indicate a feature set by creating a higher-level feature or epic to represent the group. Alternatively, you can tag the features to indicate that they belong to the same set.

As with quarterly planning, feature planning activities include determining the scope of the work, specifying goals and objectives, and developing an implementation plan. However, the scope of these activities is a single feature rather than all the features lined up for the quarter.

11.5 When Is Planning at This Level Advised and Not Advised?

Let's begin with scenarios in which it's advisable *not* to perform this level of planning. The benefit of not practicing quarterly planning is that decisions can be made on the basis of the most current information. For this reason, consider limiting planning to *shorter* planning horizons—iterations and stories—during the early phases of innovative product development, when the ability to adapt to new learning is paramount.

As a product matures, conditions begin to favor more distant planning horizons—planning for an upcoming quarter or feature. Reasons to conduct this longer-term planning include the following:

- Marketers plan on a quarterly basis and need a substantial lead time (more than a few weeks) to prepare marketing campaigns for new features.

- Sales representatives need advance notice on new, committed features so they can begin offering the features to customers as an incentive for renewals and purchases.

- The product includes numerous functions and subsystems, requiring many teams weeks or months to deliver a typical change request. Planning at the quarterly or feature level is, therefore, required so that teams can coordinate their efforts toward the solution.

- Change initiatives are ambitious, requiring effort measured in weeks, not days (e.g., reengineer a business process).

- A new feature can be implemented in small chunks (stories) but will require weeks of development until it is rich enough to be competitive.

Also, as we learned in Chapter 9, "Long-Term Agile Planning," a company may see a significant market opportunity that it can exploit successfully only if it plans for an even longer term of three to five years. In that case, it creates a long-term strategic plan and uses it to guide the quarterly plan. The long-term plan should be revised as necessary during quarterly planning to align with new information and changing priorities.

11.6 When to Use Quarterly Planning versus Flow-Based Feature Planning

The quarterly (timeboxed) and flow-based (Kanban) approaches to planning features are concerned with roughly the same planning horizon—about three months—and involve similar activities. There are significant differences, though, related to timing. When teams use quarterly planning (a timeboxed approach), they plan, prioritize and commit to *all* the features for the upcoming quarter at the same time—providing an opportunity for stakeholders to lobby for change initiatives and for the product owner (PO) to prioritize work across the product. The use of quarterly planning also means that teams are available *at the same time* to plan complex initiatives requiring multiple teams. In contrast, when organizations use a flow-based approach (e.g., Kanban), it's more difficult to find a time when all the necessary teams are available because teams aren't working to the same cadence. That's why organizations responsible for scaled, multiteam initiatives should practice quarterly planning.

The disadvantage of quarterly planning, though, is that it can impede agility: it commits teams to *all* of the features for a quarter—not just the next feature. It's true that commitment is meant to be provisional in agile planning. However, once a plan is written down, teams tend to be reluctant to change it. As a result, if a feature or story of higher value arises during the quarter, it often has to wait until the next planning cycle to be addressed. If a new feature arises toward the *end* of a quarter, it may be deferred to the next *two* quarters if commitments to the upcoming quarterly plan have already been made.

In contrast, the flow-based approach allows business stakeholders to change priorities on the fly *as each item comes up in the backlog*. That's why flow-based feature planning is preferred over quarterly planning for teams that work primarily on customer-generated requests or on innovative development—scenarios where priorities can change rapidly on the basis of customer feedback.

As a rule of thumb, it's best to adopt a mix of both approaches—allocating part of the budget to quarterly planning and the other to flow-based feature planning (Kanban approach). That way, teams can address long-term strategic initiatives while retaining the ability to respond quickly to customer feedback. Each organization should experiment to find the right mix of approaches—and it should be open to changing that mix over time.

We'll review considerations for timeboxed vs. flow-based planning in the context of scaled agile development in Chapter 17, section 17.4.

11.7 How to Conduct Quarterly Planning with Agility

An agile quarterly plan should evolve on the basis of learning and changing conditions; it should not be frozen at the start of the planning period. Despite this guideline, there is a risk that organizations that plan quarterly may slip into waterfall practices that inhibit change. If your organization has decided to plan quarterly, use the following guidelines to conduct the activity in a manner that supports rather than suppresses adaptability:

- Create a culture of change.
- Use data-informed decisioning.
- Specify outcomes, not outputs.
- View the plan as a hypothesis, not a contract.

Let's examine each of these guidelines.

11.7.1 Create a Culture of Change

Nurture a culture where stakeholders and developers embrace change. Set expectations that the plan can and should change in light of new learning and changing conditions.

See Chapter 18, "Achieving Enterprise Agility," for guidelines on creating an agile culture.

11.7.2 Use Data-Informed Decisioning

Throughout the planning period, revise the plan and revisit decisions regarding what features to include in the plan based on frequent feedback from MVPs, customers, and data analytics.

11.7.3 Specify Outcomes, Not Outputs

Evaluate success on the basis of *real-world outcomes*, not outputs. For example, evaluate success depending on whether a target churn rate is achieved, not whether the deliverables meet a set of predetermined requirements specifications.

11.7.4 View the Plan as a Hypothesis, Not a Contract

The plan is a **hypothesis**[1] about what is *likely* to be delivered based on current assumptions. The quarterly plan should not be viewed as a contract to deliver features and milestones by specified timelines. The plan includes MVPs to test assumptions and is subject to adjustment based on feedback from customers. When parties commit to the plan, it means they agree it represents the *best forecast at that point in time*.

11.7.4.1 Why It's a Forecast

Treat the plan as a forecast, not as a promise. A firm upfront commitment inhibits the organization's ability to course-correct in response to learning, data, changing market conditions, the team's performance (velocity), and unexpected technical difficulties.

11.7.4.2 And Why It's Sometimes a Promise

Sometimes, though, business stakeholders need firmer commitments from developers. As noted earlier, marketers may require a firm commitment (not just a forecast) so they can prepare customers and marketing materials for new features. Sales representatives may need it so they can use the planned features to close sales and renewals. As an agile analyst, remember that your primary goal is to do well by the business, not to do well by agile. While you should help stakeholders understand the benefits of a changeable plan, the degree of adaptability that is practical in any situation ultimately depends on net business

---

1. Mike Cohn, *User Stories Applied: For Agile Software Development* (Boston: Addison-Wesley Professional, 2004), 236.

value. As a rule of thumb, when an innovative product is in its early development, flexibility is valued over predictability. In that instance, the quarterly plan should be treated as a forecast with the full expectation of change. Once the product has matured and there is a large established customer base, predictability becomes more critical to the business, and the level of commitment required tends to increase.

Later in this chapter, we examine guidelines for satisfying the need for commitment while retaining adaptability (see section 11.11.3.3).

11.8 XP's Planning Game Guidelines

The XP guidelines for release and iteration planning are articulated in its Planning Game rules. The rules are useful for all agile planners—not just those who practice XP.

11.8.1 Overview of the Planning Game

The Planning Game was introduced in the first edition of Kent Beck's book *Extreme Programming Explained*[2] as a process for estimating and prioritizing stories. There are two versions of the game—the Release Planning Game and the Iteration Planning Game—each with its own set of rules but with the same underlying principles and steps. The Release Planning Game lays out instructions for selecting, estimating, prioritizing, and assessing risk for features in an upcoming release. In contrast, the Iteration Planning Game is concerned with the stories of an upcoming iteration. In this chapter, we focus on the Release Planning Game. XP's guidelines refer to *release planning*, but they apply equally to quarterly planning, as the term is used in this book.

The Quarterly/Release Planning Game is divided into three phases:

- Exploration
- Commitment
- Steering

The first two phases occur at the start of the quarter. In the first phase, **Exploration**, the plan is proposed. In **Commitment**, the group agrees to the plan. Section 11.11 provides XP guidelines for these phases.

The third phase, **Steering**, is triggered whenever the plan needs to be adjusted according to changing circumstances. Rules for this phase are incorporated into the guidelines in section 11.12.

---

2. Kent Beck, *Extreme Programming Explained: Embrace Change* (Boston: Addison-Wesley Professional, 1999), 51–53.

11.8.2 Overview of Roles

The Planning Game recognizes only two roles, Business and Development, each with defined responsibilities.

11.8.2.1 Business Role

Business consists of business stakeholders who make decisions about the functionality that will be included in the product. Business may be played by the sponsor, marketers, and expert users. Those in the role should have a good grasp of the needs of customers and end users.

11.8.2.2 Development Role

Development consists of those involved in all aspects of implementation, including analysis, user experience (UX), systems design, coding, and testing.

11.8.3 Overview of Planning Principles

In Beck's later writings, he dropped the game paradigm[3] but preserved its underlying concepts in the Customer's and Programmer's Bill of Rights.[4] The following planning principles are derived from XP's Release Planning Game and its Bills of Rights:

- Anyone can write a story.

- Development estimates stories.

- Business prioritizes stories.

- Anyone can ask questions.

- The plan is not static.

These principles are described in the following sections.

11.8.3.1 Anyone Can Write a Story

Anyone who sees the need for a story can write a story.[5] For example, business stakeholders and their representatives, such as business analysts, write user stories; architects and engineers write technical stories, such as a story to reduce redundancies; team analysts write functional spikes (also known as *enabler stories*).

---

3. For example, the Planning Game does not appear in the subsequent second edition of *Extreme Programming Explained*, nor is it described in another book written after the first edition, *Planning Extreme Programming* (though there is a passing reference to it).

4. Kent Beck and Martin Fowler, *Planning Extreme Programming* (Boston: Addison-Wesley Professional, 2000), 5.

5. According to the original Planning Game rules, only the business can do so. Today, agile organizations permit anyone to write a story.

11.8.3.2 Development Estimates Stories

The people doing the work—and *only* the people doing the work—are permitted to estimate the effort to perform it. XP's Programmer Bill of Rights[6] addresses the issue by stating, "You [the Programmer] have the right to make and update your own estimates."

This rule helps avoid the overcommitment that can occur if business stakeholders dictate the estimate. Overcommitment is inevitable as an occasional occurrence, but it should not be allowed to become standard practice because there are no good options if a deadline becomes threatened. You can add programmers, but it takes time to bring new developers up to speed, making matters worse. You can ask developers to work longer hours, but it leads to burnout and defections if you do it regularly. You can deliver fewer features, release the planned features with low quality, or delay the release—but none of these options will result in happy customers. The solution is to avoid the situation in the first place by relying on the estimates of those who know best: the developers doing the work.

11.8.3.3 Business Prioritizes Stories

Developers may raise risks and technical concerns, but the final decision on priorities resides with the customer (often subject to approval from the technical side). In XP's Customer's Bill of Rights,[7] this is expressed as "You [the Customer] have the right to change your mind, to substitute functionality, and to change priorities without paying exorbitant costs." This rule is so critical that I've heard an executive describe his decision to institute it as the most significant improvement the company had made to its change processes. (Previously, it was the information technology [IT] organization that prioritized changes.)

When the solution provider is internal, this rule is too often followed in the breach. The IT department tells business stakeholders when it will get around to implementing their requests—with the justification that since development understands the technical implications best, it should make the final decisions. This is a mistake.

For example, consider a technical story to redesign a database to become more efficient at handling large tables. Knowing that it will be much more costly to implement this change later, Development might want to prioritize this work even if it delays features that deliver user functionality. Nevertheless, the final decision must lie with Business, since only it knows whether the business benefit in bringing new user functionality to market quickly outweighs the added cost of delaying technical improvements.

> As an analyst, you play a crucial role in communicating the business benefits of technical stories so that business decision makers can evaluate and prioritize user and technical stories based on a common measure: value (or cost) to the business.

---

6. Beck and Fowler, *Planning Extreme Programming*, 5.

7. Beck and Fowler, 5.

11.8.3.4 *Anyone Can Ask Questions*

Everyone is encouraged to ask questions, regardless of their area of expertise. Business may ask why developers' estimates are high and challenge them to explore less costly solutions. Developers may ask business stakeholders questions about functionality and raise technical risks. The *final decision* about these issues, however, remains within each player's domain. Business has the final say on priorities, and Development has the final say on estimates.

11.8.3.5 *The Plan Is Not Static.*

An agile plan's purpose is not to tie down the team to deliver a set of features by a given deadline; it's to support *coordination* and *collaboration* using the most current information. Once a plan has been created, it should be adapted in response to change.

11.9 Quarterly Planning: Timing Considerations

As noted earlier, begin preparing features for an upcoming quarter about halfway into the previous quarter. Begin the planning process (capacity planning and roadmapping) toward the end of the previous quarter. Organizations that reserve a hardening iteration between releases (also called a stabilization iteration or IP iteration) often conduct quarterly (release) planning during the hardening iteration, but this is recommended only as a remedial practice.

The planning event may be a formal affair carried out over a dedicated block of time or may occur in an informal setting over a series of conversations. Quarterly planning may require anywhere from about four hours to two days. The longer duration is typically needed when planning the first quarters of a long-term initiative. The typical time spent on quarterly planning for a scaled initiative is one and a half to two days.

This chapter focuses on the needs of small organizations of independent teams. See Chapter 17 for guidelines on quarterly planning for a scaled organization.

11.10 Preparing for the Planning Event

The secret to the success of any meeting is preparation. Use the following guidelines to prepare for a quarterly or feature planning event.

11.10.1 Verify Entry Conditions

Ensure that all entry conditions for quarterly/feature planning are satisfied before the event. Sufficient features must be lined up and ready to accommodate the team's capacity for the quarter, with a few added ones in case features are reprioritized. A typical number of ready features is ten to twenty. To be ready, a feature must be well enough understood for planning purposes. At a minimum, it must be estimable, prioritized, valuable, and implementable within a single quarter. More formally, the feature must satisfy the feature definition of ready (DoR) if one is used.

See Chapter 6, section 6.5.7.6, for more on the feature DoR.

If the proposed change initiative began as an epic, decompose it into its initial features. Prepare the upcoming features to be ready according to the preceding guidelines. Keep in mind that features of an epic are not necessarily implemented together. The quarterly plan may include a few features of one epic followed by features of other epics.

If you're facilitating the planning event, ensure logistics (e.g., flip-charts, Post-it Notes) are available and that remote-conferencing applications are ready as needed. Other entry conditions include that a product/epic vision statement and roadmap have been specified.

See Appendix A.7 for a checklist of these and other entry conditions for quarterly and feature planning.

11.10.2 Prepare Invitation List

Invite business stakeholders and developers impacted by the change. If the teams are using a flow-based (Kanban) approach, only the teams working on the feature under consideration are invited. If the teams are conducting quarterly planning (the timeboxed approach), all teams in the product area (or SAFe ART) should be represented.

See Appendix A.8 for a comprehensive checklist of invitees to the planning event.

11.10.3 Determine the Planning Horizon

Determine the planning horizon for the event—the period that will be covered by the planning meeting. Typical options when teams are using a timeboxed approach are one quarter (three months), one PI of eight to twelve weeks, or the upcoming release cycle (often two to six months). If the teams are using a flow-based planning approach, the planning horizon equals the estimated time to implement the planned feature or feature set.

11.10.4 Prepare Inputs and Deliverables

Prepare inputs and a list of deliverables. Inputs to the event may include the product backlog with ten to twenty ready features, the long-term product roadmap, journey maps, process models, value stream maps, personas, and other analysis artifacts developed during feature preparation.

See Appendix A.9 for a comprehensive checklist of inputs to quarterly and feature planning.

Prepare a list of deliverables that will result from the meeting. Include templates and examples as appropriate. Deliverables include quarterly goals and objectives, risks, quarterly roadmap, and quarterly (release) backlog. The **quarterly backlog** lists the features committed to the upcoming planning cycle. See Appendix A.10 for a checklist of other planning deliverables.

11.10.5 Refine Features and Acceptance Criteria Incrementally

Feature analysis in agile development is an incremental process. This means that the granularity of features and their acceptance criteria increases over time. Table 11.1 provides a general guideline for incrementally refining the analysis of requirements items in an agile process. (See Shore and Warden's *The Art of Agile*.[8])

Table 11.1   *Feature Refinement over Time*

When the Feature Will Be Implemented	Associated Level of Refinement
Upcoming quarter	**Feature is ready and committed:** The feature has been identified, estimated, and prioritized. It has an owner (a designated person who will answer questions about the feature), is understood by the team and product owner, and can be implemented within a quarter. High-level feature acceptance criteria have been written. Most of the feature's component stories have been identified.
Within two to four weeks (two iterations)	**Feature is previewed:** The feature has been split into well-formed stories. Stories are being prepared to comply with the story DoR.
Within one to two weeks (one iteration)	Story acceptance criteria have been written. Story estimates (points, IDD) have been assigned.
Within one week or less	Detailed requirements have been discussed; test cases have been written; story complies with DoR.

The table describes a typical progression but should be adapted for the circumstance. For example, Table 11.1 presumes that the team follows the common practice of *actually*

---

8. James Shore and Shane Warden, *The Art of Agile*, 2nd ed. (Sebastopol, CA: O'Reilly Media, forthcoming). Early release available at https://www.jamesshore.com/Agile-Book/release_planning.html

estimating features. As we'll see later in this chapter, some organizations follow a different practice whereby, instead of estimating features to progressively higher levels of precision, they make the features increasingly *estimable*.

11.11 Planning Topics (Agenda)

Following is a suggested list of topics for facilitating a planning event when only one team is involved.

 For a product-level (multiteam) quarterly planning meeting agenda, see section 17.9.4.8 in Chapter 17.

Planning does not have to take place in a formal forum. It may take place over several informal conversations. If planning is informal, use the following list and guidelines to determine what topics to cover during the discussions. If the planning event is formal, the following items may be used as a basis for an agenda:

- Overview
  - Review business case, vision, assumptions, long-term roadmap.
  - Craft goals and objectives.
  - Review proposed features.
  - Specify planning horizon (release date) and budget.
  - Review input artifacts.
- Exploration
  - Clarify and estimate features.
- Commitment
  - Commit to quarterly goals and objectives.
  - Revise priorities.
  - Commit to scope forecast (forecast of features that will be delivered).
  - Commit to the roadmap.
  - Manage risks and dependencies.
  - Review practices.
  - Approve plan.
- Planning Retrospective
  - Convene a quarterly/feature planning retrospective.

Let's look at facilitation guidelines for each of these items.

11.11.1 Overview

Begin the event with an overview of the planning period, as described in the following sections.

11.11.1.1 *Review Business Case, Vision, Assumptions, Long-Term Roadmap*

Invite senior business executives to describe the status of the business, new developments, and customer needs. Review the business case and product or epic vision statement, as appropriate. Use the product portrait, if available, as a visual overview.

If the quarterly or feature plan is part of a longer-term initiative or epic, review the long-term plan (e.g., product roadmap, epic roadmap) and its goals and objectives so that they may guide the group during quarterly planning. This is also an occasion to revise the long-term plan if necessary (e.g., due to the emergence of new threats or opportunities).

11.11.1.2 *Craft Goals and Objectives*

Next, work with the group to specify goals and objectives for the planning horizon (e.g., the upcoming quarter or release cycle). If a long-term product roadmap exists, review the goals and objectives it specifies for the quarter and adapt them as necessary.

> Use the following guidelines when specifying quarterly goals and objectives:
>
> - Include learning goals.
> - Commit to goals and objectives over features.
> - Specify outcome-based goals.

These guidelines are described in the following sections.

Include Learning Goals

Include learning goals, especially for early development of innovative products and features (e.g., the learning goal to test the hypothesis that users will be highly engaged with the product).

Commit to Goals and Objectives over Features

Commitment to goals and objectives is higher than it is to features. Explain to stakeholders that though the *features* included in the plan are expected to change, every effort will be made to achieve the plan's goals and objectives. However, even goals and objectives might change over the course of the planning cycle.

Specify Outcome-Based Goals

As earlier advised (see section 11.7.3), express goals and objectives in terms of real-world **outcomes** rather than deliverables, actions taken, or compliance with target metrics for internal processes. Outcome-based goals keep the focus on business value while leaving room for deliverables to change on the basis of learning.

The following are examples of outcome-based goals:

- Achieve a 15 percent increase in program enrollment within two years.

- Achieve compliance with a regulation by a specified date.

- Reduce end-to-end turnaround time to one day for 90 percent of applicants within the first month of deployment.

- Reduce the number of service-desk calls/customer by 10 percent by a specified date.

Here are examples of outcome-based goals for disruptive innovations:[9]

- Increase the number of customers using products and services that didn't exist three years ago by x percent within two years.

- Increase the percentage of revenue from products and services that didn't exist three years ago by x percent within one year.

Take care to ensure that quarterly goals align with strategic goals and objectives. Goals and objectives should be SMART: specific, measurable, achievable, realistic/relevant, and timebound.

11.11.1.3 Overview of Proposed Features

Invite the customer (PO) to provide an overview of the features lined up for the planning period. Discuss the hypotheses (assumptions) that underlie the plan and the MVPs that will test them during the plan's first development cycles. See Chapter 12, "MVPs and Story Maps," for guidelines on planning MVPs.

11.11.1.4 Specify Planning Horizon (Release Date) and Budget

Work with business stakeholders and developers to gain consensus on the planning horizon—the period covered by the plan. You may specify a release date, a relative time (e.g., x weeks after event y), the number of iterations—or indicate a range of dates and firm up the date closer to release. Sometimes business constraints may determine the release date (e.g., when compliance must occur by a given deadline).

How to Forecast When a Feature Will Be Delivered

If you're planning an upcoming feature (e.g., in Kanban planning), forecast its delivery date using a burndown chart. Project the graph into the future according to the points estimated for the feature. Using the chart enables you to base the projection on past progress. Another advantage is that the conversion from story points to time is typically automated when the charts are generated by a requirements management tool. By referring to

---

9. Eric Ries, *The Lean Startup* (New York: Random House, 2011), 35.

the chart, you also reinforce to stakeholders that the completion date is a projection based on changing data, not a firm commitment.

For more on burndown charts for forecasting, see Chapter 15, section 15.7.5.5.

Nevertheless, if necessary, you can derive a quick estimate of time-to-completion using the following conversion formula (points to time).

> Time to completion [# weeks or iterations] = Total estimated effort [story points] ÷ Velocity [points per week or iteration]

Determining Capacity

The next step is to determine the team's **capacity** or **budget**. Base the capacity forecast on the team's past velocity while adjusting for changed circumstances, such as holidays, sick leave, and changes to the team's composition. Velocity can be measured in various units, such as story points delivered in an iteration, week, or month. If the team uses a time-boxed planning approach (e.g., Scrum or XP), velocity is measured as the number of story points delivered per iteration. If it's using a flow-based approach (e.g., Kanban), velocity may be measured as the number of story points or number of work items delivered per week. Kanban progress metrics include cycle time and work in progress (WIP).

For more on metrics used in Kanban, see Chapter 15, section 15.7.8.

The primary reason to measure past velocity is forecasting. You can also use velocity to flag performance issues so they can be addressed. What you should *not* do is use velocity as a metric to judge or reward a team's performance.

The velocity is best determined on the basis of "yesterday's weather" (a term coined by Alistair Cockburn) rather than on a long-term average. Recent velocity is a better predictor because the team's productivity tends to change—often improving—as development progresses. One or two weeks is too little to base a forecast on, however. Most teams take an average over the past six to eight weeks (three or four iterations). It's normal for velocity to fluctuate at first, but it should settle down after about three to six iterations (six to twelve weeks).

For guidance on determining velocity, see Chapter 6, section 6.5.7.3.

11.11.1.5 Review Input Artifacts

Review any remaining input artifacts for the event. As noted in section 11.10.4. these may include journey maps, process models, and personas. Explain how each artifact will be used to inform planning.

Also, review and discuss any items that were identified in the previous planning retrospective and quarterly retrospective. Estimate remaining work items and add them to the current quarterly backlog.

11.11.2 Exploration

Explore the features planned for the upcoming planning cycle, as follows.

11.11.2.1 Clarify and Estimate Features

Work through the proposed features in priority order (highest priority first). As each feature arises, ask business stakeholders to explain it. Review the feature description. If it is not well articulated, coach stakeholders to use the Role-Feature-Reason (Connextra) template: "As a [role] I want [feature] so that [reason]." However, don't force requirements into the template if they don't suit the format. Work with business stakeholders, testers, and developers to clarify acceptance criteria so developers understand them well enough for planning purposes. As the feature nears implementation, coach them to express AC scenarios using the Gherkin syntax.

 See Chapter 8, section 8.7, for guidelines on specifying features using the Role-Feature-Reason (Connextra) template.

See Chapter 10, section 10.9, for guidelines on specifying feature acceptance criteria.

Next, ask developers to refine the estimated effort for the feature based on a better knowledge of its requirements and acceptance criteria. Limit estimation time to about two minutes per item. Ask estimators to note the degree of confidence associated with each estimate. Guidelines for estimating features are provided in the following sections.

As an analyst, encourage the active involvement of business stakeholders during estimation. Coach stakeholders and developers to explore options for lowering unacceptable estimates by removing low-value acceptance criteria or by using a less costly solution that delivers equivalent value. If the feature cannot be estimated, split it into smaller parts and estimate the parts.

In the next sections, we explore guidelines for estimating requirements items. The guidelines apply to items of any size—features and stories.

11.11.2.2 Objectives of Estimation

Use estimates for *forward-facing* purposes. The objectives of estimation are to plan the right amount of work for the team's capacity and provide best-guess forecasts of completion timelines. Estimates should *not* be used as a means of judging a team on past performance. (Doing so only encourages estimation inflation in the future.)

11.11.2.3 How Much Time Should You Spend on Estimation?

The initial estimation at the start of the first quarter can require several days to complete. After that, for each subsequent quarter, limit the time spent on estimation to about two minutes per item. Explore the possibility of eliminating estimation entirely. (See section 11.11.2.7 on the no-estimating approach.)

11.11.2.4 What Work Is Included in the Estimate?

The estimated effort should include not only coding but *all* remaining work to deliver the feature, such as requirements elicitation and documentation by a team analyst, coding, refactoring, and testing. However, analysis work by nondedicated business analysts is excluded from the estimate because it is not counted against the team's budget. (The effort is included in general overhead.)

11.11.2.5 Estimation Best Practices

Use the following guidelines for effective feature estimation.

- Hindsight is the best foresight.
- Base the estimate on a capable developer.
- Focus on value.
- Refine the estimate over time.

Hindsight Is the Best Foresight

Dana Mitchell, agile practice lead for agile transformation at TD Bank Securities, expressed this guideline to me: Hindsight is the best foresight. Hindsight offers the most accurate measurement and learning opportunities. The best estimates are based on the team's experience tackling similar problems in the past.

Once the team has some practical experience under its belt, estimation accuracy tends to improve regardless of the estimation method used. When experienced teams do encounter estimation problems, it's usually not due to methodology but to a black swan[10] event—an atypical scenario in which the team faces impediments *vastly out of line* with expectations. For example, in one recent example, a team with an excellent track record estimating features ran into trouble when it began working on a technical story brought forward by a component team. The objective of the story was to refactor the code—centralize references to a component to make it easier to make future modifications to the component and the way it is accessed without introducing errors. Once the team began working on the story, they discovered references throughout the system that they hadn't expected. The cost was orders of magnitude greater than the original estimate.

Base the Estimate on a Capable Developer

Earlier, we saw the Planning Game rule that those doing the work should estimate the work. If developers have been assigned to the feature, they provide the estimate. If the feature is unassigned, estimators should assume that a developer with the required competencies will implement it.

Use Planning Poker to gain consensus quickly from a group of estimators. Planning Poker is discussed in section 11.11.2.8.

---

10. Nassim Nicholas Taleb, *The Black Swan, Second Edition: The Impact of the Highly Improbable* (New York: Random House, 2010).

Focus on Value

As a facilitator, ensure that if customers push back[11] against estimates, estimators aren't pressured to backtrack[12] and revise them. Enforce the rules that only those doing the work should estimate the work and that the planned effort must not exceed the budget (i.e., the team's projected capacity). Avoid conflict by focusing on value. Ask developers to explain the business value delivered by the feature. If the customer still wishes to lower the estimate, explore less-costly solutions that provide similar value. Ask developers which aspects contribute most to the feature's cost. Discuss opportunities to reduce the cost by deferring low-value requirements. In that case, split the feature and its acceptance criteria into two smaller features or stories—with high-value criteria in the planned feature and low-value criteria in the deferred feature.

Refine the Estimate over Time

Estimate an item only to the precision necessary *at the time*. As the feature approaches implementation, refine the estimate. For example, specify weeks/months or number of iterations when initially entering and preparing a feature in the product backlog. During the quarterly planning event, use more nuanced metrics such as points or IDDs to match planned work against available capacity. Re-estimate a feature whenever it changes (e.g., through the addition or removal of functionality or acceptance criteria).

11.11.2.6 Estimating Units and Methods

Commonly used estimation units include the following:

- T-shirt sizes

- Number of days, weeks, or months

- Number of iterations

- Time estimates: real time (person-days) and ideal time (IDDs)

- Story points

- Not estimating at all

T-Shirt Sizes

Use T-shirt sizes when only broad estimates are needed, such as when requirements items are first added to the backlog. Sizes may include XS, S, M, L, XL, XXL, and XXXL.

Number of Days, Weeks, Months, or Iterations

When preparing features to be ready for quarterly planning (or feature planning), refine the estimate so it is accurate enough for scoping purposes (determining the features

---

11. Mike Schultz, "4 Things to Do When Clients Pressure You for Lower Fees" [blog post], RAIN Group, 2020, https://www.rainsalestraining.com/blog/sales-objections-sales-techniques-to-fight-price-pressure

12. Schultz, "4 Things to Do."

included in the plan). The following estimation units are sufficiently precise for this purpose: number of days, weeks, or months or number of iterations to implement.

Ideal Time (IDDs)

Time-based estimation units are the most transparent, indicating the person-days or person-hours required to implement a requirements item. If the teams are practicing pair programming (an XP practice whereby programmers work in twos), effort is measured in *pair-hours* or *pair-days*—the time it would take a pair of developers to complete the story.

Time-based estimates may represent actual or ideal time. IDDs measure how long it would take a developer to implement the item assuming 100 percent of their time was dedicated to it. For example, one IDD may take three days of actual time because a developer is dedicated to the story only one-third of time.

Story Points

Story points are a *relative* measure: they don't tell us directly how *much* time a story will take. They specify how long it would take to implement it *relative* to another story.

To use story points, assemble the team at the start of the initiative to set a 1-point and (optionally) an 8-point standard. For the 1-point standard, the team selects a story that would take a dedicated developer one day to complete. It's also useful to set an 8-point standard—representing the maximum user story size, after which requirements items are classed as features.

To forecast the delivery time for an upcoming feature or story based on its points, use a burndown chart or conversion formula, as explained in section 11.11.1.4.

Should Points Measure Complexity or Effort?

There is a debate in the agile community about whether point estimates should measure relative effort or complexity. My view is that points should measure effort, since that's what you need to know for capacity planning and forecasting timelines—the primary uses for estimates. Complexity is an important variable because it affects effort and the accuracy of an estimate. (The more complex the feature, the higher the uncertainty regarding the estimate.) However, even though a feature is uncomplicated, it may require so much mundane development work that it takes longer to implement than a complex feature. It's effort, not complexity, that's matched against capacity when planning scope.

What Are the Best Estimating Units: Real Time, IDDs, or Story Points?

The short answer is that the choice of estimating units is not that consequential, because you can convert points into time whenever you need to. You can even automate that conversion, so the customer sees estimates as elapsed time regardless of the units used to track them internally. Two widely used options—story points and IDDs—are essentially equivalent. Ron Jeffries, the inventor of points estimation, believes he was likely thinking of IDDs[13] when he invented them.

---

13. Ron Jeffries, "Story Points Revisited," May 23, 2019, https://ronjeffries.com/articles/019-01ff/story-points/Index.html

There are some pros and cons to each approach (which we'll get to soon), but what's more consequential is what you base the estimate on. *Estimates should be based on experience.*

Keeping that in mind, it *is* true that the choice of units can make some difference. Let's look at the pros and cons of the available options.

The Case for Real-Time Estimates   Actual real-time estimates (vs. IDDs and points) have the virtue of transparency: their meaning is self-evident without conversion. For this reason, Kent Beck, who popularized story points in the first edition of his book on XP, reversed himself in the second edition by recommending that time estimates be used instead.[14] Similarly, Jeffries now states, in a 2019 post, "I like to say that I may have invented story points, and if I did, I'm sorry now."[15] (To be fair, Jeffries is currently predisposed against *all* estimation methods.)

Though Beck reversed himself as far back as 2004, many XP practitioners continue to follow the original guidance. As we'll see in the next section, they often have a good reason for doing so.

The Case for Story Points   One of the purported benefits of story points estimation is that if performance doesn't match expectations, you only have to change one factor, velocity. Point estimates themselves don't need to be revised because they're relative, not absolute, as is the case with real-time estimates. This benefit is not that significant, though, because the revision can be automated.

All things considered, I prefer story points. However, I was not initially a fan due to their lack of transparency. When teams used to tell me they liked story points because they provided some "wiggle room," my response used to be "I can see how that works out for the developer, but I can't see how that works for the customer."

I don't see the issue as clear-cut anymore. Experience has taught me that story points often provide cultural benefits that can override the transparency argument. Managers report that the adoption of story points estimation fosters a whole-team mentality in which everyone is focused on the success of the group rather than of the individual.

In contrast, when they've used real-time estimates, planning meetings often devolved into contentious confrontations. Stakeholders would challenge the estimates of developers; they had difficulty accepting that a request would take so many days. These tensions vanished when the teams switched to story points estimation.

One of the reasons story points reduce conflict relative to real-time estimates is that points, unlike time, are typically tracked at the team level only, not at the individual level. For example, teams track team velocity—the points delivered per iteration—but they don't track *individual* velocity. Consequently, when points estimation is used, it is the team as a whole that becomes responsible for productivity, not the individual.

---

14. Beck now states, "I prefer to work with real time estimates now." See Kent Beck, "Planning: Managing Scope," in *Extreme Programming Explained: Embrace Change*, 2nd ed., The XP Series (Boston: Addison-Wesley, 2005).

15. Jeffries, "Story Points Revisited."

Another reason story points estimation is less contentious is that points are *relative*. Stakeholders find it much easier to accept how long a story will take relative to another than the *actual time* it takes to implement. Story points estimation avoids conflict about the issue by focusing on what the team knows with confidence at the start of the quarter—*relative effort*—and postponing discussion about what it *doesn't know* as much about—absolute (real) effort.

Finally, there is a subtle but essential cultural difference between the two approaches. Story points measure the story; person-hours measure people. As TD's Mitchell explains, the use of real-time estimation for quarterly planning reinforces the notion that development staff are resources (costs), not humans.

I still have some remaining hesitation about story points because of the transparency problem. Certainly, if the issues noted here have been a concern when using real-time estimates, try using points estimation to see if it improves the dynamics.

All this, of course, assumes you're estimating. There are ways to avoid estimation entirely, as we discuss in the next section.

Fibonacci Sequence

Estimates—whether measured in points or IDDs—are commonly assigned from the Fibonacci series. In a Fibonacci series, the value of each member is equal to the sum of the previous two members. The Fibonacci series is {1, 2, 3, 5, 8, 13, 21, 34, . . .}.

Fibonacci numbers are favored for story estimation because the gaps between numbers increase as their values increase. Estimators can deliberate about whether an item is a 1 or a 2, but not whether it is a 21 or a 22. This is appropriate because the first gap represents a 100 percent difference, while the difference in the second case is only about 5 percent. Most teams use a revised form of the Fibonacci series—rounding off the higher numbers so they don't appear to be more precise than they are. The numbers in this revised sequence are as follows:

> ?, 0, 0.5, 1, 2, 3, 5, 8, 13, 20, 40, 80, 100

The values are interpreted as follows:

- ?: The story is not estimable.

- 0: No appreciable effort is required to implement the story (e.g., a small fix).

- 0.5: Some effort but less than a 1.

- 1: Standard story size against which others are measured.

- >1: Effort relative to a 1. For example, a 2 is twice as much effort as a 1.

- 5: Upper limit for most stories.

- 8: Absolute maximum for a user story. A few stories are allowed at this size if they are difficult to split.

- ≥13: A feature or epic. The item *must* be split before it is entered into an iteration plan.

You may be wondering why the cutoff for splitting work items is 8 instead of 10—the actual number of working days a developer has in a two-week period (a common iteration length). The reason is that activities other than story implementation (such as planning, demos, and retrospectives) typically consume at least two of those days.

11.11.2.7 *The No-Estimating Approach*

Ultimately, estimation is still waste, since it doesn't add to a product's value. The ideal would be to eliminate it entirely. Some teams are beginning to experiment with that approach with encouraging results. The no-estimating approach has also been endorsed by Jeffries,[16] who has argued that the added effort is better placed figuring out how to slice off thin pieces of functionality to deliver quick wins. Left unanswered is how you forecast scope if you don't have estimates on hand.

The secret to forecasting without estimating is in the preparation: If you prepare requirements items well enough for developers to have a good feel for the work involved, the stories don't actually have to be estimated. (To be fair, there is *some* estimation involved, but it's minimal.) Unlike estimation, this analysis is not overhead because the understanding is fed directly into development. Here's how you apply the approach:

During long-term planning, ask developers to provide broad estimates of features—for example, the number of iterations to complete each feature. Before quarterly planning, the PO sequences the features under consideration on the basis of their relative priorities. As the analyst, you prepare the features for planning through discussions with stakeholders, testers, and developers.

During the quarterly planning meeting, each developer silently forecasts how far down the product backlog the team will be able to reach during the quarter. When everyone has made their forecasts, they reveal their answers simultaneously and discuss their rationales.

As long as features are well prepared, forecasts are often surprisingly close to each other on the first round or two, and variances are resolved after a short discussion—especially once the team has some experience to go on. Moreover, forecasts are at least as accurate as those obtained using points—without the waste of estimating stories and tracking velocities. You can use a similar approach to determine the scope of an iteration during iteration planning.

11.11.2.8 *Planning Poker Using Delphi Estimation*

One of the challenges you face if you estimate features (as most teams do) is what to do when estimators disagree. Use Delphi estimation to address this issue. **Delphi estimation** is a method for arriving at a consensus of expert opinions, shown to result in a quick convergence of views and improved estimates.[17] The principles of Delphi estimation are as follows:

- *Anonymity:* Anonymity reduces the impact of group-think. Ask evaluators to submit responses privately—for example, online or by placing estimate cards face down.

---

16. Jeffries, "Story Points Revisited."

17. Norman Crolee Dalkey, "Delphi," Rand Corporation, 1967, 5, https://www.rand.org/pubs/papers/P3704.html

- *Controlled feedback:* Elicit feedback from evaluators who provided atypical estimates (lowest and highest). Facilitate arguments for and against the estimates.

- *Statistical group response:* At the end of each cycle, calculate the mean estimate and feed it into the next cycle. Use a mean rather than an average.

Stop the process when a predefined condition has been met (e.g., after x cycles, after consensus is achieved, or when results are unchanged). At the end of the process, use the median from the final cycle as the estimate. After a few rounds, estimates typically converge to a single value.

In agile planning, Delphi estimation often takes the form of Planning Poker. The method can be used to plan features for the quarter, plan stories for an iteration, or estimate a single work item. Typical rules of play are provided next.

Preparation

The PO has a deck of cards, each naming a feature (or story) being considered for the planning period.

Estimators are given blank cards, used for scoring. As an alternative, some teams use the calculator app on their mobile phones to record scores. Use any medium that provides anonymity.

Overview of Steps

The steps of Planning Poker can be summarized as follows:

1. Story Telling

2. Silent Estimation

3. The Reveal

4. Collaboration (Bargaining)

5. Feedback Loop

1. Story Telling   The PO picks a feature card from the deck and describes it to the estimators. Estimators ask as many questions as necessary to provide an estimate with confidence.

2. Silent Estimation   Each estimator silently estimates the feature using a Fibonacci number. Estimators write the score on the card and place it face down. An alternative is for estimators to enter estimates into the calculator app of their phones.

3. The Reveal   The facilitator asks estimators to turn their cards face up. The facilitator determines the mean estimate, low estimate, and high estimate and announces them to the group.

4. Collaboration (Bargaining)   The facilitator asks the estimators with the lowest and highest estimates to explain their evaluations. For example, an estimator may have provided an abnormally high estimate due to assumptions about the requirements, the solution, or technical difficulty not shared by the rest of the group. The group then spends a few minutes discussing counterarguments and collaborates to find alternative solutions when estimates exceed the budget.

As an analyst, you support collaboration by exploring the reasons for high estimates with the technical team and exploring low-cost alternatives. The following are examples of questions to ask estimators at this time:

- Have any of you done something very similar to this before? (An estimate from someone who has expertise is accepted over the estimate of someone who has not—assuming an expert is assigned to the feature.)

- Which aspect of the feature is contributing most to the estimate? Which acceptance criteria are the most costly?

- Which aspects of the feature and feature acceptance criteria can be implemented quickly? What are the minimum AC for the feature to be releasable?

- How are other companies implementing similar features?

- Is there a quick win that would provide similar business value?

If the estimate is higher than the budget allows, consider splitting the feature into smaller items. Distribute the acceptance criteria among the resulting features, with the highest-value acceptance criteria in the feature planned for the upcoming quarter.

5. Feedback Loop   Feed the mean estimate and arguments back into the next cycle. Return to step 1. Repeat the process until estimates converge. It typically takes up to three cycles for estimates to converge.

11.11.2.9 Estimating Other Kinds of Stories

All backlog items for the quarter should be estimated. These include user stories and features as well as work items not related to providing new capabilities, such as spikes, bug fixes, and technical stories. We examine these work items in detail in Chapter 13, "Story Preparation," but let's preview them now from an estimation perspective.

Estimating Spikes

Functional spikes represent analysis work for an upcoming feature or story. Spikes may be considered a subtype of stories. For example, SAFe refers to them as "enabler stories." There is general agreement on the value of spikes but not whether they should be estimated. A good rule of thumb is to estimate a functional spike if the analyst doing the work is a dedicated team member whose time is included in the budget. However, if the spike will be performed by someone who is not part of the team (e.g., a nondedicated business analyst), don't estimate the spike because it doesn't consume the team's budget. The work is accounted for in another way, as part of general overhead.

Estimating Bug Fixes

If a defect is deemed high priority, developers should begin work on it immediately. Don't bother estimating high-priority bug fixes unless developers believe they might cause items in the quarterly plan to be dropped.[18]

Don't track or estimate small, independent bug fixes; the overhead is not worth the time. As a general rule of thumb, create an estimate for a bug fix if it will take half a day or more to implement, since it might impact other items in the plan. Collect small bug fixes meant to be released together into a single story.

Estimating Technical Stories and Nonfunctional Requirements

So far, we've focused on the estimation of customer-facing features. Other work items that will consume the team's budget also need to be considered and estimated during planning. These include technical stories and nonfunctional requirements (NFRs). A technical story does not add user functionality but addresses a technical issue, such as removing unreachable code to avoid bugs and improve maintainability. An NFR addresses quality requirements, such as security, volume, and compliance requirements.

11.11.2.10 *Estimation for Iteration Planning Purposes*

While this chapter focuses on the estimation of features during quarterly and/or feature planning, similar guidelines apply to story estimation during iteration planning. However, the estimation units may differ, especially in the second part of iteration planning. On entry to iteration planning, story points or IDDs provide sufficient precision for initial scoping. However, in the latter part of iteration planning—the decomposition of stories into developer tasks—use real-time units (e.g., number of hours). The higher level of precision is appropriate for the smaller-sized work item (the developer task). Furthermore, concerns expressed earlier in this chapter about the impact of real-time estimates on customer–developer relations don't apply because the customer is usually absent from this part of the planning event.

11.11.3 Commitment

At the end of the planning event, business representatives and the team commit to the plan. The following actions are taken:

- Commit to quarterly goals and objectives.
- Revise priorities.
- Commit to scope forecast (delivered features).
- Construct the roadmap.
- Manage risks and dependencies.

---

18. Thanks to Ron Healy for contributing this rule in a note to the author.

- Review practices.

- Approve the plan.

These steps are described in the following sections.

11.11.3.1 Commit to Quarterly Goals and Objectives

Facilitate a final review of goals and objectives by business decision makers and developers. Revise the goals and objectives, if necessary, to gain consensus from both parties.

11.11.3.2 Revise Priorities

On entry to quarterly planning, features may be prioritized in broad terms, such as the XP priority levels: "Must have," "Adds significant value," and "Nice to have." For quarterly planning purposes, express prioritization through sequencing. Now that features have been explored and estimated, stakeholders have better information on which to refine prioritization decisions. Coach stakeholders to use the weighted shortest job first (WSJF) approach to inform sequencing decisions based on value and effort. As noted in Chapter 6, the essential aspect of the approach is how it guides decision makers to consider user and business value, time criticality, risk reduction and opportunity enablement, and estimated cost (job duration). WSJF values should *inform* sequencing decisions. However, they shouldn't *dictate* decisions because the method doesn't account for all scenarios.

 See Chapter 6, sections 6.5.4.4 and 6.5.5.5, for guidelines on calculating WSJF and cost of delay.

Ensure that there are enough ready features in the backlog after resequencing to match the team's capacity, plus a few more, in case they can be accommodated.

Balancing User Features and Debt Payment

Two conflicting priorities are often at play when planning work across the product: the prioritization of customer-facing features versus quality improvements to the system, such as technical stories to improve scalability or security. If the balance tips too far toward the former, the result can be loss of quality and an unmanageable accumulation of technical debt. To avoid this outcome, work with the PO and business stakeholders to determine an optimal target ratio of features to technical debt payment. A typical ratio of features to debt payment is about 3:1, but the organization should experiment to find the right balance.

11.11.3.3 Commit to Scope Forecast

Once the sequencing of features is confirmed, commit to the scope forecast—the features that will be delivered during the quarter. Accept features into the plan according to their priority sequence until the team's capacity is reached. The business decision maker confirms that the scope supports the goals and objectives for the quarter, and the team verifies that the total estimated effort does not exceed its capacity (the budget).

Balancing Commitment versus Adaptability

As noted earlier, in agile quarterly planning, scope commitment means that the team agrees that the planned features are the *best forecast* of what will be delivered—not a promise to deliver them. However, as also noted (see section 11.7.4.2), business constraints often require a higher commitment level. As an analyst, you support stakeholders and developers in defining a level of commitment that satisfies business constraints without unduly impairing its ability to respond to change and learning. Use the following strategies.

- **Commit to Features, Not Depth:** Developers commit to the feature but not to the *depth* of the feature that will be provided. The developers confirm that the feature's acceptance criteria are the best forecasts of what will be delivered. However, all parties agree that if time is running out, they will negotiate changes to acceptance criteria in order to deliver the feature with its highest-value requirements without postponing the release date.

- **Differentiate between Committed and Target Features:** A **committed feature** is one that the team is fully committed to delivering. A **target feature** represents a **stretch objective**—something the team is planning to provide but cannot promise. Teams commit to delivering a specified percentage of each type (e.g., 100 percent of committed features and 70 percent of target features). This practice enables teams to provide business stakeholders with predictability regarding the highest-value features while retaining flexibility concerning lower-value ones.

11.11.3.4 Construct the Roadmap

The next step is to construct the implementation plan, or roadmap—the plan for how features will be implemented across the planning horizon and the milestones that will be achieved. In this section, we examine the following artifacts used for this purpose:

- The minimal quarterly plan
- The quarterly (release) roadmap
- Program board
- Quarterly (release) Kanban board

In the next chapter, we examine a more detailed artifact used in this context—the story map.

> **Tip**
> Use the simplest planning artifact that meets the needs of teams and stakeholders.

The Minimal Quarterly Plan

The implementation plan may take many forms. The simplest is a one-dimensional list of requirements items, estimated and sequenced in order of implementation. Table 11.2 illustrates a sample template for this form. The same format may be used in release planning. The release plan indicates release goals and objectives and lists the features forecast for the release cycle.

Table 11.2 *Quarterly Plan: Minimal Template*

Delivery Date (if applicable):
Quarterly Goals and Objectives:
Milestones (Events, Dates/Timelines):
Features Forecast for the Quarter (Prioritized, Estimated):
Features Planned for Subsequent Quarter:

Use a minimal format like the one in Table 11.2 when work items in the plan represent localized changes that can be delivered in any order without diminishing their value.

Quarterly Roadmap

The minimal template described above is appropriate when each feature or story may be viewed on its own terms. However, that's not the case if the sum is worth more than its parts. If the individual features contribute to a larger value stream or goal, use one of the following templates so you can view the combination of features that will be delivered at milestones within the planning period, and plan quick wins that deliver real value:

- Quarterly roadmap
- Program board
- Story map

We cover the first two in the next sections. Story maps are covered in the next chapter. Figure 11.2 is an example of a quarterly roadmap.

The template is similar to the long-term product roadmap we saw earlier in Chapter 9, but it applies to a smaller planning horizon—one quarter. One column in Figure 11.2 is dedicated to each interval in the quarter (e.g., two weeks or an iteration). Goals, milestones, and ordered features are specified for each interval.

If the initiative involves multiple teams, the planning deliverable should also indicate which team does what. See Figure 11.4 later in this chapter for an example of a template that provides this added information.

Planning Horizon: One quarter or release cycle

Timeline	Weeks 1–2	Weeks 3–4	Weeks 5–6	Weeks 7–8
Name				
Goals and Objectives				
Assumptions Tested				
Metrics				
Milestones, Events				
Features (Ordered)				

Figure 11.2 *Quarterly (release) roadmap template*

11.11.3.5 *Manage Risks and Dependencies*

The group discusses risks and develops a plan to address them. As an analyst facilitating a risk-analysis workshop, ensure stakeholders and developers consider all risk types that might derail the plan. These include:

- Technical risks (e.g., that costly, unexpected technical problems will arise)
- Market risks (e.g., that customers won't accept the product due to privacy concerns)
- Financial risk (e.g., that the product cannot be sold at a profitable price)
- Estimation risk (e.g., that the effort turns out to be much greater than anticipated)
- Elicitation risk (e.g., that SMEs won't be available or won't respond in a timely fashion)

Assign a risk response to each risk item, describing the strategy for managing the risk. The response may be as follows:[19]

- **Void:** Treat the cause and eliminate the risk. For example, to eliminate technical risk, create a proof-of-concept to validate technical assumptions.

---

19. "Plan Risk Responses," Project Management Professional (PMP) program, GreyCampus, https://www.greycampus.com/opencampus/project-management-professional/plan-risk-responses

- **Mitigate:** Accept that the risk may occur, but put a plan B in place to reduce the impact if it does. For example, develop an alternative solution.

- **Transfer:** Transfer the risk to another body. For example, transfer financial risk to an insurance company.

- **Accept:** Accept that the risk may occur.

- **Escalate:** Escalate the risk to a higher authority level.

Identifying Dependencies

Unidentified dependencies represent risk because they can lead to unexpected integration problems and unintended consequences resulting in errors and rework. Furthermore, dependencies can result in bottlenecks and delayed releases. For example, if feature X is dependent on feature Y, and feature Y is not done, then feature X cannot be released. By specifying and tracking dependencies, you're better able to eliminate or manage these risks, coordinate teams, and plan integration testing.

One option for visualizing dependencies is to connect dependent items with a red string, as shown in Figure 11.3. This is the approach used in a SAFe program board.

 For more on the program board, see Chapter 17, section 17.9.4.6.

Planning Horizon: For example, one quarter, release cycle, program increment, or feature

Interim Planning Cycle: For example, two weeks,

Date or Period	Weeks 1–2	Weeks 3–4	Weeks 5–6	Weeks 7–8	Weeks 9–10
Name					
Goals and Objectives	Goal				
Assumptions Tested	Assumption				
Metrics	Metrics				
Milestones, Events	Milestone or event				
Features (Ordered)	Feature				

Figure 11.3 *Quarterly roadmap with dependency red strings*

You can indicate inter-team dependencies (dependencies among teams) through the use of colored cards and dots, as illustrated in Figure 11.4 (but not visible in the print edition of this book).

Planning Horizon: One quarter or release cycle

Timeline	Weeks 1–2	Weeks 3–4	Weeks 5–6	Weeks 7–8
Name				
Goals and Objectives				
Assumptions Tested				
Metrics				
Milestones, Events				
Features (Ordered)	Feature A ○ Feature B ● Feature C ○●	Feature D ○ ○ Feature E ○ Feature F ○	Feature G ○ ○ Feature H ● Feature I ○●	Feature J ○ ○ Feature K ●○ Feature L ○●

■ Red Team
■ Yellow Team
■ Blue Team

Figure 11.4 *Quarterly or release roadmap with dependency dots*

Each team in Figure 11.4 is associated with a color. The feature cards are color-coded, with the card's color indicating the primary team responsible for the feature. During planning, teams move across the cards on the roadmap, adding colored dots wherever they note a feature they are dependent on. For example, in Weeks 1–2 the yellow team is responsible for feature B; the red team is dependent on feature B.

For more on lightweight solutions for managing dependencies, see Chapter 17, section 17.11.

11.11.3.6 Review Practices

Next, work with the team to specify analysis, design, and other development practices and tools that will be used during the quarter (e.g., automated testing practices and requirements management techniques). Discuss at least one high-priority action item identified in the prior quarterly retrospective. Commit to a plan for addressing it.

Determine the means that will be used to track progress across the quarter. Table 11.3 is an example of a Kanban board template that follows work items from when they are entered into the quarterly plan until they are delivered to the customer.

Table 11.3 *Quarterly Kanban Board Template*

Initial (Entered)	Discussed	Prioritized	Assigned to team	Done	Delivered

11.11.3.7 Approve the Plan

The group ratifies the minutes and deliverables of the meeting and commits to next steps. Remind attendees that by approving the plan, they are agreeing that the goals and scope align with business goals and are attainable and that the planned features and timelines represent the best forecast at this time.

11.11.4 Planning Retrospective

At the end of the session, facilitate a retrospective about what went right and wrong during the planning session. Elicit suggestions about what to do in the future to improve the effectiveness of quarterly planning. Commit to at least one high-priority action item. Review progress on the item at the next quarterly planning meeting.

BLINK CASE STUDY PART 19
Create Release Roadmap

The Ask

After an initial meeting, business stakeholders and developers agree on a list of features for the upcoming release. You'll be facilitating a follow-up meeting to plan the incremental implementation of features across the iterations of the release cycle—with the intention of optimizing value delivery at each iteration.

The deliverable for the event will be

- **Deliverable 1:** Release roadmap indicating milestones/events and an ordered set of features for each iteration within the release cycle.

Preparation

You prepare the following event inputs based on the results of the initial release planning effort.

Event Inputs

Top sixteen features (each item is approximately two weeks' effort for one team):

1. Add BLInK to CSR calls
2. Make immediate discount available

3. Bind transaction
4. Initialize device
5. Earn rewards
6. Quick quote for preapproved applicants
7. Validate eligibility
8. Send application information to vendor
9. Add BLInK endorsement, subject to limits
10. Authorize enrollment
11. Subscriber can submit to activities online
12. Create dashboard
13. Submit Health Assessment
14. Receive recommendations
15. Analytics reports (e.g., impact on sickness, death, number of claims)
16. Summary reports to customer

You will use the quarterly roadmap template in Figure 11.3, with rows to specify milestones and features on an iteration-by-iteration basis.

What Transpires

You begin by eliciting milestones and events. The discussion results in the following list.

Milestones

- Campaign launch
- Immediate discount available
- Deployment to brokers
- Deployment to underwriters
- Quick quote deployment to customer portal

Next, you go through the list of features planned for the release and guide attendees to assign them to iterations. You coach attendees to plan quick wins, for example, by implementing a thin scenario for an entire value stream in the first iteration.

You ask the group to identify dependencies among requirements using red strings. Attendees review the plan in light of those dependencies. You direct attendees to look for features with outstanding dependencies. You facilitate the collaboration of stakeholders and developers to resolve dependencies by resequencing features and planning workarounds.

Deliverables

Deliverable 1: BLInK Release Roadmap

Figure 11.5 is a draft of the plan developed during the planning meeting. Milestones and events, such as campaign launch, are shown in the top row. Features are indicated in the rows below. The connecting strings indicate dependency relationships. For example, authorize enrollment depends on the capability to validate eligibility.

Case Study Retrospective

In this workshop, you worked with the team and stakeholders to develop a release plan that forecasts features and milestones for each iteration of the release cycle.

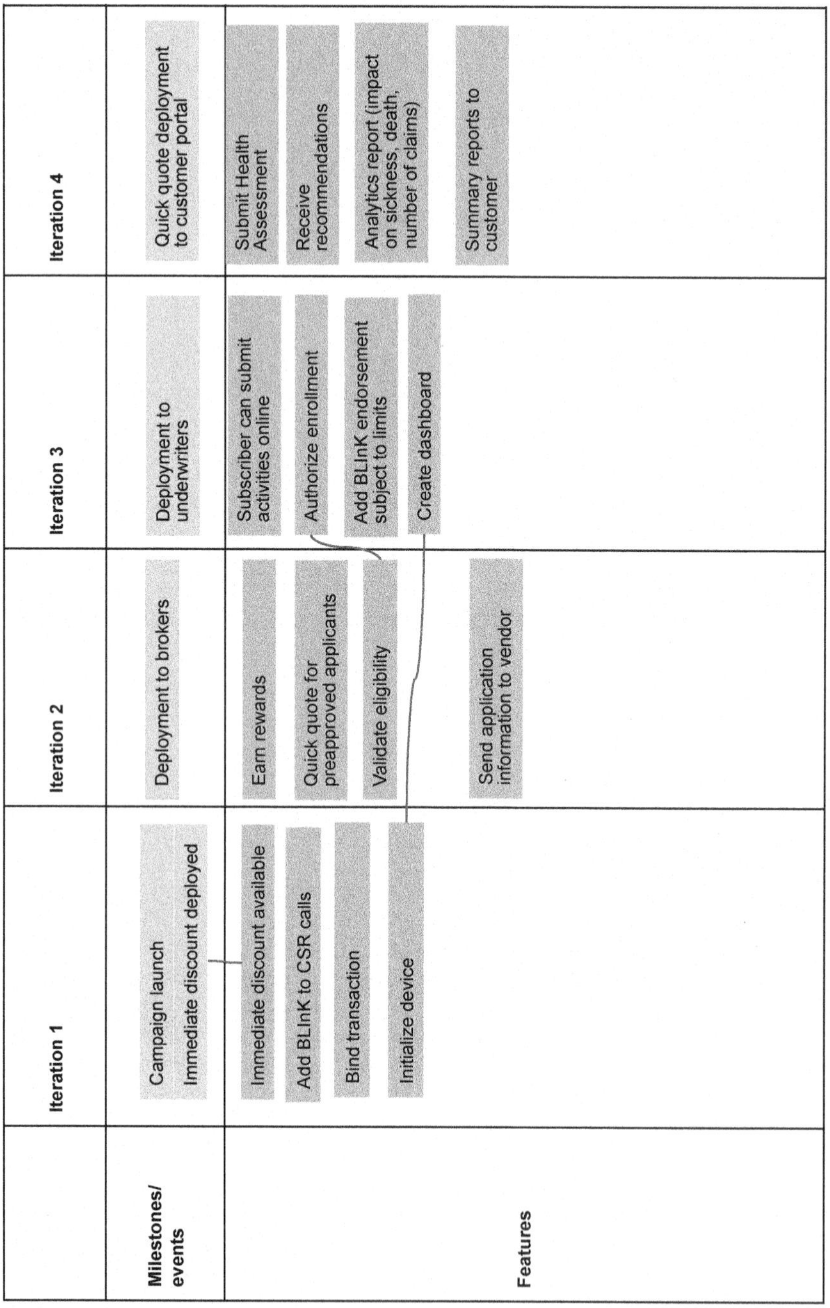

	Iteration 1	Iteration 2	Iteration 3	Iteration 4
Milestones/ events	Campaign launch Immediate discount deployed	Deployment to brokers	Deployment to underwriters	Quick quote deployment to customer portal
Features	Immediate discount available Add BLInK to CSR calls Bind transaction Initialize device	Earn rewards Quick quote for preapproved applicants Validate eligibility Send application information to vendor	Subscriber can submit activities online Authorize enrollment Add BLInK endorsement subject to limits Create dashboard	Submit Health Assessment Receive recommendations Analytics report (impact on sickness, death, number of claims) Summary reports to customer

Figure 11.5 *BLInK release roadmap with dependencies*

11.12 Reviewing the Quarterly Plan, Once the Quarter Is Underway

Review and revise the quarterly plan in accordance with changing circumstances (see sections 11.12.1–11.12.4.). This process is referred to as *steering* in XP's Planning Game. For the review, facilitate a shortened version of quarterly planning, focused on the following tasks:

- Receive updates from the PO on changes affecting the quarterly plan.

- Revise future quarters in the long-term plan.

- Review the *current* quarterly goals and objectives and revise them as necessary.

- Revise features in the quarterly plan so that remaining effort matches remaining capacity based on updated performance metrics.

- Discuss, prioritize, and estimate new features that were added to the quarterly backlog.

The following sections describe the circumstances that trigger a review of the quarterly plan.

11.12.1 Start of an Iteration

If the teams are using a timeboxed planning approach, such as Scrum, they meet for iteration planning at the start of every iteration. At or around this time, they review the quarterly plan. By reviewing the quarterly plan after the previous iteration's stories have been demonstrated, the group is able to assess and prioritize any remaining work to make stories acceptable to the customer against upcoming backlog items. Reviewing the quarterly plan at the start of the iteration planning meeting also communicates to the team the quarterly goals and objectives, so they can be considered during planning.

Revise the quarterly plan in accordance with updated estimates, performance metrics, and changed priorities. Estimate and prioritize any new stories added to the quarterly backlog.

11.12.2 Velocity Corrections

Revise the quarterly plan whenever performance diverges from the forecasted velocity to a degree that impacts the planned delivery of objectives and features. This includes lower-than-expected and higher-than-expected performance. Change the implementation schedule and milestones accordingly.

Add, split, or drop features to accord with the new velocity. If the performance is lower than expected, determine which features or acceptance criteria may be dropped from the plan without endangering the goals and objectives. If the performance is higher than expected, determine which features or acceptance criteria can be added to the plan.

11.12.3 New Features

Revisit the quarterly plan whenever features are added or expanded in the middle of a quarter. Meet with business stakeholders, developers, and testers to estimate and prioritize the new features. Determine which existing features in the quarterly plan must be dropped or reduced to make room for the new features. *No feature can be added to the plan unless it can be accommodated within the budget.*

11.12.4 The Plan Becomes Obsolete

If the whole plan has become obsolete because of changing circumstances or inaccurate forecasts, create a new quarterly plan, as described in section 11.11.

11.13 Chapter Summary

Here are the key points covered in this chapter:

- An agile quarterly plan is a hypothesis, not a firm commitment. It forecasts the goals, features, and milestones that will be completed during the planning period on the basis of what is known at the time.

- On entry to quarterly planning, features should meet the feature DoR (e.g., they have been sized to require a quarter or less to implement).

- Only those doing the work (the developers) may estimate; only the business may prioritize. Others may ask questions.

- In Planning Poker and Delphi estimation, estimators privately score items individually, then reveal their scores simultaneously. Feedback from low and high scorers is used as input to the next round.

- Options for estimating requirements items include story points and IDDs—and no estimating.

11.14 What's Next?

Chapter 12 continues quarterly planning with two essential techniques: story maps and MVPs.

One-dimensional lists of features, such as those provided on the roadmaps in this chapter, don't communicate operational sequencing—information that is important when planning features that are part of a workflow. Story maps, described in the next chapter, provide that capability. The quarterly plan's first development cycles include MVP experiments to test leap of faith hypotheses and determine the minimum marketable features in the release. The next chapter also includes extensive guidelines for planning those MVPs. The tools are complementary: story maps help planners visualize MVPs (and the delivered product) at specified intervals within the quarter.

Chapter 12

MVPs and Story Maps

This chapter continues the coverage of quarterly and feature planning, focusing on two tools used in that context: minimum viable products (MVPs) and story maps. Figure 12.1 highlights the activities covered in the chapter.

The chapter begins with MVP planning. It describes how to use MVPs to test hypotheses. It explores numerous MVP types, such as the Smoke-and-Mirrors MVP—a quick version that provides a similar frontend to that offered by the real product but uses workarounds behind the scenes. The chapter includes guidelines for using MVPs to test hypotheses, make adjustments, and decide whether to pivot or persevere. It also explores how to use MVPs to determine the smallest feature set that addresses user needs and creates the right user experience[1]—for a product, initiative, or epic.

The second part of the chapter examines story mapping—the technique used to visualize planned features within an end-to-end workflow, value stream, or user journey. The chapter explains how to use story maps to plan MVPs, deliver quick wins, and provide value to the end customer at each iteration or intermediate timeline. It includes guidelines for constructing a story map backbone—the top region of the map—using input artifacts such as journey maps, process models, and use-case models. Also included are guidelines for constructing the story map's ribs—the region specifying when features and stories will be implemented. The chapter includes guidelines for decomposing use cases (user tasks) into user stories. It also explains how to position stories on the map to indicate their operational sequence, the user tasks (features) they belong to, and when they will be implemented.

12.1 Objectives

This chapter will help you

- Plan MVPs to test leap of faith hypotheses.

- Create a story map and use it to plan the implementation and delivery of stories.

---

1. Roman Pichler, "The Minimum Viable Product and the Minimal Marketable Product," Pichler Consulting, October 9, 2013, https://www.romanpichler.com/blog/minimum-viable-product-and-minimal-marketable-product

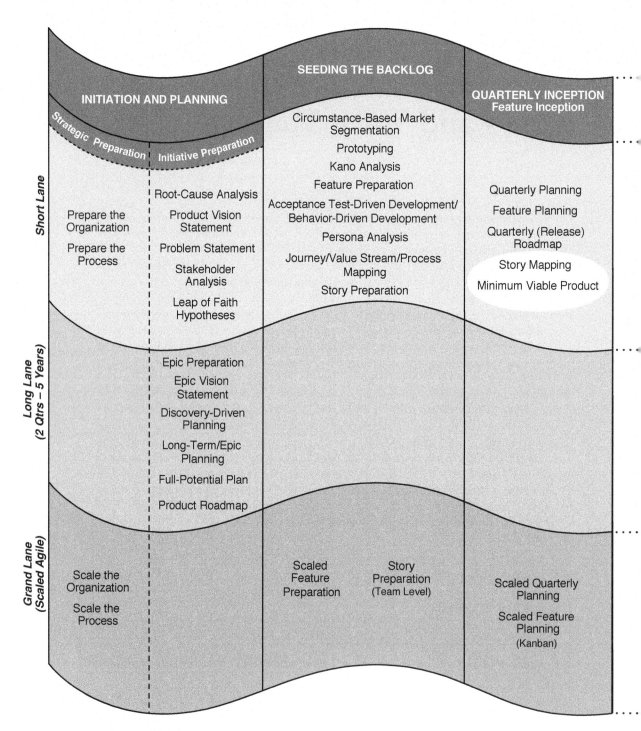

Figure 12.1   *Chapter 12 on the map*

ITERATION INCEPTION

Iteration Planning

DAILY ACTIVITIES

Daily Standup

Requirements Analysis & Documentation

Code, Build, Test, Deliver Acceptance Test-Driven Development/ Behavior-Driven Development

Minimum Viable Product, Split Testing

Epic, Feature Preparation

Story Preparation

ITERATION CLOSEOUT

Iteration Review

Iteration Retrospective

QUARTERLY CLOSEOUT
Epic, Feature Closeout

Prepare for General Availability

Quarterly Retrospective

Epic, Feature Retrospective

Pivot or Persevere

Scaled Iteration Planning

Iteration Planning (Team Level)

Product Owner Council Meetings

DevOps

User Task Force Meetings

Scaled Feature Preparation (Kanban)

Integration Meetings

Story Preparation (Team Level)

Scaled Iteration Review

Scaled Iteration Retrospective

Iteration Retrospective (Team Level)

DevOps

Scaled Quarterly/Feature Retrospective

- Indicate operational workflow on a story map backbone.

- Indicate how feature implementation will be sequenced in the story map ribs.

12.2 This Chapter on the Map

As shown in Figure 12.1, the chapter examines story mapping and MVP in the Quarterly Inception/Feature Inception zone.

12.3 MVPs and Story Mapping: How the Tools Complement Each Other

The primary objective of quarterly/feature planning (the subject of the last chapter) is to develop a plan indicating how goals and capabilities will be delivered over the planning horizon. That much is true for both agile and traditional planning. What makes an agile plan different is that its goals—especially at the start of new product development—are often *learning* goals, validated through MVPs, experimental versions of the product or feature designed to test hypotheses and deliver learning. The learning that is derived from this process is fed back into the agile plan—impacting subsequent goals and features that will be delivered.

MVPs and quick wins often require workarounds for steps that have not yet been implemented. Story maps provide a convenient way to view an end-to-end workflow at each time interval so that stakeholders and the team can visualize gaps where workarounds are required. Beyond their use for MVP planning, story maps are useful tools for planning features so that workflows are supported and meaningful value is delivered to the customer on a regular basis (e.g., at least every iteration or one- to two-week period).

Both tools are covered in this chapter. We begin with MVP planning.

12.4 MVP Planning

When a product is a new-market innovation, you can't prioritize features reliably upfront because customers themselves often won't know what they want until they see it. The lean startup approach,[2] introduced earlier in this book, addresses this problem by running experiments on customers—short-circuiting "the ramp by killing things that don't make sense fast and doubling down on the ones that do."[3]

---

2. Eric Ries, *The Lean Startup* (New York: Random House, 2011).

3. Brad Smith (CEO, Intuit), as quoted in Ries, *The Lean Startup*, 35.

12.4.1 What Is an MVP?

A minimum viable product (MVP) is a low-cost, experimental version of the product or feature used to test hypotheses and determine if it's worth fully investing in it. According to Eric Ries, the inventor of lean startup, an MVP is "that version of the product that enables a full turn of the Build-Measure-Learn loop with a minimum of effort and the least amount of development."[4] MVP is not (as often thought) the first version of the product released to the market. It's a version meant for *learning*—a means to test hypotheses and to determine the minimum set of features to include in a market-ready product. The minimal *releasable* version of the product is referred to as the **minimum marketable product** (MMP).

12.4.2 MVP Case Study: Trint

You only really understand why MVPs are so crucial to the success of innovative product development when you see a real example of the process. That was the case as I followed the story of Trint, a company founded by Emmy-winning reporter, foreign and war correspondent (and good friend) Jeffrey Kofman. Like many late-stage entrepreneurs, Kofman set out to solve a problem he understood intimately because it had bothered him throughout much of his previous professional life: every time Kofman had to transcribe an interview by hitting PLAY, STOP, TRANSCRIBE, and REWIND, he couldn't understand why he was still using a process that had remained virtually unchanged since the 1960s and 1970s. Why wasn't artificial intelligence (AI) being used to automate the speech-to-text transcription? He knew the reason: journalists can't risk inaccuracies. Since AI makes mistakes, journalists wouldn't use an AI-based product unless there was a way to verify the content. The real problem, then, was how to leverage automated speech-to-text in order to get to 100 percent accuracy.

Kofman knew that if he could solve that problem, he would have a winning product. Furthermore, he knew that if his team could solve it for journalists—whom he knew to be unforgiving—they could solve it for anybody. He concluded, therefore, that the most important leap of faith hypothesis for the product was that the company could find a way for users to correct errors in place in order to deliver transcripts that could be verified and trusted. As Kofman saw it, his team needed to create a layer on top of AI (the automated speech-to-text component) so that the AI part would do the heavy lifting of transcription, allowing the user to focus on quicker tasks: search, verify, and correct. He believed that by using this approach, he could reduce the time to perform a task that would normally take hours to complete down to minutes or even seconds. From earlier chapters of this book, you'll recognize Kofman's steps as the beginning of the MVP process: the articulation of the problem, vision, and leap of faith hypotheses for the product.

To create the MVP, Kofman gathered a team of developers with experience in audio-to-text alignment using manually entered text. He challenged them to hack together an MVP version that would automatically transcribe speech to text and allow a user to edit it.

The company's first MVP was built in just three months. Kofman decided to use some of his limited seed funding to invest in user lab testing. He brought in a group of journalists

---

4. Ries, 77.

for the testing day. Interestingly (as is often the case), the first MVP was "wrong." While the journalists liked the concept, they struggled to use the product, finding it annoying to switch back and forth between editing and playback modes. (The original design used the space bar as a toggle between modes *and* as the text space character during editing, confusing users.) As Kofman told me, "Good innovative products should solve workflow problems; this was creating new ones." And so, using feedback from the MVP, he asked the developers to build a new user experience with a better workflow.

MVP isn't just about one test; it's a process. Fifteen months into the project, in early 2016, the company developed a more refined version of the MVP. Kofman was ready to prove his hypothesis that there was a strong market for the product. At this point, the product provided much of the core functionality needed by users, such as the ability to search for text to locate key portions of an interview. However, it still lacked key components required to make it fully ready for the market. For example, there were no mechanisms for payments or pricing.

Through his extensive network of journalistic colleagues, Kofman let it be known that they would be opening up the product for free usage during one week of beta testing. When the testing began, things proceeded normally until an influential journalist at National Public Radio sent out a highly enthusiastic tweet, causing usage to soar. At ten thousand users, the system crashed. It took the company two days to get back online, but the test proved beyond a doubt that there was a market for the product.

Today, Kofman views that one day of MVP lab testing as perhaps the most important action taken by the company in its early days because it caused developers to change direction *before* spending a lot of time and money on a failed solution. The lesson, as Kofman tells it, is this: "You *have* to test your ideas out on *real* people"—the people who will actually use your product.

In previous chapters, we examined how to identify the leap of faith hypotheses that must be tested and validated for the product to be viable. Now, we focus on the next step: planning the MVPs that will test those hypotheses.

12.4.3 Venues for MVP Experiments

Since an MVP is only a test version, one of the first things to consider is where to run the test and who the MVP's testers will be. Let's explore some options.

12.4.3.1 Testing in a Lab

A user testing lab may be internal or independently operated by a third party. Testing labs provide the safest venue for testing, making them appropriate for testing in highly regulated mainstream business sectors, such as banking or insurance, where there is minimal tolerance for errors. Because the lab setting provides an opportunity to gain deep insight into users' experience of the product, it's also an ideal venue for MVP testing at the beginning of innovative product development when it's critical to understand customer motivations and the ways they use the product.

The testers should be real users. However, in cases where the requirements are stable, proxies may be used (e.g., product managers with a strong familiarity with the market).

Include testers familiar with regulations governing the product, such as legal and compliance professionals, to identify potential regulatory issues.

12.4.3.2 *Testing MVPs Directly in the Market*

The most reliable feedback comes from MVP-testing in the marketplace to a targeted group of real customers. Consider this option for *new-market* disruptions, where first adopters are often willing to overlook missing features for novelty. This option is also advised for *low-end* disruptions, where customers are willing to accept reduced quality in return for a lower price or greater convenience.

12.4.3.3 *Dark Launch*

Another way to limit negative impacts during MVP feature testing is to **dark-launch** it—to stealthily make it available to a small group of selected users before broadening its release. If the feature is not well received initially, it can be pulled back before it impacts the product's reputation; if customers like it, it is developed fully, incorporated in the product, and supported.

12.4.3.4 *Beta Testing*

A beta version is an "almost-ready-for-prime-time" version—one that is mostly complete but may still be missing features planned for the market-ready version. **Beta testing** is *real-world testing* of a beta version by a *wide range of customers* performing *real tasks*. Its purpose is to uncover bugs and issues, such as usability, scalability, and performance issues, before wide release.

Feedback and analytics from beta testing are used as inputs to fix remaining glitches and address user complaints before releasing the product or change to the market. Split testing may also be performed at this time—whereby one cohort of users is exposed to the beta version while a control group is not.

For more on split testing, see Chapter 7, section 7.11.5.2.

Beta testing is not just for MVPs; it should be a final testing step after internal alpha testing for all new features and major changes before they are widely released.

For more on beta testing, see Chapter 16, section 16.5.3.

12.4.4 MVP Types

When planning an MVP, the objective is to hack together a version of the product or feature that delivers the desired learning goals as quickly and inexpensively as possible. The following are strategies for achieving that. One MVP might incorporate any number of these strategies.

- Differentiator MVP
- Smoke-and-Mirrors MVP

- Walking Skeleton
- Value Stream Skeleton
- Concierge MVP
- Operational MVP
- Preorders MVP

These MVPs are described in the following sections.

12.4.4.1 Differentiator MVP

At the start of new product development, the most common strategy is to develop a low-cost version that focuses on the product's differentiators. This was the approach we saw taken earlier by Trint. Using existing components, the company was able to piece together an MVP demonstrating the differentiating features of its product (speech-to-text auto-transcription plus editing) and validating its value in just three months.

Another example is Google Docs, which began as Writely. Writely was an experiment by Sam Schillace to see what kind of editor could be created by combining AJAX's (JavaScript in the browser) content-editable functionality with word-processing technology.[5] Early versions focused on the product's key differentiators—its speed, convenience, and collaborative capabilities—while leaving out many other word-processing features, such as rich formatting and pagination. The hypothesis was that users would be excited enough about the differentiators to ignore the lack of richness in other areas. Interestingly, real-time collaboration on documents—which became a differentiating feature—was not seen as a primary one at the time; it was included because it seemed like the most natural way to solve the problem of documents worked on by multiple people.

The first version of the original product was pulled together quickly, using the browser for most of the editing capabilities and JavaScript to merge the local user's changes with those of other users. The client-side JavaScript amounted only to about ten pages of code.[6] Over time, the company added more word-processing features when it became apparent that they were essential to users and in order to open up new markets. Just one year after Writely was introduced, it was acquired by Google. Within the first month of its adoption, about 90 percent of Google was using it.

12.4.4.2 Smoke-and-Mirrors MVP (or Swivel Chair)

A **Smoke-and-Mirrors** MVP approach provides the user with an experience that is a close facsimile of the real thing but is, in fact, an illusion—like the one created by the magician pulling strings behind the curtain in the movie *The Wizard of Oz*.

---

5. Ellis Hamburger, "Google Docs Began as a Hacked-Together Experiment, Says Creator," *The Verge*, July 3, 2013, https://www.theverge.com/2013/7/3/4484000/sam-schillace-interview-google-docs-creator-box
6. Hamburger, "Google Docs."

One of my clients, a cable company, used this approach to provide an MVP frontend for customers to configure their own plans. The site operated in a sandbox, disconnected from operational systems. Behind the scenes, an internal support agent viewed the inputs and **swivel-chaired** to an existing internal system to process the request. The customer was unaware of the subterfuge. The MVP allowed the company to test the hypothesis that customers would *want* to customize their own plans before investing in developing the capability.

12.4.4.3 *Walking Skeleton*

A **Walking Skeleton,** or **spanning application,** validates *technical (architectural)* hypotheses by implementing a low-cost end-to-end scenario—a thin vertical slice that cuts through the architectural layers of the proposed solution. If the Walking Skeleton is successful, the business will invest in building the real product according to the proposed solution. If it is unsuccessful, the technical team goes back to the drawing board and pivots to a new technical hypothesis.

For example, in the Customer Engagement One (CEO) case study, the organization plans an end-to-end scenario for ingesting text messages from a social-network application, saving the messages using the proposed database solution, retrieving them, and viewing them as a list. Another example is Trint, whose first MVP incorporated the end-to-end scenario from speech to text to editing in order to validate the architectural design for the product.

12.4.4.4 *Value Stream Skeleton*

A **Value Stream Skeleton** implements a thin scenario that spans an operational value stream—an end-to-end workflow that ends with value delivery. It's similar to a technical Walking Skeleton except that it validates market instead of technical hypotheses. It covers an end-to-end *business* flow but does not necessarily use the proposed architectural solution.

The intuitive sequence for delivering features is according to the order in which they're used. For example, you might begin by delivering a feature to add new products to the product line for an online store and follow with features to receive inventory, place an order and fulfill an order. Not only does this sequence minimize dependency issues, but it also enables users to perform valuable work while waiting for the rest of the system to be delivered. I usually took this approach in my early programming days. The problem with it, though, is that it results in a long lag until an end customer receives value (e.g., a fulfilled order). In a business environment where there is a strong advantage in being fast to market, that kind of lag is unacceptable. Another problem is that it can delay the time until a company can begin receiving revenue from customers.

A Value-Stream Skeleton avoids these problems by delivering quick wins that implement thin versions of the end-to-end value stream, often with reduced functionality.

The first version of a Value-Stream Skeleton focuses on the value stream's endpoints—the *entry point* where the customer makes a request and the *endpoint* where the customer receives value. Workarounds are often used for the missing steps. For example, the first MVP for an online store allows a customer to purchase a few select products. The product descriptions and prices are hardcoded into the interface instead of being pulled from a database. This lowers development costs. The products are offered only in a single geographic region—simplifying the business rules and delivery mechanisms that the MVP implements. Despite the thinness of the MVP, it provides learning value to the business and real value to an end customer, who can already order and receive the products with this early version. As the business grows, the MVP evolves to handle more products and a broader geographical region.

12.4.4.5 Concierge MVP

The Concierge MVP[7] is based on the idea that it's better to build for the few than the many. Early versions are aimed at a small submarket that is *very* enthusiastic about the product, and the learning gained from the experience is used to scale the product. One example of a Concierge MVP is Food on the Table,[8] an Austin, Texas, company that began with a customer base of one parent. The company met with the parent once a week in a café to learn the parent's needs and take orders. The orders were filled manually. The process was repeated for a few other customers until the company learned enough to build the product.

As the example illustrates, you begin the Concierge MVP approach by selecting a single, real customer. The first customer can be found through market research, using analytics to determine the desired customer profile and inviting a customer who fits the profile to act as an MVP tester. Alternatively, you can select the first customer from among individuals who have previously indicated an interest in the product. This customer is given the "concierge treatment"—served by a high-ranking executive (e.g., vice president of product development) who works very closely with the customer, adding and adjusting features as more is learned.

At this stage, internal processes are often mostly manual. A company might spend a few weeks working with the first customer in this way, learning what that person does and does not want, and then select the next customer. The process is repeated until the necessary learning has been obtained and manual operations are no longer viable—at which point the product is built and deployed.

12.4.4.6 Operational MVP

An MVP isn't always created to validate software hypotheses and features; it can also be used to test operational hypotheses and changes. In a real-life example (which I'll keep anonymous to protect the company), a company created an MVP to test the impact of a price hike on sales. The MVP displayed the higher price to a select group of customers, but behind the scenes, the customers were still being charged the regular, lower price. Once the learning objective was achieved, customers received an email notifying them that they had been part of a test group and that no extra charges were actually applied.

---

7. Eric Ries, *The Lean Startup* (New York: Random House, 2011), 180.

8. Eric Ries in Lee Clifford and Julie Schlosse, "Testing Your Product the Lean Startup Way," *Inc.*, July 17, 2012, https://www.inc.com/lee-clifford-julie-schlosser/lean-startup-eric-ries-testing-your-product.html

12.4.4.7 Preorders MVP

The most reliable and cost-effective way to test a value hypothesis that customers will pay for an innovative product is to offer a means to order it before it's actually ready. The MVP can be something as simple as a promotional video or demonstration prototype. It may employ a stripped-down ordering process, such as order by email attachment, order by phone, or an online ordering site with hardcoded options. An MVP of this type might not require any stories—or it might need a few small stories (e.g., to set up a simple frontend for placing orders).

My own company, Noble Inc., used this approach when we were considering developing a product to provide a 360-degree evaluation of the business analysis practice in an organization. For the MVP, we developed a facsimile of the product and demonstrated it to our clients in an attempt to generate presales. What we learned was that there wasn't enough interest to justify building the real thing. Despite the failure of the test, I consider it money well spent. Imagine if we had learned it only after a large investment!

Dropbox's version of this MVP strategy played out much better. Dropbox posted a video of its product,[9] illustrating its main features. The video received enthusiastic and voluminous feedback from potential customers—making the case for the product and generating important suggestions about features and potential issues that were incorporated into the first marketed version.

12.4.5 MVP's Iterative Process

You don't just create an MVP and test it once. The MVP process is iterative. Its steps are as follows:

1. **Establish an MVP to test hypotheses.**

   Specify an MVP to test one or more leap of faith hypotheses (e.g., using any of the MVP types discussed in the prior section).

2. **Tune the engine.**

   Make incremental adjustments to fine-tune the product on the basis of feedback from customers as they use the product.

3. **Decision point: persevere or pivot.**

   After tuning for a while, decide whether to persevere with the business model or pivot to a different hypothesis.

12.4.6 The Pivot

A **pivot** is a switch to a different hypothesis based on a failure of the original premise. A company may decide to pivot near the start of a product's development due to the MVP process described previously. Alternatively, the pivot may occur at any time in a product's life if it becomes apparent there is no market for the product, and the product should be

---

9. Drew Houston, "Dropbox Original MVP Explainer Video," 2007, https://www.youtube.com/watch?time_continue=12&v=iAnJjXriIcw

reoriented toward a new market or usage.[10] An example of a pivot to an established product is Ryanair, once Europe's largest airline (based on passenger numbers).[11] Back in 1987, when the company realized it was failing financially, it pivoted to a low-end, disruptive revenue model based on the hypothesis that customers would be willing to pay for meals and other perks in return for cheap fares. The hypothesis was borne out when customers flocked to the airline.[12] More recently, in response to Brexit, the company has again pivoted—this time away from the United Kingdom to a business model based on growth outside of it.[13]

12.4.6.1 Constructive Failures

A pivot represents a failed premise, but, as the Ryanair example shows, the failure can often be constructive. In fact, many of today's successful companies are a result of such failures. For example, Flickr resulted from the failure of a previous offering—Game Neverending.[14] When the original product failed, the company pivoted by turning it into a successful photo-sharing app, leveraging the lessons it had learned about the value of community and the social features it had developed for the game (such as tagging and sharing). Groupon is another example. Conceived initially as an idealistic platform for social change, it then pivoted to become a platform for those seeking a bargain.

12.4.7 Incrementally Scaling the MVP

An effective way to develop a product is to start with a manual MVP and automate and scale it incrementally as the product grows. This approach was used by Zappos, an online shoe store.

Here's how the process played out, as described by the company's founder: "My Dad told me . . . I think the one you should focus on is the shoe thing. . . . So, I said okay, . . . went to a couple of stores, took some pictures of the shoes, made a website, put them up and told the shoe store, if I sell anything, I'll come here and pay full price. They said okay, knock yourself out. So, I did that, made a couple of sales."[15] In 1999, the company

---

10. Clif Gilley, "Do You Have to Build an MVP to Pivot?" [blog post], Quora, December 16, 2013, https://www.quora.com/Do-you-have-to-build-a-MVP-to-pivot

11. Thanks to my editor, Ron Healy, for informing me of this example.

12. Geoff Daigle, "Case Studies from Amazon, Yahoo, and Ryanair Reveal How Growth Teams Should Use Data + Feedback," Thinkgrowth.org, August 21, 2017, https://thinkgrowth.org/case-studies-from-amazon-yahoo-and-ryanair-reveal-how-growth-teams-should-use-data-feedback-d7b410a005f8

13. Alistair Smout and Kate Holton, "UPDATE 2—As Brexit Bites, Ryanair to Pivot Growth Away from UK for Next 2 Years," Reuters, April 6, 2017, https://www.reuters.com/article/britain-eu-ryanair-hldgs/update-2-as-brexit-bites-ryanair-to-pivot-growth-away-from-uk-for-next-2-years-idUSL5N1HE1YQ

14. Reid Hoffman, "The Big Pivot—with Slack's Stewart Butterfield," *Masters of Scale with Reid Hoffman* [podcast], November 14, 2017. https://player.fm/series/masters-of-scale-with-reid-hoffman/the-big-pivot-wslacks-stewart-butterfield

15. Jay Yarow, "The Zappos Founder Just Told Us All Kinds of Crazy Stories—Here's the Surprisingly Candid Interview," *Business Insider*, November 28, 2011, https://www.businessinsider.com/nick-swinmurn-zappos-rnkd-2011-11?op=1

signed on a dozen brands—all men's brown comfort shoes. As they added more respected brands, such as Doc Martens, the company and market grew and, in tandem, Zappos automated and scaled its business systems and processes.

12.4.8 Using MVPs to Establish the MMP

Using the MVP process, a company can quickly and inexpensively validate through experimentation which features will make the most difference. These features are referred to as the minimal marketable features (MMFs). An MMF is the smallest version of a feature (the least functionality) that would be viewed as valuable by customers if released to the market. MMFs may deliver value in various ways, such as through competitive differentiation, revenue generation, or cost savings. Collectively, the MMFs define the minimum marketable product (MMP)—the "product with the smallest feature set that still addresses the user needs and creates the right user experience."[16]

BLINK CASE STUDY PART 20

Create an MVP

Background

You convene stakeholders and developers to specify the BLInK hypotheses that will be tested during the first quarter and plan the MVPs that will be used to validate them.

The Ask

The deliverables of the workshop will be

- **Deliverable 1:** Hypothesis—Leap of faith hypothesis (or hypotheses) critical to the business case for the product
- **Deliverable 2**: MVP—High-level description of the MVP that will be used to test the hypothesis.

Inputs

- Chapter 7, Case Study Part 8, Deliverable 1: Assumptions Checklist

What Transpires

The group discusses assumptions that are most critical to the product's business case. They agree that the most urgent leap of faith hypothesis is that reluctance to sharing data can be overcome when a benefit is shown immediately (A7). Business stakeholders and developers brainstorm ways to test the hypothesis quickly and inexpensively.

---

16. Roman Pichler, "The Minimum Viable Product and the Minimum Marketable Product," October 9, 2013, https://www.romanpichler.com/blog/minimum-viable-product-and-minimal-marketable-product

Deliverables

Deliverable 1: Hypothesis

Hypothesis: Reluctance to share data can be overcome when an immediate benefit is shown (Assumption A7).

Deliverable 2: MVP

The first MVP will be a Value Stream Skeleton that allows customers to order and receive the BLInK offering. It will include a Quick Quote feature that incorporates an immediate discount to test the hypothesis about overcoming reluctance to share data.

Case Study Retrospective

The plan developed in the workshop will enable Better Living (BL) Inc. to test the leap of faith hypothesis that customers will be willing to give up some privacy in return for an immediate financial incentive. If this hypothesis isn't correct, there's no point investing further in the product, at least with its current vision. An MVP has been sketched out to test the hypothesis early and with minimal effort.

12.5 Story Mapping

A story map communicates relationships between stories through their placement on a two-dimensional plane.

12.5.1 Jeff Patton's Story Map

Jeff Patton's version of the story map—which I'll be referring to simply as a story map—provides visual cues for the *operational sequence* in which stories are executed and the *implementation sequence* in which stories will be developed. The story map helps the team visualize the end-to-end value stream at intervals within the period being planned, understand the usage context for each story, and see the dependencies between stories in the plan. Table 12.1 summarizes when and why to use a story map.

Table 12.1 *The Story Map at a Glance*

What?	Story map: A chart used in quarterly and feature planning, indicating the operational and implementation sequencing of work items (features and stories).
When?	Create a story map during quarterly and feature planning if the planned features and stories belong to a larger business process or workflow (e.g., when creating or reengineering a process). Review and revise the story map during iteration planning and whenever stories are added to or dropped from the plan.

Why?	• To plan end-to-end scenarios that deliver real value to the end customer
	• To spot gaps in the workflow where workarounds may be needed
	• To plan MVPs and quick wins
	• To visualize the usage context for stories
	• To visualize dependencies
Tips	When mapping stories, write them informally. When transferring stories from the map to the product backlog, use a formal format (e.g., Connextra).
Deliverables	*Story map* including user tasks, interim goals, and a plan for incrementally implementing features and stories across the planning horizon.

12.5.2 Benefits of a Story Map

The artifacts in the previous chapter presented requirements items as a one-dimensional list sequenced in order of planned implementation. As noted earlier, this solution is effective for planning localized changes but less so when planning a complex initiative with a broad impact.

For example, suppose you're planning to develop a meal-ordering application involving multiple users, including an end customer, restaurant workers, a dispatcher, and delivery people. As a planner, you need to visualize the whole ordering process at critical points in the plan so you can plan end-to-end scenarios for MVPs and quick wins. None of this can be communicated well with a simple list. Now, suppose the product owner (PO) is considering adding a story to the current quarterly backlog—a story to *Specify Express Delivery*. As an analyst, you would like to advise the PO on the impact of the new story on other stories further along in the operational value stream. For example, the addition of an express delivery option might impact a *Checkout* story, a *Dispatcher's* story, and a *Delivery Person's* story. Unfortunately, a simple list doesn't provide visual cues for answering these questions. A story map provides those cues by laying out the stories horizontally according to their operational sequence—the order in which they are performed—across a value stream or workflow.

Story maps help you plan a "coherent set of features"[17] at frequent intervals within the planning horizons as advised by lean software development. They do so by helping the customer and team envision how the planned features will fit together at intervals in the plan (e.g., by the end of each iteration).

Story maps make it easy to see not only what steps in a workflow *will* be implemented but also the gaps where they won't: gaps on the map point to the need to change the plan or devise workarounds.

---

17. Mary Poppendieck and Tom Poppendieck, *Lean Software Development: An Agile Toolkit* (Boston: Addison-Wesley, 2003), 29.

12.5.3 The Anatomy of a Story Map

The following sections examine the elements and regions of a story map.

12.5.3.1 Cards on the Story Map

Figure 12.2 illustrates the common elements of a story map with adaptations for MVP planning.

On the story map are cards representing stories, users, and other items of interest. The cards are color-coded according to type. The actual colors used will vary. The template in Figure 12.2 uses the following cards and colors (not displayed in the print edition of this book):

- Main cards:
  - Actor (medium blue): An **actor** card represents any person or entity (such as a software component) that interacts with the product or system, e.g., persona, user role, software service, system, subsystem, software interface, or device.
  - User task/use case (medium pink): A **user task** (or **use case**) card represents a goal that a user has for a single interaction with the product or system (e.g., *Submit an Order*).
  - Feature (light pink): A **feature** card represents a work item beyond the size limit for a story.
  - User story (yellow).
- Optional items:
  - Interim/iteration goal (pale blue): An **interim goal** is a high-level goal that will be reached during an intermediate period in the planning cycle. Within a timeboxed planning approach, the interim goal is known as the *iteration goal* or, in Scrum, the *sprint goal*.
  - Activity (green): An **activity** card represents a broad user goal (e.g., *Manage Suppliers*). Activities are optional, since their primary purpose is to derive user tasks.
  - Workaround (orange): A **workaround** card indicates where a missing task will be accomplished through a temporary fix (e.g., by manual means). Workaround cards help the business and development visualize and plan how gaps will be addressed. Don't estimate workaround cards unless they require effort from the development team.
  - Assumptions/hypotheses (beige): Assumption cards highlight the leap of faith hypotheses and other assumptions validated during the planning horizon.
  - Spike (gray): These cards represent work items to enable a future story or feature.

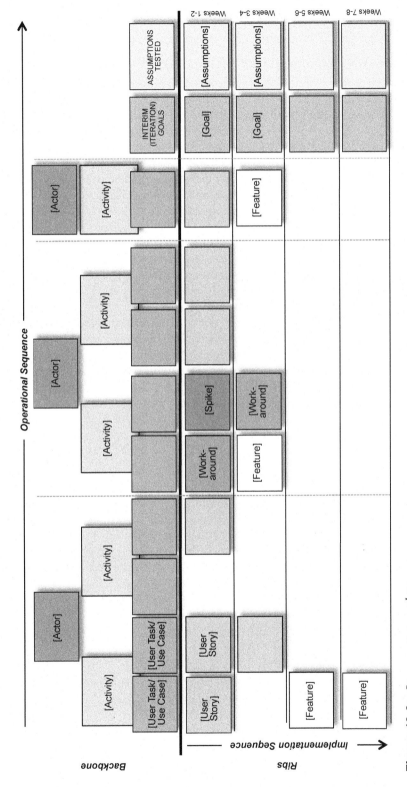

Figure 12.2 *Story map template*

12.5.3.2 Story Map Regions: Backbone and Ribs

Figure 12.2 illustrates the two regions of a story map. The upper region is the backbone, and the bottom is the ribs. The **backbone** lays out the user tasks, or use cases, that will be supported by the product, in the operational sequence—the order in which users perform them. As an agile analyst, it's your responsibility to represent user tasks in the backlog. Represent each user task (use case) as a feature, since the effort to implement all of its scenarios typically exceeds the maximum story size. The **ribs** region lays out the implementation plan for stories that support the user tasks in the backbone.

To understand the region names, picture a skeleton lying face down. The vertebrae strung out across the skeleton's backbone are analogous to the user tasks posted across the map's upper region. The ribs that fall from the vertebra correspond to the user stories positioned below the user tasks they support.

Each row in the ribs section represents an interim period within the planning horizon. The interim is any chosen timeline. If the team uses a timeboxed planning approach (e.g., Scrum, SAFe, XP), the timeline is a fixed-length iteration or sprint, typically one or two weeks long.

Within each row are the work items—stories, features, and spikes—planned for the associated timeline. Work items in higher rows are implemented before those in lower rows.

As a remedial practice, organizations that don't have the capabilities to implement full continuous integration and continuous delivery (CI/CD) may schedule a hardening iteration dedicated to prerelease work, during which no new features are developed. In that case, depict the hardening iteration as the last row in the ribs. The row should not include user stories but may contain analysis, beta testing, systems testing, final adjustments, refactoring, and other work items that don't add new functionality.

12.5.4 Dependency Relationships on the Map

Use the story map to determine and communicate dependencies between requirements items (features and stories). As a general guideline, any story within a row is dependent on those to the left because of workflow rules (the items on the left must have occurred before the story can begin) and data dependencies (the items on the left often produce data used by the story). This is only a guideline, not a rule, because the map provides a *rough approximation* of the flow, not a precise process model.

Within any column on the story map, a story may be dependent on items directly above it because the story may build on earlier implementations of the feature.

12.5.5 Story Map Example

Figure 12.3 is an example of a story map for a claims management system.

The items in the uppermost row of the backbone represent the actors (user roles) who interact with the product, laid out in the sequence in which they typically use the product or system: a customer (who submits a claim), an adjuster (who evaluates it), and a claims manager (who performs the final adjudication).

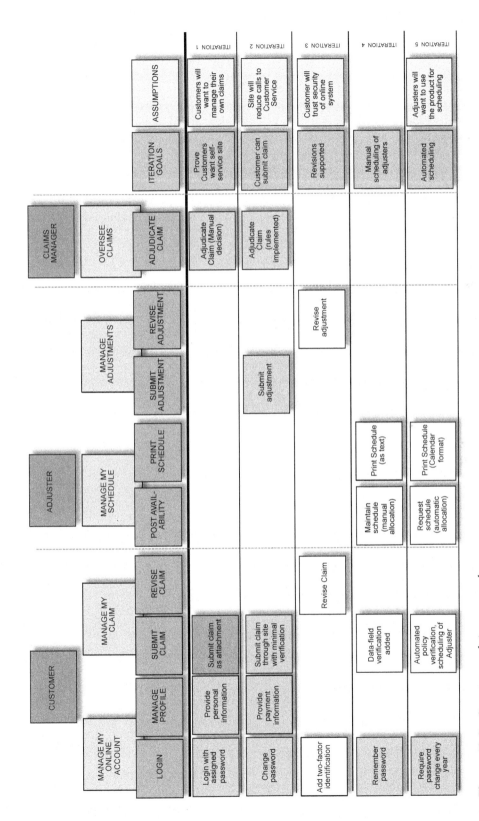

Figure 12.3 *Story map claims example*

Positioned below each actor, in the second row down, are activities—high-level jobs the actor is engaged in, laid out in the order in which they are typically executed. This row is optional. In Figure 12.3, the activities of a customer are *Manage My Online Account* and *Manage My Claim*.

Below each activity are the individual user tasks (use cases) that support it, positioned in approximate order of execution. For example, in Figure 12.3, a customer first logs in, manages her profile, submits a claim, and revises it. An adjuster posts availability (a precondition for receiving work assignments), prints a daily schedule, and submits and revises adjustments. Finally, a claims manager adjudicates the claim, ending the workflow.

12.5.6 Tips for Writing Stories on the Map

Because the placement of stories on a story map conveys so much information, you can describe them with just a few words without loss of meaning. For example, in Figure 12.3, it's clear that the story *Automated Policy Verification* (in the last row) applies while the user is submitting a claim and that the user is the customer: there's no need to spell it all out on the card. This brevity is extremely helpful while constructing the story map during planning when the map and stories are volatile.

Once planning is over, and you're ready to transcribe stories from the map to an electronic backlog, it's generally better to use a formal format, such as the Role-Feature-Reason (Connextra template), so that this contextual information is not lost during the transfer.

12.5.7 Constructing the Backbone

The following are guidelines for creating a story map backbone.

12.5.7.1 Determine the Narrative

The first step is to determine the narrative that the map will tell. A story map might cover a customer journey from prospect to loyal customer to a retired customer. Alternatively, it may describe an operational value stream or business process, such as the end-to-end process for submitting and fulfilling an order.

12.5.7.2 Inputs to Backbone Construction

Personas, journey mapping, business process modeling, stakeholder analysis, and circumstance-based market segmentation (through its analysis of "jobs" that customers do with the product) all provide valuable input in constructing the story map backbone. The next sections examine the following input artifacts: journey maps, business process models, and use-case models.

Journey Map Inputs

When using a journey map as input, transfer its stages to user activities on the story map. Translate its **touchpoint** tasks into user tasks on the story map, preserving the journey map's sequencing.

Work with stakeholders to examine the moments of truth on the journey map. Discuss adding or changing user tasks at these moments to improve the user experience, as they represent high-value opportunities to significantly impact customer attitudes.

See Chapter 10, section 10.14, for guidelines on journey mapping.

Business Process Models Inputs

To use a business process model as input to the backbone, begin by transposing the pools and lanes in the process model to actor cards on the story map. Transpose the workflow steps to activity and user task cards, depending on the scope of the step. (A user task can be accomplished in a single interaction; an activity represents a set of related user tasks.) Place each card under the appropriate actor card, as indicated by its lane in the process model.

For example, for the claims private process model described in Chapter 10, Figure 10.14, create an actor card for customer, adjuster, claim supervisor, claims manager, policy management, and finance. (The latter two might represent systems actors.) For the customer, create user tasks to log in, manage profile, submit claim, and revise claim. The resulting backbone is shown in the top portion of Figure 12.3.

See Chapter 10, section 10.16, for guidelines on process modeling.

Use-Case Model Inputs

You can also create the backbone using use-case diagrams—artifacts developed during feature preparation or a previous development effort.

See Figure 10.17 in Chapter 10 for an example of a claims use-case model.

Transpose the actors from the use-case model to actor cards on the story map. Then transfer each use case from the diagram to a user-task card on the map. Position each user task under the actor card for its primary actor, as indicated in the use-case diagram.

Keep in mind that use-case diagrams do not indicate sequencing, so you'll have to use other artifacts (e.g., a business process model) or discussion with subject matter experts (SMEs) to work that out.

12.5.7.3 Determining the Backbone Scope

Include *all* the tasks of an affected process or value stream in the backbone so that you can readily identify workflow steps that might be impacted—including ones that aren't being targeted for the change.

On scaled initiatives, use the following guidelines. When planning at the program level, as collaborating teams synchronize their quarterly plans, use an *overall* story map whose backbone covers all user tasks by all teams. This story map will provide an overview of the whole product across all teams.

Assign work items from the overall story map to individual teams. Each team conducts its own internal planning using team-level story maps or any other tool (such as road-maps) that it chooses. More on planning for scaled initiatives can be found in Chapter 17, "Scaling Agility."

12.5.7.4 *Specifying Actors on the Backbone*

The guideline for specifying actors on the backbone is to represent each user role with an actor card. Despite the simplicity of the rule, there are numerous nuances that can confuse practitioners. The following are answers to some common questions teams have asked me about actors on the map.

How Should Actors Be Sequenced on the Map?

Lay the actors out in the rough sequence in which they interact with the deployed product. The actor card should represent the **primary actor**—the one that initiates (or triggers) the activities and user tasks positioned below. Sources for these actors can be found in journey maps, process models, and user-role modeling workshops.

What If an Actor Participates at Multiple Points in the Workflow?

Don't be overly concerned about depicting the precise workflow when constructing the backbone, since the objective is only to help guide planning—not to model the business process rigorously. (There are better tools for that, such as Business Process Modeling Notation [BPMN], described in Chapter 10.) And so, even if an actor appears more than once in a workflow, you can often make do with a single actor card positioned according to the user's main contribution to the process. However, if this would confuse the viewer, add one actor card to the backbone each time the user performs an activity in the work-flow. For example, in an incident management process, a Tier 1 service desk agent registers the incident, after which the incident is handled by second- and third-tier agents. Finally, the incident is closed by the Tier 1 agent who first registered it. Because the Tier 1 agent is involved at two points in the process, you create two Tier 1 agent cards. You position one Tier 1 agent card at themap's left edge of the map, where the process begins, and one at the right edge, where the process ends.

Is the Product or System Itself an Actor?

As discussed earlier, external software components are represented as actors, but what about the system that is being built? As a *general* rule of thumb, don't represent the system under design as an actor. For example, you don't create a system actor card for an ordering system even though it is active during the *Submit Order* use case, verifying screen inputs, and storing the order. The reason is that the ordering system isn't the primary actor for the interaction. It doesn't initiate the exchange; the user does.

However, if the system under design initiates a task, post an actor card for the system and group the tasks it triggers below. For example, a release might include a feature to automatically issue a replenishment order whenever inventory levels fall below a trigger point. To model this on the map, create a *System* actor card and position the replenishment story underneath it. You need to indicate the system actor in this case because it's the primary actor—it triggered the use case. If you don't dedicate a column for the system, you won't have anywhere to place the story.

12.5.7.5 *Determining the Backbone Activities*

Lay the activities out in the approximate sequence actors carry them out, positioning each activity under the actor who initiates it.

An activity represents a broad user goal accomplished through a set of user tasks. A user task (or use case) represents a narrower user goal accomplished in a single engagement with the product or system. For example, the *Manage My Account* activity is accomplished through the user tasks *Create an Account*, *Query My Account*, *Edit My Account Information*, and *Delete My Account*. In Figure 12.3, the *Manage My Schedule* activity is accomplished through the user tasks *Post Availability* and *Print Schedule*.

Activities cards are optional because they are only a means to an end—the discovery of user tasks. However, they can be a helpful facilitation tool because it's often easier for stakeholders to first consider the big actions an actor does before analyzing specific interactions. However, if you find that activity cards do not add sufficient value, you can skip them and go straight from actors to user tasks.

12.5.7.6 *Determining the User Tasks*

Work with stakeholders to determine the user tasks in the operational workflow. Review the input artifacts with stakeholders. As discussed earlier in this chapter, user tasks are indicated at the touchpoints of journey maps, in the steps of process models, and as use cases on use-case diagrams. Position each user task under the actor who initiates it below the activity it supports.

How Broad Is a User Task?

Size a user task so that it delivers a goal that a user can carry out in a *single* interaction with the product or system.

BLINK CASE STUDY PART 21
Create Story Map Backbone

Background
You are tasked with facilitating a story mapping workshop to plan the first BLInK release in the first quarter.

The Ask
The deliverable is as follows:

- **Deliverable 1**: BLInK story map backbone

Inputs

You prepare the following inputs, developed during previous analysis efforts:

- BLInK product roadmap (see the BLInK product roadmaps in Chapter 9, "Long-Term Agile Planning," Figures 9.4 and 9.5)
- BLInK release roadmap (see the BLInK release roadmap with dependency red strings in Chapter 11, "Quarterly and Feature Planning," Figure 11.5)
- BLInK journey map (see the journey map for Aisha in Chapter 10, "Quarterly and Feature Preparation," Figure 10.9)
- BPMN private process model for the process "Enroll in BLInK program" (see Figure 10.16)
- Final user roles for upcoming release of BLInK (see Figure 10.23)
- Assumptions checklist (see Deliverable 1 of Case Study Part 8 in Chapter 7)

What Transpires

The facilitation event takes place as described next.

Review of the Product Roadmap

Using the long-term product roadmap as a guide, you review the following goals and assumptions for the release.

Release Goals

- Learn whether customers will be willing to share data when provided with the right incentive
- Enable customers to enroll in BLInK and immediately begin earning rewards

Assumptions Tested

Attendees review the assumptions checklist and select the following for testing during the planning period:

- (A7) Reluctance to share data can be overcome when benefit shown immediately.
- (A5) Customers will like the product when they see it.
- (A2) Behaviors will improve.
- (A4) Health will improve due to participation.
- (A8) Subscribers will refer others.

Attendees agree that no revisions are required to these artifacts.

Review of the Journey Map

You review the journey map. You direct attendees' attention to the *Start Trial* stage of the journey because it presents a moment of truth to overcome customers' hesitation about sharing data by offering an immediate rate reduction. You suggest an early learning objective to prove Assumption A7—that a customer's reluctance to share data can be overcome when a benefit is shown immediately. This leads to the following addition to the release goals and objectives:

- To provide the customer with a quick quote, including a rate reduction, at the time of BLInK application

Scoping the Story Map

Next, you turn to the scope of the story map backbone, asking attendees to consider how many journey map stages it should include. Attendees agree that it should cover the customer journey from the initial contact with the customer to the delivery of benefits and rewards and collection of data analytics.

Review of User-Role Modeling Workshop Deliverables

From the user role model, you identify the following actors: primary subscriber, broker/agent, vendor, actuary, and underwriter.

Review of the Process Model

From a review of the BLInK process model, you note the following users and user tasks:

- Agent tasks: Validate and submit request
- Actuary tasks: Set risk and pricing guidelines
- Underwriter tasks: Underwrite request

You learn that what had been loosely described above as "underwrite request" is actually two separate user tasks.

- Authorize enrollment
- Bind transaction

Actor Placement on the Story Map

Next, you walk through the workflow with stakeholders to determine Actor placement on the map. You decide that the map will begin with the primary subscriber who applies for BLInK. Next, you post actors in the sequence in which they are involved in the application process—the broker/agent who accepts the application, the vendor who validates eligibility, the actuary who sets risk-evaluation guidelines, and the underwriter who evaluates the application according to those guidelines. You post an additional vendor card at the right end of the map to account for device initialization for analytics collection at the end of the process.

Completing the Backbone

Finally, you discuss activities and user tasks, referring back to the sequencing indicated by the process models. Where these are not available, you discover activities and tasks through discussion.

Deliverables

The following notes outline the deliverables from the event.

Deliverable 1: BLInK Story Map Backbone

Figure 12.4 illustrates the story map backbone at the end of the workshop.
Following is a description of some of the user tasks in Figure 12.4.

- **Enter BLInK Quote and Consent (Primary Subscriber)**

   The primary subscriber enters a health assessment and obtains a quick quote. The subscriber consents to BLInK, indicating they want the device. The quote is submitted and pre-validated.

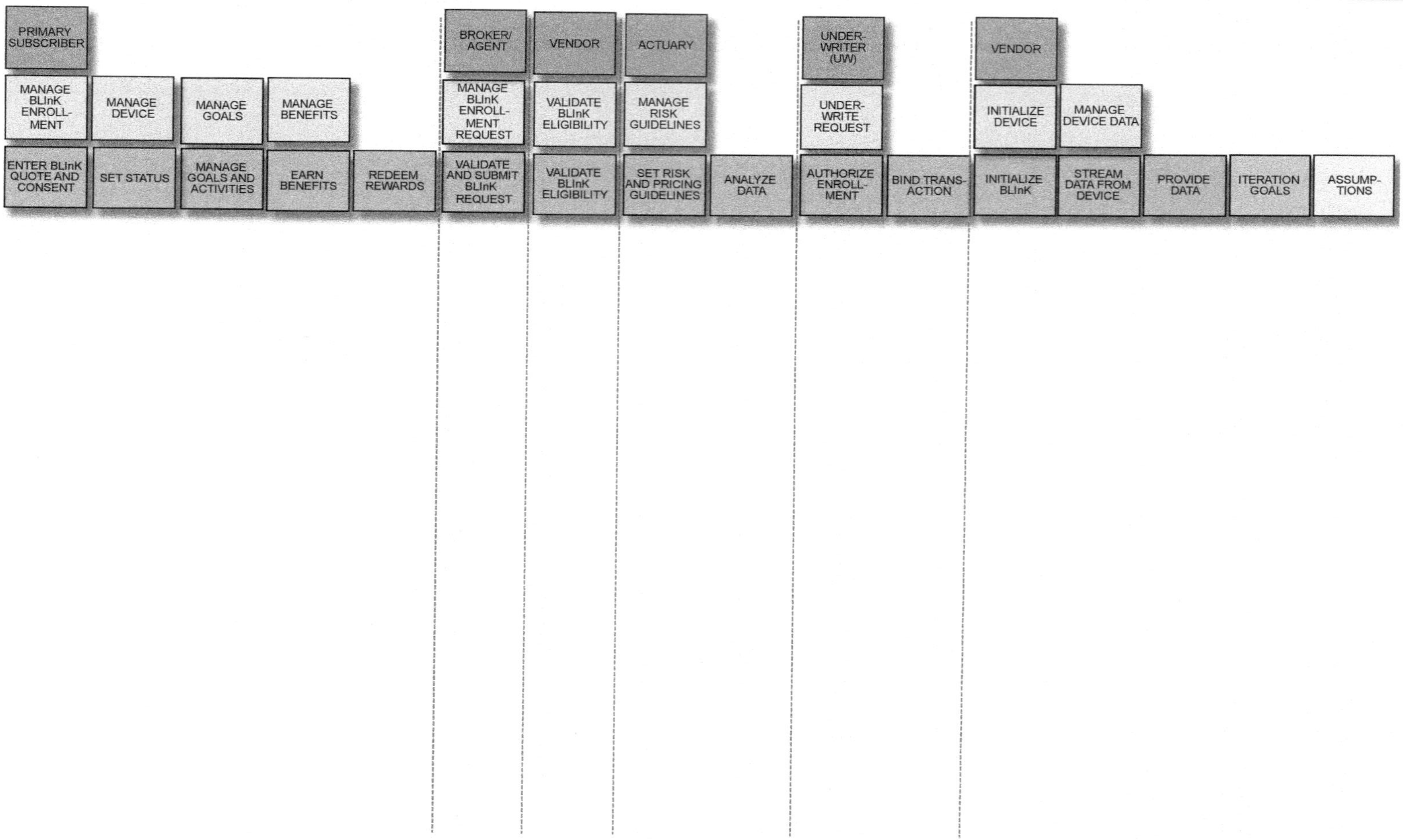

Figure 12.4 BLInK story map backbone

- **Validate and Submit BLInK Request (Broker/Agent)**

  The broker validates the application, cleans up the quote, adds endorsements, and binds the transaction.
- **Validate BLInK Eligibility (Vendor)**

  The vendor validates the applicant's eligibility for receiving the device, based on the applicant's previous history.
- **Initialize BLInK (Vendor)**

  The vendor creates a BLInK voucher, declaring that the insured is enrolled in behavior-based insurance tracking.
- **Stream Data from Device (Vendor)**

  The vendor collects detailed data from the device.
- **Provide Data (Vendor)**

  The vendor provides summary data on request.

Case Study Retrospective

In this workshop, you created a backbone that will be used as a structure for laying out the user stories in the story map according to their operational sequence.

12.5.8 Constructing the Ribs

The story map backbone provides a structure for the plan. The plan itself—describing what will be delivered and when—is expressed in the ribs. The ribs are divided into rows, with each row representing a time interval within the period being planned (e.g., one week, two weeks, one iteration [Sprint]).

Position stories in rows according to their planned implementation, with the stories scheduled for the first interval in the top row. Position each story underneath the user task it supports.

12.5.8.1 Determining Implementation Sequence

The vertical position of stories on the map indicates their planned implementation sequence. We examined the factors that inform sequencing decisions in Chapter 8, "Seeding the Backlog—Discovering and Grading Features," section 8.12. Let's review them and related considerations that inform the vertical positioning of stories on a story map:

- Weighted shortest job first (WSJF)
- Cost of delay
- Learning value (contributes to risk reduction and operations evaluation [RR&OE] and business value)
- Technological risk (included in RR&OE)
- Functional vs. nonfunctional requirements (NFRs) (impacts time criticality, RR&OE)

- "Juicy bits" first (impacts user and business value)
- Frequency (impacts user value)
- Revenue generation (included in business value)
- Dependencies (impact RR&OE)

Weighted Shortest Job First and Cost of Delay

WSJF is a widely used, effective tool for determining implementation sequence. To calculate WSJF, you assess its cost of delay (total value to the business) and then divide it by the estimated job duration (the cost to implement the item). Then sequence the items according to their WSJF values, with the highest-value item first. As noted earlier in the book, WSJF values should *inform* sequencing decisions but shouldn't dictate the position of work items in the backlog since the formula doesn't account for all scenarios. The most important aspect of the approach is in reminding decision makers to consider the factors contributing to priority-sequencing decisions: user value, business value, time criticality, risk reduction and opportunity enablement (RR&OE), and job duration. The following sections explain these factors.

See Chapter 6, sections 6.5.4.4 and 6.5.5.5, for guidelines on calculating WSJF and cost of delay.

Learning Value (RR&OE, Business Value)

One reason to prioritize a story is that it provides learning value (e.g., a story to develop an MVP that validates the hypothesis that users will pay for the service). The story contributes to risk reduction because it avoids investment in invalid hypotheses. MVPs also contribute to business and user value by identifying the highest-value features (MMFs) to invest in and include in the product.

Technological Risk (RR&OE)

Another reason to prioritize a feature or story is that it reduces technological risk. For example, a Walking Skeleton story to implement a thin scenario across the system architecture should be sequenced early because the sooner it is implemented, the earlier design errors can be revealed, and the cheaper they will be to fix.

In my early days as an analyst, the guidance at the time (e.g., according to the Rational Unified Process [RUP]) focused mostly on technical risks. Lean startup, however, typically prioritizes market risk. The general guideline I follow today is as follows: Prioritize stories that address the *highest* risk. If there is extreme uncertainty about the market for the product, prioritize market risk, because if there is no market, there will be no need to address technical issues. Prioritize technical risk if *technological uncertainty* is high because the technology is new (to the market or the team), but *market uncertainty* is low, for example, because the product type is already well established.

Functional versus Nonfunctional Requirements (Time Criticality, RR&OE)

Another consideration is whether the item is a user story to deliver a user function or is a technical story to implement nonfunctional requirements (NFRs), such as scalability, security, and performance requirements. Making matters complicated, there are often conflicting interests—with the business favoring functional stories in order to bring features to market sooner, and software engineers favoring technical stories because they know the added cost to retrofit the system later (i.e., its time criticality). In Chapter 11, section 11.11.3.2, we looked at the issue broadly with recommendations for balancing both kinds of work and achieving a target ratio. When sequencing work items for an innovative product, as a rule of thumb, prioritize functional requirements over NFRs due to the argument we made earlier about market risk. If there is no market for the product, there is no need to comply with NFRs such as scalability. Use an **emergent architecture** approach—building out just enough architecture for current conditions without going overboard planning for the future.

The situation is different for software development initiatives in heavily regulated businesses, such as finance, insurance, and telecommunications, with sizeable customer bases. In these contexts, there is often very low (or zero) tolerance for noncompliance with NFRs, including security, reliability, availability, volume, and stress requirements. Also, the solution often needs to be capable of operating at scale immediately because of the large existing customer base. In such cases, give high priority sequencing to stories that implement the necessary compliance with NFRs.

"Juicy Bits" First (User and Business Value)

Sequence stories so that some "juicy bits" are delivered early. Juicy bits (a term coined by Cohn)[18] are wow features—differentiating capabilities that generate high enthusiasm in the user community. Juicy bits not only provide user value but also deliver business value—as we saw in the case of Trint, which experienced an explosion in usage following a tweet by an influential user, which then convinced investors to support full product development.

Frequency (User Value)

All other things being equal, prioritize stories that implement functionality used frequently over functions that are used infrequently.

Revenue Generation (Business Value)

A story may be prioritized if it delivers business value even if it doesn't provide much user value (e.g., a story to implement service charges or a story that generates high-value user data).

Dependencies (RR&OE)

Another reason to prioritize a story is to prevent dependency errors. For example, suppose story A removes a parameter from the API of a component, and stories B and C exclude the dropped parameter from the component's clients. In that case, sequence B and C before A to prevent errors when story A is delivered.

---

18. Mike Cohn, *User Stories Applied: For Agile Software Development* (Boston: Addison-Wesley Professional, 2004), 101–103.

12.5.8.2 Overview of User-Task and Timeline Views

Two broad approaches, or views, can be used to construct the ribs. In the **user-task view**, you first work with the team and stakeholders to split user tasks (use cases) into smaller user stories, then you distribute the stories below the user task with highest-priority stories on top. In the **timeline view**, you proceed row by row, beginning from the top, representing the first interval (e.g., Iteration 1). First, you specify the iteration goal. Then, you work backward to plan the minimum slice of each user task required to deliver the goal.

In practice, you'll likely move back and forth between the two approaches, but for explanatory purposes, let's take them up one at a time.

12.5.8.3 User-Task View

In the user-task view, you proceed across the user tasks in the backbone. You split each user task into user stories, each within the story size limit (typically 8 points). Then you position the stories vertically in the column below the user task according to their implementation sequence. The next chapter provides extensive guidelines for splitting features into user stories. In this chapter, we focus on guidance particularly relevant for decomposing a feature representing a use case or user task.

A use case or user task is typically sized as a feature (vs. a story) because it encompasses multiple scenarios (pathways). For example, the user task *Place an order* includes scenarios for *Payment by credit card*, *Payment on account*, and various delivery options. The effort required to implement them all exceeds the maximum for a story. Assuming you're following the acceptance test–driven development practices advised in this book, you've documented the scenarios as feature acceptance criteria. When you split the feature (representing the user task), you distribute its criteria among the resulting stories.

If you're using use-case models, each user task is modeled as a use case. To split the use case, you decompose it into use-case slices or user stories. (In the use case 2.0 standard, a use case-slice is roughly equivalent to a user story.) Each slice or user story implements a scenario documented in one or more use-case flows—or a set of related scenarios. For example, you slice the use case *Place an order* into the following use-case slices/user stories:

- As a customer, I want to place an order with payment by credit card.

- As a customer, I want to pay for my order using Google Checkout.

Facilitator Tips: Plan Thin Scenarios

The first user story for a user task/use case is typically an MVP to deliver fast learning or a story that helps deliver a quick win (or both). To plan the story, ask stakeholders to first explore a thin scenario that implements the use case's **basic flow** (also called the **happy day scenario**)—a stripped-down scenario for achieving the user goal, with no options and minimal error-handling.

For example, the first story for the user task *Place an order* is a minimal version of the basic flow where the order is submitted without payment. The customer pays afterward using an email transfer.

12.5.8.4 Timeline View

Working with the timeline view, you proceed through the ribs row by row beginning at the top, as described in the following sections.

Craft the Interim Goals (Sprint Goals)

The first step is to craft the goals for each timeline (row) on the map. Each timeline represents an interim period, such as one week or one iteration. Focus most of the analysis on upcoming timelines, since goals further into the future are expected to change once development is underway. The **interim goal** is the goal that will be delivered during the timeline. In Scrum, it is referred to as the *sprint goal*.

The interim goal expresses a unifying purpose that motivates the team to work together[19] and provides guidance on what to include and exclude during the timeline. Examples of interim goals follow:

- **Learning goal to test an assumption:** If the initiative is characterized by high uncertainty, the first interim goal should be to deliver learning by validating leap of faith hypotheses (e.g., the goal to validate the hypothesis that users will engage heavily with the product).

- **Goal to implement a high-level functionality:** An interim goal can represent a high-level function that will be delivered during the timeline (e.g., enable a customer to manage a campaign).

- **Goal to achieve a business objective:** An interim goal can express a business objective (e.g., involve a new user group, increase market share).

- **Goal to address risk:** An interim goal might address architectural risk, for example, by building a spanning application.

Select Stories That Support the Goal

The next step is to select stories that support the interim goal and lay them out along the row. Position the stories under the user tasks to which they apply.

For example, a row has the interim goal, "Enable the customer to earn rewards and benefits." The team creates a user story *Award points for purchases* and places it on the row under the user task *Place an order*.

Specifying Stories for a Spanning Application

As noted earlier, specify an interim goal to address architectural risk by building a spanning application (Walking Skeleton). Lean software development recommends that the spanning application cover the complete software application even though it may implement only a small subset of scenarios. The stories in the spanning application should "drive a nail through the system"[20] by validating that the components integrate as planned for their intended purpose.

---

19. Ken Schwaber and Jeff Sutherland, *The Scrum Guide: The Definitive Guide to Scrum—The Rules of the Game*, Scrumguides.org, 2020, 11, https://www.scrumguides.org

20. Poppendieck and Poppendieck, *Lean Software Development*, 36.

For example, a group is developing a self-service site for executing financial trades. The site will support different products, each with its own business rules. For the spanning application in the first iteration, the group plans to implement stories that span the system's architectural layers from the initial booking to the trade's execution—but only for a single scenario and one product.

BLINK CASE STUDY PART 22

Specify Stories for an MVP

Background

Having constructed the backbone for the BLInK story map, you now turn to the ribs. The team is using timeboxed planning with fixed-length iterations. You convene stakeholders and developers to plan the goals and features for the first iteration, with the intention of creating an MVP to validate critical assumptions.

The Ask

The deliverable of the workshop will be

- **Deliverable 1**: BLInK story map (early draft with MVP, interim goals, and assumptions)

What Transpires

You ask the group to discuss the MVP process for the first iteration.

Crafting the Interim Goal and Assumptions

The group agrees on the following high-level goal for the iteration: "Gather market information and gauge interest."

There is consensus that the most urgent leap of faith assumptions are "(A5) Customers will like the product when they see it." and "(A7) Reluctance to share data can be overcome when benefit shown." Though less urgent, stakeholders would also like to begin testing assumption A10 in the assumption list (see BLInK Case Study Part 8 in Chapter 7) that "BLInK will lead to improved customer retention."

Planning the MVP

To achieve these learning objectives, the group plans an MVP as follows:

The MVP will be a Value Stream Skeleton that enables customers to order and receive the BLInK offering. BLInK will be marketed to the customer through messaging that provides information on how to contact a broker or agent. The broker will be provided with a Quick Quote capability to validate the hypothesis that reluctance to share data can be overcome if a benefit is immediately shown. Workarounds will be used for internal user tasks that appear on the story map but are not covered by the MVP.

Deliverables

The following outlines the deliverables.

Deliverable 1: BLInK Story Map

Figure 12.5 shows the resulting deliverable of the meeting.

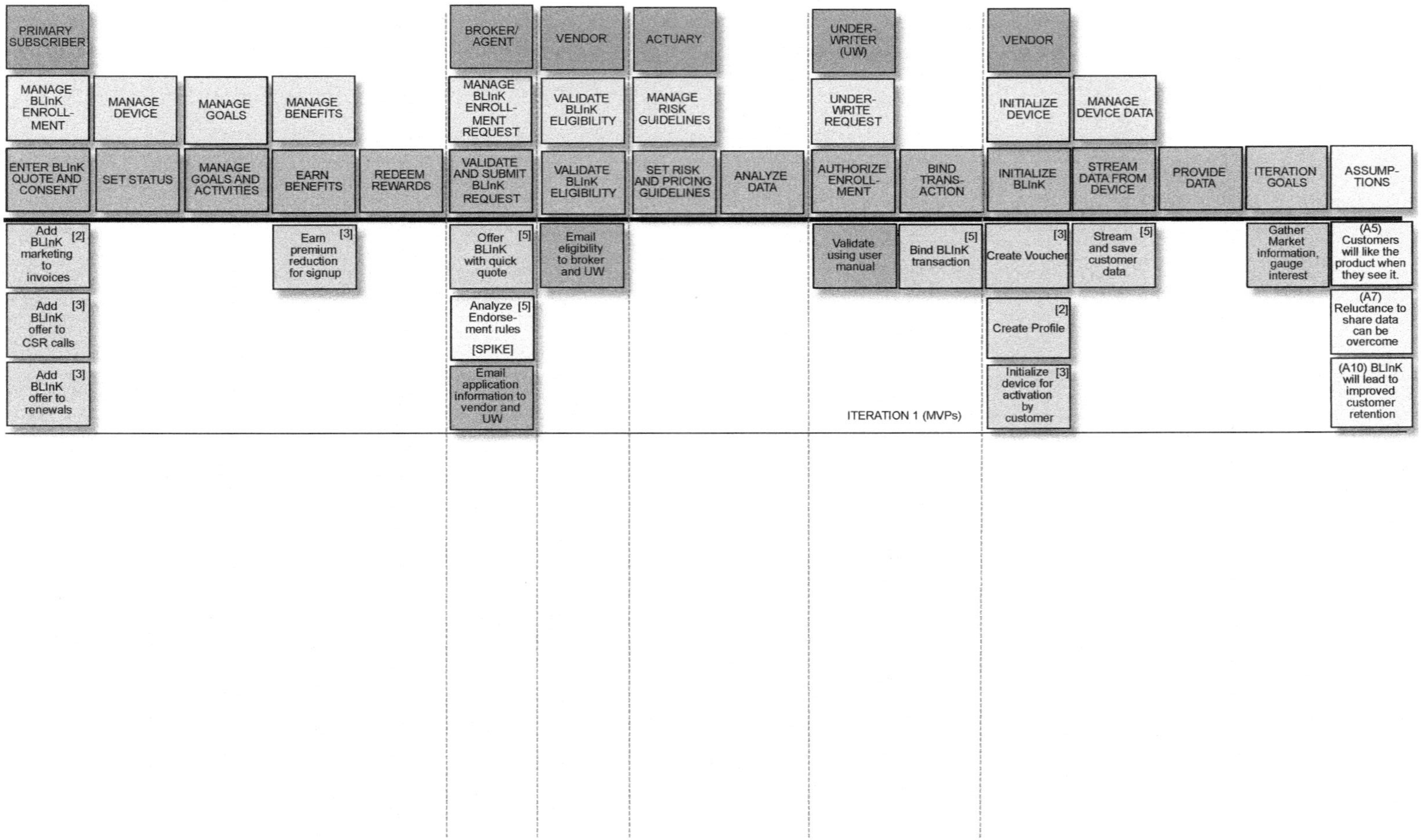

PRIMARY SUBSCRIBER

- MANAGE BLInK ENROLLMENT
  - ENTER BLInK QUOTE AND CONSENT
    - Add BLInK marketing to invoices [2]
    - Add BLInK offer to CSR calls [3]
    - Add BLInK offer to renewals [3]
- MANAGE DEVICE
  - SET STATUS
- MANAGE GOALS
  - MANAGE GOALS AND ACTIVITIES
- MANAGE BENEFITS
  - EARN BENEFITS
    - Earn premium reduction for signup [3]
- REDEEM REWARDS

BROKER/AGENT

- MANAGE BLInK ENROLLMENT REQUEST
  - VALIDATE AND SUBMIT BLInK REQUEST
    - Offer BLInK with quick quote [5]
    - Analyze Endorsement rules [SPIKE] [5]
    - Email application information to vendor and UW

VENDOR

- VALIDATE BLInK ELIGIBILITY
  - VALIDATE BLInK ELIGIBILITY
    - Email eligibility to broker and UW

ACTUARY

- MANAGE RISK GUIDELINES
  - SET RISK AND PRICING GUIDELINES
- ANALYZE DATA

UNDERWRITER (UW)

- UNDERWRITE REQUEST
  - AUTHORIZE ENROLLMENT
    - Validate using user manual
- BIND TRANSACTION
  - Bind BLInK transaction [5]

VENDOR

- INITIALIZE DEVICE
  - INITIALIZE BLInK
    - Create Voucher [3]
    - Create Profile [2]
    - Initialize device for activation by customer [3]
- MANAGE DEVICE DATA
  - STREAM DATA FROM DEVICE
    - Stream and save customer data [5]

PROVIDE DATA

ITERATION GOALS
- Gather Market information, gauge interest

ASSUMPTIONS
- (A5) Customers will like the product when they see it.
- (A7) Reluctance to share data can be overcome
- (A10) BLInK will lead to improved customer retention

ITERATION 1 (MVPs)

Figure 12.5 *BLInK story map draft with MVP*

In Figure12.5, three stories have been identified to inform the customer about the product—in invoices, renewals, and customer service representative (CSR) scripts. These have been positioned to the left of the map. The MVP includes a Broker Quick Quote feature so that the customer can benefit from a premium reduction on sign-up.

Validation of the application, which would normally require integration with the vendor, will be achieved through workarounds: the underwriter will use an offline process to assess the application and enter the assessment results into the system. Since this workaround will be replaced in upcoming iterations, a spike is planned to analyze related business rules in advance.

Steps required to activate the device and stream data are also included for quick wins so that the increment delivers real value to the customer and business.

Case Study Retrospective

In this workshop, you developed an MVP to test the assumption that customers will like the product when they see it and will be willing to overlook privacy concerns for immediate benefits. If the MVP is successful, it will provide reassurance that the company is headed in the right direction; if not, it will suggest that the company should consider changing course.

12.5.9 Other Forms of Story Maps

You can also use other kinds of story maps to indicate relationships between stories. These include persona-based maps and low-fidelity interface maps.

12.5.9.1 Persona-Based Story Maps

In a persona-based story map, stories are positioned under the persona that uses them. A similar map may be created on the basis of user roles (e.g., a bank teller, a customer). Figure 12.6 is an example of a persona-based story map.

To use this type of map as a facilitation tool, begin by posting personas or user roles on a wall. Invite attendees to brainstorm features and stories that each persona would use. Anyone may write a story. Story authors may ask developers at any time to provide a rough estimate of a work item to determine whether it qualifies as a story or feature. Distinguish between sizes by color (e.g., yellow for stories, pink for anything larger).

As the map is developing, keep cycling back to ask attendees whether each persona has all the capabilities it needs.

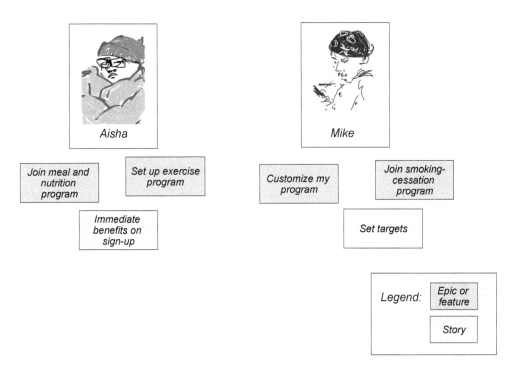

Figure 12.6 *Persona-based story maps*

12.5.9.2 Low-Fidelity Interface Maps

A low-fidelity interface map[21] is a rough workflow model of the user interface, indicating the order in which the user views interface components. An **interface component** on the map may represent any user-interface element, such as a screen, a tab, a window, or a dropdown box. Figure 12.7 is an interface map describing the user interface used by an internal support agent for the CEO case study.

The map in Figure 12.7 indicates that the user first lands on a home page, with sections for user authentication, news, and upcoming events. From the home page, the user can navigate to three components (e.g., screens): *Manage Campaign*, *Manage Customer Messages*, and *View Analytics*. From *Manage Campaign*, the user can navigate to *Create Campaign* and from there to *Create Event*; alternatively, the user can select an existing campaign from *Manage Campaign* and proceed directly to *Create Event*.

A low-fidelity interface map is used primarily for high-level design of the user interface. However, it also suggests features and stories. For example, Figure 12.7 suggests a *Manage Campaign* feature that would be composed of two smaller features or stories: *Create Campaign* and *Create Event*.

---

21. Cohn, *User Stories Applied*, 50.

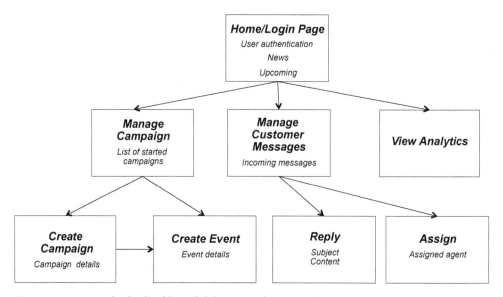

Figure 12.7   *Early draft of low-fidelity interface map for CEO case study*

12.6 Chapter Summary

Here are the key points covered in this chapter:

- An MVP is a "version of the product that enables a full turn of the Build-Measure-Learn loop with a minimum of effort and the least amount of development."[22]

- In a Concierge MVP, the business first works closely with a few select customers to learn their needs.

- A Smoke-and-Mirrors MVP provides the customer with an experience close to the real product. However, behind the scenes, workarounds are used to give the illusion of full functionality.

- Use left-to-right placement of stories on a story map to indicate operational sequence.

- Use top-to-bottom placement on a story map to indicate implementation sequence.

12.7 What's Next?

In this chapter, we examined story mapping. As the team plans work items for the interim periods (the rows), it often runs up against a sizing problem: the planned features are too large to implement within the budget for the interval and must be split into smaller stories. We look at guidelines for splitting stories in the next chapter.

---

22. Ries, *The Lean Startup*, 77.

Another concern is that you don't lose the visual information conveyed on the story map when you transfer the stories to a requirements repository at the end of the planning session. Chapter 13, "Story Preparation," includes story-writing guidelines that preserve the understanding gained during preparation and planning.

Chapter 13

Story Preparation

The secret to high-performing agile teams is effective story preparation. Well-prepared stories lead to better estimation, better iteration planning, reduced rework, and fewer impediments and delays. This chapter provides guidelines for this activity—one that begins at the start of an initiative for the first stories to be implemented and continues throughout the product's lifecycle. Figure 13.1 highlights the activities covered in the chapter.

The chapter opens with an overview of user-story fundamentals. It reviews the distinctions between stories, features, and epics and explains the Three Cs that define a story. It explores the analyst's role in story specification and provides guidelines for facilitating Triad conversations during which story preparation occurs.

The chapter provides guidelines for recording the results of those conversations using the Role-Feature-Reason (Connextra template). It explains how to write well-formed stories and specify their acceptance criteria (AC) using the behavior-driven development (BDD) Gherkin syntax. Then it extends the guidance to other kinds of stories, such as functional spikes and bug-repair stories.

Also included are extensive guidelines for splitting requirements items into small stories, based on the Richard Lawrence and Scaled Agile Framework (SAFe) patterns. The chapter concludes with guidelines for analyzing and specifying business rules and associated test scenarios for upcoming stories.

The chapter continues the case study that runs through the book, including sample solutions.

13.1 Objectives

This chapter will help you

- Craft well-written user stories that can be used effectively by the team.
- Facilitate collaboration between the customer, developers, and QA during Triad story-preparation sessions.
- Write stories using the Role-Feature-Reason (Connextra) story template.

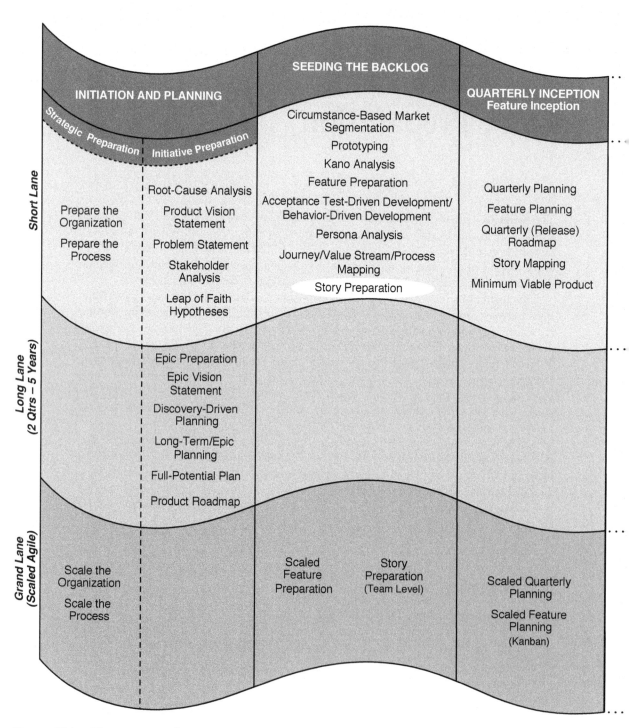

Figure 13.1 *Chapter 13 on the map*

DAILY ACTIVITIES

QUARTERLY CLOSEOUT
Epic, Feature Closeout

ITERATION INCEPTION

ITERATION CLOSEOUT

Daily Standup

Requirements Analysis & Documentation

Code, Build, Test, Deliver Acceptance Test-Driven Development/ Behavior-Driven Development

Minimum Viable Product, Split Testing

Epic, Feature Preparation

Story Preparation

Iteration Planning

Iteration Review

Iteration Retrospective

Prepare for General Availability

Quarterly Retrospective

Epic, Feature Retrospective

Pivot or Persevere

Scaled Iteration Planning

Iteration Planning (Team Level)

Product Owner Council Meetings

DevOps

User Task Force Meetings

Scaled Feature Preparation (Kanban)

Integration Meetings

Story Preparation (Team Level)

Scaled Iteration Review

Scaled Iteration Retrospective

Iteration Retrospective (Team Level)

DevOps

Scaled Quarterly/Feature Retrospective

- Specify story AC using the BDD Gherkin syntax.
- Specify nonfeature stories (e.g., nonfunctional requirements [NFRs], functional spikes, and bug fixes).
- Split large work items into stories using the Lawrence and SAFe patterns.
- Analyze business rules for stories using decision tables.

13.2 This Chapter on the Map

As shown in Figure 13.1, the chapter examines story preparation—an activity that occurs at the start of an initiative (see the Seeding the Backlog zone) and continues in a rolling fashion once development begins—as indicated by its presence in the Daily Activities zone.

13.3 Overview of Story Preparation

As an analyst, you contribute to high-performing teams by preparing upcoming stories so that they are small and well-enough understood for implementation to begin without undue delay or rework. Story preparation occurs at various times during the development cycle.

- It occurs at the start of an initiative, epic, or quarter to prepare the first stories to be implemented.
- If the team practices flow-based planning (e.g., Kanban), story preparation continues on an ongoing basis as each story nears the top of the backlog. If the team uses a timeboxed planning approach (e.g., Scrum, XP), it is carried out for the group of stories lined up for the next iteration, before each iteration planning meeting.
- Story preparation is also conducted any time new stories are added to the backlog.

Story preparation involves analysis and design. This chapter focuses on the *analysis* aspects of story preparation to bring a story to *ready*. For example, it includes guidelines for ensuring the story is testable and small.

13.4 Story Fundamentals

The story is the atomic requirements unit of agile analysis and planning—the lowest level at which we track and manage requirements. Since this chapter is focused entirely on this central unit, let's begin with a review of story fundamentals.

13.4.1 What Is a Story?

A **story** is a work item that delivers value, sized so that a single team can implement it within a short time—typically within 8 story points or ideal developer days (IDDs). Stories should be written in the language of the customer. No particular format is required. However, the Role-Feature-Reason (Connextra) format is widely used and recommended (see Section 13.9.2).

The value that a story delivers may be

- **User value**—functionality directly experienced by users, such as the ability to create autopayments.
- **Business value**, such as increased efficiencies.
- **Learning value**, such as an MVP to test a hypothesis that users will engage heavily with the product.
- **Technical benefits** that enable business opportunities, such as scalability.

There are different types of stories, differentiated by the kind of value they provide. The most common type is the user story—a story that delivers value to an end user.

13.4.2 Alternative Terminology

The term *story* originated from Extreme Programming (XP). It's so widely used in agile development that I'll be utilizing it as a default in the book for an atomic requirements unit. However, other, roughly equivalent phrases are also popular. Kanban refers to a *work item*. In Scrum, the atomic unit is called a *product backlog item (PBI)*. The term *story* is a bit more restrictive than these alternatives because a story must deliver value and be under a specified size. The term *user story* is more restrictive still because it refers, specifically, to an item that delivers value to an *end user*. The Use Case 2.0 standard uses the phrase *use-case slice*. It is roughly equivalent to a user story, as it refers to user functionality. However, the use-case slice is more formally constrained in that it must be tied to a use case (usage) of the product.

13.4.3 Size Taxonomy

As noted in the previous section, *story* infers a small size. If the work item is larger than the maximum story size, it's referred to as an epic or feature. These terms are used inconsistently in the industry. The following is an overview of the terms as I'll be using them in this book.

Epic > Feature > Story

Let's review Figure 13.2, an example that appeared in Chapter 3, "Fundamentals of Agile Analysis and Planning."

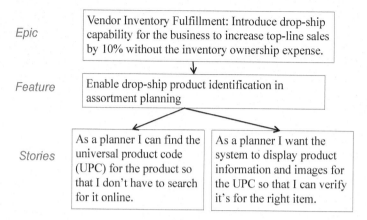

Figure 13.2 *From epic to stories*

An **epic** is an exceedingly large work item delivering business value that may require multiple quarters and multiple teams to implement, such as the epic in Figure 13.2, "Vendor Inventory Fulfillment: Introduce dropship capability for the business to increase top-line sales by 10% without the inventory ownership expense." Note how the epic involves a product-wide objective, not confined to a single department.

An epic is decomposed into features. A **feature** is a work item that one or more teams can complete within a single quarter. As stated earlier, a story is a work item that a single team can complete within a short time (e.g., one to two weeks, one iteration, 8 points or fewer).

A story can support more than one feature, and a feature can support more than one epic.

Other intermediary levels can be defined, such as epics at the program and portfolio levels, but to keep matters from getting too complicated, I'll limit the taxonomy of sizes to epic, feature, and story.

13.4.4 What's in a Name?

It's not all that important whether you call requirements units stories, PBIs, or any of the terms in use. It's *how* you slice the requirements that counts—not what you call the slices—and that's what we are mostly concerned with in this chapter.

Nevertheless, there is *some* importance to naming. Naming standards enhance communication (e.g., everyone knows what mean when you refer to an epic). And, as the following true story illustrates, terminology can sometimes improve team behaviors.

Recently, a manager complained to me that she couldn't get her teams to perform preliminary analysis because consultants had told them it wasn't "agile" to do so. As a result, many stories would get stalled during development, while people waited on analysis that should have occurred earlier. When I introduced her to functional spikes, her eyes lit up as though it was the most useful advice I could have given her. All I'd passed on to her was a term—yet it was helpful because she could now return to her teams and ask them to create *functional spikes*—an agile artifact some of the team members had heard about. That gave the analysis enough credence to be acceptable as agile by the group.

13.4.5 User Story Examples

We examine guidelines for specifying stories later in this chapter, but to give you a feel for them if you haven't used them before, here are a couple of examples:

- As a service provider, I want to post a service on the marketplace so that customers can view my offerings.

- As a service representative, I want to submit a claim with manual pre-approval so that the claim can be expedited for the customer.

The following is a specification for the bottom-right user story in Figure 13.2, elaborated with the addition of AC.

As a planner, I want the system to display product information and images for the Universal Product Code (UPC) of a dropshipping product so that I can verify it's for the right item.

Acceptance Criteria

I can see images of the product.

I can see product attributes, including color, size, rating, genre, publisher.

I can view all sellers of the product under the same listing.

13.5 The Three Cs of Stories

A user story has three components—referred to as the *Three Cs*—which, taken together, communicate the requirements for a user story:

- Card

- Conversation

- Confirmation

13.5.1 Card

A story is represented by a **card**. It can literally be a physical card (the format recommended by Kent Beck), or it may take a digital form, entered into an electronic product backlog/requirements repository. Stories typically begin as physical cards during planning and are later transferred to an electronic backlog so that they can be easily viewed and tracked from any location.

The text on the card should describe the capability in the user's terminology, from the user's point of view. As noted earlier, templates are often used to standardize the phrasing but are not required. (We look at guidelines for using templates later in this chapter.)

The story card must be **prioritized**. Prioritization is expressed through sequencing. Cards positioned at the top of the list are implemented before those below them.

13.5.2 Conversation

The textual description serves as a *reminder* to have a conversation about the requirements. The requirements themselves are communicated through **conversation** and supplementary artifacts.

13.5.3 Confirmation

Each story specifies what it will take for it to be considered "done" by the customer. Those conditions are expressed the story's **acceptance criteria (AC)**. For example, an AC for the story *Order Tickets Online* states, "Tickets ordered two weeks or more before the show receive an early-bird discount." The AC conditions for the story apply over and above those listed in the definition of done (DoD). We examine story AC further in section 13.10.

 For more on the DoD, see Chapter 6, section 6.5.7.4.

13.6 Who Is Responsible for User Stories?

The product owner (PO) has the primary responsibility for stories, has the final say on whether a story correctly reflects business needs, and is the sole person responsible for *prioritizing* stories and sequencing them in the backlog. The analyst supports the PO in carrying out these responsibilities.

13.6.1 Who Writes Stories?

Anyone on the team can create a story,[1,2] but the PO is accountable for it (Scrum).[3] (The XP guideline differs slightly in that the product manager[4]—roughly equivalent to a Scrum

---

1. Cohn states that "over the course of a good agile project, you should expect to have user story examples written by each team member." Mike Cohn, "User Stories," Mountain Goat Software, https://www.mountaingoatsoftware.com/agile/user-stories

2. Roman Pichler, "10 Tips for Writing Good User Stories" [blog post], March 24, 2016, https://www.romanpichler.com/blog/10-tips-writing-good-user-stories

3. Ken Schwaber and Jeff Sutherland, *The Scrum Guide: The Definitive Guide to Scrum—The Rules of the Game* (Scrumguides.org, 2020), 6.

4. Kent Beck, "The Whole XP Team: Product Managers," in *Extreme Programming Explained: Embrace Change* (2nd ed.), The XP Series (Boston: Addison-Wesley, 2004).

PO—writes the stories, helped by users[5] on the team.) Regardless of the story's author, it is the PO who prioritizes it.

To ensure good communication across teams and business decision makers, follow these guidelines whenever anyone adds a story:[6]

- The story must be added to the central product backlog so that it can be prioritized against other work items.

- The addition of the story must be communicated to the PO and the development team.

- The lead business analyst and PO must be notified of significant events in the story's lifecycle. The notification may be automated (e.g., by designating the business analyst and PO as watchers in Jira[7] for field changes, reassignments, and comments).

The analyst is typically responsible for writing a story's AC through collaboration between business, QA, and developers—often referred to as the Triad (see section 13.6.3). The AC are approved as correct and sufficient by the PO—often pending the consent of other stakeholders.

13.6.2 The Analyst Value Added

Teams often come to me because they are struggling with various aspects of story-writing. They find they can't get stories to be small enough for agile development, don't know how to write "good" stories, and suffer from delays when stories are not well prepared before implementation. It's asking a lot to expect POs—who may have come from the business side with little background in requirements engineering—to figure all this out. As an analyst, you provide critical support to the PO in carrying out these tasks in the following ways:

- Prior to quarterly (feature) planning, you prepare features, specify their AC, and split them into smaller stories.

- You support the PO in the negotiation, writing, and preparation of stories and enter them into a digital backlog. You continue to add and refine AC once implementation begins as new scenarios and error conditions are discovered.

- You facilitate ongoing Triad discussions between business stakeholders, testers, and developers to refine stories.

- You facilitate the development of a story-implementation plan that maximizes value delivery throughout the lifecycle.

---

5. Beck, "The Whole XP Team."

6. Ron Healy, from editing notes to the author.

7. Dan Radigan, "Using Watchers and @mentions Effectively in Jira," Jira Software, June 10, 2013, https://www.atlassian.com/blog/jira-software/using-watchers-and-mentions-effectively

- You work with developers and QA to test stories against their AC.

- The lead analyst and business analysis centers of excellence (CoEs) provide story templates and examples. They also collaborate with the team, PO, and QA to specify story DoRs.

13.6.3 The Triad

The **Triad** is a framework for carrying out backlog preparation. The Triad is not an event but an idea—the notion that there should be three players who follow the requirements around whenever they are being worked on: representatives of business, development, and QA (testing). A business analyst is often included. (See section 13.6.3.4.) When the Triad meets to discuss a story, the group collaborates to develop its essential elements: the item's AC, estimated effort, and prioritization.

13.6.3.1 Benefits of Triad

The Triad approach ensures that three key groups—business, development, and testing— are aligned whenever stories are discussed. Business knows what's needed, development creates the solution, and testers test it based on a shared understanding of the requirements. These groups can tend to drift into silos, resulting in communication breaks. The Triad is a mechanism for preventing this siloing by bringing the groups together.

The Triad reduces friction because it puts together three competencies whose responsibilities are tightly interrelated. If the business wants to add requirements to a story, doing so impacts the estimate—something the developer is responsible for. The revised cost estimate can affect the priority the business gives to the story and its sequence in the backlog. The new requirements also affect the story's AC and scenarios, about which testers have expertise. Testers are also good at thinking of edge cases that drive out the requirements that business is responsible for writing. Furthermore, any AC added to the story affect the estimate provided by the developers. Rather than bouncing between these three players whenever the story is worked on, it's better to have them in the same room at the same time.

13.6.3.2 Timing Considerations

Initial discussion about the story takes place at the time the story is written. Afterward, Triad conversations occur within two to four weeks or (if the teams are using a timeboxed framework like Scrum or XP) within one or two iterations of a story's planned implementation.

Hold a number of small meetings over time, selecting attendees according to the story under discussion. Each gathering of the Triad should be no longer than one hour.

Once the story's implementation begins, the Triad continues to meet as the story is developed and demonstrated in order to provide and gather feedback. If the implementation does not address business needs, the story is sent back to development and demonstrated until business decision makers are satisfied that the story meets its AC.

13.6.3.3 *Inputs and Deliverables*

Inputs to the Triad are as follows:

- One or more upcoming backlog items, estimated and prioritized

- DoR (if one is being used)

The deliverables of the Triad are as follows:

- Ready stories

- Updated stories, including their estimates, priorities, and AC

13.6.3.4 *Whom Should You Invite?*

Triad meetings should *not* be a whole-team event. Restrict attendance to those with an interest in the story (or stories) under discussion. The minimum number of attendees is three, each representing one of the Triad's perspectives: business, development, and testing. As an analyst, you are present to facilitate negotiation between the other parties or to represent the business. Add additional subject matter experts (SMEs) on the basis of the nature of the story under discussion (e.g., UX designer, security expert).

The *lead* roles for each perspective should be represented—for example, lead QA, lead developer, lead business analyst, PO—to ensure relevant senior stakeholders have a shared understanding of the story after the meeting. Another reason is that technical and QA leads are more likely than junior personnel to have the standing to disagree with the PO.[8] Furthermore, their consistent participation leads to familiarity with the requirements, resulting in greater efficiency.

Invite additional participants who can contribute to these perspectives regardless of their formal role (e.g., anyone else with in-depth knowledge of user needs). These attendees may change from meeting to meeting, according to the nature of the requirements being discussed.

The following sections outline the contributions of each perspective, in greater detail.

Business Perspective

The business is represented because it knows what's needed. Business stakeholders contribute an in-depth knowledge of story requirements so that developers can better estimate the story, and testers can create test cases. Stakeholders are also able to provide real AC examples. Business decision makers test the story against its AC to determine if it is done.

Testing Perspective

Testers know from experience what can go wrong as a feature is rolled out, and they often come up with edge cases that the business wouldn't think of, such as a service going down. This input, in turn, helps drive out requirements by leading to a discussion with business stakeholders about the expected system response to test scenarios.

---

8. Ron Healy, in a note to the author.

Development Perspective

Developers are present to estimate effort and collaborate with business stakeholders to explore alternative ways to deliver the story's value at less cost. Developers also help in specifying AC and test scenarios. They understand what situations are treated equivalently by the code and don't require separate testing. They know where the code is vulnerable and might need more intensive testing. As well, they know which scenarios will be covered by unit testing (e.g., validation of input fields) and do not, therefore, need to be repeated in the AC.

Analyst Perspective

As a fourth contributor, you, the analyst, facilitate Triad negotiations. You support the business in challenging assumptions about the requirements and presumed solution and ensuring alternative options are explored. You also contribute agile requirements management competencies, including story-writing, the crafting of AC, elicitation, and requirements analysis skills. You may also participate in Triad meetings as the representative of the business perspective (e.g., in place of the PO).

13.6.3.5 Guidelines for the Analyst at a Triad Event

Use the following checklist of questions during Triad meetings to explore requirements and specify AC for upcoming stories.[9]

☑ *Questions to Ask the PO*

The following is a list of questions to ask the PO:

- ☐ Why is the item needed?
- ☐ Is the item similar to anything else that's already been implemented?
- ☐ Is the item similar to anything else currently in the product backlog?
- ☐ Tell us about the essential scenarios that the system or product must handle. Can you provide specific examples?
- ☐ Have we considered every error that could occur?
- ☐ Are there any user options that we neglected to consider, such as options to select faster delivery; options available only to premium users?
- ☐ Do the AC we identified cover all the expected actions of the system?

Questions to Ask the Developer

The following is a checklist of questions to ask developers:

- ☐ What else would you need to know before coding can begin?
- ☐ Are there any dependencies that need to be addressed?

---

9. Questions incorporate guidance from Mike Cohn. See Cohn, *User Stories Applied: For Agile Software Development* (Boston: Addison-Wesley, 2004), 68.

☐ Have we considered every technical error that might occur?

☐ Do the AC duplicate tests you've already covered in unit testing (e.g., data validation tests)?

☐ Which areas of the software are most vulnerable to errors?

☐ What aspects and AC of the story are contributing most to the cost? Have you explored less costly alternatives?

☐ How have changes to the story's AC affected the estimate?

☐ What assumptions have you made about the solution when creating your estimates?

☐ Is there a less-expensive and/or faster option for delivering the story's value?

☐ Are there any outstanding tasks that need to be done up front for development to begin?

Questions to Ask QA

The following is a checklist of questions to ask testers:

☐ Are there any edge cases we haven't thought of?

☐ Do any AC or other tests duplicate scenarios that are already covered by automated testing (e.g., smoke tests)?

☐ Do you have all of the information you need to begin constructing test cases?

☐ Can you think of any test-related tasks that need to occur before implementation, such as the building of a test data bank?

☐ What is your understanding of the test scenarios covered in the story—and do others share the same understanding?

13.7 Physical versus Electronic Stories

Most development organizations working on large products record their stories electronically. There are a few important reasons for this. An electronic backlog serves as a single source of truth for all teams—making it easier to track inter-team dependencies and overall progress and to maximize value across the product. As well, businesses often require tracking of updates to stories and their attributes (e.g., estimates and AC) so that there is a verifiable record of what was agreed to. It is challenging to deliver that capability using physical cards because anyone can make changes at any time without notifying others.

However, physical cards should be used *wherever it's practical to do so* because they are more intuitive, feel less precious, and are easier to move around than their electronic counterparts. The ideal context for using physical cards is a small initiative of one to four colocated teams. Cards are also recommended during planning for large initiatives—even when teams are dispersed. Where possible, at the start of the planning period, the teams converge at a common location using physical story cards to develop the plan. After the planning event, you (the analyst) transfer the stories to an electronic backlog to provide visibility across locations.

13.8 Specifying Values for Story Attributes

In Chapter 6, you learned to define requirements attributes when preparing the requirements management process. Now, as you enter each story into the product backlog, you specify values for those attributes.

As discussed in that chapter, those attributes may include the following:

- Item type (e.g., user story, functional spike)
- Description
- Acceptance criteria
- Estimate
- Order (sequence in the backlog, assigned by the PO)
- Weighted shortest job first (WSJF)
- Cost of delay: Value of the item taking into account time criticality
- Owner
- Status (e.g., ready, done)
- Dependencies and other relationships
- Change log: Record of changes to the item

 For more on PBI attributes, see Chapter 6, section 6.5.4.3.

13.9 Writing the Story Description

Some agile practitioners don't think a story is a story unless it follows the Connextra template. In fact, there is no rule that a story's description has to follow any template—but sometimes it's a good idea to do so. Let's explore when and when not to use one.

13.9.1 When to Use a Story Template (and When Not To)

During active planning, when stories are highly volatile, don't use a template. Instead, use simple, short descriptions, such as "Offer Discount" or "Add Tip." As long as everyone understands what the stories mean, the shorter descriptions are more effective at this time because they forestall wasted time arguing over the "correct" wording. Besides, if the stories are posted on a story map (as described in Chapter 12, "MVPs and Story Maps"), much of their contextual information is communicated by their position on the map.

Use a template at the end of planning when entering stories into an electronic backlog—and any time they are added afterward. In these circumstances, it's important to consider the wording of the story because its original intent may otherwise be lost over time. While it's true that a story is only a *reminder* to have a conversation, *you can't have a conversation about a story if you can't remember what the story is supposed to be about.*

A template is advised whenever conversation alone can't be relied on to communicate requirements. These circumstances may include the following:

- Teams are non-colocated.

- Stakeholders are not freely available to answer questions.

- The developer is a third-party provider with minimal familiarity with the business.

- There will be a long delay until the story is implemented.

The lead analyst, or *CoE lead* in agile analysis, should spearhead the development and adoption of a story template and propagate its use within the organization where appropriate.

The danger with templates, though, is that they can quickly become straightjackets. No story should be *forced* into the template if it can't be naturally described in that form.

13.9.2 Role-Feature-Reason (Connextra) Template

Earlier in this book, we encountered the most commonly used template, the *Role-Feature-Reason* template—also known as the Connextra template (after the English company first known to have used it) and the *Who-What-Why*[10] template. The template is most widely used for user stories but is also recommended for other stories, such as technical stories, because it communicates the business benefit of the work item.

The Connextra template preserves and communicates a story's intent by reminding the story writer to identify key aspects at creation time—the stakeholder who wants the story, what it is they want, and why—and to express them in a clear, standardized manner.

There are several variations of the template, often differing on small matters, such as whether the word *want*, *need*, or *can* is used. A typical format is:

> As a <<who>>, I want <<what>> so (that) <<why>>.[11]
>
> For example, "As a service representative, I want to triage an incident so that high-priority items are expedited."

---

10. Mike Cohn, "Why the Three-Part User Story Template Works So Well," Mountain Goat Software, May 28, 2019, https://www.mountaingoatsoftware.com/blog/why-the-three-part-user-story-template-works-so-well

11. Cohn, "Why the Three-Part User Story Template Works So Well."

13.9.2.1 "Who" Clause

For the **Who clause**, specify the stakeholder who wants the story. Typically, a *User Role* is named. A user role is a class of users who all use the product in the same way (e.g., customer, sales agent, shipper, supervisor, or instructor). Alternatively, a *persona* may be named (e.g., "As Jodie, the Graphic Artist, I want to. . .").

13.9.2.2 "What" Clause

The **What clause** describes the capability. It should be user focused, indicating what the user wants to *do* with the product rather than describing an attribute or component of the product. For example, it's usually better to write, "As a clinical research associate (CRA), I want to see the status of a datapoint" than to write, "As a CRA, I want a traffic-light icon to indicate the status of a data item by its color (green = accepted; red = rejected)." The latter unnecessarily constrains the design: there might be a better or less expensive way to indicate status than using the suggested icon. On the other hand, if marketers have convinced the PO that the traffic-light icon is the *only* acceptable implementation, the design item becomes a *business* constraint. In that case, you should include it front and center in the story description.

Earlier in this book, I wrote about a team whose story descriptions were so poorly worded that, at times, no one (including the author) could recall their original intent. To avoid this problem, write the What clause so that it's clear what product, business object, subproduct, or usage the story is about. For example, don't specify, "As a customer, I want to search by destination." Instead, specify, "As a customer, I want to search *flights* by destination."

13.9.2.3 "Why" Clause

The **Why clause** ("so that") specifies the value of the story. The *why* expresses a higher-level goal than the *what*. It's the *reason* for the *what*, as in the following example:

- As a member, I want to view my daily usage statistics so that I can monitor my time spent online.

The goal expressed in the Why clause may be a *quality* goal—the ability to do something the user can already do but better (e.g., faster or more conveniently). The following are examples of quality goals:

- As a borrower, I want to submit a mortgage application online so that I can get an answer more quickly than through conventional means.
- As a driver, I want to renew my license online so that I don't have to waste my time waiting in line at the motor vehicles office.

Alternatively, the goal expressed in a Why clause may be to enable a subsequent user task:

- As a customer service agent, I want to view a customer's transaction history so that I can suggest changes to the customer's plan.

The Why clause is most useful before and during initial design and prioritization. It has less value once the story gets to the development team because once a story is prioritized and committed to, developers tend to have limited interest in the rationale for it. Nevertheless, I recommend the clause be preserved because it helps define the *higher-level* objectives that must be reached for the story to be done, in contrast to the lower-level conditions expressed in the AC. This becomes useful if the team needs to adjust the plan mid-flight when time is running out: the clause guides the team as it considers faster, cheaper alternatives for addressing the higher-level goal for the story. Furthermore, Why clauses remind the team and PO about the business value of remaining stories in an iteration—useful information in case some stories need to be deferred in order to meet timelines.

13.9.2.4 *"When" Clause (Optional)*

The When clause is an optional clause (not part of the standard Role-Feature-Reason template) that may be used to communicate the usage context for the requirement. This clause identifies the task (use case) the user is performing while the feature is in play. Consider the following example: "As a customer service agent, I want to view a customer's next renewal date when I respond to a service call so that I can pitch renewal incentives to customers approaching the end of their subscription period." Note how, in this example, the When clause adds context that is not obvious without it.

Some practitioners advise using the When clause as a replacement for the Who clause, contending that it provides more relevant information about the requirement. For example, "When I respond to a service call, I want to view a customer's next renewal date so that. . . ." The resulting requirement item is referred to as a **job story** as opposed to a user story.[12,13] My view is to include whatever clauses are helpful in conveying important information about a requirement and exclude those that aren't. I agree that job stories are a useful alternative to user stories in cases where the user role is obvious (e.g., the customer of an eCommerce site), but I don't see any reason why the two clauses must *always* be exclusive: sometimes it's important to communicate who needs a requirement *and* when they would use it.

13.10 Specifying Story Acceptance Criteria

The third C of a story, **confirmation**, is the shared understanding of what it will take for a story to be confirmed as done. Confirmation of a story is specified through its AC.

You specify AC on a story-by-story basis. Remember that in addition to a story's AC, the DoD must also be satisfied for a story to be done.

---

12. Alan Klement, "Replacing the User Story with the Job Story," Medium, November 12, 2013, https://jtbd.info/replacing-the-user-story-with-the-job-story-af7cdee10c27
13. Mike Cohn, "Job Stories Offer a Viable Alternative to User Stories" [blog post], Mountain Goat Software, October 29, 2019, https://www.mountaingoatsoftware.com/blog/job-stories-offer-a-viable-alternative-to-user-stories

13.10.1 Examples of Story Acceptance Criteria

Acceptance criteria may be expressed informally, or the text may follow a formal format such as the Gherkin syntax. Typically, you begin by writing a story's AC informally. Later, you specify them in feature files using Gherkin. The following are examples of informal user story AC.

> **Story:** As a service provider, I want to post a service on the marketplace so that customers can view my offerings.
>
> **Acceptance criteria**
>
> I can post a service (successful): Authenticated service provider posts a service. Posted service is viewable on the customer portal.

We saw the following example of informal AC in section 13.4.5.

> **Story:** As a planner, I want the system to display product information for the UPC of a dropshipping product so that I can verify it's for the right item.
>
> **Acceptance criteria:**
>
> I can see images of the product.
>
> I can see product attributes including color, size, rating, genre, publisher.
>
> I can view all sellers of the product under the same listing.

The Gherkin syntax is widely used for specifying AC scenarios because it is understandable to all relevant parties (business stakeholders, testers, and developers), ensures critical information is conveyed, and can be interpreted by automated testing tools. The specifications are often contained in Gherkin feature files. We examine the BDD Gherkin syntax in section 13.10.9.

 For more on specifying BDD AC in Gherkin feature files, see Chapter 10, sections 10.9.5 and 10.9.6.

13.10.2 Who Writes Acceptance Criteria?

A large part of your responsibility as an analyst revolves around AC, as they serve both as tests and requirements specifications. Typically, you are responsible for writing the AC textual descriptions and scenarios, while you or QA write the Gherkin specifications in collaboration with others. The PO has the primary responsibility for ensuring AC are correct[14] and confirming that they are satisfied, though often with the consent of other stakeholders.

---

14. See Cohn's guidance for user story testing. Cohn, *User Stories Applied*, 67–74.

For more on the analyst role in AC, see Chapter 10, section 10.9.3, where it is discussed in the context of features.

As noted in section 13.6.3, business stakeholders, QA (testers), and developers should collaborate to identify AC: business stakeholders contribute knowledge of the need and real examples; QA contributes expertise finding edge cases; developers contribute test scenarios and estimate the impact of acceptance criteria changes on cost. As an analyst, you support the business in negotiating trade-offs between AC and cost.

13.10.3 When to Create and Update Acceptance Criteria

Acceptance criteria specification occurs as part of story preparation. It should begin before the story is accepted into development and (if the team is using a timeboxed approach) before iteration planning. The reason AC must be specified early is that they influence the estimate used for planning and guide the developers' work once implementation begins.

Continue to refine and add AC right up to and during implementation. For example, for the user story "As a customer, I want to reserve a vacation property," you initially write the following AC:

- Test with payment by credit card (pass)
- Test with declined credit card payment (fail)
- Test with property unavailable on requested dates (fail)

Close to the story's implementation, you learn more about the last AC and specify the following scenario in a Gherkin feature file:

Scenario: Test with property unavailable on requested dates (fail)

> **Given** that the property is not available during the requested period
>
> **When** I attempt to reserve it
>
> **Then** I can see a list of alternate availabilities close to the requested time

Acceptance criteria may be added *whenever* the team discovers a requirements gap, including after the story has been accepted into development. Keep in mind that if a story's AC are added (or dropped), its estimate and prioritization should be reviewed and revised accordingly.

13.10.4 Specification by Example

Acceptance criteria are about more than testing; they also serve as **specifications by example**. They communicate the requirements by providing concrete examples to drive out requirements and clarify understanding.

The insight behind the specification by example guideline is that there is less chance of miscommunication if you describe *specific situations* than if you try to explain requirements by way of general rules. Since the AC act not only as inputs for testing but *as requirements specifications*, they need to be specified before coding so that they can guide the efforts of programmers.

Specification by example has several benefits:

- It avoids misunderstandings about the scope by clarifying what scenarios should be included.

- Acceptance criteria are useful for splitting stories. They provide a better basis for a split than task decomposition.

- By writing business-level AC early, testers can begin creating test cases for them before programming begins.

Focusing on AC also helps drive out waste. When specific examples are examined, it leads to meaningful discussions about whether those *scenarios should even be covered* in the story. For instance, suppose that in a meeting to discuss a story to manage incidents, developers provide a 13-point estimate. As the analyst focuses the group on specific examples, developers note that the AC that involve communication with external parties, such as ambulance services, are contributing most to the estimate. Users reveal that these scenarios occur so rarely that they can be handled manually and therefore don't need to be in the story. With the AC removed, developers estimate the story at 5 points—solving the story-size issue and eliminating low-value development at the same time.

The first AC for a story specifies a success scenario. It may be inferred, rather than written down, in order to reduce wasted effort. Alternatively, it may be specified so that it can act as a checklist item and a placeholder for more detailed test specifications. In the following example, the success scenario for the story *Submit a Claim* provides a placeholder for specifying the postconditions for a positive test. The success postconditions are that the claim status is set to preapproved and the claim is placed in a queue for items awaiting adjustment.

> **User story:** As a service representative, I want to submit a claim with manual preapproval so that the claim can be expedited for the customer.
>
> **Acceptance criteria:**
>
> Service representative manually approves claim: (Success) Claim status set to "Preapproved" and claim placed in an Adjustment queue.
>
> Service representative manually rejects the claim: (Failure) Claim status set to "Rejected."

It's common to express the first AC by rewording the story description slightly (e.g., by changing "I want" to "I can"). If you do so, make sure not to repeat the "so that" clause from the story description, as it has no relevance for AC. For example, consider the story, "As a customer, I *want* to see what timeslots are available so that I can book an appointment." Specify the AC as follows: "I *can* see what timeslots are available." Don't specify, "As a customer, I want to see what timeslots are available *so that I can book an appointment.*"

13.10.5 How Extensive Should the Acceptance Criteria Be?

Don't try to cover every possible scenario in the AC. Focus on the scenarios that best draw out and illustrate the requirements. Many of the other tests, such as detailed input-field validation tests, will be filled in by programmers and testers (e.g., through unit testing). As Dale Emery puts it, AC should cover "everything that matters and nothing that doesn't matter."[15]

The AC should not constrain the design. For example, don't specify, as an expected action, "The system displays a pop-up window showing current account balances." Instead, it's better to state, "The system displays current account balances." The latter phrasing leaves room for the customer and developers to try out various solutions to see what works best.

13.10.6 How Many Acceptance Criteria per Story?

Don't load too many AC onto a single story. A rule of thumb is to specify no more than five to seven AC per story.[16] There is also a good argument for limiting each story to a single AC so that each requirement can be prioritized and estimated separately. However, this limitation must be balanced against the added cost of managing more stories in the backlog.

If a story exceeds the maximum story size, split it and distribute the AC among the resulting stories. Group the scenarios that ought to be delivered together in the same user story. It's better to split stories by AC than by development tasks (the detailed work items to implement a story) because, with the former approach, the resulting stories implement entire user scenarios—delivering real value to the user. Also, stories split according to AC instead of tasks can be more easily prioritized because each one is characterized by functionality rather than by development work. For examples and further guidelines on splitting stories by AC, see section 13.13.3.13.

13.10.7 Characteristics of Well-Formed Acceptance Criteria

Specify story AC with the following characteristics:

- Testable
- Complete
- Concise
- Shared

Let's explore these attributes further.

---

15. As quoted by Dinwiddie in Charron, "George Dinwiddie on the Three Amigos."
16. Charron, "George Dinwiddie on the Three Amigos."

13.10.7.1 Testable

Acceptance criteria should be testable: specify AC so that it's possible to determine definitively whether or not a story has passed or failed them.

The following are examples of an untestable AC and a revised, testable AC:

User Story: Submit Transaction

Acceptance Criteria (Untestable)

Confirmed Transaction: When a transaction is accepted by the system, the user is notified.

Acceptance Criteria (Testable)

Confirmed Transaction: When a transaction is accepted by the system, the user receives a tracking number and a confirmation of transaction details.

The exception to this rule is when you deliberately want to leave wiggle room in the AC so you can pin down the conditions for acceptance once implementation begins through learning, due to the novelty of the story. See section 13.10.8 for more on this circumstance.

13.10.7.2 Complete

Acceptance criteria should cover all scenarios of importance to the business. They should include positive tests (where the user goal is successfully reached), negative tests (where the goal is not reached), and edge cases.

13.10.7.3 Concise

The AC should contain only what testers need to know to test the story. "Less is more."

13.10.7.4 "What" Not "How"

As a general rule, AC should describe what needs to happen, not how it should be done.[17] For example, the AC should state, "The user can select one of the next three available flights," not "The user can select from a dropdown list of the next three available flights." However, as noted earlier regarding user stories (see section 13.9.2.2), if the how is a constraint, you should include it. For example, if the business decision maker is insistent on a dropdown list, then you should highlight that in the AC.

13.10.7.5 Shared

It's not enough that the AC are written down. There should be a shared understanding of what they mean among business stakeholders, testers, and developers.

---

17. Steve Povilaitis, "Acceptance Criteria" [blog post], *LeadingAgile*, September 9, 2014, https://www.leadingagile.com/2014/09/acceptance-criteria

13.10.8 Emergent Acceptance Criteria

If the product or feature is innovative, the customer may not be able to say up front what qualifies as acceptable. In that case, specify *emergent* AC—criteria that provide for more leeway than usual because they will be determined through trial and error once implementation begins.

For example, an emergent AC might specify, "When I send a message successfully, I receive evidence that the message has arrived at its destination." The form of that evidence will become apparent only as the team and customer try out various approaches. In a *highly* innovative situation, the analyst may use an even more emergent formulation, "I have *confidence* the message has arrived at its destination," in order to leave maximum room for creativity in satisfying the customer's underlying need. Once implementation begins, the team tests out various options with the user to determine the solution that best provides confidence within the limits of the estimate. If sending a confirmation with the final message status is sufficient to provide confidence, then the AC is met. Alternatively, the customer may realize, through trial and error, that real-time message tracking is necessary in order to deliver confidence. If the customer wants more confidence than what is delivered by the end of the story estimate, the PO may create a new story.

13.10.9 Using the Behavior-Driven Development (BDD) Gherkin Format

Many organizations use a template for specifying AC scenarios because it formalizes the critical elements they need to know. The most popular format is the BDD Gherkin template, also called *Given-When-Then*. As noted earlier, when using Gherkin, you begin by writing informal story AC, then specify them formally in Gherkin feature files before development begins. The template also provides an added benefit: its keywords are recognized by automated testing tools. The following template incorporates its most commonly used keywords.

Gherkin Template

Scenario: <<scenario title>>
    Given <<precondition>>
    When <<trigger>>
    Then <<postcondition>>

The elements of the specification are as follows:

- The **scenario title** summarizes the test scenario.
- The **precondition** describes what must be true before the test scenario begins.
- The **trigger** describes the event or condition that starts the scenario.
- The **postcondition** describes conditions that must be true upon completion of the scenario for the test to be satisfied.
- Other useful keywords include **Feature**, to denote the beginning of a feature file, and **Background** to specify the Given steps common to all scenarios.

The following is an example of a scenario written using the Gherkin syntax.

Scenario: Renew license for tested vehicle (Success)

    Given that my insurance information is verified

    And the vehicle has passed required emissions tests

    And sufficient funds have been verified

    When I confirm submission of my license renewal application

    Then I can see my license expiration date extended for the renewal period

13.10.10 Who Tests Acceptance Criteria and When?

Acceptance criteria are tested by the customer as the story is implemented. By the time stories are demonstrated (e.g., in an iteration review), this testing should have been completed and the story deemed done.

Final integration and system tests should also be carried out continuously as each story is done, following continuous integration and continuous delivery (CI/CD) and DevOps practices. If the story's release to production will be delayed (e.g., until the feature is competitive in the marketplace), then some final testing steps may be deferred until the end of the release cycle (e.g., final beta testing).

13.11 Stories That Aren't User Stories

Generally, when agile developers speak of stories, they mean user stories—things users want. But what about all the work items that occupy a team that *aren't* about implementing users' needs? These work items include preliminary analysis and design, system upgrades, and compliance work. How do we take into account those kinds of activities when planning the team's workload?

There are two answers (and they are not exclusive). One is to accept that stories do not have to be used for every kind of requirement or work item (nor, of course, do they have to be used at all). If the organization already has processes and artifacts for managing work on NFRs and bug fixes, and they work well, there is no need to change them.

The other option is to treat all work items as stories, recognizing that the value a story delivers is not always user value. For example, a work item that implements new service charges provides business value even though it doesn't benefit the customer. A good argument for treating all work as stories is that it simplifies priortization, planning, and progress tracking, since there is only one kind of item (the story) to consider.

We've already examined one kind of story in depth: the user story—something that a user wants. Let's turn now to other types of stories.

13.11.1 What Is a Spike or Enabler Story?

A **spike**, also known as an **enabler story** "supports the activities needed to extend the architectural runway to provide future business functionality" (SAFe).[18] It's a work item to investigate what to build and how to construct it—a small investment to assess feasibility and direct resources toward future development.[19]

To avoid too much upfront analysis in the waterfall manner, encourage concurrency regarding analysis and implementation. For example, developers might be able to begin development once a small, preliminary spike has been completed—with the research continuing simultaneously with development.

13.11.1.1 Is a Spike a Story?

A spike is considered a story because it's a work item that delivers business value. However, it's not a *user story* because it doesn't deliver that value to the *user* (although it often enables future user stories to do so). Its purpose is to clarify an issue, gather information, or perform other tasks that *enable* value delivery (e.g., through future user stories).

13.11.1.2 Why Spikes Were Invented

Managers and analysts on agile teams that use stories often ask me, "How do we account for analysis time?" The answer is that it depends on when the analysis occurs. Analysis tasks carried out concurrently with development are incorporated into the total estimate for the story. They are managed like other developer tasks related to the story, such as testing and programming.

But what about the analysis that occurs *before* implementation begins as part of story preparation, such as business-rules analysis? Often, we must do at least some of this work beforehand to estimate the story reliably and—most important—to determine if the story is worth doing *at all*.[20]

Since user stories must deliver *user* value and analysis alone does not, you need another kind of placeholder for this work in the backlog. The answer is to specify a spike (enabler story) to deliver other kinds of value.

13.11.1.3 Origin of the Term Spike

Nobody seems to know for sure how the term *spike* originated. In one origin story,[21] the term is an allusion to rock climbing. Sometimes a climber drives a spike into the rock at a point somewhere ahead. While the spike does not in itself advance the climber up the

---

18. Richard Kastner and Dean Leffingwell, *SAFe 5.0 Distilled: Achieving Business Agility with the Scaled Agile Framework* (Boston: Addison-Wesley, 2020), 269.

19. Andrew Fuqua, "What's a Spike, Who Should Enter It, and How to Word It?" Leading Agile, September 13, 2016, https://www.leadingagile.com/2016/09/whats-a-spike-who-should-enter-it-how-to-word-it

20. Thanks to Ron Healy for providing this observation in an editorial note.

21. The reference is reported by attendees of the XP Universe conferences in 2001 and 2002. See http://agiledictionary.com/209/spike and https://www.quora.com/What-is-the-origin-of-the-term-spike-in-Agile-software-development-practice.

mountain, it *enables* her to do so in the future. Others[22] suggest the term may refer to the practice of newspapers to spike—or withhold—a story if it's not ready for publication. Another explanation is that it's a visual reference to a performance spike on a burndown chart.

In the following sections, we examine different kinds of spikes or enabler stories—keeping in mind that there's no consensus on what to call them. We start with functional spikes, since they most directly address how to account for business analysis work in an agile environment.

13.11.2 Functional Spike

A **functional spike** is a work item to enable other user stories through preliminary analysis (e.g., market research, exploration and evaluation of alternatives, business rules analysis, and workflow modeling). If the team uses a timeboxed planning approach (e.g., Scrum), it may strike a functional spike to prepare a feature before quarterly planning or to prepare a user story before iteration planning.

13.11.2.1 Timing Considerations

As a rule of thumb, if the team uses a timeboxed planning approach, perform the functional spike one or two iterations *before* the planned iteration for the enabled user story. There's no reason you *can't* schedule a functional spike during the same iteration as its user story (and some teams do that). However, there is rarely any good reason to do so. If you intend to perform the investigation and implement the user story in the same iteration, you don't need to create a spike; just include the analysis tasks in the story estimate as you would for other noncoding activities such as prototyping and testing.

In agile development, the term "bad smell" is sometimes used to describe a symptom of a deeper problem about agility. Some contend that overreliance on functional spikes is one of these bad smells and indicates a slide back to waterfall. However, I don't see anything wrong with the regular use of spikes. In fact, I encourage analysts to use them because teams work more efficiently when a story is well prepared going into development. Also, as noted earlier, spikes provide valuable input for estimation, planning, and prioritization—including whether or not it's worth implementing the user story being analyzed.

13.11.2.2 Describing a Functional Spike

As is the case with other stories, there are no strict rules about a functional spike's textual description. You can specify a spike informally, or use the Role-Feature-Reason (Conn-extra) template we saw earlier. For example, you may specify the following spike: As a developer, I want pricing rules to be analyzed so that I can estimate the *Place an order* user story. The "so that" clause specifies the value of the research—*why* it is needed.

---

22. Ron Healy in an editorial note to the author.

13.11.2.3 *Acceptance Criteria for Functional Spikes*

As a general rule of thumb, specify AC for a spike. The AC indicate the conditions that must be satisfied to meet the needs of the stakeholder who wants the spike. However, it's not *always* necessary to specify AC for a spike, because some spikes are considered done as soon as their time estimate runs out. If more work is required after the maximum is reached, the item is returned to the backlog so that it can be reprioritized against other work items.

Even in such cases, however, there is some value in specifying AC, because they indicate when the researcher can conclude the analysis—even if the clock has *not* run out. For example, the AC "Enough is known about the complexity of user story X to provide a reasonable estimate for capacity planning" is satisfied as soon as the story is estimable.

The following is an example of a functional spike.

Functional Spike: Research Process Workflow for the Story "Submit Mortgage Application"

Acceptance Criteria

A to-be mortgage application private process model has been created and verified by X.

13.11.2.4 *Use Qualifiers to Avoid Waterfall*

As noted in this chapter, agile development favors concurrency over waterfall's sequential approach. One way to support this practice is by adding a qualifier to a spike's AC. The qualifier describes the depth of the analysis expected during the spike—with the understanding that the remaining analysis will occur concurrently with the user story once implementation begins. For example, suppose developers need to know some but not all of the business rules regarding an incident before they can start coding. In that case, the AC might indicate, "Business rules are specified for incident types accounting for 80 percent of incidents." The following are other examples of AC with qualifiers.

Functional Spike: Research Risk-Rating for User Story "Rate a Risk"

Acceptance Criteria

A decision table indicating how risk ratings are determined has been created and verified, or the following is true:

> Enough is known to assess feasibility, and there is an illustration of how the business will research risk ratings after development begins.

Functional Spike: Research Pricing Rules for User Story "Place an Order"

Acceptance Criteria

Pricing rules are well-enough understood to estimate the story reliably during iteration planning.

13.11.2.5 Should Functional Spikes Be Estimated?

A question many teams struggle with is whether or not to assign story points to spikes. This question really has two parts: Do you estimate a spike? If so, what should you use the estimate for—capacity planning, measuring velocity, to limit the time spent on the analysis, or as input for prioritization? SAFe's guideline is as follows: Treat enablers [spikes] like all other work items, "subject to estimating, visibility and tracking, work in process (WIP) limits, feedback, and presentation of results."[23] In practice, however, the guidance should be more nuanced.

With regard to the first question—whether spikes should be estimated—provide an estimate *only* if the researcher (e.g., the analyst) is a team member whose time is counted toward capacity planning. If, as is often the case, the researcher's time is not considered in team capacity planning, then don't estimate the spike. For example, the researcher may be the PO, a nondedicated senior business analyst, or an SME. If the work needs to be done by a specified time in order to meet release timelines, you should still create the spike and prioritize it, though (even if you aren't estimating it), so that you remember to address the work in the plan.

With respect to the second question—what to use the estimate for—the following guidelines apply. Use the estimate as input for prioritizing the spike, since you can't prioritize without knowing the required effort. When setting the scope of an iteration during iteration planning, include the spike estimate if the researcher's time is included in the team's budget.

When calculating velocity, include spike points if the researcher is dedicated to the team. I should note that, despite this guidance, it is common for spike estimates *not* to be included when calculating past velocity. The reasoning often given is that only the delivery of *value to the customer* should be counted as progress—which would exclude spikes. However, though it's true that spikes don't count as progress from the customer's view, this point is irrelevant to the question of whether or not to include them in velocity calculations—since the primary purpose of measuring velocity is for *forecasting* purposes, *not* for gauging past progress.

The important thing is to be consistent: if you include spike estimates in capacity planning, you need to include them, as well, when calculating past velocities. For example, if, over a past iteration, the team delivered 45 points, 5 of which were due to spikes, their capacity for work in the next iteration is 45 points, not 40.

13.11.3 Technical Spike

A **technical spike** (or story) is a work item that deals with a technical issue. This kind of item qualifies as a story because, though technical in nature, it ultimately delivers business value, such as access to government contracts as a result of NFR compliance. Technical spikes are often created and implemented by architects and software engineers. Let's look at some subtypes.

---

23. SAFe, "Enablers," Scaled Agile Framework, last updated June 30, 2020, https://www.scaledagileframework.com/enablers

13.11.3.1 Technical Research Spike

A **technical research spike** (or story) is a work item to research a technical aspect of the solution. The following is an example of this kind of spike.

Technical Research Spike: Create Proof of Concept

Spike

Create a proof of concept to test the design architecture for the proposed intranet system.

Acceptance Criteria

A working proof of concept to pass data between nodes has been tested and can be used to evaluate the viability of the design.

13.11.3.2 Technical Debt-Payment Spike

In agile development, the rush to deliver value to the user can sometimes result in loss of quality. For example, the software may accumulate code that is redundant, poorly documented, unreachable, badly structured, or unaccompanied by automated tests. The unfinished work to fix these problems is referred to as **technical debt**. A **technical debt-payment spike** (or story) pays off this debt in order to enable future changes and capabilities.

Ideally, technical debt should never be allowed to accumulate; developers should clean up the code as they go. Nevertheless, the reality is that—even in the best-run shops—this kind of work is one of the first things to suffer when deadlines are tight. As a result, the debt piles up over time. If and when that happens, strike a technical debt-payment spike to clear it out.

13.11.3.3 Operations Infrastructure Spike

An **operations infrastructure spike** (or story) is a work item to improve the operations infrastructure to comply with NFRs and changing demand.

One of the reasons for operations infrastructure spikes is that technical NFRs such as performance and volume requirements are often deferred in agile development until the product's value has been validated in the market. As a result, agile architectures emerge organically over time—sufficient to meet current requirements and built out incrementally as needs grow. For example, the first version of a product is designed for low transaction volume. As the usage of the product increases and volume threatens to exceed capacity, you strike an operations infrastructure spike to improve the infrastructure to accommodate the expected rise in transaction volume.

13.11.3.4 Development Infrastructure Spike

A **development infrastructure spike** (or story) is a work item to improve the development environment, such as by automating the testing and deployment processes. These stories enable future stories by *greasing* the development pipeline—making it faster and safer to deliver changes to market.

13.11.4 Compliance Story

A **compliance story** is a work item to bring the organization, process, or product in line with compliance regulations, whether through software or manual means. It may include report creation, meetings with auditors, and testing activities to demonstrate compliance with compatibility requirements.[24] For example, a compliance story to comply with ISO9001:2000 and ISO9001:2008 standards might involve saving images of story cards and other agile artifacts.[25]

Use compliance stories for one-time work items—work that is scheduled once for the product. If the compliance work must be performed for *every user story*, don't create a compliance story for it. Capture it another way (e.g., by adding it to the DoD or, where appropriate, by addressing it through automated testing).

13.11.5 Bug-Repair Stories

A **bug-repair story** is a story to fix a bug or bugs. Create a bug-repair story if the bug is nontrivial (one hour or more to fix) and will be repaired in a *subsequent* iteration to that in which it was discovered. As a general rule, bug-repair stories are a half day to a few days in length. Combine small bugs that should be fixed together into a single story.

If a bug is to be fixed in the same iteration in which it is found, don't bother creating a bug-repair story. It's not worth the overhead. Fixes of this kind are accounted for indirectly: they lower the team velocity because they reduce the time available to work on functional stories.

13.12 Guidelines for Writing High-Quality Stories

It's true that the user story concept is simple—it's something a user wants—but not all stories are created equally. Peek into a product backlog and you'll find stories that are too large to be implemented within the accepted time limit, stories that have outstanding dependencies, stories that contain redundant or inconsistent requirements, and stories that have questionable value. Stories like these hinder team performance because they lead to waste—time spent on work of no (or minimal) value to the business. In the following section, we look at ways to craft stories that support high performance by avoiding these impediments.

---

24. Ivar Jacobson, Ian Spence, and Kurt Bittner, *Use-Case 2.0: The Guide to Succeeding with Use Cases*, Ivar Jacobson International, 2011, 42, https://www.ivarjacobson.com/sites/default/files/field_iji_file/article/use-case_2_0_jan11.pdf

25. Mike Cohn, *Succeeding with Agile: Software Development Using Scrum* (Boston: Addison-Wesley, 2009), 399.

13.12.1 INVEST

Analysts play a leadership role with respect to the requirements. An important part of this responsibility is to coach the customer and team to craft high-performance user stories. In this section, we explore the characteristics of well-formed stories. One of the popular mnemonics for remembering them is Bill Wake's INVEST acronym, described here with some adjustments.

A user story should have the following qualities:

- **Independent:** The user story is *minimally* dependent on other stories. (In practice, true independence is often not possible, for reasons discussed in Chapter 17, "Scaling Agility," section 17.3.1).

- **Negotiable:** The user story is understood well enough to be negotiated. It is *expected* that the story's requirements and priority will be discussed and changed over time.

- **Valuable:** The user story *delivers actual value* to the user: users can do something useful they could not do before.

- **Estimable:** The user story is well-enough understood to be reliably estimated. The story may or may not *actually* be estimated, though. It just needs to be *able* to be estimated.

- **Small:** The user story must be small enough to be implemented within a short time by a single team (e.g., estimated at 8 or fewer points, deliverable within one iteration).

- **Testable:** The AC for evaluating whether the user story is done are understood.

The INVEST qualities overlap with story DoR conditions. For more on the DoR, see Chapter 6, section 6.5.7.5.

13.12.2 INVEST IN CRUD

The INVEST acronym is a floor, not a ceiling. To enable extremely high-performing teams, craft user stories so they have the following "IN CRUD" characteristics *in addition* to the INVEST attributes.

- **Individual:** The story is individual—distinct from others in the product backlog.

- **Nonsolutionized:** The story focuses on functionality, not on solution design. (Exception: Address design *if* it is a constraint.)

- **Consistent:** The user story is consistent with other user stories in the backlog.

- **Reinforced:** The story is reinforced with supplementary artifacts as needed, e.g., wireframe, decision tables, business rules.

- **Unambiguous:** The intent of the story is clear. Avoid generic terms such as "the user" and "the product."

- **Discussed:** The story has been discussed recently by business decision makers and the team in order to confirm its value.

13.13 Patterns for Splitting Stories

A user story must be small enough to be completed in a few days. At the same time, it must deliver user value. Doing both at the same time can be a challenge. This is an occasion when an agile analyst adds considerable value—providing needed support and guidance to the team on splitting large items into small but valuable stories.

The following guidelines incorporate the Richard Lawrence[26] and SAFe[27] patterns for splitting stories.

13.13.1 How to Use the Patterns

Each of the following patterns describes a scenario in which an item's estimate exceeds the story limit. First identify the pattern that best describes the item you wish to split, then use the remedy provided to divide it into smaller stories.

13.13.2 Tie-Breakers

If there is more than one way to split an item into smaller stories (e.g., more than one pattern applies), apply the tie-breaker rules that follow.

13.13.2.1 Tie-Breaker Rule 1: Choose the Split That Creates a Low-Priority Story

Select the option that results in one or more low-priority stories because it exposes waste. Separating lower-value requirements into their own stories enables them to be costed and prioritized independently from the rest of the work item—or even removed entirely from the backlog.

Example

A Shop for Products feature is estimated at 13 points. Two proposals are being considered, each of which results in user stories within the allowable size limit.

Proposal 1

- User Story A: Shop for home products. [5 points] Priority: High

- User Story B: Shop for commercial products. [8 points] Priority: High

Proposal 2

- User Story C: Shop for non-restricted home products. [3 points] Priority: High

---

26. Richard Lawrence, "Patterns for Splitting User Stories," Agile for ALL, October 28, 2009, https://agileforall.com/patterns-for-splitting-user-stories/

27. Dean Leffingwell, *SAFe 4.5 Reference Guide: Scaled Agile Framework for Lean Enterprises,* 2nd ed. (Boston: Addison-Wesley, 2018), 487.

- User Story D: Shop for non-restricted commercial products. [5 points] Priority: High

- User Story E: Shop for restricted items. [5 points] Priority: Low

In proposal 1, restricted items are included inside stories A and B, although they are not explicitly specified. Proposal 2 separates them into story E. All other things being equal, proposal 2 is preferable because it exposes the contribution of a low-priority requirement (restricted items) to the total estimate—something that is hidden in proposal 1.

13.13.2.2 Tie-Breaker Rule 2: Choose the Split That Results in Many Small User Stories Rather than a Few Large Ones

Choose a split that creates many small stories over one that results in large stories. The benefit of small stories is that they make it easier to cost and prioritize requirements separately.

13.13.2.3 Tie-Breaker Rule 3: Choose the Split That Results in More Uniformly-Sized Stories

We know from Kanban that workflow is optimized when work items are uniformly sized because bottlenecks occur when a large work item appears in a group of small ones.

13.13.3 The Patterns

Use the following patterns to split large work items (features and epics) into smaller stories. First find the appropriate pattern; then apply the suggested remedy.

13.13.3.1 Pattern 1: Workflow Steps

In this pattern, an oversized work item encompasses the steps of an end-to-end process or value stream.

Remedy

Create one story to implement a fast, low-cost version of the process, focusing on its endpoints and using one or two thin scenarios. Rely on workarounds, if necessary, to keep the estimate low. Create additional stories to fill in the blanks. The following is an example of a work item, split according to this pattern.

Workflow Steps Pattern

Original work item (**before the split**): **Purchase a product.**

Resulting stories (**after the split**):

- Process a local order for one product offering, using a manual order-fulfillment process. The story automates order submission and delivery confirmation for one offering only and relies on workarounds for intermediate steps.

- Subsequent stories incrementally replace workarounds and add scenarios and product offerings.

13.13.3.2 Pattern 2: Business Rules

In this pattern, the work item encompasses complex business rules, resulting in a high estimate.

Remedy

Create one story for each possible scenario. Describe the required actions for the scenario (as dictated by the business rules) in the story's AC.

Business Rules Pattern

Original work item (before the split): **Register a student.**

Resulting stories:

- Register a new full-time student. (AC: New full-time student is charged the full fee.)

- Register a returning full-time student. (AC: Returning, full-time time student is charged a reduced fee for the first year.)

- Register a part-time student. (AC: Part-time student is charged a part-time fee.)

We explore business rules analysis in Section 13.14.

13.13.3.3 Pattern 3: Large Initial Effort

In this pattern, a large work item supports multiple classes of business objects, such as different types of messages, incidents, or product classes. Most of the effort will be expended implementing the first object—regardless of which one it is.

Remedy

Create and estimate a story to implement the first object—but don't specify which one. Create and estimate other stories for the remaining types.

Large Initial Effort Pattern

Original work item (before the split): **Review a claim.**

Resulting stories:

- As an adjuster, I want to review one claim type (of drug, medical, dental, approved services)

- As an adjuster, I want to review all claim types (of drug, medical, dental, approved services) given that at least one type has already been implemented.

The "given" clause in the example expresses a precondition. The second story presumes that the first story is done. Alternatively, you can communicate this precondition in the AC of the story or by tracking story dependencies.

13.13.3.4 Pattern 4: Multiple Use-Case Scenarios

In this pattern, a large work item includes multiple scenarios for the same use case. (A use case is a user task.)

Remedy

Create a story for each scenario. Begin by working with stakeholders to identify the simplest, most straightforward scenario—the **happy path** (also called the basic flow or normal flow). Create a story for it. Then create a story for each alternative scenario. (In a use-case specification, these are specified in the **alternate flows**.)

Multiple Use-Case Scenarios Pattern

Original work item (**before the split**): (Use Case) **Place a bid on an auction marketplace.**

Resulting stories:

- Place a basic bid (single value).
- Place a bid with a preset maximum.
- Place a bid with an expiry date.

13.13.3.5 Pattern 5: Data Complexity

In this pattern, most of the effort is due to the complexity of the data or data analytics. For example,

- The data comes from multiple sources (e.g., phone texts, iMessage, Facebook, IG Direct).
- The inputs are handled according to different business rules (e.g., taxation based on region).
- The data is unstructured.
- Analytics reports must support multiple views of the data.

Remedy

Create a story for the simplest data and analytics that deliver value to the customer. Then create an additional story for each data variation.

Data Complexity Pattern

Original work item (**before the split**): **Analyze voter preferences.**

Resulting stories:

- Analyze voter preferences based on aggregate metrics (e.g., total Likes).
- Analyze voter preferences based on their interactions on social media.
- Analyze voter preferences based on the behaviors of their friends.

13.13.3.6 Pattern 6: Complex UI

In this pattern, a large work item includes a complex user interface that contributes significantly to the estimate.

Remedy

Create a story for the simplest user interface that delivers the user goal. Then add stories to develop a more sophisticated interface.

Complex UI Pattern

Original work item (**before the split**): **Track my food order.**
Resulting stories:

- As a customer, I can track my order with text updates when the order's location changes.
- As a customer, I can track my order on a map that is updated in real time.

13.13.3.7 Pattern 7: NFR Implementation

In this pattern, most of the estimate is due to the story's NFRs (e.g., performance, reliability, response time, and availability targets).

Remedy

Create an initial story to provide the required functionality without satisfying the NFRs. Then add stories to comply with the NFRs.

Even if the first story is not robust enough to be formally released into the market, it still provides learning value through internal testing with users and their representatives.

NFR Implementation Pattern

Original work item (**before the split**): **Translate text image.**
Resulting stories:

- As a user, I want to convert any image of text to the language of my choice. (Note that conversion time may be slow.)
- As a user, I want the conversion to be performed in under three seconds.

13.13.3.8 Pattern 8: Multiple User Goals

In this pattern, a large work item encompasses multiple, distinct user goals. A keyword that signals this pattern is the word *manage* in a user story. For example, "Manage my order" encompasses these discrete user goals:

- Submit my order.
- Cancel my order.

Remedy

Create one user story for each discrete user goal. Use the developers' CRUD acronym (no relation to the instance mentioned earlier) to generate stories to manage the object. Create one story for each of the following:

- Create/add/insert the object.
- Read/query/view the object.
- Update/change/amend the object.
- Delete/cancel/remove the object.

Split these stories further if they still exceed the story size limit.

The following is an example of a work item split according to this pattern.

Multiple User Goals Pattern

Original work item (**before the split**): **Manage my profile.**

Resulting stories:

- Create my profile.
- View my profile.
- Update my profile.
- Remove my profile.

13.13.3.9 Pattern 9: Uncertainty

In this pattern, developers have provided a padded estimate for the item because of the high uncertainty regarding the requirements or the technology.

Remedy

Create a functional spike or technical research spike to investigate the area of uncertainty. Create another story to implement the requirements. Estimate it after the spike is complete and more is known.

Uncertainty Pattern

Original work item (**before the split**): **Offer customer discount.**

Resulting stories:

- Functional Spike: Research discount rules based on customer's transaction history.
- User Story: Offer customer discount.

13.13.3.10 Pattern 10: Integration Capabilities

In this pattern, a large work item includes integration with multiple software entities, such as internal components, third-party services, and external systems and APIs.

Remedy

Create a separate user story for integration with each entity.

Integration Capabilities Pattern

Original work item (before the split): **Fill prescription and assess eligibility for insurance coverage using three different insurance APIs.**

Resulting stories:

- Fill prescription using insurance API 1.

- Fill prescription using insurance API 2.

- Fill prescription using insurance API 3.

13.13.3.11 Pattern 11: Multiple Devices, Platforms

In this pattern, the work item is large because it must support multiple devices and software platforms.

Remedy

Create a separate user story for each device or platform.

Multiple Devices, Platforms Pattern

Original work item (before the split): **View messages.**

Resulting stories:

- As a customer, I can view my messages on my Android device.

- As a customer, I can view my messages on my iOS device.

- As a customer, I can view my messages on my Mac.

- As a customer, I can view my messages on my PC.

13.13.3.12 Pattern 12: Multiple User Roles

In this pattern, the feature requires different interfaces for different kinds of users.

Remedy

Create a story for each user role or persona that uses the feature in a unique way.

Multiple User Roles Pattern

Original work item (**before the split**): **Browse a newspaper article.**
Resulting stories:

- As a Bronze-level subscriber, I want to browse the news with limited access.
  - Acceptance criteria: Access blocked after ten views per month
- As a Silver- or Gold-level subscriber, I want to browse the news with unlimited access.
- As a Gold-level subscriber, I want to browse the news, background stories, and podcasts from leading journalists.

13.13.3.13 Pattern 13: Too Many Acceptance Criteria

In this pattern, an oversized story has numerous AC.

Remedy

Use the story's AC as a basis for splitting the item. Create a user story for each AC in the original feature, or for every group of interrelated AC that should be released together. As a rule of thumb, specify no more than five to seven AC per story.

Too Many Acceptance Criteria Pattern

Original work item (**before the split**): **Post a comment.**
Acceptance criteria:

- AC 1: I can enter and post a comment.

- AC 2: Comment passes review by the AI evaluation service (posted).

- AC 3: Comment fails the AI review (rejected).

- AC 4: Comment is flagged for manual review by the AI review (sent to the moderator for review prior to posting).

- AC 5: Comment is entered by a blocked user (rejected).

- AC 6: Comment is entered by a trusted user (comment posted without review).

Resulting stories:

- Story 1: Post a comment with no verification. (Note: In the first story, comments are posted immediately. A human moderator will regularly review the posts and manually remove them as needed.)

  Acceptance criteria:

  - AC1: I can enter and post a comment.

- Story 2: Reject blocked users from posting.

  Acceptance criteria:

  - AC 5: Comment is entered by a blocked user (rejected).

  - AC 6: Comment is entered by a trusted user (comment posted without review).

- Story 3: Pass comment through AI review.

  Acceptance criteria:

  - AC 2: Comment passes review by the AI evaluation service (posted).

  - AC 3: Comment fails the AI review (rejected).

- Story 4: Flag manual review.

  Acceptance criteria:

  - AC 4: Comment is flagged for manual review by the AI review (comment sent to the moderator for review prior to posting).

13.13.3.14 Pattern Quiz

Think you can spot a pattern? Test your understanding by examining the following cases of large work items. See if you can identify a pattern and, if you do, suggest a split using the previous guidelines.

QUIZ

Case 1: Response Team

The SMEs for a telecom have requested a feature to assign response teams to incidents. We know the business logic depends on numerous factors—but we're not sure what they are yet. Consequently, the developers have provided a high estimate just to be safe.

Case 2: Amend Policy

Insurance policy SMEs have requested a feature to amend a policy. There are many types of possible amendments. Developers estimate that the work item exceeds the maximum story size. They have tried to split it by amendment type but find it hard to estimate the effort for each story individually because whatever type is done first will be the most expensive to develop.

Case 3: Place an Order

A business SME is discussing a feature with developers during iteration planning. The feature enables a user to place an order, including scenarios for backorders and split orders. The estimate for the feature exceeds the maximum story size.

Case 4: BeeWatch

BeeWatch is developing an app to allow users to track sightings and the status of beehives around the country. The organization needs a feature to manage beehives so that users can report on a new sighting and make updates. The feature exceeds the maximum story size.

Case 5: Sentinel

Engineers at Sentinel—makers of a virus-tracking app—have implemented a capability that tracks whom users have been in close contact with, their contacts' contacts, and so on, for higher degrees of separation. The information is currently being used to send alerts to users who have been in contact with an infected person. Business stakeholders now want a feature to allow users to view their extended network as a visual map of connected dots showing who has been in contact with whom and whom those people have contacted. Users should be able to zoom in on any person in the network to see their connections to any degree of separation. The feature exceeds the maximum story size.

QUIZ ANSWERS

Please note that only one pattern and sample solution for the split is indicated, but other patterns and splits may apply.

Case 1 Response Team

Pattern 9: Uncertainty

Stories

- Spike: Research the business logic for assigning a response team.
  - Acceptance criteria: Logic is understood well enough for estimation. Input conditions are known (factors affecting the response). Possible outcomes are known. Precise rules for each scenario will be determined during the iteration.
- User story: Assign response team.

Case 2 Amend Policy

Pattern 3: Large Initial Effort

User Stories

- Amend Policy (first: Beneficiary change; add benefits; increase coverage amount)
- Amend Policy (remaining Amendments) given that the first amendment type is implemented.

Case 3 Place an Order

Pattern 4: Multiple Use-Case Scenarios

User Stories

- Place an order (basic flow).
- Place a split order.
- Place a backorder.

Case 4 BeeWatch

Pattern 8: Multiple User Goals

User Stories

- Post a new beehive.
- Find beehives in your area.
- Update information about a known hive.
- Remove a beehive from the registry.

Case 5 Sentinel

Pattern 6: Complex UI

User Stories

- View my network of contacts as text.
- View my network as a map.

13.14 Analyzing Business Rules and AC with Decision Tables

The analysis of user stories with complex business rules presents several challenges. How do you know if you've captured all the relevant scenarios in the AC? How do you verify their correctness with stakeholders? And how do you convey those rules to developers and testers in a way that can't be misinterpreted? One answer is to use a **decision table**. Decision tables have long been used by testers to specify test scenarios after coding. That's how I first used them—but I soon learned that they were *most* valuable when used beforehand as a facilitation tool during requirements elicitation.

Use decision tables for stories or features whose outcomes depend on a combination of interrelated factors. For example, in a user story to order a product, the system may offer a discount to the customer depending on the following factors:

- Quantity ordered
- Whether or not the item is featured
- Total value of the order

In this case, the system's behavior—the discount it offers—changes depending on a set of conditions. Rules of this type are referred to as *behavioral business rules*. Decision tables express these rules through specific examples rather than by describing the underlying business logic. It's a much better way to communicate rules to stakeholders, developers, and testers because the expected outcomes are unambiguous, the test scenarios and responses are laid out clearly for testers, and the math underlying the technique ensures all scenarios are addressed.

Table 13.1 provides an overview of decision tables.

Table 13.1 *Decision Tables at a Glance*

What?	A decision table documents the way that a system responds to various combinations of input conditions. Use it to describe business rules in cases where the required response depends on several factors that must all be considered together (e.g., the rules for adjudicating a request for a loan).
When?	• During elicitation, analysts use decision tables to structure interviews and document requirements for complex business rules. • During implementation, developers use the tables as input to coding. • Testers use decision tables to design test cases. The table identifies test scenarios and defines expected outcomes.
Why?	• Provides complete, consistent, and easy-to-verify documentation for complex business rules. • Simplifies and structures interviews. • Ensures all combinations of conditions have been accounted for. • Results in documentation that is highly suitable for testing.
Deliverables	• A table describing relevant scenarios and their outcomes. May be stored in a business rules Repository and referred to by a story or feature's AC.

13.14.1 Behavioral Business Rules

The International Institute of Business Analysis (IIBA) defines a **business rule** as "a specific, testable directive that serves as a criterion for guiding behavior, shaping judgments, or making decisions."[28] As discussed in Chapter 3, business rules aren't in themselves requirements, but they often underpin the requirements in that the system or product may be required to support the rules.

Business rules are categorized into two main types: definitional business rules and behavioral business rules. A **definitional business rule** specifies something that must be true or untrue[29] (e.g., the rule that each insurance policy may have one and only one policy owner). **Behavioral business rules** (the kind decision tables are used for) govern day-to-day business behavior, specifying what actions *may* or *may not* be taken in response to input conditions and events. Here is an example of an operational business rule:

> If the maximum annual payout under the insurer's policy has already been exceeded, the insurance claim is rejected.

---

28. International Institute of Business Analysis (IIBA), *BABOK v3: A Guide to the Business Analysis Body of Knowledge*, 3rd ed. (Toronto, Canada: IIBA, 2015), 240.

29. IIBA, *BABOK v3*, 241.

13.14.2 Decision Table Example

Table 13.2 is an example of a decision table for a story to reserve a vacation property on a property-sharing platform. The site is being developed by a company that currently offers other sharing services to its customers.

The business rules in Table 13.2 specify whether upfront payment is required for a reservation based on the customer's past interactions with the company.

As Table 13.2 illustrates, a decision table is divided into two regions: conditions (the top region) and actions (the bottom). Each row in the Conditions region is dedicated to an input condition—a factor that affects the outcome. For example, in Table 13.2, the first row represents the condition *frequency of late payments*, one of the factors that affects how a reservation is treated. Each row in the bottom half represents an action—a possible response. For example, in Table 13.2, the last row represents the action *Customer is required to pay a deposit to hold the reservation.*

Each column in Table 13.2 describes a unique situation, or *scenario*, and the expected system actions. For example, in the column 1 scenario, a customer has been late making payments 0 to 20 percent of the time, and the average number of days the customer has been overdue on an invoice is 0 to 15 days. The expected outcome is that the customer can hold the reservation without any payment up front. Taken together, the six scenarios in Table 13.2 represent all possible combinations of input conditions.

Table 13.2 *Decision Table for User Story: Reserve a Vacation Property*

	Scenario	1	2	3	4	5	6
Conditions	1. Frequency of late payments (0%–20%; >20%)	0%–20%	0%–20%	0%–20%	>20%	>20%	>20%
	2. Average number of days overdue per invoice in past year (0–15; 16–30; 31–365)	0–15	16–30	31–365	0–15	16–30	31–365
Actions	Customer can hold the reservation without any payment up front.	X					
	Customer is required to pay the full amount up front to hold the reservation.			X		X	X
	Customer is required to pay a deposit to hold the reservation.		X		X		

13.14.3 Benefits of a Decision Table

As Table 13.2 illustrates, decision tables provide clear specifications to multiple kinds of readers—the developer who has to code it, the tester who creates test cases from it, and any stakeholder who may be asked to verify it.

Decision tables are based on the insight that people are often better at *making* decisions than at explaining the logic behind those decisions. Using decision tables, the facilitator works around that problem by identifying all the relevant scenarios and then asking stakeholders what actions should be taken for each case. The resulting scenarios and actions are the AC for the story. Because a decision table spells out what should happen for each scenario, there is no room for misinterpretation by SMEs who verify its correctness, by developers who use it to guide coding, or by testers who use it to develop and run test scenarios.

There are additional benefits, as well. By combining rules into a central artifact, a decision table highlights opportunities to merge rules, retire them, or even indicate where they are inconsistent with each other. Most important, it provides a comprehensive list of rules and scenarios so that the business can decide which ones should be implemented and when: some scenarios may be included in the first story, some may be deferred to later stories, and others may never be implemented.

13.14.4 How to Elicit Rules Using the Table

The following sections explain how to use decision tables as a facilitation tool when eliciting business rules.

13.14.4.1 Specify Conditions

Begin by asking interviewees about the input conditions and events that affect the response. Then ask them to describe the relevant values or groups of values for each condition. Include all possible values, including valid and invalid ones. These values or groups of values are known as the **equivalence classes** for the condition. All items within an equivalence class must be treated equivalently by the system. For example, in Table 13.2, one of the equivalence classes for *average number of days overdue* is 0 to 15. This means that the outcome will be the same whether the average is 0, 4, 15, or any other number within the specified range.

List the conditions you discover and their equivalence classes in the top Conditions region of the table.

In Table 13.2, the condition *Average number of days overdue per invoice issued in the past year* has the following equivalence classes: 0–15 days, 16–30 days, and 31–365 days. These represent all possible values for the condition. What about invalid values or number of days, such as negative numbers or numbers higher than 365? In the preceding decision table, the presumption is that the input has been prescreened for these errors. However, if these invalid values are possible, you need to address two more equivalence classes: number of days overdue less than 0 and number of days overdue more than 365.

In this case, it's better to address these scenarios first in a separate table, since if the number of days overdue is invalid, there's no point evaluating the other input condition, frequency of late payment. Use a **condition-response table** for this purpose, as illustrated in Table 13.3.

Table 13.3 *Condition–Response Table for Reserve a Vacation Property*

Condition	Response (Action)
Average number of days overdue per invoice issued in the past year <0	Reject due to error
Average number of days overdue per invoice issued in the past year >365	Reject due to error
Average number of days overdue per invoice issued in the past year is 0–365	Proceed to Table 13.2 (decision table)

Table 13.3 indicates that if the input data is in error, the reservation should be rejected. If there are no errors, Table 13.2 applies.

Use a condition-response table when conditions are mutually exclusive. Use a decision table when they may occur in combination.

13.14.4.2 Specify Actions

Next, ask interviewees to list all possible actions the business might take. List these in the lower-left Actions section of the table, as shown in Table 13.2.

13.14.4.3 Specify Scenarios

The next step is to construct the scenarios. The total number of scenarios is determined according to the following formula:

Total # Scenarios = # Equivalence Classes for Condition 1 × # Equivalence Classes for Condition 2 × # Equivalence Classes for Condition 3 . . .

For example, in Table 13.2, there are two equivalence classes for the first condition and three for the second; the total number of scenarios is 2 × 3 = 6. This is the number of columns you'll need to fill.

When the conditions are simple yes/no questions, the "divide-by-two" rule works well for filling in the cells. Fill half the cells in the top row with Ys and half with Ns. For example, consider a table with three yes/no conditions and eight columns (2 × 2 × 2). Fill the first four columns in the top row with Ys, then fill in the next four with Ns. For the next row, divide by two again (4 ÷ 2 = 2). Fill in two Y cells, two Ns, two Ys, two Ns. For the third row, divide again by two (2 ÷ 2 = 1). Fill in one Y, one N, one Y, continuing until all the cells are filled.

If any of the input conditions have more than two equivalence classes, you'll need to adapt the approach. Any method is acceptable as long as, in the end, all the required columns are filled, and each scenario (column) is unique.

13.14.4.4 Specify Actions for Each Scenario

For each column in the table, describe the scenario to interviewees and ask them which action or actions apply. Mark expected actions with an X.

13.14.4.5 Specify Acceptance Criteria

Specify each column as an AC for the item. For example, the first column in Table 13.2 may be specified in Gherkin as follows:

Given that frequency of late payments is 0%–20%

And average days overdue is 0–15 days

When I request a reservation

Then I can place a hold on the reservation without payment upfront

Alternatively, an AC can simply state that the system or product responds as indicated in the decision table.

Note how the decision table serves a dual purpose. It expresses business rules unambiguously to developers, and it also specifies test scenarios for the story.

BLINK CASE STUDY PART 23

Complete the Story Map

Background

You previously created a story map backbone for the release and laid out the stories of the first iteration on the map. (For a snapshot of the story map at this point, see Chapter 12, Figure 12.5.) You meet again with the group to complete the map. You plan to focus on splitting work items in the earlier iterations of the release cycle, with the intention of addressing later features closer to implementation.

The Ask

The deliverable will be

- **Deliverable 1:** BLInK story map, release 1

What Transpires

You use the guidelines and patterns described in this and the preceding chapter to split and write stories and map them to iterations.

Deliverables

The following is the deliverable for the workshop.

Deliverable 1: BLInK Story Map, Release 1

Figure 13.3 illustrates the BLInK story map at the end of the workshop.

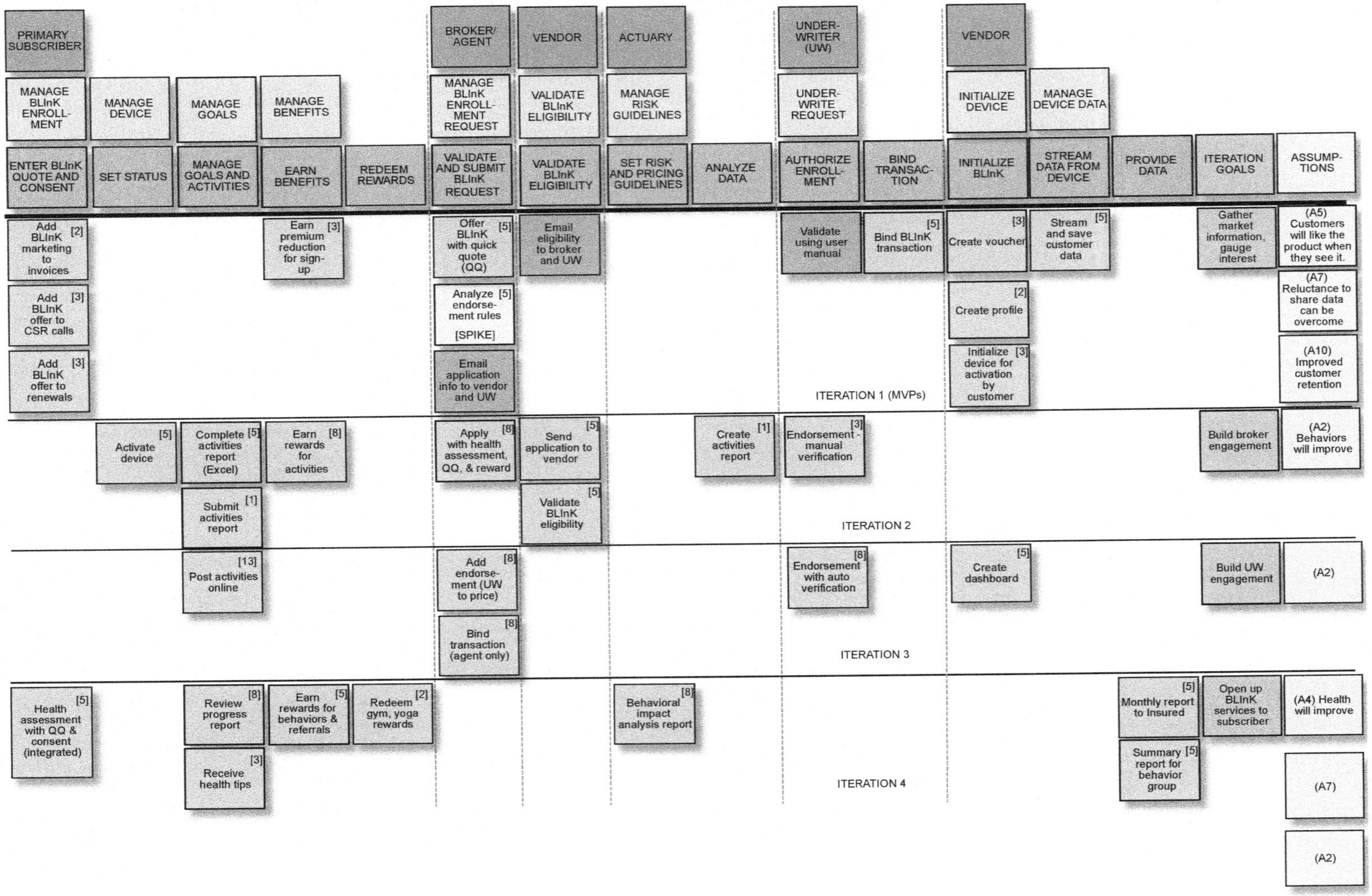

Figure 13.3 BLInK story map, release 1

Backbone (roles and activities):

- **PRIMARY SUBSCRIBER**
  - MANAGE BLInK ENROLLMENT — ENTER BLInK QUOTE AND CONSENT
  - MANAGE DEVICE — SET STATUS
  - MANAGE GOALS — MANAGE GOALS AND ACTIVITIES
  - MANAGE BENEFITS — EARN BENEFITS
  - REDEEM REWARDS
- **BROKER AGENT**
  - MANAGE BLInK ENROLLMENT REQUEST — VALIDATE AND SUBMIT BLInK REQUEST
- **VENDOR**
  - VALIDATE BLInK ELIGIBILITY — VALIDATE BLInK ELIGIBILITY
- **ACTUARY**
  - MANAGE RISK GUIDELINES — SET RISK AND PRICING GUIDELINES — ANALYZE DATA
- **UNDERWRITER (UW)**
  - UNDERWRITE REQUEST — AUTHORIZE ENROLLMENT — BIND TRANSACTION
- **VENDOR**
  - INITIALIZE DEVICE — INITIALIZE BLInK
- **MANAGE DEVICE DATA** — STREAM DATA FROM DEVICE
- **PROVIDE DATA**
- **ITERATION GOALS**
- **ASSUMPTIONS**

ITERATION 1 (MVPs)

- Add BLInK marketing to invoices [2]
- Add BLInK offer to CSR calls [3]
- Add BLInK offer to renewals [3]
- Earn premium reduction for sign-up [3]
- Activate device [5]
- Submit activities report [1]
- Complete activities report (Excel) [5]
- Post activities online [13]
- Earn rewards for activities [8]
- Offer BLInK with quick quote (QQ) [5]
- Analyze endorsement rules [SPIKE]
- Email application to vendor and UW [8]
- Email eligibility to broker and UW [5]
- Create activities report [1]
- Validate using user manual [5]
- Bind BLInK transaction [5]
- Create voucher [3]
- Stream and save customer data [5]
- Iteration goal: Gather market information, gauge interest
- Iteration goal: Build broker engagement
- Assumption (A5) Customers will like the product when they see it.
- Assumption (A7) Reluctance to share data can be overcome
- Assumption (A10) Improved customer retention
- Assumption (A2) Behaviors will improve

ITERATION 2

- Health assessment with QQ & consent (integrated) [5]
- Apply with health assessment, QQ, & reward [8]
- Send application to vendor [5]
- Endorsement - manual verification [3]
- Create profile [2]
- Initialize device for activation by customer [3]
- Build UW engagement
- Assumption (A2)

ITERATION 3

- Review progress report [8]
- Earn rewards for behaviors & referrals [5]
- Redeem gym, yoga rewards [2]
- Add endorsement (UW to price) [8]
- Bind transaction (agent only) [8]
- Validate BLInK eligibility [5]
- Behavioral impact analysis report [8]
- Endorsement with auto verification [8]
- Create dashboard [5]
- Monthly report to insured [5]
- Summary report for behavior group [5]
- Open up BLInK services to subscriber
- Assumption (A4) Health will improve

ITERATION 4

- Receive health tips [3]
- Assumption (A7)
- Assumption (A2)

Case Study Retrospective

In this workshop, you used a story map to plan the release in a manner that optimizes early delivery of value to the user. You were able to use patterns and other guidelines to split large features into valuable stories that can be implemented in a single iteration.

13.15 Chapter Summary

Here are the key points covered in this chapter:

- A user story communicates requirements using the Three Cs: card, communication, confirmation.

- The Connextra template for user stories is of the form "As a <<who>> I want <<what>> so that <<why>>."

- Use AC act as *specifications by example* to communicate requirements and as a basis for testing.

- The BDD Gherkin format for AC scenarios is as follows: Given-When-Then.

- Craft user stories following the INVEST guidelines. They should be independent, negotiable, valuable, estimable, small, and testable.

- Create a functional spike to research functional requirements.

- Use the Lawrence and SAFe Patterns to split large work items into smaller stories.

- Use a decision table to capture behavioral business rules whenever the outcome depends on a combination of input conditions.

13.16 What's Next?

If the team uses a timeboxed planning approach, iteration planning may proceed once all stories lined up for the iteration are ready. During the event, the team forecasts what will be accomplished during the planning period and determines how the stories will be implemented. If the team uses a single-item flow-based approach (e.g., Kanban), the planning process is similar but focuses on a single story at a time rather than all the stories for an iteration. Chapter 14, "Iteration and Story Planning," provides guidelines for planning stories in both contexts.

Chapter 14

Iteration and Story Planning

Chapter 13, "Story Preparation," examined how to make stories ready for short-term planning needs. This chapter focuses on that planning. Teams that practice flow-based planning (e.g., Kanban) plan each story as it comes up for development; teams that practice timeboxed planning (e.g., Scrum) schedule all of the stories for an upcoming iteration (approximately one to two weeks) together in an iteration planning meeting. This chapter covers both approaches. Figure 14.1 highlights the activities covered in the chapter.

The chapter begins with an overview of the objectives, inputs, and deliverables of iteration/story planning. Next, it takes the reader through the two aspects of planning: Part 1, the planning of *what* will be delivered (iteration goal and stories), and Part 2, the determination of *how* the work will be done. (These correspond to sprint planning topics 1–3 in the Scrum guide.)

For Part 1 of planning, the chapter explains how to determine the team's capacity in based on past progress, set the iteration goal, and forecast the stories that will be delivered. Then, it explores Part 2. It describes how to decompose stories into developer tasks and use a developer task board to track progress at the task level. Next, it explores how to use task estimates to verify the forecast and explains the analysis role in scope negotiation. The chapter also provides several Kanban board examples for tracking progress at the story level. It closes with guidelines for facilitating a feature preview (rolling lookahead) after the iteration planning meeting.

This chapter continues the case study that runs through the book, including sample solutions that can be used for individual and classroom workshops.

14.1 Objectives

This chapter will help you

- Facilitate an iteration planning meeting.
- Work with the product owner (PO) and team to craft the iteration goal.
- Forecast the stories that will be delivered.

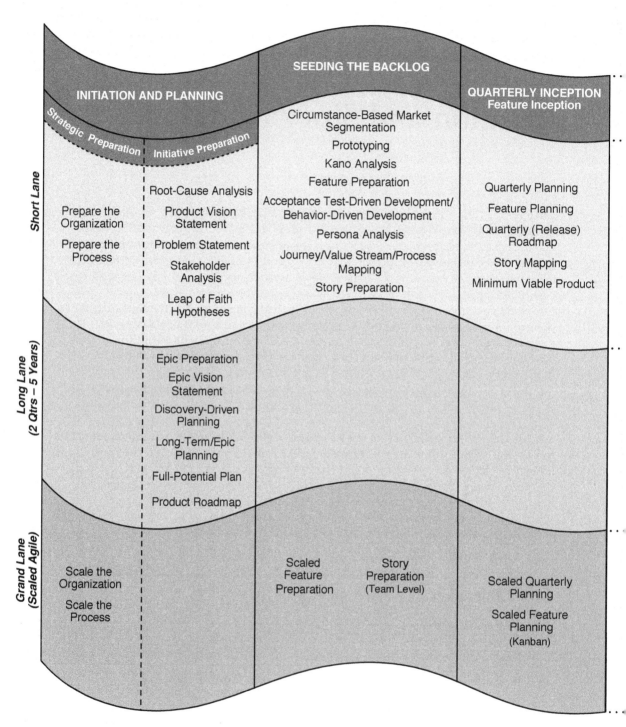

Figure 14.1 *Chapter 14 on the map*

ITERATION INCEPTION

Iteration Planning

DAILY ACTIVITIES

Daily Standup

Requirements Analysis & Documentation

Code, Build, Test, Deliver Acceptance Test-Driven Development/ Behavior-Driven Development

Minimum Viable Product, Split Testing

Epic, Feature Preparation

Story Preparation

ITERATION CLOSEOUT

Iteration Review

Iteration Retrospective

QUARTERLY CLOSEOUT
Epic, Feature Closeout

Prepare for General Availability

Quarterly Retrospective

Epic, Feature Retrospective

Pivot or Persevere

Scaled Iteration Planning

Iteration Planning (Team Level)

Product Owner Council Meetings

DevOps

User Task Force Meetings

Scaled Feature Preparation (Kanban)

Integration Meetings

Story Preparation (Team Level)

Scaled Iteration Review

Scaled Iteration Retrospective

Iteration Retrospective (Team Level)

DevOps

Scaled Quarterly/Feature Retrospective

- Coach the team in the use of agile artifacts for tracking work for the iteration, including the iteration backlog, developer task board, and Kanban board.

- Facilitate a feature preview (rolling lookahead meeting).

14.2 This Chapter on the Map

As shown in Figure 14.1, the chapter examines iteration planning, an activity in the Iteration Inception zone. It also includes the planning of individual stories within a flow-based planning framework (e.g., Kanban).

14.3 Overview of Iteration and Story Planning

When teams practice single-item flow-based planning (e.g., Kanban), they accept "ready" stories individually into development as each item comes up in the queue (presuming this does not exceed the work-in-progress [WIP] limit for development). The objective of story planning in that context is to verify that the team (or developer) has the capacity to take it on, forecast a delivery timeline, and plan the developer tasks required to implement it.

On the other hand, teams that use a timeboxed approach (e.g., Scrum, Extreme Programming [XP]) plan stories as a block at the start of each iteration during **iteration planning**. As noted previously in this book, an **iteration** is a planning period that may range from one week to one month. It is typically one to two weeks in length. (In Scrum, iterations are referred to as *sprints*, and iteration planning is known as *sprint planning*.) As a general guideline, iterations should be of fixed length so that teams work at a steady beat in synch with other teams.

Iteration planning consists of two parts (referred to, in Scrum, as Topics One, Two, and Three):

- Part 1: Forecast What Will Be Accomplished (Scrum Topic One and Two)
- Part 2: Plan the Implementation (Scrum Topic Three)

Part 1 applies mostly to teams that practice timeboxed planning (e.g., Scrum, XP). During this part, the PO and team agree on the iteration goal and forecast the stories that will be delivered over the course of the iteration. Part 1 applies only in a limited way to flow-based planning, since it's only one story that needs to be planned.

Part 2 applies equally to all teams, whether they practice flow-based or timeboxed planning. In this part, the team determines *how* the story or stories will be implemented, down to the individual developer task level. Finally, the PO and team confirm the plan.

As an analyst/planner, you contribute to iteration and story planning as a facilitator for the event and team member. Like other members of the team, you identify and estimate the tasks you'll be performing for the story. During Part 2, you support negotiations between the customer and development as they explore solution options.

14.4 Attendees

The PO and development team participate in iteration planning—including all those working on the planned stories (e.g., programmers, analysts, UX designers, and architects). Invite other attendees, such as business subject matter experts (SMEs), if their business or technical expertise will be required.

14.5 Duration

Spend up to a day[1] planning the first iteration. The event's duration should decrease as development progresses, stabilizing, over time, at around one to four hours.

14.6 Inputs for Iteration Planning

The following checklist specifies the inputs for iteration planning.

- ☐ Product backlog—with enough ready stories for about two iterations   ✔
- ☐ Quarterly (release) roadmap
- ☐ Definition of ready (DoR), where used; definition of done (DoD)
- ☐ Past performance (velocity), if available
- ☐ Availability of team members during the upcoming iteration
- ☐ Process improvement[2] tasks—added to the iteration backlog during the last iteration retrospective

---

1. *The Scrum Guide* advises a "maximum of 8 hours for a one-month sprint." (Ken Schwaber and Jeff Sutherland, *The Scrum Guide: The Definitive Guide to Scrum—The Rules of the Game*, 2020, 9, https://www.scrumguides.org. Cohn advises 1 hour to 1 day (Mike Cohn, *Succeeding with Agile: Software Development Using Scrum* [Boston: Addison-Wesley, 2010], 334).
2. Schwaber and Sutherland, *The Scrum Guide*, 11.

14.7 Deliverables of Iteration Planning

The primary deliverables of iteration planning are the iteration goal, iteration backlog, and developer task board. These are described next.

14.7.1 The Iteration Goal and Iteration Backlog

Each team has its own **iteration backlog**, consisting of three components.[3] The first two, determined during Part 1, address the **iteration goal**—the value the team will deliver—and the **iteration scope**—the stories planned for the iteration. The number of stories in the iteration backlog will vary according to story sizes, length of the iteration, and capacity of the team. A typical range is six to nine user stories for a two-week iteration.

The third component of the iteration backlog, determined during Part 2, is the plan for delivering the iteration goal and selected stories, including a breakdown of work into small, single-person developer tasks and their owners. The tasks are posted and tracked on a developer task board.

14.7.2 The Developer Task Board

A **developer task board** lists the tasks that will be performed during the planning period, along with information about each task, such as its owner, total estimated time, and remaining time. Tasks include those decomposed from stories as well as tasks not related to stories. Figure 14.2 is an example of a developer task board.

Not all stories need to be decomposed to the same level. Stories that are close to implementation (a few days away) should be decomposed into developer tasks of one day or less. Stories that are already small (one to two days) and implementable by a single team member may not need to be decomposed at all. Organizations that restrict *all* stories to that size often skip the decomposition step because their stories are already so fine-grained.

Developer tasks for a story should cover all the remaining work to implement it, including analysis, testing, prototyping, UX design, programming, and refactoring. A developer task may support more than one story—or have no relationship to the stories in the iteration. At least one developer task on the board should be a high-priority process improvement item identified in the previous Iteration's retrospective meeting.

14.7.3 The Increment

In timeboxed frameworks (e.g., Scrum), each iteration delivers value in the form of an improved product—referred to as an increment. An **increment** is a "concrete stepping stone"[4]—a usable version of the product, including all stories deemed done during the iteration. Recall that a done story satisfies both the general DoD and the story's acceptance criteria.

---

3. Schwaber and Sutherland, 11.
4. Schwaber and Sutherland, 11.

One of the mistakes practitioners sometimes make is to presume that because stories enter the iteration at the same time that they must *exit* the iteration at the same time. The recommended approach is to deliver stories *continuously* throughout the iteration to accelerate learning and expose integration problems early when they are easier to fix. Following DevOps and continuous integration/continuous development (CI/CD) practices, each story is delivered in a releasable state—coded, integrated, and fully tested—as it becomes available. The customer may decide to release it immediately (e.g., if it is a minor change) or defer deployment (e.g., if it is a significant enhancement).

For more on DevOps, CI, and CD, see Chapter 17, section 17.5.2.1.

14.8 Planning Rules

During iteration planning, the Planning Game rules we learned in Chapter 11, "Quarterly and Feature Planning," section 11.8, apply. Only the customer (i.e., the business decision maker) may prioritize stories for the iteration. Only those doing the work (the developers) may decide how much work to take on during an iteration. In the following sections, we examine how these rules play out over the course of Part 1, Forecast What Will Be Accomplished, and Part 2, Plan the Implementation, of iteration planning.

14.9 Part 1: Forecast What Will Be Accomplished

The objective of Part 1 is to forecast what the team will accomplish by the end of the upcoming iteration. The deliverables produced during this step are the following:

- Confirmed iteration goal
- Stories accepted into the iteration backlog—estimated and sequenced

The PO, analyst, and development team are present and active during Part 1. As an analyst, you facilitate and support planning and scope negotiation. The PO describes stories and priorities; the team estimates capacity and accepts stories into the iteration.

The following is a suggested list of topics for Part 1.

- Update
- Forecast capacity
- Review DoR and DoD
- Craft the iteration goal
- Discuss stories
- Forecast the stories that will be delivered

Facilitation guidelines for these items are provided in the following sections.

14.9.1 Update

The facilitator (e.g., you, the analyst, or a ScrumMaster) introduces the meeting, presents its objectives, rules, timebox, agenda, and deliverables. The PO and team provide updates about changes in the market, changed priorities, changes in team membership, technological challenges, and any other issues that might impact the work planned for the iteration.

The group reviews the quarterly plan (roadmap) and revises it, as necessary, in light of new circumstances. For example, slower-than-expected progress might require a change to timelines. The PO provides updates about issues that impact the quarterly plan, such as new items in the backlog and revised priorities. The PO and team discuss the new items, the team estimates them, and the PO reviews and sequences them in the backlog. (Feature estimation methods are described in Chapter 11, section 11.11.2.1.)

The group reviews the quarterly (release) goal for the current quarter. Then, it reviews the future quarterly goals in the long-term product roadmap.

Next, the PO introduces the iteration goal and provides an overview of the planned functionality to support that goal. The goal and scope will be reviewed and revised in greater depth during the session.

14.9.2 Forecast Capacity

The team forecasts its **capacity** for the iteration, as described in Chapter 6, "Preparing the Process" (see section 6.5.7.3). To summarize, the expected capacity is based on past velocity, adjusted for changed circumstances, as follows:

$$\text{Capacity} = \text{Velocity} \pm \text{Changed Circumstances}$$

Use the team's *recent* velocity (last three or four iterations) rather than a historical average. Adjust for changed circumstances such as holidays, illness, changes to team composition, and technical challenges. Some practitioners like to reduce planned capacity even further to allow for unknown unknowns.

For the first iteration, when there is no prior experience to draw from, the initial velocity or capacity, in person-days can be roughly estimated as follows:

$$\text{Velocity} = \text{Total Potential Person-Days} \times \text{Availability} - \text{Slack}$$

The **total potential person-days** represent the total capacity if all members are fully dedicated to the work in the plan. **Availability** is the fraction of time members can spend on the planned work versus time lost to other activities (e.g., meetings, demos, illness, vacations, unplanned bug fixes, administrative activities, and email). Following lean guidance,[5] **slack** is set aside so that members have some unplanned time in case they need to be available to pitch in and unplug bottlenecks.

---

5. Mary Poppendieck and Tom Poppendieck, *Lean Software Development: An Agile Toolkit* (Boston: Addison-Wesley, 2003), 81.

Chapter 6 also provided an alternative method for forecasting the first iteration's capacity. In that approach, the team first considers how far down the backlog it believes it will get by the end of the iteration, then sums the estimates for those stories to determine the capacity.

For more guidance on determining velocity and capacity, see Chapter 6, section 6.5.7.3.

14.9.3 Review Ready and Done Definitions

In Chapter 6, you learned to create a story DoR (see section 6.5.7.5). If you're using a story DoR, ask the PO and team to review it and revise it if necessary. Remind the group that only stories that satisfy the DoR will be accepted into iteration planning and development.

Then, facilitate a review of the DoD and revise it if necessary. For example, as CI practices are phased in, the condition "unit tests have been written" is added. Note that the addition of DoD conditions may change estimates if they require more work from the team, such as creating automated tests. In this case, the DoD changes may meet resistance from the PO if the work isn't deemed to be useful.[6]

All stories in the iteration backlog must pass the DoD in addition to their acceptance criteria before they are considered done and accepted into the product.

14.9.4 Craft the Iteration Goal

The PO proposes an iteration goal, expressing the value that the team will deliver by the iteration's end. The value delivered by the goal may be a user value (e.g., a new capability), business value (e.g., cost savings), or learning value (e.g., validation of a leap of faith hypothesis).

The iteration goal serves multiple purposes. It guides the selection of stories, unifies the efforts of team members, and guides trade-offs once the iteration is underway. The PO and development team collaborate to write the iteration goal. If the goal was previously specified during quarterly planning, it is reviewed and revised as necessary (e.g., to accommodate delays and technical challenges).

The commitment to the iteration goal is much firmer than most agile commitments. Following lean guidance, avoid thrashing[7] (overly rapid change impeding performance) by prohibiting changes to the iteration goal once implementation begins. This isn't as restrictive as it seems because iterations can be as short as one week—and the likelihood of new priorities in that period is small. But what about cases in which the team realizes midstream that it won't be able to reach the goal and wants to *shrink* it? In such cases, it's still preferable *not to cancel the iteration*. Instead, end the iteration at the designated time and carry over remaining stories into the product backlog to be prioritized against other work items. It should be noted, though, that while this is the recommended remedy,

---

6. Ron Healy, in an editorial note to the author.

7. The term *thrashing* is borrowed by lean software development from hardware, where it refers to rapid, inefficient memory swapping.

the *Scrum Guide* advises otherwise: Scrum requires that the iteration be canceled if it becomes apparent that the goal will not be met.[8]

14.9.5 Discuss Stories

The PO walks the development team through the proposed stories according to their priority sequence—describing each story and explaining how it contributes to the iteration goal. As a facilitator, initiate a discussion between the development team and PO about each story. Aim to learn just enough to be able to decompose the story into developer tasks[9] in Part 2. Make sure the group discusses at least one high-priority process improvement task identified in the last iteration retrospective meeting. Ensure the improvement task is included in the iteration backlog so that it will be addressed during the iteration.

Invite the team to raise issues that they want to work on (e.g., technical stories to improve performance and reliability). The decision about what to prioritize should involve negotiation between the business and the team, but if they can't reach a consensus, the PO decides. As a rule of thumb, plan for a three to one ratio of time spent on user-facing capabilities versus technical improvements.

14.9.5.1 The Analyst Value Added

POs from the business side can find it hard to prioritize technical work ahead of stories that deliver user value. Analysts support the PO by working with the development team to clarify the value of technical stories in business terms so that the PO can compare them on an apples-to-apples basis to user stories.

For example, the grammar-checking application I'm using to edit this text is highly functional. However, the code is inefficient—as evidenced by the whining fan whenever I use the app and the slow response time. Though I don't have any inside knowledge about the company, it seems as though it has placed a heavy emphasis on feature development at the expense of nonfunctional requirements (NFRs). This may be wise right now as it builds a new market and there isn't anywhere else for frustrated customers to go. However, this might change once the threat of competition appears. As an analyst, you can help the PO make these kinds of decisions based on a common denominator—business impact.

14.9.6 Forecast the Stories That Will Be Delivered

Next, the team determines the scope of the iteration—forecasting the stories that will be delivered and entering them into the iteration backlog. Only the team may determine its capacity. The PO may not tell the team how many stories it must commit to.

Following the lean **pull** mechanism, accept stories into the iteration until the capacity of the team is reached. This is usually done by adding stories until the total estimated story points reach the team's expected capacity. Another option is to use the **no-estimating**

---

8. Schwaber and Sutherland, *The Scrum Guide*, 8.

9. Mike Cohn, "Sprint Planning Meeting," Mountain Goat Software, September 21, 2019, https://www.mountaingoatsoftware.com/agile/scrum/meetings/sprint-planning-meeting

approach. In this case, you ask team members to forecast how far down the backlog they think they'll be able to get during the iteration. This approach works well as long as stories have been well-prepared in advance.

For more on the no-estimating approach, see Chapter 11, section 11.11.2.7.

If the PO wishes to pull more stories into the iteration after the team's capacity has already been reached, something else in the plan must be removed or reduced. For example, an entire story may be deferred to a subsequent iteration or some of a story's acceptance criteria may be split off and deferred. *As an analyst, you support this process by facilitating scope negotiation between the PO and team with the aim of maximizing the value delivered over the course of the iteration.*

14.10 Part 2: Plan the Implementation

The objective of Part 2 is to determine how the team will deliver the iteration goal and implement the stories planned for the iteration.

14.10.1 Should You Invite the PO to Part 2?

The short answer is, "Yes. Invite the PO." Here's the long answer. Some teams have told me they don't invite the PO to Part 2 because the meeting deals with internal matters. They feel the PO's presence isn't needed and, furthermore, that it can be disruptive. The argument has some merit. Nevertheless, it's better to invite POs so that they're available to answer the team's questions about design options and trade-offs as it plans its work. As an analyst, avoid the disruption this may cause by ensuring POs understand that their participation is supportive and that they are there to answer questions, not to challenge developers about how long tasks should take.

Interestingly, the question of whether to invite POs can quickly become moot. In my experience, most teams who invite them report that, after a few iterations, POs stop coming because they don't feel the time is well spent.

14.10.2 Overview of Part 2

The team decomposes the planned stories into smaller developer tasks, each of which can be performed by one member in a short period (typically, within a day or two). Team members sign up for tasks and estimate them in person-hours. Next, they add up the total time they've committed to and verify that it is within their available capacity. The scope is adjusted, if necessary, to avoid overcommitment. The deliverable produced during this part is the iteration backlog—listing the stories and developer tasks planned for the iteration.

Teams that use a flow-based planning approach (e.g., Kanban) go through the same steps as those described in the preceding paragraph—but do so for each story as it comes up in the queue rather than for all stories in an iteration.

As noted earlier, some teams limit story sizes to one day or less. In that case, the stories are often decomposed enough for iteration- and story-planning purposes and don't need to be further decomposed into tasks.

Analyst's Contribution

As an analyst, you contribute to Part 2 like other team members do—identifying and estimating developer tasks that you're responsible for. Recall that developer tasks include *all* tasks required to deliver stories, not just coding. Analysis tasks addressed during Part 2 include remaining analysis tasks for the current iteration's user stories and functional spikes to prepare for stories in upcoming iterations.

14.10.3 Part 2 Steps

The steps in Part 2 are summarized below. Be flexible. Use the following as guidance but adapt your approach to suit your needs:

- Identify developer tasks
- Sign up for tasks
- Estimate tasks
- Negotiation
- Commitment

14.10.3.1 Identify Developer Tasks

Beginning with the first story in the iteration backlog, facilitate a discussion about how the team will collaborate to implement it. The UX designer works with the PO and users at this time to develop a draft of the design that provides a cohesive, easy-to-use workflow. The team decomposes the story into developer tasks, covering all activities required to get the story to done, including analysis, design, coding, and testing. A developer task may support more than one story or no stories. If developers don't know enough about a story to decompose it, they may ask the PO and analyst clarifying questions.

Not every story and task needs to be decomposed to the same level. Developer tasks that won't be developed within the next few days need only be decomposed enough to be estimable. When the story is a few days from implementation, decompose it into tasks of one day or less.

When all the stories in the iteration backlog have been discussed, ask about any tasks that have been missed. Look out for tasks that are not story-specific. For example, a developer task to analyze the end-to-end workflow may not relate to any *specific* user story—but to a whole set of them. Tasks like this are easy to miss when you're focused on individual stories. Ensure the developer tasks also include at least one important process-improvement item identified in the previous iteration retrospective meeting.

Developer Task Board

Use a **developer task board** to plan and track development tasks for the iteration. The task board lists stories and tasks, work assignments, estimates, and measures of progress. Table 14.1 provides an overview of the artifact.

Table 14.1 *The Developer Task Board at a Glance*

What?	**Developer task board:** A planning artifact used to plan how stories will be implemented during the iteration.
When?	Create the developer task board during iteration planning, Part 2. Update it daily as work progresses. Decompose tasks to single-developer items of one day or less a few days before their execution.
Why?	• An action plan to guide development • A mechanism for tracking progress on stories once implementation begins • Decomposition, leading to a more accurate scope forecast
Tips	Use a physical board during the event. Convert it to an electronic form afterward if team members are dispersed.
Deliverables	Developer task board with estimated tasks

Figure 14.2 is an example of a developer task board.

PBI/Story	Developer Task	Owner	Estimate (Hours)	Time Spent	Time Remaining
Submit claim	Elicit data validation requirements	Barb	4	0	4
	Write test cases	Jane	1	0	1
	Create UI	Munir	8	0	8
	Search policy	Sukhi	2	0	2
	Write claims record	Sukhi	2	0	2
	Execute test	Jane	2	0	2
Assign adjuster	Create UI	Sukhi	1	0	1
	Integration with calendar	Munir	8	0	8

Figure 14.2 *Developer task board for claims*

At the beginning of the iteration, Time Spent is zero for all stories. Once the iteration is underway, team members update Time Spent and Time Remaining.

You might wonder why three Time columns are required, since you should be able to determine one from the other two. The reason is that the original estimate may have been low. In that case, the remaining time would be more than the difference between the estimate and time spent. Conversely, an overly high estimate would produce the inverse effect. By keeping track of both the forecast and actual times, members can monitor their own variances and use that information to improve future developer task estimates.

Developer Task Cards

During the planning stage, represent developer tasks using manual means, such as the developer task card in Figure 14.3.

Date:		Team Member:		Estimate:
Story ID:	Task Description	Notes		
Task Tracking				
Date	Action	Comments		

Figure 14.3   *Developer task card*

Once tasks have been identified in planning, they may be transferred to an electronic form for centralized tracking if the team is not colocated.

14.10.3.2 Sign Up for Tasks

Invite members to sign up for developer tasks. Ideally, all tasks are self-assigned. In practice, there tend to be at least some tasks that a manager has to assign because nobody wants to sign up for them.

14.10.3.3 Estimate Tasks

Next, team members estimate the time to complete the tasks they have signed up for. Estimates should be in units of hours, not points or days. The PO, if present, should take a passive role during this part of the meeting.

If a task is not understood well enough to be estimated, the facilitator asks the team to decompose it further until it is. If developers require more information about the requirements or acceptance criteria for the story in order to create an estimate, they may ask the PO questions.

I've known some teams who estimate tasks first and deal with task assignment afterward. However, it's preferable to perform task assignment first because it enables the people who will actually do the work to estimate it, resulting in a more reliable estimate. This is also consistent with XP guidance.[10]

14.10.3.4 Negotiation

Ask the team to add up the total estimated time for the developer tasks on the developer task board and verify that it is within its capacity. Also, ask team members to verify individually that the total estimated time for tasks they've signed up for is within their personal capacity. Members should also assess the *distribution* of their tasks across the iteration. For example, testers may find that testing tasks are concentrated at the end of the iteration. If an individual team member is overextended, discuss options such as reassigning the task to another team member or providing additional support. If capacity is exceeded at the team level, work with the team and PO to explore trade-offs that would deliver the same goal without overextending the team.

As an analyst, you play a critical role in supporting this collaboration and ensuring it plays out according to the rules of the Planning Game. For example, it is *not* appropriate, during negotiation, for the PO to challenge a developer's estimate. It *is* appropriate, though, for the PO to inquire about the aspects of a story that are contributing to a high estimate and negotiate an alternative way to deliver a story's value at a lower cost.

Remedies to team overextension may include the following:

- Using a less-expensive technical solution that provides similar functionality (e.g., a text UI instead of a graphic interface)

- Reducing or eliminating some developer tasks

- Decreasing the size of a story by removing acceptance criteria

- Removing entire stories from the iteration backlog and deferring them to a later time

Ensure the Planning Game rules are followed during this negotiation. Only the team may determine how much work it can take on, and only the customer may determine the stories' sequence in the backlog.

14.10.3.5 Commitment

The PO and team review the iteration goal and revise it if necessary. The team commits to delivering the iteration goal and pledges to promptly alert the customer if there is a risk the iteration goal will not be met.

---

10. Kent Beck, "Steering Phase," in *Extreme Programming Explained: Embrace Change* (Reading, MA: Addison-Wesley, 1999), 54.

The team forecasts the stories it will deliver during the iteration. The customer understands that this is a best-available forecast and that changes and trade-offs may be required once the iteration begins (e.g., due to unexpected technical difficulties).

The team commits that it will[11]

- Deliver the iteration goal.

- Deliver an increment that meets customer expectations.

- Focus on work of the highest value to the business.

- Use frequent user feedback to adapt and improve the solution.

- Collaborate with the customer throughout the development process.

- Practice continuous improvement.

The Analyst's Value Added

As an analyst, you play a crucial role in managing stakeholder expectations about the meaning of *commitment* in an agile plan so that everyone understands that the plan is a best forecast that may change—and that not all stories in the plan may be delivered.

BLINK CASE STUDY PART 24

Background

Part 1 of iteration planning has already occurred, and stories have been selected for the iteration. No changes were made to the stories indicated in the story map for iteration 1. (To view the BLInK story map, see Figure 13.3 in Chapter 13.)

The Ask

You've been asked to facilitate Part 2 of iteration planning. The deliverable from the event will be as follows:

- **Deliverable 1:** BLInK developer task board

What Transpires

You follow the facilitation guidelines for Part 2 in this chapter. The team decomposes stories into developer tasks, posts tasks on the developer task board, signs up for tasks, and estimates them. Then, you guide the team members to verify that the estimated work is within their capacity.

Deliverables

The following deliverables were produced.

Deliverables 1: BLInK Developer Task Board, Iteration One (Draft)

Figure 14.4 is a draft of the developer task board after the first two stories have been discussed.

---

11. Barry Overeem, "Myth 2: The Sprint Backlog Can't Change during the Sprint," October 30, 2017, https://www.scrum.org/resources/blog/myth-2-sprint-backlog-cant-change-during-sprint

Story	Task	Owner	Estimate (hrs)	Time Spent	Time Remaining
Receive BLInK marketing on invoices	Interview marketing SMEs on info to include	Barb	4		
	Coding, unit testing	Nabil	8		
	UAT	Sukhi	3		
Earn premium reduction for signup	Analyze premium reduction business rules	Barb	6		
	UI design	Munir	4		
	Integration with policy management system	Sukhi	8		
	Create interactive reduction rate table	Jane	2		
	Coding, unit testing	Nabil	3		
	UAT	Jane	2		

Figure 14.4 *BLInK developer task board*

Case Study Retrospective

In this workshop, the team decomposed the stories selected for the iteration into developer tasks. This gave them a better understanding of the work on which to base estimates and a detailed plan for carrying out the work.

14.11 Setting Up the Kanban Board

Use a Kanban board to manage and track the progress of stories. If your team is using the Kanban framework—or another flow-based approach—use a Kanban board to manage the flow of stories as they pass through the stages of development. If the team is using a timeboxed approach such as Scrum, SAFe, or XP, use the board to manage the stories' progress across an iteration. You can also use it to manage features across a quarter or release cycle. Table 14.2 provides an overview of Kanban boards.

Table 14.2 *Kanban Board at a Glance*

What?	**Kanban board:** A bulletin board used to manage and track workflow for stories.
When?	Use Kanban boards to track features and stories across their lifespan, across a quarter or an iteration. Update the board to reflect progress.
Why?	• Provides a transparent report on the progress of each story in the backlog • Allows a simple pull system to be used to manage work (items are pulled to the right until WIP limits reached)
Tips	Use blockers and fast track sections to highlight high-priority items.
Deliverables	Kanban board indicating the status of all stories in the planning period.

A **Kanban board** tracks **Kanbans**—placards—as they progress from left to right across its columns. In the context of agile development, each Kanban represents a feature or story. Each column on the board represents a trackable story status.

If you're using the Kanban board for Part 2 of iteration planning, begin by placing all the stories planned for the iteration in the leftmost column, To Do. Then, ask team members to select the story cards they want to work on—advancing the chosen stories to the right to indicate their new status. Once the WIP limit for any column has been reached, no more items are allowed until something has moved out of the column.

For guidance on setting up a Kanban Board and determining Kanban parameters, such as WIP limits, see Chapter 6, section 6.5.7.7.

14.11.1 Columns on the Kanban Board

There is no standard format for naming columns (states) on a Kanban board. Table 6.2 in Chapter 6 is one example of columns for tracking stories across their lifespan. Use a Kanban board of this type if the team is using a flow-based framework such as Kanban. (The table is just one example; the columns may vary.)

If your team is using a timeboxed framework such as Scrum, use a Kanban board to manage the workflow of in-flight stories during the iteration. The case study that follows includes two examples that may be used as templates for that purpose.

Figure 14.5 is the more minimalist version. There are only three primary columns: To Do, WIP, and Done. There is also a subsection under WIP for **blockers**—stories that cannot be progressed to "done" because of impediments. Notes are attached to blocked stories, indicating the nature and status of the blocker. The Blockers column alerts the team to impediments so that problems can be easily spotted and dealt with expeditiously. The figure illustrates two such blockers: the *unavailability of SMEs* blocks one story, and another is blocked by *defects*.

Figure 14.6 is an example of an expanded Kanban board with numerous status columns. All stories planned for the iteration start off in the To Do column. A team member (typically an analyst) selects a story for analysis and moves it to the BA WIP (business analysis work in progress) column. When the analysis is complete enough for development to begin, the analyst moves the story to the Dev to Do column. Intermediate To Do columns like this one make it easier to spot stories sitting in limbo, waiting to be selected by a team member. Next, a team member selects a story from the Dev to Do column and moves it to Dev WIP. If an impediment blocks the story from progressing, the story is transferred to the Blockers column.

Once a story's development is complete, the story moves through *Waiting Deployment to Testing* to *Test WIP* to *Done*.

The figure includes another feature that teams have found beneficial—a *Fast Lane* row, for stories that need to be expedited through the iteration.

- **Deliverable 1:** BLInK Kanban board—option 1 (minimalist)
- **Deliverable 2:** BLInK Kanban board—option 2 (expanded)

What Transpires

You develop two proposals—a minimalist option with a small number of states and an expanded option with much finer tracking. You present each option to the PO and team. You ask the group to discuss the kinds of workflow questions and issues that will need to be addressed and assess how well each option serves those purposes. You advise team members to use the leanest option that satisfies their needs—or combine the most useful elements into a new Kanban board design.

Deliverables

The deliverables from the workshop are as follows.

Deliverables 1: BLInK Kanban Board—Minimalist Option

Figure 14.5 presents the minimalist Kanban board for BLInK, with examples of stories as they might appear partway through the iteration.

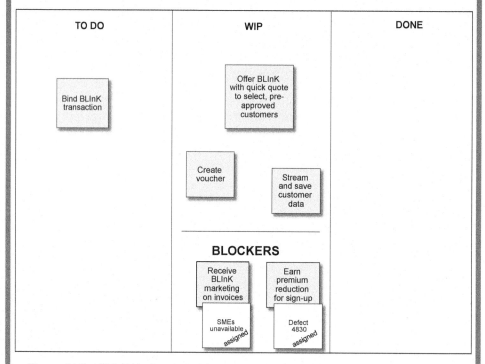

Figure 14.5 *BLInK Kanban board (minimalist option)*

Deliverables 2: BLInK Kanban Board—Expanded Option

Figure 14.6 is an option for an expanded Kanban board, as it appears at the start of the iteration.

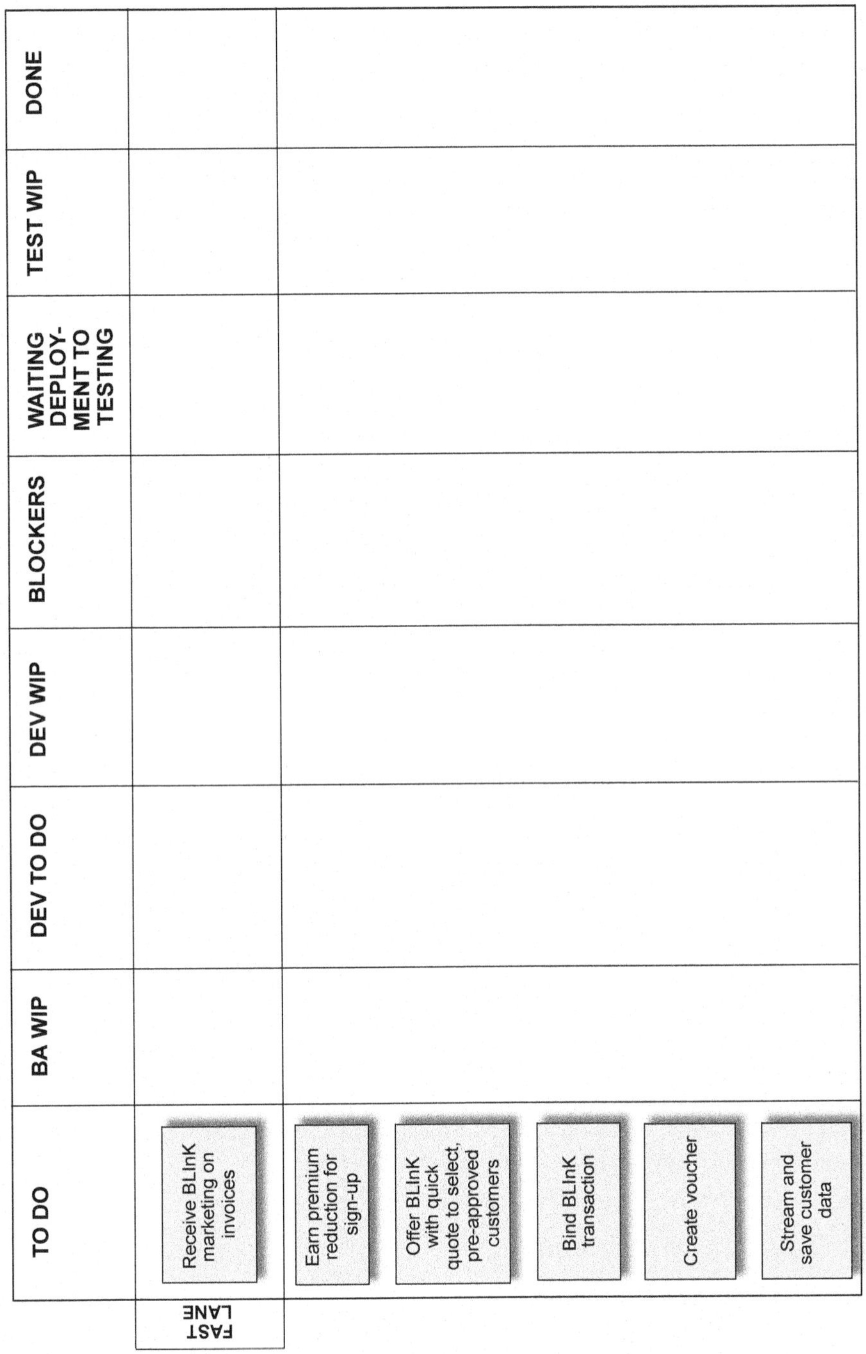

TO DO	BA WIP	DEV TO DO	DEV WIP	BLOCKERS	WAITING DEPLOY-MENT TO TESTING	TEST WIP	DONE
FAST LANE Receive BLInK marketing on invoices							
Earn premium reduction for sign-up							
Offer BLInK with quick quote to select, pre-approved customers							
Bind BLInK transaction							
Create voucher							
Stream and save customer data							

Figure 14.6 *BLInK Kanban board (expanded option)*

Case Study Retrospective

Attendees like the fact that the expanded option highlights workflow steps, allowing them to better answer questions about where work is piling up (e.g., whether in analysis, development, or testing). They also like the Fast Lane, as it helps them zero in on the progress of high-priority stories. They choose option 2.

14.12 Scaling Iteration Planning

In this chapter, our focus has been on the planning needs of single teams. What about scaled agile organizations with numerous collaborating teams? In that case, planning proceeds along much the same lines as single-team planning but with some adaptations. First, representatives of all teams meet to select stories for their teams. Next, each team plans the iteration. Finally, they all meet again to coordinate their final plans.

 For guidance on iteration planning for scaled initiatives, see Chapter 17, section 17.9.5.

14.13 Feature Preview Meeting

A **feature preview** meeting—also known as a **rolling lookahead meeting**[12]—is a short, ten-minute meeting to examine upcoming items in order to gain enough advanced knowledge of impediments, so they can be addressed in a timely fashion.

The meeting is attended by the development team and PO (customer). The inputs to the event are the team's projected capacity and a prioritized, estimable product backlog. The deliverable is a list of upcoming stories and impediments.

14.13.1 Feature Preview Objectives

The objective of a feature preview is to identify preparatory work, dependencies, and impediments that need to be considered before implementation. Discussions should remain high-level, with a focus on *raising* issues, not solving them. For example, don't decompose stories into developer tasks during this meeting.

14.13.2 Timing Considerations

If your team uses a flow-based approach, as in Kanban, conduct the feature preview on a rolling basis, looking ahead at stories queued up for the next few weeks.

---

12. Cohn, *Succeeding with Agile*, 334.

If the team uses a timeboxed framework, as in Scrum, conduct the feature preview immediately after the iteration planning meeting, looking ahead at stories one or two iterations past the current one. To find these stories, locate the first item in the product backlog past those assigned to the current iteration. Then, select stories from that point onward, summing their points until you reach *twice* the forecast velocity. These are the stories you'll discuss in the feature preview.

14.13.3 Why *Two* Iterations Ahead?

Why look two iterations ahead? Wouldn't one suffice? Let's explain by way of an example. Suppose you are in a feature preview meeting at the start of iteration 1, and the team notices an inter-team dependency. It has a story—Story X—that cannot be worked on until another team does Story Y. You alert the other team, but since they've already planned this iteration, they won't be able to get to Story Y until iteration 2. That means that your team won't be able to implement Story X until the iteration after that—iteration 3. For this reason, you preview stories *two* iterations in advance of implementation.

Note, however, that you don't need quite as much advance time if your team is using the Kanban approach because a story can be easily reprioritized *any* time before its implementation. There is no need to wait until the end of the iteration.

14.14 Chapter Summary

Here are the key points covered in this chapter:

- Iteration planning Part 1, Forecast What Will Be Accomplished, specifies the iteration goal and forecasts what will be delivered during the Iteration.

- Iteration planning Part 2, Plan the Implementation, determines how the work will be done. Stories are often decomposed into developer tasks at this time.

- The iteration backlog includes the stories selected for the iteration and the plan for implementing them.

- Use a developer task board to estimate and manage work at the task level.

- Set up a Kanban board to track the progress of stories.

- Conduct a short feature preview meeting to alert the team to upcoming impediments

14.15 What's Next?

This chapter walked you through iteration and story planning. Chapter 15, "Rolling Analysis and Preparation—Day-to-Day Activities," focuses on the day-to-day analysis activities that occur once stories are accepted into development.

Chapter 15

Rolling Analysis and Preparation—Day-to-Day Activities

The preceding chapters examined analysis and preparation at the start of an initiative. This chapter focuses on analysis tasks once implementation is underway. These tasks occur on a rolling basis as stories are accepted into development. Figure 15.1 highlights the activities covered in the chapter.

The chapter includes facilitator guidelines for updating and inspecting progress during daily standups. It explains how to track task and story progress using developer task boards, Kanban boards, burndown charts, burnup charts, and cumulative flow diagrams. It describes how to analyze customer behaviors using funnel charts and behavior-trended funnels. Also included are guidelines for implementing traceability, updating persistent business analysis (BA) information such as use-case models, and continuously integrating, testing, and delivering stories.

Next, the chapter turns to future work items, explaining how to prepare epics, features, and stories on a rolling basis in advance of their implementation.

The chapter also explains how to manage scope changes during an iteration. It ends with guidelines for closing out an iteration, including guidance on facilitating iteration reviews and retrospectives and tools for measuring and assessing progress.

The chapter continues the case study that runs through the book.

15.1 Objectives

This chapter will help you

- Conduct rolling, incremental story analysis once development is underway.
- Conduct and participate in a daily standup and follow-up meeting.

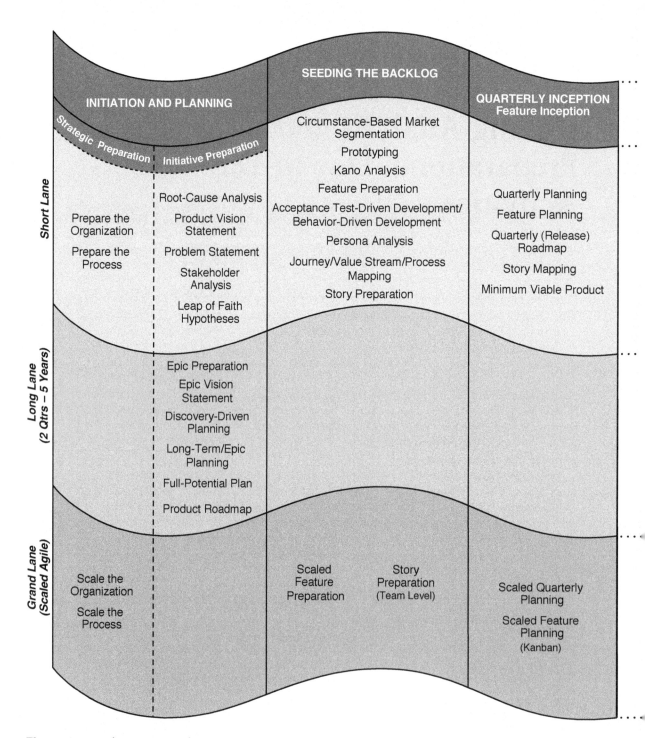

Figure 15.1 *Chapter 15 on the map*

ITERATION
INCEPTION

DAILY ACTIVITIES

ITERATION
CLOSEOUT

QUARTERLY
CLOSEOUT
Epic, Feature Closeout

Daily Standup

Requirements Analysis
& Documentation

Code, Build, Test, Deliver Acceptance
Test-Driven Development/
Behavior-Driven Development

Minimum Viable Product,
Split Testing

Epic, Feature Preparation

Story Preparation

Iteration
Planning

Iteration Review

Iteration Retrospective

Prepare for
General Availability

Quarterly
Retrospective

Epic, Feature
Retrospective

Pivot or
Persevere

Scaled
Iteration
Planning

Iteration
Planning
(Team Level)

Product
Owner
Council
Meetings

DevOps

User Task
Force
Meetings

Scaled
Feature
Preparation
(Kanban)

Integration
Meetings

Story
Preparation
(Team Level)

Scaled Iteration
Review

Scaled Iteration
Retrospective

Iteration Retrospective
(Team Level)

DevOps

Scaled
Quarterly/Feature
Retrospective

- Track the progress of requirements, diagnose problems, and forecast completion timelines.

- Understand how to interpret burndown charts, burnup charts, and cumulative flow diagrams and use them effectively.

- Know how to test stories and validate their value propositions using split testing and funnel metrics to measure outcomes and analyze behaviors.

- Manage changes to scope and priorities during an iteration.

- Prepare ongoing updates of BA information, such as process and use-case models.

- Prepare upcoming features and stories in the product backlog.

- Facilitate and participate in an iteration review/demo and iteration retrospective.

15.2 This Chapter on the Map

As shown in Figure 15.1, the chapter examines story preparation and other activities in the Daily Activities and Iteration Closeout zones. Daily Activities include daily standup; requirements analysis and documentation; code, build, test, and deliver; minimum viable product (MVP) and split testing; and epic, feature, and story preparation.

15.3 Overview of Rolling Analysis

In preceding chapters, we covered the initial seeding and preparation of the backlog at the start of an initiative. As implementation is set to begin, stories will have been prepared well enough to be reliably estimated and for development to commence without impediments. The analysis is incomplete—intentionally so, to leave room for learning and avoid waste in case the requirements change or the story is deprioritized.

Once implementation begins, you continue the story's analysis concurrent with its design and development. You also prepare upcoming stories, features, and epics in the product backlog as they advance toward the top of the queue.

To get a feel for the analysis work at this time, let's look at a typical day in your life as an agile analyst, once development is underway.

15.3.1 A Day in the Life of the Agile Analyst

Each day begins with a daily standup—a meeting to synchronize team members and report on progress. If your team is new to agile development, you may facilitate the first meetings, coaching others to take over. During the meeting, team members update the team on plans and coordinate with others—making adjustments based on changing circumstances. For example, in one session, team members speak about unexpected technical difficulties leading to delays. To address the issue, you meet with the product owner (PO) and developers during a follow-up meeting to negotiate the postponement of story acceptance criteria—or even entire stories—in order to meet timelines.

Following continuous integration and continuous delivery (CI/CD) practices, the build-test-deliver cycle occurs in a continuous manner as stories emerge from coding and unit testing. The **customer**—a user or user representative—tests each story against its acceptance criteria. If the customer is unsatisfied with the story, another round of analysis, coding, and testing occurs. Once the customer is satisfied that the story is complete enough to be released at a time of the customer's choosing, and the story satisfies the definition of done (DoD), the story is deemed **done** and is delivered to the customer. "Delivered to the customer" means the solution is reliable and in a state in which it can be released to the market or into production *at the customer's discretion.* The customer may decide, however, to delay releasing the story for various reasons (e.g., because the feature is not yet rich enough to be competitive or other necessary value stream steps are still missing).

As work on current stories nears completion, you focus on upcoming items in the product backlog. In this example, let's presume your team uses a timeboxed framework, such as Scrum or Extreme Programming (XP). In that case, the upcoming items you examine are those lined up in the backlog for the next one or two iterations. You confirm the value of these items with the PO to ensure they still have a high priority. You prepare the upcoming stories so that they are *ready* in time for planning and implementation.

From about the midway point into an epic or quarter onward, you begin to prepare for the next one (see Chapter 10, "Quarterly and Feature Preparation"). As upcoming features move closer to their implementation, you prepare them to be *feature ready.* For example, you split them into their primary stories. If your team conducts quarterly planning, you prepare all the features lined up for the quarter before the quarterly planning meeting. Throughout this process, as you discover new or changed BA information worth saving for future reference, you document it—for example, you update feature files and business process models.

You conduct the analysis in a similar manner whether the team uses a flow-based planning approach, such as Kanban, or a timeboxed approach. The main difference between the two is that in flow-based planning, the team accepts items into development *single-file*; in contrast, using timeboxed planning, it accepts a *group* of stories all at once during iteration planning. You lose some agility with the timeboxed approach because there's more resistance to change once a plan is written down. However, the advantage of timeboxed planning is that it eases coordination and prioritization of work across the product, since all teams have the same start and end times.

Finally, the team demonstrates its work and holds a retrospective meeting aimed at continual improvement. If your team uses a timeboxed approach, it conducts these events at the end of each iteration.

That's rolling analysis in a nutshell once implementation begins. In the following sections, we look at this process in greater detail.

15.3.2 Overview of Analysis Tasks

Ongoing analysis tasks may include the following:

- Further refinement of acceptance criteria and development of test cases
- Development of wireframes, low-fidelity, and high-fidelity prototypes
- Elicitation and feedback—including one-on-one and group interviews, job shadowing, questionnaires, and data analytics
- Research of existing documentation
- Requirements analysis, including specification of inputs and outputs, data verification rules, business rules analysis, process analysis, and data modeling
- Monitoring progress of tasks and stories
- Story testing and validation during the code-build-test-deliver cycle
- Managing scope changes after the iteration begins
- Updating BA information documentation (e.g., process models, use-case models)
- Requirements tracing
- Epic, feature, and story preparation

This chapter focuses on requirements analysis, progress monitoring, story testing, acceptance criteria, scope changes, BA information, and the tracing, and preparation of features, stories, and other requirements artifacts.

15.4 Updating Task Progress

Treat analysis tasks like any other developer tasks associated with a story. (Recall that developer tasks include not only coding but all remaining work that counts against the team's budget.) Decompose analysis work into developer tasks of one day or less at least a few days before performing them and track their progress on the developer task board. Update task progress on the task board regularly (at least daily). For guidelines on updating the developer task board, see section 15.7.3 in this chapter.

15.5 Triad Guideline

As you continue to elicit and analyze requirements for stories, do so within the context of **Triad** meetings, as discussed in Chapter 13, "Story Preparation." Ensure the following perspectives are present when stories are discussed: business, quality assurance (QA), and development.

 For more on the Triad, see Chapter 13, section 13.6.3.

15.6 Actions That May Be Taken against a Developer Task

You and the team may take the following actions against a developer task or story:[1]

- **Implement a task:** You can pick up a task and perform it if it is within your competency.

- **Update and inspect progress:** Update the time spent and time remaining on developer tasks on a regular basis. Update stories and work logs (short notes describing work done) daily—for example, using Jira or another electronic backlog tool.

- **Recover:** If you are overcommitted, you may request that recovery actions be taken to address the problem. Recovery actions include reducing the acceptance criteria for a story, removing developer tasks, moving tasks to another team member, providing additional support to a team member, and delaying a story to another iteration.

- **Test:** When the requirements have been implemented, the customer tests the story against its acceptance criteria. If the customer is not satisfied that the story meets its acceptance criteria, the story is sent back for further cycles of analysis, development, and testing.

- **Swarm:** If there is a risk that a high-value story will not be delivered in time, the team may swarm (converge on) the story, dropping lower-value work, if necessary. Swarming reinforces the notion that the whole team is responsible for what is delivered to the customer.[2]

15.7 Monitoring Progress

Team members update each other and inspect progress regularly through events such as the daily standup and artifacts such as the developer task board and burndown charts. Let's begin with the events.

15.7.1 The Daily Standup

Each day, the team meets for a quick meeting, known as the daily standup (also referred to, in Scrum, as the *Daily Scrum*). The **daily standup** is a short-term planning, coordination, and status-update event and a critical *inspect-and-adapt* tool. It serves as a simple daily mechanism for picking up on problems such as overworked and underutilized team members so that corrective action can be taken swiftly. Guidelines for the event follow.

---

1. I have been using these guidelines for a long time, based on XP guidance, but I no longer recall their source.
2. Ron Healy, in a note to the author.

15.7.1.1 Self-Management

The daily standup is a self-managing event; there is no leader. The team, as a whole, decides how to conduct the event and is responsible for carrying it out. An analyst or ScrumMaster may facilitate the first meeting as a way to coach the team. Afterward, any team member may act as the facilitator.

15.7.1.2 Objectives

The standup supports a *whole-team* perspective by communicating shared team goals[3] and reinforcing the principle that progress is a shared team responsibility. Its main objectives are to coordinate team efforts, discuss current impediments, and raise future risks so that issues can be addressed in a timely fashion. The purpose of the meeting is to *identify* these items, not solve them. If the team uses a timeboxed planning approach, the meeting objectives also include inspecting progress toward the iteration goal.[4]

15.7.1.3 Timing Considerations

Try to hold the meeting at the same time and place every day. The time and place may change on occasion, but this should be rare. Contrary to popular belief, the event does not need to be held in the morning—though that is a common practice as a way to set the scene for the day. Others, however, prefer to schedule their daily standups at the end of the day to review the day's work and plan the next one.

The location should be in a place where the work occurs (e.g., in front of a Kanban board or developer task board). As a general rule, the daily standup should not run over fifteen minutes, in order to keep the discussion focused and the energy high. However, more time should be allowed, if needed, to ensure each team member has an opportunity to speak. (Note, however, that this advice is contrary to Scrum guidelines, which set a fifteen-minute limit.)

15.7.1.4 Facilitation Tips

Keep the daily standup short by

- Focusing the group on identifying problems, not solving them, unless the issue can be resolved quickly.

- Moving long discussions about solutions and out-of-scope topics items off-line (e.g., to the follow-up meeting).

- Enforcing the **two-hands rule:**[5] Any team member may raise a hand to indicate that a discussion is meandering. If a second person raises a hand, it's a signal for the discussion to end.

---

3. Jason Yip, "It's Not Just Standing Up: Patterns for Daily Standup Meetings," MartinFlowler. com, February 21, 2016, https://martinfowler.com/articles/itsNotJustStandingUp.html

4. Ken Schwaber and Jeff Sutherland, "Sprint Planning," in *The Scrum Guide: The Definitive Guide to Scrum—The Rules of the Game,* 2020, 9, https://www.scrumguides.org

5. Benjamin Mitchell, "The Two Hand Rule for Meandering Stand Up," DZone, March 6, 2012, https://dzone.com/articles/two-hand-rule-meandering-stand

15.7.1.5 Who Should Attend?

Because the daily standup is an internal meeting for enhancing collaboration, all team members should be present, including testers, programmers, UX designers, and analysts. Others may also attend, but only as observers.

What about the PO?

Though the meeting is internal, the PO may attend as an observer. The benefit of including POs is that they can quickly be apprised of impediments and be available to answer questions. Some teams choose to exclude POs due to concerns that they will dominate the event and turn it into a progress report. Nevertheless, it's preferable to begin by inviting POs, and then, if their presence proves to be disruptive, discontinue the practice. The issue tends to resolve itself. Teams report that POs who initially insist on attending standups often stop coming because they realize there isn't much need for them to be there.

Interestingly, *The Scrum Guide* originally limited participation in the meeting to the "Development team,"[6] thereby *excluding* the PO. However, it has since changed its stance to allow the PO to attend under certain circumstances.[7]

15.7.1.6 Status Updates to the Team

Members update the rest of the team on the status of their work. The important aspect of the update is the discussion, not the questions. There is no obligatory agenda, but it's common for each team member, in turn, to address the following three questions:

- What did I accomplish since the last meeting?
- What will I be working on until the next meeting?
- What impediments do I foresee, whether on current or *future* work, that might prevent the team from achieving its goal?

Some teams prefer to address the impediments question first because it's the most urgent one. The inclusion of future work in the questions is to ensure that members raise issues with upcoming stories *as soon as* they become aware of them rather than wait until stories move into development.

If an issue can be resolved quickly, the team works out a solution during the meeting. Otherwise, the facilitator records it on an **improvement board** to be discussed offline (e.g., in a follow-up meeting after the standup). (See next section for guidelines.)

---

6. "The Scrum Master enforces the rule that only Development team members participate in the Daily Scrum." Ken Schwaber and Jeff Sutherland, *The Scrum Guide: The Definitive Guide to Scrum—The Rules of the Game*, Scrumguides.org, 2014, 10.

7. The 2020 version of Schwaber and Sutherland's *The Scrum Guide* states: "If the Product Owner or Scrum Master are actively working on items in the Sprint Backlog, they participate as Developers" (p. 9).

Walking the Board

An alternative way to conduct a standup is to **walk the board**. With this approach, the facilitator progresses from story to story rather than from person to person. A variant of the three questions we saw earlier may be used. For example:

- What did the team accomplish with respect to this story yesterday?
- What work will the team be doing on this story today?
- What impediments might prevent the team from delivering this story or future stories within their planned timelines?

Cover the most urgent items first. If you're using a Kanban board, begin with stories designated as blockers and high-priority items. (In the Kanban board example in Figure 15.3, these are the stories in the Blockers column and the Fast Lane.) Then, follow with the remaining stories beginning with stories closest to completion—moving across the board from right to left and from top to bottom.[8] Any member may contribute to the discussion of any story.

The benefit of this approach is that it keeps the focus on the work rather than on individual members and encourages lively team discussion and collaboration. This approach contrasts with the rote recital of "I did X. I'm going to do Y," which tends to occur using the other approach. The downside is that you may not hear from everyone, since introverted members may be reticent about contributing.

15.7.1.7 Forecasting

After the status updates, the team measures progress and updates forecasts. Various tools may be used for this purpose, including a Kanban board, developer task board, daily burndown chart, and cumulative flow diagram. These tools are discussed later in this chapter. If the team is using a timeboxed approach, such as Scrum, the team may also update the iteration backlog at this time.

Before closing the meeting, the facilitator asks if there is anything else members would like to bring up.

15.7.2 Follow-Up Meeting

One of the strategies for keeping the daily standup short is to schedule a more focused **follow-up meeting** each day. Interested team members convene in a follow-up meeting to address unresolved issues raised during the standup. Reserve about thirty to forty minutes[9] for the follow-up at the same time each day. Updates to the developer task board may also be made at this time.

Let's now turn to the artifacts used to track and inspect progress.

---

8. Jason Yip, "It's Not Just Standing Up."

9. Giora Morein, "Agile QuickTip: Schedule Follow Up Times," ThinkLouder, https://thinklouder.com/scrum-follow-ups

15.7.3 Updating the Developer Task Board

In Chapter 14, "Iteration and Story Planning," you learned to create a **developer task board** at the start of an iteration. It lists developer tasks and information items, such as total estimated task and remaining task time. Figure 14.2 in Chapter 14 is one such example, created during iteration planning. Once implementation begins, team members update the developer task board regularly—at least once per day. They may do this ad hoc as they complete tasks or at a scheduled time, such as during the daily standup or follow-up meeting.

Figure 15.2 continues the example in Figure 14.2, illustrating the developer task board once the iteration is in progress.

Story	Developer Task	Owner	Estimate (Hours)	Time Spent	Time Remaining
Submit claim	Elicit data validation requirements	Barb	4	4	4
	Write test cases	Jane	1	1	1
	Create UI	Munir	8	5	4
	Search policy	Sukhi	2	3	0
	Write claims record	Sukhi	2	0	2
	Execute test	Jane	2	0	2
Assign adjuster	Create UI	Sukhi	1	1	1
	Integration with calendar	Munir	8	1	7

Figure 15.2 *Updated developer task board*

Figure 15.2 indicates that the developer task *Create UI* is estimated at eight hours and has four hours remaining even though five have already been spent. This is not an error; the original estimate was low. Similarly, three hours have already been spent on the *Search policy* task—higher than the two hours estimated. By including the original estimates alongside the actuals, the developer task board helps team members use prior experience to improve their future forecasts.

15.7.4 Updating the Kanban Board

The **Kanban board** is another visual tool for inspecting progress. As we saw in Chapter 14, it's used to manage and track the states of stories as they advance through development. The Kanban board is useful for teams—whether they follow the flow-based Kanban framework or use a timeboxed approach such as Scrum, XP, or Scaled Agile Framework (SAFe).

If the team follows a flow-based framework, stories are pulled continuously across the columns of the Kanban board as capacity becomes available. If the team uses a timeboxed framework, the stories all enter the iteration at the same time but are pulled continuously across the board once the iteration begins. Figure 15.3 is an example of a Kanban board in the middle of an iteration for the BLInK case study.

The figure shows the states of stories at a particular point in time. For example, the story *Stream and save customer data* is in the BA WIP state (or queue), indicating BA work is in progress. *Create voucher* is in the Dev To Do state: the BA work is complete, but the story's implementation has not yet started.

15.7.4.1 Kanban Rules for Advancing Stories across the Board

The following rules apply to the movement of stories on a Kanban board:

- Rule 1: *Anyone* with the competency to advance a story may move it to the right, provided that Rule 2 is not breached.

- Rule 2: The number of items in a queue must not exceed the maximum work-in-progress (WIP) limit set for that column.

- Rule 3: Items may also move backward (e.g., when an item is returned to development after failing a test).

15.7.4.2 Lifecycle across the States of a Kanban Board (State-Transition Diagram)

The state-transition diagram in Figure 15.4 illustrates a story's lifecycle as it makes its way across the states (columns) of the Kanban board shown in Figure 15.3. The diagram is one example of how stories may progress—and regress—on the board. Actual state transitions may vary.

Each rounded rectangle in Figure 15.4 represents a state of the story—physically indicated by the Kanban queue (column) in which it sits. The figure tells the following narrative.

All stories selected for development begin in the leftmost queue—To Do. If the team uses timeboxed planning (e.g., Scrum or XP), these are the stories entered into the iteration backlog during iteration planning. Presuming that the BA WIP queue has not reached its limit, an available analyst (i.e., someone with an analysis competency) picks up the top story in the To Do column, moves it to the BA WIP queue, and begins working on it. If the BA WIP queue is full, the analyst may assist other team members.

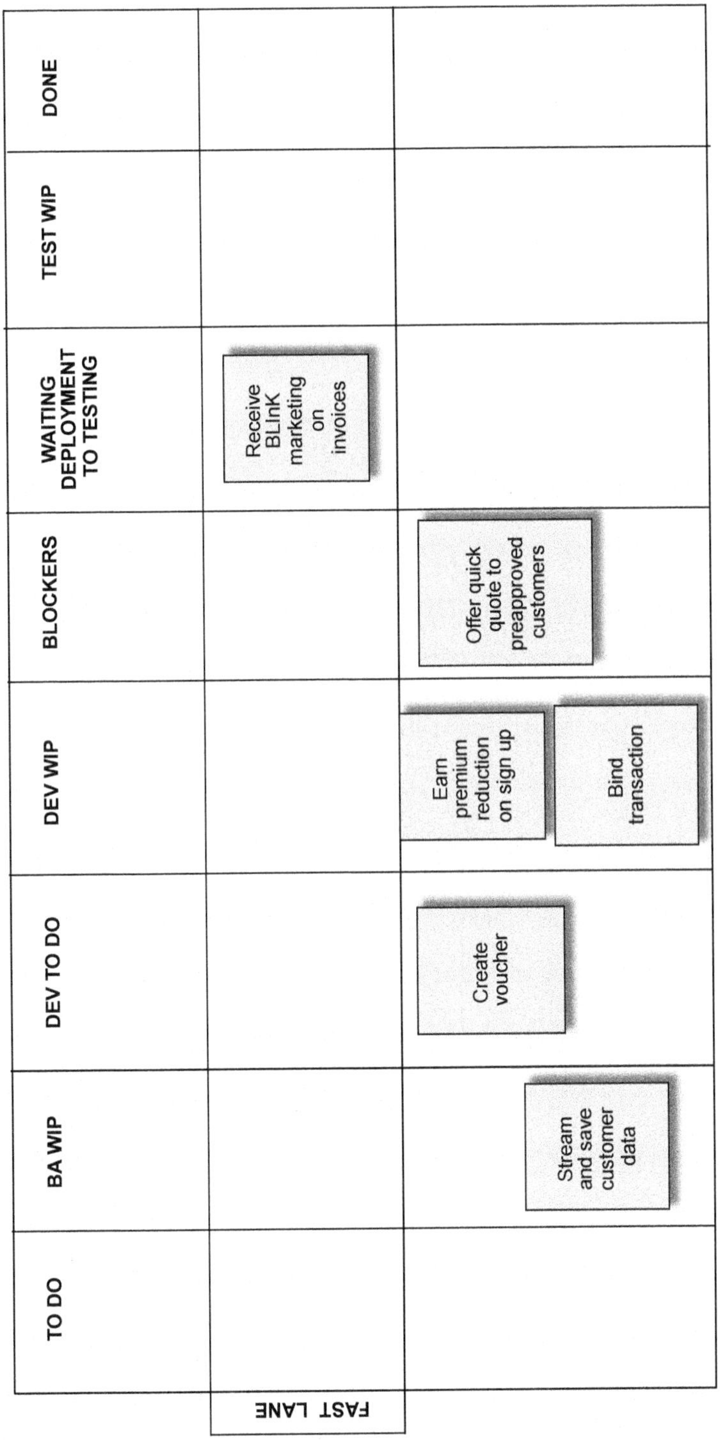

TO DO	BA WIP	DEV TO DO	DEV WIP	BLOCKERS	WAITING DEPLOYMENT TO TESTING	TEST WIP	DONE
					Receive BLInK marketing on invoices		
			Earn premium reduction on sign up	Offer quick quote to preapproved customers			
			Bind transaction				
		Create voucher					
	Stream and save customer data						

FAST LANE

Figure 15.3 *BLInK Kanban board*

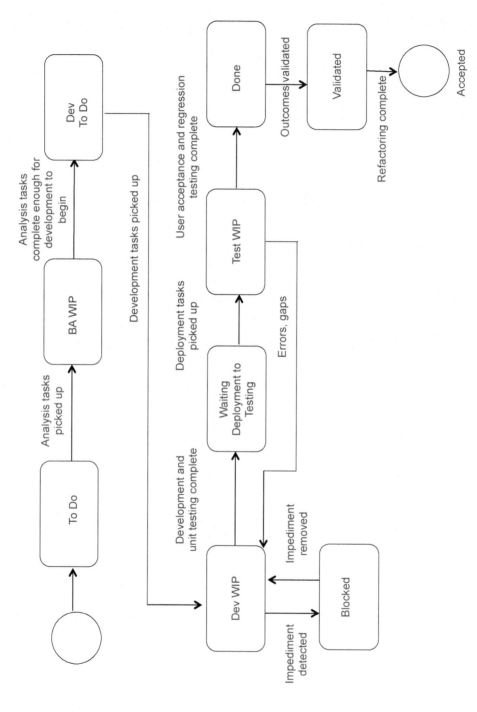

Figure 15.4 *Story state-transition diagram example*

Once the analysis on a story is complete enough for development to begin, the analyst moves the story to the Dev To Do queue, where it sits until it is picked up by a software engineer and moved to Dev WIP. While a story is in the Dev WIP queue, the analysis continues, UI prototypes are designed and presented to the user, automated tests are created, and the story is coded, unit-tested, and validated against its acceptance criteria.

If a story encounters an impediment (e.g., a technical issue or lack of access to stakeholders), it moves to the Blocked state, where it is flagged. This state corresponds to the Blockers column in Figure 15.3. Address flagged stories according to the guidelines for the Recover step, as described in section 15.6. For example, the story may be reduced in size, greater access to stakeholders may be provided, or technical assistance may be offered. Once the impediment is removed, the story moves back to Dev WIP.

When the code has passed all its lower-level technical tests, the story moves to Test WIP, where the customer—a user or user representative—tests the story against its acceptance criteria. If the customer does not feel the story is releasable yet, it is returned to Dev WIP.

After the story passes acceptance testing, it moves to the Waiting Deployment to Testing queue where it awaits final testing. Next, it is picked for deployment to testing and moved to the Test WIP column. While in that state, the story undergoes high-level integration tests, regression tests, and final system tests. Once the story complies with the DoD, it is deemed done.

Figure 15.4 illustrates a further step beyond done. After the customer has decided to deploy the story for a beta test (typically, along with other stories developed for the feature), metrics are collected to validate whether the change achieves its business objectives. For example, did it raise conversion rates of browsers to shoppers? Once the story's objectives have been validated, final work is carried out, such as performance tweaks and final testing. Once this is complete, the feature is accepted as part of the product and released for general availability (GA), where it is exposed to the broad user base.

For more on releasing stories and features, see Chapter 16, "Releasing the Product."

15.7.5 Monitoring Progress with a Daily Burndown Chart

Use a **daily burndown chart** to indicate progress, reveal trends, and forecast when the work will be completed. Elapsed time is shown along its x-axis. Remaining effort is shown along the y-axis.

The chart may be used to inspect progress at the story level or the developer task level. To track the progress of developer tasks, use real-time units. To track the progress of stories, use story estimation units (e.g., total story points or ideal developer days [IDDs]).

15.7.5.1 Main Elements

Figure 15.5 is an example of a daily burndown chart for inspecting the progress of developer tasks in an iteration backlog. The chart is updated as tasks are completed and entered.

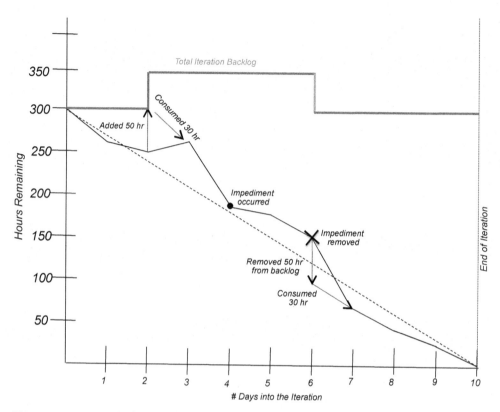

Figure 15.5 *Developer task burndown chart*

The falling solid line in Figure 15.5 (beginning at 300 hours and zigzagging to zero) indicates the hours to complete the remaining developer tasks in the iteration backlog. The dashed line illustrates the ideal path, whereby the remaining work steadily declines to zero by the end of the iteration. If the solid line lies above the dashed line, it's a sign that productivity is lagging behind expectations and that the developer tasks may not be completed in time.

To forecast the completion date for all the developer tasks in the backlog at any point in time, project the solid line on the basis of performance trends, as described in section 15.7.5.5.

15.7.5.2 Optional Elements

Figure 15.5 illustrates additional elements that can be included in the diagram to enhance understanding.

Add a **scope line** to the top of the diagram to indicate the total amount of work in the iteration backlog at any time. For example, the scope line in Figure 15.5 shows that, on day 2, the total work in the iteration backlog jumped from 200 to 250 hours due to the addition of 50 hours of work. On day 6, the same amount of work was dropped from the backlog. These scope-line changes provide a way to explain the unusual shifts in hours remaining on those days.

Critical **events** may be indicated by dots and other symbols. For example, Figure 15.5 shows an event on day 4: Impediment occurred. The removal of the impediment is indicated in the Figure by an X on day 6.

Dashed arrows may be used to explain changes. For example, in Figure 15.5, the remaining work (solid line) rose on day 3—a surprising outcome on its face. The dashed arrows explain the shift by indicating that 50 hours of work had been added, while 30 hours were performed, leading to a net *increase* of 20 hours of remaining work.

15.7.5.3 Tracking Stories on Daily Burndown Charts

In the preceding example, we used a daily burndown chart to track the progress at the task level. You can also use a daily burndown chart to track progress at the story level. The y-axis, in this case, represents the remaining story estimation units (e.g., story points or IDDs), while the x-axis represents time into the iteration. Update the graph at least once a day to reflect current progress (e.g., during the daily standup). A story must be done before it can contribute to a reduction in remaining estimation units.

Figure 15.6 is an example of a daily burndown chart used to inspect progress at the story level across an iteration.

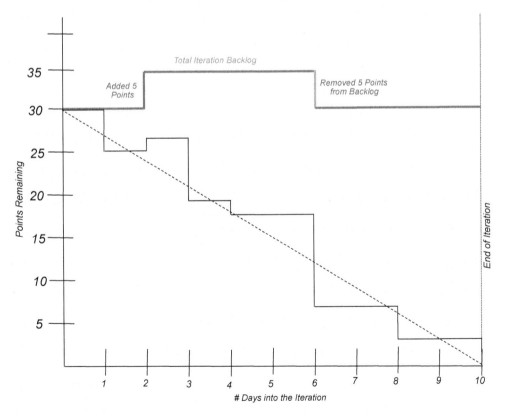

Figure 15.6 *Story daily burndown chart*

You may be wondering why, in Figure 15.6, the number of remaining points did not drop on days 5, 7, and 9. It is because no stories were *completed* on those days—even though work was done.

15.7.5.4 Is It Better to Track Developer Tasks or Stories on a Burndown?

Some teams and practice leads prefer to track progress at the developer task level (as in Figure 15.5) rather than at the story level because tasks are more granular, providing a better basis for forecasting. Others are adamant about tracking progress at the story level only (Figure 15.6) because it discourages managers from treating staff like resources. Also, since updates only occur as each story is complete, restricting tracking to the story level prevents task-level micromanagement.

To get the best of both worlds, track the total remaining task time along the y-axis but *don't update the graph as each story's task is complete.* Instead, wait until the *story* is done and sum the estimates for all of its developer tasks. For example, if a story were decomposed into two tasks estimated at four hours each, subtract eight hours from the remaining backlog work when the story is done. Using this approach, you get the more accurate forecasting that developer task estimates provide; however, the information can't be used for micromanagement, since metrics are not updated until the story is finished. This approach is equivalent to tracking stories on the graph using the sum of each story's task estimates instead of the story's points.

15.7.5.5 Using Burndowns Charts for Forecasting

The primary perspective of burndown charts is forward-looking. Use them for forecasting and to improve future performance, *not to judge past performance.*

To forecast future progress, project the progress line with the slope set to the expected velocity based on past performance. The forecast completion date is indicated by the intersection of the projected line with the x-axis.

Figure 15.7 shows the forecast for one team.

At five days into the iteration, the team has settled into a fairly steady velocity. If team members continue at that rate, though, they will reach the end of the iteration backlog on day 12, two days after the scheduled end of the iteration. To avoid missing the deadline, they'll need to improve performance or reduce the remaining work in the iteration backlog.

15.7.5.6 Using the Chart for Diagnosis: Burndown Signatures

The overall shape of a burndown chart is referred to as its *signature.* By learning to recognize signatures, you can diagnose and treat common productivity issues. The following are some of the key signatures of a burndown chart.[10]

---

10. Ken Schwaber and Mike Beedle, *Agile Software Development with Scrum* (Upper Saddle River, NJ: Prentice Hall, 2002), 76–80.

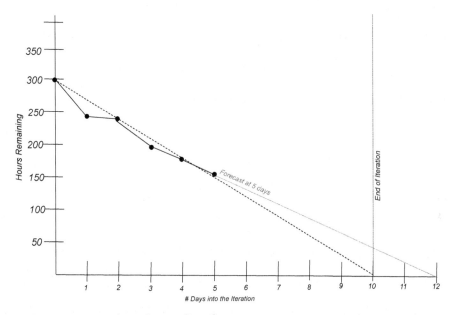

Figure 15.7   *Iteration burndown chart forecast*

Healthy Signature

Figure 15.8 is an example of a **healthy signature** for a developer task burndown chart. It zigzags a bit but stays reasonably close to the ideal path. Most of the fluctuation occurs at the left end, decreasing as the line proceeds to the right.

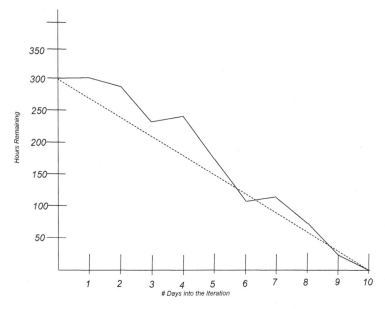

Figure 15.8   *Healthy signature*

This signature indicates that the team is working at a steady, sustainable pace that closely matches the forecast. Zigzags are expected for any team that is regularly providing progress updates, since productivity will vary due to uncontrollable events such as illness and unexpected technical difficulties. In fact, a straight line is a signal that something is amiss in the tracking system.

The initial fluctuation is expected—a sign of a team at the start of development as it gets its feet wet. Likewise, the leveling out over time is typical as a team settles into a steady pace.

Underestimating Signature

Figure 15.9 is an example of an **underestimating signature**. It looks like the outline of a mountain—rising at first until it reaches a peak, then dropping precipitously before settling into a gentle slope.

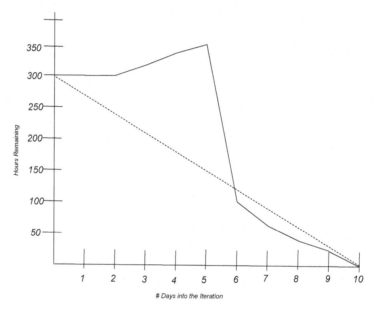

Figure 15.9 *Underestimating signature*

The initial rise is due to additional developer tasks being added to the iteration backlog. This suggests that the team had underestimated its workload and soon found itself with more work than it had bargained for. The precipitous drop afterward is unlikely to be due to sudden extreme improvements in productivity. More likely, tasks have been removed from the iteration backlog to make room for those added—resulting in the team delivering less functionality by the end of the iteration than it planned for.

It's normal for a team to exhibit this signature for the first few iterations of development when team members don't yet have a history of working together. However, if this signature persists, it suggests the team is consistently underestimating effort. As an analyst, you should investigate the causes. These may include the following:

- Certain kinds of developer tasks are consistently missed during planning.

- Stories are not adequately prepared, leading to unexpected work and stories that are not well-enough understood to be reliably estimated.

- Impediments are not being addressed promptly, creating bottlenecks once implementation begins.

Analyst's Contribution

As an analyst, you play a crucial role in addressing chronic underestimation. Create a DoR if one does not yet exist, or revise it, as necessary, if it already exists. Include conditions to fill any recurring analysis gaps you've found. For example, add conditions that the story is free from impediments and that the customer and the team understand its acceptance criteria. Ensure the team complies with the rule that a story must pass the DoR before it is accepted into development.

Overestimating Signature

Figure 15.10 is an example of an **overestimating signature**. At first, the line drops precipitously, then experiences a sharp rise, before leveling off toward the end.

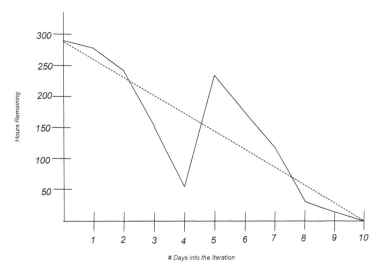

Figure 15.10   *Overestimating signature*

The signature indicates a team that started out working much more rapidly than expected. This pattern is typical for a team that is beginning to work on new problems (new technology or new business area) and, as a result, has padded the estimate as a hedge against unexpected issues. Productivity exceeds the padded estimate once the iteration begins, and the team can then take on extra work—as indicated by the sudden rise on day 5 in Figure 15.10.

If this signature persists, it's a sign of chronic overestimation by the team. As an analyst, you address this by improving estimation methods and ensuring the team understands stories better before estimating them (e.g., by investigating business rules and technological issues beforehand). Start using spikes (if you're not already doing so) to account for this work in the product backlog.

15.7.6 Burnup Charts

Figure 15.11 is an example of a burnup chart.

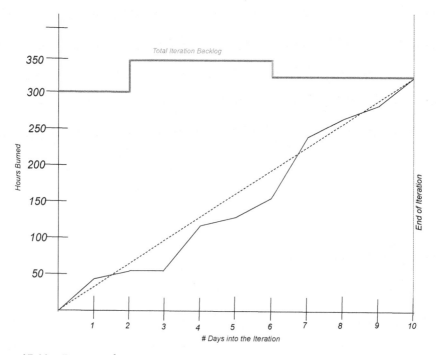

Figure 15.11   *Burnup chart*

While a burndown chart shows how much work *remains* in the iteration backlog, a **burnup chart** shows how much has been *delivered*. As with burndown charts, you can create a burnup chart to measure the progress of *stories* or *developer tasks*.

15.7.7 What Should You Use: Burndown or Burnup Charts?

If you're forecasting, use a burndown chart, since it focuses on the future and *remaining* work. A burndown chart is not ideal for diagnosing *past* patterns for process-improvement purposes because it conflates past performance with changes to the iteration backlog. A burnup chart is preferable for this purpose, since it tracks only performed work, not scope changes.

15.7.8 Cumulative Flow Diagrams

Figure 15.12 is an example of another diagram used for workflow management and process improvement: Kanban's *cumulative flow diagram*, also known as the *Newell curve*.

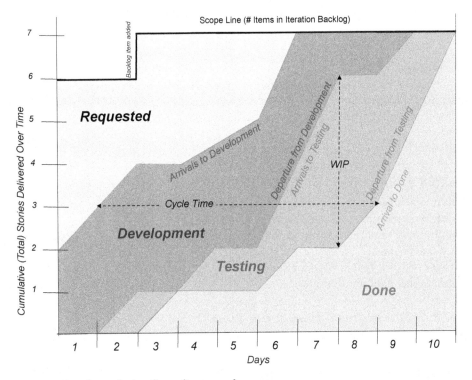

Figure 15.12 *Cumulative flow diagram elements*

The diagram tracks the cumulative total *stories* entering and exiting each stage of the development lifecycle. The following discussion looks at its use to track the flow of stories across one iteration, but it can be used to track progress over any period.

15.7.8.1 The Analyst's Contribution

The following two things are true about cumulative flow diagrams: (1) They are very useful for identifying productivity issues. (2) They are not the most intuitive of diagrams. As a business analyst conversant with cumulative flow diagrams in the context of operational workflow analysis, you can leverage your knowledge to diagnose workflow problems during product development.

15.7.8.2 Y-Axis Units

The y-axis units in a Kanban cumulative flow diagram are meant to represent a simple count of work items. When those work items are stories, however, such units are meaningful only if the stories are of uniform size. If story sizes vary appreciably, then a simple count can be misleading. A slowdown in the flow of stories through a queue may not necessarily indicate a productivity decrease, since some of the stories might be larger than usual. Consequently, a better approach is to weigh the stories by measuring story points, rather than the *number* of stories, along the y-axis.

The following discussion is based on the more widely used approach whereby the y-axis measures the number of stories under the assumption that stories are of roughly uniform size.

15.7.8.3 Regions

A cumulative flow diagram is divided into **regions** defined by **boundaries**. Each region represents a stage (Kanban column) through which a story passes. The regions are positioned from the top left of the diagram to the bottom right, in the chronological sequence in which they typically occur. For example, in Figure 15.12, the first region represents the first state, Requested, and the last represents the final state, Done.

15.7.8.4 Boundaries

Each region is bounded on its left and right sides by **boundary lines**. The boundary line on the left represents the total number of items that have arrived at that queue (state) by that point in time. Because the total is cumulative, the left boundary line never falls; it either stays level or rises.

Every region is bounded on the right by a line representing the cumulative total number of stories that have left that queue.

15.7.8.5 Interpreting a Cumulative Flow Diagram

To determine the WIP for a queue, measure the height of the corresponding region. For example, Figure 15.12 indicates that the WIP for testing at the end of day 7 is 4 (6 minus 2).

To determine the **cycle time** for the nth story arriving at the Development queue on a given day, draw a horizontal at n on the y-axis and measure its length from the first boundary line (Arrival to Development) to the last (Arrival to Done). For example, Figure 15.12 indicates that the third item to arrive into development has a cycle time of 7 days (8 minus 1).

To forecast the projected **completion date** at any point in the cycle, project the Arrival to Done line until it intersects the scope line. The time at the intersection point is the projected completion date. For example, Figure 15.13 illustrates a forecast made at the end of day 8 during a ten-day iteration.

As Figure 15.13 indicates, the forecast completion date is day 11—one day past the end of the iteration. Figure 15.13 also suggests that if the increment were released on day 10, it would include only six of the seven stories intended for the iteration.

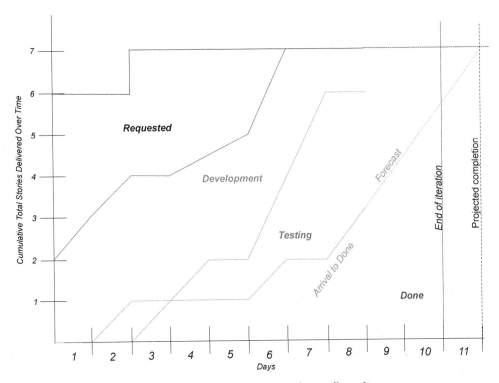

Figure 15.13   *Forecasting delivery date on a cumulative flow diagram*

Cumulative flow diagrams are useful not only for forecasting but also for diagnosing workflow problems to improve performance. The following sections described this use of the diagram.

15.7.8.6 *Diagnosing Bottlenecks*

A bottleneck occurs if items arrive at a queue faster than they can be processed. You can spot bottlenecks on the diagram by looking for areas where a region's height (WIP) increases over time. For example, in Figure 15.12, the Testing region's height increases during days 6 and 7. If you see this pattern, alert the team so they can address the bottleneck (e.g., by adding resources or reassigning other team members to assist testers).

15.7.8.7 *Diagnosing Productivity Issues*

As noted, the distance from the first to last boundary line indicates cycle time. On a healthy team, this distance should stabilize over time. If the length increases as you move to the right (as it does on day 7 in Figure 15.12), it indicates that the cycle time is rising and productivity is decreasing.

15.7.8.8 Diagnosing Sizing Problems (Stories too Big)

Figure 15.12 illustrates another pattern to watch out for—a sudden increase in the slope of the Arrival To Done line at the right end of the chart. This pattern indicates a rush of done stories at the end of the iteration. The likely diagnosis is that story sizes are too close to the maximum, causing stories to reach completion when the iteration is almost over. The remedy is to create smaller stories that are done at a more even pace over the course of the iteration.

15.8 Story Testing and Inspection (Analyze-Code-Build-Test)

Each story under development undergoes analyze-code-build-test cycles until the customer is satisfied that it meets its acceptance criteria. The following is an overview of the process.

15.8.1 Overview of the Analyze-Code-Build-Test Cycle

As an analyst, you begin testing activities before development by working with the PO, testers, and developers to determine acceptance criteria. You specify AC scenarios at the feature level, for example, in feature files using the Gherkin syntax (Given-When-Then). Following test-driven development (TDD) guidelines, programmers write unit tests that are expected to fail initially. Once coding on a unit is complete, the unit tests are rerun and are expected to pass. Low-level integration tests are also run to check the direct connections between the code and the components it communicates with. If the code fails the tests, it is sent back for changes and retested until it passes.

Once this low-level testing is complete, you support the customer—a user or user representative—in testing the solution against the story's acceptance criteria. If the acceptance criteria are met to the customer's satisfaction and other stipulations specified in the DoD are met, the story is considered done.

Following CI/CD and DevOps practices, final integration steps and system tests are carried out continuously as stories are done. They include daily build and smoke tests and automated end-to-end user acceptance testing (UAT). **Smoke tests** are quick, automated tests that verify that the main functions work and that more comprehensive testing can commence. Smoke tests can also include quick-and-dirty tests of existing functionality as the first stage of regression testing. **End-to-end UAT** examines the system or product's behavior when user tasks are strung together the way a customer uses them in a real situation. For example, UAT might include the following sequence of actions:

- For a banking application: A customer opens an account, transfers funds into the account, views the balance, and withdraws funds.

- For an insurance application: A customer submits a claim; an adjuster reviews it; a manager approves it; and payment is made to the customer.

UAT includes automated and manual tests. As noted previously, the automated UAT is performed first; if these are passed, manual UAT is carried out as a final acceptance step before release.

As each story is done, it is **delivered** to the customer—meaning it is *able* to be released into production at the customer's discretion. If the customer delays deployment (e.g., until the feature is competitive), some final tasks may be deferred to the end of the release cycle. Chapter 16 examines those tasks.

All organizations should endeavor to conduct integration and testing continuously and reliably using automation, as advised by DevOps/CI/CD. However, until an organization has these capabilities in place, it may need to postpone some of these activities. This often happens during a reserved, hardening iteration.

For more on hardening iterations, see Chapter 16, "Releasing the Product."

For more on DevOps/CI/CD practices, see Chapter 17, "Scaling Agility."

15.8.2 Validating Value

Testing against acceptance criteria proves that a feature functions as expected. But just because a solution passes its functional tests doesn't mean it was *worth developing*. For example, as a result of a change, the product might now do everything expected of it without impacting the objective to increase customer engagement. The lean startup process includes an extra level of testing to prove that the change achieved the desired outcomes. It advises that leap of faith hypotheses be tested to show that features deliver business value. If a hypothesis is found to be false, the customer must decide whether to pivot to a new hypothesis or continue to try to tweak the product. If a feature's value is validated through testing, it is accepted into the product and supported in future releases.

15.8.2.1 Split Testing

To ensure you have meaningful, actionable test results, use split testing (also known as A/B testing). With this approach, you expose one group, or **cohort**, to the change, while another group—the **control group**—is not exposed to the change. You collect metrics for both groups before and after the initiative to gauge the impact of the change. The approach may also be used to test more than one solution, each with a different user group, in order to gauge which solution is most effective.

15.8.2.2 When to Perform Split Testing

Perform split testing *early and often*. Use it as part of an MVP process to test leap of faith hypotheses in order to inform investment decisions during the early phases of innovative product development. Thereafter, use MVP split testing to test hypotheses for new features before investing heavily in them. Conduct split testing daily to gauge the impact of tweaks to stories. Perform it again when the feature is complete to determine whether to include it in the product.

15.8.2.3 *How Split Testing Works*

To explain how to use split testing to validate a feature's value, let's return to Customer Engagement One (CEO), the app that manages a company's engagements with its customers. Suppose that, in the current iteration, your team is implementing a feature to limit access for users of the free version and remind them about the premium version. The feature's objective is to improve the conversion rate of free users to paid subscribers. Now suppose that the feature has passed all the functional tests specified in its acceptance criteria. For example, reminders pop up, and user access is restricted, just as expected. But that doesn't necessarily mean the feature should be accepted into the product because you don't yet know if it achieved its objectives. To make that determination, you have to measure *outcomes*—in this case, the impact on conversion rate.

Let's assume that you expose a group of users to the changes and the conversion *does* improve. This still would not be enough to prove that the story has been validated, since there may have been other factors that caused the change, such as a drop in the price or an extraneous event that drew more interest in the premium version.

To correct for this effect, lean startup advises that you do what researchers do: isolate the effect you're trying to measure and control for environmental factors by using a control group. In the CEO example, you expose one group of users, Group A, to the changes and leave the other group, Group B, unexposed. Both groups should be similar in every other way and exposed to the same environmental influences. If Group A experiences a conversion rate increase greater than that of Group B, then the improvement must be attributable to the changes because other factors are experienced equally by both groups.

As noted earlier, when conducting split testing, you don't have to stop at two groups. You can test one interface change on Group A, another change on Group B, and have Group C as a control group.

15.8.2.4 *Using Funnel Metrics to Measure Outcomes during Split Testing*

Funnel metrics measure the flow of customers as they advance from one behavior to another in the customer-acquisition workflow. Metrics are tracked for each group involved in a split test. For example, one group experiences one solution (Group A), one group experiences a different solution (Group B), and a control group (Group C) experiences no change. The metrics are analyzed to determine what's working and where to focus future efforts.

Use conversion rate metrics when the objective is to nudge the customer toward desired behaviors (e.g., subscriptions and renewals). The **conversion rate** measures the proportion of customers who advance from one behavior to another in the customer-acquisition workflow. The number of customers at each successive stage in the flow decreases, yielding a funnel shape when illustrated on a chart, as shown in Figure 15.14. For this reason, the behaviors are referred to as **funnel behaviors**.

Let's see how to use these behaviors and metrics to support a data-driven approach that relies on learning to direct product development. The steps are as follows:

- List the behaviors
- Code-test-learn

List the Behaviors

The first step is to identify the funnel behaviors expected of new customers—from the time they come into contact with the product or company (i.e., **enter the funnel**) until they take the desired step (e.g., pay for a subscription). Returning to our previous CEO app example, the funnel behaviors along the path to subscription might be as follows:

- Behavior 1: Customer visits the website.

- Behavior 2: Customer downloads a trial version of the app.

- Behavior 3: Customer activates an account.

- Behavior 4: Customer subscribes.

Code-Test-Learn

Developers implement (code) the change—for example, they tweak a story—and introduce it to a select group of customers. The number of customers who perform each funnel behavior is recorded. A control group that does not experience the change is monitored over the same period. Other groups may also be added, each exposed to a different intervention (e.g., an alternative solution to a user story).

Funnel Chart

The results for each group are illustrated in a funnel chart. One such chart, based on the four behaviors in the previous CEO app example, is shown in Figure 15.14.

Pipeline	
Stage	Amount
Visited website	1000
Downloaded app	500
Activated account	400
Subscribed	100

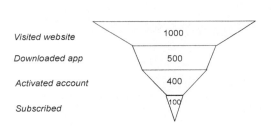

Figure 15.14 *Funnel chart*

Figure 15.14 indicates that one thousand customers entered the funnel by visiting the website. Of these, five hundred downloaded a trial version of the app, four hundred went on to activate their account, and one hundred subscribed.

Create a funnel chart for each group exposed to the changes and the control group that experiences no change. Analyze the charts, compare them with each other to determine which interventions are working, and identify bottlenecks.

Behavior-Trended Funnel

As noted in the previous sections, don't wait till *after* a story is complete to track funnel metrics; track them *over the course* of a story's implementation to test the effectiveness of alternative solutions and changes to the story.

Use a **behavior-trended funnel** to visualize funnel behavior trends as changes are applied. Figure 15.15 is an example of a behavior-trended funnel to track the impact of changes to the CEO interface.

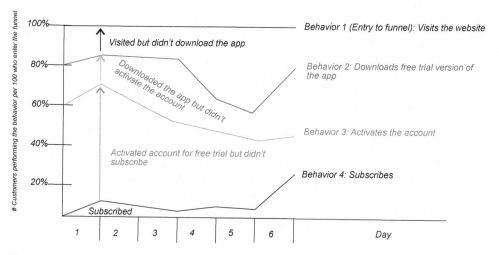

Figure 15.15   *Subscription behavior-trended funnel report*

In Figure 15.15, new tweaks are presented to a group of customers daily over a six-day period, and the impact on funnel behaviors is measured. The top line in Figure 15.15 shows the percentage of customers from the group who performed the first behavior—visited the website. Since that is the behavior that places customers into the funnel, the rate for that behavior is 100 percent.

The next line indicates the customers who performed the next behavior—downloaded a free version of the app. The vertical distance between the top two lines represents those who signed up but *didn't* download the app. A large vertical gap between any two lines indicates a bottleneck in the customer acquisition cycle.

Suppose the gap *decreases* over time (i.e., as you move to the right on the diagram). In that case, the interpretation is that the conversion rate between the behaviors is *increasing* thanks to the interventions—a positive outcome.

By the end of day 6 in Figure 15.15, the largest gap is between behavior 2 (downloading the app) and behavior 3 (activating the account), indicating a bottleneck. This suggests that future efforts should focus on nudging customers who have downloaded the app to activate their account.

15.9 Managing Scope Change during the Iteration

One of the differences between flow-based planning approaches and timeboxed approaches is how you handle scope changes once implementation begins. With flow-based frameworks, the team commits to stories one by one as they come up in the queue. Consequently, stories can be easily reprioritized right up until they are accepted into development.

There is less adaptability with timeboxed planning because an entire *block* of stories is accepted into development in advance during iteration planning—filling the team's budget for the next iteration. Changes are still possible, however, once the iteration begins. The general rule is that changes are allowed as long as the team agrees that the revised iteration backlog does not exceed its capacity or endanger the iteration goal. Now, let's look at some specific scenarios and how to manage them.

15.9.1 When Progress Is Lower or Higher than Expected

One reason to change an iteration's scope is that the team realizes it won't complete the iteration backlog by the end of the iteration. In this case, the team is responsible for promptly notifying the customer and negotiating a remedy (e.g., to delay some of the acceptance criteria for a story or use a less costly design solution). As an analyst, you play a critical role in supporting scope negotiations by exploring ways to deliver the highest-value requirements first.

Alternatively, if the team realizes it will complete the iteration backlog *early*, it should pull in new stories from the product backlog until its remaining capacity is reached.

15.9.2 When the PO Wants to Add Stories After the Iteration Begins

What about cases in which the PO wishes to *add* stories mid-iteration in response to a sudden shift in business priorities? If the team agrees that it has the capacity to take on the added work, the story should be accepted into the iteration. If not, and the PO feels strongly that a new story must be added, work with the team to estimate the new story, and support negotiations between the team and customer on ways to accommodate the work by removing an equivalent amount of work from the iteration backlog.

I should note that this scenario rarely occurs because the upfront commitment with timeboxed frameworks is so short-ranged—as short as one week. It's also not a good practice to parachute new stories into an iteration too often because it results in a loss of productivity due to **thrashing**—time lost to task-switching because the team has to drop what it's working on to take on new work. To avoid this consequence, have both sides agree on guidelines to limit the disruption. For example, require that any added story is within a specified size limit and that the addition must be requested at least two or three days before the iteration's end.

15.10 Updating Business Analysis Documentation

Many organizations know that they should reduce waste during new product development. But that's not where most of the potential waste lies: most software work actually occurs *after* an application is first delivered to the market or into production.[11] That being the case, that's where you should focus your efforts if you want to reduce overall waste. One of the ways to do that is to leverage experience and artifacts from earlier development efforts. For you as an analyst, it means transforming transient knowledge and agile artifacts into BA artifacts, such as process models, use-case models, and business rules that can later be used as references when future changes are requested. In so doing, you eliminate the waste of having to re-create them from scratch in the future. Many teams make the mistake of waiting until product release to update this information—by which time much of the original meaning may be lost. As a general rule, if something is worth documenting, it's worth documenting continuously.

> Don't document for the sake of documenting. Make sure you can identify at least one reason for creating the artifact and at least one question that it will be able to answer.

The next sections explore the types of BA information that may be documented. *BABOK v3* defines **business analysis information** as being "comprised of all the information business analysts elicit, create, compile, and disseminate in the course of performing business analysis," including "models, scope statements, stakeholder concerns, elicitation results, requirements, designs, and solution options."[12]

15.10.1 Persisting Stories

Each user story is a work item, sized to flow smoothly through the development process. When the story is done, it has served its primary purpose. Yet the story text, its acceptance criteria, and associated notes and diagrams often contain knowledge about requirements worth capturing for future reference. The act of saving this information is sometimes referred to as **persisting** the requirements (with apologies to grammarians); the resulting documentation is described as being **persistent**.

The problem with saving stories, though, is that they are too small to be useful for reference purposes. Each story describes only a small aspect of functionality. Sometimes, it represents an early, stripped-down version of something that was later replaced. What's needed for reference purposes is a requirements artifact that rolls up *all* of the user stories regarding the same user task. Two options that fit the bill are feature files and use cases. You can either use one exclusively or use the two together. Let's explore these options.

---

11. Mary Poppendieck and Tom Poppendieck, *Lean Software Development: An Agile Toolkit* (Boston: Addison-Wesley, 2003), 49.

12. International Institute of Business Analysis (IIBA), *BABOK v3: A Guide to the Business Analysis Body of Knowledge*, 3rd ed. (Toronto, Canada: IIBA, 2015), 42.

15.10.2 Feature Documentation: Organize by Features, Not Stories

The most straightforward (and widespread) approach is to document at the feature level rather than the story level. Each feature represents a user task, including the requirements for all of its user stories. As we've seen in previous chapters (see Chapter 10), you begin this process before implementation. As explained in that chapter, you can do so by creating a feature file[13] for each feature-level requirement. You specify the acceptance criteria for the feature's stories inside the feature file in natural language, for example, using the Gherkin Given-When-Then syntax. For example, a feature to introduce dropship capability may include acceptance criteria for identifying a dropship-eligible product and acceptance criteria for indicating when a dropship product is no longer for sale.

The resulting feature files with their acceptance criteria serve as reference requirements documentation and as specifications for automated and manual tests, including UAT.

For examples and guidance on specifying features, feature acceptance criteria, and the Gherkin syntax, see Chapter 10, section 10.9.

15.10.3 Updating the Use-Case Model

An alternative—or complementary—option is to document user requirements as use cases. A **use case** is a user task. It represents *"all the ways* of using a system [or product] to achieve a particular goal by a particular user."[14] A **use-case scenario** is one of those ways—one path through the use case. Examples of use cases are *Submit a claim, View newsfeed, Add a contact.* An example of a use-case scenario is *Submit a claim with incomplete information.* A **use-case diagram** shows who does what: it indicates the use cases for the product and associates them with the **actors** (user roles or external systems) who use them.

Each use case is defined in a **use-case specification.** The specification documents the use-case scenarios to varying levels of granularity. Use-case specifications provide similar information to BDD specifications, such as preconditions and postconditions. However, use cases can also include more detailed descriptions of the interaction between user and system, along with links to supplementary requirements such as NFRs and business rules.

A use-case specification is typically organized into **flows.** A **basic flow** (also called **normal flow** or **happy-day scenario**) describes an end-to-end success scenario, without optional actions or errors. Alternative flows describe steps that occur in other scenarios (e.g., when the user elects to print a receipt or when an error occurs).

Use Case 2.0 was released in 2011. Its main innovation was introducing the use-case slice as the atomic requirements unit for agile planning. A **use-case slice** represents one or more complete vertical passes through a use case. Each slice is sized like a user story. It differs from a user story, though, in the manner in which the requirements are typically represented.

For more on use cases, see Chapter 10, section 10.17.

---

13. Jens Engel, Benno Rice, and Richard Jones, "Feature Testing Setup," GitHub, https://behave.readthedocs.io/en/latest/gherkin.html

14. Ivar Jacobson, Ian Spence, and Kurt Bittner. *Use-Case 2.0 The Guide to Succeeding with Use Cases* (London: Ivar Jacobson International, SA. 2011), 4.

15.10.3.1 The Use-Case-Only Approach

The most effective way to work with use cases is to begin the model during the preliminary analysis before development and update it continuously. First, you discover the user roles (actors) and the use cases for the initiative. Then, you split the use cases into use-case slices. You use the slices for planning and managing development work. After a use-case slice is done, you save its requirements at the use-case level and discard the use-case slice.

The benefit of the use-case-only approach is that it provides one paradigm across the entire change initiative. You can address the business perspective in a **business use-case model**[15] and use that to define the system's user requirements in a **system use-case model**. There are even tools available to generate code from use-case models and associated Unified Modeling Language (UML) diagrams. Moreover, the transition from development work items (use-case slices) to reference documentation (use cases) is seamless. Use-case specifications are well suited for reference purposes because they're organized and described from the user's perspective. They're also similar in format to manual test scripts, making them ideal as a source for testing. For all of these reasons, the use-case-only approach is an excellent choice—at least in theory—yet few teams use it.

15.10.3.2 The Hybrid Approach: User Stories Plus Use Cases

The reality is that most agile teams use user stories, not use-case slices, for planning—even when they organize their persistent requirements documentation around use cases. A primary reason is that user stories were already well entrenched by the time use-case slices were introduced.[16] The ubiquity of the approach means it's easier to find team members and tools that support user stories during agile development than it is for use-case slices. Another reason teams prefer user stories during development is that they are leaner than use cases: there is less documentation to update and less formality about their format—making the approach more amenable to changes.

When teams do use use cases, it tends to be *in combination* with user stories. They use user stories to plan development, *and* they update the use-case model for future reference—either continuously (the preferable approach) or before release. The hybrid approach creates waste caused by duplicated effort yet can still provide a net benefit. The use of user stories during development keeps the process lean. Once stories are developed, their translation into use-case artifacts optimizes them for reuse on future maintenance and enhancement efforts. The costs and benefits of these approaches depend on the circumstance. Allow teams to experiment to see which works best.

In the following sections, we review the main aspects of use-case documentation.

---

15. For detailed guidance on business and system use cases, see Howard Podeswa, *UML for the IT Business Analyst*, 2nd ed. (Boston: Cengage Learning PTR, 2009).

16. User stories were invented in 1998–1999. Use-case slices weren't introduced until 2011 with the release of Jacobson, Spence, and Bittner's *Use Case 2.0*.

15.10.3.3 How to Capture Agile Artifacts in the Use-Case Model

Since most agile teams that employ use cases do so using the hybrid approach described earlier (i.e., in combination with user stories), let's explore how to transform requirements from one form into the other.

As noted previously, agile artifacts, such as user stories and story maps, are optimized for agile planning purposes, but they're not well suited for reference purposes. To illustrate how to create useful requirements documentation from them, let's return to the CEO example we've been following—the app that enables companies to manage their engagements with customers from a single interface. Figure 15.16 is a story map backbone developed to plan one of the release cycles.

The story map in Figure 15.16 indicates three tasks that are triggered internally by the system:

- *Ingest messages* (load messages from multiple sources)
- *Auto-classify messages* (use artificial intelligence to categorize messages, e.g., as a complaint)
- *Auto-triage messages* (prioritize messages)

A Tier 1 support representative can perform the following user tasks:

- View threads
- Filter messages in their inbox
- Sort messages
- Triage messages
- Assign a message to another support rep

A Tier *n* support (i.e., Tier 1, 2, or 3 support) may perform the following:

- Record an action taken against an issue
- Resolve an issue

A support manager can view analytics.

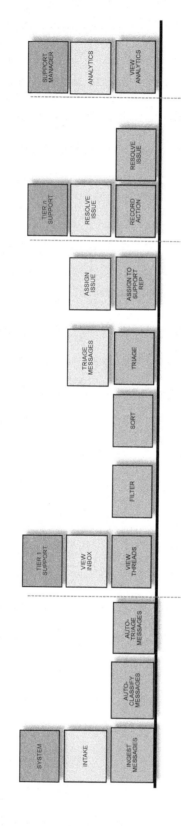

Figure 15.16 *CEO story map backbone*

Figure 15.17 is the use-case diagram that resulted from the story map backbone in Figure 15.16.

The use cases in Figure 15.17 correspond to the user tasks in the backbone of Figure 15.16 (e.g., *Assign to support rep, Record action*). Note that *Ingest messages, Auto-triage messages*, and *Auto-classify messages* represent tasks that are not triggered by a human user but by the system itself. The use cases in the model correspond to feature-level items in the product backlog. For example, the use case *Place an order* corresponds to the backlog feature *As a customer service agent, I want to place an order*.

The stick figures and boxes in Figure 15.17 represent actors—external entities (humans and external systems) that interact with the software system under discussion. A **primary actor** initiates the interaction. Indicate a primary actor by pointing an arrow from the actor to a use case. A **secondary actor** is involved only after the use case begins. To indicate a secondary actor, point an arrow from a use case to the actor.

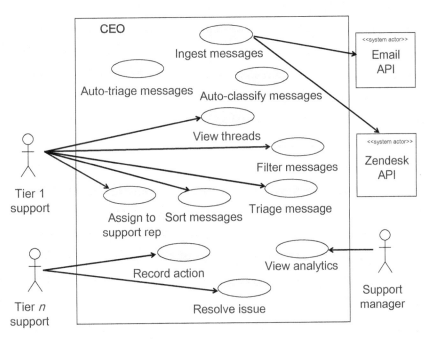

Figure 15.17 *CEO use-case diagram*

BLINK CASE STUDY PART 26

Create BLInK Use-Case Model

The Ask
As an analyst on the team, you've been tasked with creating a use-case model that teams will refer to when making future changes. The deliverable is as follows:

- **Deliverable 1**: BLInK use-case diagram

Inputs

- BLInK story map backbone (see Figure 12.4 in Chapter 12, "MVPs and Story Maps")

What Transpires

You translate the user cards and user task cards on the BLInK story map to actors and use cases on a use-case diagram, as shown in Figure 15.18.

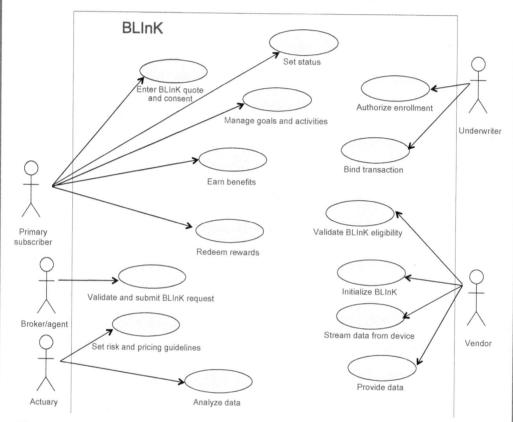

Figure 15.18   *BLInK use-case model*

Deliverables

Deliverables 1: BLInK Use-Case Model

Case Study Retrospective

The BLInK use-case diagram provides an overview of the usages that BLInK must support and the people who use them. This model will be used to organize the requirements specifications from the users' perspective, based on how they experience the system. Should any change be requested in the future to a use case in the model, the diagram will help identify the impacted user roles and interfaces to external systems. As an analyst, you'll also be able to use the diagram as a visual table of contents to locate affected use cases and find more detailed requirements in the use-case specifications to which they're linked.

15.10.3.4 Updating Use-Case Specifications

The use-case diagram is only an overview. More information is provided in the use-case specifications that lie behind the picture. Supply only as much detail as is useful. Levels of granularity may range from a **use-case brief** that provides summary information alone (trigger, preconditions, postconditions) to a full specification that describes significant scenarios in detail.

To illustrate how to roll up user stories into a use-case specification, let's examine the stories that might appear under a *Submit claim* on a story map for processing insurance claims. Figure 15.19 shows the user stories and their acceptance criteria.

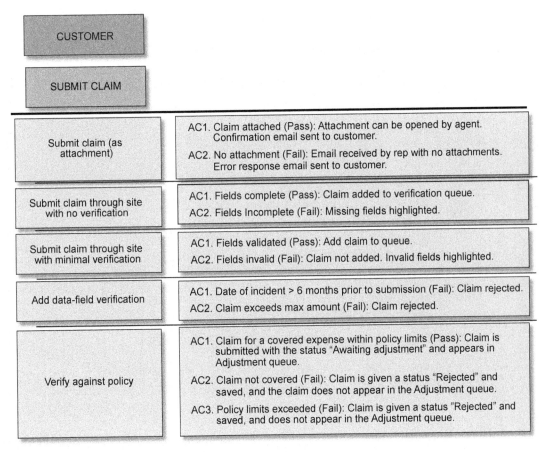

Figure 15.19   *Claims stories for the use case Submit claim*

Following is the use-case specification created from those stories:

Use Case UC023: Submit claim

Use-Case Brief

Primary Actor: Customer

Secondary Actor: Policy system (PS)

Trigger: User selects the function.

Preconditions: Customer with current policy has been authorized.

Postconditions:

Accepted Claim

- Claim has been submitted with the status "Awaiting adjustment."
- Claim appears in the Adjustment queue.

Rejected Claim

- Claim has been saved in the system with a "Rejected" status.
- Claim does not appear in the Adjustment queue.

Basic Flow: Claim submitted for a covered expense within policy limits.

1. The user identifies the policy against which the claim is being made.
2. The system verifies the policy exists and is current. (A1)
3. The user identifies the type of claim being made.
4. The system preverifies the claim against the user's insurance policy. (A2) (A3)
5. The user enters fields on the claim form.
6. The system verifies the claim form data fields. (A4) (A5)
7. The system submits the claim with a status of "Awaiting adjustment."
8. The system places the claim on the Adjustment queue.

Alternative Flows

A1. **Not a current policy:** Claim has been saved in the system, with a "rejected" status, and the claim does not appear on the Adjustment queue.

A2. **Claim not covered by policy:** Claim has been saved in the system, with a "rejected" status, and the claim does not appear on the Adjustment queue.

A3. **Policy limits exceeded:** Claim has been saved in the system, with a "rejected" status, and the claim does not appear on the Adjustment queue.

A4. **Invalid data for field type or data missing:** Invalid and missing fields (dates, postal codes, etc.) are highlighted. User can reenter data. (Claim not accepted until errors are cleared.)

A5. **Date of incident more than 6 months prior:** Claim has been saved in the system, with a "rejected" status, and the claim does not appear on the Adjustment queue.

Let's examine the components of the specification.

The Use-Case Brief

The use-case brief contains summary information about the use case. Include a description of the following elements:

- **Trigger:** The event or condition that forces the use case to begin. The trigger corresponds to the Gherkin *when* step.

- **Preconditions:** Conditions that must be true before the use case can begin. Preconditions correspond to the Gherkin *given* step.

- **Postconditions:** Summarize the outcomes of relevance. These correspond to the Gherkin *then* step.

The Flows

The basic flow describes a simple successful scenario assuming all validations are successful and no optional steps are taken. **Alternative flows** describe other pathways through the use case—such as errors and optional steps.

A flow roughly corresponds to an acceptance criterion scenario except that a flow usually highlights only a select *set* of steps taken under specified conditions, whereas a scenario covers an entire interaction. Furthermore, a scenario might pass through several flows. For example, a scenario for express delivery might begin with some basic flow steps, then veer off to an alternative flow to perform steps specific to express delivery and return to a step in the basic flow.

Keep in mind that user stories are incremental. One story might supplement or replace functionality specified in prior user stories. For example, the acceptance criteria of an early story using manual data verification might be superseded by acceptance criteria in a later story that uses system verifications. The use-case specification should reflect the *cumulative behavior* of the most recent increment.

15.10.4 Other Analysis Documentation

Other models discussed in Chapter 10, such as process models, context diagrams, data flow diagrams, and architectural diagrams, should also be created and updated continuously.

15.10.5 Tracing Analysis Artifacts

To answer requirements questions that will arise in the future, it's not enough to have persistent requirements artifacts; you also need to persist the *relationships* between them. The most important relationships to trace are those between features and their tests. If you're using Gherkin, you achieve this by creating a feature file for each feature and specifying the acceptance criteria scenarios of its subordinate user stories using the Gherkin syntax. These specifications are then used as the basis for testing.

With the use-case approach, you can trace use cases or (for more granular tracing) *use-case flows* to test scenarios. Recall that a use-case flow is a set of steps, not necessarily an entire end-to-end scenario. A flow may be part of one or more test scenarios; a scenario may incorporate one or more flows. At a minimum, every use-case flow should be traceable to at least one test scenario. Risky combinations of flows (e.g., two errors occurring during the same interaction) should also be tested.

You also trace features and use cases against artifacts other than tests. For example, suppose there is a change request to modify the feature (use case) *Submit a claim* in order to accommodate new coverages. In that case, you'd want to know if there are any dependency relationships between *Submit claim* and other features (use cases) because they flag possible impacts elsewhere in the product. For example, the dependent use case *Adjust a claim* might be affected.

We look at different ways to trace requirements items in the following sections. Keep in mind that the effort to trace these artifacts adds overhead. Determine the right degree of traceability for the situation, balancing the cost of increased overhead against the benefits of shortened cycle time to respond to future changes and increased confidence when those changes are released.

15.10.5.1 Tracing Use Cases and Features Upward (Backward Traceability)

Upward traceability links an item backward to higher-level items. For example, trace a feature back to the business goals, objectives, and processes it supports; the SMEs who provided information about it; and the personas and user roles who use it.

15.10.5.2 Tracing Horizontally (Cross-stream Traceability)

Horizontal or **cross-stream traceability** links a feature or use case to items at the same level. Use horizontal traceability to assess how a change to one feature (or use case) might impact other features (or use cases). For example, the feature (use case) *Place an order* is traced to the feature *Fulfill an order*. This signals that if *Place an order* is updated, changes to *Fulfill an order* may also be required. Furthermore, if either feature is changed, both should be tested.

15.10.5.3 Tracing Downstream (Forward Traceability)

Downward or **forward traceability** links a use case to artifacts further downstream in the development cycle. For example, you can trace features and use cases downstream to related user interfaces, databases, automated tests, and software services to flag the items that might be affected if the use case is changed in the future.

BLINK CASE STUDY PART 27

BLInK Traceability

The Ask

You've been asked to prepare for an upcoming development effort that will focus on the use case *Enter BLInK quote and consent* included earlier in the use-case model (see Figure 15.18). As part of this effort, you've decided to implement traceability mechanisms where they do not yet exist so that changes may be implemented quickly and with confidence.

What Transpires

You trace the use case *Enter BLInK quote and consent* upward to the business process and objectives it supports, the user role that uses it, and the SME who was the primary source of information. You trace it horizontally to other use cases and downstream to the test cases and components created or impacted by the use case.

Event Outputs

Figure 15.20 is a visual representation of the use case and the artifacts to which it has been traced.

Case Study Retrospective

Because of the traceability you provided, if the use-case requirements are changed in a future release, you will be able to quickly determine which SMEs to interview, which tests to rerun, and which end-to-end business processes to retest.

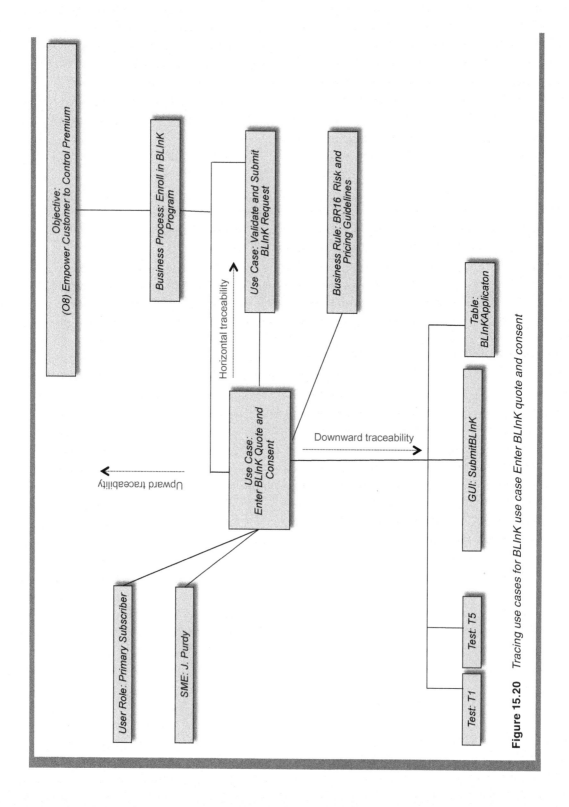

Figure 15.20 Tracing use cases for BLInK use case Enter BLInK quote and consent

15.11 Ongoing Analysis of Upcoming Epics, Features, and Stories

As work on current stories progresses, your attention as an analyst turns toward backlog preparation, referred to, in Scrum, as *product backlog refinement*: "Product Backlog refinement is the act of breaking down and further defining Product Backlog items into smaller more precise items. This is an ongoing activity to add details, such as a description, order, and size. Attributes often vary with the domain of work."[17] Technical activities are also carried out at this time—for example, preparation of the architectural runway. In this chapter, we'll be focusing on preparatory analysis activities.

Backlog preparation is an incremental activity: the closer a backlog item is to its scheduled implementation, the more detailed the analysis and the more precise the estimate.

15.11.1 How Long Should You Spend on Preparation?

As a rule of thumb, the total time spent on backlog preparation tasks should not exceed 10 percent of the team budget. However, this is only a rough guide as the actual required time will depend on multiple factors, such as the team's familiarity with the upcoming stories and the requirements' complexity.

15.11.2 Overview of Rolling Preparatory Analysis

You conduct the preliminary analysis of upcoming backlog items in a rolling fashion as their forecast implementation date comes into view.

As the end of a long-term planning period comes to a close, you begin visioning and planning for the next epic or initiative, as described in Chapters 7, 8, and 9. If the team uses flow-based planning, you prepare each feature as it approaches the top of the backlog to be feature ready. For example, you ensure it is deliverable within three months by one or more teams and begin to split it into stories. You prepare each story a few weeks before its forecast implementation date.

On the other hand, if your team uses timeboxed planning, you prepare requirements items in groups. You start preparing *all* the features intended for each upcoming quarter partway into the previous one to be ready for quarterly planning. Similarly, you prepare all the stories for an upcoming iteration to be ready in time for iteration planning.

From time to time, you also facilitate a whole-product review of the product backlog to clean out items that are no longer needed and reprioritize those that remain. This activity is referred to as **pruning and ordering**.

Feature and story preparation may sound familiar. That's because we covered them previously, in the context of the initial seeding of the backlog. First, we review feature and story preparation, focusing on how to conduct it once development is underway. Then we examine pruning and ordering.

---

17. Schwaber and Sutherland, *The Scrum Guide*, 10.

15.11.3 Feature Preparation

Feature preparation is the preliminary analysis and design of features before development. The objective of feature preparation is to produce a **ready feature**—one that is prioritized, reliably estimable, deliverable in three months or less by one or more teams, and able to be implemented without undue delay or rework. Feature preparation may include the following activities:

- Design activities (e.g., testing proofs of concept, creating wireframes, drafting a solution design)

- Preparation of the architectural runway—the "existing code, components, and technical infrastructure needed to implement high-priority, near-term features without excessive delay and redesign"[18]

- Decomposition into stories

- Specification of feature acceptance criteria

- Other analysis activities such as stakeholder and persona analysis, process analysis, use-case analysis, journey mapping, and value stream mapping

15.11.3.1 Timing

Start feature preparation at the last responsible moment, leaving just enough time to bring features to readiness before their planned implementation.

If your team uses a flow-based planning approach, start preparing each feature as it nears the top of the queue—with a lead time of about two to four weeks for a small feature and up to six weeks for a large feature. Adjust the time according to the feature's size and complexity and the team's familiarity with the feature's business and technical aspects.

If your team uses a timeboxed approach, begin preparing all the features lined up for the next quarter about halfway into the prior quarter. All of the features should satisfy the feature DoR on entry to quarterly planning (assuming the team uses a feature DoR). For example, the feature must be deliverable within a quarter by one or more teams. Perform the most granular analysis on the first features to be implemented with decreasing detail for features further back in the quarterly backlog.

 For more on feature preparation, see Chapter 10, "Quarterly and Feature Preparation."

15.11.4 Story Preparation

During feature preparation, upcoming items became feature ready. As work items in the backlog get even closer to development, they must pass a second hurdle: they must be **story-ready. Story preparation** is the work to bring stories to that state. At a minimum, to be story-ready, the item must be prioritized, estimable, deliverable by a single team within

---

18. Richard Kastner and Dean Leffingwell, *SAFe 5.0 Distilled: Achieving Business Agility with the Scaled Agile Framework* (Boston: Addison-Wesley, 2020), 263.

a short period (e.g., within 8 story points, or one iteration), and free from impediments that would delay delivery. If the team uses a story DoR, as advised in this book, then a ready story must satisfy the conditions listed in the story DoR.

All stories must be ready before they are accepted into development. If the team uses a timeboxed approach, the stories must be ready on entry to iteration planning.

15.11.4.1 Story Preparation: Analysis Activities

Preparatory analysis tasks for stories include the following:

- Specifying story acceptance criteria
- Estimating stories
- Ensuring stories have been recently discussed and prioritized
- Splitting stories
- Grouping or merging small stories that should be delivered together
- Eliciting and analyzing requirements
- Supporting collaboration between business stakeholders and developers to negotiate alternatives when the estimated effort exceeds the budget
- Implementing functional spikes
- Conducting other business analysis activities as needed (e.g., business rules analysis)
- Addressing dependencies and impediments

15.11.4.2 Addressing Dependencies and Impediments

If an upcoming item, Story A, has an unresolved dependency on Story B, work with Story B's team to explore moving B forward. If you find analysis gaps in an upcoming story, fill them. If this analysis work is nontrivial and will be performed during the iteration, add it to the developer task board. If you plan to perform it in a subsequent iteration, add the work as a functional spike to the product backlog so that it can be prioritized against other items. If you discover other impediments, bring them to others' attention (e.g., raise the lack of resources with the ScrumMaster).

For extensive guidelines on preparing stories, see Chapter 13, "Story Preparation." For guidelines on specifying functional spikes (enabler stories), see section 13.11.2.

15.11.4.3 Timing Considerations

Begin preparing upcoming stories about one to four weeks (one or two iterations) before their planned implementation. Hold a number of small Triad meetings over time, selecting attendees according to the story under discussion.

If the team uses a timeboxed framework with a two-week cadence, the first week of the iteration is usually focused on current stories and the second week on story preparation for the following iteration. When iterations are one week long, story preparation is often added to the end of the iteration planning meeting.

 For more on feature preparation, see Chapter 10, "Quarterly and Feature Preparation."

15.11.5 Pruning and Ordering

Over time, product backlogs collect old items that no longer have any value. These act as noise in the system and cause waste. The first objective of pruning and ordering is to prune these obsolete items. The second objective is to reorder the remaining items across the backlog so that they reflect current priorities.

15.11.5.1 Who Should Attend?

The primary attendees at a pruning and ordering meeting are the PO and business stake-holders. There is some disagreement about whether or not developers should be present. If the items being discussed are routine requests, some organizations exclude developers, arguing that there is no need to involve them, since prioritization is an internal business matter. However, it's often useful to have developers on hand because they can suggest innovative ways to resolve seemingly conflicting priorities.[19] For example, they might offer less costly alternatives for implementing a feature—leaving room in the budget for a technical story to improve the code's quality. In addition to the above attendees, you, the analyst, should also be present, as explained in the following section.

Analyst Contribution

As an analyst, you add value to pruning and ordering meetings in numerous ways. You may serve as the meeting's facilitator. During the meeting, you may help stakeholders and developers resolve prioritization conflicts and reach a consensus. Finally, as the role responsible for managing the backlog, you personify institutional memory regarding its items—many of which may have been there for a long time, forgotten even by their original authors. As these items are discussed, you can explain their meanings and why they were initially requested.

15.11.5.2 Frequency

Hold pruning and ordering meetings once a week to once a month, depending on how quickly business priorities change. Aside from scheduled events, the events should also be convened ad hoc whenever priorities change.

---

19. Kent Beck, "Planning: Managing Scope," *Extreme Programming Explained: Embrace Change,* 2nd ed., The XP Series (Boston: Addison-Wesley, 2005).

15.12 Accounting for Progress at the End of the Iteration

At the end of each iteration or chosen period (e.g., one week), add up the estimation units for all the delivered stories to determine the achieved velocity. For example, if 40 story points were delivered over the past iteration, the velocity is 40 points/iteration.

15.12.1 Accounting for Stories That Are Not Done

If a story was not completed during the iteration, carry the entire story and its estimation units into the next iteration. In this case, none of the story's estimation units are counted toward the current iteration because no value was delivered.

This circumstance should be rare. If it's common for stories to be incomplete at the end of an iteration, explore the root cause. Often, the reason is chronic underestimation by the development team. In this case, the team should take greater care to ensure it understands stories well enough when asked to provide estimates—and push back against the PO when it doesn't have sufficient understanding. As an analyst, you take an active part in attaining that objective through conversations with the PO, users, and business stakeholders; by communicating that understanding to the team; and by ensuring the team has considered alternative solution proposals as part of the estimation process.

15.12.2 Accounting for Progress When an Iteration Is Canceled

The Scrum guide declares that a sprint (iteration) "could be canceled" by the PO "if the Sprint Goal becomes obsolete."[20] In practice, however, cancellations rarely happen. More commonly, if the iteration goal is endangered, the PO and team readjust the iteration goal and the remaining stories in the iteration backlog according to what can be delivered by the end of the iteration.

On the rare occasion where cancellation does occur, it happens under the direction of the PO, in consultation with the development team, ScrumMaster, and other business stakeholders. The reasons to cancel an iteration may include the following:

- Unexpected technological difficulties
- A shift in the market that changes priorities
- A new opportunity that the business must address quickly

When an iteration is canceled, return all unstarted stories to the product backlog so that the PO can reprioritize them against other items. Stories that have been partially done are reviewed by the PO. If the PO determines that part of the story is potentially releasable, that part of the work is deemed done and included in the team's velocity. The remaining requirements and acceptance criteria are packaged into a new story, estimated by the team, returned to product backlog, and sequenced by the PO.

---

20. Schwaber and Sutherland, *The Scrum Guide*, 8.

15.13 The Iteration Review

An **iteration review** (also known as a sprint review/demo) is held at the end of each iteration. The iteration review is an inspect-and-adapt event to examine the increment, adjust the product backlog, and make course corrections to future plans. Its perspective should be forward looking; don't let the event become a backward-looking judgment of past performance. The iteration review is also a team motivator—a chance for developers to show off what they have been working on to stakeholders.

As a broad guideline, the iteration review is not meant to be about signoffs because the PO will have already seen the stories *during* the iteration and expressed satisfaction with them. In practice, though, agile organizations vary in how they handle signoffs in the review. For example, some teams have a two-step approvals process. In step 1, stories are initially approved during the iteration by the PO or a business SME, bringing the story to done. Step 2 occurs during the iteration review. At that time, the story is reviewed and approved by a wider group of stakeholders in the context of the entire increment, bringing the story to "done done."

In other organizations, the PO doesn't accept stories until the iteration review, at which time the PO may decide the story is done, not done—or done *enough* to be released but that more work is required. In the latter case, you add a new story for the remaining work to the product backlog.

The following attendees should be present at the review:

- PO

- Business stakeholders invited by the PO

- Development team

- Analyst: Participates as a member of the development team. May act as a facilitator.

- ScrumMaster: Responsible for ensuring the event takes place each iteration and provides coaching as needed.

The meeting's maximum duration is four hours for a one-month iteration or less for shorter iterations.

15.13.1 Inputs and Deliverable

Prepare the following inputs for an iteration review:

- Iteration backlog

- Product backlog

- Progress charts (e.g., release burndown, burnup chart)

- Completed stories

The deliverables of an iteration review are an updated record of progress (e.g., burndown chart) and a revised product backlog, including stories lined up for the next iteration.

15.13.2 Topics/Agenda

Use the following as a list of topics to discuss or as an agenda if the meeting is formal:

- Iteration overview
- Demo
- Forecast
- Collaboration
- Final review

These are discussed in the following sections.

15.13.2.1 Iteration Overview

The development lead, ScrumMaster, or someone else nominated by the team, provides an overview of the following:

- Progress toward the iteration goal
- The stories that were done
- The stories that were planned but not done
- The successes and challenges that occurred during the iteration

QA professionals and developers confirm that the stories' automated tests have been created and added to the test bank, as specified in the DoD.

15.13.2.2 Demo

In this part of the review, stories are demonstrated, and business stakeholders provide feedback about the implementation. The focus should be on collecting feedback, not on resolving problems.

There is no rule about who gives the demo. Typically, either one person, such as the analyst or development lead, presents the entire demo, or the developer who led the implementation of a story demonstrates the story. The team should experiment to see what works best.

According to the original *Scrum Guide* rules, only done items should be demonstrated in the review meeting. (The current 2020 guide is more ambiguous; it refers to inspecting the sprint's "outcome."[21]) In practice, stories that meet some but not all of their acceptance criteria are also demonstrated. This is because the customer may decide a story is

---

21. Schwaber and Sutherland, *The Scrum Guide*, 9.

complete enough for release despite lacking some of the requested functionality. In this case, the story is accepted and a new story for the unmet requirements is added to the backlog.

15.13.2.3 Forecast

The PO discusses the team's progress through the product backlog, identifies the items lined up for the next iteration, and provides updated forecasts for the remaining items in the quarterly (release) backlog. A release burndown chart and other artifacts (described in subsequent sections) may be used for forecasting purposes and to review progress. Stakeholders discuss any changes they'd like to see in the backlog with the PO and the team.

15.13.2.4 Collaboration and Final Review

Attendees collaborate to determine how they will approach the next iteration. In the final review, the PO reviews the changes to the plan, the stories planned for upcoming iterations, the resources being made available for their implementation, and the anticipated timelines for the remaining items in the backlog.

15.13.3 Iteration Review—Artifacts for Forecasting and Tracking Progress

Transparency requires that progress must be visible at any time to business stakeholders. Progress updates should be made *at least* once during the iteration in the iteration review. Workflow management software, such as JIRA, is often used for this purpose. The tools automatically generate progress artifacts such as release burndown charts.

15.13.3.1 Quarterly/Release Burndown Chart

Many of the artifacts used during the iteration review, such as quarterly (release) burndown and burnup charts, have the same form as those we saw earlier in this chapter for use during the iteration. However, their scope is an entire quarter or release cycle rather than a single iteration. Figure 15.21 is an example of a quarterly (release) burndown chart.

The solid, falling line in Figure 15.21 tracks the number of story points remaining in the quarterly (release) backlog at any time. The dashed line indicates the ideal burndown. The top line is the scope line. It shows the total story points in the backlog, including those that have—and have not—been done. The scope line's drop at iteration 2 is due to story points being removed from the backlog. The dotted lines are projections, assuming no further items are added or dropped from the backlog.

Figure 15.21 indicates that at the end of the fourth iteration, progress has been proceeding at a steady rate that is faster than expected. At this point, the diagram forecasts that the remaining points will burn down to zero early—just after the end of the fifth iteration. Based on this forecast, the development team might agree to pull in more stories into the release backlog.

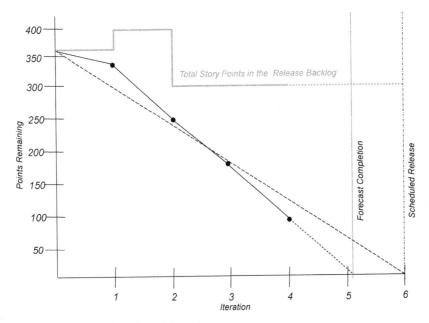

Figure 15.21   *Quarterly (release) burndown chart*

Keep in mind that charts and analytical models are useful for forecasting purposes, but they should not override experience. Developer forecasts, based on past, analogous experience, are still the best basis for prediction.

15.14 The Iteration Retrospective

Continuous improvement is a pillar of lean development and integral to any agile approach. Timeboxed planning frameworks guarantee this happens regularly by requiring an iteration retrospective (referred to, in Scrum, as a *sprint retrospective*) to be held at the end of every iteration. The meeting is an opportunity for the team to reflect on the people involved in the initiative, their relationships, the development process, and tools. Based on these reflections, the team plans actionable improvements that it can implement immediately.

15.14.1 Timing Considerations

The meeting occurs at the end of the iteration after the iteration review. The maximum duration of the event is three hours for a one-month iteration. For a two-week iteration, the maximum time is one hour; for a one-week iteration, it's thirty minutes.

15.14.2 Attendees

The following people should attend:

- PO (See section 15.14.2.1 for notes on PO attendance.)
- Development team
- Team analyst: Participates as a member of the development team; may act as a facilitator
- ScrumMaster (SM): Responsible for ensuring the event takes place each iteration and provides coaching as needed; reflects on the SM's own opportunities for self-improvement

15.14.2.1 Should the PO Attend?

The short answer is yes. The long answer is that there are varying opinions about whether the PO should attend. Scrum appears to say yes: it calls for the *Scrum team* to attend—and the PO is a member of the Scrum team. On the other hand, some of the teams I work with prefer not to invite POs because they find their presence suppresses an open discussion of problems. My view is to invite the PO because the event is about improving collaboration—and the PO is a critical partner in the collaborative relationship. However, if the PO's presence *is* disruptive, the ScrumMaster should intervene by coaching the PO to view the meeting as an opportunity for self-reflection and improvement. If that is ineffective, exclude the PO from subsequent retrospectives.

15.14.3 Inputs and Deliverables

The inputs to the meeting are the process improvement tasks created during the previous meeting. There should be no other preparation for the meeting.

The meeting's deliverables are process improvement tasks. Add high-priority improvement tasks to the iteration backlog for the upcoming iteration.

15.14.4 Topics

The meeting should be informal. Following is a sample list of topics to cover during the meeting.

- Overview
- Review: What worked and what didn't
- Create an improvement plan

These are discussed in the following sections.

15.14.4.1 Overview

Attendees reflect on the people involved in the initiative, their relationships, the development process, and the tools used by the team.

15.14.4.2 Review: What Worked and What Didn't

Attendees discuss what worked in the last iteration, what didn't work, and what they ought to be doing to improve.

The following questions may be used to drive the discussion:

- What did we do that we should *keep on doing*?

- What did we do that we should *stop doing*?

- What should we *start doing* that we aren't already doing?

- Did we meet the iteration goal?

- What metrics did we gather, and what did we find? What does the data tell us about the value of our improvements?

- What happened to the process improvement items we created in the last retrospective? What action items worked, and what did not?

As the requirements SME, you reflect and report on changes to requirements management in areas such as best practices, requirements tools, and story preparation.

> **Tips for Analyst/Facilitator**
>
> As an experienced analyst, your soft skills and background provide a wealth of techniques to draw from as a retrospective facilitator. For example, if there are strong personalities in the room, you may use **silent brainstorming** to give everyone an equal footing. To apply the technique to an iteration retrospective, post three columns on the wall: Start Doing, Stop Doing, and Continue Doing. Pass out stickies. Ask attendees to fill out the stickies silently, reflecting on these categories, and post them to the appropriate columns. Once there are no more contributions, facilitate a discussion about each category, beginning with explanations by the items' authors.

In section 15.4.5, we'll look further at facilitator techniques and games used in the context of iteration retrospectives.

15.14.4.3 Create an Improvement Plan

Attendees create an actionable plan for improvements that can be implemented *immediately* during the upcoming iteration. Add high-priority items to the upcoming iteration backlog; add other improvement items to the product backlog so that they can be prioritized against other items.

Improvements related to the BA practice may include

- Changes to the DoD, story DoR, and feature DoR
- Changes to requirements management tools and the way they are used
- Changes to the approvals process, estimation methods, and iteration length

The team will review high-priority process improvement items in the upcoming iteration planning meeting—adding developer tasks to the iteration backlog to address them. Progress on those tasks is reviewed in the next iteration retrospective meeting.

Example

During an iteration retrospective, attendees decide to experiment with eliminating team-level POs for three teams within the same product area. At the end of the retrospective, they add the following item to the upcoming iteration backlog: *Transition teams A, B, C to PO-less teams*.

During the next iteration planning event, attendees review this item, timebox it, assign it to an owner, and devolve it into tasks, such as the following:

- Develop and gain consensus on a lightweight decision-making process
- Transition POs to alternative roles (e.g., product area owner, product manager)

During the next iteration retrospective, attendees review the item. Attendees discuss how the PO-less rollout went, any issues that have arisen, and how team members and business stakeholders view the change. If the trials are successful, they roll out the practice to other product areas.

15.14.5 Iteration Retrospective Games

Several games have become popular for facilitating iteration retrospectives. Whether or not you use these games is a matter of personal style and preference. Personally, I find it unnatural to incorporate games, so I rarely use them. However, some of the organizations I work with find them useful—especially when working with large groups, as in a scaled retrospective. We'll look at two of these games: the Sailboat game and the Circles and Soup game. You can use each on its own, or you can use the two games in combination. In the latter case, begin with the Sailboat game to identify what's working and what's not, and finish with Circles and Soup to clarify what action the team can take to have the most significant impact.

15.14.5.1 Sailboat Game

The are many variations of the **Sailboat game** (also known as the *Speedboat game*). Figure 15.22 illustrates one example.

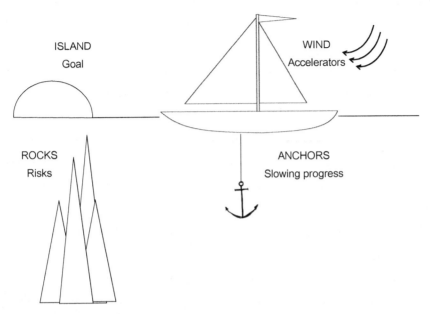

Figure 15.22   *Sailboat game elements*

The primary Sailboat game elements are as follows:

- Sailboat: Represents the initiative the team is trying to advance
- Anchors: Represent things that are slowing them down
- Wind (sails): Represent accelerators—things that are helping the team reach the goal

You may also add other elements, as shown in Figure 15.22, such as the following:

- Island: Representing the goal
- Rocks: Representing risks

If you are facilitating the Sailboat game, guide the team through the following steps:

First, ask attendees to use silent brainstorming to identify the elements in the Sailboat template—for example, Rocks (risks), Wind (accelerators), and Anchors (decelerators). Have attendees fill the cards out silently and place them on the picture in the designated areas.

When no more cards are posted, ask attendees to read out their cards. Facilitate a discussion of risks (Rocks) and how they may be managed. Next, discuss accelerators—practices the team should continue or start to adopt. Gain a consensus on relative priorities. Position the accelerators that are most important at the top of the picture.

Next, discuss the Anchors—things that are slowing the team down. If the number of anchors is large, ask attendees to group them by topic. Position the most important group at the top. Sequence the items in each group according to their relative importance.

Finally, focus on actions to improve the items posted at the top of each region. If you will be playing the Circles and Soup game, feed these actions into the game.

BLINK CASE STUDY PART 28

Iteration Retrospective—Sailboat Game

Background

You are asked to facilitate an iteration retrospective to make recommendations about practices to do or to stop doing.

The Ask

The following deliverables are to be produced during the meeting:

- **Deliverable 1:** Sailboat game board indicating Accelerators and Anchors
- **Deliverable 2:** Iteration retrospective backlog

What Transpires

The team identifies the development and deployment of an automated testing platform and the use of agile coaches as key Accelerators.

The team agrees that the Anchor topics are as follows, in order of importance: requirements management issues, lack of resources, and conflicting priorities. The top requirements management issue is that stories are not sufficiently prepared (ready) when placed into an iteration.

You follow up by discussing ways to improve the situation, such as creating a DoR and enforcing its use. The team agrees to create a high-priority task to develop a DoR. They add the task to the iteration retrospective backlog.

Deliverables

The following deliverables were created.

Deliverables 1: Sailboat Game Board Indicating Accelerators and Anchors
Figure 15.23 is the Sailboat game drawing produced during the retrospective.

Deliverables 2: Iteration Retrospective Backlog
The following high-priority item was added to the iteration retrospective backlog:

- Create and enforce a DoR

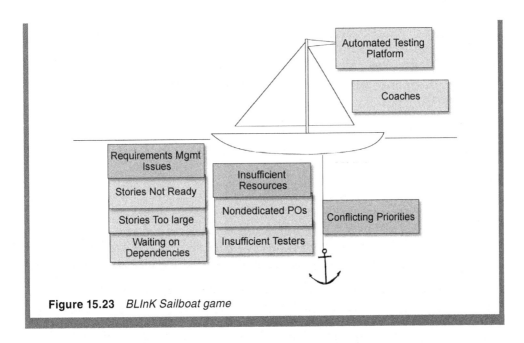

Figure 15.23 *BLInK Sailboat game*

15.14.5.2 Circles and Soup

The objective of Circles and Soup[22] is to help the team focus its efforts on areas where it has the most direct control and to recognize other instances where it should seek to influence the organization indirectly.

Circles and Soup may be used in conjunction with the Sailboat game. In this case, you use the Sailboat game to identify issues and Circles and Soup to consider the degree of impact the team can have on each one. Figure 15.24 depicts the Circles and Soup diagram used in the game.

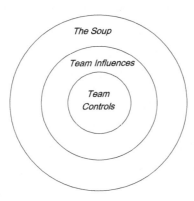

Figure 15.24 *Circles and Soup*

---

22. Diana Larsen, "Circles and Soup" [blog post], Partnerships and Possibilities Blog, July 26, 2010, https://www.futureworksconsulting.com/blog/2010/07/26/circles-and-soup

The figure illustrates one version with the following zones of influence: The Soup, Team Influences, and Team Controls. Other zones of influence may be specified (e.g., Enterprise, Product, and Team).

Facilitating the Game

Post the Circles and Soup bullseye on the wall, as shown in Figure 15.24. Guide the group to identify issues. Ask them to write each issue on a card and place it on the chart in the appropriate ring.

Ask the group to post issues in the center of the bullseye—Team Controls—that the team can take direct action on. Issues in this circle may address the artifacts the team uses to plan its work, such as story maps.

Ask the group to post issues in the Team Influences region that the team cannot affect directly but *can* impact indirectly by influencing others. Examples include increasing the resources made available to the team and purchasing a requirements management tool.

Ask the group to post in The Soup (outermost) region issues that the team has little hope of influencing. For example, these may include constraints, corporate culture, corporate standards, and the platforms that are made available. Issues in this area are ones the team must adapt to.

Finally, ask the group to review the diagram and suggest actions against each issue based on the zone it is sitting in. At first, focus on issues in the center zone and gradually move out from the center as the team matures.

15.15 Chapter Summary

Here are the key points covered in this chapter:

- Carry out analysis in a rolling fashion as features and stories rise in the backlog.

- Integrate, test, and deliver stories continually as they are completed.

- The daily standup is an inspect-and-adapt meeting, where the team plans how it will collaborate toward the iteration goal.

- Use burndown and burnup charts to view progress toward the goal, forecast the completion dates, and detect and diagnose productivity problems.

- Use cumulative flow diagrams to identify bottlenecks and other workflow problems in the product development process and to forecast completion dates.

- Validate the value delivered by features and stories through split testing. Use feedback and data from the tests, such as funnel metrics, to inform future development decisions.

- Support continual improvement by holding a retrospective at the end of every iteration or one- or two-week period. Decide on at least one high-priority improvement item that can be addressed in the next iteration.

15.16 What's Next?

In this chapter, we walked through rolling activities as stories come up in the backlog and are implemented. In Chapter 16, we focus on the final actions that occur before features and stories are released for general availability.

Chapter 16

Releasing the Product

This chapter covers the activities and guidelines for releasing software into production and the market in accordance with continuous delivery (CD) practices. The chapter reviews guidelines for determining when to defer deployment of done backlog items (e.g., to protect the brand when a feature is not yet competitive). Next, the chapter examines when to consider reserving hardening iterations before release as a remedial practice. Figure 16.1 highlights the activities covered in the chapter.

The chapter explains the stages for launching a product or major software release, including pre-alpha, alpha, and beta testing, and general availability (GA). It concludes with guidelines for facilitating two inspect-and-adapt events: quarterly (release) retrospectives aimed at continual improvement and pivot-or-persevere meetings.

This chapter continues the case study that runs through the book, including sample solutions.

16.1 Objectives

This chapter will help you

- Understand which release-preparation activities to perform continuously as stories are implemented, and which to perform closer to the release date.

- Know when a hardening iteration may be advised as a remedial practice.

- Understand the stages and activities for releasing a new product or a major change, including alpha testing, beta testing, and general availability (GA).

- Facilitate and participate in a quarterly (release) retrospective meeting.

- Facilitate a pivot-or-persevere meeting.

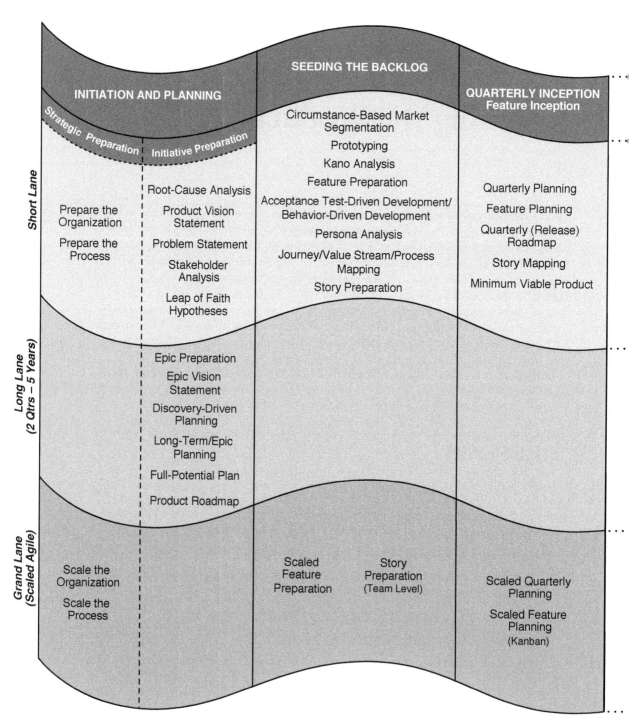

Figure 16.1   *Chapter 16 on the map*

QUARTERLY CLOSEOUT
Epic, Feature Closeout

DAILY ACTIVITIES

ITERATION INCEPTION

ITERATION CLOSEOUT

Daily Standup

Requirements Analysis
& Documentation

Code, Build, Test, Deliver Acceptance
Test-Driven Development/
Behavior-Driven Development

Minimum Viable Product,
Split Testing

Epic, Feature Preparation

Story Preparation

Iteration
Planning

Iteration Review

Iteration Retrospective

Prepare for
General Availability

Quarterly
Retrospective

Epic, Feature
Retrospective

Pivot or
Persevere

Scaled
Iteration
Planning

Iteration
Planning
(Team Level)

Product
Owner
Council
Meetings

DevOps

User Task
Force
Meetings

Scaled
Feature
Preparation
(Kanban)

Integration
Meetings

Story
Preparation
(Team Level)

Scaled Iteration
Review

Scaled Iteration
Retrospective

Iteration Retrospective
(Team Level)

DevOps

Scaled
Quarterly/Feature
Retrospective

16.2 This Chapter on the Map

As indicated in Figure 16.1, the chapter examines the Quarterly Closeout zone, including the activities Prepare for GA; quarterly, epic, and feature retrospectives; and the pivot-or-persevere meeting.

16.3 Getting Stories to Done

In the last chapter, we examined how to deliver done stories continuously to the customer. Activities performed on a continuous basis include the following:

- Story acceptance criteria specification

- Analysis and design

- Creation and execution of automated tests (e.g., unit tests, low-level and high-level integration tests, regression tests, user acceptance testing [UAT], smoke tests, and testing of non-functional requirements [NFRs], such as security, performance, stress, and reliability testing)

- Code and build

- Bug fixes

- Code cleanup—removal of technical debt (e.g., unreachable code, redundancies)

- Documentation—continual updates to user documentation, support documentation, business analysis (BA) documentation

- Manual UAT testing by the customer against acceptance criteria

Upon completion of these activities, the story is done and delivered to the customer in a *releasable* form. However, the decision about *when* to release it to the market is up to the business. For example, the product owner (PO) may decide to defer the release of an unripe feature in order to protect the brand. First, we review guidelines from Chapter 9, "Long-Term Agile Planning," on this issue. Then, we explore *how* to stage the release.

16.4 Releasing to the Market: Timing Considerations

Chapter 9 on long-term planning presented guidelines for timing the release of stories and features to the market. Now that stories are ready for deployment and the customer must decide when to release them, let's summarize the guidelines. The following guidelines presume the organization has a mature DevOps practice enabling it to deploy frequently and safely.

- If it's a bug fix or minor enhancement, release it immediately so that end customers can benefit.
- If the story is part of a major new feature that is not yet competitive, defer its release to protect the brand.
- Release a feature's stories as soon as, collectively, they would deliver a Minimum Marketable Feature (MMF)—the smallest version of the feature that would be viewed as valuable by customers if released to the market.

To illustrate how you, as an analyst, support business decision makers in this decision, let's return to a capability of the Customer Engagement One (CEO) application we saw earlier in this book—the feature to enable support agents to use automated replies when answering questions from customers. Let's presume the feature's first story has been implemented: "As a support agent, I want to save an automated reply so that I can select it in response to a customer message." In this case, you advise the PO not to release the story to the general market. Why? At this point, a support agent can save queries but can't use them. If the feature were to be released in this state, end customers would view it as an amateur-hour solution. Instead, you advise the PO to release the story for testing by users and user representatives but to defer a general release until the feature is rich enough to be competitive—at which time the company may release it or wait until the next scheduled release date arrives.

For more on when to release software changes, see Chapter 9, section 9.6.3.

16.4.1 Should You Reserve a Hardening Iteration for Prerelease Activities?

As a general rule, the steps to prepare software for release to the market should not require a dedicated iteration because, with DevOps adoption, they are mostly automated and carried out continuously. Nevertheless, some organizations reserve a dedicated iteration—often referred to as a **hardening** or **stabilizing iteration**—during which the product is prepared for general release, and no new features are developed (though bugs may be fixed). While this practice is not advised as a norm, there are certain circumstances when it is appropriate, as described in the following sections.

16.4.1.1 Hardening Iteration Due to Technical Constraints

An organization may reserve a hardening iteration as a stop-gap measure until it has the technical capability to deliver software continuously with confidence—and the culture to support it. As an analyst, it's important to meet people where they are. If a hardening iteration is necessary for these reasons, that's certainly what you should advise. At the same time, take care that teams aren't using it to delay activities they *are able* to perform continuously, such as automated unit testing. Above all, use your influence to advocate for a higher level of DevOps readiness so that, over time, a hardening iteration is no longer required.

16.4.1.2 Hardening Iteration for Quality Improvements

Even teams that work hard at practicing continuous quality can find that technical debt accumulates under the pressure to accommodate requests for customer-driven features. In such circumstances, a hardening iteration can offer a pause from feature development so that teams can focus on quality improvements, such as removing security vulnerabilities and addressing scalability issues. If a hardening iteration is necessary for this reason, encourage the team to view this as a remedial practice. At the same time, guide it to address quality improvements in a more continuous manner.

16.5 Staging the Release

A software product undergoes numerous stages on its way from coding to its release to the market. Figure 16.2 illustrates an example of these stages.

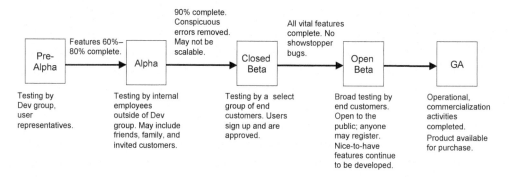

Figure 16.2 *Stages to general availability (GA)*

In Figure 16.2, the stages are as follows:

- Pre-alpha

- Alpha testing

- Closed beta testing

- Open beta testing

- General availability

The following sections describe the example in Figure 16.2. Actual stages and outputs may vary from those shown in the figure. For example, some processes involve an RC (release candidate) stage after initial beta testing and an RTM (release to manufacturing/market) stage when the software is ready for bundling and mass duplication. The steps carried out in each stage also vary—with DevOps organizations requiring less work before a general-availability release because most of it is performed continuously and automatically. Furthermore, DevOps capabilities allow features to be developed and incorporated right up to a general release, as illustrated in Figure 16.2 and described in the following sections.

16.5.1 Pre-Alpha

During the pre-alpha stage, the product is tested internally by the development group, including user representatives and the development team members. As an analyst, you write story acceptance criteria and support the customer in testing them. Pre-alpha testing typically occurs at the development organization's site. Figure 16.2 indicates that, on exit from pre-alpha, must-have features are 60 to 80 percent complete.[1]

16.5.2 Alpha Testing

Alpha testing is testing to elicit feedback and expose usability issues, requirements gaps, interoperability errors, and showstoppers. Its objective is to catch and fix these problems before sending the software out for a beta release to end customers.

Alpha testing is typically carried out by company employees and their friends and family. The company may also invite a few customers from the target market whose feedback is highly valued.

During alpha testing, feature development continues. On exit from the alpha stage, features should be 80 to 90 percent complete with no showstopper errors.

As an analyst, you contribute during this stage by eliciting and analyzing customer feedback during testing, writing stories and acceptance criteria, and updating business analysis documentation as needed. To illustrate your involvement, we return to the feature to introduce saved replies. Let's presume the following story has been accepted for alpha testing:

> **Story:** As a support agent, I want to select a saved reply.
>
> **Acceptance criteria:** When I open my menu, I can see an alphabetic, scrollable list of saved replies.

As this story is being alpha tested, you continue writing stories to enrich the feature. For example, in response to feedback from testers, you create the following story: "As a support agent, I want to search replies using keywords."

16.5.3 Beta Testing

After alpha testing, the software undergoes **beta testing**—testing by end customers to evaluate the customer experience of the product and generate buzz in advance of a release. **Beta**

---

1. Kelliann Longacre, "The Five W's of Alpha Testing," Centercode, 2020, https://www.centercode.com/blog/2017/09/five-ws-alpha-testing

testers are real customers in the target market who volunteer to test-drive the product, report bugs, and suggest new features. Features discovered at this time may be incorporated into the current release or deferred to the next one.

Beta testing may be carried out in two stages. As noted earlier, details may vary.

16.5.3.1 Closed (Private) Beta Testing

After alpha testing, **closed (private) beta testing** is carried out by a select group of end customers, invited and approved by the company. On entry to closed beta testing, the product may still lack some must-have features and may not be scalable. Monitoring begins at this stage through the use of manual log entries to track errors. Problems are visible, but automatic alerts are not yet in place.

As issues and bugs arise, the team addresses them and continues the development of the remaining features. On exit from closed beta testing, all must-have features are complete, there are no showstopper errors, and the product is ready to be exposed to the public.

16.5.3.2 Open (Public) Beta Testing

Public (open) beta testing is broad testing by real end customers. The purpose of open beta testing is to evaluate the customer experience across a wide spectrum of customers and test the "scalability, performance, and reliability"[2] of the product when it is used in real situations. Open beta testing is so called because it is open to the public: anyone may register to try out the product and provide feedback.

On entry to open beta testing, all must-have features have been implemented. During this stage, work may continue on nice-to-have stories and acceptance criteria. To illustrate, let's return to the feature to introduce saved replies. During open beta testing, users indicated they would like to see replies sorted by frequency of use. Consequently, you write the following user story:

> **Story:** As a support agent, I want to view the most common replies.
>
> **Acceptance criteria:** When I open my menu, the most frequently used replies come up first.

The team delivers the story during the open beta testing stage. You write other stories that are deferred to the next release cycle. Also, at this time, the team puts automated monitors and alerts in place.

Once beta testing is over, the PO makes a final decision regarding which features to include in the release. A feature does not have to be fully implemented to be released—just complete enough to be deemed releasable by the customer.

---

2. "Beta Test," ProductPlan, https://www.productplan.com/glossary/beta-test

16.5.4 General Availability

General availability refers to a product becoming accessible for general use and purchase.[3] A GA release typically occurs on a preset date. For a product to reach GA, all commercialization activities must have been completed. Furthermore, the product must be reliable, free of showstopper bugs, and suitable for usage in a production environment.

A GA release is often followed by numbered **maintenance releases** (MRs). For example, GA Release 5.0 is followed by MR 5.1., MR 5.2. Maintenance releases include fixes to bugs known when the product was released but not considered showstoppers, and bugs that have become apparent after release.[4]

16.5.4.1 Checklist of Activities for Reaching General Availability

The following is a checklist[5] of activities to bring a product to GA. If the organization has reached a high level of DevOps readiness (as advised), much of the work to release software reliably (e.g., documentation, regression, and security testing) occurs continuously during the pre-alpha phase as stories are done. The remaining activities should begin as early as possible during the stages leading up to GA. For example, set up manual logs during closed beta testing; set up monitors and alerts during closed beta testing, as described in the preceding sections.

Use the following checklist to plan activities for a product launch or major release. As the release date approaches, use it as a gating mechanism to determine whether the product is ready to proceed to GA.

General Availability Checklist   ☑

Perform the following tasks and satisfy the following conditions in preparation for GA:

- ☐ Stories are done and releasable (see section 16.3).

- ☐ Quality assurance (QA): Pre-alpha, alpha, and beta testing are complete (see sections 16.5.1–16.5.3). Automated tests have been created.

- ☐ Collaboration and communication:

  - ☐ Communicate release date to business stakeholders and influencers, affiliates, and partners.

  - ☐ Messaging: Position the release in terms of the product vision, the vision for the release, key features, and customer value.

---

3. "General Availability (GA)," Techopedia, February 16, 2017, https://www.techopedia.com/ definition/32284/general-availability-ga. Also see "Definition of *General Availability*," Law Insider, https://www.lawinsider.com/dictionary/general-availability

4. "What Is a GA release?" Ruckus Networks, February 24, 2015, https://support.ruckuswireless .com/articles/000002490

5. Some of the listed items have been sourced from the following: Aha! "What Is a Good Product Launch Checklist?" Aha! Labs, Inc. https://www.aha.io/roadmapping/guide/release-management/ what-is-a-good-product-launch-checklist

- ☐ The PO (customer) collaborates with developers to determine which features are complete enough to ship.
- ☐ Development group collaborates with sales marketing teams in the following areas:
  - ☐ Go-to-market strategy: Develop a strategy to sell the new features to new customers and communicate them to existing customers
  - ☐ Marketing materials
  - ☐ Launch of ad campaigns
  - ☐ Social messaging
  - ☐ Website updates
  - ☐ Media communications (e.g., interviews, release announcements)
- ☐ Operational preparations, including the following:
  - ☐ Verify system and application configurations
  - ☐ Code migrations
  - ☐ Data migrations
  - ☐ Verify auditing is enabled as required
  - ☐ Final reviews:
    - ☐ Release gate criteria met
    - ☐ Final security reviews:
      - ☐ Final review conducted. This is a *final* review only. Address and test security vulnerabilities continuously.
      - ☐ Ensure a process is in place to compel users to install security upgrades.
  - ☐ Ensure a rollback and recovery plan is in place *and has been tested.*
  - ☐ Ensure a process is in place to roll out maintenance releases after the GA release.
  - ☐ Monitoring: Set up monitors, logs, and alerts (see section 16.5.4.2).
- ☐ Commercialization activities:[6] Complete the remaining tasks required to bring the product to the market, including the following:
  - ☐ Creation of product demos and marketing materials
  - ☐ Creation of evaluation versions
  - ☐ Compliance testing
  - ☐ Localization

---

6. Carol Oles, "Go-to-Market Strategies for Successful Software Commercialization," *Devpro Journal*, July 2, 2018, https://www.devprojournal.com/business-operations/sales/go-to-market-strategies-to-successful-software-commercialization

- ☐ International availability

- ☐ Multichannel distribution (e.g., app stores, website, auto-updates)

- ☐ Licensing, pricing models (e.g., site license, individual license, volume-based pricing)

- ☐ Complete documentation:

  - ☐ User guides

  - ☐ Technical specifications

  - ☐ Support documentation

  - ☐ Analysis and testing documentation (e.g., feature specifications, process models, use-case models, business rules specifications, and manual test cases)

- ☐ Traceability mechanisms have been implemented and satisfy regulatory and compliance requirements.

- ☐ Training:

  - ☐ Develop instructional videos.

  - ☐ Create and implement training programs for sales agents and marketers.

  - ☐ Train customer service agents to use the new features and support the end customer in their use.

- ☐ Value validation and feedback from end customers: Track success metrics. Elicit customer feedback, success scenarios, and failures.

- ☐ Continuous improvement: Plan and execute continuous improvement actions to improve the organization's release capabilities, with a strong focus on DevOps readiness[7] in the following areas:

  - ☐ Cultural: Take steps to foster a culture of collaboration between development and operations.

  - ☐ Continuous integration (CI)

  - ☐ Automated testing

  - ☐ Early incorporation of security testing

  - ☐ Automation of the build process and infrastructure resourcing

- ☐ Release retrospective: Review lessons learned.

- ☐ Pivot or persevere: Determine whether continue in the same direction or radically shift course.

---

7. Allana Brown, Nicole Forsgren, Jez Humble, Nigel Kersten, and Gene Kim, 2016: *State of DevOps Report*, Puppet+Dora DevOps Research and Assessment, 2016, https://services.google.com/fh/files/misc/state-of-devops-2016.pdf

We explore monitoring, analysis documentation, value validation, the release retrospective, and pivot-or-persevere meetings in the following sections.

16.5.4.2 Monitoring

In the operational preparations described in the preceding checklist, one of the activities is setting up systems for logs, monitors, and alerts. The purpose of these systems is to inform developers as soon as possible when a problem occurs so that the team can act quickly to correct it. Examples of problems tracked and detected by these means include load-related issues, high error rates, high CPU spikes, and availability and latency issues.

The following are the main elements of a monitoring system.

- A **log** is a textual description of an event—typically an error.

- A **monitor** gathers metrics on error rates.

- **Metrics** are counts or timing measurements. An example of a count is the number of production incidents. Timing metrics include *page download time, availability, mean time between failures (MTBF)*, and *cycle time*.

- An **alert** is sent by a monitor when metrics are not within an acceptable range.

Begin setting up logs, monitors, and alerts early to be ready in time for the release date. See section 16.5.3 for guidelines on introducing these elements during beta testing.

16.5.4.3 Analysis Documentation

As noted previously, if an analysis artifact is worth keeping, it's worth updating continuously. For example, in Chapter 15, "Rolling Analysis and Preparation—Day-to-Day Activities," we saw how to update feature files and use-case models during feature preparation and development.

As the release cycle comes to a close, you might wonder what to do with the story map. Since its primary purpose is to plan the implementation, should you discard it once the plan is complete or preserve it?

If your team is about to head into another release cycle that impacts the same process or value stream as the last one, preserve the story map backbone and use it to begin the next story map. However, remove the stories in the ribs section, since those will be different in the new release cycle.

If the team will be working on a different process or value stream, save the backbone for future reference—as an image, in virtual form, or by converting it to another format (e.g., a high-level process model).

 For guidelines on persisting story maps, see Chapter 15, sections 15.10.3.3 and 15.10.3.4. For guidelines on documenting features and acceptance criteria in feature files, see section 15.10.2.

16.5.4.4 *Value Validation*

In Chapter 15, you learned how to use split (A/B) testing to measure the effects of changes to the software during implementation (see section 15.8.2). Once a feature is complete enough to be released, you perform split testing to validate that it delivers its business and customer objectives. If the feature is validated, you include it in the release and support it as part of the product.

You also conduct split testing to validate hypotheses at the epic and product level. You use metrics and feedback from the tests to inform whether to pivot or persevere with the current hypotheses. (See section 16.7 for guidance on facilitating a pivot-or-persevere meeting.)

16.6 Quarterly (Release) Retrospective

Conduct a quarterly, release, epic, or feature retrospective to review the status of a long initiative, celebrate big wins, validate assumptions, and review impacts and outcomes that take a long time to manifest. For simplicity, I'll refer to the meeting as a *quarterly retrospective*, since the goals and format are similar for the other contexts.

During the quarterly retrospective, attendees discuss what went well and didn't go well during the quarter and make recommendations for improvement. The meeting's length varies from one hour to a couple of days depending on the duration of the period under review and the scale of the initiative. This section focuses on team retrospectives. For guidelines on quarterly retrospectives for scaled organizations, see Chapter 17, "Scaling Agility," section 17.9.17.

Deliverables from a quarterly (release) retrospective include the following:

- Recommendations: What to keep doing, stop doing, and start doing

- Risk management plan

- Action plan including a timeline

- Addition of at least one high-priority work item to the next quarterly (release) backlog

16.6.1 Facilitation Guidelines

As a retrospective meeting facilitator, you should be someone with a strong vision for DevOps and acceptance test–driven development (e.g., a lead in DevOps, CI/CD, business analysis, or agile practice). Invite the following people to attend:

- Senior management

- ScrumMaster (if applicable)

- Current and potential customers

- Stakeholders
- POs, product managers
- Development team managers
- Development team representatives

Keep the meeting focused by steering the group away from lengthy narratives about past events toward problem solving. Avoid generalized questions about what went right and wrong. Instead, lead the discussion toward issues that the team has the power to influence—either directly or indirectly, through persuasion.

> Use the following guidelines to achieve an effective quarterly retrospective:
>
> - Prepare
> - Concentrate on problem areas
> - Focus on DevOps/CI/CD practices
> - Discuss metrics, not opinions
> - Use a checklist

Let's examine these guidelines.

16.6.1.1 Prepare

The quarterly (release) retrospective is most effective if the facilitator and attendees prepare beforehand.[8] Before the event, discuss what did and did not go well during preliminary discussions with stakeholders and developers. Prepare a timeline of major events. Distribute it to the development team so they can review and annotate it before the meeting. See section 16.6.2 for guidance on preparing the timeline.

16.6.1.2 Concentrate on Problem Areas

Don't try to boil the ocean. Direct the discussion toward areas that you know are problems within your organization.

16.6.1.3 Focus on DevOps/CI/CD Practices

An organization must have a strong focus on DevOps/CI/CD readiness to release software on demand with confidence. As a quarterly retrospective facilitator, you should have deep expertise in these practices. Organize the retrospective discussion around DevOps readiness, concentrating on what you know is working well and not working well concerning DevOps adoption.

---

8. Naresh Jain, "Release Retrospective vs. Sprint Retrospective" [blog post], Managed Chaos, June 20, 2012, http://blogs.agilefaqs.com/2012/06/20/release-retrospective-vs-sprint-retrospective

16.6.1.4 Discuss Metrics, Not Opinions

As noted, during a retrospective, attendees review what went well and what did not. One of the greatest challenges in doing so is that people's opinions are unreliable. One person can believe something went well, while another thinks the opposite is true. Furthermore, people may believe something went well only because they aren't aware of better options. To avoid these pitfalls, focus on outcome-based metrics, not opinions.[9] Support this emphasis by posting metrics on the timeline (both good and bad) along with improvement interventions to highlight which interventions are and are not having the desired effect. Use *actionable metrics* that measure meaningful outcomes, such as revenue increases, rather than internal yardsticks, such as the number of lines of code.

Metrics for evaluating the success of DevOps/CI/CD adoption include the following:

- Deployment frequency
- Percentage of successful deployments: Ensure the meaning of *successful deployment* is clearly defined by the organization (e.g., deployments without outages)
- Lead time for changes
- Number of production incidents
- Availability

16.6.1.5 Use a Checklist

Use a checklist to help you prepare questions. The wrong way to use the checklist is to run through it during the retrospective, asking every question. The right way is to use it to ensure you *consider* all relevant issues from all relevant perspectives. You should focus, however, on those areas that are problematic. Perspectives to consider include:

- DevOps and supporting practices
- Technology
- Productivity
- QA
- Program/portfolio
- Marketplace

See Appendix A.11 for a checklist of quarterly retrospective questions addressing each of these perspectives.

---

9. Dan Holloran, "Top Metrics for Measuring DevOps Delivery Value," Splunk, November 14, 2019, https://victorops.com/blog/top-metrics-for-measuring-devops-delivery-value

16.6.2 Preparing the Timeline

Use a **timeline** to illustrate when events and milestones occurred during the planning period under review. As noted earlier, you draft the timeline before the retrospective, posting improvement efforts alongside positive and negative metrics to highlight the impact of interventions. Figure 16.3 illustrates the elements of a timeline. (Note that the colors indicated by this figure will not be displayed in the print edition of this book.)

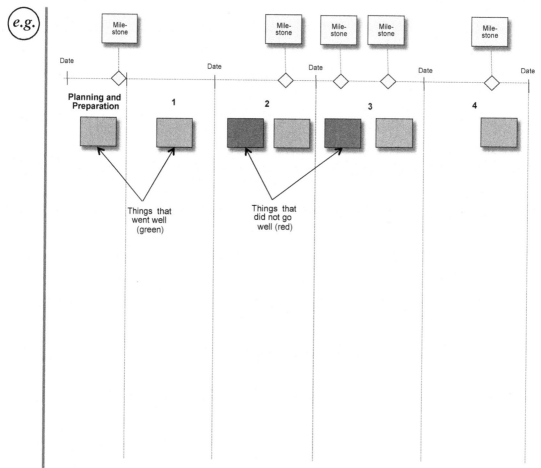

Figure 16.3 *Elements of a timeline*

The timeline should span the period under review (e.g., the quarter, release cycle, or epic). In the example in Figure 16.3, the numbers 1, 2, 3, and 4 represent iterations. Other interim periods, such as weeks, may also be used. The following elements are included:

- **Milestones:** Points in time at which significant **events** occurred (indicated by diamonds).
- **Events:** Noteworthy occurrences (e.g., an iteration begins or ends, a review is held, an objective is met, a feature is delivered, outcomes are measured). Events are indicated as milestones and color-coded cards. **Green cards** represent things that went well. **Red cards** represent things that did not go well.

Ask attendees to prepare notes regarding significant events, successes, and failures and update the timeline accordingly. Ask technical members (e.g., software engineers, architects) to address development successes and failures (e.g., features that were planned but not released and internal efforts to improve the development process). Ask QA professionals to address defects that occurred, test-automation efforts, and quality metrics. Invite data analysts to address usage patterns, metrics gathered from A/B testing, and key performance indicators (KPIs), such as conversion and retention rates.

16.6.3 Walkthrough of a Quarterly Retrospective

Unlike sprint (iteration) retrospectives, quarterly retrospectives are not included in the Scrum framework. Guidelines for conducting the meeting vary.[10,11] As a general guideline, the meeting should be informal and not overly constrained by a preplanned agenda. In the following sections, we walk through one such event.

16.6.3.1 Introduction

As the event facilitator, you introduce the quarterly retrospective as an opportunity for continual improvement—emphasizing that the objective is to mine past experience for guidance about the future. You reinforce to attendees that the purpose of the meeting is *not* to judge (or be judged by) past performance.

16.6.3.2 Updating the Timeline

You review the timeline draft with the group, focusing on DevOps-related issues and areas known as problems. You ask attendees to update the timeline with things that went well and things that did not go well, using metrics to inform their evaluations.

16.6.3.3 Mining the Timeline

You work with the group to mine the timeline by using it to explore the impact of changes. For example, the group examines a milestone on the timeline indicating when new DevOps practices were adopted—exploring the improvements that followed with respect to the frequency of successful deployments and MTBF.

---

10. Madhavi Ledalla, "The Significance of Release Retrospectives" [blog post], 2018, https://lmadhavi.wordpress.com/2018/04/10/the-significance-of-release-retrospectives
11. Singapore Management University (SMU), "Project Timeline," https://wiki.smu.edu.sg/is480/ IS480_Team_wiki%3A_2013T1_Prime_Factor_Project_Schedule

16.6.3.4 Recommendations

Next, you turn the focus to recommendations. You ask attendees to consider the following questions, focusing on problems and successes raised in the preceding discussion:

- What are we doing that we should keep doing?

- What are we doing that we should stop doing?

- What are we not doing that we should start doing? Are there any new practices or conventions we should adopt?

You might use the Sailboat (Speedboat) game during this part of the meeting—asking attendees to post things they should keep doing or start doing on the sail, and things they should stop doing on the anchor.

 For more on the Sailboat game, see Chapter 15, section 15.14.5.1.

Next, you ask attendees to prioritize the issues and problems that have been identified. Then, you facilitate a discussion focused on high-priority items. You ask attendees to consider these items from the following points of view:

- What problems and issues are within our sphere of influence?

- What problems do we need to escalate to someone who does have influence?

You may use the Circles and Soup game for this part of the meeting, asking attendees to position items on a bullseye based on the associated sphere of influence.

 For more on the Circles and Soup game, see Chapter 15, section 15.14.5.2.

Finally, you work with the group to develop an action plan for implementing the recommendations—guiding them to include at least two or three things that can be done immediately. You add these actions to the upcoming quarterly backlog.

16.7 Pivot-or-Persevere Meeting

With the pivot-or-persevere meeting, we return to where we began—with the leap of faith hypotheses behind the vision for a product or change initiative. Conduct **pivot-or-persevere meetings** on a regular basis to validate those hypotheses. Use leading indicators and actionable metrics to inform the decision about whether to pivot, persevere, or stop all work on the initiative. To **persevere** is to continue in the current direction. To **pivot** is to make a radical shift toward a new hypothesis.

 For more on planning MVP experiments to test hypotheses, see Chapter 12, section 12.4. For guidance on specifying actionable metrics, see Chapter 7, section 7.11.5.

16.7.1 Data-Informed—Not Data-Driven

As a pivot-or-persevere meeting facilitator, you'll be asking attendees to review metrics collected during MVP experiments and feature development. The pivot-or-persevere decision should be *informed* by this data but not driven by it. While metrics influence the decision, they are not the only determining factor. Business leadership's gut feeling about the product, sense of where the market is moving, and conversations with customers also contribute to the decision. The objective of data-*informed* decision-making is to come to a *better* decision through data, not to use data as the sole determining factor.

16.7.2 Timing Considerations

Schedule a pivot-or-persevere meeting every couple of weeks to every few months and whenever it becomes apparent that a leap of faith hypothesis is likely to be false.[12] One recommended time is during the quarterly retrospective because relevant stakeholders are already assembled.

16.7.3 Attendees

Invite the following people to attend the pivot-or-persevere meeting:[13]

- Development team representatives (e.g., engineering leads, team analyst)
- Business analysts, PO: Provide an overview of vision, customers, leap of faith hypotheses, MVP experiments, and results
- Data analysts: Report on MVP results; summarize KPI metrics over an extended period, comparing actual metrics against targets
- Business leadership teams: Report on the market, potential markets, feedback, conversations with customers
- External advisers: Provide an external perspective on the success or failure of the product or initiative

16.7.4 Walkthrough of a Pivot-or-Persevere Meeting

To illustrate a pivot-or-persevere meeting, let's return to the example discussed earlier in this book: Trint, an app used in journalism to transcribe interviews. Since we're about to diverge from the company's true-life history, we'll presume a similar company and app exists—DCyphr. DCyphr's leap of faith hypothesis is that journalists will value the product for its ability to transcribe interviews reliably without the tedium and time requirements of current manual methods. According to this hypothesis, enough journalists and news organizations will subscribe for the company to be profitable within seven years. The company holds pivot-or-persevere meetings every month to evaluate the hypothesis as it continues to apply improvements.

---

12. Eric Ries, *The Lean Startup* (New York: Random House, 2011), 164.
13. Ries, *The Lean Startup*, 164.

One year after the product was launched, the company holds a pivot-or-persevere meeting to assess long-term outcomes and determine whether to continue with the original hypothesis. Data analysts at the event note that, at current growth rates, the company is not forecast to reach profitability by the target date. However, there is a potential bright spot in the data. While growth in the target market (journalists) is below expectations, there has been steady growth among a small subgroup—librarians. The marketing team has reached out to customers in this group to gain a deeper understanding of their reasons for purchasing the product. The librarian users report that they like the way the app makes the libraries' videos and audio recordings searchable. They use the app to transcribe audio to text automatically; then, they search the text for keywords.

Based on these insights, decision makers agree to abandon the original hypothesis and pivot to a new one—that customers will use the product to search existing video content. They decide to begin by focusing on the needs of librarians and researchers. The founder expresses a gut feeling that search-engine developers will become a key driver of growth in this area in the future. Product developers agree to begin developing an API with auto-transcription and search capabilities aimed at third-party search-engine developers.

Several years after this pivotal meeting, the product has become the leading provider of video and audio search capabilities to third-party developers. One year later, Google buys the company. While this story is hypothetical, it's not atypical. Successful companies are often the result of a pivot resulting from the failure of an earlier hypothesis.

BLINK CASE STUDY PART 29

Pivot or Persevere

Background

It's a few years into the BLInK program. The company wishes to assess whether to continue with BLInK as initially conceived or pivot to a new hypothesis.

The Ask

You've been tasked with facilitating a pivot-or-persevere meeting for the BLInK initiative with the aim of guiding future investment in the product.

What Transpires

You review two of BLInK's key value hypotheses:

- The accuracy of risk forecasts will improve as a result of reduced deviation in actual versus expected loss ratios.
- Health will improve as a result of a customer's participation in BLInK programs, as measured by a reduction in annual claims.

Data analysts report on two key metrics used to test these hypotheses:

- Loss-ratio deviation, calculated as the absolute value of (Expected loss ratio – Actual loss ratio) / Actual loss ratio
- Change in average total annual claim amount per customer

The analysts used a split-testing approach to compare outcomes for BLInK subscribers versus a control group of nonsubscribers with similar health profiles and claims histories.

The results of their analyses are as shown in Table 16.1.

Table 16.1 *BLInK Data Analysis for Pivot-or-Persevere Meeting*

Metric	Year 1	Year 2	Year 3	Year 4
Reduction in Loss-Ratio Deviation (Measuring Improved Accuracy of Loss-Ratio Forecast)				
Target	0%	1%	1%	2%
Actuals: BLInK vs. control group	0%	0%	2%	8%
Reduction in Total Annual Amount Claimed per Customer (Measuring Improved Health Outcomes)				
Target	0%	1%	5%	10%
Actuals: Blink vs. non-BLInK	0%	0%	1%	0%

You facilitate a review of the results. Loss-ratio accuracy did not improve appreciably during the first two years. However, it improved more than expected in the third year and even more in the fourth year. Data analysts explain that personal data used in the forecasts began accumulating much faster than expected in Year 3. The data bonanza is now resulting in higher accuracy improvements than had been initially envisioned.

On the other hand, concerning the second metric, there is almost no reduction in total annual claim amounts per customer when adjusted for the control group, suggesting that the program does not improve customers' health outcomes.

Case Study Retrospective

As a result of the meeting, business leadership has concluded that the product's first hypothesis has been validated—that BLInK would improve loss-ratio forecasts due to the wealth of personal data provided by the program. At the same time, leadership has also concluded that the hypothesis regarding improved health outcomes has *not* been validated. They decide to double down on BLInK features that generate the greatest amount of actuarial data from customers while reducing investment in health-improvement features that don't generate useful data.

16.8 Chapter Summary

Here are the key points covered in this chapter:

- When a product reaches GA, it becomes widely available for purchase and use.

- As a normative practice, perform build-test steps continually, as stories are completed; don't wait until a hardening iteration.

- Prerelease activities include alpha and beta testing; setting up logs, monitors, and alerts; and commercialization activities.

- Hold a quarterly (release) retrospective at the end of the planning cycle to inspect what worked and what didn't and make improvement recommendations.

- Hold pivot-or-persevere meetings to make data-informed decisions about whether or not to continue in the same direction or pivot to a new hypothesis.

16.9 What's Next?

In the preceding chapters, we've walked through agile analysis in the context of a small initiative. If the initiative is scaled, containing multiple teams, you'll need additional tools to synchronize their work and support inter-team collaboration. That's the subject of the next chapter.

Chapter 17

Scaling Agility

This chapter focuses on the challenges faced by scaled agile organizations and the practices for addressing them. Figure 17.1 highlights the activities covered in the chapter. The chapter begins by examining why we need scaled agile techniques—and why agile practices designed for small organizations of independent teams are usually insufficient at scale.

Next, the chapter provides guidelines for choosing a scaled agile approach. It compares and contrasts the flow-based approach (e.g., Kanban) and the timeboxed approach (e.g., Scrum, Scaled Agile Framework [SAFe]), and explains when to use which one in a scaled organization.

To successfully scale agility, a product development organization must have the capability to integrate and deliver software changes continuously, reliably, and sustainably at scale. The chapter explores essential practices for achieving that—including DevOps, continuous integration (CI), continuous delivery (CD), acceptance test–driven development (ATDD), test-driven development (TDD), and behavior-driven development (BDD).

Success at scaling agility also depends on culture. The chapter examines key cultural practices, including the leader-as-coach and leader-who-serves (servant-leadership) models, and a focus on quality. (This chapter introduces the topic. For a more extensive treatment of agile culture, see Chapter 18, "Achieving Enterprise Agility.")

Next, the chapter explains how to scale the requirements repository—including guidelines for specifying the product backlog, subproducts, team backlogs, and the definition of done (DoD) at scale.

The chapter then focuses on the scaled agile organization. It explains why component teams are usually necessary and how they interact with feature teams. It explains how to organize teams into leveled product areas and how to organize by portfolio and program. The chapter also describes additional roles and organizations in a scaled organization, such as area POs, extended teams, competency groups, user task forces, and product owner councils (POC).

Next, the chapter explains how to scale the process. First, it provides an overview of scaled planning and analysis events and activities. Then it explores those items and provides detailed guidance for carrying them out. Scaled events discussed in the chapter include the scaled quarterly (release) planning meeting, scaled feature preparation, POC meetings, scaled iteration planning (also known as *big room sprint planning*), and the

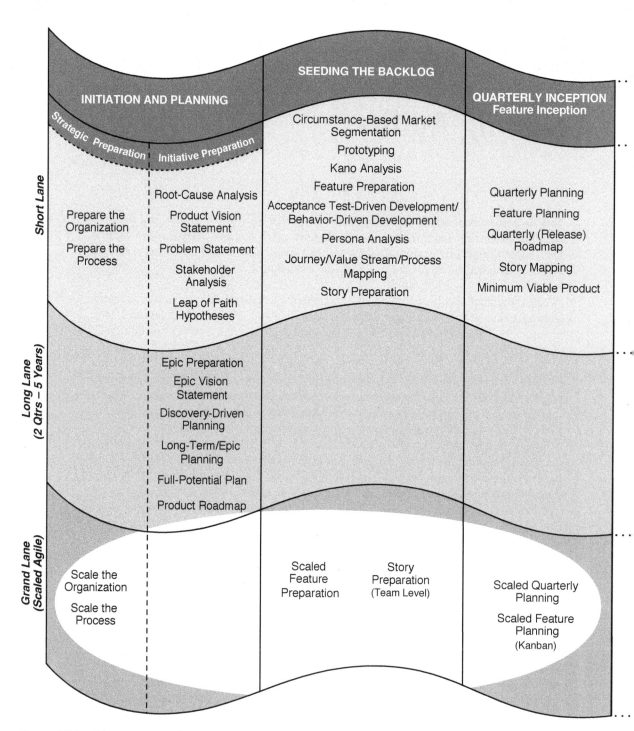

Figure 17.1   *Chapter 17 on the map*

DAILY ACTIVITIES

ITERATION INCEPTION

ITERATION CLOSEOUT

QUARTERLY CLOSEOUT
Epic, Feature Closeout

Daily Standup

Requirements Analysis
& Documentation

Code, Build, Test, Deliver Acceptance
Test-Driven Development/
Behavior-Driven Development

Minimum Viable Product,
Split Testing

Epic, Feature Preparation

Story Preparation

Iteration
Planning

Iteration Review
Iteration Retrospective

Prepare for
General Availability

Quarterly
Retrospective

Epic, Feature
Retrospective

Pivot or
Persevere

Scaled
Iteration
Planning

Iteration
Planning
(Team Level)

Product
Owner
Council
Meetings

DevOps

User Task
Force
Meetings

Scaled
Feature
Preparation
(Kanban)

Integration
Meetings

Story
Preparation
(Team Level)

Scaled Iteration
Review

Scaled Iteration
Retrospective

Iteration Retrospective
(Team Level)

DevOps

Scaled
Quarterly/Feature
Retrospective

scaled iteration retrospective. The chapter provides guidelines for selecting software tools to support collaboration among teams. It also offers lightweight solutions, such as using roamers and scouts.

The chapter concludes with guidance for addressing potential problems and challenges when scaling an agile organization, such as coordinating with waterfall teams.

17.1 Objectives

This chapter will help you

- Understand how DevOps, CI, CD, and ATDD enable frequent, reliable delivery of value to the end user.

- Understand how to structure a scaled development organization into portfolios, programs, product areas, feature teams, and component teams.

- Know when to use timeboxed and when to use flow-based planning approaches.

- Conduct scaled agile events, such as scaled quarterly and iteration planning meetings.

- Conduct rolling analysis (feature and story preparation) on a scaled agile initiative.

17.2 This Chapter on the Map

As indicated in Figure 17.1, the chapter focuses on the Grand Lane of the planning and analysis map, cutting across all activity zones from Initiation and Planning to Quarterly Closeout.

17.3 Why Do We Need a *Scaled* Agile Approach?

It's common, in agile circles, to hear that a scaled agile organization should be composed of self-sufficient, independent teams.[1,2] If agile teams were, in fact, totally independent at scale, there would be no need for scaled agile frameworks (or this chapter); you would simply follow team-level agile practices and multiply them across the organization without any additional processes or roles. (As we'll see, this is roughly the approach of

---

1. For example, the Scrum Guide declares that "members have all the skills necessary to create value each Sprint" and are "self-managing." Ken Schwaber and Jeff Sutherland, "The Scrum Team," in *The Scrum Guide: The Definitive Guide to Scrum—The Rules of the Game*, 2020, 5, https://www.scrumguides.org

2. As another example, Ron Jeffries writes, "Much of the work of any company can be done by single cross-functional teams." See Ron Jeffries, "Issues with SAFe," April 2, 2014, http://ronjeffries.com/xprog/articles/issues-with-safe

the Large Scale Scrum [LeSS] framework.) Yet, in practice, dependencies among teams are the norm, not the exception, in scaled agile organizations. These persistent dependencies aren't a bug. They're a feature of a well-scaled organization, and it is neither possible nor *desirable* to eliminate them. Because agile teams in scaled organizations are interdependent—not independent—we need effective solutions for coordinating and integrating their work at scale.

First, we examine why teams are interdependent in a scaled agile organization. Then, we look at the following strategies for addressing that interdependence:

- **Planning:** Choosing an agile planning approach that supports inter-team collaboration
- **Continuous Delivery:** Integrating, testing, and delivering software continuously, safely, and sustainably at scale (DevOps/CI/CD)
- **Scaled Agile Culture:** Creating a culture that supports innovation at scale
- **Scaling the Backlog:** How to structure the product backlog in a scaled agile environment
- **Scaling the Organization:** How to structure a scaled agile organization
- **Scaling the Process:** Scaling the agile process to promote collaboration across teams
- **Scaling Tools:** Tools and techniques for supporting scaled agile development and team coordination
- **Potential Issues in Scaling Agility:** How to address challenges scaling agility, such as non-colocated teams and coordination with waterfall developers

17.3.1 Why Scaled Agile Teams Are Interdependent

Scaled agile teams tend to be dependent on each other because of the interconnectedness of a product's features, technical complexity, and shared components. Let's explore these issues.

17.3.1.1 *Interconnected Features*

Consider a mobile phone and the subproducts—or high-level features—it encompasses, such as a camera, photo-editing, messaging, and social-network capabilities. In a scaled agile organization, each of these subproducts is maintained by a feature team or team of teams.

The user can use each subproduct on its own, but the product's full value lies in how all its subproducts work with *each other*. For example, customers can access photo-editing and messaging directly from the camera—enabling them to shoot, edit, and send images seamlessly. Because subproducts are *designed* to work together this way, rather than as standalones, they will inevitably have dependencies on each other—and so will the teams that develop and maintain them.

The same applies when the product is not a physical object but a software system. Consider Z-News, a fictional, digital news service. Z-News's teams are organized by business areas (e.g., an order-processing team, a service-delivery team, a billings team). Now suppose that stakeholders have requested a new subscription service to deliver personalized news hourly to readers. This single request will require numerous teams working in concert with each other. The order-processing team will add the capability to order the new subscription, the service-delivery team will implement the delivery of customized news each hour, and the billings team will implement the monthly subscription charges for the new service. Across the value stream—from the subscription order to service delivery—each team relies on data produced by other teams. For example, the order-processing team captures subscription details, such as topics and sources, and the service-delivery team uses that information to determine what news items to deliver. Because the teams are interdependent, they need to coordinate their plans at the frontend of the development cycle, collaborate throughout development, and integrate and test their work continually as stories are done. *How* they do that effectively is the subject of this chapter.

17.3.2 Product Complexity

Another reason for team dependencies is that the competencies required to implement a feature for a complex product are usually too numerous to be accommodated in a small agile team of no more than ten members. Expertise is typically needed in UI design and coding, cloud services, the deployment framework, automated testing, the application stack, the software stack (infrastructure), open-source tools, database management, and business domain knowledge. Since a small team usually can't cover all these competencies, the competencies are typically distributed among a group of interdependent teams.

17.3.3 Shared Components

Another reason that team dependencies can't, and shouldn't, be eliminated is that multiple teams often share software components and are dependent on the team that manages them. As we'll explore later in this chapter, if we let feature teams change a component as they see fit, the result will be inconsistency in design and quality across the component. To ensure this doesn't happen, a **component team** takes primary responsibility for it. However, component teams introduce dependencies—because if a feature team requires a change to a component, it's dependent on the component team to implement it. Similarly, if the component team changes a component, the feature teams that depend on it are potentially impacted.

17.4 Planning: Choosing an Approach That Supports Inter-team Collaboration

There are two necessary but distinct coordination issues to address in a scaled organization: What approach will the organization use to plan work across multiple teams, and how will it time the integration and delivery of software across multiple teams? In answering those questions, it's essential to realize that the solutions to the two problems are not necessarily the same. In fact, it's usually best to use a mixed approach—a timeboxed or hybrid approach to plan large features at the frontend and a flow-based approach at the back end to continuously implement, integrate, and deliver improvements to the customer. We addressed the issue of flow-based versus timeboxed approaches earlier in this book. Let's revisit it now with a focus on scaled agile organizations.

17.4.1 Review of the Two Approaches

In a **flow-based** approach, each work item moves from step to step in the development lifecycle at its own pace, provided that work-in-progress (WIP) limits at each step are not exceeded. The aim is to achieve a continuous flow of each item without bottlenecks—from initiation through delivery. This is the approach used by the Kanban framework.

In contrast, with **timeboxed** planning, teams commit to *all* of the work items for a specified period (the timebox) at the start of the period. Two common timeboxes are the quarter and the iteration. A quarter refers to three months, but (as noted elsewhere) I use the term in this book as a shorthand for a release cycle, a SAFe program increment (PI), or any period of two to six months. An **iteration** is a shorter timebox, typically one or two weeks. Frameworks that incorporate iterations include Scrum, Extreme Programming (XP), LeSS, and SAFe. In Scrum, this period is referred to as a *sprint*. The maximum duration of a sprint is one month.

17.4.2 Which Approach Should You Use at the Frontend?

As a general guideline, feature teams benefit most from a mixed planning approach at the frontend, using flow-based (Kanban-style) planning for customer-driven features and quarterly (timeboxed) planning for large, strategic initiatives.

17.4.2.1 *When to Use a Flow-Based Approach to Accept Requirements into Development*

The flow-based portion of the budget enables teams to respond quickly to learning, rather than waiting a quarter or more to apply newly gained knowledge. This part of the budget should be set aside for small efforts that can be handled by a single team with minimal help from others. For example, the team might be exploring options to improve the conversion rate of browsers to subscribers or looking at different ways for a user to filter or sort content. To do so, they try out different options with customers and adapt them based on customer feedback. Since customers' responses drive each inspect-and-adapt cycle, there is no sense in trying to predict and prioritize their preferences too far in advance. Consequently, a flow-based approach is advised.

17.4.2.2 *The Pitfalls of Relying Solely on a Flow-Based Approach*

However, many organizations with which I work have discovered that when they rely *solely* on flow-based planning, the product becomes fractured because the approach encourages teams to think locally about their aspect of the product instead of having a whole-product orientation. Moreover, they're finding that an overdependence on flow-based planning makes it difficult to get big, product-wide changes off the ground. The reason is that, with each team working according to its own timetable, it's rare for all teams required for a large initiative to be free at the same time. Also, because there is no designated time when all teams meet to consider the next planning cycle, there is no obvious opportunity for stakeholders to gather and make their case for major initiatives so that they can be compared and prioritized.

17.4.2.3 Why You Should Reserve Some of the Budget for Timeboxing

To avoid these problems, an organization should reserve some of its teams' budgets for preplanned, timeboxed work—large product-wide work items that teams commit to before each quarter. The timeboxed portion of the budget ensures that there *will* a designated time—the quarterly planning meeting—when all teams will be free for product-wide initiatives, and stakeholders can lobby for large work items. Examples of large initiatives that benefit from quarterly planning include

- An initiative to change the way a user navigates through a product

- The implementation of a consistent user experience (UX) across the product

- Integration of the product with a third-party platform

As I write this chapter, a development group is working on an epic to support the needs of customers with visual disabilities. This change affects every area of the product that has a UI. It's also a strategic initiative that delivers a high-value business outcome because it will help their sales teams close government contracts. Significant changes such as this one, or those described in the preceding examples, require the upfront commitment of a large number of teams—something that is easier to achieve when all teams are free at the start of a quarter than it is with flow-based planning.

Quarterly planning also offers other advantages for large initiatives. First, it allows for better coordination with those outside of the IT organization, such as marketing and sales teams who plan by the quarter when developing go-to-market strategies, and Internet of Things (IoT) vendors who require significant lead time for development, integration, and integration testing. At the iteration level (one or two weeks), timeboxed planning has motivational benefits: it sets all teams to the same beat as they progress toward a common short-term goal; it also provides an opportunity for a group of collaborating teams to show off the value of their collective efforts to stakeholders on a regular basis (e.g., during a biweekly demo).

As an illustration of a company that has gone through an evolution on this issue, consider Hootsuite, a social media management tool. I recently spoke with a lead developer at the company (who also happens to be my son, Yasha Podeswa). He noted that teams have moved from a flow-based approach to one that is currently about 80 percent timeboxed and 20 percent flow-based. He expects the organization to settle down to something closer to a 50/50 split. Like this company, each organization should find its own optimal ratio through experimentation.

17.4.2.4 Why Feature Teams Shouldn't Overrely on Timeboxing

It is sometimes advisable (as in the preceding example) to *temporarily* overcorrect in favor of timeboxed planning to shock an organization accustomed to thinking short-term into developing a longer-term perspective. However, as a general practice, it's better not to tilt too far in this direction, because it significantly lengthens the learning cycle. For example, with quarterly planning, it can take as long as two quarters until development is able to act on learning discovered late in a quarter because the upcoming quarter may have already been planned by that time.

There are also cultural downsides to an overreliance on timeboxed planning: when almost all work is preplanned, teams inevitably start to view success in terms of outputs (delivering what was promised) instead of improving business outcomes. It is true that these shortcomings can be addressed somewhat by communicating a shared understanding that quarterly plans are not hard commitments (see Chapter 11, "Quarterly and Feature Planning"). However, it's also true that teams tend to be reluctant to change a plan once it's written down and committed to. For these reasons, as a general guideline, feature teams should use the flow-based approach for customer-driven features and reserve quarterly planning for large product-wide initiatives.

17.4.2.5 What About Non–Feature Teams?

The trade-off is different, though, for teams whose customers are other developers (e.g., coders who use an API) rather than end users. In this case, the balance often tips in favor of timeboxed planning.

Always keep in mind that there is no one-size-fits-all approach. Experiment to find out what works best for your organization, and be open to changing your practice over time. Because both approaches have their place in scaled agile development, I address both in this chapter (as I have elsewhere in this book).

17.4.3 Overview of the Analyst Contribution to Scaled Planning and Implementation

As an analyst, you contribute to agile planning and team collaboration at scale in numerous ways. You help collaborating teams schedule their work using lightweight tools, such as group-level story maps. You prevent dependencies from becoming impediments by using a variety of techniques: identifying and flagging dependencies and issues early during feature and story preparation, specifying end-to-end user acceptance tests (UAT) using ATDD/BDD, specifying and enforcing a feature definition of ready (DoR), and using business analysis (BA) techniques such as business process modeling to analyze workflow and data dependencies.

You are also an essential part of the solution to the widespread problem of insufficient POs. By acting as a proxy PO or a team analyst, you take on daily interactions with the team so that the PO can focus on outward-facing activities. Furthermore, you increase team productivity by reducing time otherwise spent searching out stakeholders and subject matter experts (SMEs) whenever the team has requirements-related questions. You also play an essential role in communicating a broad understanding of the business's medium-term plans and priorities beyond the team's natural focus on more immediate priorities.[3]

17.5 Continuous Delivery: Delivering Software Continuously, Safely, and Sustainably at Scale

In the previous sections, we examined guidelines for accepting stories into development, with recommendations for when to use a flow-based approach such as Kanban and when a timeboxed approach such as Scrum is the appropriate choice. The guidance was nuanced, with scenarios and arguments for each option. That's not the case once a story's implementation begins. Use a flow-based approach to advance the story continuously through the stages from coding to delivery. Don't gate the backend of development by waiting until the end of an iteration or release cycle to deliver stories. (Keep in mind that although stories are *delivered* continuously, the customer may decide to defer the release to the market for business reasons.)

Using a continuous, flow-based approach for implementation and delivery provides the following benefits:

- It provides the capability for a business to react quickly to changes in the market and customer behavior.

- It accelerates learning by enabling short feedback loops.

- It enables immediate deployment of bug fixes, small enhancements , and quick wins.

- It results in more reliable systems through earlier and more frequent testing.

In continuous development, each story proceeds smoothly through the code-build-test-deliver steps. First, the developer writes automated unit and low-level integration tests for the story. Then, the story is coded and tested. Next, it is merged with other development branches (stories by other developers and teams) and the master branch (the main product) and undergoes higher-level testing. Finally, it is delivered continuously to the customer in a releasable form. This process contrasts with the noncontinuous practice of waiting until the end of an iteration or an even longer long planning cycle (e.g., three months) to deliver software.

17.5.1 Overview of Automation in the Test-Build-Deploy Steps

The reason that not every large organization is following this approach today has to do with culture and automation (or lack thereof). You can't deliver frequently and safely at scale unless you have a culture that values that capability and is prepared to invest in automating the build, test, and deployment steps.

Figure 17.2 illustrates the steps that a change request goes through.

---

3. Thanks to Ron Healy.

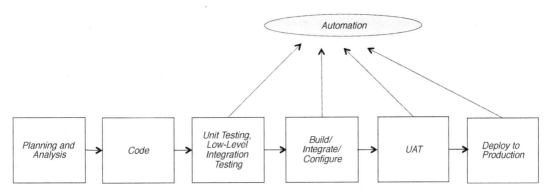

Figure 17.2   *Automation overview*

In low-performing organizations, the steps in Figure 17.2 are mostly manual. High-performing organizations automate the steps from unit testing through deployment to production. By automating these steps, an organization can deliver changes quickly *and* safely to the market. Scaled agile organizations that successfully achieve those objectives follow the DevOps approach, described in the next section.

17.5.2 DevOps, CI/CD

The most effective guidelines today for delivering continuously and safely at scale are encompassed in the DevOps approach. The following is a summary of its practices.

17.5.2.1 DevOps

DevOps is a software delivery approach aimed at delivering software frequently and reliably so that a business can respond quickly to change. It incorporates automation of the build-test-deploy-monitor steps and the dynamic provisioning of virtual environments and software services.

Collaborative Culture

The term *DevOps*—a combination of development and operations—reflects the approach's focus on collaboration and the removal of silos[4] among groups that have traditionally been separated. In a siloed organization, development teams, operations groups, and business stakeholders often work at cross-purposes. For example, business stakeholders and feature teams prioritize fast delivery of customer-facing features, whereas operations groups and component teams favor quality improvements. In a DevOps organization, these groups work closely together. For example, developers collaborate with operations to automate the integration, test, and provisioning steps (see "Shift Left" below).

---

4. Andrea Crawford, "DevOps Is the Modern Way of Delivering Applications Faster and with Higher Quality" [blog post], IBM, March 14, 2019, https://www.ibm.com/cloud/blog/what-is-devops

Benefits

With DevOps practices in place, an IT organization can get code from *committed* to running safely in production in about an hour, as opposed to a month or more, which is common in many traditional waterfall organizations. Because of the fast cycle time and reliability, software updates can occur multiple times per day.[5] Yet, despite the accelerated pace, quality does not suffer; in fact, it improves because of the increased testing enabled by automation.

DevOps Practices

Many of the practices in DevOps come from other frameworks and approaches, such as CD, CI, and Kanban. DevOps includes the following practices and guidelines:

- Shift left
- Build loosely coupled systems and components
- Lightweight change management
- CI/CD

Let's explore these guidelines further.

Shift Left   Shift left means to take quality assurance (QA) and other steps that are generally thought of as *latter* steps in the development process and move them to earlier stages of the lifecycle. With this approach, the DevOps competency group focuses on mentorship and support and nurturing team members who can adapt creatively to change. They provide testing tools, share automated tests, and attend reviews and demos to ensure that quality and automation issues are effectively addressed.

Build Loosely Coupled Systems and Components   Build software systems, subsystems, services, and components that are loosely coupled: they should be as self-contained as possible and communicate with each other in limited, well-defined ways. Loose coupling enables faster, safer improvement to one part of a system by minimizing the impact on other parts.

Lightweight Change Management   Research has shown that requiring teams to seek approval for changes from an external body, such as a change advisory board (CAB), slows down delivery without resulting in better outcomes (as measured by metrics such as change fail rate and time to restore).[6] The best outcomes result from using a lightweight review process that relies primarily on automation to ensure quality and create change records for auditing purposes.

---

5. As noted elsewhere in this book, bug fixes and small changes are often released to the market at this frequency, but major features are usually released at a slower rate.

6. Nicole Forsgren, Jez Humble, and Gene Kim, *Accelerate: Building and Scaling High Performing Technology Organizations* (Portland, OR: IT Revolution, 2018), 78–80.

CI/CD   DevOps incorporates CD and CI practices for integrating, testing, and delivering software quickly and reliably. We'll explore these practices in the following section.

17.5.2.2 Continuous Delivery and Continuous Integration

Continuous delivery is a defined set of practices and principles for getting features, fixes, experiments, and other changes into production or the hands of users, quickly, reliably, and sustainably. It incorporates and extends CI practices. Successful CD adoption requires strong leadership and a data-informed process. The primary principles of CD are described next.

Build Quality In

Build quality into the product during development. Don't accept code unless it includes automated tests, and has passed them. Address end-to-end integration issues early through ATDD practices—by identifying integration points, specifying end-to-end integration tests before development begins, and updating and conducting tests continuously as stories are implemented. (For more on ATDD, see section 17.5.4.)

Work in Small Batches

Following Kanban guidance, keep batch sizes small to enable fast delivery cycles and accelerated learning. Do this by limiting the size of user stories and splitting them, as necessary, before development.

It is true that there is an administrative cost to managing many small-sized work items compared to managing fewer large ones, but it is more than compensated for by reduced waste. The reason is that small story sizes accelerate learning—quickly informing the team about where to invest resources. Furthermore, by splitting work items into small stories that are prioritized and estimated separately, you expose wasteful aspects of a story that may not be worth implementing at all.

Use Computers for Repetitive Work

Use automation for mundane tasks such as testing and deployment; use people to improve repetitive processes and for decision-making. For example, let humans decide that a solution is ready to be deployed, but once they've indicated their approval, implement the deployment automatically.

Continuous Improvement

Foster a culture where everyone is relentless in the pursuit of improvement.

Everyone Is Responsible

See quality and system stability as product-level goals shared by all teams—not as the sole concern of QA or operations. Everyone should feel responsible for the *whole* product—not just the subproduct they are focused on.

Comprehensive Configuration Management

Use automation to provision environments and build, test, and deploy software based on information stored in a version control system.

Continuous Integration and Trunk-Based Development

As noted earlier, CD incorporates and extends **continuous integration** practices. CI was developed by Grady Booch as a practice for integrating separate branches of software development frequently into a single, integrated master branch—or **trunk**—through the use of automation.

In a CI organization today, integrations and builds occur multiple times per day. The lifespan of a development branch typically ranges from a few hours to one day.[7] No more than two days should pass before it is merged with the master branch.

Continuous, Automated Testing

Testing—from unit testing to end-to-end user acceptance testing (UAT)—should be continuous and largely automated. All automated tests should be written, run, and passed before a feature is considered done. Feature teams should do their own testing—including integration testing. QA should play a supporting, rather than an active role, coaching the team to create automated tests for relevant scenarios and providing automated test cases, test data, and testing tools.

Automated Provisioning

Automate the build and provisioning of software services and virtual environments. Take advantage of cloud services and other technologies to enable automation of these steps because, by doing so, you shorten time to market and facilitate on-demand scaling.

17.5.2.3 More on DevOps

As this book focuses on analysis and planning, I've included only a brief summary of DevOps' technical aspects. For detailed guidance on technical and other aspects of DevOps, please see *The DevOps Handbook*,[8] *Applying DevOps Principles at Scale*,[9] and *Accelerate: Building and Scaling High Performing Technology Organizations*.[10]

17.5.3 Test-Driven Development

Test-driven development is an approach to software development whereby tests are written before coding. In the original TDD process (focusing on low-level tests), a developer performs the following steps:[11]

---

7. Forsgren, Humble, and Kim, *Accelerate*, 215.

8. Gene Kim, Patrick Debois, John Willis, Jez Humble, and John Allspaw, *The DevOps Handbook: How to Create World-Class Agility, Reliability, and Security in Technology Organizations* (Portland, OR: IT Revolution Press, 2016).

9. Gary Gruver, Gene Kim, and Tommy Mouser, *Leading the Transformation: Applying Agile and DevOps Principles at Scale* (Portland, OR: IT Revolution Press, 2015).

10. Forsgren, Humble, and Kim, *Accelerate*.

11. "Red, Green, Refactor," Codecademy, https://www.codecademy.com/articles/tdd-red-green-refactor

- Write unit tests before coding the software unit.
- Run the tests. The tests are expected to fail (turn "red"), since the solution has not yet been written.
- Write the code.
- Run the tests. They should now pass (turn "green").
- If they don't pass, keep fixing and testing until they do.
- Clean up the code once it passes.

17.5.4 ATDD and BDD

Acceptance test–driven development extends TDD to include the testing of higher-level system behaviors that occur in response to requests from the UI. ATDD test specifications are developed through the collaboration of the customer, testers, and developers—often referred to as the *Triad*.

As an analyst, you support Triad discussions and write specifications for the test scenarios. Following ATDD practice, you write the initial test specifications before implementation begins—not after it is complete. In this way, the specifications act not only as test cases but also as **specifications by example**—instances that clarify the requirements to developers. All automated tests, including high-level integration tests, must be written, run, and passed for a feature to be accepted as done.

Behavior-driven development (BDD) / Gherkin is often used to specify the test scenarios because it results in concrete examples that are readily understood by all the perspectives (the Triad) involved in the discussions. At the same time, the specifications can be used by testing tools as input to automated testing. BDD refers to the approach. Gherkin is the language commonly used to write the specifications. The template is the one we saw earlier in Chapter 13, "Story Preparation," section 13.10.9.

Gherkin Template
Scenario: <<scenario title>>
    Given <<precondition>>
    When <<trigger>>
    Then <<postcondition>>

Following this approach, you collaborate with the Triad to specify AC scenarios at the feature level in feature files using the Gherkin syntax—tagging different parts of the file to control which ones are activated. This enables end-to-end tests to be specified up front before all the parts are available.[12]

Your organization may use alternative mechanisms to specify and run these tests. The important thing is *that* you specify them and *when* you specify them (i.e., before

---

12. For more on writing BDD scenarios, see Jens Engel, Benno Rice, and Richard Jones, "Feature Testing Setup," GitHub, https://behave.readthedocs.io/en/latest/gherkin.html

development). You don't necessarily have to use feature files and the Gherkin syntax to achieve that.

For more on BDD and the specification of feature acceptance criteria, see Chapter 10, section 10.9.

For more on Triad meetings, see Chapter 15, section 15.5.

17.6 Scaled Agile Culture: Creating a Culture That Supports Innovation at Scale

To be successful at scaling agility, it's not enough for an organization to address technology. Culture and leadership are at least as important, as explained in the following sections.

17.6.1 Effective Agile Leadership

Effective leadership has been shown to have a "measurable impact" on "profitability, productivity and market share."[13] To be successful at scaling agility, an organization requires effective leadership at all levels—from the whole-product level down to the team-level PO. Key features of successful agile leadership[14] include the following:

- Leader-as-coach
- Servant leadership / leaders who serve
- Vision with accountability
- Model the behavior you wish to see

17.6.1.1 Leader-as-Coach

Instead of a centralized command-and-control model, agile organizations follow a **leader-as-coach**[15] approach. The leader-as-coach focuses on mentorship and support—nurturing team members who can adapt to changing circumstances in ways that unleash their creativity[16]and support the vision. As an analyst, you support this objective by coaching developers in elicitation, analysis, and requirements management competencies (e.g., teaching them to split requirements into small stories that deliver value).

17.6.1.2 Servant Leadership

Servant leadership is closely related to the leader-as-coach model. The term **servant-leader** was introduced by Robert K. Greenleaf in a 1970 essay. In his book *Servant Leadership:*

13. Steve Bell and Karen Whitely Bell, "High-Performance Leadership and Management," in Forsgren, Humble, and Kim, *Accelerate*, 179–197.

14. Bell and Bell, "High-Performance Leadership."

15. Herminia Ibarra and Anne Scoular, "The Leader as Coach," *Harvard Business Review* (November–December 2019), https://hbr.org/2019/11/the-leader-as-coach

16. Ibarra and Scoular, "The Leader as Coach."

A Journey into the Nature of Legitimate Power and Greatness, Greenleaf relates that the idea came from reading Hermann Hesse's novel *A Journey to the East.* Hesse introduces the central figure, Leo, as a servant to a band of men on a mythical journey. Leo performs menial tasks for them but also sustains them spiritually. After he disappears, the group disbands. The narrator eventually discovers that Leo, whom he had known as a servant, was the leader of the order that had sponsored the journey.[17]

Servant leadership is self-described as "a philosophy and set of practices that enriches the lives of individuals, builds better organizations and ultimately creates a more just and caring world."[18] A **servant-leader** is a servant first—not a leader-first person driven by power or greed.

Recognizing that caring is mediated through institutions, Greenleaf also advocated for the **institution-as-servant** to society. Today, the principle of institution-as-servant seems more critical than ever as enterprises realize that, to survive, they must take action to serve the society they depend on as it faces unprecedented challenges from climate change and human expansion, uneven wealth distribution, and rapid technological and political change.

17.6.1.3 *Leaders Who Serve: Vision with Accountability*

Servant leadership sometimes gets a bad reputation because it's best known for the first part of the term—*servant.* However, there is an important second part, *leader,* that relates to vision and direction. To better capture this aspect, the term **leader who serves** has been suggested (Scrum).[19] As Ken Blanchard has pointed out,[20] unless people know where the leader wants to go and what needs to be accomplished to get there, there is little chance of arriving at the desired destination. Leaders should have a product-wide vision for their domain of expertise (e.g., quality, DevOps) and be *accountable* for translating that vision into action. As an analyst, you support the leader in communicating that vision to team members.

According to Blanchard, a compelling vision addresses the following aspects:

- **Why?:** What business are we in? Why are we doing what we're doing?
- **The Future:** If we do a good job, what will happen?
- **Values:** What values will guide the journey?
- **Goals:** What should we focus on doing right now?

---

17. Robert K. Greenleaf, *Servant Leadership: A Journey into the Nature of Legitimate Power and Greatness,* 25th Anniversary Edition (New York: Paulist Press, 2002).

18. "What Is Servant Leadership?" Robert K. Greenleaf Center for Servant Leadership, 2016, https://www.greenleaf.org/what-is-servant-leadership

19. The Scrum Guide describes Scrum Masters as "leaders who serve" the team and organization. Ken Schwaber and Jeff Sutherland, *The Scrum Guide: The Definitive Guide to Scrum—The Rules of the Game* (Scrumguides.org, 2020), 6, https://www.scrumguides.org

20. Ken Blanchard, "Servant Leadership: Vision and Direction" (PennState, 2016), https://sites.psu.edu/leadership/2016/04/01/servant-leadership-vision-and-direction-by-ken-blanchard

17.6.1.4 Model the Behavior You Wish to See

Effective leaders model the behavior they wish to see in others. This is especially true concerning experimentation and continual improvement. Leaders should demonstrate, by example, that they are willing to challenge and test our their own established ways of thinking.

17.6.2 Prioritize Quality

An agile culture prioritizes quality and everyone understands its importance. Decision-makers are willing to spend the time and resources to make quality improvements—even if it means slowing down feature development.

17.6.3 Remove Silos; Foster Collaboration

An agile culture removes silos and fosters collaboration between all parties involved in product development, including business stakeholders, developers, testers, and operation teams.

17.6.4 Foster a Culture of Rapid Learning

In an agile culture, people are encouraged to come up with their own improvement ideas and test them out. The organization uses the lean startup approach to validate improvement ideas for the product and the internal processes used to develop it. The following is a brief review of the steps:

- Make sure you're solving the right problem. Use root-cause analysis to determine the underlying cause or need.

- Form a hypothesis about a solution.

- Plan an experiment (the minimum viable product [MVP]) that will be used to test the hypothesis.

- Conduct the experiment. Use customer feedback and metrics to evaluate the MVP against the hypothesis. Use leading indicators to forecast the likely outcome.

- If the experiment is successful, adopt the improvement and continue monitoring and adjusting.

- If it is unsuccessful, decide whether to persevere and continue making adjustments, as described in the preceding steps; pivot to a new hypothesis; or stop all work on the initiative.

17.7 Scaling the Backlog

Next, we explore how to scale the product backlog for multiple teams. Before introducing new terminology and concepts for answering this question, let's review some terms we've been using throughout the book.

- An **epic** is an initiative that can encompass multiple teams over multiple quarters.

- A **feature** is a work item that can be implemented by one or more teams in one quarter (three months) or less.

- A **story** is a work item that can be implemented by a single team within a single iteration (if the team uses a timeboxed approach) or one or two weeks (if it uses a flow-based approach). Typically, the maximum size for a story is 8 story points, but some teams limit stories to 1 point.

17.7.1 Overview

Figure 17.3 is an overview of the product backlog in a scaled agile organization and its relationships to teams, team backlogs, components, and POs.

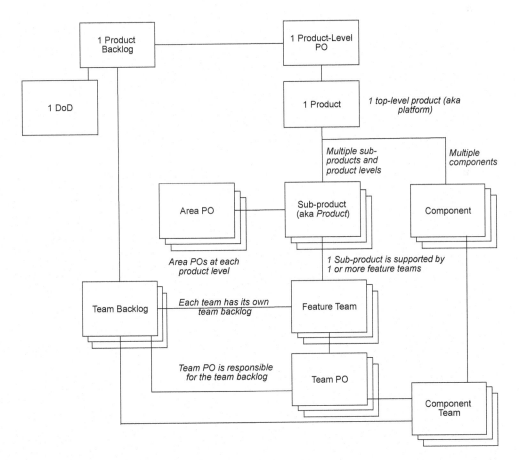

Figure 17.3 *Product backlog and team relationships*

We'll explore Figure 17.3 in the following sections.

17.7.2 One Top-Level Product

At the top level, there is only one **whole product**, commonly referred to as a **platform**. The top-level product represents a complete end-to-end good or a service, as viewed by the customer; it is *not* a software component. For example, a customer experiences a social network app as a complete, integrated product, not its parts, such as newsfeed and contacts. Everyone, regardless of their area of specialization, should be working to improve the whole product—not just one part of it.

17.7.3 Multiple Subproducts

The whole product encompasses multiple **subproducts**, or **product areas**, each representing a high-level usage. These may also be referred to as products, but to avoid confusion, I'll refer to the top-level only as the product (or whole product) to clearly distinguish it from sublevels. Each subproduct can have sub-subproducts for multiple levels.

The subproducts of a social network app might include a profile, home page, and newsfeed. A bank might have more than twenty subproducts at the first level with multiple levels of subproducts underneath.

17.7.4 One Product-Level PO

There is one PO at the top level, responsible for managing the whole product. This role may go by various names, such as chief product owner (CPO). In this chapter, I'll refer to the role as the **product-level PO**.

The product-level PO makes decisions with a whole-product view in mind and has ultimate responsibility for the *contents* of the backlog at the product level, prioritizing its items, and *maximizing the value of the product and work across the product at all times*. The product-level PO does not act alone in carrying out these duties. Other stakeholders are typically required for approvals and signoffs. Furthermore, the authority to make local decisions should be divested to lower-level POs.

The perspective of the product-level PO is mostly outward-facing, focusing on strategic issues and market differentiation. To stay abreast of developments on the ground, the product-level PO should practice **management by walking around**—dropping in from time to time on daily standups. The product-level PO often acts, as well, as a lower-level PO for one of the subproducts.

17.7.5 One Backlog at the Whole-Product Level

There is only one product-level backlog, containing product-level backlog items (epics and large features). Each product-level item is decomposed into team-level work items before its implementation begins. Each team can only accept backlog items that fall within its area of expertise.

The use of a single product-level backlog across all teams makes it easier for the product-level PO to view and assess priorities across the product and ensure that the highest-value items are always being worked on. It also simplifies the tracking of dependencies across teams.

17.7.6 Multiple Team Backlogs

Each team has a team backlog that includes its view of the product-level backlog and finer-grained work items specific to the team. As a rule of thumb, the number of items in a backlog should not exceed 100 to 150.[21] The guideline is based on the Dunbar number[22]—a suggested limit on the number of relationships a person can keep track of. Keep the total number of items low by entering far-off items as large epics and features. Split them into smaller-sized items only as they approach the top of the backlog. Hold pruning and ordering sessions regularly to remove obsolete items. (For more on pruning and ordering, see Chapter 15, section 15.11.5.)

17.7.7 Feature Teams

Each team should be a long-lived entity dedicated to a subproduct or software component. Most of these teams should be **feature teams**, focusing on a subproduct, product area, or feature set.

Each team should be as self-sufficient as possible, containing the business and technical competencies required to complete features in its area of expertise. However, as we saw earlier in this chapter, in most large IT organizations, it is neither possible nor desirable for teams to achieve *full* self-sufficiency for reasons that include technical complexity, the interoperability of subproducts, and dependencies on component teams.

17.7.8 Component Teams

A complex product will typically contain shared components—core microservices used across multiple teams and subproducts. If each feature team were given free rein to apply changes to these components, the result would be components without any unifying design vision or consistent quality level. To avoid these problems, create component teams. The team should be guided by a leader with a strong vision for the component. Its members should have the expertise to make changes efficiently, uniformly, and safely to the component. Component-team members may do this work within the component team. Alternatively, to reduce team dependencies, they may be sent out to feature teams as full-time, part-time, or extended team members. In that capacity, they may execute changes to the component themselves or coach feature teams to modify it in line with the component vision.

17.7.9 One Definition of Done (DoD)

To ensure a consistent quality level, specify only one DoD across the whole product.

---

21. Mike Cohn, *Succeeding with Agile: Software Development Using Scrum* (Boston: Addison-Wesley, 2010), 332.

22. David Edmond, Nigel Warburton, and Robin Dunbar, "Robin Dunbar on Dunbar Numbers," *Social Science Bites*, November 4, 2013, https://www.socialsciencespace.com/2013/11/robin-dunbar-on-dunbar-numbers

17.8 Scaling the Agile Organization

As noted earlier in this chapter, an organization developing a complex product will inevitably require multiple interdependent teams in order to cover all the necessary competencies for all of its subproducts and components. For example, the top-level product for a large company might easily include more than twenty subproducts. Each of these, in turn, might be delivered over multiple channels (e.g., Web, mobile), each of which requires specialized technical competencies. For a company such as SAP (a vendor of enterprise resource planning software), this can require, in total, more than two thousand agile teams.[23] In this section, we explore how to structure agile organizations of that size.

17.8.1 Scaling by Subproduct and Product Area: MyChatBot Case Study

The solution is to structure the organization by subproducts, also known as product areas. Let's look at a fictional example, MyChatBot. MyChatBot is an innovative company and product based on the hypothesis that customers will want to use chatbots for common customer-engagement tasks in order to increase sales and customer outreach at minimal cost. The company has identified ten primary high-level tasks customers would use MyChatBot for, including Sales, Marketing, Customer Support and Engagement, Analytics. In circumstance-based market segmentation, these are identified as the **jobs** customers hire the product to do.

 See Chapter 8, section 8.4, for more on circumstance-based market segmentation.

Figure 17.4 depicts how the MyChatBot organization is structured into levels of subproducts. For illustration purposes, I've included only four of its subproducts.

As indicated in Figure 17.4, MyChatBot is the top-level product. Below are its subproducts—one for each primary usage of the product. Four of these usages are highlighted: Sales, Marketing, Customer Support and Engagement, and Analytics.

Each of these subproducts has numerous sub-subproducts, referred to as *product areas*. For example, the Customer Support and Engagement subproduct includes a product area for each of the following sub-subproducts:

- **Collaboration Tool Automation:** To facilitate the collaboration of support staff

- **Ingest Content:** To load Chatbot messages originating on social media and elsewhere

- **User Efficiency:** To optimize the efficiency of customer-support users

Each product area is divided up into **feature sets**—groups of related product features. For example, Collaboration Tool Automation has one team for each of the following feature sets: tagging, triaging, and assigning messages using automation. In a larger organization, there might be multiple teams devoted to each feature set.

---

23. Darrell K. Rigby, Jeff Sutherland, and Andy Noble, "Change Management: Agile at Scale," *Harvard Business Review* (May–June 2018), https://hbr.org/2018/05/agile-at-scale

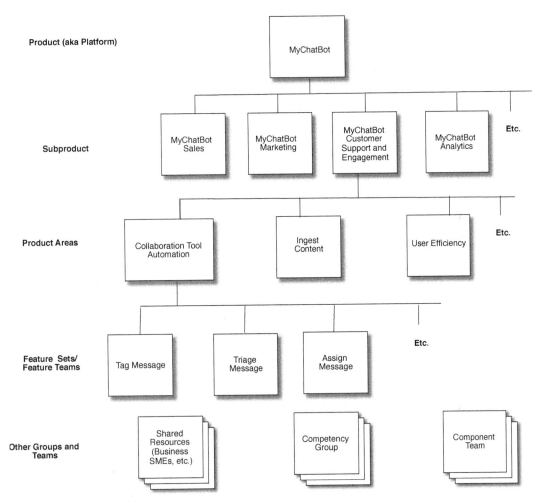

Figure 17.4 *MyChatBot organization*

In addition to the feature teams, Figure 17.4 indicates component teams dedicated to commonly used components. For example, MyChatBot might have a component team dedicated to an API that manages outgoing messages to third-party products, such as social networks. Figure 17.4 also indicates **competency groups**—associations that supply the teams with members, shared resources, and support within a particular area of expertise, such as UX design.

17.8.2 Scaling the PO Role

As mentioned earlier in this chapter, high-performing organizations require leadership at every level. A product-level PO is responsible for the whole product, while area POs are assigned at all the intermediate subproduct levels down to the individual team. Each of these teams is led by a team PO or proxy PO. We've discussed the product-level PO. Let's examine the other roles.

17.8.2.1 Area POs

An **area PO** should be assigned to each subproduct or sub-subproduct down to the level above the team level. (At the team level, a team PO or proxy PO is assigned, as described shortly.) Each area PO is responsible for a subproduct—a high-level use case, or job, customers hire the product to do. The role may be filled by a portfolio manager, program manager, product manager, or SAFe Release Train Engineer (RTE). Area POs have ultimate responsibility for prioritization decisions in their area—though (as noted earlier) other stakeholders are typically required for signoffs and approvals, and local decision-making should be devolved to lower-level POs. An area PO may also act as a PO for one of the lower levels.

17.8.2.2 Team POs

Each team is led by a team PO or proxy PO (described in the next section). The PO's outward-facing activities include speaking with business executives to understand strategic objectives, interacting with salespeople and customers, attending trade shows, conducting surveys to understand the market, and talking to data analysts to understand how people are using the product. Inward-facing duties involve close day-to-day interactions with the team—requiring about ten hours or more per week.

The full complement of PO-related responsibilities is often too excessive for a single person, so the work is often distributed among roles. If there is a team-level PO, the team PO focuses on outward-facing activities, while the team analyst focuses on inward-facing responsibilities. If the team is led by a proxy PO, the area PO focuses outward, and the proxy PO takes on inward-facing tasks.

17.8.2.3 Proxy PO and Business Analyst

It's hard enough for a PO to find sufficient time to work day-to-day with *one* team while fulfilling external-facing responsibilities. In practice, a PO is often required to support *more* than one team because of a scarcity of resources. An effective solution in this case is to use a **proxy PO** or business analyst at the team level to take on some of the PO's responsibilities. The proxy PO or business analyst works full time with the team to answer detailed questions about the requirements and communicate higher-level goals to the team so that the PO can focus on external responsibilities.

Formally, this can play out in several ways. An area PO may be assigned to preside over a group of teams, with proxy POs at the team level. Alternatively, a team-level PO may be shared by a few teams, with team analysts taking on inward-facing responsibilities at the team level.

17.8.3 Portfolio and Program Structure

Another way to structure a scaled organization is by portfolios and programs. This structure is especially well-suited to initiatives that span departments or entire products. Figure 17.5 depicts the organizational structure for XComm, a fictional company loosely based on a real telecommunications company.

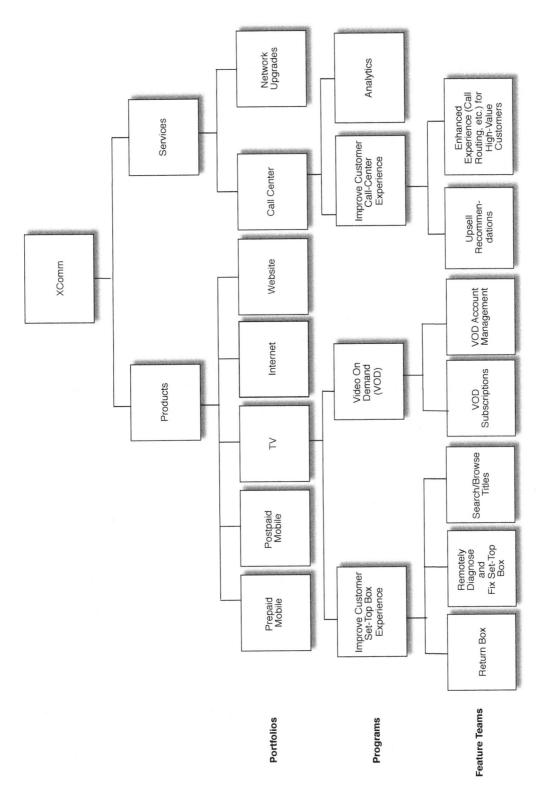

Figure 17.5 *Portfolio and program organizational structure*

As depicted in Figure 17.5, the organization is divided into products and services. The products division focuses on initiatives to improve the products XComm sells to its customers (e.g., mobile and Internet products). The services side focuses on quality improvements to its support services (e.g., call center improvements and network upgrades).

17.8.3.1 Portfolio Level

A **portfolio** is a broad initiative that may span departments, business areas, products, and systems. Figure 17.5 indicates that the products division contains prepaid mobile, TV, and Internet portfolios, each representing a line of business.

The portfolio is the largest organizing unit in SAFe, responsible for strategy and investment. Lean portfolio management (LPM) practices should be used. The focus of LPM is on providing resources to long-lived teams of teams[24] so that they can realize strategic objectives and achieve desired outcomes. This contrasts with the traditional practice of funding one-time projects with specified outputs. LPM includes the lean startup practices covered in this book, such as MVP, pivot or persevere, lean techniques for eliminating waste, and cultural practices such as servant-leadership (discussed in this chapter).

Portfolio Epics

In SAFe, long-lived initiatives at the portfolio level are classified as **portfolio epics**. A portfolio epic can span multiple teams of teams—referred to in SAFe as *Agile Release Trains* (ARTs). The following format may be used to specify the hypothesis statement for a portfolio epic:[25]

Epic description: For [customers] who [perform some activity], the [solution] is a [what] that [delivers this value]. Unlike [competition/existing solution or non-existing solution], our solution [does something better].

Business outcomes (measurable benefits)

- <benefit 1>
- <benefit 2>

Leading indicators

- <indicator 1>
- <indicator 2>

---

24. John May, "Lean Portfolio Management: How to Build a Better Enterprise by Being More Lean," Atlassian, https://www.atlassian.com/agile/agile-at-scale/lean-portfolio-management
25. Richard Kastner and Dean Leffingwell, *SAFe 5.0 Distilled: Achieving Business Agility with the Scaled Agile Framework* (Boston: Addison-Wesley, 2020), 154.

Nonfunctional requirements (NFRs)

- <NFR 1>
- <NFR 2>

17.8.3.2 Program Level

Each portfolio is responsible for a group of programs. A **program** is a long-lived mission—a theme or business objective around which teams are organized. For example, in Figure 17.5, the TV portfolio includes a program to improve customer set-top box experience and a program dedicated to video-on-demand products. The call center portfolio includes a program to improve the customer call-center experience. Each program is overseen by a program manager, analogous to the area PO we've been discussing.

Program Epics

Manage the work within a program using **program epics**. While a portfolio epic can span ARTs, a program epic is confined to a single team of teams or ART.

17.8.3.3 Feature-Team Level

Each feature team at the bottom level focuses on a related set of features. For example, the program to improve customer set-top box experience has feature teams dedicated to "return box" and to "remotely diagnose and fix set-top box".

17.8.3.4 What about Projects?

High-performing agile organizations today tend not to organize around projects because the overhead in winding them up and down is too high. Instead, they maintain long-term, stable feature teams that gather expertise in a subset of the product, enabling them to respond quickly to change requests.

That doesn't mean you won't find *any* projects in agile organizations. For example, projects can still be an effective mechanism for managing large, strategic initiatives.

17.8.4 Forming the Feature Teams

Figure 17.6 illustrates a typical team at MyChatBot.

Figure 17.6 is based on an actual company, but details will vary for each organization. Each feature team has a full-time proxy PO or business analyst and three or four full-time members. Many team members have specialized expertise, but at least one or two on each team should be jacks-of-all-trades—people who can pitch in to unblock bottlenecks as needed.

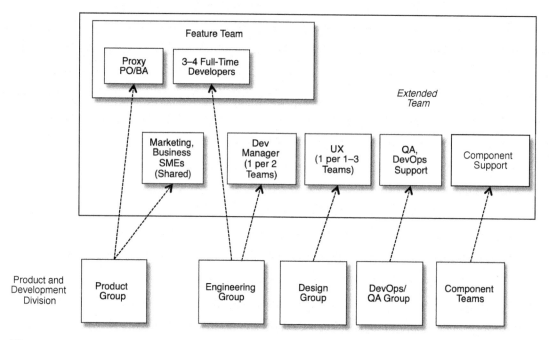

Figure 17.6   *Example of feature team with extended team*

Everyone on the team, regardless of competency, should understand that they work for the *customer*, not the IT department, and for the benefit of the *whole* product, not a component or aspect of the product.

17.8.5 The Extended Team

As noted earlier, if we included all of the necessary competencies for delivering value on every team, each team would need numerous members (e.g., those with competencies in automated integration testing, failure mode and effects analysis [FMEA], component testing, and *infrastructure-as-code* tools such as AWS CloudFormation). This usually adds up to too much expertise to contain within one small agile team of dedicated members, so some competencies are accounted for in the *extended* team. This group extends the core team with additional members *shared* across teams.

In Figure 17.6, the extended team includes marketing and business SMEs, a shared development manager, a shared UX designer, QA support to help the team with automated testing, and component support to assist the team in the use of components.

17.8.6 Component Teams

Figure 17.6 also indicates component teams, discussed earlier in section 17.7.8. Component teams contribute component support to the extended team—offering coaching and expertise in core microservices and shared components.

17.8.7 Competency Groups

A **competency group** is an organization for continuous improvement in an area of expertise—typically responsible for hiring, training, and maintaining a pool of individuals skilled in the competency. It should be led by a person with a strong vision for the competency across the product.

It's inefficient for each feature team in a large organization to seek out expertise on its own for the capabilities it requires. Instead, feature teams should approach competency groups for support and coaching services in their areas of expertise.

Competency groups may supply full-time members to teams (e.g., security SMEs and UX designers). Alternatively, they may loan out members to a group of teams. For example, the QA group may send out QA professionals to coach a group of teams in testing and share automated tests. Figure 17.6 shows that the engineering competency group provides developers to feature teams and development managers to the extended team. The following sections describe the competency groups in Figure 17.6. Actual competency groups will vary by organization.

17.8.7.1 Product Group

The **product group** members determine *what* should get built. Its members are accountable for ensuring that the *right* product is developed and understanding the needs of customers and the market. As a general rule, product group members are nontechnical and come from the business side (e.g., product managers, business SMEs, and others from within sales and marketing).

The product group contributes POs, program managers, CPOs, business analysts, proxy POs, and marketing and other business SMEs to feature teams as full-time members or shared among teams as part of the extended team.

17.8.7.2 Engineering and Component Group

The **engineering and component group** is responsible for implementation. Its members include software developers, engineering managers, technical architects, and business systems analysts (BSA). It may contain subgroups for specialized areas of expertise, for example, in frontend client apps, backend servers, third-party APIs (used to access third-party services), and the product's APIs. The engineering and component group feeds and supports the feature teams and component teams.

17.8.7.3 Design Group

The **design group** is responsible for ensuring a cohesive user experience. It contributes UX designers to feature teams.

17.8.7.4 DevOps/QA Group

The **DevOps/QA group** is responsible for coaching teams to automate the integrate-build-test-deploy steps and for assigning people to help teams develop deployment pipelines. The group should be led by someone with a strong vision for DevOps adoption across the product.

It may include a **QA subgroup**, whose primary responsibility is to the product's quality assurance function. The QA professionals' objective should not be to write and run tests on behalf of the team, but rather to *support* teams so they can do it themselves. QA support includes the following:

- Coaching the team to write automated tests
- Sharing automated tests with the team
- Providing the team with test tools and a test data bed
- Providing support for ATDD/BDD
- Attending planning and preparation sessions (e.g., Triad events) to ensure all essential scenarios and exceptions are covered

The role of the DevOps/QA competency group is particularly important regarding integration and integration testing—as these activities cut across all teams. While the teams themselves should be carrying out these tasks, it's not enough to rely on the teams alone to get it right. The DevOps competency group should provide vision and leadership on integration practices at the product level—guiding teams across the organization in the adoption of CD/CI best practices.

Other sub-groups may include a **cloud (AWS) competency group**, providing leadership, coaching, and tools in cloud-based Web services, and an **information security (Infosec) group** responsible for information protection across the product.

17.8.7.5 To Whom Do Competency Group Members Report When Sent Out?

If a competency group member is sent out to a feature team, to whom does the person report—the group or the feature team? The answer depends on whether the member is lent out on a full-time or part-time basis and whether that person plays an active or supporting role. As a rule of thumb, full-time, active members report to the feature team; part-time, supporting roles report to the competency group.

For example, suppose the engineering competency group sends out a developer with Hadoop experience to work full time with a team on big-data analysis. In this case, the developer reports to the team PO as a full-fledged member. On the other hand, suppose the QA group supplies one of its members to play a supporting role, coaching feature teams in automated testing. In this case, the QA professional reports to the QA competency group leader, not the feature team PO. Similarly, a cloud competency group may supply an SME to a group of feature teams to support them in the use of cloud services. In that case, the SME works closely with the teams and attends daily standups but has a primary responsibility to the cloud competency group leader.

17.8.8 The Product Owner Council

As noted throughout this chapter, some team dependencies can't be avoided, nor should they be. As a result, scaled organizations need to coordinate plans across teams. While lean, bottom-up measures for coordinating teams are helpful, they are usually insufficient to ensure a whole-product vision prevails or efficiently resolve coordination issues on a complex project. Instead, a coordinating body synchronizes the priorities and schedules of interdependent teams. This body goes by various names; I'll use the one most often used by the organizations I work with—the **product owner council** (POC). A POC is responsible for coordinating the teams within its area (e.g., a subproduct, product area, or feature set).

17.8.8.1 Composition of the POC

The POC should include representatives from all teams and levels of management underneath it. Figure 17.7 is an example of a POC based on a real organization. Other council compositions may differ.

The following sections discuss the POC members shown in Figure 17.7.

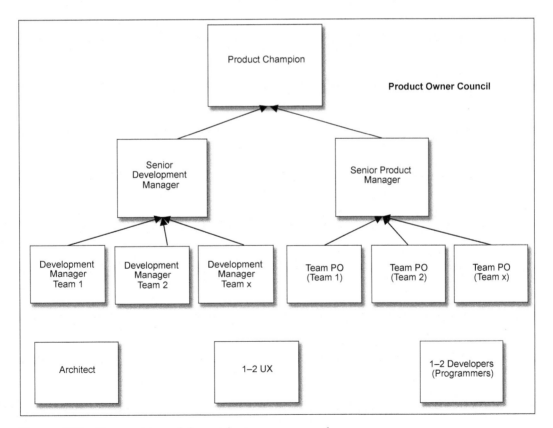

Figure 17.7 *Composition of the product owner council*

Product Champion

To speed decision-making and ensure a whole-product view prevails, the POC has only one ruler, the **product champion**. Product champions should have a grounding in both the business and technical aspects of the product, as they will be called on to balance priorities from both areas.

The product champion is a first among equals. The ruler has the ultimate responsibility for decisions but does so with the approval of stakeholders in collaboration with development and operations teams. Also, as noted earlier, some local decision-making responsibilities are devolved to lower-level POs.

The champion role is played by the PO at the corresponding product level. In a single-level organization, the product-level PO (above the team level) plays the role of product champion. When the organization is multileveled by product area, as illustrated in Figure 17.4, the area PO is the product champion for the product area's POC. For example, in Figure 17.4, the area PO for collaboration tool automation acts as the product champion for the POC overseeing the product area.

Team-Level PO/Proxy PO

Team-level POs and proxy POs contribute knowledge of customer features and customer-reported bugs to the POC.

Development Managers

Development managers bring technical issues such as technical debt and security issues to the POC.

Senior Product Manager

The senior product manager manages the team-level POs in the product area.

Senior Development Manager

The senior development manager manages the development managers across the teams in the product area.

Architect

Technical architects contribute guidance and suggestions for architectural improvements.

Developers (Engineers)

One or two developers are included in the POC to provide expertise regarding feasibility, estimate complexity and effort, and suggest more cost-effective alternatives for delivering similar value.

UX Designers

If they are required, one or two UX designers are included in the POC.

17.8.9 User Task Force

As a general rule, it's preferable for the development team to speak directly with real users. However, when a product has a large user base, a **user task force** is often needed to act as a sounding board for the user community and raise new ideas and customer-requested features.

The user task force members should be real users who understand the nuances of usage.

The person heading the group is referred to as a **user proxy**. This person may be a business analyst, a former user, or a manager of those who use the product, such as a customer service representative (CSR) manager representing CSR users. The user proxy meets regularly with the user task force to obtain a comprehensive and up-to-date view of the needs of the user community.

17.8.10 Release Management Team

Release management is the process of managing the deployment of a release across its lifecycle from planning, development, build, verification, deployment into production and support.[26] A **release management team** may be formed to set standards for the build-test-release process and implement release and version controls. Alternatively, these responsibilities may be covered by other teams (e.g., DevOps and CI teams).

In a mature scaled agile organization, the release management team plays a visionary and supportive role—helping teams carry out automated build-and-test activities on their own. As a transitional practice in a less mature organization, the release management team may also be directly involved in release management tasks in collaboration with feature development teams.[27] However, as the feature teams gradually take over release management functions, the release management team's role should evolve to focus on continuous improvement in the development organization's capability to deliver software changes frequently and safely at scale.

17.9 Scaling the Agile Process

We've focused on technical and organizing principles and practices that are key to successfully scaling an agile organization. Let's now turn to the planning and analysis process. How do you scale it in a way that supports innovation, collaboration, and coordination across teams?

---

26. Gabriel Gutierrez, "Everything You Need to Know to Master Release Management," Smartsheet, https://www.smartsheet.com/release-management-process

27. Scott Ambler, Glen Little, Mark Lines et al., "Disciplined Agile Release Management: A Goal-Driven Approach," ProjectManagement.com, July 18, 2015, https://www.projectmanagement.com/blog-post/61824/Disciplined-Agile-Release-Management--A-Goal-Driven-Approach

17.9.1 Scaled Agile Frameworks

There are several popular scaled agile frameworks offering solutions to this question. Most of the companies I work with, though, are framework-agnostic. That's appropriate because there *is* no one-size-fits-all framework that works well for all cases. Instead, take an experimental, evidence-driven approach and use what works best.

Each of the frameworks offers useful guidance. Many are popular enough that a planner or analyst working in a large organization should have a least a passing familiarity with them. The following sections provide a summary of some of the more widely used ones you're likely to encounter.

17.9.1.1 SAFe

If you're an agile business analyst, it probably won't be long before you run into SAFe. A primary reason is that it's popular among the same kinds of organizations that tend to hire business analysts. Another is that many SAFe concepts, such as PIs and program epics, are widely used—even by organizations that haven't adopted the framework as a whole.

Teams in SAFe are organized into **Agile Release Trains**—each ART being a long-lived team of teams dedicated to delivering end-user value for an operational value stream (end-to-end business process). SAFe also includes useful guidance concerning LPM and program management, as described in section 17.8.3.

One of SAFe's key concepts is the **program increment**—a "planning interval during which an Agile Release Train (ART) delivers incremental value in the form of working, tested software and systems."[28] The most common PI cycle is composed "four development iterations followed by one innovation and planning (IP) iteration."[29] SAFe does not proscribe a specific length for a PI, but it notes that "a typical PI duration is 8–12 weeks."[30]

SAFe is controversial in agile circles. For example, Ron Jeffries, one of the originators of XP, argues that while SAFe plays lip service to agile practices such as CD, it actually normalizes antipatterns that work against them[31]—such as its acceptance of a late-stage hardening iteration between PIs. Some of this criticism is misplaced. For example, SAFe doesn't *require* a hardening iteration—though it does (at least at the time of this writing) require that an IP iteration be reserved for each PI cycle. Moreover, SAFe's hardening iteration is not intended as a mechanism for deferring integration and testing activities.

Despite the controversies, some SAFe concepts and practices, such as planning and coordinating at the PI level, are useful whether you adopt the whole framework or not. The most effective way to benefit from SAFe is to apply its practices where they are helpful but to focus less on its formal structures and events.

---

28. Richard Kastner and Dean Leffingwell, *SAFe 5.0 Distilled: Achieving Business Agility with the Scaled Agile Framework* (Boston: Addison-Wesley, 2020), 274.

29. Leffingwell et al., *SAFe Reference Guide*, 274.

30. Leffingwell et al., 274.

31. Ron Jeffries, "Issues with SAFe," April 2, 2014, https://ronjeffries.com/xprog/articles/issues-with-safe

17.9.1.2 LeSS: Large Scale Scrum

LeSS was developed in 2005 by Craig Larman and Bas Vodde as "a set of rules combined with guides for applying Scrum in a multiteam context."[32] There are two versions of LeSS. The smaller LeSS framework applies to organizations of two to eight teams. **LeSS Huge** applies to organizations with eight or more teams.

The guiding principle behind LeSS is that "Large Scale Scrum is Scrum"[33]—and that extra roles and processes should not be required in a scaled agile organization. Synchronization of teams is meant to be achieved through transparency and continual collaboration rather than through added ceremony. While some of the companies I work with are experimenting with LeSS, none have adopted it at scale. The chief reason is that they find that its hypothesis doesn't hold up—and that they do, in fact, need additional processes and roles (as advised in this chapter).

17.9.1.3 Nexus

Nexus was created by Ken Schwaber (one of the originators of Scrum) as an agile framework to extend Scrum to larger initiatives of three to nine Scrum teams working on the same product backlog. The term *Nexus* has two meanings. It refers to the framework itself and to a team of teams—a group of "multiple cross-functional Scrum teams working together to deliver a potentially releasable integrated increment at least by the end of each Sprint."[34] Like Scrum, Nexus is a timeboxed approach based around the sprint, a period of one month or less (typically one to two weeks) during which an increment is created.

17.9.1.4 DAD

DAD is a hybrid framework developed by Scott Ambler that builds upon other frameworks. It is non-prescriptive—offering several variations based on circumstances—including Scrum-based, Kanban-based, and lean startup–based lifecycles.

17.9.2 Overview of Scaled Activities and Events

Let's now turn to the activities and events used for planning, coordination, and preparation in a scaled agile organization. Figure 17.8 is an overview of these items. Please note that the **meetings** and **events** in the following discussion indicate any occasion when people communicate—whether informal or formal.

Figure 17.8 is simplified for clarity. Though the figure does not show loops, the process is iterative. The left side shows the overall sequence in which items first appear. The events on the right are held throughout the development cycle.

---

32. Craig Larman and Bas Vodde, "Introduction to LeSS," in *Large Scale Scrum: More with LeSS* (Boston: Addison-Wesley, 2016).

33. Larman and Vodde, "Introduction to LeSS," 5.

34. Ken Schwaber, *NexusTM Guide, The Definitive Guide to Scaling Scrum with Nexus: The Rules of the Game* (Scrum.org, January 2018), 5, https://scrumorg-website-prod.s3.amazonaws.com/drupal/2018-01/2018-Nexus-Guide-English_0.pdf

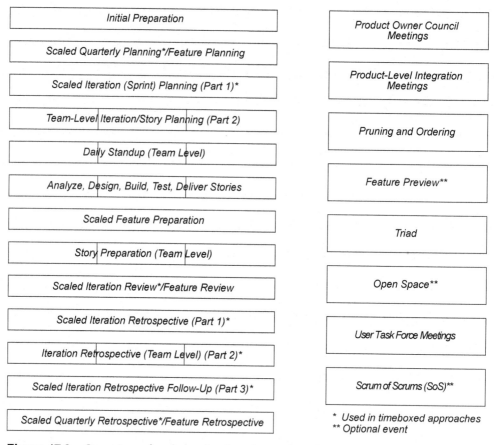

Figure 17.8 *Overview of scaled agile planning and analysis events*

We walk through the scaled agile development process in the upcoming sections, focusing on the following activities and events. (For guidance on other events, such as pruning and ordering, see Chapter 15, "Rolling Analysis and Preparation—Day-to-Day Activities.")

- Initial preparation
- Scaled quarterly planning/feature planning
- Scaled iteration (sprint) planning meetings (product and team levels)
- Feature preview
- Integration meetings
- Daily standup
- Scrum of Scrums (SoS)
- Product owner council (POC) meeting
- Scaled feature preparation

- Story preparation (team level)
- User task force meetings
- Scaled iteration review/feature review
- Scaled iteration retrospective (product and team levels)
- Scaled quarterly retrospective/feature retrospective
- Open Space events

17.9.3 Initial Preparation

To prepare for a scaled initiative, you perform the visioning and backlog-seeding tasks outlined in Chapter 7, "Visioning," and Chapter 8, "Seeding the Backlog—Discovering and Grading Features." To summarize, the steps are as follows:

- Perform a root-cause analysis to determine the source of the problem.
- Develop a vision for the product or change initiative.
- Identify the leap of faith hypothesis for the proposed product, epic, or feature.
- Use MVPs to test the hypothesis with real customers.
- Pivot or persevere—assess whether to continue in the same direction toward the vision or abandon the hypothesis and make a radical shift.

At the feature level, you follow this process to test the feature's hypothesis and determine the minimum marketable feature (MMF)—the smallest version of the feature that would be viewed as valuable by customers if released to the market. If the hypothesis is proven, the feature is added to the product backlog to be more fully developed.

17.9.3.1 Initial Feature and Story Preparation

As an analyst, you contribute to the preparation of the backlog's first features and stories at the start of the initiative. Feature preparation activities include determining the MMF, matching work items to teams, identifying integration points and risks, and drafting the technical architecture and user experience.

Story preparation occurs at the team level. It includes splitting work items into small stories and specifying story acceptance criteria.

Once development is underway, you prepare work items in a rolling fashion, as described in sections 17.9.12 and 17.9.13.

17.9.3.2 Preparing the Architectural Runway

The technical work involved in feature and story preparation is sometimes referred to as preparing the **architectural runway**. As the term suggests, the runway lays the groundwork for development to "take off" at its scheduled time. Runway preparation activities include identifying existing components and services that will be accessed, determining the protocols used by services to communicate with each other, creating the required infrastructure, and providing guidance on best practices.[35]

17.9.4 Scaled Quarterly and Feature Planning

In the following sections, we examine the planning of upcoming features in a scaled organization. In a timeboxed planning context, this occurs as part of quarterly planning.

The objectives of quarterly and feature planning are as follows:

- Review and align business and technical goals and objectives across teams for the upcoming quarter or feature.

- Review and revise future quarterly goals.

- For quarterly planning, determine what features will be included in the planning cycle; estimate and prioritize items in the quarterly backlog.

- Coordinate and align team-level plans for the quarter or feature.

- Verify that the planned features are sufficiently prepared for implementation to begin without delay or unnecessary rework.

17.9.4.1 Timing Considerations

If the teams use a flow-based planning approach such as Kanban, they conduct scaled feature planning on each feature as it approaches the top of the backlog. Only those teams affected by the feature need to attend the planning session.

If the teams use a timeboxed approach, all of the product area's teams gather for a scaled quarterly planning meeting to commit to the goals and features for the upcoming quarter. Quarterly planning should occur concurrently with ongoing development *during* the latter half of the previous quarter; don't dedicate an iteration to it. (Note, though, that this conflicts with SAFe guidance requiring an Innovation and planning iteration before each PI.)

That said, organizations that can't build, test, and deploy in a continuous, safe fashion may need to reserve a hardening iteration at the end of a release cycle as a remedial practice until they achieve DevOps/CD readiness. In that case, the hardening iteration may be used to complete the previous planning cycle and prepare for the next one.

17.9.4.2 Preconditions for Quarterly and Feature Planning

On entry to planning, each feature under consideration has been prepared and is *feature ready* (i.e., sufficiently prepared so it can be implemented without undue delay or rework). To be feature ready, a feature must satisfy the following conditions:

- It complies with the feature definition of ready (DoR) if one has been specified.

- It can be implemented within a quarter by one or more teams.

---

35. Ben Morris, "What Should a Scaled Agile 'Architectural Runway' Actually Look Like?" October 12, 2017, https://www.ben-morris.com/what-does-a-scaled-agile-architectural-runway-actually-look-like

- Its integration points and issues have been identified.

- A solution for the feature has been drafted.

- UX design has begun.

- The architectural runway is prepared.

- All teams on which delivery of the feature is dependent have been tentatively assigned to the feature.

17.9.4.3 Checklist of Attendees

Use the checklist in Appendix A.12 when considering whom to invite. Actual invitees will vary by organization and initiative. If the organization uses flow-based planning (e.g., Kanban), invite representatives from the teams that will collaborate on the feature. If it uses a timeboxed approach, invite representatives from *all* the teams in the product area.

17.9.4.4 Overview of Quarterly and Feature Planning

You conduct quarterly planning at two levels: the team level and the scaled, multiteam level (also known as product level, product-area level). Teams first gather for an overview of the vision, goals, and upcoming features. Then, they break out into teams for team-level planning before reconvening to resolve inter-team dependencies and address impediments.

The planning process may be informal, involving a few short, one- or two-hour meetings during the last weeks of the previous quarter or feature. Alternatively, it may take place as a formal gathering of teams at the start of the quarter or feature being planned. The typical duration of a scaled quarterly planning event is one and a half to two days.

Teams should be colocated for the event—assuming it is safe and practical to do so.[36] Colocation makes it easier to synchronize plans when dependencies are discovered, build cross-team relationships, and prevent siloing. Furthermore, it supports collaboration and a whole-product culture. If physical colocation isn't possible, use a virtual equivalent. Select a virtual meeting application that supports breakout rooms (e.g., Microsoft Teams or Zoom).

> **Tip**
> You can hack tools that don't include breakout rooms to provide equivalent functionality. Set up several conversations or meetings in separate windows—one for the entire group (multiple teams) and one for each team. To change rooms, attendees transfer back and forth from the group conversation to their team conversation.

---

36. Due to the pandemic being experienced at the time of this writing, I have to add the caveat that in-person guidance should only be utilized when it does not risk the health of attendees.

17.9.4.5 *Inputs and Deliverables*

The primary inputs to quarterly planning and feature planning are the proposed features (or feature). For quarterly planning, prepare enough ready features to meet the capacity for all teams during the quarter, plus a few extra features in case they can be accommodated. The actual number will depend on the number of teams in the product area (or ART) and team sizes. A general rule of thumb is to prepare ten to fifteen features per quarter (or PI), but larger product areas can accommodate twenty to thirty features.

Other inputs include the long-term, strategic product roadmap, journey maps, process maps, high-level solution architecture, projected team velocities, and high-priority process-improvement items identified in the previous quarterly retrospective.

The main deliverables of the event include the following:

- The goals and objectives

- Planned date or date range when the feature or features will be released

- Milestones

- Multiteam quarterly (release) backlog containing features

- Team-level quarterly (release) backlogs containing stories and tasks

17.9.4.6 *The Program Board*

SAFe's **program board** is a useful artifact for planning and coordinating work across multiple teams. It is similar to the quarterly roadmap we saw in Chapter 11, Figure 11.3, but adapted for multiple teams. You can use a program board to plan all features for an upcoming quarter, or to coordinate teams collaborating on a feature. Figure 17.9 illustrates the elements of a program board.

	Iteration 1	Iteration 2	Iteration 3	Iteration 4
Milestones/events	Milestone or event			
Team 1	Feature / Dependency			
Team 2				
Team 3				
Team 4				

Figure 17.9 *Program board template*

In the example in Figure 17.9, the planning cycle is subdivided into four fixed-length iterations. Typical durations for an iteration are one week and two weeks.

The figure contains a row for milestones and a row for each team within the product area (or SAFe ART). Color-coded cards are used as follows (which are not visible in the print edition of this book):

- Orange cards denote milestones and events
- Blue cards denote features
- Red cards indicate dependencies

Indicating Dependency Relationships

In Figure 17.9, a string between two items indicates a dependency between them. Another option for showing dependencies is to utilize color-coded cards and dots, where the color denotes the team. For example, a feature or event that belongs to the Yellow team is written on a yellow card. A blue dot on a card denotes a dependency on the Blue team. This scheme may be used to indicate dependencies on other multiteam artifacts as well, such as timelines and story maps. For an example of dot-dependencies, see Figure 11.4.

17.9.4.7 Facilitation Guidelines

The meeting location should contain one large common area where the teams can convene to discuss common issues and breakout areas where teams can conduct team-level planning sessions. If the event is virtual, set up virtual breakout rooms before the meeting—one room per team—plus one main room for everyone to convene in.

Encourage teams to be transparent while working on team-level plans so that dependencies can be easily spotted. Hold a multiteam checkpoint every hour so that teams can synchronize plans. At the checkpoint, teams update each other on progress since the last checkpoint and notify others of any impediments and dependencies they've discovered.

17.9.4.8 Topics (Agenda)

The following is a list of topics for the meeting. If you are holding informal meetings, use it as a general guide for what to discuss. If the meeting is formal, use it as the basis for an agenda. For a more detailed agenda, see SAFe PI planning guidelines.[37]

Day 1

Morning: Updates

- Business and backlog update
- Architecture vision
- Practices and tools update
- Set release date/date range, cadence, budget

---

37. Kastner and Leffingwell, *SAFe 5.0 Distilled*, 104–107.

Afternoon: Exploration and Planning

- Part 1: Team-level exploration and planning (3 hours)
- Part 2: Inter-team collaboration (multiteam) (2 hours)

Day 2

Morning: Team-Level Commitment

- Part 1: Product-area synchronization (multiteam) (1 hour)
- Part 2: Team-level planning and commitment (3 hours)

Afternoon: Product-Level Commitment

- Part 1: Product-area synchronization (multiteam) (3 hours)
- Part 2: Quarterly planning meeting retrospective

Let's walk through these items.

Day 1 Morning: Updates

The morning of the first day is devoted to issues that affect all teams, including reviewing the product vision, objectives and the features (or feature) under consideration.

Business Update A senior business executive updates the group on the product's positioning in the market, recent challenges and opportunities, current needs, the current product vision, goals and objectives, and quarterly goals and objectives.

Backlog Update The area PO summarizes the features under consideration. The group reviews high-priority process improvement items identified in the previous quarterly retrospective. Work items identified for the quarter during the updates are added to the quarterly backlog.

Architecture Vision The technical architect explains the vision for the system architecture and updates the group on current and future changes.

Practices and Tools Update Development managers update the group on practices and tools to support agility at scale (e.g., automated testing practices, requirements management tools, changes to the DoR and DoD).

Set Release Date/Date Range, Cadence, Budget The group sets and confirms a date or *date range* to release the changes to customers and app stores. If the organization uses fixed iterations, the group agrees on a common cadence (iteration length). Each team submits its budget based on projected capacity.

 For guidelines on determining the team capacity, see Chapter 11, section 11.11.1.4.

Day 1 Afternoon: Exploration and Planning

The afternoon of day 1 is devoted to team-level planning, followed by cross-team coordination, as described in Part 1 and Part 2 below.

Part 1: Team-Level Exploration and Planning (3 Hours)   Teams meet in breakout areas to conduct team-level planning sessions. Encourage teams to be transparent: teams should be able to view the plans of other teams.

Each team determines what features it will be able to implement on the basis of its capacity and matches them to iterations (or weeks) in the planning cycle, according to the guidelines in Chapter 11. The team also identifies milestones, dependencies, and impediments in the plan.

Checkpoints (SoS)

Every hour, the facilitator calls for a five- to ten-minute checkpoint (or SoS).[38] Teams meet in the group area to coordinate plans. You may use the following three questions to structure the conversation:

- What has my team done since the last checkpoint that could affect other teams? For example, my team encountered unexpected technical difficulties in implementing a feature that others depend on.

- What is my team planning to do before the next checkpoint that could affect other teams' plans? For example, my team will be implementing or postponing a service used by other teams.

- What impediments is my team experiencing? How can other teams help? Examples of impediments include the following:
  - My team needs subject-matter expertise from another team to estimate the next set of features.
  - My team depends on another team to deliver a feature, but the other team has not committed to the necessary work.

Part 2: Inter-team Collaboration (Multiteam) (2 Hours)   Following team-level planning, the teams gather to present their plans to each other. They also describe the dependencies, impediments, and risks that were raised during the team breakouts. The teams may spend up to an hour negotiating and collaborating to address coordination issues, readjusting their schedules as necessary to reduce impediments.

Day 2 Morning: Team-Level Commitment

The morning of day 2 is focused on team-level planning and commitment.

Part 1: Product-Area Synchronization (Multiteam) (1 Hour)   The teams gather to describe the adjustments they made to their team-level plans at the end of the previous day.

---

38. Cohn, *Succeeding with Agile*, 341.

Part 2: Team-Level Planning and Commitment (3 Hours)   Next, the group breaks out into team sessions to continue the team-level planning begun on day 1. Each team commits to its team-level quarterly plan and goal.

Day 2 Afternoon: Product-Level Commitment

In the afternoon of day 2, the teams gather to discuss risks and impediments and agree on a plan to address them. The meeting ends with a confidence vote on the product-level quarterly or feature plan. A planning retrospective is held afterward to assess the event and suggest improvements. Details follow.

Part 1: Product-Area Synchronization (Multiteam) (3 Hours)   Each team presents its plans and describes any remaining dependencies, impediments, and risks. Attendees discuss these issues and come to a consensus on how to address them. As each plan is reviewed and approved by business decision makers, it is posted in the room alongside other team plans.

As the event facilitator, look for opportunities to consolidate artifacts from individ -ual team plans into group-level artifacts to support inter-team planning and coordination. Merge team-level quarterly (release) roadmaps into a product area (ART) program board. Merge team-level story maps into a multiteam story map. Create a consolidated list of dependencies, risks, and impediments.

The group commits to quarterly (feature) goals and objectives at the product area level. If some teams are unable to commit to the goals, discussions and negotiations continue until a consensus is reached.

Part 2: Quarterly Planning Meeting Retrospective   The meeting closes with a discussion of what worked, what did not work during the session, and next steps.

BLINK CASE STUDY PART 30

Create a Program Board

The Ask

The BLInK development organization has grown to include product areas. You've been asked to facilitate a release planning meeting for the four teams in your product area.

The release cycle will include four 2-week iterations. Each team has primary responsibility for an aspect of the product, as follows:

- Team 1 specializes in customer self-service features.
- Team 2 focuses on features for customer service representatives (CSRs).
- Team 3 focuses on BLInK business operations features, such as features used by adjusters.
- Team 4 focuses on features tied to the vendor of the BLInK device.

The expected deliverable is as follows:

- **Deliverable 1**: Program board

Inputs

The following inputs have been identified.

Milestones

The following milestones will be included in the plan:

- New campaign launch
- Immediate discount available
- Deployment to brokers
- Deployment to underwriters
- Quick quote deployment to customer portal

Features Lined Up for the Release

The following features are being considered for the quarter. Each is estimated to require about two weeks' effort by a single team.

- Add BLInK information to CSR call screens
- Immediate discount available to customers
- Bind transaction
- Initialize device
- Customer can earn rewards
- Quick quote for preapproved applicants
- Validate eligibility
- Send application information to the vendor
- Add BLInK endorsement, subject to limits
- Authorize enrollment
- Subscriber can submit activities online
- Create a customer dashboard
- Submit a Health Assessment
- Receive health recommendations
- Analytics report to the business (impact on sickness, death, number of claims)
- Summary reports to customer

What Transpires

The group discusses timeliness for the milestones and events and posts the items on the program board.

You walk through the list of features lined up for the release cycle. The teams tentatively select most of the features on the list according to their areas of expertise. A senior development manager assigns the final items. As features are assigned to iterations, you post them on a group-level program board.

Using the program board as a visual reference, you invite teams to consider dependencies between items on the board and mark them with red strings.

Deliverables 1: Program Board

Figure 17.10 is a draft of the program board as it appears after the session. Milestones and events, such as Campaign launch, are indicated in the top row. Features for each team are shown in the rows below. The connecting strings indicate

Milestones/events	Iteration 1	Iteration 2	Iteration 3	Iteration 4
	Campaign launch	Deployment to brokers	Deployment to underwriters	Quick-quote deployment to customer portal
	Immediate discount deployed			
Team 1	Immediate discount available		Subscriber can submit activities online	Submit Health Assessment
Team 2	Add BLInK to CSR calls	Earn rewards	Authorize enrollment	Receive recommendations
		Quick quote for pre-approved		
Team 3	Bind transaction	Validate eligibility	Add BLInK endorsement subject to limits	Analytics report (impact on sickness, death, number of claims)
Team 4	Initialize device	Send application info to vendor	Create dashboard	Summary reports to customer

Figure 17.10 *BLInK program board*

dependency relationships. For example, there is a dependency shown between the feature to Validate eligibility and the one to Authorize enrollment. The reason for the dependency is that you can't authorize enrollment unless eligibility has been validated.

Case Study Retrospective

Team plans in the product area have been synchronized, and impediments have been identified. Features, milestones, events, and dependencies have been planned and communicated on a program board—a centralized artifact that the teams will continue to use to coordinate their work.

17.9.5 Scaled Iteration (Sprint) Planning Meetings

If the organization uses timeboxed planning, the teams hold an iteration planning meeting at the start of each iteration. Planning is carried out in two parts: in Part 1, the team of teams forecasts what it will deliver in the upcoming iteration; in Part 2, each individual team determines how it will do the work. Note that teams that use a flow-based approach don't perform Part 1, since they don't have iterations. Teams that use timeboxed planning carry out both parts.

If possible, bring all the product area teams to one physical location for Parts 1 and 2. The teams convene in a common area for area-level planning (Part 1), then disperse into breakout areas for team-level planning in Part 2.

If the teams cannot gather physically at one location, they should meet virtually for Part 1, perform Part 2 locally, and follow up with a virtual meeting to update each other and synchronize plans.

Let's examine Parts 1 and 2 in greater detail.

17.9.5.1 Part 1: Forecast What Will Be Accomplished (Multiteam)

In iteration planning Part 1, the team of teams forecasts what it will accomplish in the next iteration. Attendees should represent the business and all of the development teams in the product area. These include the following:

- Facilitator: As an analyst, you may fill the role, or it may be filled by the area PO, a development manager, or ScrumMaster.

- Team representatives: For early iterations, all members of all teams should be present. Later in the release cycle, each team may send one or two representatives.

- Area PO

- Team-level POs, proxy POs

Inputs and Deliverables

The inputs to the meeting are as follows:

- Product backlog
- The increment—the most recent, integrated version of the software
- Past team velocities, used to forecast future team capacities.

Each story lined up for iteration planning must be *story ready*. Conditions for readiness include the following:

- The story is estimable.
- The story is small (can be implemented in one iteration; is estimated at no more than 8 story points).
- The story is prioritized.
- The story's value has been confirmed recently.
- The team that will be working on the story has been identified.
- If a story DoR has been specified, the story meets the DoR.

The deliverables from the meeting are as follows:

- Iteration goal, shared by the group
- Iteration backlog—an ordered list of stories accepted into the iteration, matched with teams

Agenda

The following agenda may be used.

Introduction and Update (Approximately 10 Minutes) As the facilitator, you explain the purpose of the event. The area PO updates the group on recent trends, opportunities, risks, and changes in the marketplace as well as conversations with customers, users, data analysts, marketers, and the product-level PO. Features, strategic objectives, and future improvements are also reviewed.

Forecast Capacity Each team pulls stories into its team iteration plan, summing the story estimates until the team's capacity is reached. The capacity is based on the team's recent performance with adjustments due to changed circumstances.

 For guidance on forecasting a team's capacity for an iteration, see Chapter 14, section 14.9.2.

Review Readiness and Done Definitions   As the analyst, you review the DoD with the group and gain agreement that the definition will apply to all requirements items (product backlog items).

If a story DoR has been specified, you review it with the group and revise it as necessary. The teams agree they will only accept stories that satisfy the DoR into the iteration plan.

Craft the Common Iteration Goal   The area PO and team representatives craft an iteration goal for the group.

Present Backlog Items   The area PO describes the focus areas for the next iteration and their relative priorities. A **focus area** may be a business theme or objective (e.g., to penetrate a new market) or a large feature, like compliance reports.

Next, the area PO presents the upcoming stories lined up for the iteration and posts them by focus area, sequenced according to priority.

Match Items with Teams   Going into the meeting, the teams should have a good idea which items they will be selecting because of previous feature and story preparation. During the meeting, the teams accept the stories and negotiate and trade stories with other teams. Any remaining stories that have not been self-assigned are allocated to teams. Typically, this is done by a group-level development manager or the area PO.

Problem-Solving   During the **problem-solving** part of the event, you promote the use of visualization tools such as story maps to resolve team-coordination issues. Integration issues are also addressed at this time. Recall that in preparing features and stories, the teams will have met with the architect, QA professional, and CI and technical SMEs to draft a solution, identify integration points, and flag integration issues (see sections 17.9.3.1 and 17.9.3.2). During problem solving, DevOps and CD/CI SMEs coach the teams to manage those issues through ATDD/BDD, CD/CI, and DevOps practices, including continual, automated testing.

Review and Commitment   As the facilitator, you or a development manager reviews team commitments to ensure that high-priority items are evenly distributed among the teams and that no team's capacity is exceeded. The area PO readjusts priorities as needed.

The teams commit to a common iteration goal, the common iteration backlog, and the stories that each team will deliver in the upcoming iteration.

17.9.5.2 Part 2: Plan the Implementation (Team Level)

In Part 2, each team determines how it will do the work. Part 2 is carried out individually by each team or jointly if teams are tightly connected. However, despite the internal team focus of Part 2, teams should, ideally, be colocated when conducting it (see the next section on big room planning for details).

The goal of Part 2 is to lay the groundwork for the selected stories to begin without impediments, delays, or unnecessary rework. Details may vary, but typically, by the end of Part 2, the following objectives are achieved:

- Stories have been decomposed into single-person developer tasks.
- Developer tasks have been matched with team members.
- Developer tasks have been estimated by the people who will be doing the work.
- A solution has been drafted.

Practices and objectives may vary. For example, some teams limit their stories to single-person, single-day work items. In that case, the stories are already so small and estimable that little is gained by decomposing them further.

During Part 2, the UX designer works with the analyst, team PO or proxy PO and with stakeholders to develop a user-friendly design with a cohesive workflow. The technical team begins preliminary work on the architecture and technical design.

17.9.6 Big Room Iteration Planning

In big room iteration planning, all of the teams in the product area or ART gather in the main room for Part 1, forecasting the group-level iteration goal and features that they will deliver (see section 17.9.5.1 for details). Then, they disperse into breakout areas to conduct Part 2—team-level implementation planning. As the event facilitator, coach teams that are closely related to locate their breakout areas next to each other and send scouts to each other's meetings. Advise the scouts to report back regularly to their teams.

When physical colocation is not possible, use a virtual equivalent. In this case, teams gather in a virtual main room for product-wide discussions and move to breakout rooms for team-level planning.

17.9.6.1 Benefits of Colocation

Although Part 2's focus is internal, the proximity to other teams in a big room planning event provides numerous benefits over non-colocated meetings. Inter-team dependencies are easier to address because if a team discovers one, a member can simply move to the other team's room to negotiate adjustments to the plan. Moreover, shared team members and stakeholders can move back and forth between breakout areas as their expertise is needed. This solves the problem of shared contributors not being able to be in two places simultaneously when the teams plan at separate locations. As this is one of the key benefits of colocation, you should monitor the breakout rooms to ensure shared team members and SMEs (e.g., a shared technical architect or PO) are circulating between the groups as necessary.

17.9.6.2 Walkthrough of Part 2

During part 2 of big room iteration planning, each team crafts a team-level iteration goal to support the group goal, plans developer tasks, matches each task with a team member.

and estimates the tasks. Guide the team to match people with tasks *before* task estimation so that the person doing the work can be the one to estimate it.

If a team discovers a dependency on another team, one of its members moves to another team's breakout room to request assistance and collaborates with them to resolve dependencies—for example, by resequencing their stories or adding developer tasks.

Every hour, you call a checkpoint (or SoS). You ask each team to send representatives to the checkpoint to tell others what the team has done since the last one, what it is planning to work on till the next checkpoint that might affect other teams, and on any newly detected dependencies on other teams. Then, teams update each other about the current state of their team-level plans.

Following Part 2, if there is sufficient interest, representatives from related teams meet for a deep dive on shared design problems.

For more on team-level meetings for iteration planning Part 2, see Chapter 14, section 14.10.

17.9.7 Feature Preview

A **feature preview** is a team-level meeting to identify upcoming backlog items and dependencies so that they can be addressed in time to avoid bottlenecks. Mike Cohn refers to the meeting as a rolling lookahead. The point of the meeting is to raise issues, not solve them. The meeting is held as described for a nonscaled organization in Chapter 14, except that it is concerned with inter-team dependencies—not just those within the team.

If your team uses Kanban or another flow-based approach, conduct the feature preview on a rolling basis about once a week. If it uses a timeboxed approach (e.g., Scrum), convene the meeting following iteration planning and each week thereafter.

The meeting should be short—about ten minutes. The PO and team inspect the product backlog to identify stories that will be developed during the next two to four weeks (in the case of a Kanban team) or the two iterations that follow the current one (if the team uses a timeboxed approach). This leaves enough time for both collaborating teams to readjust their plans and address the dependency before it becomes an impediment.

For more on the feature preview, see Chapter 14, section 14.13.

17.9.8 Integration Meetings

During development, the teams' engineering leads meet regularly to address integration issues through design modifications and automated integration testing. The meetings should focus on problem solving; they should not be rote updates—as is often the case with the "What has my team done?" format of an SoS.

During the meeting, integration, DevOps, and CI SMEs provide coaching in test automation and other CD/CI practices as required. The objective is to coach others to do the work themselves—not for an integration team to perform it.

17.9.9 Daily Standup

In a scaled agile organization, each team conducts team-level daily standups in the same manner as that described for a non-scaled organization.

 For more on the daily standup, see Chapter 15, section 15.7.1.

Some scaled agile frameworks also advise that multiteam standups be held at the product area level to address integration issues and provide updates. These meetings are also known as SoS meetings (see next section). However, these meetings are not generally advised. The reason is that integration issues are better handled through the focused, problem-solving integration meetings described in the previous section. Furthermore, updates to other teams are more effectively communicated through other means. These include automated tracking of changes to the repository and the use of chat rooms by collaborating teams.

On a more fundamental level, the problem with the multiteam standup and SoS is that they are a self-organizing solution to the integration problem. In practice, self-organization is not generally effective for addressing integration issues—*unless* the effort is led by someone with an overarching vision for how integration should be managed and automated across the product.

17.9.10 Scrum of Scrums (SoS)

Despite the preceding remarks, many organizations conduct SoSs, and the event is compulsory in SAFe. Let's examine it briefly in case you're asked to participate in one.

The purpose of a **Scrum of Scrums** event is for teams to self-organize to raise and address cross-team dependencies and integration issues.

The event's frequency is based on the needs of the organization. One to three times per week is common, as are daily SoS meetings. The duration of the event may range from fifteen minutes to an hour. The first fifteen minutes are reserved for updates by the teams; the remaining time is used to resolve issues that arose in the first part.

Each team sends one representative to the SoS. This person should be someone best positioned to deal with the issues being raised. Attendees at the SoS are expected to change over time as new issues come forward. Team POs may attend as observers.

If there are multiple product areas (or ARTs), each product area/ART holds SoSs for the teams in its group. Whole-product SoS meetings are also held, attended by representatives from each product area.

During the SoS, representatives from each team (or product area) update each other on progress and perceived impediments. There is no proscribed agenda, but the following three questions are widely used:

- What did my team do since we last met that might have an impact on the other teams? For example, a team may report that it delayed a story, implemented a story ahead of schedule, or changed a software interface.

- What will my team do until we meet again that might have an impact on other teams?

- What impediments does my team foresee that other teams should know about or can help us with?

- What else do we need to share with other teams?

As a rule of thumb, no more than fifteen minutes should be spent on the updates. After the updates, if impediments have come to light, interested attendees stay to work on a solution.

17.9.11 Product Owner Council Meeting

The goal of a POC meeting (referred to in SAFe as the PO Sync)[39] is to align the vision and prioritize work across teams, and resolve conflicts. Upcoming work items may also be prepared. The attendees are the POC members listed in section 17.8.8. These may include the area PO, team POs, development managers, technical architects, and a few developers and designers as needed. The area PO typically plays the product champion role (first among equals).

To understand prioritization conflicts and how they can be addressed in the meeting, let's examine a scenario loosely drawn from a real case study.

A telecom company is working on a feature to plan its communication towers using three-dimensional location data. Team A is working on the user-facing aspects of the feature.

The current geographical information system (GIS) only provides 2D data, but a new GIS is being phased in to support 3D coordinates. A component team will be updating the outgoing GIS API so that it sends location requests to the new GIS in order to access 3D location data. A prioritization conflict arises when the component team decides to delay the API update so that it can do it together with other related work.

The teams meet to resolve the issue in the POC. In one scenario, they agree to a workaround: Team A will temporarily bypass the API and access the GIS directly until the component team updates the API. Alternatively, the component team might agree to move the API updates forward to satisfy the needs of Team A.

17.9.11.1 Frequency and Timing

Convene a POC meeting before implementing a multiteam feature to ensure that all teams that will be needed will be available. POC events need not be long, formal meetings. For example, they may take the form of a few one- or two-hour discussions before an upcoming quarter.

If the organization uses a flow-based planning approach such as Kanban, hold POC meetings in a rolling fashion as each feature approaches the top of the backlog. Continue holding them as needed once feature implementation begins.

---

39. Kastner and Leffingwell, *SAFe 5.0 Distilled*, 108.

If the organization uses timeboxed planning, hold a POC meeting before each quarter to negotiate and prioritize the features that will be included. Once the quarter begins, convene POC meetings as needed. A common frequency is two or three POC meetings per week. SAFe recommends they be held at least once per week.[40] The duration of the meeting (or set of meetings) is typically thirty to sixty minutes.

17.9.11.2 Walkthrough

Let's walk through an example of a POC event.

Progress Check

The POC event begins with a progress check by the product champion. The champion notifies the POC of new, unexpected work that has come in. Then, representatives from each team describe their team's progress and impediments (e.g., prioritization conflicts with other teams).

Problem Solving

The team representatives work with each other and the product champion to resolve prioritization issues—balancing customer-facing features prioritized by feature team POs, technical efficiencies and debt-payment work advanced by development managers and architects, and strategic priorities presented by senior product managers. If a conflict cannot be resolved collaboratively, the product champion may impose a decision.

Both feature development and quality improvements should be included in the plan. A rule of thumb is to aim for a ratio of about 3:1 for features to quality improvements.

The POC meeting may also be used for feature preparation. This activity is described in the following section.

17.9.12 Scaled (Quarterly) Feature Preparation (Multiple Teams)

Backlog preparation is carried out in a rolling fashion as features approach the top of the backlog. Although this preparation is an incremental, continuous activity, it helps to think of two points along the continuum: **feature preparation** (the preparation of multiteam features) and **story preparation** (the readying of team-level stories). We've discussed these activities before in the context of single teams. In the upcoming sections, we focus on how you carry them out in a scaled agile organization. Let's begin with feature preparation.

The objective of feature preparation is to do enough prework that the feature can be developed without undue delay or rework. During feature preparation, multiteam features are split into team-level work items, each of which can be completed within one quarter, and the items are tentatively matched with teams. All of the teams needed for a feature must commit to it before implementation begins. As a general guide, each team should plan to work on no more than two features at a time.

As part of feature preparation, the teams also carry out some light architectural work and initial whiteboarding of the technical and visual design. They meet with the architect,

---

40. Kastner and Leffingwell, *SAFe 5.0 Distilled*, 108.

QA, and CI and technical SMEs to draft a solution, identify integration points, and flag integration issues. When an integration problem is identified, the technical leads begin work on a design solution.

Developers assess the level of uncertainty concerning the feature's estimate. If the uncertainty is high, they may decide to create a spike to analyze the feature further and improve the estimate—or increase the estimate to account for the uncertainty.

17.9.12.1 Timing Considerations

Begin preparing features with enough lead time to get them ready in time for development. A **ready** feature is one whose integration issues have been identified and for which preliminary design has begun. Furthermore, the feature has been sized to be implementable by one or more teams in a product area (or ART) within one quarter (or SAFe PI). If a feature DoR has been specified, the feature must comply with it.

If the teams are using a flow-based planning approach (e.g., Kanban), they prepare each multiteam feature or feature set as it comes into view—with a lead time of about six weeks for large features and two to four weeks for smaller ones.

If the teams use a timeboxed approach, they prepare all of the features planned for a quarter in advance, starting about halfway into the preceding quarter. Experiment to see which lead times work best.

Once implementation begins, the team technical leads hold integration meetings on a regular basis to work out integration issues as they arise and address them through design changes and automated integration testing (see section 17.9.8).

17.9.12.2 Participants

Participants in feature preparation include the following:

- Area POs (or SAFe Release Train Engineer): Responsible for end-to-end value; meets with stakeholders, developers, and QA to analyze the value streams affected by the feature and identify integration points and team dependencies.

- POs: Team-level POs for the teams involved in the feature.

- Integration and testing SMEs (CI, DevOps, QA): Provide leadership and coaching in continuous delivery and automation of the integrate-build-test-deploy steps. Help design solutions for integration issues.

- Technical architect: Prepares the architectural runway. Helps design solutions for integration issues.

- Team technical leads: Team technical leads work together to resolve integration and other cross-team issues by roughing out a design solution.

- Developers: Developers involved in the feature ask questions and estimate effort.

- Team analyst: Splits work items into single-team features and stories. Specifies the features and their acceptance criteria in accordance with ATDD/BDD practices.

17.9.12.3 Inputs and Postconditions of Feature Preparation

The main inputs to feature preparation are:

- The product backlog, containing sequenced features
- The feature DoR
- Projected team capacities

The postconditions (outcomes) of feature preparation are as follows:

- Features are ready and satisfy the feature DoR (if one is used).
- Features are split into single-team work items that can be implemented within a quarter.
- Features have been tentatively matched with teams, and all teams required for the feature are committed to it.
- The architectural runway has been prepared.
- Cross-team design and analysis issues have been addressed.
- Integration points and tests have been identified.
- Each team has begun to decompose its work into stories that are within the story size limit.

17.9.12.4 Walkthrough

The area PO discusses the upcoming feature or features with the teams. Details follow.

Prioritization

Organizations that use flow-based planning prepare each feature as it arises in the backlog—waiting until the last responsible moment in order to minimize waste in case priorities change. However, as noted earlier, teams that use a timeboxed approach prepare *all* of the features lined up for the upcoming quarter in advance to be ready in time for quarterly planning. In this case, the area PO and the team of teams collaborate to prioritize the group of features intended for the quarter. Factors to consider include the following:

- The feature's impact on profit
- The feature's impact on the end customer
- The strategic objectives supported by the feature
- Business and technical risks associated with the feature
- Opportunities addressed by the feature
- Cost of delay and Weighted Shortest Job First (WSJF)

For more on determining the cost of delay and WSJF, see Chapter 6, sections 6.5.4.4 and 6.5.4.5.

If priorities conflict, the group should attempt to come to a collaborative decision. Typically, they reach a consensus, but if necessary, the area PO decides with consent from approvers.

Developers ask questions to understand what is needed. As an analyst, you work with the teams to split multiteam features into smaller features that can each be accomplished by a single team in a quarter.

Tentative Acceptance

The resulting single-team features are then tentatively matched with teams. Each team accepts features until it reaches its capacity. To spread the risk, the senior development manager should ensure that high-priority work is evenly distributed among teams. A senior development manager or area PO assigns any remaining features that have not been matched with teams.

As a team analyst, you work with the team to split upcoming features into their main stories, focusing on features and stories that will be implemented first.

Feature Estimation

The team that will be working on a feature estimates it. Use Planning Poker to guide estimators toward a consensus.

You can use story points to estimate features, but it's usually adequate to use a looser estimation approach at this point. For example, the team assigned to a feature may estimate that it will take the full team (or half the team) x number of weeks to complete.

For guidance on Planning Poker, see Chapter 11, section 11.11.2.8.

Managing Dependencies

The teams raise inter-team dependencies that threaten to impede the timely delivery of the upcoming feature or features. Teams work under the leadership and coaching of the architect and technical leads in DevOps, CI, CD, and ATDD/BDD to design solutions for integration issues.

17.9.13 Team-Level Story Preparation

Once a feature has been prepared, decomposed into team-level work items, and matched with teams, further preparation is carried out at the team level. The aim of this activity, which I've been referring to as *story preparation*, is to arrive at small stories that are "ready" for development, estimable, prioritized, and testable. If a story DoR was specified, the stories are brought into compliance with it.

You carry out story preparation in the context of Triad meetings. The Triad comprises the people who represent the perspectives of the business, development, and QA. (Triad meetings are discussed in Chapter 13, section 13.6.3.) The business perspective may be represented by a team-level PO or proxy PO (if assigned), a business analyst, or business stakeholders, such as SMEs and approvers.

The inputs to story preparation are the story DoR (if specified) and the product backlog, containing upcoming work items that are feature ready (meet the feature DoR).

If your team uses a flow-based approach, you perform story preparation on a story-by-story basis, starting one or two weeks before the story's planned implementation. If the team uses a timeboxed approach, prepare all the stories for the upcoming iteration in advance, beginning about halfway into the previous iteration.

To ensure that all stories are sufficiently prepared, specify a story DoR and require that all stories must comply with it before implementation begins. If the team uses timeboxed planning, go further and require that the story DoR be satisfied for all stories on entry to iteration planning in order to enable a short and efficient meeting.

For more on story preparation, see Chapter 13 and Chapter 15, section 15.11.4.

17.9.14 User Task Force Meetings

As noted in section 17.8.9, when a product has a large and diverse user population, a user task force may be used to stay abreast of issues arising in the user community. The group is headed by a user proxy, who takes the community's concerns back to the teams.

In the first part of a user task force meeting, attendees discuss issues raised by end users, such as bugs and feature requests. These issues are added to a **user task-force issues backlog** and allocated to task-force members. In the second part, attendees review previous items in the issues backlog and report on their status since the last task-force meeting.

17.9.15 Scaled Iteration Review or Feature Review

A **scaled iteration** or **feature review** (also called *iteration demo* or *feature demo*) is a multiteam meeting to demonstrate new or changed functionality delivered through the collaboration of stakeholders and the team of teams (e.g., the teams within a product area or ART). (In Scrum and LeSS, this event is known as the **sprint review**.) Attendees include development team members and key stakeholders invited by the area PO and team POs. The review is intended to "inspect the outcome of the Sprint and determine future adaptations,"[41] obtain feedback from stakeholders, and motivate the teams.

Upcoming backlog items are also discussed during the meeting and reprioritized, if necessary, to optimize value delivery. The iteration/feature review contributes to motivation by providing an opportunity for collaborating teams to demonstrate their collective accomplishments on a frequent basis.

---

41. Schwaber and Sutherland, *The Scrum Guide*, 9.

17.9.15.1 Considerations for Teams Using Flow-Based versus Timeboxed Planning

If the teams use a flow-based planning approach (e.g., Kanban), they hold a feature review when the feature is complete enough to be released. All teams involved in delivering the feature attend the review. All Done stories that support the feature are included.

If the teams use a timeboxed approach, like Scrum, they hold an iteration review at the end of each iteration. All of the teams in the product area are invited to attend. All stories brought to Done by all teams in the product area are included in the review.

Guidelines for conducting a scaled iteration (feature) review are similar to those for single-team reviews except that multiple teams are present.

For more on the iteration review, see Chapter 15, section 15.13.

17.9.16 Scaled Iteration Retrospective

In a scaled iteration retrospective, all teams in the product area gather in one location for group-level and team-level meetings. The retrospective may be carried out in parts, as follows:

- Part 1 (optional): Scaled iteration retrospective (multiteam)
- Part 2: Team-level iteration retrospectives
- Part 3: Scaled iteration retrospective follow-up (multiteam)

Team-level meetings focus on internal areas for improvement; multiteam meetings focus on issues that cut across teams.

17.9.16.1 Part 1: Scaled Iteration Retrospective (Multiteam) (Optional)

Part 1 is a multiteam event with representatives from all teams in the product area. The purpose of Part 1 is to identify issues and impediments that span teams. Limit the event to about thirty minutes for a two-week iteration review and fifteen minutes for 1-week iterations. If possible, bring the teams together physically, but virtual meetings are also effective if that is not possible.

Attendees include representatives from all teams, team-level POs (if assigned), the area PO, and business owners, as appropriate. Although this is primarily an internal development event, business attendees are included because of their potential to remove impediments outside the control of the development teams.[42]

During the meeting, attendees identify issues and impediments that cut across teams. Use the following checklist as a source of questions.

- What should teams start doing to get better at collaborating?
- What coordinating mechanisms should we be using?

---

42. This guidance was included in an earlier version of SAFe. See Dean Leffingwell, *SAFe® 4.0 Reference Guide: Scaled Agile Framework® for Lean Software and Systems Engineering* (Boston: Addison-Wesley, 2016), 216–218.

- What decision-making processes should we use?
- How can we get better at prioritizing work across teams in a way that maximizes value delivery?
- What tools should we be using?
- What events and meetings should we be conducting?
- What roles and functions should we include?
- How can teams communicate better with each other?
- How can we do better at promoting a Whole-Product approach?
- What are teams already doing that we want to *continue* doing?
- What should we *stop* doing?

Team representatives bring these issues and recommendations back to their teams.

17.9.16.2 Part 2: Team-Level Iteration Retrospectives

Attendees move to team-breakout areas for Part 2. Teams that work closely together should be situated near each other so that they can confer about common issues.

During this part, each team spends about 30 minutes carrying out a team-level iteration retrospective focused on improving the team's practices. The team-level retrospectives are conducted as described earlier in this book.

 For more on team-level iteration retrospectives, see Chapter 15, section 15.14.

17.9.16.3 Part 3: Scaled Iteration Retrospective Follow-Up (Multiteam)

Following team-level iteration retrospectives, the teams gather for a follow-up to review their recommendations. Attendees include the area PO, team-level POs/proxy POs, rotating team representatives, and (if Scrum is used) the ScrumMasters. Part 3 should last about ninety minutes[43] for a two-week iteration and forty-five minutes for a one-week iteration.

During the follow-up, attendees feed intelligence gained from the team-level retrospectives back to the group. Team representatives discuss the impediments and improvements brought up at the team retrospectives that have an impact beyond the team. Topics may include recommendations for prioritizing stories, coordinating work across teams, managing inter-team dependencies, and mechanisms for increasing transparency between teams.

17.9.16.4 Virtual Iteration Retrospectives

If the organization is vast and attendees cannot be colocated, virtual retrospective games can help manage feedback from large numbers of people in real time.[44] These online

---

43. Larman and Vodde, "Introduction to LeSS," 13.

44. Luke Hohmann, "How to Run HUGE Retrospectives across Dozens of Teams in Multiple Time Zones!" Innovation Games, June 5, 2014, https://www.innovationgames.com/2014/06/how-to-run-huge-retrospectives

tools can be used by moderately large organizations (10 teams with 60 or more people) to extremely large organizations (250 or more teams with thousands of people) to identify common problems and the improvements likely to have the most significant impact.

Following is an outline for facilitating a scaled virtual iteration retrospective, with attendees participating on a shared platform.[45] The description is tool-agnostic; details will differ depending on the application.

Walkthrough

The retrospective begins with each team meeting individually to reflect on the past cycle. This part of the retrospective should take place at a time convenient for its members and last about one or two hours. If retrospective games are used, the teams play them individually at this time.

Next, attendees across all teams go online to identify what's currently working across the group, what's not, and what the group should start doing. An online version of the Sailboat (or Speedboat) game (described in Chapter 15) may be used for this purpose.

As the facilitator, you ask attendees to rate each item they've identified in the game (both positive Sail items and negative Anchor items) in terms of impact.

You pick the highest-ranked positive and negative items and discuss them with the group. You ask attendees to assign a zone of control for each item (e.g., whether it is within the control of the enterprise, product, or team). They post each item in the corresponding zone using an online version of the Circles and Soup game. Then, you ask attendees to assess who or what is affected by these issues (e.g., whether people, process, or technology). You use analytical software to illustrate and identify response patterns.

For more on the Sailboat game, see Chapter 15, section 15.14.5.1. For more on Circles and Soup, see section 15.14.5.2.

Figure 17.11 illustrates the responses for a large retrospective.

Each dot in Figure 17.11 represents an item that was raised during the retrospective. The dot's placement indicates the item's zone of control (along the x-axis) and the entity it impacts (on the y-axis). The colors signify severity (but note they are not visible in the print edition of this book). A red dot indicates a high-negative impact; yellow represents a medium-negative impact; blue indicates a medium-positive impact; and green signifies a high-positive impact. The figure shows clusters of negatives (lots of reds and some yellows) in the Team/Technology cell and Team/People cell—indicating that technology and people issues *within* the team are the areas with the greatest impediments, where intervention is likely to have the most significant effect. On the other hand, the Process zones across all scales—Enterprise (Product), Product Area (Program), and Team—are predominantly green, indicating satisfaction with process issues at all organization levels.

17.9.17 Scaled Quarterly/Feature Retrospective

The iteration retrospective is an effective inspect-and-adapt mechanism for reviewing short-term efforts at continual improvement. However, it's also useful to conduct retrospectives

---

45. Hohmann, "How to Run HUGE Retrospectives."

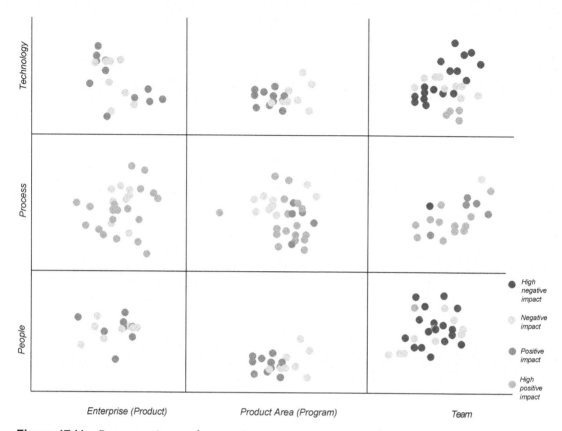

Figure 17.11 *Retrospective results overview*

to review progress on longer-term improvement efforts that may not show results for some time.

If the teams use a flow-based approach, convene a scaled feature retrospective at the end of a multiteam feature. If they use a timeboxed approach, hold a scaled quarterly retrospective at the end of the quarter with representatives from all teams in the product area (or ART). Attendees review how the past quarter went and begin preparations for the next.

17.9.17.1 Walkthrough of the Session

As noted in Chapter 16, "Releasing the Product," a retrospective should be an informal event focused on providing solutions to issues known to be problems. It should not be a formal event that follows a preset agenda. To describe the event, let's walk through one with you as the facilitator.

 For more on quarterly (release) retrospectives, see Chapter 16, section 16.6.

Part 1: Identify Issues (30 Minutes)
In Part 1, you identify the main issues, as described here.

Brainstorm Problems Before the meeting, you hold preliminary discussions as described in Chapter 16, section 16.6, so that you have an idea going into the retrospective what the main problems are. Once the meeting begins, attendees gather to brainstorm cross-team issues that should be addressed. You post the items you know to be problems as seed words for the discussion. The goal at this stage is to generate as many ideas as possible. No idea goes into the garbage can.

Clarify the Problem Attendees discuss each problem from multiple points of view:

- **What** was the initial problem? What event brought it to our attention?
- **When** did it occur?
- **Where** did it occur?
- **Why** do we care? What was the impact? What was the cost to the business?

You use root-cause analysis to determine the underlying causes of the observed symptom (the originally identified problem). Attendees reach a consensus on the most important cause contributing to the problem. You work with the group to restate the problem so that the root cause is clearly identified, using the following template: "The problem of [root cause] affects [impacted stakeholders] when [triggering event] [where] the impact of which is [observed symptoms]."

Part 2: Discuss Solutions (30 Minutes)
Attendees brainstorm solutions to the problems discovered in Part 1. The focus is on generating as many solutions as possible.

Next, attendees come to a consensus on the three most promising solutions to the problems raised. They add work items for implementing these solutions to the quarterly backlog for the upcoming quarter. These process improvement items will be used as input to the next quarterly planning event.

17.9.18 Open Space

An **Open Space** event is a self-organizing meeting for large groups. Attendees create their own agendas to address issues related to a central theme.[46] Open Space events are held to foster inter-team coordination, collaboration, and learning. Everyone needed to address the theme of the event should attend. The total number of participants in an Open Space may range from a few people to over a thousand.

---

46. Open Space Technology was created by Harrison Owen. For more on Open Space, see https://openspaceworld.org/wp2

17.9.18.1 Timing Considerations

Hold an Open Space at the start of a quarter, release cycle, or PI. Convene additional, shorter events as appropriate once development begins (e.g., one-hour events once a week).

The duration of an Open Space event may range from a short meeting (forty-five minutes) to two and half days. For Open Space events that are limited to discussion, one day is usually sufficient. For events that produce deliverables, two days are usually adequate. Two and half days may be needed if the intention is to create a plan to deal with the issues raised during the event.

17.9.18.2 The Four Basic Mechanisms

The four basic mechanisms in an Open Space are Marketplace, Circle, Bulletin Board, and Breathing.

Marketplace

The **Marketplace** is a place where topics are pitched and discussed. It consists of a large meeting room divided into breakout areas where an attendee can **shop** by exchanging ideas or **window-shop** by being a passive listener.

Circle

The **Circle** is where the group meets as a whole for discussion and updates. Arrange chairs in a large circle or concentric circles, with flipchart paper and markers placed in the middle.

Bulletin Board

The **Bulletin Board** is a public board of issues and opportunities posted by participants.

Breathing

Breathing refers to the pulsating flow of individuals back and forth between group sessions and smaller breakout sessions.

Inputs

The four required inputs to an Open Space are as follows:

- **Invitation:** A letter expressing an important purpose or theme for the event
- **Invitation list:** A list of everyone needed to address the theme
- **Spacetime:** A location and time for the event
- **Footprints:** Support on-the-ground for implementing the recommendations resulting from the event

17.9.18.3 Open Space Guidelines

The following guidelines govern an Open Space event.

Law of Two Feet

During an Open Space event, discussions in the breakout areas of the Marketplace go on simultaneously. The **Law of Two Feet** applies: if attendees are not benefiting from a discussion, they are encouraged to *vote with their feet* and move—either to a different breakout area or to take a break from the meeting.

The Four Principles

Four underlying principles guide an Open Space.

- Whoever comes are the right people: The people who care enough to show up are those who are most effective at addressing the theme.

- Whatever happens is the only thing that could have: There's little value in ruminating about the past. Focus on what can be done right now to improve things.

- When it starts is the right time: Creativity doesn't run according to a schedule. Valuable ideas come up at any time.

- When it's over, it's over: It's more important to address issues fully than to stick to a schedule.

17.9.18.4 Walkthrough

Following is an example of a walkthrough of an Open Space event, where you are the facilitator.

Introduction

You ring a bell. Attendees assemble in the Circle. The leader of the sponsoring group introduces you. You describe the theme and explain the principles and ground rules of an Open Space event, including the Law of Two Feet, the four principles, and the process. After the introduction, you move into the background. From this point onward, your focus will be on promoting a conducive environment for self-organization.

Create Agenda (1 Hour)

You invite each interested attendee to come to the center of the Circle and announce a topic to the group. The attendee posts the topic on the Bulletin Board, indicating its breakout area and timeslot. Topics might include proposals

- For new requirements management tools

- For technical spikes to test the viability of a new technology

- To eliminate team POs

- To experiment with the no-estimating approach
- To hold quarterly hackathons
- To change from timeboxed to flow-based planning

Registration
Attendees sign up for topics on the Bulletin Board.

Breakouts
As each topic comes up in the schedule, the person who posted it and those who signed up for it assemble at the arranged time and place. The poster introduces the topic to the group, then takes notes once the discussion is underway. Attendees follow the Law of Two Feet: if they aren't receiving value, they leave the conversation.

Debriefing
Every forty-five minutes, the entire group convenes in the Circle for a thirty-minute debriefing on what transpired during the breakouts.

News Updates
If the event is spread over several days, hold a News session at the start and end of each day to announce new topics on the Bulletin Board, communicate important insights from the breakouts, and discuss logistics.

Final Debriefing and Post-event
At the end of the event, the group gathers in the Circle for a final debriefing. Ideas, recommendations, and insights from the breakouts are reviewed, documented, and distributed after the event to attendees.[47]

17.9.19 Triad

Feature and story preparation should occur in the context of Triad meetings. The Triad is a reference to the three perspectives that should be represented when stories are discussed: QA, the customer (PO/proxy PO), and development. Triad meetings are discussed in Chapter 13.

For guidelines on Triad meetings, see Chapter 13, section 13.6.3.

---

47. "Open Space Technology," Wikipedia, April 22, 2019, https://en.wikipedia.org/wiki/Open_Space_Technology

17.10 Agile Requirements Management Software Tools

The early agile guidance was for stories to be written on and managed as physical cards. Cards work well as long as the organization is small and colocated. However, if it is scaled, use cards primarily for initial planning; afterward, transfer stories to a software requirements repository to provide access across teams and locations.

Let's look at some guidelines for choosing a requirements tool.

17.10.1 Requirements Management Tool Checklist

Following is a checklist of qualities to seek out when selecting an agile requirements management tool:

- Supports the requirements types and units defined by the organization (e.g., business requirements, stakeholder requirements, user stories, use cases)
- Supports the agile artifacts used by the organization (e.g., story maps, Kanban boards, burndown charts)
- Provides required levels of traceability
- Provides views at different levels: portfolio, program, product area, team
- Supports user-defined attributes defined for product backlog items
- Provides a platform for cross-team collaboration
- Supports visualization of requirements (e.g., through wireframes, process models, prototypes)
- Is sufficiently scalable for the needs of the organization
- Integrates well with other tools used by the organization
- Is easy to learn, maintain and use

17.10.2 Overview of Agile Requirements Management Tools

Appendix A.13 is an overview of requirements management and collaboration tools for agile initiatives, including JIRA, Blueprint, JAMA, and Rational Team Concert (RTC). Things may change by the time you read this.

17.11 Lightweight Tools for Supporting Inter-team Collaboration

Earlier in this chapter, we examined DevOps/CI/CD/ATDD practices to enable inter-team collaboration by continuously integrating and testing work across teams. In the following sections, we look at some simple, lightweight techniques for supporting team collaboration that complement those practices. Some of these tools are discussed earlier in the book; this section brings them together in one place.

17.11.1 Team Structure

As noted earlier in this chapter, team dependencies can rarely be eliminated in a large organization. One effective way to manage them is to reduce them through team structure, so there are fewer of them to deal with in the first place. To do so, organize cross-functional, full-stack feature teams that are as self-sufficient as possible, as described in Chapter 5, "Preparing the Organization," section 5.7.

17.11.2 Visualization

Use visual means, where possible, to communicate team dependencies on planning artifacts (e.g., through the physical placement of stories on a group-level story map; red strings or dots on a program board).

Communicate plans and progress to other teams through transparent information radiators (e.g., product-level and team-level story maps, program boards, product roadmaps, release roadmaps).

17.11.3 "Just Talk"

"Just Talk" is the LeSS guideline for lateral, peer-to-peer communication between people across teams. Encourage team members to communicate directly—in person, virtually, by phone or email (in that order of preference) to anyone on any team whenever they need help rather than wait for a formal event.

17.11.4 Scouts

Use **scouts** to keep two teams that are closely related updated on each other's plans. The scout should be someone with a view of the big picture beyond the team perspective—typically a PO, proxy PO, or business analyst.

For example, suppose Team A sends a scout to Team B to act as a silent observer during its daily standups. The scout reports back to the home team (Team A) about decisions that Team B has made that impact Team A and advises Team A about impacts its decisions might have on Team B.

17.11.5 Roamers

Roamers are team members who switch teams at every iteration. They typically have technical or business competencies that are under-resourced and in high demand. Roamers are cross-pollinators: they act as physical conduits for sharing knowledge and stories, strengthen the informal bonds between teams, and upgrade the skills of others through mentorship and teaching.

17.11.6 Shared Team Members

With this option, two closely linked teams share a team member. For example, consider a team whose features use a service maintained by a component team. In this case, one member of the component team may join the feature team as a shared team member to enhance collaboration. This person shares not only technical expertise across teams but other information as well. For example, the shared member tells the feature team about the component team's plans and changes, and reports to the component team about the feature team's plans to use the component service.

17.11.7 Implement Work Items Sequentially, Not Concurrently

Follow lean guidance[48] and keep the number of concurrent items each team works on small, so there are less items to track and therefore fewer dependencies to manage. As a rule of thumb, each team should be working on no more than two features at a time.

17.11.8 Enforce a Definition of Ready

Eliminate undue delays and rework by specifying and enforcing a feature DoR, with the condition that all teams needed for the feature must be committed to it before it can be accepted into the quarterly (release) plan. At the story level, specify a story DoR condition that all dependencies on other teams have been addressed before the story's acceptance into iteration planning and development.

17.12 Potential Issues and Challenges in Scaling Agility

Let's now turn to potential issues and challenges that may arise as you scale the organization and review guidelines for addressing them.

17.12.1 Guidelines for Non-colocated Teams

Even before the pandemic, it was common for most scaled development organizations to be non-colocated. For example, many of the companies I work with have work-from-anywhere policies, driven mainly by the high cost of commercial real estate. The COVID-19 pandemic has accelerated this practice. Additional guidelines for coordinating geographically dispersed teams follow.

---

48. Mary Poppendieck and Tom Poppendieck, *Lean Software Development: An Agile Toolkit* (Boston: Addison-Wesley, 2003), 8.

17.12.1.1 *Reduce Communication Challenges*

Reduce communication challenges as much as possible (e.g., by forming groups where all teams share a common time zone and working language).

17.12.1.2 *Treat All Locations Equally*

Don't make logistical decisions that consistently favor one team over another. For example, if teams are in different time zones, don't schedule meetings that regularly prefer one zone.

17.12.1.3 *Encourage Regular Site Visits*

To foster personal inter-team connections, encourage regular site visits to non-colocated teams.

17.12.1.4 *Always Use the Highest Quality Communication Available*

Use the highest quality communication possible. Conference phone calls are at the low end of quality and should be reserved for one-way communication (e.g., for status reports). In order of preference, use the following:

- Virtual meeting or video conference
- Asynchronous communication: wikis, SharePoint, messaging services, email
- Conference call

Use collaborative tools such as Google Docs and CardBoardIt to allow teams to work together in real time.

17.12.1.5 *Score Quick Wins*

Plan to deliver changes that demonstrate real value as early as possible (about two to four weeks) to build confidence and promote a whole-product culture across teams.

17.12.1.6 *Commit to Communication Quality Standards*

Have each team commit explicitly to quality standards regarding communication with other teams (e.g., maximum time to respond to an email, availability to other teams).

17.12.1.7 *Bring Everyone Together at the Beginning and End*

Bring all teams together at the start of the quarter or release cycle for a few days, or even an entire iteration, to provide an opportunity for people to form personal relationships.[49] Once team members return to their home locations, these relationships will speed the development process through fast, direct communication.

Toward the end of the release cycle (e.g., during the last iteration or two before the release date) bring the teams together for a final push.

---

49. Cohn, *Succeeding with Agile*, 368.

17.12.1.8 More Documentation

There is no getting around the need for more documentation when teams are dispersed than when they are colocated, since less information can be communicated verbally. Expect to create more extensive and detailed written requirements specifications and more status reports than you would need for colocated teams.

17.12.2 Guidelines for Working with Waterfall Teams

Many scaled initiatives today are a heterogeneous mix of agile and waterfall teams. Typically, agile teams work on a frontend system, while waterfall teams work on the backend. This mixed arrangement represents additional challenges because waterfall teams work with much longer cadences and often don't use the same requirements units, techniques, and tools as agile teams. Use the following guidelines when working with a waterfall team.

17.12.2.1 Resolve Waterfall Dependencies First

To ensure an agile team is never bottlenecked while waiting for a waterfall team, require that a feature may be pulled into an agile planning cycle only if the waterfall team has already completed the necessary work. Ensure this rule is enforced by including it in the DoR.

17.12.2.2 Integrate According to the Waterfall Schedule

Continuously integrate the agile teams' work, as described in this chapter, but plan integration testing with the waterfall teams based on the waterfall schedule.

17.12.2.3 Waterfall Scouts

Arrange for a scout from the waterfall team to attend agile planning events (e.g., iteration planning meeting, daily standups) so that the waterfall team can stay up to date with changing plans.

17.12.2.4 Encourage Baby Steps

You may not be able to get waterfall teams to change their entire processes overnight. However, you may be able to nudge them to take baby steps toward agility—for example, to shorten the delivery cycle from once every few months to once every few weeks.

17.12.2.5 Align Cycles

Align the end of the waterfall cycle with the end of an agile iteration. For example, if the waterfall team runs on a twelve-week cadence, and the agile teams' iterations are two weeks long, all teams (agile and waterfall) will be aligned once every six iterations. At the end of the cycle, hold a quarterly (release) retrospective with all teams, immediately followed by a quarterly (release) planning meeting for the next cycle.

17.12.2.6 Educate and Proselytize

Run courses in agile development for the waterfall teams so they can understand how the agile teams will be working. Bring waterfall teams to iteration reviews.

17.12.3 Inability to Deploy Frequently and Reliably

One of the most common difficulties I hear about from organizations transitioning to agile practices is that they are unable to achieve the fast deployment cycles required by the approach—or, at least, they can't do so safely at scale. The most effective solution is to automate the build-test-deploy steps by adopting DevOps/CI/CD practices, as described in this chapter. Until the organization has reached the necessary level of DevOps readiness, it should look for ways to shorten the learning and delivery cycle as much as it currently can. For example, instead of waiting until a prerelease testing phase at the end of the quarter, the development organization releases changes into a testing environment every two weeks or less so that users can try them out and provide feedback on a frequent basis.

17.12.4 Recurring Integration Errors and Dependency Issues

Another problem I see frequently occurs when individual teams deliver stories that pass their acceptance criteria but fail end-to-end UAT at the end of the release cycle. We've seen solutions to this problem throughout this book. Let's pull them together here.

The most critical part of the solution is to adopt the DevOps/CI/CD/ATDD practices described in section 17.5.4. To summarize, you specify the end-to-end tests up front at the feature level, as described earlier in this chapter. The specifications guide the development teams and are used for automated testing when stories are Done. DevOps/CI/CD practices enable development branches from separate teams to be merged frequently and safely. This catches integration issues early when they are easier to fix.

The other part of the solution is at the frontend. Before accepting a multiteam feature into the quarterly (release) plan and before its development begins, you prepare the feature, as described in this chapter and in Chapter 10, "Quarterly and Feature Preparation." As part of this preparation, you analyze the end-to-end value streams and processes affected by the feature and their integration points with other components and services. This analysis informs your specification of the feature's integration tests. Architects and developers use the analysis to prepare a design solution for any potential integration issues that were flagged. The analysis work is done up front so that all teams will be able to share a common architectural and design vision as they begin to implement their solutions. Once implementation begins, the team technical leads meet on a regular basis to work out integration issues as they arise and address them through design changes and automated integration testing. See section 17.9.8 for more on integration meetings.

17.12.5 Conflicting Priorities

Another issue often encountered in scaled agile organizations is conflicting priorities—team-level POs working at cross-purposes, each pushing development in their own business domain or technical area. What's often missing in these situations is strong leadership from the product-level PO. To be effective, the product-level PO must own the product vision and have prime responsibility (with consent from other stakeholders) for making decisions with a whole-product view in mind. A scaled organization with multiple levels (e.g., subproducts, sub-subproducts) should have intermediary PO levels as well, all the way down to team POs—each granted authority (or partial authority) to make decisions within their domain. In this chapter, I've referred to these as *area POs*—each of which is responsible for a product area. For guidelines on assigning area POs, see section 17.8.2.

To resolve prioritization issues, the higher-level PO should meet regularly with lower-level POs and the other stakeholders who need to buy into the decision. This may happen in various forums, such as the POC and quarterly planning meetings, discussed earlier in this chapter.

17.12.6 Insufficient Business Resources

Another common issue faced by scaled agile organizations is that the business side often doesn't have enough SMEs to dedicate to the development teams to answer questions about requirements. The solution is for these SMEs to become *extended* team members—a pool of experts shared among a group of teams. Guidelines for forming extended teams can be found in section 17.8.5.

A related HR issue is insufficient product managers and other business SMEs to fill the team-level PO roles. An effective solution is to allocate these scarce leadership resources to PO roles *above* the team level (e.g., area PO, CPO) and to assign business analysts to work at the team level as proxy POs, as discussed in section 17.8.2.3.

Some of my clients have been experimenting with a different solution to this problem—eliminating team-level POs entirely, in favor of team self-organization. This approach is advocated by some lean scaled agile frameworks (e.g., LeSS), but the results have been mixed, at best. When a PO is assigned only above the team level, that person is too removed from the team for effective communication. As a result, the team suffers from the loss of the broader perspective and vision that a PO would provide. Moreover, in the absence of a formal leader, an *informal* one tends to emerge—and not always of the right kind for an effective agile team.

To avoid these consequences, assign POs at *all* levels of the organization, down to *and including* the team level. As an alternative to a team PO (if one is not available), a proxy PO may be assigned. This role is often filled by a business analyst.

Team POs and proxy POs should meet regularly with area POs to receive updates on the big-picture perspective so that they can communicate it down to the teams—and can communicate knowledge gained at the team level upward through the organization.

17.13 Chapter Summary

Here are the key points covered in this chapter:

- Use DevOps/CI/CD/ATDD/BDD practices to deliver software continuously, reliably and sustainably at scale.

- In a scaled agile organization, there is one whole product, one product-level backlog, one DoD, one product-level PO, and one integrated increment across all teams.

- In scaled quarterly (release) planning meetings, the team of teams meets to forecast the features will be delivered and synchronize plans.

- In big room iteration (sprint) planning, all teams in the group meet first to determine what will be done, then split into breakout areas to determine *how* the work will be done. The close proximity of teams allows dependencies to be addressed immediately.

- Product-level feature preparation is a multiteam activity in which upcoming features are tentatively matched with development teams, analysis is performed and the architectural runway is prepared. Story preparation is performed at the team-level to bring upcoming stories into compliance with the story DoR before implementation and iteration planning.

- Lightweight mechanisms for managing inter-team dependencies include organizing teams by value, Just Talk, sending scouts to other teams' planning sessions, and sharing a team member.

17.14 What's Next?

This chapter has expanded the agile approach from the individual team out to a scaled development organization. What about going further—and applying an agile approach beyond software development to the enterprise as a whole? That's the topic of the next chapter.

Chapter 18

Achieving Enterprise Agility

This chapter explores agile planning and analysis from the enterprise perspective—beyond the IT context that has been the main focus of the rest of this book. It leverages lessons learned from agile software development to benefit other industries. Readers do not require a background in software development or agile concepts to benefit from the chapter. It is relevant to any business reader—particularly those responsible for, or interested in, corporate culture management, including senior executives, HR directors, and business relationship managers (BRM). Figure 18.1 highlights the activities covered in the chapter.

The chapter begins with an overview of enterprise agility, including an explanation of its importance in today's business environment and a summary of its primary practices. A recurring theme in the chapter is the critical importance of an agile corporate culture for successful innovation. The chapter provides practical guidelines for developing and sustaining an agile culture based on three principles for applying the guidance and thirteen essential practices. Among the thirteen practices are iterative experimentation, embracing change, acceleration, empathy, distributed authority, busting silos, and data-informed decision-making. The chapter concludes with guidelines for agile financial planning, including Real Options and discovery-driven planning. A detailed case discovery-driven planning case study is included in Appendix B.

18.1 Objectives

This chapter will help you

- Understand the goals and properties of an agile enterprise.
- Learn three principles and thirteen practices for an agile enterprise culture.
- Differentiate between a new-market disruption, a low-end disruption, and a sustaining innovation.
- Protect islands of innovation using tools such as purpose branding.

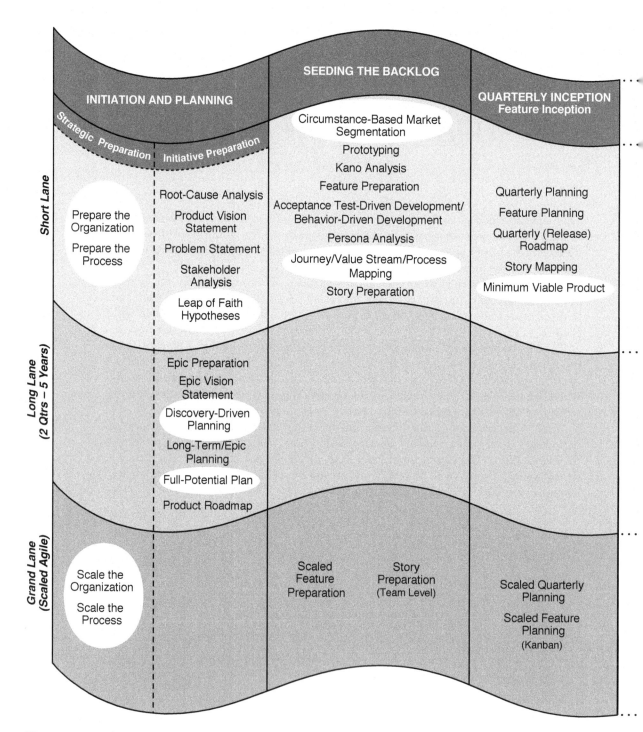

Figure 18.1 *Chapter 18 on the map*

**QUARTERLY
CLOSEOUT**
Epic, Feature Closeout

DAILY ACTIVITIES

**ITERATION
INCEPTION**

**ITERATION
CLOSEOUT**

Daily Standup

Requirements Analysis
& Documentation

Code, Build, Test, Deliver Acceptance
Test-Driven Development/
Behavior-Driven Development

Prepare for
General Availability

Quarterly
Retrospective

Epic, Feature
Retrospective

Iteration
Planning

Iteration Review

Iteration Retrospective

Minimum Viable Product,
Split Testing

Epic, Feature Preparation

Story Preparation

Pivot or
Persevere

User Task
Force
Meetings

DevOps

Product
Owner
Council
Meetings

Scaled
Iteration
Planning

Integration
Meetings

Scaled Iteration
Review

Scaled
Quarterly/Feature
Retrospective

Scaled
Feature
Preparation
(Kanban)

Iteration
Planning
(Team Level)

DevOps

Story
Preparation
(Team Level)

Scaled Iteration
Retrospective

Iteration Retrospective
(Team Level)

- Understand the importance of empathy and how to practice it in the context of business operations and product development.

- Know guidelines for establishing and sustaining communities of practice to support continual improvement.

- Understand why traditional financial planning methods don't work for highly innovative businesses and why discovery-driven planning is more effective in those circumstances.

- Using the appendixes referred to in this chapter, you'll also learn to apply discovery-driven planning and create a reverse income statement, pro forma operations specifications, and milestone planning charts.

18.2 This Chapter on the Map

As shown in Figure 18.1, the chapter addresses the following analysis and planning activities and techniques across the zones on the map:

- Prepare the organization

- Scale the organization

- Prepare the process

- Scale the organization

- Leap of faith hypotheses

- Minimum viable product (MVP)

- Pivot or persevere

- Discovery-driven planning

- Full-potential plan

- Circumstance-based market segmentation

- Journey mapping

- Value stream mapping

- DevOps

Cross-references are provided for topics covered in greater detail in earlier chapters.

18.3 Overview of Enterprise Agility

In the previous chapters, the term *agile* was used to describe a development process and an IT organization. But what does it mean for the *enterprise* as a whole to be agile?

18.3.1 Definition of an Agile Enterprise

An **agile enterprise** can be defined as a business, company, or association that aims to continuously improve its competitiveness by optimizing its ability to anticipate and respond quickly to changing conditions. It uses an iterative, empirical approach to translate learning into continuous value delivery to the customer and enterprise.

Another way to think about it is that an agile enterprise follows the guidance of the Manifesto for Agile Software Development—except that it does so in the context of *any* product or service, not just software. This guidance's chief elements include valuing individuals over process, working products over specifications, collaboration over contractual relationships, and responsiveness to change over predefined plans.

Beyond the Manifesto, the ideas and practices in this section have a variety of origins. These include full-potential planning, lean startup, lean thinking, Six Sigma, *The Innovator's Dilemma*,[1] and *The Innovator's Solution*.[2] However, this chapter owes its strongest debt to the lessons learned through working with my clients, such as Abhijeet Mukherjee, chief experience officer at Nirveda Cognition; Andre Franklin at Covance; Dana Mitchell, agile practice lead for agile transformation at TD Bank Securities; and Alain Arseneault, the Senior Manager Strategic Initiatives, Practice Standards, and Support Group at BMO Financial Group, when we first worked together, and later, IIBA Acting President and CEO.

18.3.2 Why It Matters

We might ask what is to be gained by defining and describing an agile enterprise. After all, no such ideal exists (or should), since every company faces different challenges, each of which requires an individualized solution. Nevertheless, it's valuable to have a picture of what an enterprise committed to optimizing its agility looks like, so an organization may then decide which practices to adopt and which to omit in favor of *other* attributes, like predictability. A clear view of an alternative can also help reluctant executives overcome their apprehension about agile adoption by providing a vivid contrast to the picture they may be experiencing daily in their organizations—such as long decision chains that result in choices made too late to be of value, unacceptable response times to change requests and incidents, siloed business units within the organization, and, at the end of the day, products that may meet every specification yet miss the mark.

---

1. Clayton M. Christensen, *The Innovator's Dilemma: When New Technologies Cause Great Firms to Fail (Management of Innovation and Change)* (New York: HarperCollins, 2003).

2. Clayton M. Christensen and Michael Raynor. *The Innovator's Solution: Creating and Sustaining Successful Growth* (Boston: Harvard Business Review Press, 2003), 49–50.

18.3.3 The Business Analysis Contribution

One of the core responsibilities of agile business analysis at the senior level is to help the organization meet its strategic goals and respond effectively to change by leveraging lessons learned from previous initiatives, the way change was received in the past, an understanding of the market, customer behaviors, and the company's competitive positioning. A key component of that knowledge is the agile planning and analysis approach itself—a set of principles and practices incorporating lessons learned about what works in a rapidly changing environment, including a wealth of proven tools for understanding customer needs and translating that understanding into products.

Though the agile approach has its roots in manufacturing, it matured in software development. As master communicators and critical linchpins between vision and execution, senior agile analysts are particularly well positioned to return agile practices in their updated form to their original, non-IT context and disseminate them to the broader enterprise from the executive level on down.

Agile Processes: From Business to IT and Back

The agile approach has come full circle. Many of its practices started in the manufacturing sector, were later adapted for software development, and are now finding their way back into the non-IT world at large. The *lean* family of practices is one such example. The practices were introduced at Toyota by Kiichiro Toyoda, Taiichi Ohno, and others in the 1930s, as part of the Toyota Production System. They were later described in *The Machine That Changed the World: The Story of Lean Production* (1990) by Daniel Womack, James P. Roos, and Daniel T. Jones, and *Lean Thinking* (1996).[3] Lean software development—an adaptation of lean ideas to software development—was introduced at a 1992 international conference in Germany and later popularized in the book *Lean Software Development: An Agile Toolkit* (2003).[4] The lean approach later reemerged in a nontechnical business context as *The Lean Startup* (2011).[5]

18.3.4 Drivers for Enterprise Agility

Often, an enterprise's first exposure to agile approaches comes from teams within its IT department, then spreads to the business divisions they interact with, such as Finance and Marketing and upward to the organization's executive levels.

At the same time, the drive to transform may also come from the top down. Established corporations, such as IBM, are undergoing top-down transformations, "deliberately

---

3. James P. Womack and Daniel T. Jones, *Lean Thinking: Banish Waste and Create Wealth in Your Corporation*, 2nd ed. (New York: Simon and Schuster, 2003).

4. Mary Poppendieck and Tom Poppendieck, *Lean Software Development: An Agile Toolkit* (Boston: Addison-Wesley, 2003).

5. Eric Ries, *The Lean Startup: How Today's Entrepreneurs Use Continuous Innovation to Create Radically Successful Businesses* (New York: Currency, 2011).

designing the whole organisation around agile, everything from how the workplace is designed with open spaces even for the most senior leadership, to the rewards system, to assessments, to their recruitment, learning and development, their communications process. **They are a 100% agile organisation.**"[6]

Whether it's a trucking company using real-time monitoring of trucks or an insurance company developing usage-based insurance (UBI) products, enterprises across a broad range of sectors are seeking to gain a competitive advantage by developing innovative products that customers are excited about, and by anticipating and responding quickly to changing markets. Executives in these companies are looking for some of the agile "secret sauce" that has made smaller, younger new-technology companies adept at pivoting on a dime. That secret sauce is the subject of this chapter.

18.3.5 Agility in Heavily Regulated Sectors

It's one thing to apply agile principles such as fail fast when an organization is a startup company in a loosely regulated industry. It's much more challenging if the enterprise is an established organization in a highly regulated business sector—such as a financial institution, government agency, or an insurance company. Nevertheless, it's a challenge that is not insurmountable. In my own professional work, I've seen (and assisted) established companies in each of these sectors make the transition, including the US Food and Drug Administration, TD Bank, Canada Mortgage and Housing Corporation (CMHC), Intact Insurance, TELUS, Rogers Cable, and LabCorp. They've used agile approaches to develop highly innovative products in their industries, such as customizable services for TV cable service and personalized car insurance products based on customer behaviors. They've *also* leveraged agile approaches to develop services that are *not* so innovative—such as incident management systems and compliance projects—because they like the way agile product development delivers value quickly to the customer, exposes technical risk early, and results in solutions users are much happier using.

18.4 Foundational Practices

The elements of an agile process for enterprises are encompassed in practices such as lean startup/MVP. The following is an overview of some of the frameworks and guidance that inform enterprise analysis and this chapter: lean startup/MVP, full-potential plan, circumstance-based market segmentation, and the practices for disruptive innovation advanced by Clayton Christensen, Michael Raynor, and Rory McDonald.

---

6. "Has Agile Management's Moment Arrived?" Knowledge@Wharton, Wharton School, August 1, 2017, http://knowledge.wharton.upenn.edu/article/agile-managements-moment-arrived (my emphasis).

18.4.1 Lean Startup/MVP

Lean startup, developed by Eric Reis, uses validated learning to make decisions based on feedback and data from controlled experiments in the marketplace.[7] The idea is to invest a small amount in order to learn whether to invest a much larger amount to develop a product. To use the approach, you identify leap of faith hypotheses—critical assumptions that must be true for the innovation to succeed. For example, consider a proposed personal health device (like the BLInK example that runs through this book) whose business model is based on leveraging customer behavior data to drive revenue.[8] A leap of faith hypothesis for the venture is that people will engage heavily with the product—because, if they don't, insufficient data will be generated for the innovation to be financially viable.

To validate a hypothesis, you create an MVP—a minimal version designed for learning—and expose it to real customers for testing. Then, you examine the feedback from the MVP tests to determine whether to persevere and develop the product under the current hypothesis, pivot to a radically new direction, or stop all work on the initiative.

For more on lean startup and MVP, see Chapter 7, section 7.11, and Chapter 12, section 12.4.

18.4.2 Full-Potential Plan

The **full-potential plan** is an approach to achieving bold goals within three to five years (e.g., to grow an acquired company rapidly after an acquisition).

The steps of the approach can be summarized as follow:

- In Phase 1, you define **bold targets** for the next three to five years and select three to five high-priority initiatives—or **Big Bets**—that will deliver a significant or fast impact.

- In Phase 2, you create a detailed plan to develop and sustain the Big Bets.

- Phase 3 delivers quick wins using the MVP approach.

See Chapter 9, section 9.4, for more on the full-potential plan.

18.4.3 Circumstance-Based Market Segmentation

Circumstance-based market segmentation is a process for identifying the **jobs** that customers hire the product to do. A job represents what the customer hopes to accomplish (e.g., to increase one's social circle, adopt healthier habits, or relieve anxiety). You determine the jobs through field research (e.g., by asking customers who have purchased or rejected the product why they made their decisions). Then, you segment the market by the jobs customers do rather than by demographics or the products they buy. You analyze each segment to determine their needs, and develop products and features to serve them.

---

7. Eric Ries, *The Lean Startup* (New York: Random House, 2013).

8. Gary DeAsi, "How to Use Customer Behavior Data to Drive Revenue (Like Amazon, Netflix & Google)" [blog post], Pointillist, https://www.pointillist.com/blog/customer-behavior-data

See Chapter 7, section 7.10.1, and Chapter 8, section 8.4, for more on circumstance-based market segmentation.

18.4.4 Disruptive Innovation

The guidelines and practices for disruptive innovation were developed by Clayton M. Christensen, Michael Raynor, and Rory McDonald in *The Innovator's Dilemma*,[9] *The Innovator's Solution*,[10] and related articles in the *Harvard Business Review*.[11] The idea is that incumbents tend to disregard the low end of the market as they chase the more profitable high end with bells and whistles most customers don't need. This opens an opportunity for a new entrant (the **disruptor**) to offer a product that fills the customer's need in a radically different way that meets or exceeds the target market's expectations in attributes they care about (e.g., price and convenience)—though other qualities that they care less about may suffer. The disruptor grows so quickly that by the time incumbents respond, it is often too late and the new entrant has transformed or captured the market. We'll do a deeper dive into disruptive innovation in section 18.8.1.1.

Even a great innovative idea will fail if the necessary internal cultural conditions are not present in the enterprise.[12] This is especially so for disruptive innovation because it occurs under conditions of extreme uncertainty—conditions that call out for an aggressively agile culture. We look further into the elements of an agile culture in section 18.6.

18.5 Overview of the Agile Process for Developing Innovative Products

The guidelines of circumstance-based market segmentation, the lean startup/MVP process, and disruptive innovation theories can be broadly summarized in the following nine steps for developing innovative products using an agile process.

1. **Identify the needs:** Perform field research to determine customers' *underlying motivation* in deciding to make a purchase—the need they are trying to meet. (In circumstance-based market segmentation, a need is referred to as a **job** customers want to do.) Ask customers who purchased the product—and different products that serve a similar need—why they made their choices. Ask those who decided *not* to purchase to explain their decisions.

9. Clayton M. Christensen, *The Innovator's Dilemma: When New Technologies Cause Great Firms to Fail (Management of Innovation and Change)* (New York: HarperCollins, 2003).

10. Clayton M. Christensen and Michael Raynor. *The Innovator's Solution: Creating and Sustaining Successful Growth* (Boston: Harvard Business Review Press, 2003), 49–50.

11. Clayton M. Christensen, Michael E. Raynor, and Rory McDonald, "What Is Disruptive Innovation?" *Harvard Business Review* (December 2015), https://hbr.org/2015/12/what-is-disruptive-innovation

12. Alain Arseneault, in a note to the author.

2. **Identify the opportunities:** Ask customers what needs aren't being met well today. What services and products are too costly, too inconvenient, or too inaccessible? What difficulties are customers experiencing *that they don't even think of as problems* because there is currently no alternative? Which of these problems can the company solve through innovation?

3. **Separate customers by needs:** As Theodore Levitt, a professor at Harvard Business School, has said, "People don't want to buy a quarter-inch drill. They want a quarter-inch hole."[13] In other words, it's not the tool or product that counts to the customer; it's the outcome. Divide customers into groups by their needs (also referred to as jobs)—a problem they want to solve or a need they have that is not being met—not by demographics, product, or market size. Then seek to understand and address the needs of each group.

4. **Determine the vision:** Articulate the vision for the product or improvement. If it's a disruptive innovation, specify a vision for performing a job in a way that meets or outperforms expectations in the target group's critical areas of concern (e.g., cost, convenience)—even though initial versions might underperform in areas they care less about.

5. **Identify the leap of faith hypotheses:** Identify the leap of faith hypotheses that must be true for the business model to be successful.

6. **Conduct MVP testing:** Test the leap of faith hypotheses through rounds of MVP experiments with real customers, making adjustments based on feedback and metrics. Use leading indicators to forecast the likely outcome.

7. **Pivot or persevere:** Use the results of MVP testing to identify the Minimum Marketable Product (MMP)—the smallest version of the product that would be viable in the market. Use feedback from MVP testing to determine whether to commit to the vision or make a radical change in direction.

8. **Continuously improve:** Use the results of MVP testing to identify the Minimum Marketable Product (MMP)—the smallest version of the product that would be viable in the market. Use an iterative process to implement the MMP and continuously improve the product. Use data, frequent feedback, and MVP testing to inform decisions.

9. **Accelerate:** If the innovation is disruptive, accelerate rapidly to capture the market before incumbents and competition can respond.

18.6 Agile Corporate Culture

Successful innovation is not just about having a good idea—or even the right processes. It's about culture. Everyone involved in developing a product deemed "innovative" in

---

13. As quoted in Christensen and Raynor, *The Innovator's Solution: Creating and Sustaining Successful Growth*, chapter 3.

their industries—especially if it's a disruptive innovation—must share an organizational culture that embraces, supports, and encourages innovation. Failing to do so can result in disappointing failure.

Let's begin by defining corporate culture; then we'll look at what it means for that culture to be agile.

18.6.1 Definition of Corporate Culture

Culture is the sum total of beliefs and ideas that guide behavior. Adam Grant defines it as "repeated patterns of behavior that reveal norms and values."[14] Perhaps the most succinct way to explain culture is that it's *"what people do when no one's watching."*[15]

Corporate culture is "the beliefs and ideas that a company has and the way in which they affect how it does business and how its employees behave."[16]

18.6.2 Definition of Agile Corporate Culture

An **agile corporate culture** is a set of behaviors and ideas that guide an organization and its employees *in ways that optimize the organization's ability to anticipate and respond to change.* Agile cultures embed collaboration, empowered decision-making, and cognitive empathy in the organization—elements we explore further in this chapter.

Jeremy Gutsche defines the following prerequisites for an innovative culture:

- **Urgency:** A necessary condition for reinvention and innovation is that people have a sense of urgency about the need for change.

- **Perspective:** When the organization's perspective is based on past accomplishments, the result can be complacency and a loss of urgency. An agile organization's perspective is not focused on the past or exclusively on the present; it's oriented toward future needs and trends.

- **Experimental Failure:** The enterprise must value and nurture a culture of experimentation. People should *expect* failure to occur—as a natural and necessary part of innovation.

- **Customer Obsession:** The company must be obsessed with understanding its customers and creating an emotional, cultural connection with them.

- **Intentional Destruction:** The organization understands that existing hierarchies must be destroyed as a necessary precondition for reinvention, and it supports that process.

---

14. Adam Grant, "The Science of Leadership" [podcast], *Stay Tuned with Preet*, December 27, 2018.

15. Grant, "The Science of Leadership."

16. "Corporate culture," *Cambridge Dictionary*, http://dictionary.cambridge.org/dictionary/english/corporate-culture

These elements underlie the guidance in the following sections. For more on Jeremy's model, I urge readers to explore *The Innovation Handbook*[17] and *Exploiting Chaos*.[18]

18.7 Overview of Principles and Practices for an Agile Corporate Culture

Many existing agile and agile-adjacent frameworks and practices touch on agile corporate culture, even if they don't always call it out in those terms. These include lean thinking, Six Sigma, lean startup, the GE Beliefs,[19] DevOps, the Agile Manifesto, as well as lessons learned from transitioning companies.[20] The following synthesizes this guidance into a set of principles and practices for an agile culture.

The three principles for applying agile practices are as follows:

- Tailor the approach to the circumstance.

- Protect islands of innovation.

- Invest aggressively in enterprise agility.

The thirteen practices for an agile corporate culture are as follows:

- Iterative experimentation (fail fast)

- Embrace change

- Acceleration

- Empathy

- Responsible procrastination

- Distributed authority

- Let those who do the work estimate the effort

- Collaboration

---

17. Jeremy Gutsche, *Create the Future + the Innovation Handbook: Tactics for Disruptive Thinking* (New York: Fast Company, 2020).

18. Jeremy Gutsche, *Exploiting Chaos: 150 Ways to Spark Innovation in Times of Change* (New York: Gotham Books, 2009). Available as an ebook at http://cdn.trendhunterstatic.com/EXPLOITING-CHAOS-by-Jeremy-Gutsche-TrendHunter.pdf

19. Jeffrey Immelt, "Letter to Shareholders," in *GE 2014 Annual Report*, 10–11, https://www.annualreports.com/HostedData/AnnualReportArchive/g/NYSE_GE_2014.pdf

20. See, for example, Steve Blank, "Corporate Acquisitions of Startups—Why Do They Fail?" *Forbes*, April 22, 2014, https://www.forbes.com/sites/steveblank/2014/04/22/corporate-acquisitions-of-startups-why-do-they-fail. Also see Peter Nowak, "Video Streaming in Canada," September 27, 2016, http://www.alphabeatic.com/video-streaming

- Commit to outcomes, not outputs

- Transparency

- Bust silos

- Data-informed innovation

- Monitor adjacent and low-end markets

18.8 Three Principles for Applying Agile Practices

Let's begin with the principles for applying the practices.

18.8.1 Tailor the Approach to the Circumstance

The core meaning of agility is *adaptability*, and nowhere is this attribute more apt than for the agile approach itself. As in *Fight Club* (the novel and film by the same name), the first rule of an agile corporate culture is that *there is no agile culture*—or no *single* one for all situations. The agile practices that an organization adopts must be tailored to fit the mission of the enterprise and the values that matter most to it—and those practices should evolve as the mission changes over time. For example, Apple's original mission was "To make a contribution to the world by making tools for the mind that advance humankind."[21] A corporate culture tailored to this mission would embrace most, if not all, of the agile practices discussed in this chapter, such as fail fast. In contrast, Apple's mission today is the more prosaic and product-focused statement that "Apple designs Macs, the best personal computers in the world, along with OS X, iLife, iWork, and professional software. Apple leads the digital music revolution with its iPods and iTunes online store. Apple has reinvented the mobile phone with its revolutionary iPhone and App Store, and is defining the future of mobile media and computing devices with iPad."[22] A corporate culture aligned with the new mission's emphasis on past and current products and successes would lean more toward predictability and reliability and less toward experimentation and transformational change than one aligned with the first. It's not a question of what's right—but what's right *for the organization at that time.*

Culture can also vary *within* an organization. Suppose an established enterprise has created a new business unit to develop an innovative service. Even while the rest of the enterprise adopts a culture that supports predictability, the new business unit would be wise to adopt a highly agile culture that promotes learning and embraces change due to the novelty of the product.

---

21. "How Apple's Current Mission Differs from Steve Jobs' Ideals," Investopedia, June 22, 2019, https://www.investopedia.com/ask/answers/042315/what-apples-current-mission-statement-and-how-does-it-differ-steve-jobs-original-ideals.asp

22. "How Apple's Current Mission Differs."

18.8.1.1 Disruptive Innovation

> "Remember that the things that they fire you for when you're young are the same things that they give lifetime awards for you when you're old."
>
> —Francis Ford Coppola[23]

One of the most important factors that determine the appropriate level of agility for an organization is the degree to which it is (or is not) involved in disruptive innovation. For that reason, it's essential to determine whether the product being developed is—or has the potential to be—a disruptive innovation.

To understand disruptive innovation, let's examine one that many people use in their daily lives—Crest 3D Whitestrips, a fourteen-day teeth-whitening system introduced by Procter & Gamble in August 2000.[24] Before Whitestrips, teeth-whitening was a professional procedure requiring a visit to the dentist—something that many people could not afford. Whitestrips disrupted this status quo by offering a low-cost alternative that anybody could use at home. By getting the job done more conveniently and at a lower cost than a dental procedure, Whitestrips took existing business away from the professional dental industry. Note that Whitestrips didn't do the job of whitening teeth *as well* as a dentist; it did it *well enough* for consumers unwilling to pay a premium for extra quality they didn't need. This situation is typical of **low-end disruptions**.

The product also created new customers—people who hadn't used whitening products and services before because of the cost. Furthermore, it transformed the oral-care-product market, previously associated almost exclusively with toothpaste, by creating a new product category—teeth-whitening products—and a vibrant demand for those products. Consequently, Whitestrips can also be characterized as a **new-market disruption**.

Crest's disruption was so successful that three years after the introduction of Whitestrips, teeth-whitening products were responsible for almost 20 percent of Crest's sales and had captured "almost two-thirds of the entire tooth-whitening category" according to Information Resources.[25]

The determination of whether a product is disruptive not only informs investment decisions but also affects how we plan and develop the product. This is because disruptive innovation occurs under conditions of extreme uncertainty on multiple fronts. Since the business is doing things that have never been done before, there's no way to know in advance how customers will react, how they will use the product, and whether the business model itself is realistic and sustainable. Agile methodologies are a means for addressing this uncertainty through practices that optimize learning and adaptability.

---

23. Quoted in Robert Rodriguez, "Robert Rodriguez and Robert Zemeckis Talk Failure in *The Director's Chair*," May 19, 2015, http://www.indiewire.com/2015/05/watch-robert-rodriguez-and-robert-zemeckis-talk-failure-in-the-directors-chair-61710

24. Mukund R. Dixit and D. Karthik, "Proctor & Gamble v/s Colgate—2003: An Exercise in Competitive Dynamics," *Emerald Insight*, August 28, 2013, https://www.emerald.com/insight/content/doi/10.1108/CASE.IIMA.2019.000012/full/html

25. As quoted in Lisa Biank Fasig, "After Its Market Share Started to Decay, P&G's Crest Team Fought Back," *Cincinnati Business Courier*, January 30, 2004, https://www.bizjournals.com/cincinnati/stories/2004/02/02/story2.html

We'll begin by defining innovation. Next, we'll explain what it means for an innovation to be *disruptive* and the different kinds of disruptive innovation that can occur.

What Is an Innovation?

To determine whether a particular innovation is disruptive, you first need to define innovation. An **innovation** is a new idea, design, product,[26] or service or the evolution of an existing thing that fulfills an unmet need—whether conscious or unconscious.[27] Note that this definition (and the ones that follow for innovation *types*) may not apply to all industries, and different organizations may define those terms differently. Also, keep in mind that while the definition focuses on the *idea* or product, any concept—even a great one—will fail if the necessary cultural conditions for innovation are not present within the organization.

Types of Innovation

Every company must continuously innovate—but not every innovation is (or needs to be) a disruptive innovation. It may be a sustaining innovation. Please note that these categories are a convenient over-simplification of a complex issue and that there is no hard line separating the two types. Nevertheless, they provide a useful framework for considering an idea or product proposal, its potential to transform the market and the strategies that should be used to develop and market it—or defend against it, if you're an incumbent.

What Is Sustaining Innovation?

Sustaining innovation is the type of innovation incumbents tend to be good at. It refers to the continual improvement of *established* products and services. (This definition differs from Christensen's formulation, which includes progress leaps under certain conditions—not just incremental changes.[28]) For example, CDs were a sustaining innovation when they were introduced because, while they were an improvement, they didn't change the underlying business and distribution model in the music industry. CDs were distributed to retail outlets that sold them to customers—just like vinyl records.

One way to think of sustaining innovation is as a business equivalent to the natural world's evolutionary process—small, incremental changes leading to continual improvement. Like its evolutionary counterpart, the general drift of sustaining innovation in business is toward higher and higher levels of quality.

What Is Disruptive Innovation?

Disruptive innovation refers to the development of novel products and services that transform their industries in some way (e.g., through innovative features, how they deliver value to the customer, or the benefits they provide to their customers, such as low cost and greater convenience). (Note that this definition differs from Christensen's, as discussed in

---

26. "Innovation," *Cambridge Dictionary*, https://dictionary.cambridge.org/dictionary/english/innovation

27. Alain Arseneault, in a note to the author.

28. Christensen, Raynor, and McDonald, "What Is Disruptive Innovation?"

an upcoming section.) Disruptions can also disrupt *other* industries, as was the case with Crest 3D Whitestrips, which disrupted not only the oral-care industry of which P&G was a part but the dentistry profession as well.

Often, a disruptive innovation introduces an entirely new way to get a job done that is more convenient or cheaper than the available alternatives. For example, Whitestrips performs the job of whitening teeth without requiring an expensive and inconvenient visit to the dentist. We'll be exploring Flickr later in this chapter: it's also an example—though a less obvious one. Flickr performs the job of building a social community in a way that is different (and more profitable for the company developing it) than its founder's original venture—Game Neverending.

The disruption often solves a pressing problem by hacking together existing services in unexpected ways. The problem may be global—such as a pandemic or climate change—or one that a market or submarket cares strongly about.

An example of the latter is Trint (discussed in Chapter 12, section 12.4.2)—an automatic transcription service. It began when its founder, a former journalist, realized he could eliminate the tedium of transcribing videos by combining a manual user interface with an automated speech-to-text AI component. In his vision, the AI part would do the heavy lifting of transcription, leaving the user to focus on quicker tasks that needed human intervention, such as verifying and correcting text. Trint's customers were not new to the market; they were already consumers of transcription services. Moreover, many weren't even *aware* they had a problem until Trint provided a solution. Today Trint claims to be the leading speech-to-text platform for content production and has recently received additional funding from the *New York Times* and other outlets.[29]

Disruption as an Evolutionary Leap

We can find biological analogies to disruptive innovation in the evolutionary leaps that occur in response to

- Extreme environmental stressors

- Random mutations (experiments) that yield outsize results

- Convergence

Extreme Environmental Stressors   An example of an **extreme environmental stressor** leading to an evolutionary disruption is the Cretaceous-Tertiary, or K-T, extinction event. According to a prevailing theory, a meteor crashed into the earth 65.5 million years ago on the edge of the Yucatán Peninsula,[30] causing global wildfires, earthquakes and volcanic eruptions, and other cataclysmic changes that wiped out many forms of life, including the dinosaurs. Small mammals that could burrow under the ground survived and filled

---

29. Michael Nelson-Wolter, "Trint Announces New Investment from The New York Times Company," Trint, September 9, 2020, https://trint.com/resources/7l8yv28v/trint-announces-new-investment-from-the-new-york-times-company

30. History.com editors, "Why Did the Dinosaurs Die Out?" History.com, June 7, 2019, https://www.history.com/topics/pre-history/why-did-the-dinosaurs-die-out-1

the ecological niches left behind. A similar dynamic is at play when a company's competitors suddenly disappear (e.g., when more than 450 banks failed during the global financial crisis in 2007–2008 and the five years that followed). Another is businesses closing en masse during a pandemic—as is currently occurring at the time of this writing. Like the post-K-T mammals, those who will thrive in the new environment will be the entities that can quickly adapt and transform themselves to fill the niches that will open up due to the event.

Random Mutations (Experiments) That Yield Outsize Results   Genetic mutations can be thought of as nature's experiments. Sometimes a mutation or set of mutations yields an outsize result (e.g., the mutations for an opposing thumb enabled humans to use tools—a capability no other mammal has had before or since to a comparable degree). In the business world, organizations should mimic nature and conduct experiments. As with genetic mutations, those experiments often lead to incremental improvement, but every so often, one of those improvements or innovations has far-reaching effects. A business example is the invention of computers, which created new markets and opportunities in multiple industries.

Convergence   This happens when several smaller improvements combine to create a sum that is greater than its parts. An example from the natural world is the convergence of two improvements—language and an opposing thumb—which contributed to early Homo sapiens' ability to convey knowledge across generations and greatly accelerating the advance of human civilization, art, and technology. A business example is the convergence of touch-screen technology, Wi-Fi, mobile data services, and an innovative business model (the app store), transforming the mobile device from a telephone into a personal digital assistant (PDA).

Updates to Christensen's Disruptive Model

It's worth noting that the preceding definition for disruptive innovation differs in significant ways from that advanced by Christensen, Raynor, and McDonald, the originators of the concept. They define disruption as "a process whereby a smaller company with fewer resources is able to successfully challenge established incumbent businesses." In their view, the innovation must gain a foothold first in a fringe market—either at the low end of an existing market or in a new market (customers who have never used the product before). Furthermore, the disruptive product must "initially be considered inferior by most of an incumbent's customers."[31] According to this understanding, Uber does not qualify as disruptive to the cab industry because it did not emerge in a low-end or new market; it targeted mainstream cab customers from the start. Moreover, the authors argue that Uber was not considered inferior to traditional cabs by most customers.

As the authors explain, they created this definition to describe a phenomenon they'd noticed—companies transforming their industries before competitors had a chance to react. When they realized that their first draft, focusing on low-end disruptions, failed to

---

31. Christensen, Raynor, and McDonald, "What Is Disruptive Innovation?"

take into account new-market disruptions, they adapted the definition.[32] Why stop there, though, when there are other scenarios where new products and services have successfully disrupted traditional ways of doing business? The problem, in my opinion, is that the authors' definition and conditions for disruptive innovation are too restrictive in the first place.

Let's begin with the first restriction—that the disruptor must be a small company with limited resources. Nevertheless, the authors accept that Apple's iPhone was *disruptive* to the laptop industry because it "was able to challenge laptops as mainstream users' device of choice for going online."[33] This belies their definition of disruption because Apple was by no means a small company with limited resources.

Similarly, by all practical measures, Crest's Whitestrips was disruptive to dentistry because it offered a profoundly new way to do the job of whitening teeth without the inconvenience and expense of going to a dentist. Yet Crest, too, is far from being a small company. It seems clear that though disruptors may *often* be small, they don't have to be.

What about the condition that a disruptive innovation must target low-end or new-market customers? Again, this is a common occurrence but not a necessary condition. For example, the authors consider Netflix to have been a disruptor of Blockbuster, yet it targeted existing customers, not new ones, and did not focus on the low-end market. What's clear, therefore, is that the authors' definition is not only overly restrictive but is even inconsistent with their own usage.

Is Uber Disruptive?

As noted previously, by the authors' reckoning, Uber is not disruptive to the taxi industry because it started in San Francisco, where the cab market was well-served. Furthermore, it would be disqualified because it didn't target the service to low-end markets; its first customers already used cabs. Yet, Uber has transformed the cab business and done so in a textbook disruptive fashion. Christensen, Raynor, and McDonald tacitly acknowledge this problem by arguing that artificial legislative constraints explain why Uber has all the hallmarks of a disruptive company without being a "disruptor." At best, it's a distinction without a difference.

In contrast, the definition I'm using sees disruptive innovation as development that *transforms the way business is done* (e.g., by creating a new business model or making changes in the value stream, the way the product is developed, its features or benefits). According to this understanding, we would quickly recognize Uber as a disruptor because it has radically changed every aspect of the cab industry. These changes include its relationship to customers and providers, its underlying business model, how it delivers its services, the benefits it provides, and the technology it uses. Unlike traditional taxi companies, Uber is based on a marketplace model; its value is derived from connecting people who need a ride with people who have underutilized cars and want to earn more income

---

32. "For example, we originally assumed that any disruptive innovation took root in the lowest tiers of an established market—yet sometimes new entrants seemed to be competing in entirely new markets. This led to the distinction . . . between low-end and new-market footholds." See Christensen, Raynor, and McDonald, "What Is Disruptive Innovation?"

33. Christensen, Raynor, and McDonald, "What Is Disruptive Innovation?"

with flexible hours. Moreover, the company's ultimate vision is an even more transformative one—to replace cab drivers entirely with automation.

Besides, Uber would likely qualify as a disruptor even by the authors' restrictive definition. For example, Uber's initial release *was* a new-market disruption in the sense that it changed what it *meant* to be a customer: in Uber's sharing economy, the company's customers are not just riders but drivers, too. More recently, Uber has brought other new customers into the fold, including restaurants and people looking for micro-mobility transportation solutions, such as scooters.

Why Disruptions Do Not Have to Be of Low Quality

What about the contention that the disruptive product must initially be considered inferior by most customers? I would argue that while a disruptive innovation is *often* of lower quality, it's wrong to insist that it *must* be. For example, Trint offers verifiable voice-to-text automated transcription with similar reliability to traditional, manual services and with much faster turnaround times. In other words, the product offers comparable or *enhanced* quality by the yardsticks used by its most demanding customers. Nevertheless, it is successfully disrupting its industry.

Types of Disruptions

With the preceding adaptations to the theory, most disruptive innovations can be characterized by the following types:

- Low-end disruptions
- New-market disruptions
- Mainstream disruptions
- Business-model disruptions

Low-End Disruptions

Low-end disruptions target customers who currently use the product but would be willing to pay less for an acceptable but inferior product if it provided other advantages they care more about.

Over time, low-end disruptive innovations often improve—to the point that they can capture the middle and high end of the market as well. Digital cameras are one such example. The first versions available in the general market were inferior to film and didn't appear to pose a direct threat to higher-end film-based cameras. Despite the low quality of digital cameras, new customers who wouldn't have purchased an analog camera bought digital ones because of other attributes: ease of use by an untrained photographer and the ability to view images instantly at no cost. Today, digital cameras have improved to the point that they have taken over not only the consumer market but most of the high-end art market as well.

Once digital cameras produced acceptable images for the mainstream, they were incorporated into mobile phones. This is an interesting case of one disruption providing the opportunity for a second disruption:[34] the inclusion of a digital camera helped transform the mobile phone from a device used to make calls to a personal digital assistant and media device—a Swiss Army knife for the modern consumer.

New-Market Disruptions

The next type of disruption—a **new-market disruption**—opens up entirely *new* markets, customers who have never before used the product or service. The PC is one example because it brought computing for the first time to individuals. Another example is online brokerages, which attract customers who had never purchased stocks before.

Mainstream Disruptions

A **mainstream disruption** is one that targets *existing mainstream* customers—as opposed to low-end or new-market customers. Typically, a mainstream disruption solves a problem that most customers have learned to live with and may not even recognize as problems. When the disruptor offers a solution, customers' expectations change, transforming the industry. Trint is an example of a mainstream disruption: it solves the journalist's problem of having to hit pause-rewind-play repeatedly when transcribing interviews.

Because this type of disruption is directed at the incumbents' primary customer base, it is less likely to enter the market under the radar. Consequently, when considering a mainstream disruption, it is particularly essential that the organization have a plan for rapidly scaling the product and growing the customer base.

Business Model Disruptions

A **business-model disruption** is any other innovation that transforms the fundamental business model in its industry. After the disruptor introduces the disruptive business model, competitors follow suit until even established incumbents soon must adapt to the new model or disappear. As noted earlier, one example is music streaming, which transformed the business model for the music industry. Another is the transition from one-time software sales to the Software as a Service (SaaS) model.

The trigger for a business-model disruption is often a transformative event that affects the entire industry, such as the COVID-19 pandemic that is rapidly transforming the retail sector (and many others) as people look for online solutions and alternatives to in-person shopping. The trigger may also be a revolutionary technology, such as the inventions of 5G and CRISPR genome editing—each of which has the potential to transform multiple business sectors.

Any aspect of the business model may be transformed by a business-model disruption, including the following:

- **Production process** (e.g., from manually produced prescription glasses to methods that rely heavily on robotics and automation)[35]

---

34. Thanks to Ron Healy for extending this example.

35. Julie Bos, "The Need for Speed," Labtalk Online, June 2020, https://www.labtalkonline.com/articles/81741

- **Service delivery** (e.g., from delivery of hard-goods to digital delivery). The disruption involves a radical shift in how a customer receives and interacts with a service (e.g., medical services delivered online).

- **Product distribution** (e.g., from retail stores to an app store or from Netflix's release of its content to its streaming platform vs. traditional studio release to theaters)

- **Revenue streams** (e.g., from sales to subscription fees or Airbnb's replacement of traditional hospitality revenue with a revenue stream based on service fees to renters and hosts)

18.8.1.2 *Is It a Disruption? The Litmus Test*

This understanding of disruption can be summarized in a litmus test for determining whether an innovation has the potential to be disruptive. Keep in mind that business strategy cannot be boiled down to a simple formula. The litmus test (adapted from Christensen's formulation) is a useful *first cut* at determining whether an innovation has the potential to replace existing market leaders but is only a rough guide.[36]

According to this scheme, to be a disruptive innovation, a venture, product, or feature must pass *either* test 1, 2, or 3—and it *must* pass test 4.

Test 1. Is it a *new-market* disruption?

Are there many people who need the service but manage without it (e.g., because they would have to pay a skilled person to do it or have to go to an inconvenient location to use it)?

Test 2. Is it a *low-end* disruption?

Are there customers who would purchase a lower-quality, lower-priced product in this category than is currently available—and can the company make a profit serving these customers under those conditions?

Test 3. Is it a *main-stream* disruption?

Does it solve a problem that current customers have learned to live with but would appreciate a solution for—if one were available?

The final test is based on one advanced by Peter Thiel (discussed further in section 18.9.3):

Test 4. Does the business possess a credible plan for accelerating growth shortly after the product's release and for scaling up its operating capacity quickly enough to outrun incumbents if they launch a counterattack? If not, it might be more prudent to wait until they do.

It's important to note that the disruptive nature of a product or service may change over time. It may be disruptive when first introduced but, once established in the market,

---

36. Christensen and Raynor, *The Innovator's Solution*, 49–50.

become the incumbent—at which point the relative predictability of the circumstances argues for a more plan-based, less agile culture.

18.8.1.3 Adapting the Culture for Disruptive versus Sustaining Innovations

Once you've determined the type of innovation the organization is involved in, you can adapt the target agility level accordingly. For example, an organization that embarks on a disruptive venture knows very little at the start about who its customers are, how best to market and deliver the product to them, how customers will incorporate the product into their lives, or what features they will find most useful. These conditions of extreme uncertainty call out for an aggressively agile culture.

In contrast, a sustaining innovation is an improvement to a *well-established* product or service. Because there is less uncertainty than is the case with disruptive innovation, the business culture can afford to be more plan-based. Furthermore, business forces in an established enterprise are more likely to lean toward minimizing risk than experimentation and acceptance of failure because of the *gravity of past success*, as we discuss later in this chapter. All of these factors lean toward more planning and less agility than for disruptive innovation.

It's important to clarify three things, though, about enterprises in this established, sustaining stage of development. First, established business units also benefit from some level of agile adoption—because even if an innovation is only a sustaining one, the sooner it is brought out to the market, the better. That is best accomplished using agile approaches.

Second, agile approaches provide essential guidance, even for sustaining innovations, on responding to unexpected challenges. For example, if progress toward a new product version is lagging, the agile approach recommends slicing off high-value pieces for immediate delivery rather than prolonging the release date.

Third, the survival of incumbents today often hinges on getting ahead of the startups nipping at their heels *before* they become a threat. As a result, it's safe to say that there should be at least *some* agile in every enterprise.

18.8.2 Protect Islands of Innovation

As an enterprise establishes itself, it accumulates forces that inhibit agility—influences from which agile business units must be vigorously protected. Christensen provides the basis of today's understanding of these forces in his book, *The Innovator's Dilemma*[37]—I urge all readers to read that book, as well as its sequel, coauthored with Raynor, *The Innovator's Solution*.[38] The picture that emerges can broadly be described as follows: When a company first introduces a disruptive product or service into the market, everything is in a state of flux. The product is undergoing rapid development; the company is just discovering who its customers are and how they use the product—and both investors and first adopters tend to have a high tolerance for risk. Taken together, these conditions are a natural fit for a highly agile culture that values experimentation and iterative prod-

---

37. Christensen, *The Innovator's Dilemma*.
38. Christensen and Raynor, *The Innovator's Solution*.

uct development over excessive planning. In this environment, an agile corporate culture can thrive—for a time.

18.8.2.1 The Gravity of Past Success

Once a business matures, however, it begins to suffer from what former chess champion Garry Kasparov has referred to as "the gravity of past success"[39]—and it becomes increasingly difficult to maintain the innovative, risk-taking edge of the early years. Christensen has analyzed why this is so for mature enterprises.[40] The gravity of existing markets, channels, and customers is so consequential that any new revenue promised by the innovation tends to pale in comparison. As a result, the venture fails to attract the necessary investment. Furthermore, as time goes on, legislation tends to catch up to new-market disruptions. As a result, even companies that started out with a high tolerance for failure eventually find themselves in an environment less conducive to experimentation. What the *gravity of success* tells us, then, is that even a once-innovative company will eventually experience a reduced tolerance for risk and for experimenting with real customers in the marketplace and will be less likely to invest in the research and development (R&D) required for transformational innovation. To sustain innovation once a disruptor has become the incumbent, the enterprise must protect its agile business units from this force.

18.8.2.2 Autonomy for Agile Business Units within Non-Agile Enterprises

Because of the gravity of past success, an agile business unit existing within an established enterprise has a relationship with its parent that is both a blessing and a curse. The established enterprise is a potential source of resources, information, channels, and customers—advantages not available to small startups. But these benefits come with strings attached—the proximity to a *sustaining* (vs. innovative) culture with built-in forces that discourage high-risk innovation.

The answer is to find the sweet spot, where the enterprise's resources are made available to the disruptive unit but not to the *exclusion* of other options. The aim is to leave the business unit with the autonomy to find its own market, delivery channels, and revenue models while benefiting from its privileged relationship with its parent.

18.8.2.3 How Much Autonomy?

The more disruptive the innovation, the greater the autonomy that should be given to the business unit. Autonomy can extend to the business's legal structure, funding sources, and physical housing in a location removed from the parent organization.

Failure to provide enough autonomy to an agile business unit can doom it. According to an analysis by Steve Blank,[41] when an established enterprise acquires a startup, the

---

39. Preet Bharara, "Putin, Pawns and Propaganda (with Garry Kasparov)" [podcast], *Stay Tuned with Preet* (Café and Pineapple Media and WNYC Studios), December 7, 2017.

40. Christensen, *The Innovator's Dilemma.* Also see Clayton Christensen, *The Innovator's Dilemma: When New Technologies Cause Great Firms to Fail* (Boston: Harvard Business Review Press, 2016).

41. Blank, "Corporate Acquisitions of Startups."

purchase frequently ends in failure because "what gets lost when a large company looks at the rationale for an acquisition (IP, team, product, users) is that startups are run by founders *searching for a business model . . .* with a *continual customer discovery process, iterating, pivoting and building incremental MVP's.*" In other words, every aspect of a startup organization is agile—adaptive, iterative, and experimental—down to the fundamental business model. When an enterprise impinges on the unit's autonomy to innovate in these areas, it kills the goose that laid the golden egg—removing the very qualities that made it successful.

Instead, the agile business unit needs to be given the autonomy to continue as it had before it was acquired—to iterate toward "the right combination of product, market, revenue, costs, etc."[42] While Blank's guidance referred to a corporation *acquiring* a startup, the recommendation that innovative business units need broad autonomy to iterate in *every* area is just as relevant when the unit is developed internally within the enterprise.

18.8.2.4 *Autonomous Branding: The Purpose Brand*

The concept of extending autonomy to innovative business units extends to branding. It's often advantageous for an established company launching a disruptive product to create an *autonomous* brand distinct from that of the parent company. One such scenario is when an established business attempts to compete directly against new-market disruptors—products that create markets that didn't previously exist and new customers with new expectations. The new entrant already disrupting the market has often built a loyal following by the time an incumbent responds—by which time the priorities of customers are often more strongly aligned with the disruptor (a headwind well known to the taxi and hotel industries). When launching its own disruptive challenge, an incumbent can avoid its own brand's negative associations by creating an autonomous, distinct brand for the new business. In Toronto, Loblaw successfully did this when it introduced its small, independently run stores into communities as separately branded Independent City Markets—thereby avoiding the negative associations toward chain stores in the eyes of downtown customers.

Another scenario calling for autonomous branding occurs when an established company introduces a *low-end disruption*. In this case, after having spent a long time burnishing a reputation for high quality, the company risks devaluing its brand by associating it with a low-cost, low-quality product. The solution is to create a **purpose brand**[43] for the innovation—one that refers to the main brand name in order to leverage its *positive* associations with customers but includes a qualifier that marks the products for a distinct usage. Care should be taken, especially when licensing is involved, to ensure the purpose brand is of a *high enough* quality to protect the primary brand. One such example is Karl Lagerfeld Pour H&M, a purpose brand for Lagerfeld's low-end, disruptive product line produced for H&M, offering designer goods at chain-store prices.

Pierre Cardin offers a cautionary tale about what happens when the purpose brand's quality is not well monitored and the purpose brand is not well-enough separated from

---

42. Blank, "Corporate Acquisitions of Startups."
43. Christensen, *The Innovator's Solution.*

the primary brand.[44] In the 1960s and 1970s, the Pierre Cardin brand had a prestigious reputation. Cardin's clients included the Beatles and Eva Peron, and the designer had won coveted awards such as the Gold Thimble of French Haute-Couture. Yet, by 1989, after licensing issues and an inability to control quality across the brand, Cardin's reputation had fallen so far that *The Economist* described his signature as being "as devalued as the dollar bills that he signs."[45] In 2011, he tried unsuccessfully to sell the brand for 1 billion euros, when its actual value was estimated at about 200 million euros.

18.8.2.5 *Autonomous Internal Business Unit*

The formal business structure for providing autonomy will vary according to the situation—from an independent internal business unit to a separately owned company.

An autonomous but *internal* unit is appropriate when an established enterprise seeks to create an innovative business alongside its established business. One example is the disruptive subscription maintenance service developed by the Otis Elevator Company. The service is based on monitoring and responding to Internet of Things (IoT) sensors as an alternative to regularly scheduled service calls.

Another scenario[46] calling for an autonomous internal unit is when an established company acquires a startup to gain access to its products or customers—but not for the other aspects of its business model, such as its channels or management structure.

On the other hand, if the acquiring company *does* wish to gain access to all aspects of the startup's business model, the startup should be preserved as a separate business entity, as discussed in the following section.

18.8.2.6 *The Agile Unit as Separate Business Entity*

In other cases, the degree of autonomy required for success is so high that the new business should be structured as a legally separate business entity. This occurs when an established company acquires a startup while the startup is still in the early stages of developing its business model, such as identifying its customers, channels, and suppliers. Absorbing the acquired company into the enterprise at this phase would risk short-circuiting that development due to the pressure to use the purchasing company's resources, such as its established delivery channels and existing customer base. In order to give the new unit the latitude to freely develop these aspects of the business—even when they *conflict* with the priorities of the established enterprise—the established company is better advised to preserve the startup as a separate legal entity, with its existing CEO.[47] The incumbent supports the startup by partnering with it or investing in it while leaving the startup full independence to develop its own business model.

---

44. Jason Dike, "Digging Deeper: Pierre Cardin's Demise to Licensing King," *Highsnobiety*, 2015, https://www.highsnobiety.com/p/digging-deeper-pierre-cardin

45. Dike, "Digging Deeper."

46. Blank, Corporate Acquisitions of Startups."

47. Blank, Corporate Acquisitions of Startups."

18.8.3 Invest Aggressively in Enterprise Agility

The benefits of agility—like rapid response and accelerated learning—are not cost-free. While some benefits can be achieved at a low cost (e.g., by focusing on organizational structure and practices), more significant benefits can only be realized if these actions are backed up by aggressive investment in enabling technology. I remember first learning this lesson years ago as a programmer when I transitioned from mainframes to mini-computers. The new technology provided my colleagues and me, for the first time, with an interactive, real-time development environment. This change alone sped up the cycle time from coding to testing by orders of magnitude—and led us to adopt a new way of working. It was so easy to rewrite and retest code in the new environment that, instead of planning everything meticulously in advance, we started using a more iterative, experimental approach. We came to this agile approach *naturally* because the technology enabled us to do so. Since then, I've been convinced that the two go hand in hand: agile transformation at the people and process levels must come alongside investment in the enabling technology with the active and visionary support of leadership. The technical investment tends to be of three kinds:

- R&D investment in technology to deliver disruptive services

- Investment in technology to accelerate product development

- Investment in technology to enable rapid growth

18.8.3.1 R&D Investment in Technology to Deliver Disruptive Services

Established companies often have a poor record of providing the levels of investment in R&D necessary for the technology to deliver transformative services to the customer. Unsurprisingly, this leads to preventable failures when they try to challenge a disruptor. In my local area, this played out in the struggle between Rogers Corporation (a provider of cable services) and Netflix for streaming-services customers. According to a postmortem analysis by Peter Nowak,[48] the cable company's investment in R&D for its streaming service, Shomi, never came close to matching Netflix's $300-million-per-year investment in R&D to provide high reliability over a broad range of devices. Having lost this battle over a disruptive service (streaming) the cable company now faces a possible existential threat to its core business (cable services). One effective way to prevent this fate is for incumbents to fund disruptive service-delivery innovation, at least as aggressively as their major startup competitor. Other strategies, as noted earlier, include buying or partnering with a competitor.

18.8.3.2 Investment in Technology to Accelerate Product Development

In order to respond quickly to changing market conditions and learning, an enterprise needs to be able to make last-minute changes to the product, *even while it is being developed.* That requires investment—because legacy processes often require a much longer lead time. To create products that customers love, a business needs the technology to

---

48. Nowak, " Video Streaming in Canada,"

quickly prototype and test the product on customers and generate and mine customer feedback.

This is much more difficult to achieve with hard goods than with software, but not impossible, given some ingenuity. For example, a car manufacturer may collaborate with a component-maker to develop processes enabling it to specify high-level requirements upfront (e.g., the overall dimensions of a metal block component) but delay detailed specifications until later in the manufacturing process.

Increasingly, even hard goods—from washing machines to toothbrushes—are enabled by software. A successful agile enterprise should be committed to investing in the capabilities needed to improve its products' enabling software in a continuous, reliable, and sustainable manner. Best practices toward those goals are encompassed in the DevOps approach.

For more on DevOps, see Chapter 17, section 17.5.2.1.

18.8.3.3 *Investment in Technology to Enable Growth*

When a company's business and market grow quickly, so, too, must its operating capacity. The business' IT systems need more computing power to handle larger volumes of transactions per unit time and greater storage capacity for long-term retention of customer and transaction data. If a company is in an accelerated growth phase, it needs all of this to happen very quickly. At the same time, if the business contracts, an agile enterprise needs to be able to quickly divest the unrequired IT infrastructure. The same is true of its non-IT product development and business operations as they scale up and down in response to business needs.

Fortunately, today, at least with respect to IT services, adaptable technology of this kind is much easier to obtain than in the past due to the availability of services such as Amazon Web Services (AWS), which provides a ready-to-go, scalable infrastructure for companies.

When Should an Established Company Transition to Scalable IT Services?

If the enterprise is a large, established company with complex legacy systems, the costs involved in adapting existing code to use external services such as AWS or internal components are often too high to justify the change. For these organizations, the transition to scalable services is often not practical until the entire system is overhauled or replaced. When these organizations *do* incorporate scalable services, it's usually when developing a new product.

Outsourced or In-House Adaptable Infrastructure?

An enterprise that's decided to use the enabling technology we have been discussing must consider whether to develop the capabilities in-house or outsource them to a third party. The benefits of an outsourced infrastructure (e.g., AWS) are that it accelerates time to market for new products and services and decreases upfront investment and associated risk. Furthermore, an outsourced infrastructure enables operational capacity and costs to expand and contract dynamically with the business. All of these are critical to a startup company and to an established enterprise wishing to get a new, disruptive business quickly off the ground. But these benefits must also be weighed against future costs. Outsourcing can lock a company into services that will become *more* expensive than equivalent in-house services once the business has scaled.

18.9 The Thirteen Practices for an Agile Corporate Culture

Now that we've examined the preconditions and principles for applying an agile approach, let's turn to the practices. The following are thirteen practices for an agile corporate culture.

18.9.1 Iterative Experimentation (Fail Fast)

> "Ever failed. No matter. Try again. Fail again. Fail better."
> —Samuel Beckett, *Endgame*

At the core of agile product development is its **iterative** practice—a repetitive, experimental approach for testing out ideas in short cycles of planning and implementation. The terms *adaptive, empirical,* and *emergent* are also used to describe this approach. As I've noted earlier in this book, I believe that this practice is so central to an agile approach that an organization cannot credibly refer to itself as "agile" without using it. What's wrong with the alternative—relying on careful planning to get it right the first time?

The answer is that there *isn't* anything wrong with it—as long as everything that needs to be known up front *can* be known with an acceptable level of certainty. This is often the case for a company making small improvements to an established product. But it's not so for companies that are developing entirely new kinds of markets and products, are using novel technology, or are operating within a highly changing business environment. Extensive planning is of limited value in these situations because the basis of any such plan is highly subject to change. Instead, businesses must learn to wean themselves off of the false sense of control that a plan-based approach *appears* to provide toward one that recognizes that, since knowledge evolves organically over time, so, too, must solutions. Businesses in these circumstances need to emulate innovators in the creative industries—sectors in which the iterative, experimental approach is the dominant way of working.

At the beginning of this book, I wrote that people who view my paintings (e.g., Figure 1.5 in Chapter 1, "The Art of Agile Analysis and Planning") often assume that I plan them extensively beforehand, when, in fact, that's rarely the case. More typically, I begin with a rough vision, try something out, see how it works, adjust my approach, and repeat—learning from each iteration about what needs to go into the next. This repeated cycle of ideation, implementation, evaluation, and adjustment is the same one used by innovators in other fields I've been involved in, like chemical engineering and software development. It's also the approach used by Airbnb's creators, as they worked closely with their first customers to figure out how to resolve issues of trust between property owners and renters. Through iterative experimentation, they arrived at a solution based on community-generated customer and property ratings.

18.9.1.1 *See Failure as an Opportunity for Learning*

One way to gauge an organization's commitment to experimentation is by its attitude toward failure. An enterprise with a culture of experimentation sees failure as an opportunity for growth and learning. As I wrote earlier in this book, the successful Flickr[49] app was born out of the collapse of a previous venture, Game Neverending. Despite the game's failure, it provided learning about the underlying desire of customers for a sharing platform to build communities. This insight led the company to pivot toward a photo-sharing app—thereby saving the company from collapse and leading to the innovation of many of the features used on today's social networks, such as tagging and sharing.

An agile enterprise uses iterative experimentation not only for product development but for other areas of the business, including market, product, service delivery, and channel development. In general, the more uncertainty there is about an aspect of the business, the more critical it is to develop it in an iterative, experimental way.

18.9.1.2 *What Is the Optimum Failure Rate?*

According to Donald Reinsertsen, "It is necessary to have a reasonable failure rate in order to generate a reasonable amount of information"[50]—but what does *reasonable* mean? Research has shown that "the maximum amount of information is generated when the probability of failure is 50%."[51] The specific numbers will vary because each organization must weigh the benefits of learning from failures against the costs of managing those failures, including increased quality assurance (QA) costs, increased post-release monitoring, and increased rework.

18.9.1.3 *Experimentation in the Mainstream*

One of the most difficult cultural adjustments for an established company transitioning to an agile culture is *getting used to the idea of putting something out that's not perfect.*

Many executives have shared with me the "one great difficulty" they have with following an agile approach, and it usually boils down to this: Experimentation and failure are fine for startups, but not for highly regulated mainstream companies whose customers and regulators have little or no tolerance for failure. The counterargument is that if these companies aren't going to cede true innovation to their startup competitors, there's no way to *avoid* failure. This is because failure is an intrinsic part of the experimental process, and experimentation is the *only* viable approach when uncertainty is high. How do you square the circle?

---

49. Reid Hoffman, "The Big Pivot—with Slack's Stewart Butterfield" [podcast], *Masters of Scale with Reid Hoffman*, November 14, 2017.

50. Donald Reinsertsen, *Managing the Design Factory: A Product Developer's Toolkit* (New York: Free Press, 1998). As quoted in Mary Poppendieck and Tom Poppendieck, *Lean Software Development* (Boston: Addison-Wesley, 2003), 19.

51. Poppendieck and Poppendieck, *Lean Software Development*, 19.

For a description of this process, see Christensen, Clayton, and Raynor, *The Innovator's Solution*, 228–229.

The answer is that experimentation does not have to occur in the wild. If an experiment cannot be conducted in the market, conduct it as a closed beta test with a volunteer group of customers in a testing lab. While not as reliable as a true field test, even a limited test of this type provides opportunities for early and frequent feedback throughout product development so that resources can be guided in a timely fashion toward the most promising solutions.

Another way to overcome resistance to experimentation is to nurture a culture that accepts that no products are perfect out of the gate—and that there would be no version 2.0s if such perfection existed. The point of an agile approach is that learning acquired from market testing can guide the business toward addressing the *imperfections that matter* more quickly than extensive upfront planning can.

18.9.2 Embrace Change

Multiple studies have shown that transformative changes often fail and that the human, cultural element is a critical success factor. For example, mergers and acquisitions (M&As) have been shown to have failure rates anywhere from 50 percent[52] to 70 or even 90 percent.[53] A study by the *International Journal of Innovation and Applied Studies* found the integration stage to be the most problematic due in large part to "the human factor (the employees—coping with cultural differences, politics, lack of effective communication, etc.)."[54] M&As are only one example. The typical enterprise is reported to have undergone "five enterprise-wide changes in the past three years and 73% expect change to accelerate."[55] This was the situation even before the pandemic. With the prospect of even *more* radical change as people's worlds are upended by medical, economic, and climate challenges, it's more crucial than ever that leadership adopts a culture based on the expectation of change.

Beth Comstock, a director of Nike Inc. and former CEO of Business Innovations at General Electric Company, has written about key practices for embracing change.[56] These are summarized in sections 18.9.2.1 through 18.9.2.5.

18.9.2.1 Articulate a Change Vision

To counteract resistance to change, leadership needs to communicate an inspirational reason for the change and be actively engaged in ensuring everyone is committed to making the change happen.

---

52. Godfred Koi-Akrofi, "Mergers and Acquisitions Failure Rates and Perspectives on Why They Fail," *International Journal of Innovation and Applied Studies* 17, no. 1 (2016), 150–158.

53. Clayton M. Christensen, Richard Alton, Curtis Rising, and Andrew Waldeck, "The Big Idea: The New M&A Playbook," *Harvard Business Review* (March 2011).

54. Koi-Akrofi, "Mergers and Acquisitions Failure Rates."

55. Edith Onderick-Harvey, "5 Behaviors of Leaders Who Embrace Change," *Harvard Business Review* (May 18, 2018), https://hbr.org/2018/05/5-behaviors-of-leaders-who-embrace-change

56. Beth Comstock, "The Age of Emergent Change," *Rotman Management Magazine* (Spring 2019).

18.9.2.2 Make the World Your Classroom

Get out into the world, observe what's happening, and seek out opportunities in the trends and changes you discover. Apply Comstock's guideline of "focusing on threes":[57] The first time you notice something, take note. The second time, ask if it's coincidental. The third time, recognize it's a trend that may represent an opportunity for the business.

18.9.2.3 Make Time to Think about the Future

Follow the 70/20/10 rule. Focus 70 percent of resources and time on the present—the core business. Focus 20 percent on the next three to five years. Reserve 10 percent for innovation—thinking about and imagining something truly new. Especially today, in a time of rapid change and an uncertain environment, the eyes and ears of leaders must be trained on the future so they can *anticipate* needs and adapt accordingly.[58]

18.9.2.4 Make a Safe Space for Bad News

I once worked as a consultant for an organization undergoing a major change to its technical architecture. Its leader was so intimidating that his subordinates concealed problems from him and each other—a prime example of what happens when people don't feel safe being the bearers of bad news. Successful change leaders create safe spaces where people can talk openly about what's working and what's not working.

18.9.2.5 Don't Ask Why, Ask Why Not

In a culture that embraces change, leaders don't ask, "Why?" They ask, "Why not?" Provide the means and opportunities for people to experiment with new ideas. Foster a culture of goalkeepers, not gatekeepers. **Gatekeepers** guard the status quo. **Goalkeepers** help people accomplish goals, even when it means breaking the status quo.

18.9.3 Acceleration

An agile organization values and has the capacity for rapid acceleration with respect to time to market, growth, and operational capacity, as described in the following sections.

18.9.3.1 Accelerating Time to Market

As I noted at the beginning of this book, one of the most common reasons I hear from executives for wanting to transition to an agile approach is the promise of accelerated time to market. Agile organizations achieve this miracle by using data-informed methods, such as data mining and the MVP process, to quickly identify high-value features for early delivery. In addition, they use highly automated quality-control systems that make it possible to deliver product improvements frequently and reliably to the market.

For more on the MVP process, see Chapter 12.

---

57. Comstock "The Age of Emergent Change."
58. Alain Arseneault, in a note to the author.

18.9.3.2 Accelerating Growth and Operational Capacity

Any disruptive innovation should expect stiff competition as soon as a product's success becomes apparent. The best defense is to be prepared to scale quickly so that the innovation dominates the market before competitors have a chance to mount an effective response.

The agile organization must have the capacity to quickly accelerate **market penetration** and ramp up its **operational capacity** to service the growing volume. This capacity is so crucial to the success of an innovative product that Peter Thiel[59] abandoned his own plan to grow PayPal when it became apparent the company wouldn't be able to grow fast enough to outrun eBay, its main customer and competitor. Thiel's viral-marketing plan had been to grow the market by offering a ten-dollar rebate for referrals. When he realized he couldn't sustain the plan long enough to dominate the market before eBay could mount an effective response, he decided to sell the company to eBay.

Why Startups Must Be Able to Accelerate Growth

A new startup that is not targeting an incumbent's primary customer base (e.g., when the startup is a low-end or new-market disruptor) often has a small window of time when it can operate under the radar. During this short period of grace, it must be able to grow quickly enough that by the time the incumbent and other competitors mount an effective response, the disruptor has reached **escape velocity**—the point where competitors no longer constitute a threat.

On the other hand, if the innovation targets an incumbent's primary market, the incumbent will likely notice it quickly because of the impact on revenue streams. In this case, there is no period of grace, and the innovator must be prepared to accelerate *immediately* upon the product's release into the market.

Why Incumbents Must Be Able to Accelerate Growth

Incumbent businesses are not startups—but they do increasingly find themselves in startup *situations* whenever they introduce game-changing products and services into the marketplace. Just as in the case of their smaller competitors, these businesses need to be able to scale quickly after the product is first introduced in order to capture the market before competitors—other incumbents and new startups—rush in to replicate the innovation.

Acceleration Affects Every Division

To fend off competition once an innovation is introduced, every division in the enterprise—not only product development—needs to be prepared to quickly scale up its activities and attune itself to an accelerated pace. This includes testing, deployment, marketing, training, support, finance, channel development, and supply-chain management.

---

59. Based on Reid Hoffman's interview with Thiel. See "Escape the Competition—with PayPal's Peter Thiel" [podcast], *Masters of Scale with Reid Hoffman*, November 7, 2017.

Accelerate by Removing Impediments

A commitment to acceleration means working hard to remove roadblocks that slow down processes without adding value. These are the areas of friction referred to, in lean thinking, as **waste**, or **muda** (e.g., excessive red tape and wasteful documentation).

18.9.4 Empathy

Empathy is "the action of understanding, being aware of, being sensitive to, and vicariously experiencing the feelings, thoughts, and experience of another of either the past or present."[60] It's "an attempt to better understand the other person by getting to know their perspective."[61]

In today's world, every company needs to integrate empathy for the customer as an enterprise-wide value into its culture. Indeed, empathy should extend beyond the customer to the company's relationships with everyone it impacts, including its employees. For example, by trusting and empowering its employees to make decisions, a company reduces friction in the customer experience, leading to higher satisfaction.[62]

Empathy is critical to successful product development. Satya Nadella of Microsoft has said, "Empathy makes you a better innovator. If I look at the most successful products we [at Microsoft] have created, it comes with that ability to meet the unmet, unarticulated needs of customers."[63]

Empathy should extend beyond the product-development process. An empathic company has a keen awareness of customer sensibilities *at all times*, enabling it to meet—and even anticipate—expectations, leading to successful customer experiences in all of the customer's engagements with the product, the company, and its employees.

It's clear today that the quality of those customer experiences is critical to a company's success. For example, a 2020 PwC report[64] based on a sample of fifteen thousand people from twelve countries and previous studies, published the following findings:

- Seventy-three percent of respondents specified customer experience as an important factor influencing their decisions, and 42 percent would pay a premium for a successful experience.

- More American customers specified "friendly, welcoming service" (48 percent) than "state-of-the-art technology" (32 percent) as a critical success factor.

---

60. "Empathy," *Merriam-Webster*, https://www.merriam-webster.com/dictionary/empathy

61. Justin Bariso, "There Are Actually 3 Types of Empathy. Here's How They Differ—and How You Can Develop Them All," *Inc.* (September 19, 2018), https://www.inc.com/justin-bariso/there-are-actually-3-types-of-empathy-heres-how-they-differ-and-how-you-can-develop-them-all.html

62. David Clarke and Ron Kinghorn, "Experience Is Everything: Here's How to Get It Right," PwC, 2018. https://www.pwc.com/us/en/advisory-services/publications/consumer-intelligence-series/pwc-consumer-intelligence-series-customer-experience.pdf

63. Michal Lev-Ram, "Microsoft CEO Satya Nadella Says Empathy Makes You a Better Innovator," *Fortune* (October 3, 2017), https://fortune.com/2017/10/03/microsoft-ceo-satya-nadella-says-empathy-makes-you-a-better-innovator

64. Clarke and Kinghorn, "Experience Is Everything."

The key ingredients for a successful customer experience were found to be *speed, convenience,* consistency, *friendliness,* and a *human touch.*[65] By practicing empathy internally and empowering its employees to make decisions, an organization improves speed, convenience, friendliness, and a human touch—four of the five key ingredients for a successful customer experience (the other being consistency).[66]

A company that practices empathy in its customer relationships receives multiple benefits. According to the PwC report, US customers who felt appreciated were "more likely to recommend or endorse a brand on social media, . . . make repeat purchases, . . . [and] try additional services or products."[67]

Organizations express empathy through their values and the individuals (managers and employees) who practice it. An agile organization should make empathy central to its culture: it should train its people to be empathetic and develop empathic leaders who use their understanding of people to provide them with what they need for success.[68]

18.9.4.1 *The Three Types of Empathy*

Daniel Goleman, one of the founders of emotional intelligence, lists three types of empathy: cognitive, emotional, and compassionate empathy.[69] These are described in the following sections, along with their implications for organizations.

Cognitive Empathy

Cognitive empathy (also known as **perspective taking**) means "knowing how the other person feels and what they might be thinking." Cognitive empathy should be an enterprise value. It is a critical attribute for successful negotiation and a proven motivating factor: Goleman quotes a University of Birmingham study finding that managers who exhibited the strongest cognitive empathy were best at motivating their employees to do their best. Moreover, cognitive empathy is a critical success factor in product development, as it enables the organization to understand customers' underlying reasons for making a purchase and anticipate the features and products they will want in the future.

Emotional Empathy

Cognitive empathy on its own is not sufficient for successful leadership, since a person can use his or her knowledge of others' feelings to manipulate them in a way contrary to their interests. **Emotional empathy** is *actually sharing* the feelings of another person—to "cry when they're crying"—something human beings (narcissists excluded) can do because of the mirror neuron system.

---

65. Clarke and Kinghorn, "Experience Is Everything."

66. Clarke and Kinghorn, "Experience Is Everything."

67. Clarke and Kinghorn, "Experience Is Everything."

68. Tanveer Naseer, "Empathy in Leadership—10 Reasons Why It Matters," Tanveer Naseer Leadership, 2020, https://www.tanveernaseer.com/why-empathy-matters-in-leadership

69. Daniel Goleman, "Emotional Intelligence, Social Intelligence," originally published June 1, 2007, http://www.danielgoleman.info

Emotional empathy is beneficial in people management, but it must be matched with sufficient detachment to avoid burnout and be accompanied by *compassionate* empathy. Emotional empathy is a critical component of success in customer support, sales, and marketing (e.g., in **emotional marketing** where emotions are used to influence customers' decision to purchase or recommend the product).

Compassionate Empathy

When customers have problems, it's not enough for the company to feel their pain. Customers want those feelings to lead to action. That's where **compassionate empathy** (also known as **empathic concern**) comes in: a person is moved to help another. Compassionate empathy toward customers is a more challenging level of empathy for a for-profit corporation to embrace, as it requires a much more intimate relationship with the individual than is the norm; it's a more natural goal for charitable organizations. Nevertheless, the recognition of compassionate empathy's importance by for-profit corporations is growing, as companies realize that their survival is increasingly bound up with the health of the economic and social ecosystems that support them. In recognition of that fact, Greenleaf has adapted his original servant-leadership[70] model to also include the **institution as servant**—the organization as a servant to society and the entity through which compassionate empathy is mediated. Today, the principle of institution as servant seems more critical than ever as society faces unprecedented challenges from climate change and human expansion, uneven wealth distribution, and rapid technological and political change. (For more on this topic, see Greenleaf's book *The Institution as Servant*.[71])

18.9.4.2 Practical Tools

Empathy should be an enterprise-level value practiced throughout the organization. The following are practical tools and guidelines for incorporating empathy in various aspects of a business.

Circumstance-Based Market Segmentation

As noted earlier, cognitive empathy means understanding a person's feelings and underlying motivations for making purchasing decisions. One useful tool for understanding those motivations is **circumstance-based segmentation**—a market-analysis and product-development approach introduced at the top of this chapter. The motivations for purchasing a product are referred to as *jobs*. Following the approach, you analyze the jobs customers would *hire* the product for, identify competing products that they currently use for those jobs and develop new products that perform those jobs in novel ways.[72]

The story of Game Neverending (noted in section 18.9.1.1) illustrates the central tenet of the approach—to focus on motivations (jobs), not the features of the product. Founder

---

70. "What Is Servant Leadership?" Robert K. Greenleaf Center for Servant Leadership, 2016, https://www.greenleaf.org/what-is-servant-leadership

71. Robert K. Greenleaf, *The Institution as Servant* (Cambridge, MA: Center for Applied Studies, 1972).

72. Christensen and Raynor, *The Innovator's Solution*, 77–79.

Stewart Butterfield developed Flickr from an analysis that the job people were *really* hiring boardgames for had little to do with games per se but was about providing a platform for community and social interaction. When his first attempt to fill that job through an online game was unsuccessful, he pivoted to a new way to satisfy customers' underlying desire for community: he repurposed the original game's social aspects, such as chatting and sharing, to create Flickr.

Empathy in the Context of Product Development and Improvement

As noted earlier, the integration of cognitive empathy into the corporate culture is fundamental to the success of an agile enterprise and for successful agile product development. For the enterprise, it means being aware at all times of what customers are feeling and what they might be thinking. One effective way to foster cognitive empathy toward customers is by obtaining frequent feedback about the product during and after product development. The best feedback comes from the customer actively *using* the product, not through questionnaires. Create prototypes and incremental versions often. Use customer feedback and analytics to continually improve the product during development, and once it is out in the market.

Marketing analytics can be hard to absorb and internalize by product designers and the business. One way to foster empathy is to personalize the data by inventing personas—fictional avatars who stand in for market segments.

 For more on personas, see Chapter 10, section 10.12.

Empathy in Business Operations

Practice empathy during business *operations* using the **voice of the customer (VoC)**—a Six Sigma technique[73] for capturing customer feedback (e.g., through surveys and observations) in order to understand and anticipate customer needs. Support VoC when improving operations by using **value stream analysis**—a technique that analyzes the full end-to-end business process from the customer's perspective in order to improve cycle times and optimize efficiencies.

 For more on value stream analysis, see Chapter 10, section 10.15.

Use **journey mapping** to understand the customer experience from the time customers become interested in the brand until they become loyal customers (or, even further, until they retire), in order to identify **moments of truth** along that path—critical moments when customers form lasting impressions of the brand and where interventions can be most fruitful.

Customer journey analytics (CJA) is defined as "the process of tracking and analyzing the way customers use combinations of channels to interact with an organization and

---

73. "Six Sigma DMAIC Process—Define Phase—Capturing Voice of Customer," Six Sigma Institute, 2019, https://www.sixsigma-institute.org/Six_Sigma_DMAIC_Process_Define_Phase_Capturing_Voice_Of_Customer_VOC.php

covers all channels present and future which interface directly with the customer."[74] Use CJA to help visualize the customer journey and identify submarkets. CJA also enable the organization to recognize customer behavior patterns that affect critical key performance indicators (KPIs) in order to segment customers and determine the right engagement strategy for them.[75,76]

For more on journey mapping, see Chapter 10, section 10.14.

18.9.5 Responsible Procrastination (Last Responsible Moment)

Responsible procrastination means postponing decisions and activities until the *last responsible moment (LRM)*—the moment when the cost of further delay becomes unacceptably high (e.g., when an important solution option expires).

While the practice is a counterintuitive reversal of the maxim "Don't put off till tomorrow what you can do today," it's appropriate for organizations operating under volatile conditions because it means that actions and decisions will be based on the highest-quality data available—that which is most current.

Responsible procrastination can also lead to significant waste reduction for change requests that are ultimately abandoned. The reason is that it reduces the amount of upfront work on the request—work that becomes valueless if the request is canceled.

Note that responsible procrastination does not *always* mean that actions are postponed. For example, credible threats from disrupters should be acted on *immediately* because the cost of a delay—domination of a new market by the disrupter before the incumbent can respond—would be unacceptably high.

For guidance on calculating the cost of delay, see Chapter 6, section 6.5.4.4.

18.9.6 Distributed Authority

An organization can be committed to iterative experimentation but still suffer slowdowns because one level (e.g., a product development team) has to wait for approval from a higher level up the chain to make an important decision. This delay not only introduces friction into the process but also causes decisions to be made by a person with less direct knowledge of local conditions. An agile organization averts these problems by practicing distributed authority.

---

74. David Roe, "Gartner Report Highlights Emerging Customer Journey Analytics Market," CMS Wire, July 20, 2016, https://www.cmswire.com/customer-experience/gartner-report-highlights-emerging-customer-journey-analytics-market

75. DeAsi, "How to Use Customer Behavior Data."

76. Roe, "Gartner Report."

18.9.6.1 Benefits of Distributing Authority

A corporate culture of distributed authority gives local entities the autonomy to make decisions within their domains. Not only does distributed authority reduce friction and speed the organization's response to change, it improves the quality of the response as well.

Research has shown that leaders who empower their employees are more effective at encouraging creativity and voluntary community behavior than those who do not, are more likely to be trusted by their subordinates, and are more effective at influencing employee performance.[77]

It is particularly crucial, in today's uncertain environment, for organizations to practice distributed authority in the ways they organize their workforce and make decisions. Leaders must empower people to make their own decisions (even if it may be risky) so that the business can move quickly when required. Please note, though, that we are speaking of handing down the *authority* to make decisions and take action to the local level—not the devolution of *accountability* for the consequences of those actions.

18.9.6.2 Distributed authority = Localized Decision-Making + Clear Span of Influence + Vision

Distributed authority is effective only if it is composed of three elements: localized decision-making, clear span of influence, and vision. Local entities make local decisions within a clearly understood span of influence in support of the corporate vision—within a culture that supports local empowerment. Executives make the big, strategic decisions while operational decisions are left to functional managers and employees.[78]

The leader provides vision and serves as a coach. Managers may sit in on the discussions that lead to a decision—or they may have a fast reporting channel—so that they can be apprised of changes and ask for clarification in real time, guide teams, and provide feedback. This approach works only if leaders have people whom they can trust to make good decisions in line with their vision—something that can be achieved by following the *leader-as-coach* model.

 For more on agile leadership see Chapter 17, section 17.6.1. For more on the leader-as-coach model, see section 17.6.1.1.

While writing this chapter, I had a conversation with a frustrated local arts committee member at a large Canadian law firm that bore out this truth. He complained to me that the firm had put a rule in place requiring all art purchases to be approved at the corporate level rather than by local committees, as had previously been the case. By his account, the speed and the quality of decisions were much better when local committees made them because locals had on-the-ground knowledge regarding the contribution the company's collection was making to the local community. Whether it's about art-buying

---

77. Allan Lee, Sara Willis, and Amy Wei Tian, "When Empowering Employees Works, and When It Doesn't," *Harvard Business Review* (March 2, 2018), https://hbr.org/2018/03/when-empowering-employees-works-and-when-it-doesnt

78. Alain Arseneault, in a note to the author.

or product development, distributed authority works better than centralization because it puts decisions in the hands of those who have the firmest grasp of local conditions and the necessary expertise—while leaving strategic decisions to a central body that has a broad overview of the business.

18.9.6.3 Be Like the Octopus

One way to think about distributed, autonomous authority structures is to consider the octopus. It has been proposed that, in addition to a central brain for strategic decisions, an octopus has a "brain" at each tentacle, each of which is empowered to make local decisions within its area of control.

According to this view, each tentacle brain receives inputs and builds its own procedures based on local experience. For example, while the central brain makes a strategic decision to obtain food, each tentacle brain has the autonomy to decide how best to carry out that objective according to what it finds in its immediate surroundings.[79] This mechanism is quite different from the human nervous system, which, for the most part, is centrally controlled by a single brain. Traditional organizations whose control is concentrated at the center are structured like humans—but an agile organization is more like an octopus: strategic decisions are made at the executive level, but the authority for local decisions is made on the ground—with each role responsible for making decisions in its span of control.

18.9.6.4 When Should Authority Be Not Only Localized but Individualized?

To ensure that decision-making is as frictionless as possible, some organizations go one step further and not only localize decision-making but invest that authority in an individual rather than a group. An example of this is the PO role in Scrum—an individual accountable for prioritizing a team's work items. In a large agile organization, a single PO may be accountable for prioritization decisions across the whole product, while a single area PO is responsible for resolving conflicts within a product area.

The guideline to individualize decision-making authority is a good rule of thumb to follow when speed is paramount. There are circumstances, though, when it's better to spend the extra time it takes to gain consensus from a group in order to arrive at a higher-quality decision. One of those occurred while I've been writing this book when I was asked to sit on an arts council jury. Our objective was to prioritize a long list of art proposals. After spending two or three days on my own, reviewing and scoring 125 proposals, I spent another two days working with the other jurors to arrive at a consensus. The council could have saved the last two days by simply averaging our initial individual scores. What I learned from the experience, however, was that the added time and cost were more than

---

79. Andrea Michelson, "Octopus Arms Have Minds of Their Own," *Discovery*, January 14, 2020, https://www.discovery.com/science/Octopus-arms. Recent research, however, indicates that the arms and central brain may be more connected than previously thought. See https://www.sciencedaily.com/releases/2020/11/201102120027.htm

compensated for by the result: a much higher-quality decision about where to invest the council's funds. Our group had been tasked with evaluating proposals from almost every imaginable art practice—video, performance art, dance, community art, and costume design—and no juror could possibly have had enough expertise in all of those areas to arrive at a knowledgeable decision. With the help of a skilled facilitator (Peter Kingstone), we were able to reach a consensus on the qualities we were looking for in a proposal and, ultimately, on which proposals to fund. Most important, we all walked away feeling a sense of ownership over the result—so that if we ran into headwinds within our own communities of practice, we would be more likely to stand by the decisions that were made.

This scenario is not unlike that faced by a product owner council (or any other coordinating group) when prioritizing and funding proposals covering a broad range of groups whose concerns are not always aligned. In such cases, it's worth taking a little extra time to reach a consensus rather than force a decision. In many cases, the product champion (POC leader) and other stakeholders may still need to ratify the decision—but it would be rare for them to change the recommendations.

A caveat: Consensus-based decision-making works well *as long there is a skilled facilitator guiding the effort*—one who is able to use and adapt consensus-building techniques according to the situation. Furthermore, to be an effective consensus builder, the facilitator must be trusted by all parties and seen as having no "skin in the game."

While facilitators should be neutral about decisions, they *should* take an active role with respect to *process*—ensuring all evaluators have an equal opportunity to make their case.

18.9.6.5 The Holacratic Approach to Distributed Authority

Holacracy is an attempt to formalize the practice of distributed authority. I'm not recommending the approach; it's a little out there for many organizations and has its issues—but it does provide a number of practical ideas worth considering. A central guidance is that each role in an organization be formally defined, with respect to its purpose, domain (the areas it is allowed to control and regulate), and accountabilities (expectations others have of the role). These role definitions are used to define how authority is distributed across the organization, according to the following rule:

> When you fill a role, you gain the authority to take any action you deem reasonably useful to express the role's Purpose or energize one of its Accountabilities, as long as you don't violate the Domain of another role.[80]

This approach enables distributed authority by clarifying who may do what without waiting for consent from a higher authority. It's a good fit for some organizations because it provides a clear line of accountability while still allowing for fast decisions to be made locally. On the other hand, its formalization of roles goes against the grain of another agile principle, whereby each individual contributes according to their abilities.

---

80. Brian Robertson, "Rule of Law & Property Rights in Organizations: The Keys to Holacracy's Distribution of Power" [blog post], Blog.holacracy.org, April 4, 2016, https://blog.holacracy.org/rule-of-law-property-rights-in-organizations-89d5bde5ef4

A variation on the Holacratic approach is to assign a proxy role to support the primary role in order to avoid delays:[81] when the primary decision maker is unavailable to make a decision, the proxy may decide on that person's behalf. This is the approach used in software development, whereby a proxy PO (often a business analyst) makes decisions on behalf of the PO.

18.9.7 Let Those Who Do the Work Estimate the Effort

Another agile cultural practice that can be difficult for transitioning companies is asking workers to estimate their own work—and then *believing* them.

In many traditional companies, management sets goals and milestones, and their employees are expected to follow them. On those occasions when workers *are* asked to provide cost and time estimates, they are often overridden (e.g., when the company makes sales commitments to clients that aren't in line with the estimates). This situation is rarely sustainable. The organization will either gain a reputation for missed deadlines or try unsuccessfully to meet its deadlines through last-minute infusions of resources (a tactic that has been shown to be ineffective). Alternatively, it may overwork its employees, ultimately resulting in high attrition rates and a slowing down of development as new recruits are brought on board.

In order to avoid these consequences, do the opposite: ask those who will do the work to estimate the work—and believe them. Actively work with them to refine those estimates by providing additional information as it becomes available and encouraging them to explore alternative ways of achieving the desired outcome.

18.9.8 Collaboration

Collaboration is critical in today's industry, where the pace of change is accelerating and the solutions to problems are cross-disciplinary. Collaboration unleashes the collective problem-solving abilities of the organization. Any agile enterprise should embed collaboration in its corporate culture and values, employee training, and recognition and rewards systems. When training employees about the concept of collaboration, address how collaboration fits into the broader corporate culture, how to apply it in different contexts (e.g., within the organization and in relation to outside entities) and how to adapt the approach based on the different ways people like to collaborate (e.g., introverts vs. extraverts).

The following sections provide guidelines for practicing collaboration within and beyond the boundaries of the enterprise.

18.9.8.1 *Internal Collaboration (within the Enterprise)*

A few years ago, I worked with an international company whose CEO seemed not only to tolerate conflict between factions in the enterprise but to *encourage* it in the apparent belief that the Darwinian environment would enable the best ideas and people to survive and flourish. More often than not, this kind of competitive environment led, instead, to

---

81. Ron Healy, in a note to the author.

disruptive and wasteful behaviors. For example, while I was helping the company evaluate prospective team members for a new initiative, one faction actually asked me to exclude a candidate because he belonged to another group, and they were worried he would be a Trojan horse. As outlandish as those fears sounded, the crazy part was that *they weren't even unfounded*—such was the lack of collaborative spirit that prevailed at the company. This mentality spread all the way down to individuals—many of whom were more concerned with their own goals and reputation than those of the team or the company.

On the other hand, I've experienced highly collaborative cultures in other workplaces. This was the case, for example, at Tnuva Computers, where I would meet regularly with my boss, Yossi, as he mentored me in architectural design for IBM's CICS systems. I enjoyed the same conditions at Cherniak and Gottlieb, where I would often confer with my colleague, Jason Weiss, for guidance on the thornier design challenges of assembling packets of information for an intranet system. In cases like these, I was able to achieve much more than I could have on my own and deliver a faster, more reliable result because I felt comfortable walking over to a colleague's desk or picking up the phone to ask for help. It was a win-win-win: my more experienced managers and colleagues were able to focus on higher-level issues, I was able to punch above my weight, and the company benefited from the improved outcomes. This is what happens when an enterprise creates a culture that encourages collaboration and a sense of common purpose toward a shared goal.

A culture of collaboration should also be encouraged both inside and outside organizational units—across *teams* working on the same initiative, across *different levels* in the corporate hierarchy, and across *business areas* in the organization.

Use Generic Job Titles

One simple but highly effective way to embed collaboration in the culture is to use generic titles and role names, rather than specific titles, wherever possible so that members feel free to contribute to the group goal as best they can regardless of role. Examples are *product developer* and *team member*—used to refer to anyone contributing to the development of a product, including business analysts, testers, and product designers.

Collaboration-Building Events

Another way to develop a collaborative culture is to hold events, such as weekend retreats and marathon sessions, where people collaborate on pet projects. Collaboration-building events encourage team solidarity and assist in the forming of relationships. Connections informally forged during the events make it much easier for people to pick up the phone later when assistance is needed.

Collaboration-Enhancing Architecture

Even the physical architecture can be designed to promote collaboration. Foot traffic may be designed, as it is at Apple's campus, to encourage impromptu meetings. Provide areas for employees to socialize after work—for example, to play boardgames, listen to music, play table tennis, or exercise. Group classes such as aerobics and lunch-time yoga classes deliver health benefits while providing an opportunity to build relationships that contribute to a shared, collaborative spirit in the company.

In Defense of Solitude

There are some creative workers (myself included) who perform best when they have the time and place to work things through on their own. Such people are apt to find that the open-office concept does not work for them—the environment being too chaotic and public for the kind of undistracted, deep thinking they need to be great at their jobs. Even personalities that are more naturally extroverted need a place for quiet reflection at times. The employer should ensure that these needs are accommodated. For example, at Hootsuite, a company with many of the open-office, collaboration-positive features discussed previously, there are also private rooms that can be reserved as needed—including an actual log cabin inside the building for those who really need to retreat. (This is in Canada, after all.)

18.9.8.2 Collaboration outside the Enterprise

An agile enterprise also values[82] collaborative relationships with entities *outside* the organization—preferring contractual terms with service providers, suppliers, solution providers, and others that promote ongoing cooperation and partnership, in contrast to an adversarial relationship based on adherence to a predetermined plan.

It's especially important that relationships with external solution providers be collaborative if the product or service is innovative, since little is known up front about how customers will use it and what features they will find most useful. A collaborative approach affords the greatest chance of success in these circumstances because it provides the flexibility for all parties to work together and adapt the plan as they move toward an emergent solution.

18.9.8.3 The Dutch Polder Model

The Dutch polder model is a consensus-based approach to decision-making, originally designed in the Netherlands during the oil crisis (1979–1982) as part of an agreement in which "social partners agreed to moderate wages in exchange for reduced working hours."[83] In a broader sense, it is associated with a cultural tradition that dates back to the Middle Ages—born in a place whose geographical challenges could be solved only through collaborative efforts. There is much in the polder model that agile enterprises can learn and benefit from.

The Whole Team Is Responsible for Success or Failure

The connection between agile practice and the polder model was suggested to me by an opera designer, whom I'll refer to as M.—as I was discussing this book with him and what it has to say about culture and the ways we interact with each other. He was reminded of a couple of incidents that had happened to him recently. He told me of a show he'd designed that was traveling across Europe. At the Netherlands location, a nonlocal

---

82. I say "values" because this type of relationship is not always achievable in practice. There needs to be a certain level of trust between the parties for the approach to be successful.

83. Fabian Dekker, *Challenges for the Dutch Polder Model*, Flash Report 2017-40, June 2017, European Social Policy Network (ESPN), European Commission.

director became angry about a mistake and demanded that the lead crew member tell him who was responsible for it. The lead refused, and the director kept insisting until, finally, the lead said to him, "Sir, you will have to find another way to address us, or leave until you understand how we work. With us, *it is not the individual who is responsible; it is the whole team.*" This illustrates one principle of the polder model: the *whole* team takes on the responsibility to do the work—and the whole team is accountable for the outcome.

The Whole Team Collaborates to Solve Problems

M.'s second story began in a different country in Europe. He thought it would be a nice touch to have liquid stream down from the wall at a point in the performance, so he asked the crew if they could execute it. The reaction was quite different from that in the previous story: the lead immediately stepped forward and said it couldn't be done. Yet, when the performance was later held in the Netherlands, M. got an entirely different response when he made the same request. The crew first went off to confer as a team. Then, they came back to tell him that, yes, they thought they *could* come up with something. Working collaboratively with the set designer, they were able to devise an ingenious scheme using backstage pulleys to lift a sack of liquid and, at the right moment, tip it into a hole in the wall. This story illustrates another tenet of the polder model: *The whole team collaborates to solve problems.*

18.9.9 Commit to Outcomes, Not Outputs

In traditional planning, the solution provider commits to delivering specified deliverables (the scope) at a specified cost within a given time frame. This approach doesn't work when requirements are volatile because it locks all parties into predetermined specifications that are likely to be outdated by the time the product is delivered. Instead of focusing on predetermined deliverables, agile enterprises focus on desired *outcomes*, such as increased revenues and increased customer loyalty.

18.9.10 Transparency

I remember walking into a situation room at one my clients' sites. Displayed across its walls were the plans and milestones for all the teams working on an insurance initiative. Anyone from any team could walk into that room and quickly see what each team was planning for the upcoming weeks. It was a textbook example of **transparency**—frictionless information-sharing.

Schnackenberg and Tomlinson have defined transparency as follows: "Transparency is the *perceived* quality of intentionally *shared information* from a sender."[84] This definition is broad enough to apply to any business area but precise enough to identify the key

---

84. Andrew K. Schnackenberg and Edward C. Tomlinson, "Organizational Transparency: A New Perspective on Managing Trust in Organization-Stakeholder Relationships," *Journal of Management* 42, no. 7 (2017): 1784–1810, https://doi.org/10.1177/0149206314525202

aspects of transparency: that it is primarily about *information*-sharing; and that it is the receiver's *perceived* quality of the information that matters—not the sender's intentions.

The *quality* of transparency is determined by several factors, including the *availability*, *timeliness*, *accuracy*, and *comprehensibility* of the shared information to the receiver.

Transparency is also important because it enables other agile practices. For example, a customer may be comfortable with a loosely committed *collaborative* relationship only because there is full transparency with regard to progress.

18.9.11 Bust Silos

Siloing is the flip side of transparency: the hoarding of information. Bust silos because they undermine a whole-product culture. They impede the leveraging of knowledge across the enterprise, make it more difficult to synchronize teams, and encourage polarization. Replace them with cross-functional groups organized around value delivery so that the seamless flow of information enables rapid decision-making.

I noted in an earlier chapter the remarks made by a retiring VP. His one regret, he said, was that he'd structured the organization by competency instead of by value—and that this had led to regrettable siloing between groups, resulting in conflicting priorities and allegiances. Were he to start all over, he said, he would have organized teams around value. This remark demonstrates two essential truths about siloing. The first is that siloing is corrosive to an organization. The second is suggested by the VP having been aware of the problem for some time yet unable to address it. *Siloing can be difficult to dislodge once it's engrained in the culture.* For silo-busting to be successful, it requires a strong sponsor with enough authority to communicate that siloing will not be tolerated in the organization.

18.9.11.1 Everyone Works for the Business

An executive of an IT department described siloing in his organization this way to me: "The problem today is that you often see business bonding together against IT. You see IT bonding together against business. But you never see business and IT bonding together for or against anything!"

The most straightforward structural solution for this problem, he suggested, would see the product engineering group disappear entirely as a formal organization within the enterprise. Since that is often not feasible, the next best solution is to establish clear lines of reporting so that the foremost alignment of all members (whether they have business or technical functions) is to the *business*. For example, in a cable company, everyone tasked with improving a customer's set-top box experience would report to the business—regardless of whether they were from the technical side or the business side.

Note that *working for the business* includes addressing customers' needs as well as company objectives that may or may not line up with those of the customer. For example, service fees support a financial company's profit-making objectives but run counter to customers' priorities.

18.9.11.2 *Business* **Can** *Lead a Technical Team*

There's a widespread belief among many of the organizations I work with that business stakeholders are not capable of leading their technical, product-engineering teams. Because of this assumption, people with a technical background often end up acting as team leads, standing in for the business (e.g., as proxy POs or business systems analysts). With little *direct* input to product development from the business side, the company's entire engineering division becomes viewed, in time, as if it's an outsourced organization—even when it is internal. In contrast, in an agile enterprise culture, not only *can* business people lead technical teams, but as a general rule, they *should*.

In the context of agile software development, the person responsible for setting team priorities—the PO—should come from the business side (e.g., a product manager or a business stakeholder who is an SME). In order to assist in daily communication with product developers, the leader should be supported, as needed, by a team analyst trained at bridging the gap between business and engineering. The analysts themselves should be a mix of those with business and technical backgrounds. Those with backgrounds in both areas should be especially prized.

18.9.11.3 *Organize Cross-functional Teams around Value; Form Communities of Practice (Guilds) around Competencies*

To bust silos, minimize friction and accelerate value delivery, organize teams around value delivery[85]—*not* by competency. At the same time, form communities of practice (CoPs)—also known as guilds or competency groups—around competencies.

Let's begin with team organization; then, we'll examine CoPs. Organize cross-functional teams so that, to the degree possible, each team includes all of the capabilities (business *and* technical) needed to deliver value to the customer, with minimal reliance on other teams. The value the cross-functional team creates may be **operational** (e.g., the delivery of a purchased product or service to the customer) or **developmental** (e.g., the creation of a new product).

18.9.11.4 *Job-Based Organization (High-Level Use Cases)*

To organize product-development teams around value, create teams according to the **jobs** the customer hires the product to do, using circumstance-based market segmentation. As noted earlier, the circumstance-based approach uses research to identify the jobs that people hire the product to do. Each job represents a high-level use case for the product—a need that it satisfies. You structure the product development organization so that each of these jobs is owned by a team or a team of teams (also known as a **product area** or **Agile Release Train [ART]**). If the organization is scaled, you create a leveled organization by decomposing large jobs into smaller jobs for as many levels as necessary.

Figure 18.2 is an example of organization by jobs for MyChatBot, a software product that uses ChatBot technology to enable a company to expand its outreach to customers at minimal cost.

---

85. Richard Kastner and Dean Leffingwell, *SAFe 5.0 Distilled: Achieving Business Agility with the Scaled Agile Framework* (Boston: Addison-Wesley, 2020), 184.

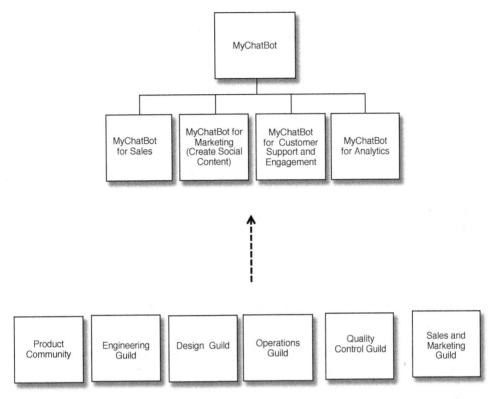

Figure 18.2 *MyChatBot, organized by job*

In Figure 18.2, there is a team (or team of teams) to develop capabilities for each job a customer may hire a ChatBot to do: sales, marketing (generation of social content), customer support and engagement, and analytics. For a more complex example, see Chapter 17, Figure 17.4. It illustrates a multilevel ChatBot product-development group once the product has become more complex and requires a larger organization to support it.

18.9.11.5 Form Communities of Practice (Guilds) around Competencies

Organize CoPs, or guilds, around competencies. CoPs engage in continual improvement in their areas of expertise, enable information-sharing, and maintain a well-trained bench of professionals to supply to the organization. For example, in Figure 18.2, there are CoPs and guilds for product, engineering, design, operations, quality control, and sales and marketing competencies.

CoP Case Studies

To understand CoPs and how they benefit an organization, let's look at two case studies.

Case A: Agile BA CoP   Andre Franklin, senior manager, business systems analysis, describes his experience with CoPs as follows: "Our team was created out of a more traditional business analysis role. Our organization sought to separate analysts into business-centric and systems-centric disciplines within IT. I was granted the opportunity to lead the systems side of the practice. This newly formed team came with varying years of experiences and an even wider gap in our experience leveraging 'agile-like' approaches to software development. We needed to develop an agile BA community with a common set of expectations and a vernacular to describe what we do and how. This common set of expectations would be the starting point of engaging in our new role and most importantly, it would allow us to learn from one another as we worked through challenges across the various projects.

"One of the most significant outcomes of this effort has been the continued growth and self-organizing of our analysis community of practice—a group that includes business and systems analysts from across the enterprise. The knowledge, tools, and practices shared amongst this group is a great value add to our organization, reducing the amount of re-work on projects and eliminated in-efficiencies in our processes that were causing delays."[86]

Case B: Agile BA CoP   In the second case study, True Innovation Inc. worked with a globally distributed, resource-sector firm to establish an operational excellence CoP. The aim of the CoP was to address strategic integration challenges accompanying the adoption of a complex new global production system. Company executives were very concerned that cultural and language differences across regions and the diversity of affected departments and operating sites would render this extremely difficult, if not impossible. The CoP developed digital collaboration tools and convened in-person planning conferences with an emphasis on design choices that fostered the shared interests and motivations of operational excellence practitioners. It also experimented with just-in-time peer production and sharing of digital learning media. Tim Lloyd, True Innovation managing director, reports that not only did the CoP succeed in accelerating the resolution of complex challenges while significantly reducing the effort demanded of centralized program leaders; those same executives were at times surprised to discover that the anticipated collaboration and problem-solving barriers seemingly dissolved. Furthermore, Lloyd observed that the intervention demonstrated how "the egalitarian attitudes inherent in CoPs offer a powerful force for breaking through hierarchical interaction patterns that can impede rapid and complex adaptations." With respect to lessons learned from the experience, Lloyd says, "It's important to discover those processes and tools that successfully build on the community of practice's collegial spirit to amplify it and *project effective open innovation collaboration styles* across the affected regions and departments. *Self-organization, decentralized decision-making*, and *responsibility-driven peer-to-peer learning*—these are powerful tools for sustaining and building on natural aspects of a CoP to accomplish significant strategic and operational objectives, despite distinct cultures and differences in governance, strategy and performance across collaborating organizations."[87]

---

86. Andre Franklin, in an email to the author.

87. Tim Lloyd, in a personal communication with the author.

CoP Roadmap

The following steps provide a roadmap for building and cultivating a CoP, based on guidelines by Buckner,[88] Wenger,[89] and others:

1. **Obtain executive support:** For a CoP to be effective, it requires the active support of a strong executive sponsor.

2. **Focus on value:** The CoP should always be focused on the value it delivers to the organization. Make a habit of discussing the CoP's value during meetings (e.g., by discussing scenarios where using a CoP tool or technique provided benefits to the company). Start by focusing on the CoP's contribution to current issues. Then, consider the value the CoP will be able to deliver over time.

1. **Build the CoP:** In an alive CoP, members can contribute at various levels of participation, according to their interest, availability, and capabilities—for example,

   - CoP program manager represents the community; guides, coaches, evangelizes, and resolves issues.

   - CoP managers determine the community's strategy, inform the community, and schedule meetings.

   - Core team members manage community resources, support CoP managers, and assist in meeting preparation.

   - Members attend meetings, and share content and best practices.

2. **Grow the CoP organically:** Begin with a simple structure. Add elements (e.g., a website or initiatives to define best practices) as membership and engagement grows.

3. **Maintain a knowledge repository:** Maintain a knowledge repository containing tools, examples, templates, and other content that members can easily share. Meet about twice a year to prune the repository by removing outdated items.

4. **Engage in regular communication inside and outside of the community:** Schedule meetings at least once a month. Develop public spaces for information-sharing, such as group meetings and chat rooms. Have regularly scheduled meetings and events, but pepper them with conferences, special events, workshops, and invited speakers. Meet regularly enough to maintain a sense of community but not so often as to lead to member fatigue. Encourage real-time peer-to-peer communication within the community (e.g., using messaging apps). Invite external perspectives by seeking input from other CoPs on how to build effective communities.

---

88. Tracy Buckner, "Building a Community of Practice in 5 Steps," Red Hat, February 18, 2020, https://opensource.com/open-organization/20/2/building-community-practice-5-steps
89. Etienne Wenger, Richard McDermott, and William M. Snyder. *Cultivating Communities of Practice: A Guide to Managing Knowledge* (Boston: Harvard Business Review Press, 2002). Also see Wenger, McDermott, and Snyder's "Seven Principles for Cultivation Communities of Practice," *Working Knowledge* (March 25, 2002), https://hbswk.hbs.edu/archive/cultivating-communities-of-practice-a-guide-to-managing-knowledge-seven-principles-for-cultivating-communities-of-practice

This is just a brief overview of CoPs. To learn more about building and cultivation of CoPs, read *Cultivating Communities of Practice.*[90]

18.9.12 Data-Informed Innovation

Any organism that demonstrates agility, whether it's a cat chasing its prey or an enterprise trying to capture a market, relies on data—specifically, the ability to detect timely information and immediately make use of it to affect its actions. An agile organism uses data not only to respond to change but to predict behaviors and events on the basis of patterns and trends.

The opportunities today to capitalize on data are high due to the bounty of data that has become available in recent years thanks to the widespread use of Internet browsers, mobile apps, and IoT devices. In addition, **sentiment analysis** enables a company to learn a customers' likes and dislikes, make personalized recommendations, and create targeted marketing campaigns by determining and categorizing the feelings (e.g., anger) expressed in pieces of text using machine learning.

Agile enterprises continually seek ways to capture, generate, and leverage this data. They use data *operationally* to deliver innovative products and services. For example, Otis Elevator Company's subscription service (mentioned earlier) uses data from its elevators' sensors to determine when to service the elevators. Agile enterprises also seek to leverage data for *product development*—using it to detect and forecast market trends in order to inform development decisions.

18.9.12.1 The BA Contribution to Data-Informed Innovation

Currently, the roles responsible for data analytics activities include the **data analyst**, responsible for analyzing existing data, the **data engineer**, responsible for generating it, and the **data scientist**, who is expected to be a master-of-all-trades from programming to statistics to business. All of these roles require technical competencies, making them inaccessible to nontechnical businesspeople. This is a significant drawback because it excludes from this important role those who understand the business best.

The role of the business analyst, as technology concierge to the business side, becomes crucial in this context because he or she is well placed to identify and communicate opportunities where data analytics can transform a business, detect trends, and guide strategic investment. This is also an argument for a new subspecialty within business analysis—the **business data strategist**—perhaps the subject of another book. The International Institute of Business Analysis has started down this road by creating a certification in Business Data Analytics (IIBA-CBDA)—a less senior counterpart to what is being proposed.

18.9.12.2 Data-Informed Financial Planning

When a business is developing a product under conditions of uncertainty—either because the product is innovative or the market is volatile—it can't use traditional financial

---

90. Wenger, McDermott, and Snyder, *Cultivating Communities of Practice.*

planning methods because so many of the financial fundamentals are unknown and unknowable at the outset. In such cases, organizations are advised to use data-informed planning methods in which planned market experiments are used to test financial assumptions and direct ongoing investment. We return to agile financial planning a bit later in this chapter and the appendix.

18.9.13 Monitor Adjacent and Low-End Markets

Pay close attention to the low end of the market and adjacent markets because that's where disruptive threats are most likely to come from. Let's examine each of these threats.

18.9.13.1 Threats from Adjacent Markets

Be alert to threats from new, adjacent markets that disrupters seek to exploit by relying on convenience and other properties. These niche markets are often viewed by incumbents as too small to be a threat or unlikely to survive—until they surround the incumbent. One well-known example is Apple, which used its dominance of niche markets such as education to eventually capture the personal computing market. Apple repeated the performance when it leveraged its early dominance of the emergent *personal* mobile-phone market to overtake the incumbent, Blackberry, on its own turf—the *business* mobile-phone market.

Fast Follower

A common strategy relied on by incumbents to fend off threats from adjacent markets is to adopt a *fast-follower* approach. With this strategy, the incumbent waits to see how a disruption will turn out. If the disruption becomes a real threat, the full resources of the incumbent are unleashed to quickly duplicate the new product and overwhelm the competition.

Unfortunately (see Bartman),[91] in the case of new-market disruptions, the fast-follower approach is often unsuccessful because the established company's past experience and technology are not relevant to the new market it is now competing in.

18.9.13.2 Threats from the Low End

Be alert to threats from the low-priced end of the existing market. As noted by Christensen, incumbents often fail to respond forcefully to these threats because they have little interest in the low-quality, commodified end of the business where profit margins are low. By the time an incumbent company wakes up, the disrupter has taken over the low-end market. Eventually, technical improvements combined with lowered customer expectations conspire to threaten the incumbent's primary market as well.

---

91. Tom Bartman, "Confronting a New-Market Disruption: When Disrupting the Disruptor Is the Only Way to Succeed," Medium, November 8, 2015, https://medium.com/@tom_bartman/confronting-a-new-market-disruption-when-disrupting-the-disruptor-is-the-only-way-to-succeed-f02355ad919b

18.9.13.3 *Identify Threats Early*

The only way to fend off these threats is to identify potential attacks early and vigorously defend against them—innovating preemptively, *even when there is no appreciable threat to the bottom line*, and *even when the innovation has the potential to disrupt and cannibalize the company's own primary business*. While it seems counterintuitive for a company to be sowing the seeds of its own demise, it's more relevant to think of such actions as a necessary pivot—for if indeed a disruption is on the horizon, the established company needs to be on the right side of that change to survive.

To catch threats early, closely monitor the edges of the market. Pay close attention to the loss of customers for the company's lower-priced items, since this is often an early warning sign of a *low-end disruption* that could ultimately threaten the company. Monitor new *adjacent* markets. If startups in these markets appear to be growing a customer base that was not previously active, they have the potential to become new-market disrupters that eventually threaten the incumbent's primary market.

New-market disruptions are difficult to detect by examining existing customers because this kind of innovation targets *new* customers—those who are not yet in the market. Nevertheless (as noted by Bartman), the company can pick up an early warning signal by monitoring losses of its *low-frequency* customers, since they will be most ripe for the picking by a new-market disruption that offers something new or different.

Once a threat is detected, the incumbent should respond quickly. On an ongoing basis, the company should maintain an innovation unit devoted to seeking new ways to use technology to innovate and "disrupt the disruptor."[92]

18.9.13.4 *What Not to Do*

The taxi industry is an example of an incumbent whose very existence is being threatened today by low-end disruption. When Uber first appeared, I wondered why the established taxi companies didn't immediately begin developing their own version of the app, even as they fought legislative battles against the disruptors encroaching on their business. The first cab companies I saw responding this way were in Italy. Depending on whether you ordered the cab in the traditional way or used the app, the pricing was different—with the app option priced to be competitive with Uber. Some taxi companies in North America are now doing the same thing, but they were much slower to respond—and it remains to be seen whether their late intervention will be enough to stave off the threats to the industry.

18.9.13.5 *A Positive Case Study of a Response to a Threat*

Netflix is an example of a company that has used the strategy of closely monitoring markets to guide two successful pivots. The company began as an online provider of DVD rentals and sales. Once adjacent markets for streaming technology began to appear, Netflix acted quickly to transform itself into the leading distributor of streamed content, leveraging its position in the movie rental business to overtake its new-market competitors—and proving that the gravity of past successes *can* be turned to the company's advantage.

---

92. Bartman, "Confronting a New-Market Disruption."

As its new business matured and other content bundlers entered the streaming market, Netflix reacted preemptively *again*. It created its own content and made it available exclusively on its service—disrupting the new streaming market by bypassing the existing studio systems.

18.10 Agile Financial Planning

One of the conundrums that planners face is how to carry out financial planning under conditions of extreme uncertainty. The traditional approach uses historical data to analyze historical trends and forecast financial outcomes, such as return on investment. Unfortunately, when planning the development of a new-market innovation, little may be known up front about the market for the product, costs, or other financial fundamentals required to build a traditional business case.

18.10.1 Real Options

One lean tool used when planning under uncertain circumstances is **Real Options**. It's a formal financial technique that includes complex mathematical formulae. However, at its heart, it means that one should keep one's options open as long as possible so that commitments can be based on the highest quality data available—that which is most current. With this approach, commitments are postponed until the last responsible moment (LRM)—the moment when the cost of a further delay is no longer acceptable.

The cost of delaying a decision is determined by comparing the option to commit early against the option of delaying the commitment. A profit and loss statement is created for each option—forecasting profits at regular intervals after the product is introduced. Monthly economic impact statements are also prepared, indicating the ongoing value of each option to the customer. Detailed guidance on these approaches can be found in Mary and Tom Poppendieck's *Lean Software Development*.[93]

For guidance on calculating the cost of delay, see Chapter 6, section 6.5.4.4.

18.10.2 Discovery-Driven Planning

Discovery-driven planning addresses the uncertainty issue by turning traditional planning on its head. Instead of working forward toward the bottom line, you begin by asserting what outcomes need to occur for the venture to be worthwhile. Then, you work your way backward to determine the assumptions that need to be made for those outcomes to happen. Next, you create a plan that uses an iterative process to test assumptions early.[94] See Appendix B for a detailed case study using the methodology. The appendix also includes

93. Poppendieck and Poppendieck, *Lean Software Development*, 83–91.

94. For a description of this process, see Christensen, Clayton, and Raynor, *The Innovator's Solution*, 228–229.

guidance on creating pro forma operations specifications that describe the activities and associated costs required for the new business.

18.11 Chapter Summary

Here are the key points covered in this chapter:

- An agile enterprise is one that aims to increase competitiveness by anticipating and responding quickly to changing market conditions and by creating products loved by customers. It uses an empirical approach that optimizes the translation of learning into delivered value.

- A *new-market* disruption attracts those who were not previously customers.

- A *low-end* disruption grabs existing market share by providing lower-quality items at low cost.

- Traditional planning methods are not appropriate for innovative businesses because of the high uncertainty around business fundamentals.

- *Circumstance-based market segmentation* is an approach that focuses on the *jobs* customers "hire" the product for.

- To optimize response time and the quality of decisions, distribute decision-making authority downward to local bodies.

- Bust silos within the enterprise by organizing around value.

- Discovery-driven planning is a data-informed financial approach used for innovative products, developed under conditions of extreme uncertainty.

Appendix A

Additional Resources and Checklists

A.1 Mapping of Book Chapters to IIBA and PMI Guides

Table A.1 maps chapters in this book, *The Agile Guide to Business Analysis and Planning*, to the following guides:

- *BABOK v3: A Guide to the Business Analysis Body of Knowledge*[1]
- *Agile Extension to the BABOK Guide v2*[2]
- *The PMI Guide to Business Analysis*[3]
- *The Agile Practice Guide (PMI)*[4]

---

1. International Institute of Business Analysis (IIBA), *BABOK v3: A Guide to the Business Analysis Body of Knowledge*, 3rd ed. (Toronto, Canada: IIBA, 2015).

2. IIBA and Agile Alliance, *Agile Extension to the BABOK Guide V2* (Toronto, Ontario: IIBA, 2017).

3. Project Management Institute (PMI), *The PMI Guide to Business Analysis* (Newtown Square, PA: PMI, 2018).

4. Project Management Institute (PMI), *The Agile Practice Guide* (Newtown Square, PA: PMI, 2017).

Table A.1 Chapters in This Book Mapped to Chapters in IIBA and PMI Guides

Book Chapter	BABOK v3 (IIBA)	Agile Extension to the BABOK Guide v2 (IIBA/ Agile Alliance)	PMI Guide to Business Analysis	Agile Practice Guide (PMI/Agile Alliance)
1, "The Art of Agile Analysis and Planning"	2, "Business Analysis Key Concepts"	1, "Introduction"	Part 1, Section 1, "Introduction"	2.3, "Lean and the Kanban Method"
2, "Agile Analysis and Planning: The Value Proposition"	2, "Business Analysis Key Concepts"	1, "Introduction"	Part 1, Section 1, "Introduction"	2, "An Introduction to Agile"
3, "Fundamentals of Agile Analysis and Planning"	2, "Business Analysis Key Concepts"	1, "Introduction"	Part 1, Section 1, "Introduction," Section 3, "The Role of the Business Analyst" Part 2, Section 1, "Introduction"	2, "An Introduction to Agile"
4, "Analysis and Planning Activities across the Agile Development Lifecycle"	3, "Business Analysis Planning and Monitoring"	3, "Analysis at Multiple Horizons"	Part 2, Section 4, "Planning"	3, "Life Cycle Selection"
5, "Preparing the Organization"	6, "Strategy Analysis"	4, "Strategy Horizon"	Part 1, Section 2, "The Environment in Which Business Analysis Is Conducted"	4, "Implementing Agile: Creating an Agile Environment"

Book Chapter	BABOK v3 (IIBA)	Agile Extension to the BABOK Guide v2 (IIBA/Agile Alliance)	PMI Guide to Business Analysis	Agile Practice Guide (PMI/Agile Alliance)
6, "Preparing the Process"	3, "Business Analysis Planning and Monitoring"	3, "Analysis at Multiple Horizons" 4, "Strategy Horizon"	Part 1, Section 5.4, "Conduct Business Analysis Planning" Part 2, Section 4.5, "Determine Analysis Approach"	3, "Life Cycle Selection"
7, "Visioning"	6, "Strategy Analysis"	4, "Strategy Horizon"	Part 1, Section 4, "Needs Assessment" Part 1, Section 5, "Stakeholder Engagement" Part 1, Section 9, "Solution Evaluation"	5, "Implementing Agile: Delivering an Agile Environment"
8, "Seeding the Backlog—Discovering and Grading Features"	7, "Requirements Analysis and Design Definition"	4, "Strategy Horizon" 5, "Initiative Horizon"	Part 1, Section 7, "Analysis"	5, "Implementing Agile: Delivering an Agile Environment"
9, "Long-Term Agile Planning"	6, "Strategy Analysis"	4, "Strategy Horizon" 7, "Techniques"	Part 1, Section 4, "Needs Assessment"	5, "Implementing Agile: Delivering an Agile Environment"

Continues

Table A.1 *Chapters in This Book Mapped to Chapters in IIBA and PMI Guides (Continued)*

Book Chapter	BABOK v3 (IIBA)	Agile Extension to the BABOK Guide v2 (IIBA/Agile Alliance)	PMI Guide to Business Analysis	Agile Practice Guide (PMI/Agile Alliance)
10, "Quarterly and Feature Preparation"	7, "Requirements Analysis and Design Definition"	5, "Initiative Horizon" 7, "Techniques"	Part 1, Section 7, "Analysis"	5, "Implementing Agile: Delivering an Agile Environment"
11, "Quarterly and Feature Planning"	5, "Requirements Lifecycle Management"	5, "Initiative Horizon" 7, "Techniques"	Part 1, Section 4, "Needs Assessment" Part 1, Section 5, "Stakeholder Engagement"	5, "Implementing Agile: Delivering an Agile Environment"
12, "MVPs and Story Maps"	5, "Requirements Lifecycle Management"	5, "Initiative Horizon" 7, "Techniques"	Part 1, Section 7, "Analysis"	5, "Implementing Agile: Delivering an Agile Environment"
13, "Story Preparation"	4, "Elicitation and Collaboration" 7, "Requirements Analysis and Design Definition"	6, "Delivery Horizon"	Part 1, Section 8, "Traceability and Monitoring"	5, "Implementing Agile: Delivering an Agile Environment"
14, "Iteration and Story Planning"	5, "Requirements Lifecycle Management"	6, "Delivery Horizon"	Part 1, Section 7, "Analysis" Part 2, Section 6, "Monitoring and Controlling"	5, "Implementing Agile: Delivering an Agile Environment"

Book Chapter	BABOK v3 (IIBA)	Agile Extension to the BABOK Guide v2 (IIBA/Agile Alliance)	PMI Guide to Business Analysis	Agile Practice Guide (PMI/Agile Alliance)
15, "Rolling Analysis and Preparation—Day-to-Day Activities"	7, "Requirements Analysis and Design Definition"	6, "Delivery Horizon"	Part 1, Section 7, "Analysis" Part 1, Section 8, "Traceability and Monitoring"	5, "Implementing Agile: Delivering an Agile Environment"
16, "Releasing the Product"	8, "Solution Evaluation"	5, "Initiative Horizon" 6, "Delivery Horizon"	Part 1, Section 9, "Solution Evaluation" Part 2, Section 7, "Releasing"	5, "Implementing Agile: Delivering an Agile Environment"
17, "Scaling Agility"	3, "Business Analysis Planning and Monitoring"	4, "Strategy Horizon"	Part 1, Section 2, "The Environment in Which Business Analysis Is Conducted"	6, "Organizational Considerations for Project Agility"
18, "Achieving Enterprise Agility"	6, "Strategy Analysis"	2, "The Agile Mindset" 4, "Strategy Horizon"	Part 1, Section 2, "The Environment in Which Business Analysis Is Conducted"	6, "Organizational Considerations for Project Agility"

A.2 Rules of Thumb in Agile Analysis and Planning

Table A.2 provides an overview of rules of thumb in agile analysis and planning. Keep in mind that these are only broad guidelines. Once the agile process has been up and running for a while, use experience to guide you because practices will vary according to circumstances.

Table A.2 *Agile Business Analysis Rules of Thumb*

Item	Rule of Thumb
Quarterly Planning	
How much effort (general guideline)?	According to need—often up to 10% of planning horizon (e.g., 1-day planning for 10-day iteration).
Initial preparation	Approximately 1 month preparation time, not to exceed 2 months. Start about 1.5 months prior to the quarter being planned.
Quarterly (release) planning	1–2 days; for multiple teams, 1.5–2 days.
Timebox for a quarter, release cycle, or program increment (PI)	8–12 weeks but may vary. In SAFe, one PI cycle often consists of four 2-week iterations plus one innovation and planning iteration.[a]
Iteration planning	May range from 1 hour to 1 day[b,c]
Developer tasks	Normally, up to a day per task; may range from half a day to 2 days.
Feature preview	Held after iteration planning; thereafter, every couple of days. Duration: 10 minutes.
Cadence (iteration length)	Typically 1–2 weeks. In Scrum, may be up to one month.
Estimating and Splitting Epics and Stories	
When to prepare and split a feature	With flow-based planning, consider each feature about 6 weeks prior to implementation for large features and 2–4 weeks prior for smaller features. With quarterly planning, begin preparation of features halfway into the prior quarter.
When to prepare stories	Begin Triad conversations to prepare a story 1–4 weeks prior to its implementation. If you're using timeboxed planning, begin one to two iterations before its planned iteration.
Story point: Translation to time	Initially, set 1 story point equal to 1 day's work by one developer, including all work required to implement the story: analysis, design, coding, testing, etc. Duration will change thereafter, depending on the velocity of the team.
Acceptable story point values	Use adjusted Fibonacci series: 0, 0.5, 1, 2, 3, 5, 8, 13, 20, 40, 80, 100

Item	Rule of Thumb
Maximum size for a user story	Maximum is 8 (points or ideal developer days). Most stories should be at 5 or below.
Team velocity	Velocities may vary widely by teams, from about 20 to the 60s, depending on team size, the length of an iteration, and the way points are allocated. At first, forecast velocity (team capacity) to about 60 percent of total developer days available to the team in the iteration. Thereafter, revise forecasts on the basis of prior iterations with adjustments for changing circumstances.
Number of stories completed per iteration	Approximately 6–10.[d]
Acceptance criteria (AC)	
Maximum number of AC for a story?	As a rule, no more than 5–7 AC per story
Who specifies AC?	AC are developed in collaboration with the members of the Triad: business, QA, and development, with primary accountability belonging to the product owner or designated stakeholder.
When are AC specified for a user story?	Initially specified prior to implementation during story preparation; may be refined and added to during implementation.
Backlog Preparation (Refinement):[e] *Adding Detail, Estimates, Acceptance Criteria, and Prioritization*	
Backlog preparation	Time spent varies according to circumstances. As a general guideline, does not exceed 10% of total budget for the iteration.[f]
Pruning and ordering	Frequency ranges from once a week to once a month. PO and stakeholders review, remove, re-sequence backlog items.
General Availability	
Deployment frequency to production or the market	May be 2–6 months for major releases, continuous (multiple times per day) for small changes.

[a] Richard Kastner and Dean Leffingwell, *SAFe 5.0 Distilled: Achieving Business Agility with the Scaled Agile Framework* (Boston: Addison-Wesley, 2020), 274.

[b] Mike Cohn, *Succeeding with Agile* (Boston: Addison-Wesley, 2010), 334.

[c] XP recommends up to 1 day for first 1-week iteration, gradually reduced to 1 hour. Scrum recommends up to 8 hours of planning for a 1-month iteration. See Ken Schwaber and Jeff Sutherland, *The Scrum Guide. The Definitive Guide to Scrum: The Rules of the Game*, Scrumguides.org, 2020, 9.

[d] Cohn reports an average of "six to nine user stories per 2-week sprint" for a 6-person team (see Cohn, *Succeeding with Agile*, 240). This accords roughly with the estimate provided for 7-person teams.

[e] Schwaber and Jeff Sutherland, *The Scrum Guide*, 10.

[f] See an earlier version of the Scrum Guide: Ken Schwaber and Jeff Sutherland, *The Scrum Guide. The Definitive Guide to Scrum: The Rules of the Game*, Scrumguides.org, 2017, 15.

A.3 Facilitation Tips

- *Prepare.* The secret to a successful meeting—whether formal or informal— is preparation. Prepare an agenda or list of topics, clearly articulated objectives, background notes, questions, input artifacts, lists, and samples of deliverables.

- *Meet with attendees one on one before the meeting.* Premeetings provide an opportunity to get a heads-up on the "elephants in the room" that people may be reluctant to discuss in public.

- *Use the highest-quality communication possible.* For real-time group events, in order of preference, use colocated events, video-conferencing and virtual meetings, conference call. Consider using asynchronous alternatives, such as chat rooms, where team members and stakeholders can check in at any time to review and respond to issues raised by other members in the group.

- *Use a combination of question styles.* Use closed-ended questions (e.g., "Will the product offer a member area or something similar?") and open-ended questions (e.g., "What else do you want to tell me about?").

- *Keep it short.* Always start on time. If key attendees have not arrived within a few minutes, postpone the meeting. Once the meeting begins, stick to the timebox for each agenda item.

- Be *impartial* about content; be *strict* about process.

- *Open with a clear statement of purpose.* Clarify why the meeting was called. What will it accomplish?

- *Use a parking lot.* Add out-of-scope items that come up to a **parking lot**— a reserved area of the whiteboard for issues not on the agenda. Address parking-lot items if there is time left at the end of the event, or assign them as post-event action items.

- *Use flipcharts, not modeling tools, during the meeting.* Use whiteboards, flipcharts, and sticky notes. They're easy to create and alter, don't "feel" like they should be permanent, and can be seen at a glance. Defer use of software tools until *after* the meeting.

- *Break large groups into subgroups.* Ask each subgroup to conduct its own separate meeting in a breakout area and report back to the larger group.

- *Keep devices off.* Ask participants to put aside their devices and laptops during the meeting.

- *Make a mess.* Creativity is messy. Encourage noisy discussions and rough sketches. Drawings don't have to be neat.

- *Place a time limit on the discussion of contentious issues.* If stakeholders can't agree within that time, they may continue the conversation as long as there is consensus on what to remove from the agenda to make up for the lost time. Otherwise, record the issue on the parking lot for future discussion.

- *Be prepared to deal with resistance or opposite views.*
- *Review decisions and action items.* At the end of the meeting, review deliverables and decisions. Create and review action items for any issues that were not resolved during the meeting, and assign them to individuals.

A.4 Visioning Checklist

Use the following checklist to determine whether your organization has missed any visioning steps. Then use the guidelines in Chapter 7, "Visioning," to carry out steps that are missing.

- ☐ Business case is available: business context, root-cause analysis, problem statement, market analysis.
- ☐ Product vision statement has been created and disseminated.
- ☐ Stakeholder analysis has been performed.
- ☐ Customer and business objectives have been identified.
- ☐ Leap of faith hypotheses have been identified.
- ☐ Metrics and leading indicators have been agreed upon for validating hypotheses.

A.5 Stakeholder Checklist

Table A.3 *Stakeholder Checklist*

Stakeholder Type	Contribution
Customers	Provide insight into problems with current service offerings.
Users	Ensure that requirements meet the needs of end users of the IT system.
High-level management	Ensures that business needs are met and that management control, tracking, and reporting requirements are included.
Line management (internal users)	Ensures that solution improves line operations for internal users.
Product champion	Has a broad vision for the product. Is an agent of change, a motivator.
Service desk agents	Have firsthand knowledge of customer complaints, interruptions of service, etc., with the current system. Have their own requirements whenever a change occurs: e.g., new procedures, training, scripts.
Executive sponsor and steering group	Conflict resolution. The early and continuing involvement of sponsors and the steering group (approval boards) promotes buy-in.
Business process owners	Understand problems and issues with the current business process. Ensure that the proposed process is fit for purpose and undergoes continual improvement.
Service owner	Ensures that business objectives for the service are addressed and realized.
Service manager	Ensures tactical, operational needs for the service are met. Responsible for continual service improvement and for evaluating emerging needs of customers.
Service-level manager	Ensures that service-level agreements are defined, agreed on, and met.
Product manager	Provides input regarding the impact on the business if the proposed changes are made or not made. Provides insight regarding the impact of the change on existing services. Defines the overall risk profile and costs across lines of service.
Business relationship manager	Provides a consolidated view of costs and risks across customers and contracts. Provides insight into how proposed changes will impact other services currently supplied to customers.

Continues

Table A.3 *Stakeholder Checklist (Continued)*

Stakeholder Type	Contribution
Change manager	Responsible for the final step in the approval process for deploying changes. Primarily concerned with protecting the production environment and ensuring that the change does no harm (i.e., that change-related incidents are minimized).
Subject matter experts	Provide deep knowledge in their area of expertise (business, technical, or other).
Business architects	Ensure that business standards and guidelines are followed and that changes are consistent with the business model.
Standards and guidelines organizations	Experts in standards and guidelines that constrain development.
Solution providers	Provide a reality check to ensure that requirements are realistic and of sufficient quality to be used for design and coding purposes. Provide solution options and estimates.
Supplier manager	Ensures that all contracts with suppliers support the needs of the business and that suppliers meet their contractual commitments.
Testers (QA)	Ensure that requirements are testable. Provide guidance to team in automated testing. Involved in the specification of test scenarios and acceptance criteria.
Maintenance programmers	Have firsthand knowledge of bugs in current system.

A.6 NFRs and Constraints Checklist

Use the following checklist to make sure you haven't forgotten any important nonfunctional requirements (NFRs) or constraints.

- ☐ **Usability:** Requirements related to the user interface, such as user-friendliness, ✔ accessibility, look and feel, online help, and visual design guidelines.

- ☐ **Reliability:** The ability of the system to perform under specified routine and nonroutine conditions for a specified period of time. Includes the following:

  - ☐ MTBF (mean time between failures): Mean time between service failures of the same service

  - ☐ MTBSI (mean time between system/service incidents): Mean time between failures

  - ☐ MTTR (mean time to repair): Mean elapsed time to fix and restore a service from the time an incident occurs

- ☐ **Performance:** Describes how the system must behave with respect to time and resources. Includes the following:

  - ☐ Speed

  - ☐ Efficiency

  - ☐ Availability

  - ☐ Accuracy

  - ☐ Response time

  - ☐ Recovery time

  - ☐ Start-up time

  - ☐ Resource usage

  - ☐ Throughput (transactions per unit time)

- ☐ **Supportability:** Requirements related to the ability to monitor and maintain the system. Includes abilities to test, configure, install, and upgrade the system.

- ☐ **Plus (+):** Additional constraints on the system, including the following:

  - ☐ Design requirements

  - ☐ Implementation requirements: Constraints on the coding and construction of the system; includes constraints on platforms, coding languages, and standards

  - ☐ Interface requirements: Capability to interact with specified external systems and the nature of those interactions (e.g., protocols, formats)

  - ☐ Physical requirements: Physical constraints on the hardware; includes requirements related to size, temperature control, materials, and so on

  - ☐ Legal, compliance, regulatory, and copyright requirements and constraints

A.7 Readiness Checklist for Quarterly Planning

Use the following checklist to verify readiness for quarterly planning. The checklist may also be used to assess the readiness of an epic or feature.

☑ A.7.1 Analysis Readiness

Consider the following checklist to verify that sufficient analysis has occurred for planning to begin.

- ☐ Has a product or epic vision been articulated? Has it been widely communicated?
- ☐ Is there a product roadmap?
- ☐ Are there sufficient ready features lined up in the product backlog (e.g., ten to twenty ready features prior to quarterly/release planning)? At a minimum, to be ready, a feature must be estimable, prioritized and implementable within a single quarter by one of more teams in a product area (or SAFe ART). More formally, the feature(s) must satisfy the feature definition of ready (DoR), if one is being used.
- ☐ Has a release timeline been proposed?
- ☐ If timeboxed planning is practiced (e.g., SAFe, Scrum, XP), has a cadence been set for the iterations (sprints) within the release cycle or program increment?
- ☐ Do all teams understand which aspects of the requirements and solution they are responsible for?
- ☐ Have the users affected by the next release been identified? Are user goals for the product well understood (e.g., through personas)?
- ☐ Is the high-level solution architecture ready? Do design proposals exist? Have proofs of concept been created?

A.7.2 Logistics Readiness

Use the following checklist to verify logistics for the planning event.

- ☐ Projector, connectors available
- ☐ Presentation laptop or connector for facilitator's laptop
- ☐ Compatible display apps (e.g., PowerPoint)
- ☐ Technical support contact number
- ☐ WiFi account sign-on information, where required (e.g., for connection to projector, for Web access)
  - ☐ Supporting applications installed
  - ☐ Sign-on tested

☐ Flipcharts, whiteboards, Post-it charts

☐ Name IDs (tents, tags)

☐ Stationery: pens, markers, paper

☐ Room where all groups can meet together for collective meeting

☐ Smaller gathering places for breakout groups

☐ Remote participants, broadcasts: remote conferencing applications (e.g., WebEx, Zoom, Microsoft Team, Google Hangouts, video, recording services) are installed, configured, and tested

A.8 Checklist of Invitees for Quarterly Planning

Use the following checklist of invitees to ensure you've considered all relevant perspectives. Keep in mind that not all invitees in the list will be relevant for every situation.

> **Note**
>
> This list is for non-scaled organizations. For an expanded list for scaled agile planning, see Appendix A.12.

- ☐ Product owner: Contributes understanding of features needed by customers and customer-reported bugs. Accountable for prioritization.

- ☐ Development manager: Raises technical work items, such as technical debt payment, security issues.

- ☐ Analyst: May be senior business analyst, senior business systems analyst, or another member. Helps ensure work of highest value is addressed in the plan (e.g., by slicing off high-value parts of stories). Contributes requirements analysis competency; facilitates planning sessions; supports collaborative negotiations between customer (PO) and developers.

- ☐ Solution engineers: Point person to the customer from presales to acceptance. Outlines requirements and works with developers to create a solution that meets customer needs.

- ☐ Technical architect: Designs the solution structure and provides technical leadership to the team.

- ☐ At least one or two developers: Assess feasibility, provide estimates, and suggest alternative ways of doing things.

- ☐ Up to two user experience designers (if needed).

- ☐ Business owners: Primary responsibility for business outcomes (goals): For example, return on investment, compliance. Coordinate with other departments.

A.9 Checklist of Quarterly and Feature Planning Inputs

Prepare the following inputs, as required, in advance of quarterly/feature planning:

- ☐ Delivery/release date, date range, or timeline.   ✔

- ☐ Iteration cadence (for timeboxed planning, e.g., Scrum).

- ☐ Product vision, epic vision (if applicable), product portrait.

- ☐ Long-term product roadmap (strategic plan).

- ☐ Stakeholder analysis artifacts (user roles, personas, etc.).

- ☐ Journey maps, process maps as appropriate, and other preparatory analysis and design artifacts.

- ☐ For quarterly planning: Approximately ten to twenty ready features in the product backlog, roughly estimated to collectively require one quarter to implement, including a few extra features in case they can be accommodated.

- ☐ Design: High-level solution architecture, summary of changed services, etc.

- ☐ High-priority improvement items identified in prior quarterly retrospective.

A.10 Checklist of Quarterly and Feature Planning Deliverables

The deliverables of quarterly/feature planning include the following:

- ☑ ☐ Confirmed delivery/release date, date range or timeline.
- ☐ Confirmed iteration cadence (where timeboxed planning is practiced).
- ☐ Confirmed goals and objectives for the planning period.
- ☐ Risks.
- ☐ Feature dependencies.
- ☐ Confirmed scope: Features committed to the upcoming planning cycle, also known as the quarterly (or release) backlog. Features may be grouped into two subsets: committed features (features that will definitely ship) and target features (features the group plans to deliver but does not fully commit to).
- ☐ Work items for the first two to four weeks have been split and meet the story DoR.
- ☐ Quarterly/feature implementation plan (quarterly roadmap) has been agreed upon, indicating features, events, and milestones across the planning period.

A.11 Checklist of Quarterly (Release) Retrospective Questions

Use the following checklist to prepare questions for a quarterly (release) retrospective and to ensure you *consider* every important perspective when developing your questions. However, focus on areas known to be problematic.

A.11.1 DevOps and Supporting Practices Perspective ✔

- ☐ What are the impressions of team members and the customer regarding DevOps, continuous integration and continuous delivery (CI/CD), and acceptance test–driven development (ATDD) practices?

- ☐ What have been the biggest benefits of the practices? What do the metrics indicate? For example, did deployment frequency increase? Did failure rate and downtime decrease?

- ☐ What DevOps, CI/CD, and ATDD practices can we introduce immediately? What practices should we plan to adopt over time?

- ☐ What are the impediments to greater adoption of the practices?

A.11.2 Technology Perspective

- ☐ What technological changes went well?
- ☐ What technological changes did not go well?
- ☐ What architectural initiatives are underway or being planned?
- ☐ What should we be doing to improve the infrastructure?
- ☐ What performance improvements did we implement?

A.11.3 Productivity Perspective

- ☐ Review product-development productivity metrics and indicators. This may include a review of the following items:
  - ☐ Key performance indicators (KPIs): Review KPIs (e.g., churn rate, conversion rate, engagement rate, customer satisfaction, and loyalty metrics) to determine whether development efforts improved outcomes.
  - ☐ Number of planned features versus number of delivered features.
  - ☐ Number of features that were actually used by the customer.

☐ Burnup charts, internal performance metrics: Review charts, velocity metrics, and other internal metrics such as number of lines of code. Facilitate a discussion of the reasons for the variations and suggestions for improving outcomes. Internal metrics are less instructive than outcome KPIs, but they can provide a more granular picture of when productivity rose and when it dipped in order to analyze and diagnose problems. See Chapter 15, "Rolling Analysis and Preparation—Day-to-Day Activities," section 15.7.5.6, for instruction on how to use burndown charts for diagnosis of productivity issues.

☐ What features were we able to deliver?

☐ What features did we plan but were unable to deliver?

☐ Were the features delivered in order of priority?

☐ Were stakeholders available when we needed them?

☐ Did we receive sufficient resources for the planned work?

A.11.4 Quality Assurance (Testing) Perspective

☐ How are we collecting and measuring customer feedback—the voice of the customer?

☐ How are we testing and measuring whether our efforts are achieving the desired business outcomes?

☐ Are the metrics we are collecting actionable? Do they provide unambiguous guidance about where to focus future efforts?

☐ Are service level requirements (NFRs) being met?

☐ Review of quality metrics, such as the following:

    ☐ Number of issues reported by the customer

    ☐ Turnaround time to fix issues

    ☐ Number of defects shipped into production

    ☐ Number of defects due to previous changes

☐ In what ways is quality improving? How is it deteriorating?

    ☐ Are we successful at addressing quality improvements continuously?

    ☐ Did technical debt accumulate?

    ☐ What technical debt was paid off?

    ☐ Was software released with decreased or increased maintainability, reliability, or performance?

☐ Were there any issues implementing test automation? Are feature teams taking on more automated testing responsibilities?

A.11.5 Program/Portfolio Perspective

☐ Review of status across the full portfolio of projects.

☐ How are we progressing toward long-term strategic goals and objectives?

☐ Have there been any missed release dates?

☐ Was a release date extended? Why?

A.11.6 Marketplace Perspective

☐ When did market challenges occur? When are they anticipated?

☐ Has the business changed any of its strategic priorities? What impact does this have on the prioritization of new work?

A.12 Checklist of Invitees for Scaled Quarterly and Feature Planning

Use the following checklist when considering who to invite. Actual invitees will vary by organization and initiative. If the organization uses flow-based planning (e.g., Kanban), invite only representatives from the teams that will collaborate on the feature. If it's using a timeboxed approach, invite representatives from *all* of the teams in the product area.

- ☐ Senior analyst: Facilitates planning sessions, supports collaborative negotiation between customer (PO) and developers.

- ☐ Leader: Area PO—may be Release Train Engineer (SAFe), CPO, shared PO

- ☐ Team-level POs, proxy POs from all affected development teams: Responsible for understanding customer features, customer-reported bugs and local decision-making.

- ☐ Business owners: Own financial and planning responsibilities. (In SAFe, there are three to five business owners per Agile Release Train [ART].)

- ☐ Solution engineer: Point person to the customer from presales to acceptance. Outlines requirements and works with developers to create a solution that meets customer needs.

- ☐ QA: Help teams create and run their own automated tests. Suggest test scenarios to help ensure adequate test coverage.

- ☐ Operations: Support deployment automation, cloud services, tooling, and so on.

- ☐ Development managers from all affected teams (where assigned): Raise technical debt work items, security requirements, quality improvements, and so on.

- ☐ Senior product manager (where assigned): Manages team-level POs.

- ☐ Senior development manager (where assigned): Manages team-level development managers.

- ☐ Technical architect: Designs the solution structure and provides technical leadership to the team.

- ☐ Developers: Discuss feasibility, provide estimates, and suggest easier ways of doing things.

- ☐ UX designers, as needed.

A.13 Overview of Agile Requirements Management Tools

Following is an overview of software tools that are widely used at the time of this writing for requirements management on agile initiatives. Things may change by the time you read this.

A.13.1 JIRA

JIRA is one of the most popular tools used by agile teams. Add-ons are available to scale it to the portfolio level. JIRA provides the capability to automatically generate Scrum artifacts, like burndown charts. It supports the Kanban process, including Kanban boards and automated determination of flow metrics (e.g., cycle times). For more on JIRA, see https://www.atlassian.com/software/jira/agile.

A.13.2 Blueprint

Blueprint's Storyteller is used by large organizations. It supports stories, visual models, Kanban, product backlog management, and Scrum. One of its benefits is that it supports the SAFe framework, including support for value streams, portfolio epics, and PI planning. For more on Blueprint, see https://www.blueprintsys.com.

A.13.3 JAMA Software

JAMA provides requirements traceability for a broad range of requirements items, including user stories and features. The tool is not agile-specific but is configurable for agile frameworks. JAMA may be used in combination with JIRA. For more on JAMA, see https://www.jamasoftware.com.

A.13.4 Other Requirements Management and Collaboration Tools

Other tools in use include the following:

- **Asana:** Asana is a tool for managing work. It is especially well suited to agile's self-managing teams. It can be used to manage the iteration backlog, allowing team members to either self-assign or be assigned to developer tasks. For more on Asana, see https://asana.com.

- **Cardboard:** Cardboard allows remote users to collaborate remotely in real time to create and revise story maps. Users across locations can create cards and drag and drop them anywhere on the map. For more information, see https://www.cardboardit.com.

- **Microfocus ALM Octane:** ALM Octane (formerly Hewlett Packard Enterprise [HPE]), is used for agile development at scale and is well integrated with DevOps. For more on ALM, see https://software.microfocus.com/en-us/products/alm-octane/overview.

- **Rational Team Concert (RTC):** RTC is a collaboration tool used for agile planning and tracking work items. Key features include collaborative story-mapping capabilities and its ability to integrate with the large-scale requirements tool IBM DOORS Next. For more on RTC, see https://www.ibm.com/support/knowledgecenter/ SSYMRC_6.0.6.1/com.ibm.team.concert.doc/topics/c_product-overview.html.

- **IBM Doors Next:** IBM Doors Next is a requirements management tools within the Rational family. Because SAFe is embedded in the tool, it's a good fit for organizations that follow that framework. For more, see https://www.ibm.com/ca-en/ marketplace/cloud-requirements-management.

- **CA Technologies with Rally Software:** CA Technologies (which acquired Rally Software in 2015), has a family of products that support agile team collaboration across time zones, portfolio views, project views, and scaled agile frameworks (SAFe, LeSS).

- **Confluence:** Confluence is often used by my clients in combination with other tools, such as JIRA, to provide a single source of truth for requirements—consolidating items from JIRA with code reviews, team meeting notes, release notes, and other artifacts. For more on Confluence, see https://www.atlassian.com/software/ confluence.

- **Caliber:** Caliber is a full-featured requirements management tool that supports traceability, requirements attributes, visualizations through storyboards, wireframes, and so on, as well as the creation of stories. For more information on Caliber, see https://www.microfocus.com/products/requirements-management/caliber/features.

- **Google Docs:** Google Docs is a widely used application for creating and modifying collaborative documents. Writers are able to collaborate simultaneously on the same document in real time, greatly simplifying version control because there is only one version to keep track of. Google Docs may be used to edit retrospective backlogs, analysis artifacts, or any document shared across the group. For more on Google Docs, see https://www.google.com/docs/about/.

- **Stormboard:** Stormboard is a tool for brainstorming. See https://stormboard.com.

- **Innovation Games:** Innovation Games offers a number of collaborative games useful for iteration and quarterly retrospectives, such as the Speedboat Game, where participants identify accelerators (sails) and impediments (anchors) that slow down the development process. For more information, see http://www.innovationgames.com.

- **Visio:** Visio is a widely used application for creating diagrams (e.g., business process models and use-case diagrams). It's not a smart modeling tool: it's strictly for drawing and doesn't recognize diagramming errors or ensure consistency in the naming of diagram elements. Nevertheless, it's a useful tool when something more sophisticated is not available.

Appendix B

Discovery-Driven Planning Case Study: BestBots

The following case study illustrates how to perform discovery-driven planning, using the approach described by McGrath and MacMillan in the *Harvard Business Review*.[1] The case study uses publicly available data regarding the global wet-floor robotics industry,[2] but dates have been shifted forward three years for didactic purposes. The subject of the case study, BestBots, is a fictional company.

B.1 Background: BestBots Case Study

BestBots is a US-based company with an established business providing robotic products to the aerospace industry. The company's founder believes the company's experience developing best-in-class mapping and navigation technology, human–machine interfaces, and reliable mission-performance solutions would position it to become a market leader in the new-growth industry of domestic robotics. Consequently, she wishes to establish a new business in this area, focusing on robots for cleaning tasks within the home that customers most wish to avoid, such as mopping, toilet cleaning, and vacuuming. Company executives project that BestBot will be able to dominate the sector by producing robots at lower cost and higher reliability than those currently available on the market.

For its initial line of products, the company plans to produce robotic wet-floor mops. This sector is currently small (the third-largest category of domestic robots) but is quickly gaining momentum, especially in countries in which floors are largely uncarpeted, such as countries in Asia. The year is 2021 as the company asks you, a senior analyst, to help prepare a study of the viability of the proposal and a plan for proceeding that minimizes financial risk for the company.

---

1. Rita Gunter McGrath and Ian MacMillan, "Discovery-Driven Planning," *Harvard Business Review*, July–August 1995, https://hbr.org/1995/07/discovery-driven-planning

2. Andrew Murphy, "Domestic: Robotics Outlook 2025," Loop Ventures, International Federation of Robotics, June 7, 2017, http://loupventures.com/domestic-robotics-outlook-2025

You choose discovery-driven planning because traditional financial planning methods are not viable owing to the high level of uncertainty surrounding the venture.

B.2 Initial Market Analysis

To prepare for the planning process, you begin with some initial research into the market opportunity. The business category for the product, wet-floor robotics, is currently a small market and does not in itself present a strong case for the venture. However, the business case is based on the product's longer-term potential. The outlook on that score seems very promising since, by 2028, the market is expected to grow appreciably. The question now before the company is whether those future projections are strong enough to justify investment today.

B.2.1 Market Estimates (Past and Future)

You research estimates regarding the current and future global market for wet-floor robots and find them to be as indicated in Table B.1.[3]

Table B.1   *Estimated 2021 and 2028 Global Market for Wet-Floor Robots*

	2021 (Current)	2028 (Projected)
Units Sold (Million)	1.17	6.00
Average Selling Price	$125	$110
Market Value ($ Billion)	0.15	0.66

B.2.2 Compound Annual Growth Rate

Your next step is to use the above figures to calculate the compound annual growth rate (CAGR), a measure of how quickly the market is expected to expand.

To calculate CAGR backward from values at the beginning and end of a period requires some difficult mathematics, because this kind of relationship is exponential. Here's the mathematical formula:

$$\text{CAGR} = 10^{(1/n \times \log(\text{Final/Initial}))} - 1,$$

where

n = number of years between final and initial dates
Final = projected final value after n years
Initial = value at the start of the period

---

3. Figures based on the following source, with dates shifted two years, for use in the example: Murphy, "Domestic: Robotics Outlook 2025."

B.2.3 Spreadsheet Fix

If you don't have access to a mathematical calculator, you can obtain the CAGR by using online tools or by creating a spreadsheet and entering data into its cells as indicated in Table B.2.

Table B.2   *Using a Spreadsheet to Calculate CAGR*

Cell	Instruction
A1	Enter the initial value for the attribute (e.g., units sold)
A2	Enter the projected final value
A3	Enter the following formula to obtain the CAGR: =(POWER(10,(1/n*LOG10(A2/A1))))-1

Using the figures in Table B.1 for years 2021 and 2028, you calculate the CAGR for units sold, the CAGR for average selling price (ASP), and CAGR for market value. These are indicated in Table B.3.

Table B.3   *CAGR for Units Sold, Average Selling Price, and Market Value Based on 2021 Data and 2028 Projection*

	2021 (Current)	2028 (Projected)	Compound Annual Growth Rate (CAGR) (Calculated)
Units sold (Million)	1.17	6.00	26%
Average Selling Price	$125	$110	–1.8%
Market Value ($ Billion)	0.15	0.66	23.6%

B.3   Determine Constraints (Required Outcomes)

Rather than try to project overall profits and returns, discovery-driven planning works in the opposite direction by *beginning* from the required outcomes that need to be delivered to justify the venture.

In our case study, there are two such constraints that relate to this proposal. First, BestBots has a policy that any strategic investment must increase the total profits of the company by 10 percent to be worth pursuing. Second, it has a policy regarding investment in new-market innovation: because of the high level of uncertainty surrounding such ventures, BestBots demands a *premium* of 33 percent on return on sales (ROS) over and above the ROS it is currently getting for existing products and services.

You note the following constraints on the venture:

B.3.1 Constraints

C1: Increase in total company profits for strategic ventures: 10 percent

C2: Risk premium on ROS for new-market innovation: 33 percent

Return on Sales: ROS

ROS is the profit generated from every dollar in sales. The formula for ROS is

ROS = Profit ÷ Sales,

where Profit = Sales – Expenses

For example, if in one year there was $1 million in sales, generating $200,000 in profits, the ROS = $200,000 ÷ $1M = 20%.

Having researched these policies, you next seek to turn these constraints into hard numbers. To do that, you need to know the current total profit for the enterprise and the required ROS for sustaining innovation. Table B.4 indicates the total sales and expenses for BestBots in the year 2021.

Table B.4 *Company Sales and Expenses, 2021*

Total Sales	$1 billion
Total Expenses	$880 million

Constraint C1 requires that the venture increase profits by 10 percent. To turn that into a hard number, you first determine the current profit, as follows:

Current Total Profit = Total Sales – Total Expenses = $1B – $880M = $120M

The required profit from the venture is therefore as follows

Required Profit from Venture = 10% × Current Total Profit = 10% × $120M = $12M

The second constraint requires a premium over and above the current ROS. You first calculate current ROS as follows:

Current ROS (2021) = Total Profit ÷ Total Sales = $120M ÷ $1B = 12%

Since new-market innovations are required to provide a premium of 33 percent over and above the regular ROS, you calculate the required ROS from the venture as follows:

Required ROS for new Venture = Current ROS + (33% × Current ROS) = 12% + (33% × 12%) = 16%

To summarize, the financial constraints can now be expressed as follows:

C1: Required profit from venture = $12M

C2: Required ROS for new venture = 16%

B.4 Create Draft of Reverse Income Statement

A reverse income statement works its way backward from the end of a traditional statement, beginning with the outcomes that are required in order for the venture to be successful—its financial constraints. You then work backward from these outcomes to determine the financial factors (unit costs, sales volumes, etc.) required to achieve them. As you work your way through the process, you take note of any financial assumptions so that you can later devise a plan to test them. These are noted below as they occur. See Table B.5 for a summary of the assumptions used in the reverse income statement. The first draft for the reverse income statement is as follows:

Reverse Income Statement (Draft)	
Constraint 1, Strategic venture premium: Venture increases total enterprise profits by 10% Constraint 2, Risk premium on return on sales (ROS) for new-market innovation: 33%	
Required profit to increase total profits 10%	= **$12M**
Required ROS for new venture with 33% risk premium	= **16%** (Assumption 1)
Required sales revenue to deliver 16% ROS	= Required profit ÷ Required ROS = $12M ÷ 16% = **$75M** (Assumption 2)
Total allowable costs to deliver 16% ROS	= Required sales – Required profit = $75M – $12M = **$63M**
Required Unit Pricing	
Table B.1 indicates the projected global unit price for wet-floor robots in 2028 to be $110. The company believes that, as a new entrant to the market, it will require a lower price of $90 per unit to entice customers away from the dominant brands in the market.	
Competitive unit pricing to entice customers to new entrant, 2028	$90 (Assumption 3)
Required unit sales (total units sold)	
Required unit sales at $90/unit	= Required sales revenues ÷ Unit price = $75M ÷ $90 per unit = **833,333 Units**

Required Market Share	
Projected global market (units sold), 2028	= 6M units (Assumption 4; see Table B.1)
Required market share of unit sales	= Required unit sales ÷ World market units sold
	= 833,333 ÷ 6M
	= 14%
Cost per Unit	
Allowable costs per unit for 16% ROS	= Total allowable costs ÷ Required units
	= $63M ÷ 833,333
	= $75.60

B.4.1 Conclusions from the Reverse Income Statement Draft

For the initiative to satisfy investment constraints, BestBots's wet-floor robots must be able to capture 14 percent of the world market by 2028 and have the capacity to produce and sell more than 833,333 units per year at a unit cost of $75.60. If these figures prove unachievable, the venture is not worth investing in.

B.5 Create Pro Forma Operations Specifications

Next, you create pro forma operations specifications. This document describes the activities and associated costs required for the new business. For the business to be feasible, the estimated costs must be at or below $75.60 per unit.

Pro Forma Operations Specifications	
1. Sales Costs	
Required wet-floor robot unit sales per year	= 833,333 units
Average order size	= 30 units (Assumption 5)
Required number orders per year	= Required units ÷ Average order size
	= 833,333 ÷ 30
	= 27,778 Orders
Number sales calls required per sale	= 3 (Assumption 6)
Total required calls per year	= Sales calls per sale × Required orders per year
	= 3 × 27,778 = 83,334
Calls per day per salesperson	= 10 (Assumption 7)

Required salesperson days per year	= Total required calls per year ÷ Calls per day per person = 83,334 ÷ 10 = **8,333**
Number workdays per year each salesperson available	= 250 (Assumption 8)
Required salespersons for 250 workdays per year	= Required person days per year ÷ Workdays per person = 8,333 ÷ 250 = **33**
Salesperson salary	$50,000 (Assumption 9)
Total sales salary cost	= Salary × Required number salespeople = $50,000 × 33 = **$1.65M**

2. Manufacturing

Reliability	20% fewer negative incidents than leading competitor (Assumption 10)

Production staffing costs

Capacity per production line per year	40,000 units (Assumption 11)
Required production lines	= Required units sold per year ÷ Capacity per line per year = 833,333 ÷ 40,000 = **21**
Number of staff required per line	10 (Assumption 12)
Total required production line staff	= Number production lines × Number staff per line = 21 × 10 = **210**
Salary per production staff	$20,000 (Assumption 13)
Total production salaries	= Salary × Total required production line staff = $20,000 × 210 = **$4.2M**

Material and packaging costs

Material costs per unit	$10 (Assumption 14)
Total material costs	= Material costs per unit × Number units = $10 × 833,333 = **$8.33M**
Packaging cost per unit	$1 (Assumption 15)
Total packaging costs (833,333 units @ $1/unit)	$833,333

3. Shipping	
Number shipping containers required per order (average order size, 30 units)	= 1 (Assumption 16)
Number containers required	= Number orders × Number containers per order = 27,778 × 1 = 27,778
Shipping cost for 1 container	= $50 (Assumption 17)
Total shipping costs	= Shipping cost per container × Number containers = $50 × 27,778 = **$1.39M**
4. Equipment and Depreciation	
Equipment investment	$150M (Assumption 18)
Equipment lifespan	5 years (Assumption 19)
Annual depreciation	= $150M ÷ 5 years = **$30M**

B.6 Create Assumptions Checklist

Next, you list the assumptions you made while creating the previous deliverables. These are indicated in Table B.5.

Table B.5 *Financial Assumptions Checklist*

ID	Assumption	Measurement
1	Return on sales	16%
2	Annual sales revenue	$75M
3	Unit sales price that will entice customers to a new entrant	$90
4	2028 global market, wet-floor robots	6M units sold
5	Average order size	30 units
6	Sales calls per order	3
7	Calls per day per salesperson	10
8	Workdays per salesperson per year	250
9	Salesperson salary	$50,000

ID	Assumption	Measurement
10	Reliability required to attract customers to new entrant: percentage fewer negative incidents than leading competitor	20%
11	Production line capacity	40,000 units per line per year
12	Number of staff required per line	10
13	Salary per production staff	$20,000
14	Material costs per unit	$10
15	Packaging cost per unit	$1
16	Number of containers per order (30 units)	1
17	Shipping cost, 1 container (30 units)	$50
18	Equipment investment	$150M
19	Equipment lifespan	5 years
20	Allowable overhead costs (see revised reverse income statement)	$16.6M

B.7 Revise Reverse Income Statement

With a more detailed analysis now available, you update the original draft of the reverse income statement to create the revised reverse income statement:

Reverse Income Statement (Revised)	
Constraints	
Required return on sales	16%
Required sales revenue	$75M
Required profit	$12M
Allowable costs (revenue – profit)	$63M
Estimated Costs to Deliver Required Outcomes	
Sales salaries	$1.65M
Production salaries	$4.2M
Material costs	$8.33M
Packaging costs	$833,333

Shipping costs	$1.39M
Annual depreciation	$30M
Total estimated cost	**$46.4M**
Allowable overhead (Allowable costs – Estimated cost)	= $63M – 46.4M: $16.6M (Assumption 20)
Per-Unit Figures	
Sales price	$90
Allowable cost per unit	$75.60
Material costs	$10

The newly revised information in the reverse income statement indicates that for this venture to be viable, the *overhead must not exceed $16.6 million*.

B.8 Create Milestone Planning Chart

The next step is to create a plan to test assumptions at various milestone events. A milestone event is a point in time when an event must be completed. At each of these milestones, a pivot-or-persevere decision may be made—to either persevere with the venture if test results justify further investment, or pivot to a different business model.

The following is the milestone planning chart created for BestBots. Dates have not yet been assigned, as they will be determined in consultation with the business and product development team.

BestBots Milestone Planning Chart for Testing Financial Assumptions

Milestone Event Completed	Assumption ID to Be Tested
1. Feasibility study	4: 2028 global market, wet-floor robots
	5: Average order size
	6: Sales call per order
	7: Calls per day per salesperson
	8: Workdays per salesperson per year
	9: Salesperson salary
	13: Salary per production staff
	16: Number of containers per order (30 units)
	17: Shipping cost, 1 container (30 units)

Milestone Event Completed	Assumption ID to Be Tested
2. Prototypes created	3: Unit sales price to entice customers to new entrant in the market
	10: Reliability required to attract customers to new entrant
3. Pilot Production Plant	1: Return on sales
	2: Annual sales revenue
	5: Average order size
	6: Sales calls per order
	7: Calls per day per salesperson
	9: Salesperson salary
	10: Reliability required to attract customers to new entrant
	11: Production line capacity
	12: Number of staff required per line
	13: Salary per production staff
	14: Material cost per unit
	16: Number of containers per order (30 units)
	17: Shipping cost, 1 container (30 units)
	18: Equipment Investment
4. Pilot market analysis and product revision	1: Return on sales
	2: Annual sales revenue
	3: Unit sales price to entice customers to new entrant in the market
	4: 2028 global market, wet-floor robots
	14: Material costs per unit
	15: Packaging cost per unit
	19: Equipment lifespan
	20: Allowable overhead costs

Bibliography

Christensen, Clayton M. *The Innovator's Dilemma: When New Technologies Cause Great Firms to Fail (Management of Innovation and Change)*. Boston: Harvard Business Review Press, 2016.

Christensen, Clayton M., and Michael Raynor. *The Innovator's Solution: Creating and Sustaining Successful Growth*. Boston: Harvard Business Review Press, 2013.

Cohn, Mike. *Succeeding with Agile: Software Development Using Scrum*. Boston: Addison-Wesley, 2010.

Comstock, Beth. *Imagine It Forward: Courage, Creativity, and the Power of Change*. New York: Currency, 2018.

Forsgren, Nicole, J. Humble, and G. Kim. *Accelerate: Building and Scaling High Performing Technology Organizations*. Portland, OR: IT Revolution, 2018.

International Institute of Business Analysis (IIBA) and Agile Alliance. *Agile Extension to the BABOK Guide V2*. Toronto: IIBA, 2017.

Kim, Gene, Patrick Debois, John Willis, Jez Humble, and John Allspaw. *The DevOps Handbook: How to Create World-Class Agility, Reliability, and Security in Technology Organizations*. Portland, OR: IT Revolution Press, 2016.

Lawrence, Richard, with Paul Rayner. *Behavior-Driven Development with Cucumber: Better Collaboration for Better Software*. Boston: Addison-Wesley, 2019.

Leffingwell, Dean, and Richard Kastner. *SAFe 5.0 Distilled: Achieving Business Agility with the Scaled Agile Framework*. Boston: Addison-Wesley, 2020.

Project Management Institute (PMI). *The Agile Practice Guide*. Newtown Square, PA: PMI, 2017.

Podeswa, Howard. *The Business Analyst's Handbook*. Boston: Course Technology, 2008.

Poppendieck, Mary, and Tom Poppendieck. *Lean Software Development: An Agile Toolkit*. Boston: Addison-Wesley, 2003.

Ries, Eric. *The Lean Startup*. New York: Random House, 2011.

Taleb, Nassim Nicholas. *The Black Swan, Second Edition: The Impact of the Highly Improbable*. New York: Random House, 2010.

Wenger, Etienne, Richard McDermott, and William M. Snyder. *Cultivating Communities of Practice: A Guide to Managing Knowledge*. Boston: Harvard Business Review Press, 2002.

Index

A

Noble Inc. offers a comprehensive suite of practical training programs in business analysis and agile planning. Our focus is on the needs of the business analyst, product owner, and product and program manager. We provide a unique learning experience, where training is interspersed with coaching, during practical team workshops on a live project or case study. Clients tell us that this not only provides better learning outcomes, it results in artifacts that they are immediately able to use on current projects.

> "[T]he workshops and use-cases made the course a big success . . . everyone found the course very valuable and I know it will provide consistency to our process mapping going forward."
>
> —*P.T., Mawer Investment Management Ltd., Dec. 24, 2020*

To view our course offerings, see:

http://www.nobleinc.ca/courses.html

To book a workshop for your company or organization, contact: info@nobleinc.ca

Nobleinc

Agile Development
Books, eBooks & Video

Whether are you a programmer, developer, or project manager InformIT has the most comprehensive collection of agile books, eBooks, and video training from the top thought leaders.

- Introductions & General Scrum Guides
- Culture, Leadership & Teams
- Development Practices
- Enterprise
- Product & Project Management
- Testing
- Requirements
- Video Short Courses

Visit **informit.com/agilecenter** to read sample chapters, shop, and watch video lessons from featured products.